The Official CompTIA Network+ Study Guide (Exam N10-008)

Course Edition: 1.0

Acknowledgments

CompTIA.

James Pengelly, Author

Thomas Reilly, Senior Vice President, Learning

Katie Hoenicke, Senior Director, Product Management

Evan Burns, Senior Manager, Learning Technology Operations and Implementation

James Chesterfield, Manager, Learning Content and Design

Becky Mann, Director, Product Development

Katherine Keyes, Content Specialist

Notices

Table of Contents

Lesson 1: Comparing OSI Model Network Functions................................ 1

    Topic 1A: Compare and Contrast OSI Model Layers......................... 2

    Topic 1B: Configure SOHO Networks.. 10

Lesson 2: Deploying Ethernet Cabling.. 19

    Topic 2A: Summarize Ethernet Standards 20

    Topic 2B: Summarize Copper Cabling Types 25

    Topic 2C: Summarize Fiber Optic Cabling Types........................... 34

    Topic 2D: Deploy Ethernet Cabling... 41

Lesson 3: Deploying Ethernet Switching.. 51

    Topic 3A: Deploy Networking Devices... 52

    Topic 3B: Explain Network Interfaces 58

    Topic 3C: Deploy Common Ethernet Switching Features............... 65

Lesson 4: Troubleshooting Ethernet Networks.................................... 75

    Topic 4A: Explain Network Troubleshooting Methodology 76

    Topic 4B: Troubleshoot Common Cable Connectivity Issues......... 85

Lesson 5: Explaining IPv4 Addressing.. 97

    Topic 5A: Explain IPv4 Addressing Schemes 98

    Topic 5B: Explain IPv4 Forwarding 106

    Topic 5C: Configure IP Networks and Subnets 115

Lesson 6: Supporting IPv4 and IPv6 Networks.................................... 125

    Topic 6A: Use Appropriate Tools to Test IP Configuration 126

    Topic 6B: Troubleshoot IP Networks 133

    Topic 6C: Explain IPv6 Addressing Schemes................................. 139

Lesson 7: Configuring and Troubleshooting Routers 149

    Topic 7A: Compare and Contrast Routing Concepts 150

    Topic 7B: Compare and Contrast Dynamic Routing Concepts 156

    Topic 7C: Install and Troubleshoot Routers 171

Lesson 8: Explaining Network Topologies and Types 185

    Topic 8A: Explain Network Types and Characteristics 186

    Topic 8B: Explain Tiered Switching Architecture 194

    Topic 8C: Explain Virtual LANs 200

Lesson 9: Explaining Transport Layer Protocols 207

    Topic 9A: Compare and Contrast Transport Protocols 208

    Topic 9B: Use Appropriate Tools to Scan Network Ports 216

Lesson 10: Explaining Network Services 225

    Topic 10A: Explain the Use of Network Addressing Services 226

    Topic 10B: Explain the Use of Name Resolution Services 233

    Topic 10C: Configure DNS Services 241

Lesson 11: Explaining Network Applications 247

    Topic 11A: Explain the Use of Web, File/Print, and Database Services 248

    Topic 11B: Explain the Use of Email and Voice Services 256

Lesson 12: Ensuring Network Availability 267

    Topic 12A: Explain the Use of Network Management Services 268

    Topic 12B: Use Event Management to Ensure Network Availability 274

    Topic 12C: Use Performance Metrics to Ensure Network Availability 284

Lesson 13: Explaining Common Security Concepts................................... 295

    Topic 13A: Explain Common Security Concepts 296

    Topic 13B: Explain Authentication Methods.................................... 304

Lesson 14: Supporting and Troubleshooting Secure Networks 317

    Topic 14A: Compare and Contrast Security Appliances 318

    Topic 14B: Troubleshoot Service and Security Issues.................................... 329

Lesson 15: Deploying and Troubleshooting Wireless Networks 341

    Topic 15A: Summarize Wireless Standards.................................... 342

    Topic 15B: Install Wireless Networks 350

    Topic 15C: Troubleshoot Wireless Networks.................................... 358

    Topic 15D: Configure and Troubleshoot Wireless Security 366

Lesson 16: Comparing WAN Links and Remote Access Methods........................... 375

    Topic 16A: Explain WAN Provider Links.. 376

    Topic 16B: Compare and Contrast Remote Access Methods 383

Lesson 17: Explaining Organizational and Physical Security Concepts................. 395

    Topic 17A: Explain Organizational Documentation and Policies 396

    Topic 17B: Explain Physical Security Methods................................... 408

    Topic 17C: Compare and Contrast Internet of Things Devices 416

Lesson 18: Explaining Disaster Recovery and High Availability Concepts 423

    Topic 18A: Explain Disaster Recovery Concepts................................ 424

    Topic 18B: Explain High Availability Concepts.................................. 431

Lesson 19: Applying Network Hardening Techniques.................................... 439

    Topic 19A: Compare and Contrast Types of Attacks.................................... 440

    Topic 19B: Apply Network Hardening Techniques.. 453

Lesson 20: Summarizing Cloud and Datacenter Architecture................................ 463

Topic 20A: Summarize Cloud Concepts.. 464

Topic 20B: Explain Virtualization and Storage Area Network Technologies.. 471

Topic 20C: Explain Datacenter Network Architecture........................... 478

Appendix A: Mapping Course Content to CompTIA Network+ (N10-008)...............A-1

Solutions S-1

Glossary G-1

Index I-1

About This Course

CompTIA is a not-for-profit trade association with the purpose of advancing the interests of IT professionals and IT channel organizations, and its industry-leading IT certifications are an important part of that mission. CompTIA's Network+ Certification is an entry-level certification designed for professionals with 9-12 months' work experience in roles such as a junior network administrator or network support technician.

The CompTIA Network+ certification exam will verify the successful candidate has the knowledge and skills required to:

- Establish network connectivity by deploying wired and wireless devices.

- Understand and maintain network documentation.

- Understand the purpose of network services.

- Understand basic datacenter, cloud, and virtual networking concepts.

- Monitor network activity, identifying performance and availability issues.

- Implement network hardening techniques.

- Manage, configure, and troubleshoot network infrastructure.

CompTIA Network+ Exam Objectives

Course Description

Course Objectives

This course can benefit you in two ways. If you intend to pass the CompTIA Network+ (Exam N10-008) certification examination, this course can be a significant part of your preparation. But certification is not the only key to professional success in the field of network support. Today's job market demands individuals have demonstrable skills, and the information and activities in this course can help you build your network administration skill set so that you can confidently perform your duties in any entry-level network support technician role.

On course completion, you will be able to:

- Deploy and troubleshoot Ethernet networks.

- Support IPv4 and IPv6 networks.

- Configure and troubleshooting routers.

- Support network services and applications.

- Ensure network security and availability.

- Deploy and troubleshooting wireless networks.

- Support WAN links and remote access methods.

- Support organizational procedures and site security controls.

- Summarize cloud and datacenter architecture.

Target Student

The Official CompTIA Network+ Guide (Exam N10-008) is the primary course you will need to take if your job responsibilities include network administration, installation, and security within your organization. You can take this course to prepare for the CompTIA Network+ (Exam N10-008) certification examination.

Prerequisites

To ensure your success in this course, you should have basic IT skills comprising nine to twelve months' experience. CompTIA A+ certification, or the equivalent knowledge, is strongly recommended.

The prerequisites for this course might differ significantly from the prerequisites for the CompTIA certification exams. For the most up-to-date information about the exam prerequisites, complete the form on this page: www.comptia.org/training/resources/exam-objectives.

How to Use The Study Notes

The following sections will help you understand how the course structure and components are designed to support mastery of the competencies and tasks associated with the target job roles and will help you to prepare to take the certification exam.

As You Learn

At the top level, this course is divided into **lessons,** each representing an area of competency within the target job roles. Each lesson is composed of a number of topics. A **topic** contains subjects that are related to a discrete job task, mapped to objectives and content examples in the CompTIA exam objectives document. Rather than follow the exam domains and objectives sequence, lessons and topics are arranged in order of increasing proficiency. Each topic is intended to be studied within a short period (typically 30 minutes at most). Each topic is concluded by one or more activities, designed to help you to apply your understanding of the study notes to practical scenarios and tasks.

Additional to the study content in the lessons, there is a glossary of the terms and concepts used throughout the course. There is also an index to assist in locating particular terminology, concepts, technologies, and tasks within the lesson and topic content.

In many electronic versions of the book, you can click links on key words in the topic content to move to the associated glossary definition, and on page references in the index to move to that term in the content. To return to the previous location in the document after clicking a link, use the appropriate functionality in your eBook viewing software.

Watch throughout the material for the following visual cues.

Student Icon	Student Icon Descriptive Text
	A **Note** provides additional information, guidance, or hints about a topic or task.
	A **Caution** note makes you aware of places where you need to be particularly careful with your actions, settings, or decisions so that you can be sure to get the desired results of an activity or task.

As You Review

Any method of instruction is only as effective as the time and effort you, the student, are willing to invest in it. In addition, some of the information that you learn in class may not be important to you immediately, but it may become important later. For this reason, we encourage you to spend some time reviewing the content of the course after your time in the classroom.

Following the lesson content, you will find a table mapping the lessons and topics to the exam domains, objectives, and content examples. You can use this as a checklist as you prepare to take the exam, and review any content that you are uncertain about.

As A Reference

The organization and layout of this book make it an easy-to-use resource for future reference. Guidelines can be used during class and as after-class references when you're back on the job and need to refresh your understanding. Taking advantage of the glossary, index, and table of contents, you can use this book as a first source of definitions, background information, and summaries.

Lesson 1

Comparing OSI Model Network Functions

LESSON INTRODUCTION

Computer networks are complex systems that incorporate multiple functions, standards, and proprietary technologies. The Open Systems Interconnection (OSI) model is used to try to simplify some of this complexity. It divides network technologies between seven functional layers. This makes it easier to separate and focus on individual concepts and technologies while retaining an understanding of relationships to the functions of technologies placed in other layers.

This lesson uses the OSI model to give you an overview of the technologies that you will be studying in the rest of the course. You will compare the functions of these layers in the OSI model and apply those concepts to the installation and configuration of a small office/home office network.

Lesson Objectives

In this lesson, you will:

- Compare and contrast OSI model layers.

- Configure SOHO networks.

Topic 1A

Compare and Contrast OSI Model Layers

EXAM OBJECTIVES COVERED
1.1 Compare and contrast the Open Systems Interconnection (OSI) model layers and encapsulation concepts.

Networks are built on common standards and models that describe how devices and protocols interconnect. In this topic, you will identify how the implementation and support of these systems refer to an important common reference model: the Open Systems Interconnection (OSI) model. The OSI model breaks the data communication process into discrete layers. Being able to identify the OSI layers and compare the functions of devices and protocols working at each layer will help you to implement and troubleshoot networks.

Open Systems Interconnection Model

A network is two or more computer systems that are linked by a transmission medium and share one or more protocols that enable them to exchange data. You can think of any network in terms of nodes and links. The nodes are devices that send, receive, and forward data and the links are the communications pathways between them.

The International Organization for Standardization (ISO) developed the **Open Systems Interconnection (OSI) reference model** (iso.org/standard/20269.html) to promote understanding of how components in a network system work. It does this by separating the function of hardware and software components to seven discrete layers. Each layer performs a different group of tasks required for network communication.

7	Application
6	Presentation
5	Session
4	Transport
3	Network
2	Data Link
1	Physical

The OSI model.

Although not all network systems implement layers using this precise structure, they all implement each task in some way. The OSI model is not a standard or a specification; it serves as a functional guideline for designing network protocols, software, and appliances and for troubleshooting networks.

 To remember the seven layers, use the following mnemonic: All People Seem To Need Data Processing.

Data Encapsulation and Decapsulation

A network protocol is a set of rules for exchanging data in a structured format. A network protocol has two principal functions:

- **Addressing**—Describing where data messages should go. At each layer, there are different mechanisms for identifying nodes and rules for how they can send and receive messages.

- **Encapsulation**—Describing how data messages should be packaged for transmission. Encapsulation is like an envelope for a letter, with the distinction that each layer requires its own envelope. At each layer, the protocol adds fields in a header to whatever data (payload) it receives from an application or other protocol.

A network will involve the use of many different protocols operating at different layers of the OSI model. At each layer, for two nodes to communicate they must be running the same protocol. The protocol running at each layer communicates with its equivalent (or peer) layer on the other node. This communication *between* nodes at the same layer is described as a same layer interaction. To transmit or receive a communication, *on* each node, each layer provides services for the layer above and uses the services of the layer below. This is referred to as adjacent layer interaction.

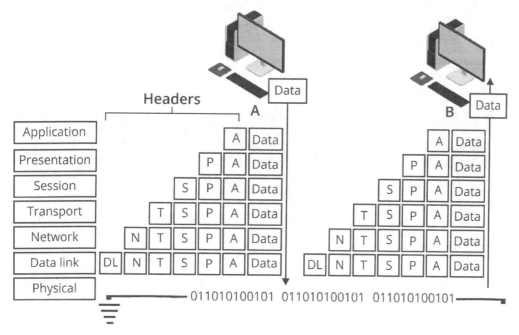

Encapsulation and decapsulation. (Images © 123RF.com.)

When a message is sent from one node to another, it travels down the stack of layers on the sending node, reaches the receiving node using the transmission media, and then passes up the stack on that node. At each level (except the physical layer), the sending node adds a header to the data payload, forming a "chunk" of data called a protocol data unit (PDU). This is the process of encapsulation.

For example, on the sending node, data is generated by an application, such as the HyperText Transfer Protocol (HTTP), which will include its own application header. At the transport layer, a Transport Control Protocol (TCP) header is added to this application data. At the network layer, the TCP segment is wrapped in an Internet Protocol (IP) header. The IP packet is encapsulated in an Ethernet frame at the data link layer, then the stream of bits making up the frame is transmitted over the network at the physical layer as a modulated electrical signal.

The receiving node performs the reverse process, referred to as decapsulation. It receives the stream of bits arriving at the physical layer and decodes an Ethernet frame. It extracts the IP packet from this frame and resolves the information in the IP header, then does the same for the TCP and application headers, eventually extracting the HTTP application data for processing by a software program, such as a web browser or web server.

 You might notice that this example seems to omit some OSI layers. This is because "real-world" protocols do not conform exactly to the OSI model.

Layer 1—Physical

The **physical layer (PHY)** of the OSI model (layer 1) is responsible for the transmission and receipt of the signals that represent bits of data from one node to another node. Different types of transmission media can be classified as cabled or wireless:

- **Cabled**—A physical signal conductor is provided between two nodes. Examples include cable types such as copper or fiber optic cable. Cabled media can also be described as bounded media.

- **Wireless**—Uses free space between nodes, such as microwave radio. Wireless media can also be described as unbounded media.

The Physical layer specifies the following:

- **Physical topology**—The layout of nodes and links as established by the transmission media. An area of a larger network is called a segment. A network is typically divided into segments to cope with the physical restrictions of the network media used, to improve performance, or to improve security. At the Physical layer, a segment is where all the nodes share access to the same media.

- **Physical interface**—Mechanical specifications for the network medium, such as cable specifications, the medium connector and pin-out details (the number and functions of the various pins in a network connector), or radio transceiver specifications.

- The process of transmitting and receiving signals over the network medium, including modulation schemes and timing/synchronization.

Devices that operate at the Physical layer include:

- **Transceiver**—The part of a network interface that sends and receives signals over the network media.

- **Repeater**—A device that amplifies an electronic signal to extend the maximum allowable distance for a media type.

- **Hub**—A multiport repeater, deployed as the central point of connection for nodes.

- **Media converter**—A device that converts one media signaling type to another.

- **Modem**—A device that performs some type of signal modulation and demodulation, such as sending digital data over an analog line.

Layer 2—Data Link

The **data link layer (layer 2)** is responsible for transferring data between nodes on the same logical segment. At the Data Link layer, a segment is one where all nodes can send traffic to one another using hardware addresses, regardless of whether they share access to the same media. A layer 2 segment might include multiple physical segments. This is referred to as a logical topology.

Relatively few networks are based on directly connecting hosts together. Rather than making hosts establish direct links with one another, each host is connected to a central node, such as a switch or a wireless access point. The central node provides a forwarding function, receiving the communication from one node and sending it to another. The addresses of interfaces within the same layer 2 segment are described as local addresses or hardware addresses.

 Nodes that send and receive information are referred to as end systems or as host nodes. This type of node includes computers, laptops, servers, Voice over IP (VoIP) phones, smartphones, and printers. A node that provides only a forwarding function is referred to as an intermediate system or infrastructure node.

The data link layer organizes the stream of bits arriving from the physical layer into structured units called frames. Each frame contains a network layer packet as its payload. The data link layer adds control information to the payload in the form of header fields. These fields include source and destination hardware addresses, plus a basic error check to test if the frame was received intact.

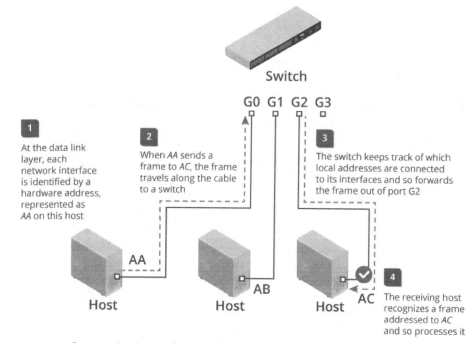

Communications at layer 2 of the OSI model. (Images © 123RF.com)

Devices that operate at the data link layer include:

- **Network adapter or network interface card (NICs)**—An NIC joins an end system host to network media (cabling or wireless) and enables it to communicate over the network by assembling and disassembling frames.

- **Bridge**—A bridge is a type of intermediate system that joins physical network segments while minimizing the performance reduction of having more nodes on the same network. A bridge has multiple ports, each of which functions as a network interface.

- **Switch**—An advanced type of bridge with many ports. A switch creates links between large numbers of nodes more efficiently.

- **Wireless access point (AP)**—An AP allows nodes with wireless network cards to communicate and creates a bridge between wireless networks and wired ones.

Layer 3—Network

The **network layer (layer 3)** is responsible for moving data around a network of networks, known as an internetwork or the Internet. While the data link layer is capable of forwarding data by using hardware addresses within a single segment, the network layer moves information around an internetwork by using logical network and host IDs. The networks are often heterogeneous; that is, they use a variety of physical layer media and data link protocols. The main appliance working at layer 3 is the **router**.

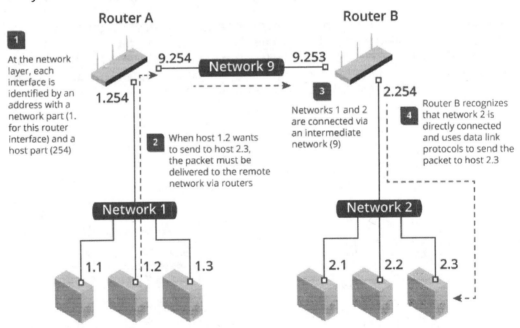

Communications at layer 3 of the OSI model. (Images © 123RF.com)

The network layer forwards information between networks by examining the destination network-layer address or logical network address. The packet is forwarded, router by router (or hop by hop), through the internetwork to the target network. Once it has reached the destination network, the hardware address can be used to deliver the packet to the target node.

 The general convention is to describe PDUs packaged at the network layer as packets or datagrams, and messages packaged at the data link layer as frames. Packet is often used to describe PDUs at any layer, however.

It is usually important for traffic passing between networks to be filtered. A basic firewall operates at layer 3 to enforce an access control list (ACL). A network ACL is a list of the addresses and types of traffic that are permitted or blocked.

Layer 4—Transport

The first three layers of the OSI model are primarily concerned with moving frames and datagrams between nodes and networks. At the **transport layer**—also known as the end-to-end or host-to-host layer—the content of the packets becomes significant. Any given host on a network will be communicating with many other hosts using many different types of networking data. One of the functions of the transport layer is to identify each type of network application by assigning it a port number. For example, data requested from an HTTP web application can be identified as port 80, while data sent to an email server can be identified as port 25.

At the transport layer, on the sending host, data from the upper layers is packaged as a series of layer 4 PDUs, referred to as segments. Each segment is tagged with the application's port number. The segment is then passed to the network layer for delivery. Many different hosts could be transmitting multiple HTTP and email packets at the same time. These are multiplexed using the port numbers along with the source and destination network addresses onto the same link.

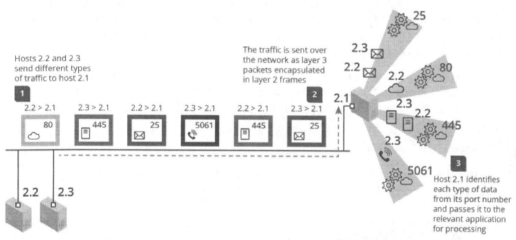

Communications at layer 4 (transport) of the OSI model. (Images © 123RF.com)

At the network and data link layers, the port number is ignored—it becomes part of the data payload and is invisible to the routers and switches that implement the addressing and forwarding functions of these layers. At the receiving host, each segment is decapsulated, identified by its port number, and passed to the relevant handler at the application layer. Put another way, the traffic stream is de-multiplexed.

The transport layer can also implement reliable data delivery mechanisms, should the application require it. Reliable delivery means that any lost or damaged packets are resent.

Devices working at the transport layer include multilayer switches—usually working as load balancers—and many types of security appliances, such as more advanced firewalls and intrusion detection systems (IDSs).

Upper Layers

The upper layers of the OSI model are less clearly associated with distinct real-world protocols. These layers collect various functions that provide useful interfaces between software applications and the transport layer.

Layer 5—Session

Most application protocols require the exchange of multiple messages between the client and server. This exchange of such a sequence of messages is called a session or dialog. The **session layer (layer 5)** represents functions that administer the process of establishing a dialog, managing data transfer, and then ending (or tearing down) the session.

Layer 6—Presentation

The **presentation layer (layer 6)** transforms data between the format required for the network and the format required for the application. For example, the presentation layer is used for character set conversion, such as between American Standard Code for Information Interchange (ASCII) and Unicode. The presentation layer can also be conceived as supporting data compression and encryption. However, in practical terms, these functions are often implemented by encryption devices and protocols running at lower layers of the stack or simply within a homogenous application layer.

Layer 7—Application

The **application layer (layer 7)** is at the top of the OSI stack. An application-layer protocol doesn't encapsulate any other protocols or provide services to any protocol. Application-layer protocols provide an interface for software programs on network hosts that have established a communications channel through the lower-level protocols to exchange data.

More widely, upper-layer protocols provide most of the services that make a network useful, rather than just functional, including web browsing, email and communications, directory lookup, remote printing, and database services.

OSI Model Summary

The following image summarizes the OSI model, listing the PDUs at each layer, along with the types of devices that work at each layer.

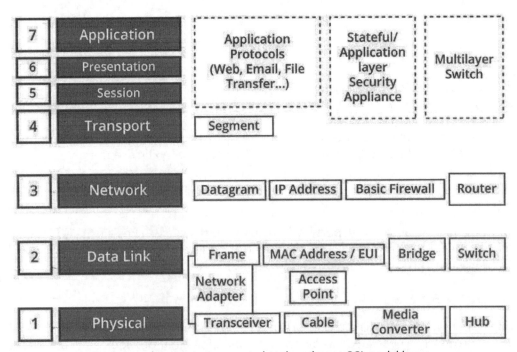

Devices and concepts represented at the relevant OSI model layer.

Review Activity:

OSI Model Layers

Answer the following questions:

1. At which OSI layer is the concept of a port number introduced?

2. At which layer of the OSI model is no header encapsulation applied?

3. What component performs signal amplification to extend the maximum allowable distance for a media type?

4. Which OSI layer packages bits of data from the Physical layer into frames?

5. True or False? The Session layer is responsible for passing data to the Network layer at the lower bound and the Presentation layer at the upper bound.

Topic 1B

Configure SOHO Networks

EXAM OBJECTIVES COVERED
1.1 Compare and contrast the Open Systems Interconnection (OSI) model layers and encapsulation concepts.

The OSI model involves quite a lot of abstraction. As a practical example, it is worth examining how a basic network is implemented. In this topic, you will learn the connection and configuration options for components within a typical small office/home office (SOHO) router.

SOHO Routers

Networks of different sizes are classified in different ways. A network in a single location is often described as a **local area network (LAN)**. This definition encompasses many different sizes of networks with widely varying functions and capabilities. It can include both residential networks with a couple of computers, and enterprise networks with hundreds of servers and thousands of workstations.

Small office/home office (SOHO) is a category of LAN with a small number of computing hosts that typically rely on a single integrated appliance for local and Internet connectivity.

Networks such as the Internet that are located in different geographic regions but with shared links are called **wide area networks (WANs)**. The intermediate system powering SOHO networks is usually described as a SOHO router because one of its primary functions is to forward traffic between the LAN and the WAN. However, routing is actually just one of its functions. We can use the OSI model to analyze each of these in turn.

Physical Layer Functions

Starting at layer 1, the SOHO router provides the following physical connections:

- A number of RJ-45 ports (typically four) to connect to a local cabled network. These are typically labeled as the LAN ports.

- Radio antennas to transmit and receive wireless signals.

- A type of modem (typically cable or digital subscriber line) to connect to the Internet Service Provider's (ISP's) network. This is typically labeled as the WAN port. On the example in the diagram, the interface is another RJ-45 port, designed to connect to a fiber to the premises Internet service using the same Ethernet technology as the local network. On other SOHO routers, there may be a different type of WAN modem, such as an RJ-11 port to connect to a digital subscriber line (DSL) service.

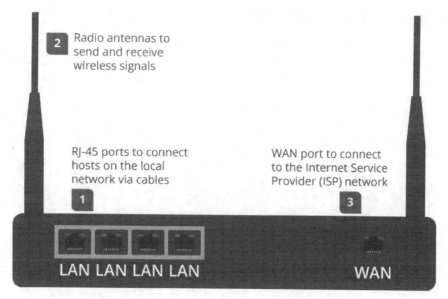

Physical layer connectivity options on a SOHO router.

Data Link Layer Functions

At layer 2, the SOHO router implements the following functions to make use of its physical layer adapters:

- **Ethernet switch**—the RJ-45 jacks are connected internally by an Ethernet switch.

- **Wireless access point**—the radio antennas implement some version of the Wi-Fi standard. The access point functions as a wireless hub, allowing stations (PCs, tablets, smartphones, and printers) to form a wireless network. The access point it also wired to the Ethernet switch via an internal port. This forms a bridge between the cabled and wireless segments, creating a single logical local network.

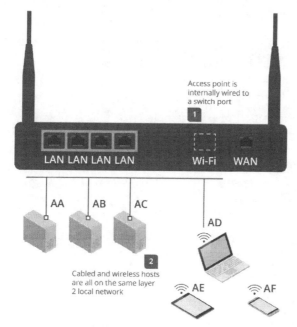

Data link layer local network segment. (Images © 123RF.com)

At this layer, each host interface is identified by a media access control (MAC) address.

Network Layer Functions

At layer 3, the network layer, the routing part of the SOHO router makes forwarding decisions between the local private network and public Internet. These zones are distinguished by internet protocol (IP) addresses. The local network uses a private IP address range, such as `192.168.1.0/24`. The SOHO router itself is identified by an address in this range, such as `192.168.1.1` or `192.168.1.254`.

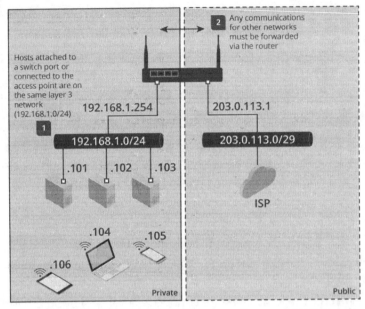

Network layer private and public segments. (Images © 123RF.com)

The router runs a dynamic host configuration protocol (DHCP) server to allocate a unique address to each host that connects to it over either an Ethernet port or via the wireless access point. The addresses assigned to clients use the same first three octets as the router's address: `192.168.1`. The last octet can be any value from 1 to 254, excluding whichever value is used by the router.

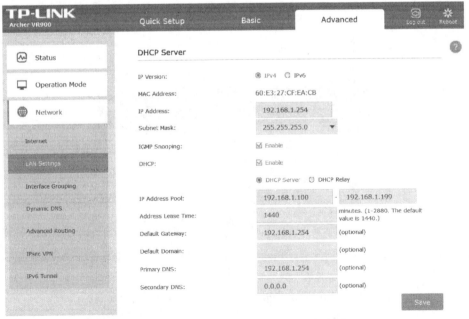

Configuring the LAN addresses using DHCP on a wireless router.
(Screenshot courtesy of TP-Link Technologies Co., Ltd.)

The SOHO router's WAN interface is allocated a public IP address, say
`203.0.113.1`, by the internet service provider. When a host on the local
network tries to access any valid IP address outside the `192.168.1.0/24`
range, the router forwards that packet over its WAN interface and directs any
replies back to the host on the LAN.

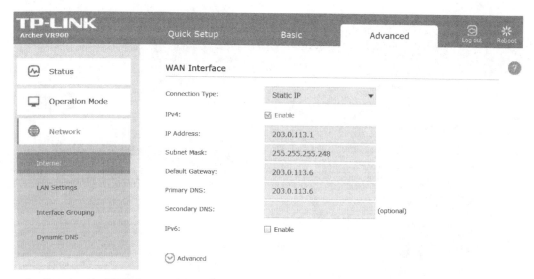

*Configuring the WAN (internet) interface on a wireless router. These parameters are supplied by
the ISP. Many ISP services use DHCP to allocate a dynamic WAN address, but some offer static
addressing. (Screenshot courtesy of TP-Link Technologies Co., Ltd.)*

Transport and Application Layer and Security Functions

There is no separate OSI model layer for security. Instead, security issues can arise
and solutions are needed at every layer. Network security is essentially a matter
of allowing or preventing devices, users, and services (applications) from using the
network. The WAN interface is the network perimeter. The SOHO router can apply
filtering rules to traffic sent between the public and private zones, implementing
a firewall. The firewall can be configured to block traffic based on source or
destination IP addresses and also on the type of application.

At layer 4, each application is identified by a port number, such as 80 for hypertext
transfer protocol (HTTP) web traffic or 25 for Simple Mail Transfer Protocol (SMTP)
email traffic.

The firewall in the router can be configured with rules specifying behavior for each
port. For example, computers on the network might use the server message block
(SMB) protocol to share files. It would not be appropriate for hosts on the Internet
to be able to access these shared files, so the SMB port would be blocked by default
on the WAN interface but allowed on the LAN and WLAN interfaces.

Any host can connect to the RJ-45 ports on the router and join the network. The
wireless network is usually protected by an encryption system that requires each
station to be configured with a passphrase-based key to join the network.

Access to the router's management interface and its configuration settings is
protected by an administrative account passphrase. As the router is connected to
the Internet, it is critical to configure a strong passphrase.

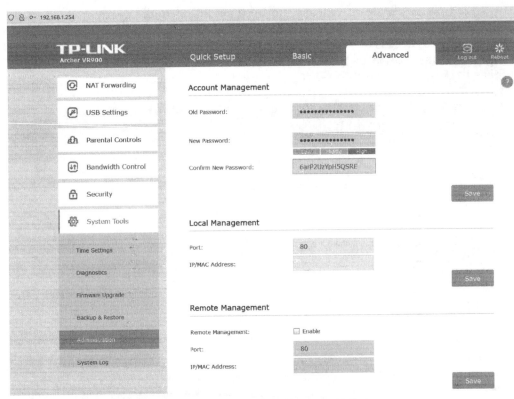

Configuring a management interface on a wireless router.
(Screenshot courtesy of TP-Link Technologies Co., Ltd.)

The Internet

The WAN interface of the router connects the SOHO network to the Internet.

The Public Switched Telephone Network

Most SOHO subscriber Internet access is facilitated via the **public switched telephone network (PSTN)**. The SOHO router is described as customer premises equipment (CPE). More widely, this is any termination and routing equipment placed at the customer site. Some of this equipment may be owned or leased from the telecommunications company (or telco); some may be owned by the customer.

The CPE is connected via its modem and WAN port to the local loop. This is cabling from the customer premises to the local exchange. The point at which the telco's cabling enters the customer premises is referred to as the demarcation point (often shortened to demarc).

Internet Service Providers

The major infrastructure of the Internet consists of high bandwidth trunks connecting Internet eXchange Points (IXPs). Within an IXP datacenter, ISPs establish links between their networks, using transit and peering arrangements to carry traffic to and from parts of the internet they do not physically own. There is a tiered hierarchy of ISPs that reflects to what extent they depend on transit arrangements with other ISPs.

Internet Standards

Although no single organization owns the Internet or its technologies, several organizations are responsible for the development of the internet and agreeing common standards and protocols.

- **Internet Assigned Numbers Authority (IANA) (iana.org)**—manages allocation of IP addresses and maintenance of the top-level domain space. IANA is currently run by Internet Corporation for Assigned Names and Numbers (ICANN). IANA allocates addresses to regional registries who then allocate them to local registries or ISPs. The regional registries are Asia/Pacific (APNIC), North America and Southern Africa (ARIN), Latin America (LACNIC), and Europe, Northern Africa, Central Asia, and the Middle East (RIPE NCC).

- **Internet Engineering Task Force (IETF) (ietf.org)**—focuses on solutions to Internet problems and the adoption of new standards, published as Requests for Comments (RFCs). Some RFCs describe network services or protocols and their implementation, while others summarize policies. An older RFC is never updated. If changes are required, a new RFC is published with a new number. Not all RFCs describe standards. Some are designated informational, while others are experimental. The official repository for RFCs is at rfc-editor.org.

References to RFCs in this course are for your information should you want to read more. You do not need to learn them for the certification exam.

The OSI model has a stricter definition of the Session, Presentation, and Application layers than is typical of actual protocols used on networks. The Internet model (tools. ietf.org/html/rfc1122) uses a simpler four layer hierarchy, with a link layer representing OSI layers 1 and 2, layer 3 referred to as the Internet layer, a Transport layer mapping approximately to layers 4 and 5, and an Application layer corresponding to layers 6 and 7.

Hexadecimal Notation

To interpret network addresses, you must understand the concept of base numbering systems. To start with the familiar; decimal numbering is also referred to as base 10. Base 10 means that each digit can have one of ten possible values (0 through 9). A digit positioned to the left of another has 10 times the value of the digit to the right. For example, the number 255 can be written out as follows:

    (2 x 10 x 10) + (5 x 10) + 5

Binary is base 2, so a digit in any given position can only have one of two values (0 or 1), and each place position is the next power of 2. The binary value 11111111 can be converted to the decimal value 255 by the following sum:

    (1 x 2 x 2 x 2 x 2 x 2 x 2 x 2) + (1 x 2 x 2 x 2 x 2 x 2 x 2) + (1 x 2 x 2 x 2 x 2 x 2) +
    (1 x 2 x 2 x 2 x 2) + (1 x 2 x 2 x 2) + (1 x 2 x 2) + (1 x 2) + 1

As you can see, it takes 8 binary digits to represent a decimal value up to 255. This number of bits is called a byte or an octet. The four decimal numbers in the SOHO router's WAN IP address 203.0.113.1 are octets.

While computers process everything in binary, the values make for very long strings if they have to be written out or entered into configuration dialogs. Hexadecimal notation (or hex) is a convenient way of referring to the long sequences of bytes used in some other types of network addresses. Hex is base 16 with the possible values of each digit represented by the numerals 0 through 9 and the characters A, B, C, D, E, and F.

Use the following table to help to convert between decimal, binary, and hexadecimal values.

Decimal	Hexadecimal	Binary
0	0	0000
1	1	0001
2	2	0010
3	3	0011
4	4	0100
5	5	0101
6	6	0110
7	7	0111

Decimal	Hexadecimal	Binary
8	8	1000
9	9	1001
10	A	1010
11	B	1011
12	C	1100
13	D	1101
14	E	1110
15	F	1111

As you can see from the table, every hex digit lines up neatly with four binary digits (a nibble). Each byte or octet can be expressed as two hex digits. For example, the decimal value 255 is FF in hex. This would sometimes be written as 0xFF for clarity.

Review Activity:

SOHO Networks

Answer the following questions:

1. True or false? The WAN port on a SOHO router is connected to the LAN ports by an internal switch.

2. What type of address is used by the switch to forward transmissions to the appropriate host?

3. True or false? The DHCP server in the SOHO router assigns an IP address to the WAN interface automatically.

4. What function or service prevents an Internet host from accessing servers on the LAN without authorization?

5. How is the decimal value 12 expressed in hex?

6. How is the decimal value 171 expressed in hex?

Lesson 1

Summary

You should be able to compare and contrast OSI model layers and encapsulation concepts and apply them to analyzing the function of networks and networking components.

Guidelines for Comparing OSI Model Network Functions

Follow these guidelines to make effective use of the OSI model:

- Use characteristics of physical layer media and devices to plan wiring topologies and identify potential performance issues.

- Use the data link layer to plan logical segments to isolate groups of hosts for performance or security reasons.

- At the network layer, map data link segments to logical network IDs and work out rules for how hosts in one network should be permitted or denied access to other networks.

- Evaluate service requirements at the transport layer to determine which ports a host should expose.

- Use the session, presentation, and application layers to determine performance and security requirements for the services that the network is providing.

Lesson 2

Deploying Ethernet Cabling

LESSON INTRODUCTION

At the physical layer, networks are made from different cabling types and their connectors and transceivers. These establish direct links between nodes in a local segment. At the data link layer, nodes in these segments are given a standard means of exchanging data as frames.

As they are closely related, networking products often define standards for both the physical and data link layers. While plenty of products have been used in the past, many cabled networks are now based on the Ethernet standards. Understanding the options and specifications for Ethernet is essential to building and supporting networks of all sizes.

In this topic, you will summarize standards for deploying Ethernet over copper and fiber optic media types and identify the tools and techniques required to deploy Ethernet cabling.

Lesson Objectives

In this lesson, you will:

- Summarize Ethernet standards
- Summarize copper cabling types.
- Summarize fiber optic cabling types.
- Deploy Ethernet cabling.

Topic 2A

Summarize Ethernet Standards

EXAM OBJECTIVES COVERED
1.3 Summarize the types of cables and connectors and explain which is the appropriate type for a solution.
2.3 Given a scenario, configure and deploy common Ethernet switching features. (CSMA/CD only)

In this topic, you will identify the components used in an Ethernet network implementation. Ethernet dominates the wired LAN product market. Its popularity is largely based on its ease of installation and upgradability. Large and small networks use Ethernet technology to provide both backbone and end-user services. Due to the wide deployment of Ethernet today, you will undoubtedly be required to manage and troubleshoot Ethernet networks.

Network Data Transmission

All network signaling uses electromagnetic radiation of one type or another. Electromagnetic radiation means transmitting signals as electric current, infrared light, or radio waves. The electromagnetic radiation forms a carrier wave with a given bandwidth or range of frequencies. A signal is transmitted over the wave by modulation and encoding schemes. One example of encoding is transitioning between low and high voltage states in an electrical circuit, making use of a characteristic of the wave called amplitude. These voltage changes can encode digital information—ones and zeroes or bits. The more bandwidth available in the media, the greater the amount of data that can be encoded.

The narrow definition of bandwidth is a frequency range measured in cycles per second or Hertz (Hz), but the term is very widely used in data networking to mean the amount of data that can be transferred, measured multiples of bits per second (bps). Encoding methods mean that, for instance, a signal with 100 MHz frequency bandwidth can transfer much more than 100 Mbps.

Copper Cable

Copper cable is used to transmit electrical signals. The cable between two nodes creates a low voltage electrical circuit between the interfaces on the nodes. There are two main types of copper cable: twisted pair and coaxial (coax). Copper cable suffers from high attenuation, meaning that the signal quickly loses strength over long links. Twisted pair cable is rated to Cat standards.

Fiber Optic Cable

Fiber optic cable carries very high frequency radiation in the infrared light part of the electromagnetic spectrum. The light signals are also not susceptible to interference or noise from other sources and less effected by attenuation.

Consequently, fiber optic cable supports higher bandwidth over longer links than copper cable. Fiber optic cabling is divided into Single Mode (SMF) and MultiMode (MMF) types, and MMF is categorized by Optical Mode designations (OM1, OM2, OM3, and OM4).

Ethernet Standards

Over the years, many protocols, standards, and products have been developed to implement the functions of the physical and data link layers of the OSI model. The most important of these are the Institute of Electrical and Electronics Engineers (IEEE) **802.3 Ethernet standards** (ieee802.org/3).

Ethernet standards provide assurance that network cabling will meet the bandwidth requirements of applications. The standards specify the bit rate that should be achieved over different types of media up to the supported distance limitations. These Ethernet media specifications are named using a three-part convention, which is often referred to as xBASE-y. This describes:

- The bit rate in megabits per second (Mbps) or gigabits per second (Gbps).

- The signal mode (baseband or broadband). All mainstream types of Ethernet use baseband transmissions, so you will only see specifications of the form xBASE-y.

- A designator for the media type.

For example, 10BASE-T denotes an early implementation that works at 10 Mbps (10), uses a baseband signal (BASE), and runs over twisted pair copper cabling (-T).

Media Access Control and Collision Domains

Ethernet is a multiple access area network, which means that the available communications capacity is shared between the nodes that are connected to the same media. Media access control (MAC) refers to the methods a network technology uses to determine when nodes can communicate on shared media and to deal with possible problems, such as two devices attempting to communicate simultaneously.

Ethernet uses a contention-based MAC system. Each network node connected to the same media is in the same **collision domain**. When two nodes transmit at the same time, the signals are said to collide and neither signal can reach its destination. This means that they must be resent, reducing available bandwidth. The collisions become more frequent as more nodes are added, and consequently the effective data rate is reduced.

The Ethernet protocol governing contention and media access is called **Carrier Sense Multiple Access with Collision Detection (CSMA/CD)**. A collision is the state when a signal is present on an interface's transmit and receive lines simultaneously. On detecting a collision, the node broadcasts a jam signal. Each node that was attempting to use the media then waits for a random period (backoff) before attempting to transmit again.

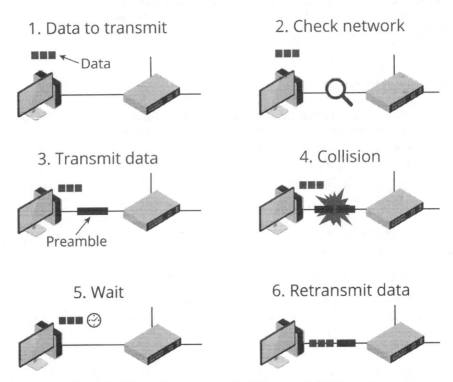

The CSMA/CD media access method. (Images © 123RF.com.)

The collision detection mechanism means that only half-duplex transmission is possible. This means that a node can transmit or receive, but it cannot do both at the same time.

In the 10BASE-T wiring topology, each node is cabled to an Ethernet hub. The hub repeats incoming signals to each connected node. Consequently, every host connected to the same hub is within the same collision domain. The 10BASE-T standard dates from 1990. You are very unlikely to find it deployed to any networks.

100BASE-TX Fast Ethernet Standard

The Fast Ethernet standard uses the same CSMA/CD protocol as 10BASE-T but with higher frequency signaling and improved encoding methods, raising the bit rate from 10 Mbps to 100 Mbps. 100BASE-TX refers to Fast Ethernet working over Cat 5 (or better) twisted pair copper cable with a maximum supported link length of 100 meters (328 feet).

100BASE-TX can be implemented with a hub, but most networks started to replace hubs with switches as the connection point for end systems. The contention-based access method used by a hub does not scale to large numbers of end systems within the same collision domain. Where a hub works only at the physical layer, a switch uses information about source and destination addresses carried in layer two frames to establish a temporary circuit between two nodes. Unlike a hub, each switch port is a separate collision domain. By eliminating the effect of contention, switches allow for full-duplex transmissions, where a node can transmit and receive simultaneously, and each node can use the full 100 Mbps bandwidth of the cable link to the switch port.

To support compatibility with hosts still equipped with 10 Mbps Ethernet interfaces, Fast Ethernet introduced an autonegotiation protocol to allow a host to choose the highest supported connection parameters (10 or 100 Mbps and half or full duplex). 10BASE-T Ethernet specifies that a node should transmit regular electrical pulses when it is not transmitting data to confirm the viability of the link. Fast Ethernet codes a 16-bit data packet into this signal advertising its service capabilities. This is called a Fast Link Pulse. A node that does not support autonegotiation can be detected by one that does and sent ordinary link integrity test signals, or Normal Link Pulses.

Fast Ethernet would not be deployed on new networks, but you may need to maintain it in legacy installations.

Gigabit Ethernet Standards

Gigabit Ethernet builds on the standards defined for Ethernet and Fast Ethernet to implement rates of 1000 Mbps (1 Gbps). Over copper wire, Gigabit Ethernet is specified as 1000BASE-T, working over Cat 5e or better. Gigabit Ethernet does not support hubs; it is implemented only using switches. The maximum distance of 100 m (328 feet) applies to cabling between the node and a switch port, or between two switch ports.

Gigabit Ethernet is the mainstream choice for new installations of access networks; that is, cabling to connect client workstations to a local network. The main decision would be whether to use copper or fiber optic cable. Fiber gives give better upgrade potential in the future, while copper cable is cheaper to install and far more hosts are installed with network cards that support copper than support fiber.

10 Gigabit Ethernet (10 GbE) multiplies the nominal speed of Gigabit Ethernet by a factor of 10. Because of the higher frequencies required, 10 GbE can only run at reduced distances over unshielded twisted pair. Longer runs require higher categories of cable with some type of shielding. There are also specifications for 40 Gbps operation:

Specification	Cable	Maximum Distance
10GBASE-T	UTP (Cat 6)	55 m (180 feet)
	F/UTP (Cat 6A)	100 m (328 feet)
	S/FTP (Cat 7)	100 m (328 feet)
40GBASE-T	S/FTP (Cat 8)	30 m (100 feet)

10/40 GbE Ethernet is not deployed in many access networks, as the cost 10/40 GbE compatible network adapters and switch transceiver modules is high. It might be used where a company's business requires very high bandwidth data transfers, such as TV and film production.

Review Activity:

Ethernet Standards

Answer the following questions:

1. With CSMA/CD, what will happen if a host has data to transmit and there is already data on the cable?

2. Which Ethernet standard works at 100 Mbps over Cat 5 or better copper cable?

3. Which copper Ethernet standard meets the bandwidth requirements for clients in an office network while minimizing costs?

4. A network designer wants to run a 10 gigabit backbone between two switches in buildings that are 75 m (246 feet) apart. What is the main consideration when selecting an appropriate copper cable?

Topic 2B

Summarize Copper Cabling Types

 EXAM OBJECTIVES COVERED
1.3 Summarize the types of cables and connectors and explain which is the appropriate type for a solution.

Copper wire twisted pair cabling is the most popular choice for access networks in offices. You are likely to work with this network media daily as part of your duties as a network professional. Understanding the characteristics of twisted pair will enable you to properly install and service your networks.

Unshielded Twisted Pair Cable Considerations

Twisted pair is a type of copper cable that has been extensively used for telephone systems and data networks. One pair of insulated wires twisted together forms a balanced pair. The pair carry the same signal but with different polarity; one wire is positive, and the other is negative. This allows the receiver to distinguish the signal from any noise more strongly. The cable is completed with an insulating outer jacket.

Twisted pair cable—Each color-coded pair is twisted at a different rate to reduce interference.
(Image by Thuansak Srilao © 123RF.com.)

The pairs are twisted at different rates to reduce external interference and crosstalk. Crosstalk is a phenomenon whereby one pair causes interference in another as a result of their proximity.

Twisted pair can use either solid or stranded conductor wires. Solid cabling uses a single thick wire per conductor and is used for cables that run behind walls or through ducts. Stranded cabling uses thin filament wires wrapped around one another and is used to make flexible patch cords for connecting computers to wall ports and switch ports to patch panel ports. Copper wire thickness is measured using American Wire Gauge (AWG). Increasing AWG numbers represent thinner wire.

Solid cable uses thicker 22 to 24 AWG, while the stranded cable used for patch cords is often 26 AWG. The attenuation of stranded wire is higher than solid wire, so it cannot be used over extended distances.

Most twisted pair cable used in office networks is **unshielded twisted pair (UTP)**. Modern buildings are often flood-wired using UTP cabling. This involves cables being laid to every location in the building that may need to support a telephone or computer.

Shielded and Screened Twisted Pair Cable Considerations

Shielded cable is less susceptible to interference and crosstalk. This type of cable is required for some Ethernet standards and may also be a requirement in environments with high levels of interference.

Shielded cable can be referred to generically as **shielded twisted pair (STP)**, but there are actually several types of shielding:

- Screened cable has one thin outer foil shield around all pairs. Screened cable is usually designated as screened twisted pair (ScTP) or foiled/unshielded twisted pair (F/UTP), or sometimes just foiled twisted pair (FTP).

- Fully shielded cabling has a braided outer screen and foil-shielded pairs and is referred to as shielded/foiled twisted pair (S/FTP). There are also variants with a foil outer shield (F/FTP).

Legacy STP cable could be complex to install, as it required bonding each element to ground manually, but modern F/UTP and S/FTP solutions (using appropriate cable, connectors, and patch panels) reduce this complexity by incorporating bonding within the design of each element.

 Using screened or shielded cable means that you must also use screened/shielded connectors. Screened/shielded cable elements should not be mixed with unscreened/unshielded elements.

Cat Cable Standards

The American National Standards Institute (ANSI) and the Telecommunications Industry Association (TIA)/Electronic Industries Alliance (EIA) have created **categories of cable standards** for twisted pair to simplify selection of a suitable quality cable. These categories, along with other aspects of telecommunications wiring best practices, are defined in the ANSI/TIA/EIA 568 Commercial Building Telecommunications Cabling Standards (tiaonline.org/standard/tia-568). Similar standards are also maintained by the ISO (ISO/IEC 11801), which refers to categories of components and classes of permanent links (incorporating both cable and termination).

Cat/Class	Cable Type	Network Application	Max. Distance	Frequency	Connector
3	UTP	10BASE-T	100 m (328 ft)	16 MHz	RJ-45
5	UTP	100BASE-TX	100 m (328 ft)	100 MHz	RJ-45
5e (Class D)	UTP or F/UTP	1000BASE-T	100 m (328 ft)	100 MHz	RJ-45
6 (Class E)	UTP, F/UTP, or U/FTP	1000BASE-T	100 m (328 ft)	250 MHz	RJ-45
		10GBASE-T	55 m (180 ft)		
6a (Class Ea)	UTP, F/UTP, U/FTP, or S/FTP	10GBASE-T	100 m (328 ft)	500 MHz	RJ-45
7 (Class F)	S/FTP or F/FTP	10GBASE-Tv	100 m (328 ft)	600 MHz	GG45/ TERA
8/8.1 (Class I)	U/FTP or F/UTP	40GBASE-T	30 m (100 ft)	2000 MHz	RJ-45
8.2 (Class II)	F/FTP or S/FTP	40GBASE-T	30 m (100 ft)	2000 MHz	GG45/ TERA

For 1000BASE-T, Cat 5 is also acceptable (if properly installed), but Cat 5 cable is no longer available commercially. Unlike Ethernet and Fast Ethernet, Gigabit Ethernet uses all four pairs for transmission and is thus more sensitive to crosstalk between the wire pairs.

Here are some details about the categories used for network media:

- Cat 5 cable is no longer available. Cat 5e is tested at frequencies up to 100 MHz (like Cat 5 was) but to higher overall specifications for attenuation and crosstalk, meaning that the cable is rated to handle Gigabit Ethernet throughput. Cat 5e would still be an acceptable choice for providing network links for workstations.

- Cat 6 can support 10 Gbps but over shorter distances—nominally 55 m, but often less if cables are closely bundled together.

- Cat 6A is an improved specification cable that can support 10 Gbps over 100 m. Cat 6A cable is bulkier than Cat 5e, and the installation requirements more stringent, so fitting it within pathways designed for older cable can be problematic. TIA/EIA standards recommend Cat 6A is recommended for use in health care facilities, with Power over Ethernet (PoE) 802.3bt installations, and for horizontal connections to wireless access points.

- Cat 7 cable is always of a screened/shielded type and is rated for 10GbE applications up to 100 m (328 feet). Cat 7 is not recognized by TIA/EIA but appears in the cabling standards created by the ISO (ISO/IEC 11801). It must be terminated with GG45 or TERA connectors rather than standard RJ-45 connectors.

Cabling is not the only part of the wiring system that must be rated to the appropriate category. For faster network applications (Gigabit Ethernet and better), the performance of connectors becomes increasingly critical. For example, if you are installing Cat 6A wiring, you must also install Cat 6A patch panels, wall plates, and connectors.

- Cat 8 is intended for use in datacenters only for short patch cable runs that make top-of-rack connections between adjacent appliances. ISO define two variants; 8.1 (Class I) is equivalent to TIA/EAI Cat 8 and uses RJ-45 connectors while 8.2 (Class II) must use outer shielding or screening and GG-45 or TERA connectors.

Twisted Pair Connector Types

Twisted pair copper cabling uses **Registered Jack (RJ)** connectors for the physical interface. There are many different types of RJ connector, identified by numbers (and sometimes letters). Some are physically different, while others are identical but wired differently for different applications.

RJ-45 Connectors

RJ-45 connectors are used with 4-pair (8-wire) cables. The connectors are also referred to as 8P8C, standing for 8-position/8-contact. This means that all eight "potential" wire positions are supplied with contacts, so that they can all carry signals if needed. RJ-45 is used for Ethernet twisted pair cabling.

RJ-45 jack and plug. (Image © 123RF.com.)

 RJ-45 plugs have a plastic retaining clip. This is normally protected by a rubber boot. This type of cable construction is also referred to as snagless.

RJ-11 Connectors

The smaller RJ-11 connectors are used with 2- or 3-pair UTP. There is room for six wires, but the four center wires are most commonly used. Typically, the innermost pair, wired to pins 3 and 4, carries the dial tone and voice circuit. These are also called the Tip and Ring wires after the way older phone plugs were wired. The other pair is usually unused but can be deployed for a secondary circuit. RJ-11 connectors are used for telephone systems—for example, to connect a modem to a phone jack.

RJ-11 jack and plug. (Image © 123RF.com.)

An RJ-11 connector has only two contacts (6P2C). To use more pairs, the jack can be wired as RJ-14 (6P4C) or RJ-25 (6P6C).

Copper Termination Standards

Each conductor in a 4-pair data cable is color-coded. Each pair is assigned a color (Blue, Orange, Green, or Brown). The first conductor in each pair has a predominantly white insulator with strips of the color; the second conductor has an insulator with the solid color. The ANSI/TIA/EIA 568 standard defines two methods for terminating Ethernet connectors: **T568A and T568B**. The wiring for both standards is shown in the following figure.

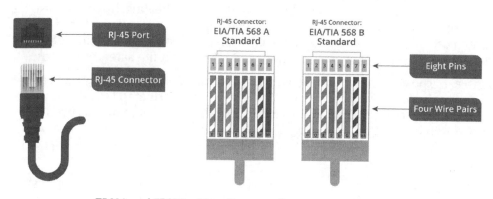

T568A and T568B wiring diagrams. (Images © 123RF.com.)

In T568A, the green pairs are wired to pins 1 and 2 and the orange pairs are wired to pins 3 and 6. In T568A, these pairs swap places, so orange is terminated to pins 1 and 2 and green to 3 and 6. Organizations should try to avoid using a mixture of the two standards. T568A is mandated by the US government and by the residential cabling standard (TIA 570), but T568B is probably the more widely deployed of the two.

Pin	Wire Color (T568A)	Wire Color (T568B)	10/100 Mbps	1/10/40 Gbps
1	Green/White	Orange/White	Tx+	BixA+
2	Green	Orange	Tx-	BixA-
3	Orange/White	Green/White	Rx+	BixB+
4	Blue	Blue		BixB-
5	Blue/White	Blue/White		BixC+
6	Orange	Green	Rx-	BixC-
7	Brown/White	Brown/White		BixD+
8	Brown	Brown		BixD-

 Cat 7 and Cat 8 are so sensitive to noise that the secondary wire in each pair is solid white with no stripe, as the coloring process reduces the effectiveness of the insulation.

Plenum- and Riser-rated Cable

Basic cable consideration decisions include the category, unshielded versus shielded, and the appropriate use of solid versus stranded cable. Another consideration is how cable installation must conform to any national or local building regulations.

A **plenum** space is a void in a building designed to carry heating, ventilation, and air conditioning (HVAC) systems. Plenum space is typically a false ceiling, though it could also be constructed as a raised floor. As it makes installation simpler, this space has also been used for communications wiring in some building designs. Plenum space is an effective conduit for fire, as there is plenty of airflow and no fire breaks (such as walls or doors). If the plenum space is used for heating, there may also be higher temperatures. Therefore, building regulations require the use of fire-retardant plenum cable in such spaces. Plenum cable must not emit large amounts of smoke when burned, be self-extinguishing, and meet other strict fire safety standards.

General purpose (nonplenum) cabling uses PVC (polyvinyl chloride) jackets and insulation. Plenum-rated cable uses treated PVC or Fluorinated Ethylene Polymer (FEP). This can make the cable less flexible, but the different materials used have no effect on bandwidth. Data cable that is plenum-rated under the US National Electrical Code (NEC) is marked CMP/MMP. General purpose cables are marked CMG/MMG or CM/MP.

Cabling that passes between two floors is referred to as riser. Conduit for riser cabling must be fire-stopped. This means that fire cannot spread through the opening created by the conduit. Riser cabling (in conduit or in spaces such as lift shafts) should also conform to the appropriate fire safety standards. These are similar to the requirements for plenum spaces but not quite as strict. Data cable that is riser-rated under the NEC is marked CMR/MPR.

Coaxial and Twinaxial Cable and Connectors

Coaxial (or coax) cable is made of two conductors that share the same axis, hence the name ("co" and "ax"). The core conductor of the cable is made of copper wire (solid or stranded) and is enclosed by plastic insulation (dielectric). A wire mesh (the second conductor), which serves both as shielding from EMI and as a ground, surrounds the insulating material. A tough plastic sheath protects the cable.

Coax cable. (Image by destinacigdem © 123RF.com.)

Coax cables are categorized using the Radio Grade (RG) standard, which represents the thickness of the core conductor and the cable's characteristic impedance. RG-6 is 18 AWG cable with 75 ohm impedance typically used as drop cable for Cable Access TV (CATV) and broadband cable modems. For this application, coax is usually terminated using **F-type connectors**, which are secured by screwing into place.

F-type connector. (Image created by Colin and reproduced under the Creative Commons Attribution ShareAlike 3.0 license.)

Twinaxial (or twinax) is similar to coax but contains two inner conductors. Twinax is used for datacenter 10 GbE (unofficially referred to as 10GBASE-CR) and 40 GbE (40GBASE-CR4) interconnects of up to about 5 meters for passive cable types and 10 meters for active cable types. Twinax for 10/40 GbE is terminated using SFP+ Direct Attach Copper (DAC) and QSFP+ DAC transceivers.

Direct Attach Copper (DAC) twinax cabling with SFP+ termination. (Image created by Labsy and reproduced under the Creative Commons Attribution ShareAlike 4.0 license.)

Review Activity:

Copper Cabling Types

Answer the following questions:

1. **What is the measurement standard for wire thickness?**

2. **What are the characteristics of S/FTP cable?**

3. **Which categories of U/UTP cable are certified to carry data transmission faster than 100 Mbps?**

4. **True or False? Cat standards apply only to wiring.**

5. **100BASE-T transmit pins are 1 and 2. What color code are the wires terminated to these pins under T568A and T568B?**

6. **Why is plenum-rated cable used when cable is run in an area where building air is circulated?**

7. **Which cable type consists of a single core made of solid copper surrounded by insulation, a braided metal shielding, and an outer cover?**

Topic 2C

Summarize Fiber Optic Cabling Types

 EXAM OBJECTIVES COVERED
1.3 Summarize the types of cables and connectors and explain which is the appropriate type for a solution.

Fiber optic media can support higher bandwidths over longer distances than copper wire. These advantages make it a popular choice for long-distance telecommunications networks and for reliable, high-speed networking within datacenters. Understanding the characteristics of fiber optic media will help you to support existing installations and upgrades.

Fiber Optic Cable Considerations

The electrical signals carried over copper wire are subject to interference and attenuation. Fiber optic signaling uses pulses of infrared light, which are not susceptible to interference, cannot easily be intercepted, and suffer less from attenuation. Consequently, fiber optic cabling supports higher bandwidth over longer cable runs (that can be measured in kilometers, rather than meters).

A single optical fiber is constructed from three elements:

- Core provides the transmission path for the light signals (waveguide).

- Cladding reflects signals back into the waveguide as efficiently as possible so that the light signal travels along the waveguide by multiple internal reflections. The core and cladding can be made from glass or plastic. The cladding is applied as a thin layer surrounding the core. While made of the same material, the cladding has a different refractive index to the core. The effect of this is to create a boundary that causes the light to bounce back into the core, facilitating the process of total internal reflection that guides the light signal through the core.

- Buffer is a protective plastic coating. It may be of a tight or loose configuration, with the loose format using some form of lubricant between the strand and the sheath.

In basic operation modes, each fiber optic strand can only transfer light in a single direction at a time. Therefore, multiple fibers are often bundled within a cable to allow simultaneous transmission and reception of signals or to provide links for multiple applications.

There are many different outer jacket designs and materials suited for different installations (indoor/plenum, outdoor, underground, undersea, and so on). Kevlar (Aramid) strands and sometimes fiberglass rods (strength members) are often used to protect the fibers from excessive bending or kinking when "pulling" the cable to install it. For exposed outdoor applications, a steel shield (armor) may be added to deter rodents from gnawing the cable.

Single Mode Fiber and Multimode Fiber

Fiber optic cables are specified using the mode, composition (glass/plastic), and core/cladding size; for example, 8.3 micron core/125 microcladding single mode glass or 62.5 micron core/125 microcladding multimode plastic. Fiber optic cables fall into two broad categories: single mode and multimode.

- **Single Mode Fiber (SMF)** has a small core (8 to 10 microns) and a long wavelength, near infrared (1310 nm or 1550 nm) light signal, generated by a laser. Single mode cables support data rates up to 100 Gbps and cable runs of many kilometers, depending on the quality of the cable and optics. There are two grades of SMF cable; OS1 is designed for indoor use, while OS2 is for outdoor deployment.

- **Multimode Fiber (MMF)** has a larger core (62.5 or 50 microns) and shorter wavelength light (850 nm or 1300 nm) transmitted in multiple waves of varying length. MMF uses less expensive optics and consequently is less expensive to deploy than SMF. However, it does not support such high signaling speeds or long distances as single mode and so is more suitable for LANs than WANs.

Optical transceivers for SMF are now only slightly more expensive than ones for MMF. Consequently, SMF is often used for short range applications in datacenters, as well as for long distance links. SMF still comes at a slight price premium, but it provides better support for 40 Gbps and 100 Gbps Ethernet standards.

MMF is graded by **Optical Multimode (OM)** categories, defined in the ISO/IEC 11801 standard:

- **OM1/OM2**—62.5-micron cable is OM1, while early 50-micron cable is OM2. OM1 and OM2 are mainly rated for applications up to 1 Gbps and use LED transmitters.

- **OM3/OM4**—these are also 50-micron cable, but manufactured differently, designed for use with 850 nm Vertical-Cavity Surface-Emitting Lasers (VCSEL), also referred to as laser optimized MMF (LOMMF). A VCSEL is not as powerful as the solid-state lasers used for SMF, but it supports higher modulation (transmitting light pulses rapidly) than LED-based optics.

Fiber Optic Connector Types

Fiber optic connectors are available in many different form factors. Some types are more popular for multimode and some for single mode.

Straight Tip

Straight Tip (ST) is an early bayonet-style connector that uses a push-and-twist locking mechanism. ST was used mostly for multimode networks, but it is not widely used for Ethernet installations anymore.

Two ST connectors. (Image by Aleh Datskevich © 123RF.com.)

Subscriber Connector

The **Subscriber Connector (SC)** is a push/pull design, allowing for simple insertion and removal. It can be used for single- or multimode. It is commonly used for Gigabit Ethernet.

Local Connector

The **Local Connector (LC)** is a small-form-factor connector with a tabbed push/pull design. LC is similar to SC, but the smaller size allows for higher port density. LC is a widely adopted form factor for Gigabit Ethernet and 10/40 GbE.

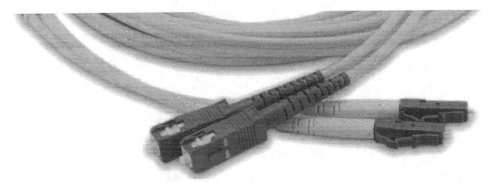

Patch cord with duplex SC format connectors (left) and LC connectors (right). (Image by YANAWUT SUNTORNKIJ © 123RF.com.)

Mechanical Transfer Registered Jack

Mechanical Transfer Registered Jack (MTRJ) is a small-form-factor duplex connector with a snap-in design used for multimode networks.

MTRJ connector. (Image by Aleh Datskevich © 123RF.com.)

Fiber Ethernet Standards

Ethernet standards over fiber set out the use of different types of cable for 100 Mbps, 1 Gbps, and 10 Gbps operation. There are variants for long wavelength optics, required for long distance transmission, and short wavelength optics.

Specification	Optics	Cable	Maximum Distance	Connectors
100BASE-FX	1300 nm	MMF (OM1) MMF (OM2)	2 km (1.2 miles)	ST, SC, MT-RJ
100BASE-SX	850 nm	MMF (OM1) MMF (OM2)	550 m (1804 feet)	ST, SC, LC
1000BASE-SX	850 nm	MMF (OM1)	275 m (902 feet)	ST, SC, LC, MT-RJ
		MMF (OM2) MMF (OM3)	550 m (1804 feet)	
1000BASE-LX	1300 nm 1310 nm	MMF (OM1/ OM2/OM3) SMF (OS1/OS2)	550 m (1804 feet) 5 km (3.1 miles)	SC, LC
10GBASE-SR	850 nm	MMF (OM1)	33 m (108 feet)	SC, LC
		MMF (OM2)	82 m (269 feet)	
		MMF (OM3)	300 m (984 feet)	
		MMF (OM4)	400 m (1312 feet)	
10GBASE-LR	1310 nm	SMF (OS1/OS2)	10 km (6.2 miles)	SC, LC

Fiber is often used for backbone cabling in office networks and for workstations with high bandwidth requirements, such as video editing. The principal applications of 10 GbE (and better) are:

- Increasing bandwidth for server interconnections and network backbones, especially in datacenters and for storage area networks (SAN).

- Replacing existing switched public data networks based on proprietary technologies with simpler Ethernet switches (Metro Ethernet).

Fiber Optic Cable Installation

Fiber optic can be installed in the same topology as copper cable using distribution frames and switches. Long distance cables are typically laid as trunks or rings with repeaters or amplifiers between cable segments to strengthen the signal.

Normally, strands are installed in pairs (duplex) at each device, with one strand for transmit (Tx) and one strand for receive (Rx).

Fiber Optic Patch Cords

Patch cables for fiber optic can come with the same connector on each end (LC-LC, for instance) or a mix of connectors (LC-SC, for instance). Duplex patch cords must maintain the correct polarity, so that the Tx port on the transmitter is linked to the Rx port on the receiver and vice versa. The TIA/EIA cabling standard sets out A to B patch cord to port orientations. Each element in the link must perform a crossover, and there must be an odd number of elements, such as two patch cords and a permanent link (three elements).

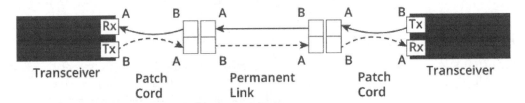

Fiber patch cord polarity.

Most connectors are keyed to prevent incorrect insertion, but if in doubt, an optical power meter can be used to determine whether an optical signal is being received from a particular fiber.

 Transmitted optical signals are visible as bright white spots when viewed through a smartphone camera. This can be used to identify which adapter on an optical interface is transmitting and which fiber patch cord is receiving a signal from the other end of the cable.

Finishing Type

The core of a fiber optic connector is a ceramic or plastic ferrule that holds the glass strand and ensures continuous reception of the light signals. The tip of the ferrule can be finished in one of three formats:

- **Physical Contact (PC)**—The faces of the connector and fiber tip are polished so that they curve slightly and fit together better, reducing return loss (interference caused by light reflecting back down the fiber).

- **Ultra Physical Contact (UPC)**—This means the cable and connector are polished to a higher standard than with PC.

- **Angled Physical Contact (APC)**—The faces are angled for an even tighter connection and better return loss performance. APC cannot be mixed with PC or UPC. These connectors are usually deployed when the fiber is being used to carry analog signaling, as in Cable Access TV (CATV) networks. They are also increasingly used for long distance transmissions and for Passive Optical Networks (PON), such as those used to implement Fiber to the x (FTTx) multiple subscriber networks.

It is important to match the finishing type when you are selecting a connector type. APC finishing is often not supported by the patch panels, transceivers, and switch ports designed for Ethernet.

Where there are multiple strands within a single cable, the strands are color-coded (TIA/EIA 598) to differentiate them. Also, by convention, cable jackets and connectors use the following color-coding:

Type	Jacket Color	Connector Color
OM1	Orange	Beige
OM2	Orange	Black
OM3/OM4	Aqua	Aqua
SMF PC/UPC	Yellow	Blue
SMF APC	Yellow	Green

Review Activity:

Fiber Optic Cabling Types

Answer the following questions:

1. **What type of fiber optic cable is suited for long distance links?**

2. **Which grade or grades of fiber have a 62.5 micron core?**

3. **Which fiber Ethernet standard is best suited to implementing backbone cabling that does not exceed 200 m (656 feet) and can achieve at least 4 Gbps throughput?**

4. **What maximum distance is defined in standards documentation for 1000BASE-LX running over MMF?**

5. **You need to provision a fiber patch panel to terminate incoming cabling with green LC connectors. What type of ports should be provisioned on the patch panel?**

Topic 2D

Deploy Ethernet Cabling

EXAM OBJECTIVES COVERED
1.3 Summarize the types of cables and connectors and explain which is the appropriate type for a solution.
5.2 Given a scenario, troubleshoot common cable connectivity issues and select the appropriate tools.

The networking industry has developed a standard model for deploying a structured cabling system. The model is adaptable to both small and large networks. In this topic, you will learn how a distribution system can provision network access throughout a building or site.

Structured Cabling System

Cabled networking for client access in an office building will use a structured cabling scheme, such as that set out in the ANSI/TIA/EIA 568 Commercial Building Telecommunications Wiring Standard. ANSI/TIA/EIA 568 identifies the following subsystems within a structured cabling system:

- **Work Area**—The space where user equipment is located and connected to the network, usually via a wall port.

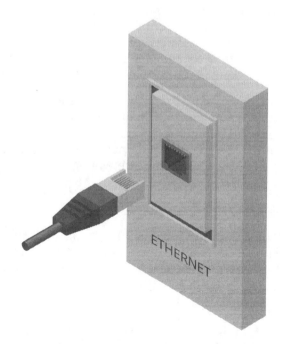

Modular wall plate. (Image by Nikolai Lebedev © 123RF.com.)

- **Horizontal Cabling**—Connects user work areas to the nearest horizontal cross-connect. A cross-connect can also be referred to as a distribution frame.

Horizontal cabling is so-called because it typically consists of the cabling for a single floor and so is made up of cables run horizontally through wall ducts or ceiling spaces.

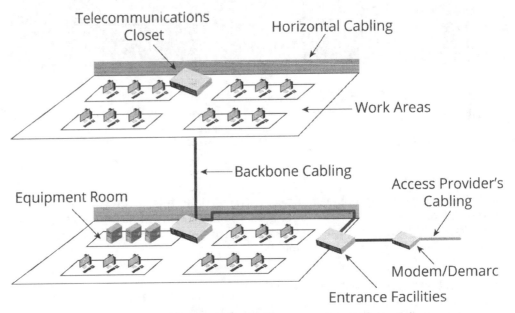

Wiring distribution components. (Images © 123RF.com.)

- **Backbone Cabling**—Connects horizontal cross-connects (HCCs) to the main cross-connect (optionally via intermediate cross-connects). These can also be described as vertical cross-connects, because backbone cabling is more likely to run up and down between floors.

- **Telecommunications Room**—Houses horizontal cross-connects. Essentially, this is a termination point for the horizontal cabling along with a connection to backbone cabling. An equipment room is similar to a telecommunications room but contains the main or intermediate cross-connects. Equipment rooms are also likely to house "complex" equipment, such as switches, routers, and modems.

- **Entrance Facilities/Demarc**—Special types of equipment rooms marking the point at which external cabling (outside plant) is joined to internal (premises) cabling. These are required to join the access provider's network and for inter-building communications. The demarcation point is where the access provider's network terminates and the organization's network begins.

Cable Management

Cable management techniques and tools ensure that cabling is reliable and easy to maintain. Copper wiring is terminated using a distribution frame or **punchdown block**. A punchdown block comprises a large number of **insulation-displacement connection (IDC)** terminals. The IDC contains contacts that cut the insulation from a wire and hold it in place. This design allows large numbers of cables to be terminated within a small space. Several different punchdown block and IDC formats have been used for telecommunications and data cabling.

66 Block

A 66 block is an older-style distribution frame used to terminate telephone cabling and legacy data applications (pre-Cat 5). A 66 block comprises 50 rows of 4 IDC terminals. The 25-pair cable from the access provider is terminated on one side of the block. On the other side of the block, the terminals terminate the wiring from the PBX. A jumper (bridging clip) is installed over the middle two terminals to complete the connection.

A private branch exchange (PBX) is a telephone system serving the local extensions of an office.

110 Block

The 110 block (developed by AT&T) is a type of distribution frame supporting 100 MHz operation (Cat 5) and better. A 110 wiring block is arranged horizontally rather than vertically, offering better density than a 66 block. There is also more space for labeling the connectors and each column of connectors is color-coded, making management simpler. The incoming wire pairs are fed into channels on the wiring block, then a connector block or wafer is installed to terminate the incoming wiring. Outgoing wire pairs are then punched into the terminals on the connector blocks to complete the circuit.

BIX and Krone Distribution Frames

Where a 110 block uses a two-piece design where wafer blocks are installed over the main block, competing formats BIX and Krone use a single module. 110 blocks and BIX blocks (developed by Nortel) are common in North America, while some European vendors often prefer Krone. As well as the differences in block design, the IDCs are angled differently in each format, requiring a different termination blade to be used to ensure a reliable connection.

Patch Panel/Patch Bay

In data networks, numerous moves, adds, and changes (MACs) would require reterminating the wiring. To simplify MACs, a **patch panel** or patch bay is a type of distribution block with IDCs on one side and pre-terminated RJ-45 modular ports on the other. This allows incoming and outgoing connections to be reconfigured by changing the patch cable connections, which is much simpler than reterminating punchdown blocks.

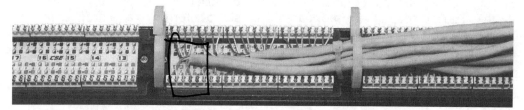

IDCs at the rear of a patch panel. (Image by plus69 © 123RF.com.)

The structured cabling (running from the work area or forming a backbone) is terminated at the back of the patch panel on the IDCs. An RJ-45 patch cord is used to connect the port to another network port, typically a switch port housed in the same rack. This greatly simplifies wiring connections and is the most commonly installed type of wiring distribution where connections need to be changed often.

Patch panel with prewired RJ-45 ports. (Image by Svetlana Kurochkina © 123RF.com.)

Wiring Tools and Techniques

Installing fixed cable from a bulk spool is referred to as pulling cable because the cable must be pulled, carefully, from the telecommunications closet to the work area. Cable is normally routed through conduits or wall spaces, avoiding excessive bends and proximity to electrical power cables and fittings, such as fluorescent lights, as these could cause interference. The main fixed cable run can be up to 90 m (295 feet). Stranded-wire patch cords (between the PC and wall port) and jumpers (a stranded-wire cable without connectors used on cross-connects) can be up to 5 m each (16 feet) and no more than 10 m (33 feet) in overall length. This is because the attenuation of stranded cable is higher than solid cable.

Starting at the patch panel, label the end of the cable with the appropriate jack ID, then run it through to the work area. This is also referred to as a drop, as in most cases you will be dropping the cable from the ceiling space through a wall cavity. If several cables are going to roughly the same place, you can bundle them and pull them together. Leave enough slack at both ends (a service loop) to make the connection and to accommodate future reconnections or changes, cut the cable, and label the other end with the appropriate ID. Electrician's scissors (**snips**) are designed for cutting copper wire and stripping insulation and cable jackets. Alternatively, there are dedicated **cable stripper** tools that have replaceable blades for different data cable types. Cable cutting blades should be rounded to preserve the wire geometry. Stripping tools should have the correct diameter to score a cable jacket without damaging the insulation wires. Heavy duty cutters are required for armored cable.

Termination Tools

Fixed cable is terminated using a **punchdown tool**. This tool fixes conductors into an IDC. There are different IDC formats (66, 110, BIX, and Krone), and these require different blades. Many punchdown tools have replaceable blades, though. Blades are double-sided; one side pushes the wire into the terminal while the other side cuts the excess. Make sure the blade marked "cut" is oriented correctly to cut the excess wire.

Alternatively, a block tool terminates a group of connectors in one action. For a 110 format panel, there are four position blocks (suitable for terminating 4-pair data cabling) and five position blocks (for 25-pair telephony cable).

A patch cord is created using a **cable crimper**. This tool fixes a plug to a cable. The tools are specific to the type of connector and cable, though some may have modular dies to support a range of RJ-type plugs.

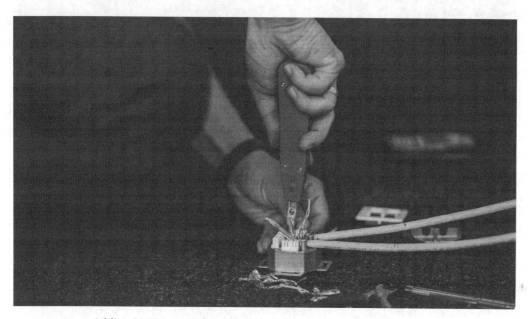

Adding RJ-45 terminals to a network cable using a punchdown tool.
(Image by dero2084 © 123RF.com.)

 You must untwist the ends of the wire pairs and place them into the connector die in the correct order for the wiring configuration (T568A or T568B) you want to use. You must not untwist the wires too much, however. Cat 6 is demanding in this respect and requires no more than 0.375" (1 cm) of untwisting.

For shielded and screened cable, termination must be made to shielded IDCs or modular plugs. On an IDC, a metal clip placed over the exposed foil or braided shield bonds the cable to the housing. A shielded modular plug has a metal housing and is not terminated using a standard crimper. There are several different designs, but all follow the principle of connecting the cable shield to a bonding strip.

Fiber Distribution Panels and Fusion Splicing

A modern build or refurbishment might replace copper wiring with fiber optic cabling. The structured links are installed in a similar way to copper cabling, however, because continually reconnecting fiber optic cables risks wear and tear damage, and you do not want to have to replace cable runs through conduit. Permanent cables are run through conduit to wall ports at the client access end and a **fiber distribution panel** at the switch end. Fiber patch cables are used to complete the link from the wall port to the NIC and from the patch panel to the switch port.

Fiber distribution panel. (Image by Aleh Datskevich © 123RF.com.)

Using connectors does reduce the overall performance of the cable. Each connector will "cost" a certain amount of insertion loss (typically budgeted as 0.5 dB) and reflection loss. Consequently, in some circumstances it may be preferable to splice two cables together, either to repair damage or to extend the cable run. Cables can be spliced mechanically using an adhesive junction box containing index matching fluid that ensures a continuous path between the two fiber strands. A **fusion splicer** achieves a more permanent join with lower insertion loss (>=0.1 dB). The fusion splicing machine performs a precise alignment between the two strands and then permanently joins them together using an arc weld. A fusion splicer is a high-precision instrument and must be kept clean and maintained following the manufacturer's guidelines.

Splicing may also be used to attach a pigtail (a segment of cable with a factory-fitted connector at one end only) or to field terminate to a connector (splicing a factory-prepared SC or LC connector to an incoming cable). A spliced cable or pigtail must be protected with a special cover and supported by a splice tray. Connectors for field terminated splicing do not require a tray and the protective cover is built into the connector.

Transceivers

A network might involve the use of multiple types of cabling. When this occurs, switch and router equipment must be able to terminate different cable and connector types, and devices must convert from one media type to another. Enterprise switches and routers are available with modular, hot-swappable **transceivers/media converters** for different types of fiber optic patch cord connections.

There are also transceiver modules for copper wire cabling.

Historically, transceiver modules were based on the Gigabit Interface Converter (GBIC) form factor, which used SC ports and was designed (as the name suggests) for Gigabit Ethernet. GBIC was very bulky and has largely been replaced by **Small Form Factor Pluggable (SFP)**, also known as mini-GBIC.

SFP/SFP+

SFP uses LC connectors and is also designed for Gigabit Ethernet. Enhanced SFP (SFP+) is an updated specification to support 10 GbE but still uses the LC form factor. There are different modules to support the various Ethernet standards and fiber mode type (10GBASE-SR versus 10GBASE-LR, for instance). Consequently, a transceiver is designed to support a specific wavelength. The transceivers must be installed as matched pairs.

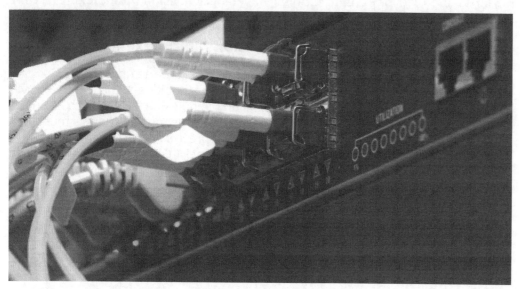

Switch with hot-pluggable SFP fiber transceivers. (Image by Zdenek Maly © 123RF.com.)

 You will often see the term MSA in conjunction with modular transceivers. Multi-Source Agreement (MSA) is intended to ensure that a transceiver from one vendor is compatible with the switch/router module of another vendor.

QSFP/QSFP+

Quad small form-factor pluggable (QSFP) is a transceiver form factor that supports 4 x 1 Gbps links, typically aggregated to a single 4 Gbps channel. Enhanced quad small form-factor pluggable (QSFP+) is designed to support 40 GbE by provisioning 4 x 10 Gbps links. QSFP+ is typically used with parallel fiber and multi-fiber push-on (MPO) termination. An MPO backbone ribbon cable bundles 12 or more strands with a single compact terminator (the cables are all manufactured and cannot be field terminated). When used with QSFP+, four strands transmit a full-duplex 40 Gbps link, four strands receive, and the other four strands are unused.

QSFP+ can also be used with Wavelength Division Multiplexing (WDM) Ethernet standards.

Wavelength Division Multiplexing

Ordinary (or "grey") SFP/SFP+ are duplex interfaces with one transmit port and one receive port that require two fiber strands. Each strand is a single channel. Wavelength Division Multiplexing (WDM) is a means of using a strand to transmit and/or receive more than one channel at a time.

BiDirectional Wavelength Division Multiplexing

Bidirectional (BiDi) transceivers support transmit and receive signals over the same strand of fiber. This uses WDM to transmit the Tx and Rx signals over slightly shifted wavelengths, such as 1310 nm for Tx and 1490 nm for Rx. BiDi transceivers must be installed in opposite pairs, so the downstream transceiver would have to use 1490 nm for Tx and 1310 for Rx. **Bidirectional wavelength division multiplexing (WDM)** links are documented in Ethernet standards (1000BASE-BX and 10GBASE-BX).

Coarse and Dense Wavelength Division Multiplexing

Coarse Wavelength Division Multiplexing (CWDM) supports up to 16 wavelengths and is typically used to deploy four or eight bidirectional channels over a single fiber strand. Dense Wavelength Division Multiplexing (DWDM) provisions greater numbers of channels (20, 40, 80, or 160). This means that there is much less spacing between each channel and requires more precise and expensive lasers. CWDM and DWDM transceivers support multi-channel 1 G, 10 G, and 40 G Ethernet links. As with BiDi, the transceivers must be installed in opposite pairs for each channel.

In a point-to-point WDM topology, each transceiver is cabled to a multiplexer/demultiplexer (mux/demux). The single fiber strand is run to a mux/demux at the other site. Alternatively, devices called optical add/drop multiplexers (OADM) can insert and remove signals for a particular wavelength channel on a ring topology.

Review Activity:

Ethernet Cabling

Answer the following questions:

1. **Which types of distribution frame are best suited to 100 MHz or better operation?**

2. **What type of distribution frame is best suited to cabling wall ports to Ethernet switches in way that best supports futures changes?**

3. **What tool is used to terminate wiring at a 110 block?**

4. **At what layer of the OSI model does a fiber distribution panel work?**

5. **You need to provision modular SFP+ transceivers to support a 10 gigabit link between two switches using an existing fiber cable. What two characteristics must you check when ordering the transceivers?**

6. **You have selected an SFP+ 1310 nm Tx and 1490 nm Rx transceiver to implement a BiDi link between two switches. Should you provision a second SFP+ 1310 nm Tx and 1490 nm Rx for the other switch?**

Lesson 2

Summary

You should be able to summarize the properties of copper and fiber optic media and connectors and match them to an appropriate Ethernet standard for a particular solution.

Guidelines for Deploying Ethernet Cabling

Consider these best practices and guidelines when you are installing Ethernet networks:

- Select an Ethernet standard, media type, connectors, and transceivers that meet the requirements for different types of network segment:

    - 1000BASE-T over Cat 5e or Cat 6 for client access/office networks or 10GBASE-T over Cat 6A or better for very high-bandwidth requirements.

    - 10GBASE-CR/40GBASE-CR4 twinax or 10GBASE-SR MMF for datacenter applications.

    - 1000BASE-SX or 10GBASE-SR over MMF for backbones.

    - 1000BASE-LX or 10GBASE-LR for site-to-site links.

    - Wave division multiplexing to get more bandwidth from existing fiber.

- Consider the factors that can affect the performance of network media, such as electromagnetic interference and attenuation and whether shielded copper or fiber optic cable will be required to ensure reliable performance.

- Follow the 568 Commercial Building Telecommunication Cabling Wiring Standard to apply a structured cabling design with patch panels to distribute cabling from communications closets to work areas. Use either T568A or T568B termination consistently.

- Use plenum cables in designated plenum spaces of a building to comply with fire codes and use PVC in non-plenum spaces.

- Use appropriate tools to prepare cable and terminate to either punchdown blocks or to connectors.

Lesson 3
Deploying Ethernet Switching

LESSON INTRODUCTION

Cabling establishes the links between nodes on the network, but each node also requires a network interface. Not many networks are established by directly connecting each end system to every other local system. Cabling and support costs are reduced by using intermediate systems to establish local networks. These intermediate systems are deployed as network appliances such as hubs, bridges, and switches. Installing and configuring, these devices will be a regular task for you during your career in network administration.

Lesson Objectives

In this lesson, you will:

- Deploy networking devices.

- Explain network interfaces.

- Deploy common Ethernet switching features.

Topic 3A

Deploy Networking Devices

 EXAM OBJECTIVES COVERED
2.1 Compare and contrast various devices, their features, and their appropriate placement on the network.

Most networks use intermediate systems to reduce cabling costs and complexity. In this topic, you will summarize the functions of various connectivity devices working at the physical and data link layers.

Repeaters and Media Converters

The attenuation of signals passing over copper or fiber cable imposes a distance limitation on links. A link where the cable length exceeds the distance limitation may not achieve the required speed or may be unreliable. A **repeater** overcomes the distance limitation by boosting the signal at some point along the cable run. A repeater works at the physical layer (Layer 1) of the OSI model and is transparent with regard to the rest of the network infrastructure (the link is treated as one length of cable). A repeater is always powered and represents a single point of failure for the link. Repeaters are available for both copper and fiber links, with the latter also described as an optical-electrical-optical (OEO) repeater.

Where a repeater connects two cable segments of the same type, a **media converter** is used to transition from one cable type to another. Media converters also work at the Physical layer of the OSI model. They may be supplied as standalone appliances or rack-mounted appliances. The following media conversions are typical:

- **Single mode fiber to twisted pair**—These powered converters change light signals from SMF cabling into electrical signals carried over a copper wire Ethernet network (and vice versa).

- **Multimode fiber to twisted pair**—A different media converter model is required to convert the light signals carried over MMF media.

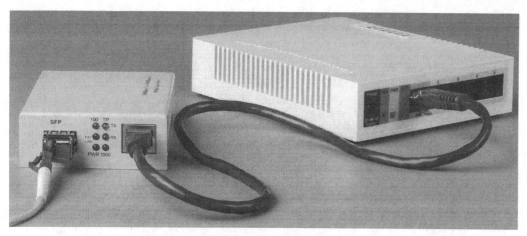

Single mode fiber to UTP media converter. (Image by ironstealth © 123RF.com.)

- **Single mode to multimode fiber**—These passive (unpowered) devices convert between the two fiber cabling types.

Hubs

Most Ethernet networks are implemented so that each end system node is wired to a central intermediate system. In early types of Ethernet, this function was performed by a **hub**. While hubs are no longer widely deployed as standalone appliances, it is important to understand the basic functions they perform.

A hub acts like a multiport repeater so that every port receives transmissions sent from any other port. As a repeater, the hub works only at the Physical layer. Electrically, the network segment still looks like a single length of cable. Consequently, every hub port is part of the same shared media access area and within the same collision domain. All node interfaces are half-duplex, using the CSMA/CD protocol, and the media bandwidth (10 Mbps or 100 Mbps) is shared between all nodes.

When Ethernet is wired with a hub there needs to be a means of distinguishing the interface on an end system (a computing host) with the interface on an intermediate system (the hub). The end system interface is referred to as **medium dependent interface (MDI)**; the interface on the hub is referred to as MDI crossover (MDI-X). This means that the transmit (Tx) wires on the host connect to receive (Rx) wires on the hub.

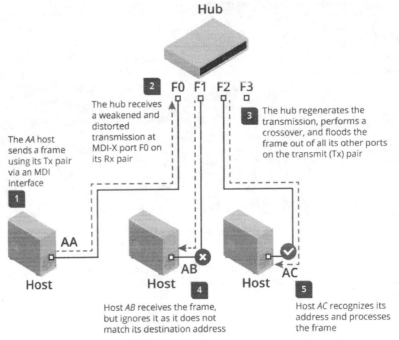

Hub-based Ethernet communications. (Images © 123RF.com.)

There are no configuration options for a hub. You just connect the device to a power source and then connect the network cables for the hosts that are going to be part of the network segment served by the hub.

Bridges

An Ethernet **bridge** works at the data link layer (layer 2) to establish separate physical network segments while keeping all nodes in the same logical network. This reduces the number of collisions caused by having too many nodes contending for access.

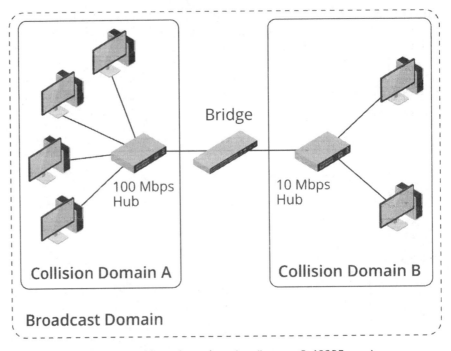

Collision and broadcast domains. (Images © 123RF.com.)

This figure shows how a bridge creates separate collision domains. Each hub is a shared access media area. The nodes connected to the hubs share the available bandwidth—a 100 Mbps Ethernet for domain A and a 10 Mbps Ethernet for domain B—because only one node within each collision domain can communicate at any one time. The bridge isolates these segments from each other, so nodes in domain B do not slow down or contend with nodes in domain A. The bridge does allow nodes to communicate with the other collision domain, by forwarding only the appropriate traffic. This creates a single logical network, referred to as a layer 2 **broadcast domain**.

An Ethernet bridge builds a MAC address table in memory to track which addresses are associated with which of its ports. When the bridge is initialized, the bridging table is empty, but information is constantly added as the bridge listens to the connected segments. Entries are flushed out of the table after a period to ensure the information remains current.

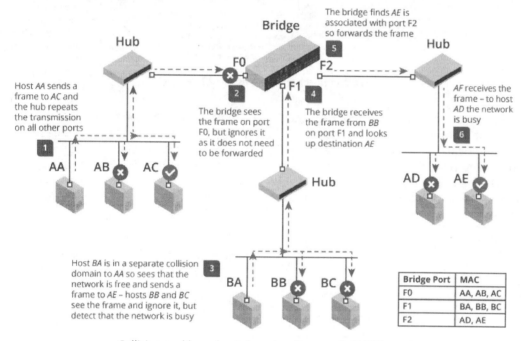

Collision and broadcast domains. (Images © 123RF.com.)

If no record of the hardware address exists or the frame is a broadcast or multicast, then the bridge floods the frame to all segments except for the source segment (acting like a hub).

Layer 2 Switches

The problems created by contention can be more completely resolved by moving from a shared Ethernet system to switched Ethernet. Hubs and bridges are replaced with switches. Gigabit Ethernet and Ethernet 10 GbE cannot be deployed without using switches.

An Ethernet layer 2 **switch** performs the same sort of function as a bridge, but in a more granular way and for many more ports than are supported by bridges. Each switch port is a separate collision domain. In effect, the switch establishes a point-to-point link between any two network nodes. This is referred to as **microsegmentation**.

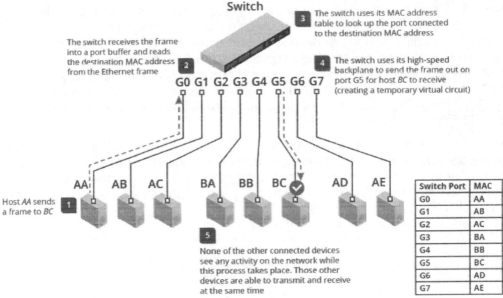

Switch operation. (Images © 123RF.com.)

Because each port is in a separate collision domain, collisions can occur only if the port is operating in half-duplex mode. This would only be the case if a legacy network card or a hub is attached to it. Even then, collisions affect only the microsegment between the port and the connected interface; they do not slow down the whole network. As with a bridge, though, traffic on all switch ports is in the same broadcast domain, unless the switch is configured to use virtual LANs (VLANs).

Review Activity:

Networking Devices

Answer the following questions:

1. **You need to run UTP cable between two switches at opposite ends of a warehouse that is 140 m (459 feet) long. What additional device (if any) is required for the installation to be compliant with 1000BASE-TX Ethernet standard?**

2. **True or false? All the nodes shown in the following figure are in the same collision domain.**

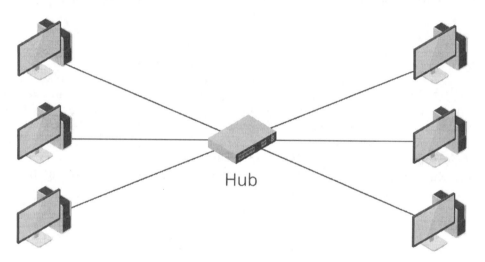

3. **True or False? A computer with a 10BASE-T Ethernet adapter cannot be joined to a 100BASE-T network.**

4. **True or False? Devices can only transmit on an Ethernet network when the media is clear, and the opportunity to transmit becomes less frequent as more devices are added. Also, the probability of collisions increases. These problems can be overcome by installing a hub.**

5. **True or false? A bridge does not forward broadcast traffic.**

Topic 3B

Explain Network Interfaces

EXAM OBJECTIVES COVERED
1.1 Compare and contrast the Open Systems Interconnection (OSI) model layers and encapsulation concepts.
5.2 Given a scenario, troubleshoot common cable connectivity issues and select the appropriate tools. (Tap only)
5.3 Given a scenario, use the appropriate network software tools and commands. (tcpdump only)

A network interface is the means by which a node is connected to the media and exchanges data with other network hosts. As a network technician, you will frequently be involved with installing, configuring, and troubleshooting network interfaces. You must also be able to capture and analyze network traffic, using a packet sniffer.

Network Interface Cards

The transceiver component responsible for physically connecting the node to the transmission medium is implemented in a network interface card/controller (NIC). Most Ethernet adapters designed for use with copper cabling are capable of 10/100/1000 operation, meaning that they support Gigabit Ethernet, Fast Ethernet, and 10BASE-T. A different kind of adapter would have to be provisioned for a fiber link. Adapters that support 10 GbE or 40 GbE come at a considerable price premium over basic Gigabit models. A NIC may also provision multiple ports on the same card. This allows either connections to different networks or aggregating the separate links into a higher bandwidth channel.

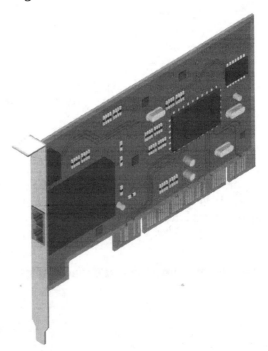

Network Interface Card (NIC) with two RJ-45 ports. (Image © 123RF.com.)

Each Ethernet network interface port has a unique hardware address known as the **Media Access Control (MAC) address**. This may also be referred to as the Ethernet address (EA) or, in IEEE terminology, as the **extended unique identifier (EUI)**. A MAC address is also referred to as a local or physical address.

Ethernet Frame Format

Ethernet encapsulates the payload from higher layer protocols within a protocol data unit (PDU) called a **frame**. The basic format of an Ethernet frame and **Ethernet headers** is shown in the following figure.

Header fields in an Ethernet frame.

Preamble

The preamble and Start Frame Delimiter (SFD) are used for clock synchronization and as part of the CSMA/CD protocol to identify collisions early. The preamble consists of 8 bytes of alternating 1s and 0s with the SFD being two consecutive 1s at the end. This is not technically considered to be part of the frame.

Error Checking

The error checking field contains a 32-bit (4-byte) checksum called a **Cyclic Redundancy Check (CRC)** or Frame Check Sequence (FCS). The CRC is calculated based on the contents of the frame; the receiving node performs the same calculation and, if it matches, accepts the frame. There is no mechanism for retransmission if damage is detected nor is the CRC completely accurate at detecting damage; these are functions of error checking in protocols operating at higher layers.

Media Access Control Address Format

A MAC/EUI address is a 48 bit (6 byte) identifier. The format of the number differs depending on the system architecture. It is often displayed as 6 groups of 2 hexadecimal digits with colon or hyphen separators or no separators at all (for example, 00:60:8c:12:3a:bc or 00608c123abc) or as 3 groups of 4 hex digits with period separators (0060.8c12.3abc, for instance).

 An EUI-64 is a 64-bit hardware address. A translation mechanism allows a 48-bit MAC address to be converted to an EUI-64. EUI-64 addresses can be used with IPv6.

Burned-in Addresses

The IEEE gives each card manufacturer a range of numbers, and the manufacturer hard codes every interface produced with a unique number from their range. This is called the burned-in address or the universal address. The first six hex digits (3 bytes or octets), also known as the Organizationally Unique Identifier (OUI), identify the manufacturer of the adapter. The last six digits are a serial number.

An organization can decide to use locally administered addresses in place of the manufacturers' universal coding systems. This can be used to make MACs meaningful in terms of location on the network, but it adds a significant amount of administrative overhead. A locally administered address is defined by changing the U/L bit from 0 to 1. The rest of the address is configured using the card driver or network management software. It becomes the network administrator's responsibility to ensure that all interfaces are configured with a unique MAC.

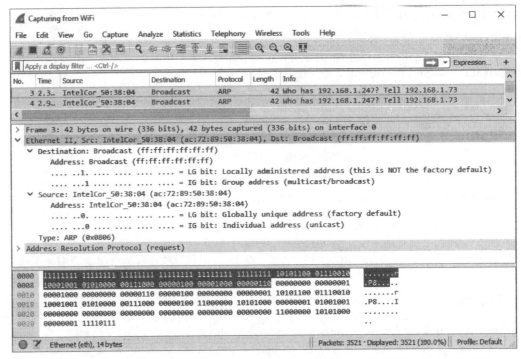

Captured Ethernet frame showing the resolved OUI and I/G and U/L bits in the destination (broadcast) and source addresses. (Screenshot courtesy of Wireshark.)

Broadcast Address

The I/G bit of a MAC address determines whether the frame is addressed to an individual node (0) or a group (1). The latter is used for broadcast and multicast transmissions. A MAC address consisting entirely of 1s is the broadcast address (ff:ff:ff:ff:ff:ff) and should be processed by all nodes within the same broadcast domain.

Frame Length and Maximum Transmission Unit

The official IEEE 802.3 standard defines a 2-byte field to specify the size of the data field or payload. The payload can normally be between 46 and 1500 bytes. The upper limit of the payload is also referred to as the **maximum transmission unit (MTU)**. However, most Ethernet products follow the original DIX specification, referred to as Type II frames, and use the field to indicate the type of network layer protocol contained in the frame—IPv4 or IPv6, for instance. These EtherTypes are values of 1536 or greater; anything less than that is interpreted as the data length. For example, IPv4 is coded as the hex value 0x0800, or 2048 in decimal, while IPv6 is 0x86DD.

To comply with CSMA/CD, the minimum length of an Ethernet frame is 64 bytes, so the payload must be at least 46 bytes. If this is not the case, it is automatically padded with redundant data. The maximum size of an Ethernet frame is normally 1518 bytes, excluding the preamble. Some Gigabit and 10 GbE Ethernet products support jumbo frames with much larger MTUs. Such products are not standardized, however, making interoperability between different vendors problematic.

Packet Sniffers and Taps

One of the most important tools used for network support is a protocol analyzer. This is the tool that allows inspection of traffic received by a host or passing over a network link. A protocol analyzer depends on a **packet sniffer**. A sniffer captures frames moving over the network medium.

 Often the terms sniffer and protocol analyzer are used interchangeably but be aware that they might be implemented separately.

A basic software-based sniffer installed to a host will simply interrogate the frames received by the network adapter by installing a special driver. This allows the frames to be read from the network stack and saved to a file on disk. They also support filters to reduce the amount of data captured.

There are three main options for connecting a sniffer to the appropriate point in the network:

- **SPAN (switched port analyzer)/mirror port**—this means that the sensor is attached to a specially configured port on the switch that receives copies of frames addressed to nominated access ports (or all the other ports). This method is not completely reliable. Frames with errors will not be mirrored and frames may be dropped under heavy load.

- **Passive test access point** (TAP)—this is a box with ports for incoming and outgoing network cabling and an inductor or optical splitter that physically copies the signal from the cabling to a monitor port. There are types for copper and fiber optic cabling. Unlike a SPAN, no logic decisions are made so the monitor port receives every frame—corrupt or malformed or not—and the copying is unaffected by load.

- **Active TAP**—this is a powered device that performs signal regeneration (again, there are copper and fiber variants), which may be necessary in some circumstances. Gigabit signaling over copper wire is too complex for a passive tap to monitor and some types of fiber links may be adversely affected by optical splitting. Because it performs an active function, the TAP becomes a point of failure for the links in the event of power loss.

A TAP will usually output two streams to monitor a full-duplex link (one channel for upstream and one for downstream). Alternatively, there are aggregation TAPs, which rebuild the streams into a single channel, but these can drop frames under very heavy load.

tcpdump

tcpdump is a command-line packet capture utility for Linux, providing a user interface to the libpcap library. The basic syntax of the command is:

```
tcpdump -i eth0
```

Where eth0 is the interface to listen on (you can substitute with the keyword any to listen on all interfaces of a multi-homed host). The utility will then display captured packets until halted manually (by pressing `Ctrl`+`C`). The operation of the basic command can be modified by switches. For example, the `-w` and `-r` switches write output to a file and read the contents of a capture file respectively. The `-v`, `-vv`, and `-vvv` can be used to increase the amount of detail shown about each frame while the `-e` switch shows the Ethernet header.

tcpdump is often used with some sort of filter expression:

- **Type**—filter by `host`, `net`, `port`, or `portrange`.

- **Direction**—filter by source (`src`) or destination (`dst`) parameters (`host`, `network`, or `port`).

- **Protocol**—filter by a named protocol rather than port number (for example, `arp`, `icmp`, `ip`, `ip6`, `tcp`, `udp`, and so on).

Filter expressions can be combined by using Boolean operators:

- `and (&&)`

- `or (||)`

- `not (!)`

Filter syntax can be made even more detailed by using parentheses to group expressions. A complex filter expression should be enclosed by quotes. For example, the following command filters frames to those with the source IP 10.1.0.100 and destination port 53 or 80:

```
tcpdump -i eth0 "src host 10.1.0.100 and (dst port 53
or dst port 80)"
```

 Refer to tcpdump.org for the full help and usage examples. ngrep (github.com/jpr5/ ngrep) is another useful packet capture and analysis tool. As well as the standard filter syntax, it supports use of regular expressions (regexr.com) to search and filter capture output. You can also use the netcat tool (nmap.org/ncat) to copy network traffic from one host to another for analysis.

Wireshark

Wireshark (wireshark.org) is an open source graphical packet capture and analysis utility, with installer packages for most operating systems. Having chosen the interfaces to listen on, the output is displayed in a three-pane view, with the top pane showing each frame, the middle pane showing the fields from the currently selected frame, and the bottom pane showing the raw data from the frame in hex and ASCII.

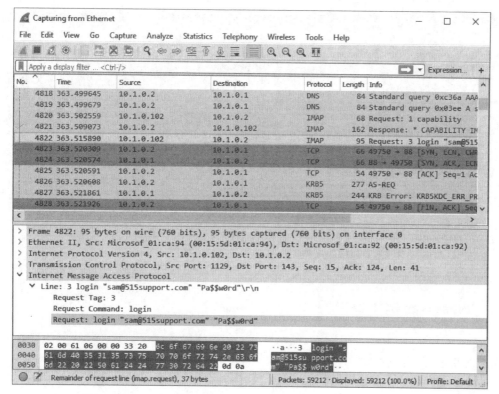

Wireshark protocol analyzer. (Screenshot courtesy of Wireshark.)

There is also a command-line version of Wireshark called Tshark wireshark.org/docs/ wsug_html_chunked/AppToolstshark.html.

Review Activity:

Network Interfaces

Answer the following questions:

1. True or False? The CRC mechanism in Ethernet allows for the retransmission of damaged frames.

2. What is an I/G bit?

3. What is an MTU?

4. On a switched network, what configuration changes must be made to allow a host to sniff unicast traffic from all hosts connected to a switch?

5. Write the command to use tcpdump to capture traffic from the IP address 172.16.16.254 on the interface eth0 and output the results to the file router.pcap.

Topic 3C

Deploy Common Ethernet Switching Features

EXAM OBJECTIVES COVERED
2.3 Given a scenario, configure and deploy common Ethernet switching features.
5.3 Given a scenario, use the appropriate network software tools and commands.

Switches are now used in almost all Ethernet networks, so you are certain to encounter them in the environments that you support. There are many models of Ethernet switches, however. Understanding the range of capabilities of these devices will prepare you to support a wide variety of network environments.

Ethernet Switch Types

Ethernet switches from different vendors come in a variety of ranges to support various sizes of networks. While a basic model might feature 12 to 48 ports and little scope for expansion, advanced switches support interconnections via high-speed backplanes and expandable capacity through plug-in modules plus power supply redundancy, management consoles, and transceivers for fiber optic connectivity.

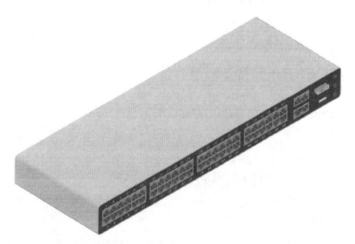

An example of a workgroup switch. (Image © 123RF.com.)

The market is dominated by Cisco's Catalyst and Nexus platforms (over 55% of sales), but other notable vendors include HP® Enterprise, Huawei, Juniper®, Arista, Linksys®, D-Link, NETGEAR®, and NEC.

Ethernet switches can be distinguished using the following general categories:

- **Unmanaged versus managed**—On a SOHO network, switches are more likely to be unmanaged, standalone units that can be added to the network and run without any configuration. The switch functionality might also be built into an Internet router/modem. On a corporate network, switches are most likely to be managed. This means the switch settings can be configured. If a managed switch is left unconfigured, it functions the same as an unmanaged switch does.

- **Stackable**—Switches that can be connected together and operate as a group. The switch stack can be managed as a single unit.

- **Modular versus fixed**—A fixed switch comes with a set number of ports that cannot be changed or upgraded. A modular switch has slots for plug-in cards, meaning they can be configured with different numbers and types of ports.

- **Desktop versus rack-mounted**—Simple unmanaged switches with five or eight ports might be supplied as small freestanding units that can be placed on a desktop. Most larger switches are designed to be fitted to the standard-size racks that are used to hold networking equipment.

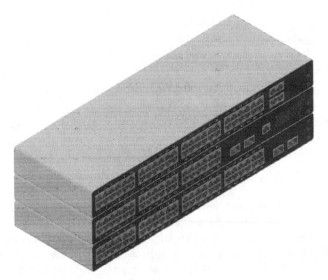

An example of a modular chassis that allows provisioning multiple access switches. (Image © 123RF.com.)

Switch Interface Configuration

Configuration of a managed switch can be performed at a command line interface (CLI). Once you have established a connection to the switch's management interface, you can configure settings for each of the switch port interfaces. These settings control the network link configured for each client device attaching to the switch. Most switch operating systems work in multiple command modes or hierarchies. For example, Cisco IOS has three principal modes:

- **User EXEC mode**—This is a read-only mode where commands can be used to report the configuration, show system status, or run basic troubleshooting tools.

- **Privileged EXEC mode/enable mode**—This allows the user to reboot or shut down the appliance and to backup and restore the system configuration.

- **Global configuration mode**—This allows the user to write configuration updates.

Most switch CLIs also support `TAB` and/or use of `?` to list different ways to complete a partial instruction.

In user mode, a variety of **show commands** can be used to display the current configuration. There are usually many `show` commands, but two of particular importance are as follows:

- `show config` displays the switch's configuration. The startup configuration (`show startup-config`) could be different from the running configuration (`show running-config`). If there has been some undocumented change to the switch, using these commands and comparing the output may reveal the source of a problem.

- `show interface` lists the state of all interfaces or the specified interface. Interfaces are identified by type, slot, and port number. For example, GigabitEthernet 0/2 (or G0/2) is port #2 on the first 10/100/1000 slot (or only slot). An interface has a line status (up if a host is connected via a good cable) and a protocol status (up if an Ethernet link is established). Down indicates a fault while administratively down indicates that the port has been purposefully disabled. show interface will also report configuration details and traffic statistics if the link is up/up.

 Stackable switches precede interface identifiers with a module ID. For example, GigabitEthernet 3/0/2 is the second port on first slot in the third module in the stack. Note that this numbering does vary between manufacturers. Also, some start from zero and some from one.

```
FastEthernet1/0/1 is up, line protocol is up (connected)
  Hardware is Fast Ethernet, address is f41f.c253.7103 (bia f41f.c253.7103)
  MTU 1500 bytes, BW 100000 Kbit/sec, DLY 100 usec,
     reliability 255/255, txload 1/255, rxload 1/255
  Encapsulation ARPA, loopback not set
  Keepalive set (10 sec)
  Full-duplex, 100Mb/s, media type is 10/100BaseTX
  input flow-control is off, output flow-control is unsupported
  ARP type: ARPA, ARP Timeout 04:00:00
  Last input 00:00:51, output 00:00:00, output hang never
  Last clearing of "show interface" counters never
  Input queue: 0/75/0/0 (size/max/drops/flushes); Total output drops: 0
  Queueing strategy: fifo
  Output queue: 0/40 (size/max)
  5 minute input rate 0 bits/sec, 0 packets/sec
  5 minute output rate 0 bits/sec, 0 packets/sec
     18 packets input, 1758 bytes, 0 no buffer
     Received 4 broadcasts (2 multicasts)
     0 runts, 0 giants, 0 throttles
     0 input errors, 0 CRC, 0 frame, 0 overrun, 0 ignored
     0 watchdog, 2 multicast, 0 pause input
     0 input packets with dribble condition detected
     111 packets output, 13828 bytes, 0 underruns
     0 output errors, 0 collisions, 1 interface resets
     0 unknown protocol drops
```

Viewing interface configuration on a Cisco switch. (Image © and Courtesy of Cisco Systems, Inc. Unauthorized use not permitted.)

Switches normally support a range of Ethernet standards so that older and newer network adapters can all be connected to the same network. In most cases, the port on the switch is set to autonegotiate **speed** (10/100/1000) and full- or half-**duplex** operation. A static configuration can be applied manually if necessary.

Auto MDI/MDI-X

Under 100BASE-T, an end system uses media dependent interface (MDI) to transmit on pins 1 and 2 and receive on pins 3 and 6. This is also referred to as an uplink port. As an intermediate system, a switch port uses MDI-X and receives on pins 1 and 2 and transmits on pins 3 and 6. The cable between the host interface port and switch interface port should be straight through (either T568A on both ends or T568B on both ends).

When a switch needs to be connected to another switch, communications would fail if both interfaces used MDI-X. Historically (in the days of hubs and very early 10/100 switches), dedicated uplink ports and/or crossover cables were used to make these connections. A crossover cable has T568A termination at one end and T568B termination at the other end. Nowadays, most switch interfaces are configured to use **auto-MDI/MDIX** by default. This means that the switch senses the configuration of the connected device and cable wiring and ensures that an MDI uplink to an MDIX port gets configured. This will also ensure a link if a crossover cable is used to connect an end system by mistake.

 The same principle applies to Gigabit Ethernet and faster. While all four pairs carry bidirectional signals, the interfaces still use an MDI to MDI-X link. In practical terms, all Gigabit Ethernet interfaces must support auto MDI/MDI-X.

MAC Address Table and Port Security

A switch learns MAC addresses by reading the source address when a frame is received on a port. The address mapping for that port is normally cached in a **MAC address table**. The address table is implemented as content addressable memory (CAM), a special type of memory optimized for searching, rather than random access. Consequently, the MAC address table is often also referred to as the CAM table. Entries remain in the MAC address table for a period before being flushed. This ensures problems are not encountered when network cards (MAC addresses) are changed.

If a MAC address cannot be found in the MAC address table, then the switch acts like a hub and transmits the frame out of all the ports, except for the source port. This is referred to as flooding.

You can query the MAC address table of a switch to find the MAC address or addresses associated with a particular port using a command such as:

```
show mac address-table
```

```
NYACCESS1#show mac address-table dynamic
            Mac Address Table
-------------------------------------------------

Vlan      Mac Address        Type        Ports
----      -----------        --------    -----
   1      000a.8aa2.135e     DYNAMIC     Fa0/23
   1      08cc.683e.fd18     DYNAMIC     Fa0/23
   1      08cc.683e.fd40     DYNAMIC     Fa0/23
   1      18e7.285f.0c28     DYNAMIC     Fa0/24
   1      44ad.d916.2598     DYNAMIC     Fa0/24
   1      5006.04be.159d     DYNAMIC     Fa0/1
Total Mac Addresses for this criterion: 6
```

Displaying dynamic entries in the MAC address table of a Cisco switch. (Image © and Courtesy of Cisco Systems, Inc. Unauthorized use not permitted.)

A **port security** configuration validates the MAC address of end systems that connect to a switch port. In most scenarios, you would not expect the MAC address of servers and workstations to change often, except for predictable upgrade cycles. Unknown or frequently changing host MAC addresses might indicate an intrusion attempt. A port security configuration has two elements:

- Specify a static MAC address or allow the port to learn and accept a certain number of sticky addresses.

- Specify an enforcement action when a policy violation is detected (alert only or shutdown the port, for instance).

Port Aggregation

Port aggregation means combining two or more separate cabled links into a single logical channel. From the host end, this can also be called NIC teaming. The term bonding is also widely substituted for aggregation. For example, a single network adapter and cable segment might support 1 Gbps; bonding this with another adapter and cable segment gives a link of 2 Gbps.

Port aggregation is often implemented by the **Link Aggregation Control Protocol (LACP)**. LACP can be used to autonegotiate the bonded link between the switch ports and the end system, detect configuration errors, and recover from the failure of one of the physical links.

Port Mirroring

Unlike a hub, a switch forwards unicast traffic only to the specific port connected to the intended destination interface. This prevents sniffing of unicast traffic by hosts attached to the same switch. There are circumstances in which capturing and analyzing network traffic is a legitimate activity, however, and **port mirroring** provides the facility to do this. Port mirroring copies all packets sent to one or more source ports to a mirror (or destination) port. On a Cisco switch, this is referred to as a switched port analyzer (SPAN).

Configuring port mirroring on a switch. (Screenshot courtesy of Nvidia.)

The mirror port would be used by management or monitoring software, such as a packet sniffer, network analyzer, or intrusion detection system (IDS) sensor. Either ingress or egress traffic, or both, can be captured. Optionally, in order to avoid overloading the monitoring system, packets may be filtered based on criteria such as protocol ID or TCP/UDP port number.

> *Port mirroring demands a lot of processing and can lead to the switch hardware becoming overloaded and consequently crashing. If possible, test any security solution that requires port mirroring under typical loads before deploying it on a production network.*

Jumbo Frames and Flow Control

Some types of hosts, such as those implementing storage area networks (SANs) have special requirements. Traffic processed by these hosts can be optimized by configuring port settings for jumbo frames and flow control.

Jumbo Frames

Ordinarily, an Ethernet frame can carry a data payload or maximum transmission unit (MTU) of up to 1,500 bytes. When you are transferring data around a storage network with a 10 Gbps switching fabric, a 1500-byte limit means using a lot of frames. A **jumbo frame** is one that supports a data payload of up to around 9,000 bytes. This reduces the number of frames that need to be transmitted, which can reduce the amount of processing that switches and routers need to do. It also reduces the bandwidth requirement somewhat, as fewer frame headers are being transmitted. The benefits of jumbo frames are somewhat disputed, however.

When implementing jumbo frames, it is critical that all hosts and appliances (switches and routers) along the communications path be able and configured to support them. It is also vital to ensure that each device supports the same MTU. Also, it can be complex to calculate the MTU if any additional headers are used (for IPSec, for instance).

The MTU value in the `show interface` output will indicate whether jumbo frames are accepted on a particular port.

Flow Control

IEEE 802.3x **flow control** allows a server to instruct the switch to pause traffic temporarily to avoid overwhelming its buffer and causing it to drop frames. A switch port can be configured to enable or disable (ignore) use of PAUSE frames. The 802.3x global PAUSE mechanism does not distinguish between traffic types, however, which can pose problems with voice/video traffic and infrastructure-critical traffic, such as routing protocol updates. Class of service (CoS) and quality of service (QoS) mechanisms ensure reliable performance for these time-sensitive applications by marking and policing traffic. The updated priority flow control (PFC) mechanism (IEEE802.1Qbb) allows PAUSE frames to apply to certain traffic classes only.

Power Over Ethernet

Power over Ethernet (PoE) is a means of supplying electrical power from a switch port over ordinary data cabling to a connected powered device (PD), such as a VoIP handset, IP camera, or wireless access point. PoE is defined in two IEEE standards (now both rolled into 802.3-2018):

- **802.3af**—Powered devices can draw up to about 13 W over the link. Power is supplied as 350mA@48V and limited to 15.4 W, but the voltage drop over the maximum 100 feet of cable results in usable power of around 13 W.

- **802.3at (PoE+)**—Powered devices can draw up to about 25 W, with a maximum current of 600 mA.

- **802.3bt (Ultra PoE)**—Supplies up to about 51 W (Type 3) or 73 W (Type 4) usable power.

PoE switches are referred to as endspan (or endpoint) power sourcing equipment (PSE). If an existing switch does not support PoE, a device called a power injector (or midspan) can be used.

When a device is connected to a port on a PoE switch, the switch goes through a detection phase to determine whether the device is PoE-enabled. If not, it does not supply power over the port and, therefore, does not damage non-PoE devices. If so, it determines the device's power consumption and sets the supply voltage level appropriately.

Powering these devices through a switch is more efficient than using a wall-socket AC adapter for each appliance. It also allows network management software to control the devices and apply schemes, such as making unused devices go into sleep states and power capping.

Review Activity:

Common Ethernet Switching Features

Answer the following questions:

1. You need to verify whether a switch port is misconfigured by checking the number of collisions being reported. What general command could you use at a CLI to report this information?

2. True or false? A managed switch should have auto MDI/MDI-X enabled by default.

3. A technician configures a switch port with a list of approved MAC addresses. What type of feature has been enabled?

4. A server has a four-port gigabit Ethernet card. If a switch supports port aggregation, what bandwidth link can be achieved?

5. What port configuration feature allows a server to smooth incoming traffic rates?

6. Can you safely connect a server to a PoE+ enabled port or should you disable PoE first?

Lesson 3

Summary

You should be able to identify the features of network devices operating at layers 1 and 2 and determine their appropriate placement on the network. You should be able to deploy and configure Ethernet switches with appropriate port configurations.

Guidelines for Deploying Network Devices

Follow these guidelines to deploy switches and other networking devices:

- Identify a switch model that will meet current and future needs, taking into account port density, management features, and any requirement to use Power over Ethernet.

- Configure appropriate port settings for high-bandwidth hosts, such as link aggregation, jumbo frames, and flow control.

- Identify any hosts that require nonstandard configuration, such as disabling auto-negotiation of speed and duplex settings or disabling auto MDI/MDI-X.

- Create a management plan for legacy hub and bridge appliances to ensure they do not impact overall network performance.

- Identify any need for physical layer repeater or media converter functions that cannot be met by installing a switch.

- Make a plan for capturing network traffic at strategic points in the network, either through port mirroring or via a network TAP.

- Optionally, use known or locally administered MAC addresses and port security to mitigate the risk of unknown devices connecting to the network.

Lesson 4
Troubleshooting Ethernet Networks

LESSON INTRODUCTION

Whether you are dealing with support cases or validating an installation or configuration, problem solving is a critical competency for all network technicians. Effective problem solving requires a mixture of technical knowledge, soft skills, and intuition, plus the discipline to apply a structured approach.

In this lesson you will explain the steps in CompTIA's Network+ troubleshooting methodology and apply these steps to solving common cable and connectivity issues.

Lesson Objectives

In this lesson, you will:

- Explain network troubleshooting methodology.

- Troubleshoot common cable connectivity issues.

Topic 4A

Explain Network Troubleshooting Methodology

 EXAM OBJECTIVES COVERED
5.1 Explain the network troubleshooting methodology.

Network problems can arise from a variety of sources outside your control. As a network professional, your users, your managers, and your colleagues will all look to you to identify and resolve those problems efficiently. To do that, you will need a strong fundamental understanding of the tools and processes involved in troubleshooting a network. Being able to resolve problems in these areas is a crucial skill for keeping your network running smoothly.

Troubleshooting requires a best practice approach to both problem solving and customer/client communication. A troubleshooting model provides you with proven processes on which to base your techniques and approach.

Network Troubleshooting Methodology

When you encounter a network problem, you must try to get it resolved as quickly as you reasonably can. However, you must also take enough time to determine what has caused the problem so that you can avoid a recurrence.

You should make sure you familiarize yourself with the order of the steps in the CompTIA® Network+® **troubleshooting methodology**. These steps are explained in more detail in the following topics.

1. Identify the problem:

    - Gather information.

    - Duplicate the problem, if possible.

    - Question users.

    - Identify symptoms.

    - Determine if anything has changed.

    - Approach multiple problems individually.

2. Establish a theory of probable cause:

    - Question the obvious.

    - Consider multiple approaches.

    - Top-to-bottom/bottom-to-top OSI model.

    - Divide and conquer.

3. Test the theory to determine cause:

   • Once theory is confirmed, determine next steps to resolve problem.

   • If theory is not confirmed, reestablish new theory or escalate.

4. Establish a plan of action to resolve the problem and identify potential effects.

5. Implement the solution or escalate as necessary.

6. Verify full system functionality, and if applicable, implement preventive measures.

7. Document findings, actions, and outcomes.

Identify the Problem (Gather Information)

The first step in the troubleshooting process is to identify the problem. There are several techniques and approaches that can assist with this step.

Gather Information

At the outset, define the scope of the problem (that is, the area affected). This is helpful in two ways. First, if it's a single user, then it's not as urgent as the other outstanding call you have. But if it's the whole third floor, then it's more urgent. In addition, the fact that the problem affects a wider area means that it is unlikely to be a problem with one user's workstation. Knowing the scope of the problem can help to identify its source and prioritize the issue in relation to other incidents.

As well as the information-gathering techniques discussed here, consider what indirect sources of information there may be:

• Check the system documentation, such as installation or maintenance logs, for useful information.

• Check recent job logs or consult any other technicians who might have worked on the system recently or might be working on some related issue.

• Use vendor support sites (knowledge bases) and forums.

Information gathering is the first step in troubleshooting. (Image by rawpixel © 123RF.com.)

Identify Symptoms and Duplicate the Problem

Symptoms are facts and clues in the affected system that can be correlated with known causes and issues. To identify symptoms, complete the following tests:

- Make a physical inspection; look for something out of the ordinary.

- Check system logs or diagnostic software for information.

- Duplicate the problem on the user's system or a test system. You will need to try to follow the same steps as the user. Issues that are transitory or difficult to reproduce are often the hardest to troubleshoot.

Identify the Problem (Question Users)

If you cannot identify symptoms or duplicate the problem, there are additional techniques that you can use to diagnose the issue.

Question Users

The first report of a problem will typically come from a user or another technician, and they will be one of the best sources of information, if you can ask the right questions. The basis of getting troubleshooting information from users is asking good questions. Questions are commonly divided into two types:

- Open questions invite someone to explain in their own words. Examples are: "What is the problem?" or "What happens when you try to switch the computer on?" Open questions are good to start with, as they help to avoid making your own assumptions about what is wrong, and they encourage the user to give you all the information they can.

- Closed questions invite a Yes/No answer or a fixed response. Examples include: "Can you see any text on the screen?" or "What does the error message say?" Closed questions can be used to drill down into the nature of the problem and guide a user toward giving you information that is useful.

Determine If Anything Has Changed

There are two key questions to ask when trying to identify the cause of a problem:

- Did it ever work? Hopefully, your users will answer the question truthfully, because the correct answer is important—two different approaches are required. If the system worked before 9:00 a.m., you must ask what happened at 9:00 a.m. If the system never worked, then you are not looking for something that stopped working, but for something which was never working in the first place.

- What has changed since it was last working? The change that caused the problem may not be obvious. Maybe the window cleaners were in the building, and one of them tripped over a cable and now the user can't log in. Maybe someone has moved the user's workstation from one end of his desk to another and plugged the cable into a different port. Check for documented changes using the system inventory, but if this does not reveal anything, look for undocumented changes in the local area of the incident.

Approach Multiple Problems Individually

When you start to investigate symptoms, you might discover symptoms of more than one problem. Perhaps a user has reported that a machine has lost Internet connectivity, and you discover that it has also not been receiving maintenance updates. The issues could be related, or one might be incidental to the other.

If the problems do not seem to be related, treat each issue as a separate case. If they seem to be related, check for outstanding support or maintenance tickets that might indicate existing problems.

It may also be the case that a user reports two different problems at the same time, often preceded by "While you're on the line..." sort of statements. Treat each problem as a separate case. In most cases, you should advise the user to initiate a separate support ticket.

Establish a Theory of Probable Cause

If you obtain accurate answers to your initial questions, you will have determined the severity of the problem (how many users or systems are affected), a rough idea of where to look (workstation or server end), and whether to look for a recent change or an oversight in configuration.

You diagnose a problem by identifying the symptoms. From knowing what causes such symptoms, you can test each possible cause until you find the right one. Sometimes symptoms derive from more than one cause; while this type of problem is rarer, it is much harder to troubleshoot.

A network system comprises many components. Fault finding needs to identify which component is causing the issue. For difficult problems, be prepared to consider multiple approaches. If one approach does not identify the problem, use a different one. For example, you could consider two different styles of approaching troubleshooting:

- Question the obvious. Step through what should happen and identify the point at which there is a failure or error. This approach can quickly identify obvious oversights, such as a network cable not being plugged in.

- Methodically prove the functionality of each component in sequence. This approach is more time consuming but may be necessary for a difficult problem.

Top-to-Bottom/Bottom-to-Top OSI Model Approach

Methodical validation of network components can be approached by testing at each layer of the OSI model in sequence. There are many components which go to make up a network.

Some, or several, of these components may be at fault when a problem is reported to you. It is important that you tackle the problem logically and methodically. Unless a problem is trivial, break the troubleshooting process into compartments

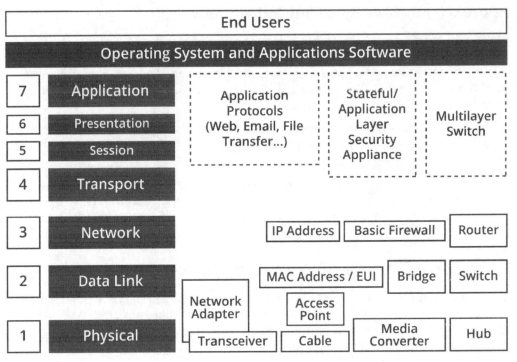

Troubleshooting top-to-bottom or bottom-to-top using the OSI model.

or categories, using the OSI model as a guide. Start from either the top or bottom and only move up or down when you have discounted a layer as the source of the problem. For example, when troubleshooting a client workstation, you might work as follows:

1. Decide whether the problem is hardware or software related (Hardware).

2. Decide which hardware subsystem is affected (NIC or cable).

3. Decide whether the problem is in the NIC adapter or connectors and cabling (cabling).

4. Test your theory (replace the cable with a known good one).

When you have drilled down like this, the problem should become obvious. Of course, you could have made the wrong choice at any point, so you must be prepared to go back and follow a different path.

 If you are really unlucky, two (or more) components may be faulty. Another difficulty lies in assessing whether a component itself is faulty or if it is not working because a related component is broken.

Divide and Conquer Approach

In a divide and conquer approach, rather than starting at the top or bottom, you start with the layer most likely to be causing the problem and then work either down or up depending on what your tests reveal. For example, if you start diagnosis at layer 3 and cannot identify a problem, you would then test at layer 4. Conversely, if you discovered a problem at layer 3, you would first test layer 2. If there is no problem at layer 2, you can return to layer 3 and work from there up.

Test the Theory to Determine the Cause

By questioning the obvious or by using one or more methodical diagnostic approaches, hopefully you will have gathered enough data to come to an initial theory about the probable cause. Remember that you might be wrong! Without jumping to conclusions, set out to prove or disprove your suspicions by using your troubleshooting skills and toolkit.

If you cannot prove the cause of the problem, you will either need to develop and test a new theory or decide to escalate the problem. **Escalation** means referring the problem to a senior technician, manager, or third party. You may need to escalate a problem for any of these reasons:

- The problem is beyond your knowledge or ability to troubleshoot.

- The problem falls under a system warranty and would be better dealt with by the supplier.

- The scope of the problem is very large and/or the solution requires some major reconfiguration of the network.

- A customer becomes difficult or abusive or demands help on an unsupported item.

Some of the alternatives for escalation include:

- Senior staff, knowledge experts, subject matter experts, technical staff, developers, programmers, and administrators within your company.

- Suppliers and manufacturers.

- Other support contractors/consultants.

When you escalate a problem, you should have established the basic facts, such as the scope of the problem and its likely cause and be able to communicate these clearly to the person to whom you are referring the incident.

If you can prove the cause of the problem, you can start to determine the next steps to resolve the problem.

Establish a Plan of Action

Assuming you choose not to escalate the issue, the next step in the troubleshooting process is to establish an action plan. An action plan sets out the steps you will take to solve the problem. There are typically three solutions to any problem:

- **Repair**—You need to determine whether the cost of repair/time taken to reconfigure something makes this the best option.

- **Replace**—Often, this is more expensive and may be time-consuming if a part is not available. There may also be an opportunity to upgrade the device or software.

 A basic technique when you are troubleshooting a cable, connector, or device is to have a known good duplicate on hand (that is, another copy of the same cable or device that you know works) and to test by substitution.

- **Ignore**—Not all problems are critical. If neither repair nor replace is cost-effective, it may be best either to find a workaround or just to document the issue and move on.

When you consider solutions, you must assess the cost and time required. Another consideration is potential effects on the rest of the system. A typical example is applying a software patch, which might fix a given problem but cause other programs not to work. This is where an effective configuration management system comes into play, as it should help you to understand how different systems are interconnected and cause you to seek the proper authorization for your plan.

Implement the Solution

The solution to a problem might just involve resetting a system to its baseline configuration. Perhaps a user installed some unauthorized software, disabled a necessary service, or unplugged a cable. If you are reverting to a known good configuration, you may be able to implement the solution directly. If the solution requires a change to the system or the network environment, you are likely to have to follow a change management plan.

If you do not have authorization to implement a solution, you will need to escalate the problem to more senior personnel. If applying the solution is disruptive to the wider network, you also need to consider the most appropriate time to schedule the reconfiguration work and plan how to notify other network users. When you change a system as part of implementing a solution, test after each change. If the change does not fix the problem, reverse it and then try something else. If you make a series of changes without recording what you have done, you could find yourself in a tricky position.

Verify Full System Functionality and Implement Preventive Measures

When you apply a solution, validate that it fixes the reported problem, and that the system as a whole continues to function normally. In other words, identify the results and effects of the solution. Ensure that you were right and that the problem is resolved. Can the user now log in properly? Is there any way you can induce the problem again?

Before you can consider a problem closed, you should be satisfied in your own mind that you have resolved it and you should get the customer's acceptance that it has been fixed. Restate what the problem was and how it was resolved, then confirm with the customer that the incident log can be closed.

To fully solve a problem, you should try to eliminate any factors that may cause the problem to recur. For example, if a user plugs his or her laptop into the wrong network jack, ensure that the jacks are clearly labeled to help users in the future. If a faulty server induces hours of network downtime, consider implementing failover services to minimize the impact of the next incident.

Document Findings, Actions, and Outcomes

Most troubleshooting takes place within the context of a ticket system. This shows who is responsible for any given problem and what its status is. This gives you the opportunity to add a complete description of the problem and its solution, including findings, actions, and outcomes.

This is massively useful for future troubleshooting, as problems fitting into the same category can be reviewed to see if the same solution applies. It also helps to analyze IT infrastructure by gathering statistics on what type of problems occur and how frequently.

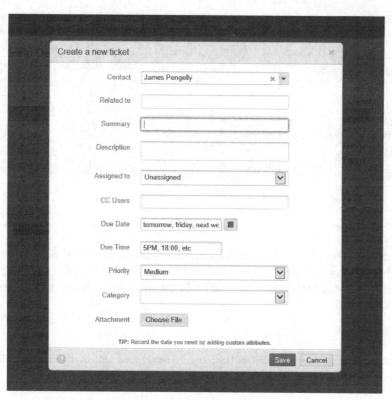

Creating a ticket in the Spiceworks IT Support management tool.
(Screenshot courtesy of Spiceworks.)

When you complete a problem log, remember that people other than you may come to rely on it. Also, logs may be presented to customers as proof of troubleshooting activity. Write clearly and concisely, checking for spelling and grammar errors.

Review Activity:

Network Troubleshooting Methodology

Answer the following questions:

1. **Which step has been omitted from the following list of activities related to identifying the problem? Gather information • Duplicate the problem, if possible • Question users • Identify symptoms • Determine if anything has changed**

2. **Which three means of establishing a theory of probable cause refer to the OSI model?**

3. **When should you escalate a problem?**

4. **Which step follows "Implement the solution or escalate as necessary" in the troubleshooting methodology?**

5. **True or False? Documentation should be created only at the end of the troubleshooting process.**

Topic 4B

Troubleshoot Common Cable Connectivity Issues

EXAM OBJECTIVES COVERED
5.2 Given a scenario, troubleshoot common cable connectivity issues and select the appropriate tools.

Applying a layer-by-layer approach to network troubleshooting can greatly assist with isolating symptoms and causes. In this topic, you will investigate some common issues that can affect cabled networks and identify the tools and techniques that can be used to solve problems at the physical and data link layers.

Specification and Limitations

When troubleshooting a link, you will need to compare the expected performance with the actual current performance. To do this, you must understand how to assess and distinguish speed, throughput, and distance specifications and limitations.

Speed versus Throughput

At the physical layer, a signal transmitted over a communications channel consists of a series of events referred to as symbols. A symbol could be something like a pulse of higher voltage in an electrical current or the transition between the peak and the trough in an electromagnetic wave. The number of symbols that can be transmitted per second is called the baud rate. The baud rate is measured in hertz (or MHz or GHz).

At the data link layer, the nominal bit rate—or bandwidth—of the link is the amount of information that can be transmitted, measured in bits per second (bps), or some multiple thereof. In order to transmit information more efficiently, a signaling method might be capable of representing more than one bit per symbol. This also helps to overcome noise and detect errors. The use of these encoding methods means that the bit rate will be higher than the baud rate. In Ethernet terms, the **speed** is the expected performance of a link that has been properly installed to operate at 10 Mbps, 100 Mbps, 1 Gbps, or better.

The nominal bit rate will not often be achieved in practice. **Throughput** is an average data transfer rate achieved over a period of time excluding encoding schemes, errors, and other losses incurred at the physical and data link layers. Throughput can be adversely affected by link distance and by interference (noise).

Throughput is typically measured at the network or transport layer. Often the term goodput is used to measure an averaged data transfer rate at the application layer. This takes account of the effect of packet loss. Throughput is also sometimes measured as packets per second.

As well as bandwidth or throughput and packet loss, the speed at which packets are delivered is also an important network performance characteristic. Speed is measured as a unit of time—typically milliseconds (ms)—and is also referred to as latency, or delay. Latency can occur at many layers of the OSI model. It is not usually a critical factor on local Ethernets, however.

The term speed is also used to describe how well or badly a link is performing in terms of throughput but do be aware of the distinction between bandwidth and latency.

Distance Limitations, Attenuation, and Noise

Each type of media can consistently support a given bit rate only over a defined **distance**. Some media types support higher bit rates over longer distances than others. Attenuation and noise enforce distance limitations on different media types.

- Attenuation is the loss of signal strength, expressed in decibels (dB). dB expresses the ratio between two measurements; in this case, signal strength at origin and signal strength at destination.

- Noise is anything that gets transmitted within or close to the channel that isn't the intended signal. This serves to make the signal itself difficult to distinguish, causing errors in data and forcing retransmissions. This is expressed as the signal to noise ratio (SNR).

Cable Issues

When troubleshooting cable connectivity, you are focusing on issues at the physical layer. At layer one, a typical Ethernet link for an office workstation includes the following components:

- Network transceiver in the host (end system).

- Patch cable between the host and a wall port.

- Structured cable between the wall port and a patch panel (the permanent link).

- Patch cable between the patch panel port and a switch port.

- Network transceiver in the switch port (intermediate system).

The entire cable path (patch cords plus permanent link) is referred to as a channel link.

Verifying patch cord connections. (Image by Kjetil Kolbjornsrud © 123RF.com.)

Assuming you are investigating link failure (complete loss of connectivity), the first step is to check that the patch cords are properly terminated and connected to the network ports. If you suspect a fault, substitute the patch cord with a known good cable.

If you cannot isolate the problem to the patch cords, test the transceivers. You can use a loopback tool to test for a bad port.

 If you don't have a loopback tool available, another approach is to substitute known working hosts (connect a different computer to the link or swap ports at the switch). This approach may have adverse impacts on the rest of the network, however, and issues such as port security may make it an unreliable method.

If you can discount faulty patch cords and bad network ports/NICs, you will need to use tools to test the structured cabling. The solution may involve installing a new permanent link, but there could also be a termination or external interference problem.

Loopback Plugs, Status Indicators, and Interface Configuration

A network **loopback adapter** (or loopback plug) is a specially wired RJ-45 plug with a 6" stub of cable. The wiring pinout is pin 1 (Tx) to pin 3 (Rx) and pin 2 (Tx) to pin 6 (Rx). This means that the packet sent by the NIC is received by itself. This is used to test for bad ports and network cards.

Another approach when you are troubleshooting a suspected cable problem is to check the link lights or network connection **LED status indicators** on the NIC at one end and the switch/router port at the other. You will need the vendor documentation to interpret the LEDs. There may be two LEDs for status and for link. On a switch port, the following LED link states are typical:

- **Solid green**—The link is connected but there is no traffic.

- **Flickering green**—The link is operating normally (with traffic).

- **No light**—The link is not working or is disconnected at the other end.

- **Blinking amber**—A fault has been detected (duplex mismatch or spanning tree blocking, for instance).

- **Solid amber**—The port is disabled.

If there are no obvious hardware failure issues, you should verify the settings on the switch port and NIC. Most adapters and switches successfully autonegotiate port settings. If this process fails, the adapter and port can end up with mismatched speed or duplex settings. In most cases, this will be because either the adapter or the switch port has been manually configured. If a host is set to a fixed configuration and the switch is set to autonegotiate, the switch will default to 10 Mbps/half-duplex because the host will not negotiate with it! So, if the host is manually configured to 100 Mbps/full duplex, the link will fail. Setting both to autonegotiate will generally solve the problem. A speed mismatch will cause the link to fail, while a duplex mismatch will slow the link down (it will cause high packet loss and late collisions).

```
cumulus@cumulus:mgmt:~$ net show interface swp5
      Name  MAC                    Speed  MTU    Mode
      ----  ----                   -----  ---    ----
DN    swp5  0c:7a:75:b5:c8:05      1G     9216   Access/L2

All VLANs on L2 Port
--------------------
100

Untagged
--------
100

cl-netstat counters
-------------------
RX_OK  RX_ERR  RX_DRP  RX_OVR  TX_OK   TX_ERR  TX_DRP  TX_OVR
-----  ------  ------  ------  -----   ------  ------  ------
66     0       0       0       1227    0       0       0

Routing
-------
  Interface swp5 is up, line protocol is down
  Link ups:        2    last: 2021/08/06 18:20:21.82
  Link downs:      8    last: 2021/08/06 18:35:42.62
  PTM status: disabled
  vrf: default
  index 7 metric 0 mtu 9216 speed 1000
  flags: <UP,BROADCAST,MULTICAST>
  Type: Ethernet
  HWaddr: 0c:7a:75:b5:c8:05
  Interface Type Other
  Master interface: bridge
  protodown: off
```

Viewing interface configuration on a Cumulus VX switch. (Screenshot courtesy of Nvidia.)

Cable Testers

When troubleshooting a permanent link, you should verify that the cable type is appropriate to the application. For example, you cannot expect 10 GbE Ethernet to run over an 80 m Cat 5e link. You may also need to verify that unshielded cable has not been installed where shielded or screened cable would be more suitable. Using an incorrect cable type might result in lower-than-expected speed and/or numerous checksum errors and link resets. Check the identifier printed on the cable jacket to verify the type that has been used.

From a safety point -of -view, you must also ensure that the cable jacket type is suitable for the installation location, such as using plenum-rated cable in plenum spaces and riser-rated cable in riser spaces.

If the cable is not accessible, cable testing tools can also be used to diagnose intermittent connectivity or poor performance issues. The best time to verify wiring installation and termination is just after you have made all the connections. This means you should still have access to the cable runs. Identifying and correcting errors at this point will be much simpler than when you are trying to set up end user devices.

A **cable tester** reports detailed information on the physical and electrical properties of the cable. For example, it can test and report on cable conditions, crosstalk, attenuation, noise, resistance, and other characteristics of a cable run. Devices classed as certifiers can be used to test and certify cable installations to a performance category—for example, that a network is TIA/EIA 568 Category 6A compliant. They use defined transport performance specifications to ensure an installation exceeds the required performance characteristics for parameters such as attenuation and crosstalk.

Technician using a cable certifier. (Image by Wavebreak Media © 123RF.com.)

A cable tester might incorporate the function of a **time domain reflectometer (TDR)**. A TDR is used to measure the length of a cable run and can locate open and short circuits, kinks/sharp bends, and other imperfections in cables that could affect performance. A TDR transmits a short signal pulse of known amplitude and duration down a cable and measures the corresponding amplitude and time delay associated with resultant signal reflections. A TDR analyzes these reflections and can display any problems found and their location. The TDR measures the amount of time taken for the signal to bounce back and can therefore calculate the distance to the cable fault to within a meter, which makes isolating the problem simpler.

Wire Map Testers and Tone Generators

If a dedicated cable tester or certifier device is not available, a **multimeter** can be used to check physical connectivity. The primary purpose of a multimeter is for testing electrical circuits, but it can test for the continuity of any sort of copper wire, the existence of a short, and the integrity of a terminator. To perform useful tests, you need to know the readings that are expected from a particular test. For example, if the resistance measured across UTP Ethernet cable is found to be 100 ohms, then the cable is okay, but if the resistance between the two ends of a cable is infinity, the cable has a break. Many multimeters designed for ICT use incorporate the function of a **wire map tester**. These are also available as dedicated devices. Wire map testers can identify the following problems:

- **Continuity (open)**—A conductor does not form a circuit because of cable damage or because the connector is not properly wired.

- **Short**—Two conductors are joined at some point, usually because the insulating wire is damaged, or a connector is poorly wired.

- **Incorrect pin-out/incorrect termination/mismatched standards**—The conductors are incorrectly wired into the terminals at one or both ends of the cable. The following transpositions are common:

  - **Reversed pair**—The conductors in a pair have been wired to different terminals (for example, from pin 3 to pin 6 and pin 6 to pin 3 rather than pin 3 to pin 3 and pin 6 to pin 6).

  - **Crossed pair (TX/RX reverse)**—The conductors from one pair have been connected to pins belonging to a different pair (for example, from pins 3 and 6 to pins 1 and 2). This may be done deliberately to create a crossover cable, but such a cable would not be used to link a host to a switch.

Another potential cable wiring fault is a split pair. This is where both ends of a single wire in one pair are wired to terminals belonging to a different pair. This type of fault can only be detected by a wire map tester that also tests for excessive crosstalk. This is generally the kind of functionality associated with a cable tester or certifier.

A network **tone generator** and probe are used to trace a cable from one end to the other. This may be necessary when the cables are bundled and have not been labeled properly. This device is also known as a Fox and Hound or tone probe. The tone generator is used to apply a signal on the cable to be traced where it is used to follow the cable over ceilings and through ducts.

Attenuation and Interference Issues

If a cable link is too long, **decibel (dB) loss** (or insertion loss) may mean that the link experiences problems with high error rates and retransmissions (frame or packet loss) resulting in reduced speeds and possibly loss of connectivity. Insertion loss is measured in decibels (dB) and represents the ratio of the received voltage to the original voltage.

A dB expresses the ratio between two values using a logarithmic scale. A logarithm is a mathematical tool for performing complex multiplication and division exponential operations as simpler additions and subtractions. The essential point is that a logarithmic scale is nonlinear, so a small change in value represents a large change in the performance measured. The following reference points are useful to remember:

- +3 dB means doubling, while -3 dB means halving.

- +6 dB means quadrupling, while -6 dB relates to a quarter.

- +10 dB means ten times the ratio, while -10 dB is a tenth.

 For a longer primer on dB math, view the presentation at internetsociety.org/wp-content/uploads/2017/10/dB-Math.pdf.

The maximum value allowed for insertion loss depends on the link category. For example, Cat 5e at 100 MHz allows up to 24 dB, while Cat 6 allows up to 21.7 dB at 250 MHz. When you are measuring insertion loss itself, smaller values are better (20 dB insertion loss is better than 22 dB, for instance). A cable certifier is likely to report the margin, which is the difference between the actual loss and the maximum value allowed for the cable standard. Consequently, higher margin values are better. For example, if the insertion loss measured over a Cat 5e cable is 22 dB, the margin is 2 dB; if another cable measures 23 dB, the margin is only 1 dB, and you are that much closer to not meeting acceptable link standards. Higher grade or shielded cable may alleviate the problem; otherwise, you will need to find a shorter cable run or install a repeater or additional switch.

Careful cable placement is necessary during installation to ensure that the wiring is not subject to interference from sources such as electrical power cables, fluorescent lights, motors, electrical fans, radio transmitters, and so on. **Electromagnetic interference (EMI)** is something that should be detected when the cable is installed, so you should suspect either some new source that has been installed recently or some source that was not taken into account during testing (machinery or power circuits that weren't activated when the installation testing took place, for instance). Interference from nearby data cables is also referred to as alien crosstalk.

 Radio frequency interference (RFI) is EMI that occurs in the frequencies used for radio transmissions.

Crosstalk Issues

Crosstalk usually indicates a problem with bad wiring (poor quality or damaged or the improper type for the application), a bad connector, or improper termination. Check the cable for excessive untwisting at the ends and for kinks or crush points along its run. Crosstalk is also measured in dB, but unlike insertion loss, higher values represent less noise. Again, the expected measurements vary according to the cable category and application. There are various types of crosstalk that can be measured:

- **Near End (NEXT)**—This measures crosstalk on the receive pairs at the transmitter end and is usually caused by excessive untwisting of pairs or faulty bonding of shielded elements.

- **Attenuation to Crosstalk Ratio, Near End (ACRN)**—This is the difference between insertion loss and NEXT. ACR is equivalent to a signal-to-noise ratio (SNR). A high value means that the signal is stronger than any noise present; a result closer to 0 means the link is likely to be subject to high error rates.

- **Attenuation-to-Crosstalk Ratio, Far End (ACRF)**—Far End Crosstalk (FEXT) is measured on the receive pairs at the recipient end. The difference between insertion loss and FEXT gives ACRF, which measures cable performance regardless of the actual link length.

- **Power sum**—Gigabit and 10 GbE Ethernet use all four pairs. Power sum crosstalk calculations (PSNEXT, PSACRN, and PSACRF) confirm that a cable is suitable for this type of application. They are measured by energizing three of the four pairs in turn.

 Complete loss of connectivity indicates a break in the cable (or a completely faulty installation), while intermittent loss of connectivity is more likely to be caused by attenuation, crosstalk, or noise.

Cable Application Issues

When dealing with patch cords and legacy network equipment, you need to account for the proper cable application.

Straight Through and Crossover Cables

There are two main formats for patch cords:

- **Straight through**—the cable is terminated with either T568A at both ends or T568B at both ends. This type of cable is used for an uplink (MDI port to MDIX port).

- **Crossover**—the cable is terminated with T568A at one end and T568B at the other. This type of cable is used to connect an end system (host) to another host or a hub to a hub.

In fact, crossover cable is no longer required for this type of application, as switches either have an uplink port for this purpose or can autodetect and select between an uplink and straight-through connection. This is referred to as auto-MDI/MDI-X. All Gigabit Ethernet ports support auto-MDI/MDI-X.

Rollover Cable/Console Cable

A console cable is used to connect a PC or laptop to the command line terminal of a switch or router. The console port connection on the appliance is a standard RJ-45 jack (but wired in a different way to Ethernet). A legacy console cable has a serial DB-9 connector for the PC end. As almost no computers come with DB-9 ports anymore, modern cables use a USB connector and port. Console cable is traditionally colored pale blue.

A program such as PutTTY on the PC is used to establish the connection using the appropriate settings for the serial link. Usually these are 9,600 bps (baud), 8 data bits/1 stop bit, and no parity or flow control. On some newer appliances, a USB cable can be used.

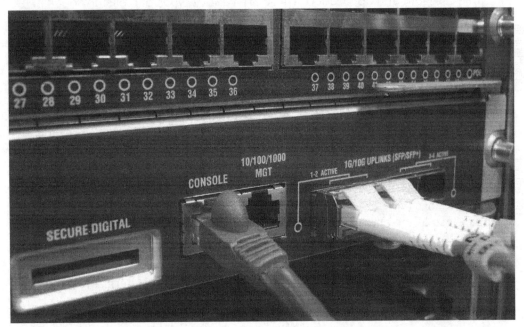

RJ-45 console port with cable connected. The Secure Digital slot for firmware updates and the MGT port next to the console port. (Image by Sorapop Udomsri © 123RF.com.)

 Routers typically have console and AUX ports. The AUX port is used to connect to the router over a dial-up modem. The console port just uses a serial (or null modem) link.

Power over Ethernet

Cat 3 or better is required to support PoE, while PoE+ must be Cat 5e or better. Drawing power down the cable generates more heat. If this heat is not dissipated, it can affect data rates. Thermal performance is improved by using pure copper cabling with larger conductors. A thin conductor will generate more heat through resistance. Shielded cabling is capable of dispersing heat more efficiently, too.

Fiber Optic Cable Testing Tools

Although fiber optic cable does not suffer from attenuation in the same way as copper cable or to the same extent, there will still be some loss of signal strength from one end of the connection to the other. This is due to microscopic imperfections in the structure of the glass fiber and in the smoothness of the edge of the core, leading to some small fraction of the light within the core being scattered or absorbed. As with attenuation in copper cables, the signal loss is increased with increasing cable length. The EIA/TIA 568 specification for fiber allows for a signal loss of between 0.5 dB/km and 3.5 dB/km, depending on the type of fiber used and the wavelength of the light.

Attenuation can be tested using an optical source and optical power meter (or fiber light meter), which may be purchased together as a fiber testing kit. If a break is identified in an installed cable, the location of the break can be found using an **optical time domain reflectometer (OTDR)**. This sends light pulses down the cable and times how long it takes for any reflections to bounce back from the break. A broken cable will need to be repaired (spliced) or replaced. An OTDR can also be used to verify that new splices are sound.

An **optical spectrum analyzer (OSA)** is typically used with wavelength division multiplexing (WDM) to ensure that each channel has sufficient power. At very long distances, the attenuation of different wavelengths can vary. This is referred to as spectral attenuation. An OSA can determine whether existing cable is suitable for reuse with WDM and which wavelengths will support the link distance required.

When you are working with fiber optic cabling, it is important to understand that any mismatch between the cables coupled together will result in data loss. This can occur if the fiber cables are not properly aligned, are different sizes, or may have suffered damage (broken/misshaped fiber strands) during transport.

Dirty Optical Cables

Dirt, dust, or grease in the transmission path will greatly reduce signal strength or block transmission completely. Most commonly, this occurs at a connector. Connectors should be covered with a dust cap when removed and the surrounding area should be dust free before performing a disconnection. Connectors should be cleaned using solvent designed for fiber optics, taking care not to apply excess solvent. The wet to dry method applies a drop of solvent to a lint-free cloth and moving the connector from the wet drop across a dry part. Contamination could also be introduced when a cable is spliced. Ensure splicing equipment is cleaned according to the manufacturer's instructions before every splice operation.

Incorrect Transceivers

The transceivers used in each optical interface (whether SFP, GBIC, or other media converter) are designed to be used with a specific type of optical fiber. For example, transceivers designed for single mode fiber use lasers while multimode fiber transceivers typically use LEDs. Different transceivers are designed to work at different optical wavelengths (typically 850 nm, 1300 nm, or 1550 nm). This means it is important to check the manufacturer's documentation for the interface to ensure the correct fiber type is used, not only for the fiber optic cable, but also for the fiber patch cords used to connect to it at each end. Mismatches between cable, patch cords, and interfaces may lead to significant signal loss.

Review Activity:

Common Cable Connectivity Issues

Answer the following questions:

1. **What cabling faults would a wire map tester detect?**

2. **How would you test for excessive attenuation in a network link?**

3. **What is the reason for making power sum crosstalk measurements when testing a link?**

4. **Your network uses UTP cable throughout the building. There are a few users who complain of intermittent network connectivity problems. You cannot determine a pattern for these problems that relates to network usage. You visit the users' workstations and find that they are all located close to an elevator shaft. What is a likely cause of the intermittent connectivity problems? How might you correct the problem?**

5. **You have connected a computer to a network port and cannot get a link. You have tested the adapter and cable and can confirm that there are no problems. No other users are experiencing problems. The old computer also experienced no problems. What cause would you suspect, and what is a possible next step?**

Lesson 4

Summary

You should be able to apply the CompTIA Network+ troubleshooting methodology and use appropriate tools to diagnose symptoms and causes of common cable connectivity issues.

Guidelines for Troubleshooting Ethernet Networks

Follow these guidelines to make effective use of troubleshooting tools and procedures for Ethernet networks:

- Use the process of identify, theorize, test, plan, implement, verify, and document to structure all troubleshooting activity.

- Prepare for troubleshooting by developing questioning skills and building reference documentation.

- Use top-to-bottom/bottom-to-top/divide-and-conquer with reference to the OSI model to isolate problems to layers.

- Document expectations of speed/throughput over link distances to identify when performance is reduced. Verify that cables are being used for their proper application, given factors such as shielding against external interference, crossover, rollover/console, and plenum/riser.

- Test the connectivity path (ports, patch cords, structured links) methodically.

- Use loopback adapters, status indicators, and CLI tools to verify port status.

- Use multimeters, wire mappers, toner generators, and cable testers to identify faults in copper cable. Use power meters, OTDRs, and spectrum analyzers for fiber optic plant.

Lesson 5
Explaining IPv4 Addressing

LESSON INTRODUCTION

The physical and data link layers covered in the previous lessons establish local links between nodes. At the network layer (layer 3) these individual networks can be connected together into a network of networks, or internetwork.

In this lesson, you will identify the addressing and data delivery methods of the Internet Protocol (IP). IP is at the heart of most modern networks, and consequently one of the most important topic areas for a network professional to understand and apply.

Lesson Objectives

In this lesson, you will:

- Explain IPv4 addressing schemes.

- Explain IPv4 forwarding.

- Configure IP networks and subnets.

Topic 5A

Explain IPv4 Addressing Schemes

EXAM OBJECTIVES COVERED
1.1 Compare and contrast the Open Systems Interconnection (OSI) model layers and encapsulation concepts. (IP header only)
1.5 Explain common ports and protocols, their application, and encrypted alternatives. (IP protocol types only)

The Transmission Control Protocol/Internet Protocol (TCP/IP) suite consists of complementary protocols and standards that work together to provide the functionality of the vast majority of modern networks. The Internet Protocol (IP) stands at the heart of this protocol suite, providing logical addressing and packet forwarding between different networks. In this topic, you will start to investigate the characteristics of IP by examining the structure of IPv4 packets and the format of IPv4 addresses.

There are two versions of IP; version 4 is more widely adopted and is the version discussed in the following few topics. IPv6 introduces a much larger address space and different means of configuring clients and is discussed later in the next lesson.

IPv4 Datagram Header

Ethernet works at the Physical and Data Link layers of the OSI model (layers 1 and 2). An Ethernet is a single network segment, or layer 2 broadcast domain. Ethernet, and other layer 1/layer 2 products, have no concept of multiple networks or of logical subdivisions within a network. This function is implemented at the Network layer (layer 3). As a layer 3 protocol, the Internet Protocol (IP) provides logical network addressing and forwarding.

The **Internet Protocol (IP) header** contains fields to manage the logical addressing and forwarding function.

The Version field indicates the version of Internet Protocol in use (4), while the Length fields indicate the size of the header and the total packet size (including the payload). The maximum theoretical size is 65,535 bytes, but actual packets would typically be much smaller to avoid fragmentation when transported as the payload of Ethernet frames.

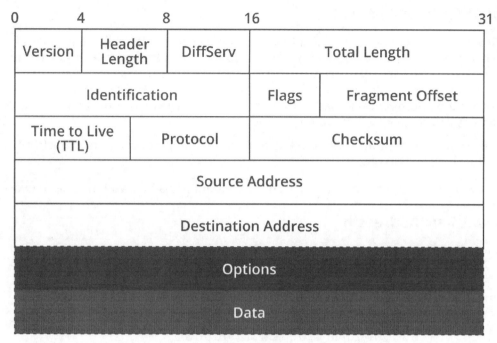

IPv4 header.

The Protocol field describes what is contained (encapsulated) in the payload so that the receiving host knows how to process it. For most packets, the **IP protocol type** value in the Protocol field will indicate a Transmission Control Protocol (TCP/6) segment or a User Datagram Protocol (UDP/17) datagram, which work at the Transport layer. The values assigned to protocols (such as 6 for TCP and 17 for UDP) are managed by IANA.

Those are the values in decimal. You are also likely to see them in their hex forms (0x06 and 0x11). Both formats ultimately represent 8-bit binary values (00000110 and 00010001).

Some protocols run directly on IP (rather than at the Transport layer). These IP protocol types include the following:

- Internet Control Message Protocol (ICMP/1) is used for status messaging and connectivity testing.

- Internet Group Messaging Protocol (IGMP/2) is used with multicasting.

- Generic Routing Encapsulation (GRE/47) is used to tunnel packets across an intermediate network. This is used (for example) in some virtual private network (VPN) implementations.

- Encapsulating Security Payload (ESP/50) and Authentication Header (AH/51) are used with the encrypted form of IP (IPSec).

- Enhanced Interior Gateway Routing Protocol (EIGRP/88) and Open Shortest Path First (OSPF/89) are protocols used by routers to exchange information about paths to remote networks.

IPv4 Address Format

Networks in an internetwork must have a way of uniquely identifying each logical network and each individual host within those networks. At the Data Link layer, an interface is identified by using a MAC or hardware address. This type of address can be used only for local delivery of frames. At the Network layer, IP source and destination addresses are used to forward packets to the proper destination. An IP address provides two pieces of information:

- **The network number (network ID)**—This number is common to all hosts on the same IP network.

- **The host number (host ID)**—This number identifies a host within an IP network.

32-bit IPv4 Addressing

An IPv4 address is 32 bits long. In its raw form, it appears as follows:

`11000110001100110110010000000001`

The 32 bits are subdivided into four groups of 8 bits (1 byte) known as octets. The previous IP address could therefore be written as:

`11000110 00110011 01100100 00000001`

It is almost impossible for people to use binary formats as configuration values. To make an IP address easier to use, it is formatted using **dotted decimal notation**. This notation requires each octet to be converted to a decimal value. The decimal numbers are separated using a period. Converting the previous number to this notation gives:

`198.51.100.1`

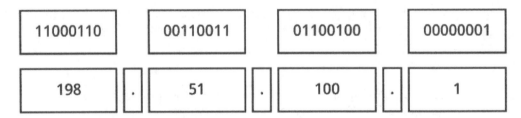

Dotted decimal notation.

Binary/Decimal Conversion

The following examples demonstrate the process of converting between binary and decimal notation.

In base 2 (binary), digits can take one of two different values (0 and 1). The place values are powers of 2 (2^1=2, 2^2=4, 2^3=8, 2^4=16, and so on). You should memorize these values to be able to perform binary/decimal conversions using the columnar method. Consider the octet `11101101` represented in base 2. This image shows the place value of each digit in the octet in the first two rows, with the binary octet in the third row. Rows four and five show that where there is a 1 in the octet, the decimal place value is added to the sum:

2^7	2^6	2^5	2^4	2^3	2^2	2^1	2^0	
128	64	32	16	8	4	2	1	
1	1	0	0	0	1	1	0	
128*1	64*1	32*0	16*0	8*0	4*1	2*1	1*0	
128	+64	+0	+0	+0	+4	+2	+0	= 198

Binary to decimal conversion.

You can use the same columnar method to convert from decimal to binary. For example, the number 51 can be converted as follows:

	2^7	2^6	2^5	2^4	2^3	2^2	2^1	2^0
	128	64	32	16	8	4	2	1
51 =	0	+0	+32	+16	+0	+0	+2	+1
	0	0	1	1	0	0	1	1

Decimal to binary conversion.

If all the bits in an octet are set to 1, the number obtained is 255 (the maximum possible value). Similarly, if all the bits are set to 0, the number obtained is 0 (the minimum possible value). Therefore, theoretically an IPv4 address may be any value between 0.0.0.0 and 255.255.255.255. However, some addresses are not permitted or are reserved for special use.

Network Masks

An IP address represents both a network ID and a host ID. A 32-bit **network mask** (or netmask) is used to distinguish these two components within a single IP address. The mask conceals the host ID portion of the IP address and thereby reveals the network ID portion.

The mask and the IP address are the same number of bits. Wherever there is a binary 1 in the mask, the corresponding binary digit in the IP address is part of the network ID. The 1s in the mask are always contiguous. For example, this mask is valid:

11111111 11111111 11111111 00000000

But the following string is not a valid mask:

11111111 00000000 11111111 00000000

The network ID portion of an IP address is revealed by ANDing the mask to the IP address. When two 1s are ANDed together, the result is a 1. Any other combination produces a 0.

For example, to determine the network ID of the host IP address 198.51.100.1 with a mask of 255.255.255.0, the dotted decimal notation of the IP address and mask must first be converted to binary notation. The next step is to AND the two binary numbers. The result can be converted back to dotted decimal notation to show the network ID (198.51.100.0). The only difference between the host IP address and the network ID lies in the last octet, which is not masked.

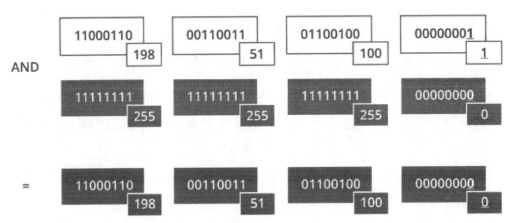

ANDing IP address and subnet mask to derive the network ID.

Instead of the dotted decimal mask, this network can be identified using prefix or slash notation. The prefix is simply the number of bits set to 1 in the mask. The network can therefore be referred to as 198.51.100.0/24.

The default masks align with octet boundaries. This means that the values in the mask will be 255 or zero. For example, the default 24-bit mask is as follows:

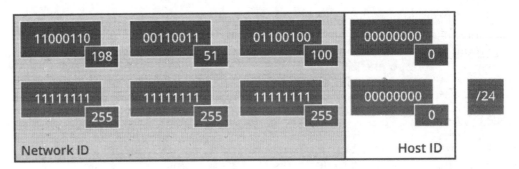

Network ID and host ID portions when using a 24-bit mask.

An 8-bit mask is 255.0.0.0 and a 16-bit mask is 255.255.0.0.

A longer network portion, such as 255.255.255.0, allows for more network IDs within the overall internetwork, but with fewer available host addresses per network. A short netmask (255.0.0.0) allows for millions of hosts per network, but only 126 possible network addresses.

Subnet Masks

The relative sizes of the network and host portions determine how many networks and hosts per network an addressing scheme can support. The conventional addressing technique has IP addresses with two hierarchical levels, namely the network ID and host ID. This scheme of using whole octet boundaries is inflexible, so a system of dividing networks into subnetworks or subnets was devised.

Subnet addressing has three hierarchical levels: a network ID, subnet ID, and host ID. To create logical subnets, bits from the host portion of the IP address must be allocated as a subnetwork address, rather than part of the host ID.

This means the subnet ID lies within an octet boundary. For example, a binary mask with 28 bits could use all the octets, with the network prefix boundary lying within the fourth octet:

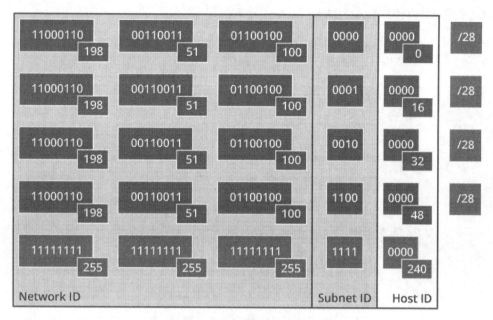

Subnet addressing.

This leaves only 4 bits for the host ID range.

The network ID and subnet ID use different masks. The mask for the whole network is still 255.255.255.0. Hosts within the network use the subnet mask 255.255.255.240.

It is important to understand that only one mask is ever applied to the IP address on each interface. The mask containing the subnet information is only used *within* the IP network. External IP networks continue to address the whole network by its network ID (198.51.100.0/255.255.255.0). Hosts within the network use the longer subnet mask to differentiate the subnets. These are 198.51.100.0/255.255.255.240, 198.51.100.16/255.255.255.240, 198.51.100.32/255.255.255.240, 198.51.100.48/255.255.255.240, and so on).

Because the 1s in a mask are always contiguous, each octet in decimal in an IPv4 mask will always be one of the following.

Octet Mask Bits	Binary Octet	Decimal Equivalent
1	10000000	128
2	11000000	192
3	11100000	224
4	11110000	240
5	11111000	248
6	11111100	252
7	11111110	254
8	11111111	255

Try to memorize these values to make converting masks between binary and decimal formats easier. For example, a shorter mask with 14 bits has the following mask:

```
11111111  11111100  00000000  00000000  255 252 0 0
```

Host Address Ranges

The IP network `198.51.100.0/24` allows for 254 possible host IDs. The host ID portion is 8 bits long:

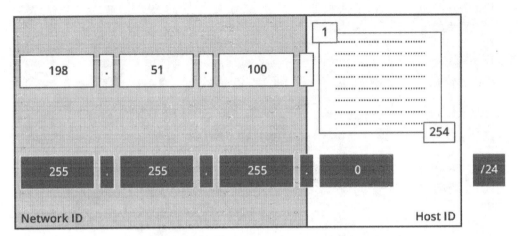

Host address range for a /24 network.

8 bits can express 256 possible values (2^8). However, the first address (`198.51.100.0`) cannot be assigned to a host because it is the network address. Similarly, the last address (`198.51.100.255`) is reserved (for use as a broadcast address).

Using some of these 8 host bits as a subnet ID creates extra networks, but each of those subnets has fewer host addresses (14 in this example):

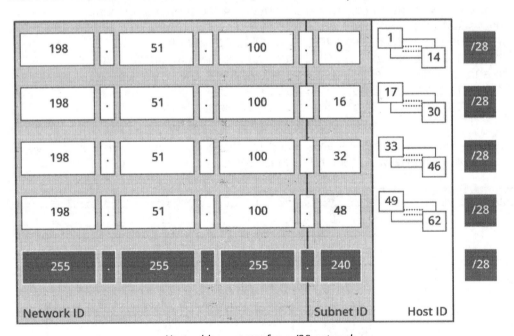

Host address range for a /28 network.

The purpose of subnetting is to create layer 3 broadcast domain segments with fewer hosts. The trick with subnet design is to fit the scheme to the requirements for number of subnetworks and number of hosts per subnet. Each bit added to the mask approximately halves the number of available host addresses.

Review Activity:

IPv4 Addressing Schemes

Answer the following questions:

1. **Convert the binary value 11110010 to decimal.**

2. **Convert the decimal value 72 into binary.**

3. **What is the dotted decimal representation of an 8-bit netmask?**

4. **What is the dotted decimal representation of an 18-bit netmask?**

5. **Given an 18-bit netmask, are the IP addresses 172.16.1.10 and 172.16.54.10 on the same network?**

6. **If the network ID is 10.1.0.0/22, how many IP addresses are available for allocation to host interfaces?**

Topic 5B

Explain IPv4 Forwarding

EXAM OBJECTIVES COVERED
1.4 Given a scenario, configure a subnet and use appropriate IP addressing schemes.

The core function of IP is to facilitate the creation of a group of logically distinct but interconnected networks, referred to as an internetwork. This means that some packets addressed to hosts on remote networks must be forwarded via one or more of the intermediate systems that establish paths between networks.

In this topic, you will identify the basic principles by which IP distinguishes local and remote hosts and networks, plus the methods by which a packet can be addressed to more than one host.

Layer 2 versus Layer 3 Addressing and Forwarding

When designing or supporting an IP network, it is important to understand how the logical addressing scheme of network, subnet, and host IDs at the network layer maps to forwarding at the data link layer. Forwarding at layer 3 is referred to as routing, while forwarding at layer 2 is described as switching.

The following figure illustrates how both switching and routing components might be used in a typical network. The whole network is connected to the wider Internet via the WAN interface on the router. The router's other interfaces are used to divide

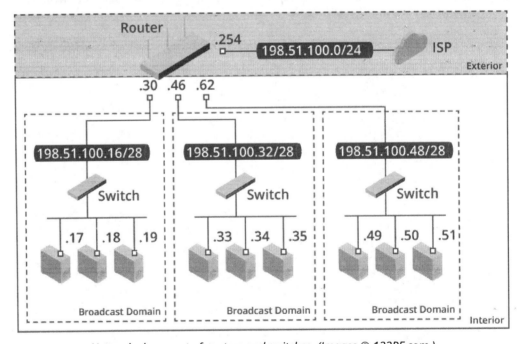

Network placement of routers and switches. (Images © 123RF.com.)

the network into three logical subnetworks. These subnets are mapped to layer 2 segments, each implemented using a switch.

Nodes within each subnet can address one another directly (they are in the same broadcast domain), but they can only communicate with nodes in other subnets via the router.

Within each subnet or broadcast domain, nodes use MAC addresses to forward frames to one another, using a mechanism to translate between layer 3 IP addresses and layer 2 MAC addresses.

The Network layer can also accommodate forwarding between different types of layer 1/layer 2 networks. The private zone is implemented using Ethernet, but the link between the router's public interface and the ISP might use a different technology, such as digital subscriber line (DSL).

IPv4 Default Gateways

When two end system hosts attempt to communicate via IPv4, the protocol compares the source and destination address in each packet against the netmask. If the masked portions of the source and destination IP addresses match, then the destination interface is assumed to be on the same IP network or subnet.

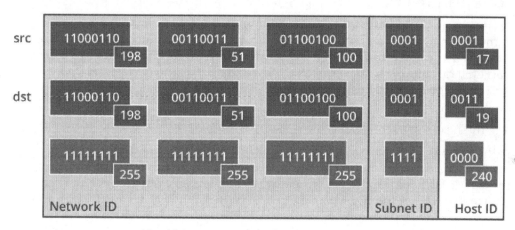

Matching source and destination network IDs.

In the figure, the first 28 bits of the source and destination address are the same. Therefore, IP concludes the destination IPv4 address is on the same IP network and tries to deliver the packet locally.

If the masked portion does not match, as in the following figure, IP assumes the packet must be routed to another IP network:

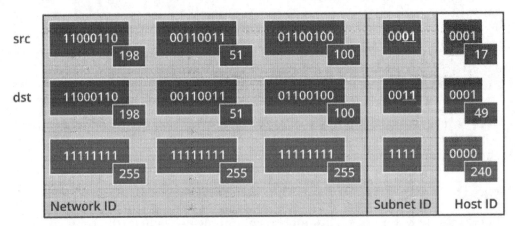

Different source and destination network IDs.

When the destination IPv4 address is on a different IP network or subnet, the host forwards the packet to its **default gateway**, rather than trying to deliver it locally. The default gateway is a router configured with a path to remote networks.

The router determines what to do with the packet by performing the same comparison between the source and destination address and netmask. The router then uses its routing table to determine which interface it should use to forward the packet. If no suitable path is available, the router drops the packet and informs the host that it could not be delivered.

If the message is destined for yet another network, the process is repeated to take it to the next stage, and so on.

Paths to other IP networks can be manually configured in the routing table or learned by a dynamic routing protocol. Dynamic routing protocols allow routers to share information about known networks and possible paths to them. This information allows them to choose the best routes to any given destination and select alternate routes if one of these is unavailable.

Address Resolution Protocol

When two hosts communicate over an Ethernet network using TCP/IP, an IP address is used at the Network layer to identify each host interface. However, transmission of data must take place at the Physical and Data Link level using the local or hardware/MAC address of the interface. The TCP/IP suite includes the **Address Resolution Protocol (ARP)** to perform the task of resolving an IP address to a hardware address.

When both sending and receiving hosts are within the same broadcast domain or subnet, local address resolution takes place using ARP requests and ARP replies, as shown in the figure:

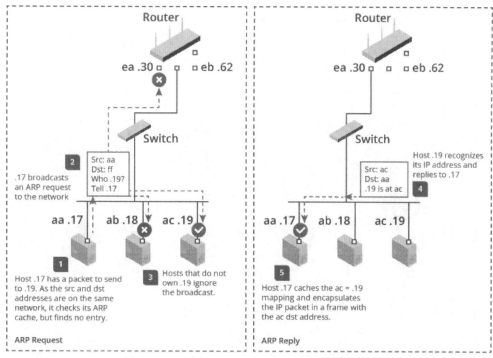

ARP requests and replies. (Images © 123RF.com.)

If the destination address is on a remote network, then the local host must use its default gateway to forward the packet. Therefore, it must determine the MAC address of the default gateway using ARP.

The router also uses ARP messaging for its Ethernet interfaces. ARP messaging is only used with Ethernet, however. A router's public interface might use a different type of framing and local addressing.

Unicast and Broadcast Addressing

IPv4 uses several mechanisms with which to communicate with other hosts. When an IPv4 host wants to send a packet to a single recipient, it uses a **unicast** packet, addressed to the IP address of the destination host. If, however, the local host needs to communicate with multiple hosts, it can use a different scheme.

One means of addressing multiple hosts is to perform a **broadcast**. A broadcast can be performed by sending a packet to the network or subnet's broadcast address. The broadcast address is the last address in any IP network, or put another way, the address in any IP network where all the host bits are set to 1.

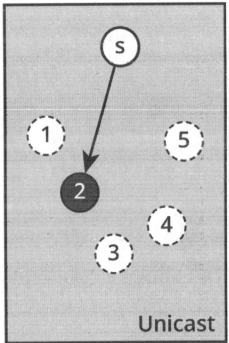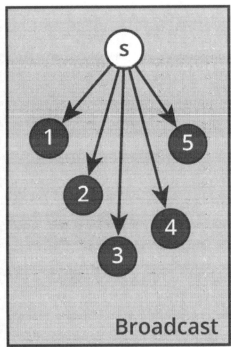

Unicast and broadcast addressing.

For example, if the subnet mask is 255.255.240.0, the last four digits of the last octet in the IP address is the host ID portion. If these digits are set to all 1s, that is the last possible address before the next subnet ID, and therefore the network broadcast address:

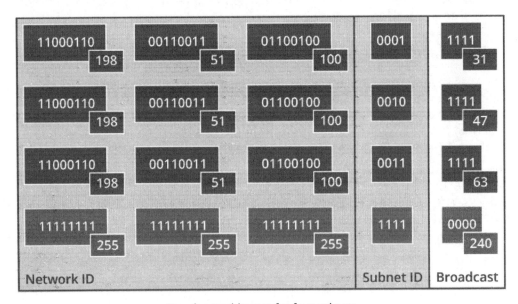

Broadcast addresses for four subnets.

All hosts that share the same broadcast address receive the packet. They are said to be in the same layer 3 broadcast domain. Broadcast domain boundaries are established at the Network layer by routers. Routers do not forward broadcasts, except in some specially configured circumstances.

As with unicast traffic, IP packets must be delivered to hosts using layer 2 MAC addresses. At layer 2, broadcasts are delivered using the group MAC address (ff:ff:ff:ff:ff:ff). This means that there is also a broadcast domain scope at layer 2. With legacy devices such as hubs and bridges, every port on all physically connected nodes is part of the same layer 2 broadcast domain. This is also the case with a basic or unmanaged switch. By default, a switch floods broadcasts out of every port except the source port.

Multicast and Anycast Addressing

While the majority of IPv4 traffic is unicast or broadcast, other addressing schemes are used in special circumstances.

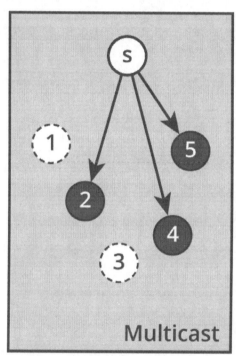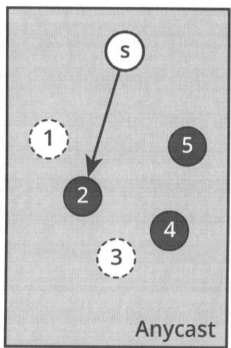

Multicast and anycast addressing.

Multicast Addressing

IPv4 **multicasting** allows one host on the Internet (or private IP network) to send content to other hosts that have identified themselves as interested in receiving the originating host's content. Multicast packets are sent to a destination IP address from a special range configured for use with that multicast group.

At layer 2, multicasts are delivered using a special range of MAC addresses. The switch must be multicast capable. If the switch is not multicast-capable, it will treat multicast like a broadcast and flood the multicast transmissions out of all ports.

The intent to receive multicasts from a particular host is signaled by joining a multicast group. The **Internet Group Management Protocol (IGMP)** is typically used to configure group memberships and IP addresses.

Anycast Addressing

Anycast means that a group of hosts are configured with the same IP address. When a router forwards a packet to an anycast group, it uses a prioritization algorithm and metrics to select the host that is "closest" (that will receive the packet and be able to process it the most quickly). This allows the service behind the IP address to be provisioned more reliably. It allows for load balancing and failover between the server hosts sharing the IP address.

Review Activity:

IPv4 Forwarding

Answer the following questions:

1. **Given the subnet mask 255.255.255.128, are the IP addresses 192.168.0.1 and 192.168.1.1 on the same network?**

2. **If a packet is addressed to a remote network, what destination MAC address will the sending node use to encapsulate the IP packet in a frame?**

3. **Assuming unmanaged switches, how many broadcast domains are present in the following figure?**

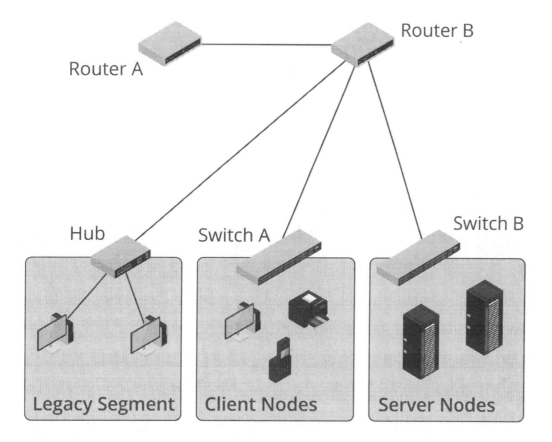

4. **If a host is configured with the IP address 10.0.10.22 and mask 255.255.255.192, what is the broadcast address of the subnet?**

5. **What type of addressing delivers a packet to a single host from a group without using unicast?**

Topic 5C

Configure IP Networks and Subnets

EXAM OBJECTIVES COVERED
1.4 Given a scenario, configure a subnet and use appropriate IP addressing schemes.

Organizations with large networks need to divide those networks up into smaller segments to improve performance and security. A network segment is represented at the Network layer by a subnet. Understanding basic principles of segmentation and subnetting will be critical to progressing a career in networking.

Virtual LANs and Subnets

Modern Ethernet networks are built using switches. In its default configuration, every port on a switch will be in the same local segment or, put another way, in the same broadcast domain. Any host within a broadcast domain can contact any other host using the same logical addressing scheme (IP subnet) and by hardware/MAC addressing.

If too many hosts are attached to the same switch, broadcast traffic can become excessive and reduce performance. At layer 2, **virtual LANs (VLANs)** are a means of addressing this issue. Each interface on a managed switch can be assigned a VLAN ID. Using VLANs means that different groups of computers on the same cabling and attached to the same switch(es) can appear to be in separate LAN segments. Each VLAN is a separate broadcast domain.

At layer 3, subnetting is the process of logically dividing an IP network into smaller subnetworks (subnets), with each subnet having a unique address. A subnetting scheme can be applied to represent the VLAN design in the layer 3 topology.

For example, the following subnet design allocates separate subnets (10.0.1.0 and 10.0.2.0) for the two VLANs configured on Switch A and for the serial WAN links configured between Router A and Routers B and C (10.0.3.0 and 10.0.4.0). Routers B and C also have a subnet each for their local networks (10.0.5.0 and 10.0.6.0).

Apart from breaking up broadcast domains, subnets can be used to achieve other network design goals:

- Many organizations have more than one site with WAN links between them. The WAN link normally forms a separate subnet.

- It is useful to divide a network into logically distinct zones for security and administrative control.

- Networks that use different physical and data link technologies, such as Token Ring and Ethernet, should be logically separated as different subnets.

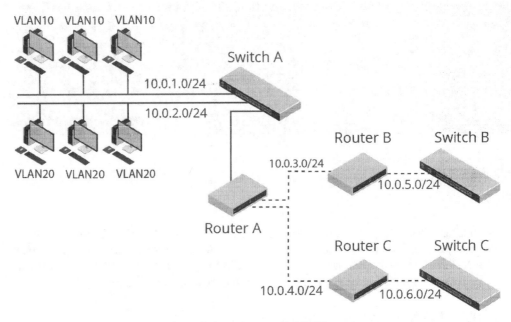

Subnet design. (Images © 123RF.com.)

Classful Addressing

So far, we have considered IP network and subnet IDs using masks or network prefixes. This is referred to as classless addressing. A **classful addressing** scheme was employed in the 1980s, before the use of netmasks to identify the network ID portion of an address was developed. Classful addressing allocates a network ID based on the first octet of the IP address.

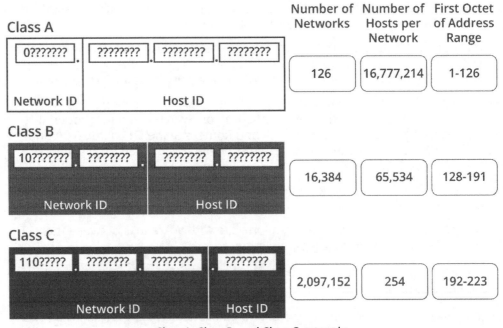

Class A, Class B, and Class C networks.

Class A network addresses support large numbers of hosts—over 16 million. However, there are only 126 Class A network addresses. There are 16,000 Class B networks, each containing up to about 65,000 hosts. Finally, Class C networks support only 254 hosts each, but there are over 2 million of them.

When considering classful addressing, you need to be able to identify the address class from the first octet of the IP address. This table shows how to identify an address class from the first octet of the IP address in decimal.

First Octet	Class
1–126	Class A
128–191	Class B
192–223	Class C

While routers have performed classless routing for years, the class terminology is still very widely used. Even under classless addressing, the old classes are often used as names for the netmasks that align to whole octet boundaries:

- Class A: 255.0.0.0 (/8)

- Class B: 255.255.0.0 (/16)

- Class C: 255.255.255.0 (/24)

Classful addressing is also important because it established some IP address ranges that cannot be used for ordinary host addressing or for addressing over the Internet.

Public versus Private Addressing

A **public IP address** is one that can establish a connection with other public IP networks and hosts over the Internet. The allocation of public IP addresses is governed by IANA and administered by regional registries and ISPs. Hosts communicating with one another over a LAN could use a public addressing scheme but will more typically use private addressing.

Private IP Address Ranges

Private IP addresses can be drawn from one of the pools of addresses defined in RFC 1918 as non-routable over the Internet:

- 10.0.0.0 to 10.255.255.255 (Class A private address range).

- 172.16.0.0 to 172.31.255.255 (Class B private address range).

- 192.168.0.0 to 192.168.255.255 (Class C private address range).

Any organization can use private addresses on its networks without applying to a registry or ISP, and multiple organizations can use these ranges simultaneously. Internet access can be facilitated for hosts using a private addressing scheme in two ways:

- Through a router configured with a single or block of valid public IP addresses; the router translates between the private and public addresses using a process called Network Address Translation (NAT).

- Through a proxy server that fulfills requests for Internet resources on behalf of clients. The proxy server itself must be configured with a public IP address on the external-facing interface.

Automatic Private IP Addressing (APIPA)

A host's IP configuration can either be applied statically or it can use an autoconfiguration method. Autoconfiguration on an IPv4 network usually means using a Dynamic Host Configuration Protocol (DHCP) server.

Automatic Private IP Addressing (APIPA) was developed by Microsoft as a means for clients that could not contact a DHCP server to communicate on the local network anyway. If a Windows host does not receive a response from a DHCP server within a given time frame, it selects an address at random from the range 169.254.1.1 to 169.254.254.254.

 These addresses are from one of the address ranges reserved for private addressing (169.254.0.0/16). The first and last subnets are supposed to be unused.

This type of addressing is referred to as link local in standards documentation (RFC 3927). Link local addressing mechanisms can also be implemented on other operating systems, such as Bonjour® for the macOS® platform or Avahi for Linux®.

Other Reserved Address Ranges

There are two additional classes of IP address (D and E) that use the values above 223.255.255.255:

- Class D addresses (224.0.0.0 through 239.255.255.255) are used for multicasting.

- Class E addresses (240.0.0.0 through 255.255.255.255) are reserved for experimental use and testing.

Loopback Addresses

While nominally part of Class A, the range 127.0.0.0 to 127.255.255.255 (or 127.0.0.0/8) is reserved. This range is used to configure a **loopback address**, which is a special address typically used to check that TCP/IP is correctly installed on the local host. The loopback interface does not require a physical interface to function. A packet sent to a loopback interface is not processed by a network adapter but is otherwise processed as normal by the host's TCP/IP stack. Every IP host is automatically configured with a default loopback address, typically 127.0.0.1. On some hosts, such as routers, more than one loopback address might be configured. Loopback interfaces can also be configured with an address from any suitable IP range, as long as it is unique on the network. A host will process a packet addressed to a loopback address regardless of the interface on which it is received.

Other

A few other IPv4 address ranges are reserved for special use and are not publicly routable:

- **0.0.0.0/8**—Used when a specific address is unknown. This is typically used as a source address by a client seeking a DHCP lease.

- **255.255.255.255**—Used to broadcast to the local network when the local network address is not known.

- **100.64.0.0/10, 192.0.0.0/24, 192.88.99.0/24, 198.18.0.0/15**—Set aside for a variety of special purposes.

- **192.0.2.0/24, 198.51.100.0/24, 203.0.113.0/24**—Set aside for use in documentation and examples.

IPv4 Address Scheme Design

The following factors must be weighed when planning an IPv4 network addressing scheme:

- The number of IP networks and subnetworks required.

- The number of hosts per subnet that must be supported.

- The network ID must be from a valid public or a private range (not from the loopback, link local reserved range, multicast range, or reserved/experimental range, for instance).

- The network and/or host IDs cannot be all 1s in binary—this is reserved for broadcasts.

- The network and/or host ID cannot be all 0s in binary; 0 means "this network."

- Each host ID must be unique on the IP network or subnet.

- The network ID must be unique on the Internet (if you are using a public addressing scheme) or on your internal system of internetworks (if you are using a private addressing scheme).

When you are performing subnet calculations, try to think in terms of the number of mask bits. It helps to remember that each power of 2 is double the previous one:

2^2	2^3	2^4	2^5	2^6	2^7	2^8
4	8	16	32	64	128	256

Also memorize the decimal values for the number of bits set to 1 in an octet within a mask:

1	2	3	4	5	6	7	8
128	192	224	240	248	252	254	255

In the following example, the network designed is subnetting the network address 172.30.0.0/16. The process of designing the scheme is as follows:

1. Work out how many subnets are required (remembering to allow for future growth), then round this number up to the nearest power of 2.

    For example, if you need 12 subnets, the next nearest power of 2 is 16. The exponent is the number of bits you will need to add to your default mask. For example, 16 is 2^4 (2 to the power of 4), so you will need to add 4 bits to the network prefix. In dotted decimal format, the subnet mask becomes 255.255.240.0.

2. Work out how many hosts each subnet must support and whether there is enough space left in the scheme to accommodate them.

    For example, the network address is in the /16 range, and you are using 4 bits for subnetting, so you have 32 − 20 = 12 bits for hosts in each subnet. The number of hosts per subnet can be expressed using the formula 2^n-2, where *n* is the number of bits you have allocated for the host ID. 12 bits is enough for 4094 hosts in each subnet.

You subtract 2 because each subnet's network address and broadcast address cannot be assigned to hosts.

Wherever a 1 appears in the binary mask, the corresponding digit in the IP address is part of the network or subnet address. When you are planning what your mask will be, remember this rule. Allocate more bits in the mask if you need more subnets. Allocate fewer bits in the mask if you need more hosts per subnet.

Just for comparison, if you have a /24 (or Class C) network address and try to allocate 16 subnets, there will be enough space left for only 14 hosts per subnet (2^4-2).

3. Work out the subnets. The easiest way to find the first subnet ID is to deduct the least significant octet in the mask (240 in this example) from 256. This gives the first subnet ID, which, in full, is 172.30.16.0/20.

    The subsequent subnet IDs are all the lowest subnet ID higher than the one before—32, 48, 64, and so on.

4. Work out the host ranges for each subnet. Take the subnet address and add a binary 1 to it for the first host. For the last host, take the next subnet ID and deduct two binary digits from it. In this case, this is 172.30.16.1 and 172.30.31.254, respectively. Repeat for all subnets.

Review Activity:

IP Networks and Subnets Configurations

Answer the following questions:

1. **True or False? The IP address 172.24.0.1 is routable over the Internet.**

2. **What is a Class D address?**

3. **What is the significance of the address 127.0.0.1?**

4. **A host is configured with the IP address 10.0.10.22 and subnet mask 255.255.255.192. How many hosts per subnet would this addressing scheme support?**

5. **If the IP address 10.0.10.22 were used with an /18 mask, how many subnets and hosts per subnet would be available?**

Review Activity:

Design an IP Subnet

At the 515support branch office, you have been asked to implement an IP network. Your network ID is currently 198.51.100.0/24. You need to divide this in half (two subnets) to accommodate hosts on two separate floors of the building, each of which is served by managed switches. The whole network is served by a single router.

Using the above scenario, answer the following questions:

---

1. **To divide the network in half, what subnet mask do you need to use?**

2. **What are the subnet IDs for each network?**

3. **What is the broadcast address for each subnet? 198.52.100.127 and 198.51.100.255.**

4. **What is the range of assignable IP addresses for each subnet?**

5. **Your manager has considered his original plan and realized that it does not accommodate the need for a WAN link to the head office or a separate segment for a team that works with sensitive data. What mask will you need to accommodate this new requirement, and how many hosts per subnet will it allow?**

Lesson 5

Summary

You should be able to use an appropriate IPv4 addressing scheme to plan a subnetted network.

Guidelines for Planning IPv4 Addressing Schemes

Follow these guidelines to configure subnets and use appropriate IP addressing schemes:

- Ensure good understanding of IPv4 addressing concepts to facilitate network design and support:

  - The use of 32-bit IPv4 addresses and netmasks or network prefixes to identify networks and subnets within networks.

  - The role of the Address Resolution Protocol (ARP) in mapping layer 3 to layer 2 IP:MAC addresses

  - The importance and uses of unicast, broadcast, multicast, and anycast addressing schemes.

  - The impact of legacy classful addressing features on address selection and usage, especially as regards private versus public ranges and loopback, class D, and class E ranges.

- Work out the topology of switches, virtual LANs (VLANs), and routers to create broadcast domain network segments that meet requirements for performance, security, and physical/data link network technologies.

- Allocate more bits to the netmask to create more subnets with fewer hosts per subnet, or fewer bits to the netmask to create fewer subnets with more hosts per subnet.

- Ensure that each host is configured with an appropriate IP address/subnet mask and default gateway for its subnet.

Lesson 6
Supporting IPv4 and IPv6 Networks

LESSON INTRODUCTION

IP is implemented on network hosts using a wide variety of configuration interfaces and tools. You must be confident about selecting an appropriate tool to use to complete a particular support or troubleshooting task.

This lesson also introduces IPv6 addressing concepts and highlights some key differences between IPv6 and IPv4.

Lesson Objectives

In this lesson, you will:

- Use appropriate tools to test IP configuration.

- Troubleshoot IP networks.

- Explain IPv6 addressing schemes.

Topic 6A

Use Appropriate Tools to Test IP Configuration

 EXAM OBJECTIVES COVERED
1.5 Explain common ports and protocols, their application, and encrypted alternatives. (ICMP only)
5.3 Given a scenario, use the appropriate network software tools and commands.

TCP/IP command line utilities enable you to gather information about how your systems are configured and how they communicate over an IP network. When used for troubleshooting, these utilities can provide information about communication issues and their causes.

IP Interface Configuration in Windows

Each host adapter must be allocated an appropriate IP address and subnet mask, plus the IP address of the default gateway (router) for its network. Typically, a host is also configured with the addresses of domain name system (DNS) servers that can resolve IP address to name labels, making identification of hosts and services simpler.

These IP configuration values can be assigned statically or dynamically. Configuring large numbers of hosts with a valid static addressing parameters is a complex management task. Most hosts are configured to obtain an address automatically, using a service called the Dynamic Host Configuration Protocol (DHCP).

Under Windows, each Ethernet adapter is assigned a name. In early Windows versions the first adapter was named "Local Area Connection," but recent versions just use the label "Ethernet." Additional adapters are identified as "Ethernet2," "Ethernet3," and so on. A new name can be applied if necessary. The IP configuration for each adapter interface is often set using the GUI Properties dialog accessed via the Network Connections applet. However, you can also configure interfaces using `netsh` commands.

```
netsh interface ip set address "Ethernet" dhcp

netsh interface ip set address "Ethernet" static
10.1.0.1 255.255.255.0 10.1.0.254
```

In Windows, all changes to the network interface configuration are persistent, meaning that they continue to apply when the system is rebooted.

You can also use `netsh` to report the IP configuration (`netsh interface ip show config`, for example).

`netsh` is implemented in the legacy command prompt interface. Script-based configuration is now more likely to use PowerShell cmdlets. The `Get-NetAdapter` and `Get-NetIPAddress` cmdlets can be used to query the existing configuration. A new configuration can be applied using `New-NetIPAddress` or an existing one can be modified using `Set-NetIPAddress`.

ipconfig

While netsh and PowerShell offer a lot of granular functionality, the **ipconfig** command is still widely used for basic configuration reporting and support tasks. ipconfig can be used as follows:

- `ipconfig` without any switches will display the IP address, subnet mask, and default gateway (router) for all network interfaces to which TCP/IP is bound.

- `ipconfig /all` displays complete TCP/IP configuration parameters for each interface, including whether the Dynamic Host Configuration Protocol (DHCP) is enabled for the interface and the interface's hardware (MAC) address.

- `ipconfig /renew interface` forces a DHCP client to renew the lease it has for an IP address.

- `ipconfig /release interface` releases the IP address obtained from a DHCP Server so that the interface(s) will no longer have an IP address.

- `ipconfig /displaydns` displays the Domain Name System (DNS) resolver cache.

- `ipconfig /flushdns` clears the DNS resolver cache.

- `ipconfig /registerdns` registers the host with a DNS server (if it supports dynamic updates).

```
PS C:\Windows\system32> ipconfig /all

Windows IP Configuration

    Host Name . . . . . . . . . . . . : PC10
    Primary Dns Suffix  . . . . . . . : corp.515support.com
    Node Type . . . . . . . . . . . . : Mixed
    IP Routing Enabled. . . . . . . . : No
    WINS Proxy Enabled. . . . . . . . : No
    DNS Suffix Search List. . . . . . : corp.515support.com

Ethernet adapter Ethernet:

    Connection-specific DNS Suffix  . : corp.515support.com
    Description . . . . . . . . . . . : Microsoft Hyper-V Network Adapter
    Physical Address. . . . . . . . . : 00-15-5D-00-65-31
    DHCP Enabled. . . . . . . . . . . : Yes
    Autoconfiguration Enabled . . . . : Yes
    IPv6 Address. . . . . . . . . . . : fdf0:2413:6d1c:30:997b:634e:5b90:7e(Preferred)
    Link-local IPv6 Address . . . . . : fe80::997b:634e:5b90:7e%9(Preferred)
    IPv4 Address. . . . . . . . . . . : 10.1.24.101(Preferred)
    Subnet Mask . . . . . . . . . . . : 255.255.255.0
    Lease Obtained. . . . . . . . . . : Wednesday, August 4, 2021 12:11:31 AM
    Lease Expires . . . . . . . . . . : Thursday, August 12, 2021 12:11:30 AM
    Default Gateway . . . . . . . . . : fe80::215:5dff:fe00:6510%9
                                        10.1.24.254
    DHCP Server . . . . . . . . . . . : 10.1.16.1
    DHCPv6 IAID . . . . . . . . . . . : 67114333
    DHCPv6 Client DUID. . . . . . . . : 00-01-00-01-27-E6-CC-0C-00-15-5D-00-65-31
    DNS Servers . . . . . . . . . . . : 10.1.16.1
    NetBIOS over Tcpip. . . . . . . . : Enabled
PS C:\Windows\system32> _
```

Identifying the current IP configuration with ipconfig. (Screenshot used with permission from Microsoft.)

 There are also `/release6` and `/renew6` switches for use with DHCPv6 (a DHCP server supporting IPv6).

ifconfig and ip

In Linux, Ethernet interfaces are classically identified as `eth0`, `eth1`, `eth2`, and so on, although some network packages now use different schemes, such as `en` prefixes. In Linux, you need to distinguish between the running configuration and the persistent configuration. The persistent configuration is the one applied after a reboot or after a network adapter is reinitialized. The method of applying an IP configuration to an adapter interface is specific to each distribution. Historically, the persistent configuration was applied by editing the `/etc/network/interfaces` file and bringing interfaces up or down with the `ifup` and `ifdown` scripts. Many distributions now use the NetworkManager package, which can be operated using a GUI or the nmcli tools. Alternatively, a network configuration might be managed using the systemd-networkd configuration manager. Additionally, recent distributions of Ubuntu use netplan to abstract some of this underlying complexity to configuration files written in **YAML ain't markup language (YAML)**. The YAML configuration files are rendered by either systemd-networkd or NetworkManager.

When it comes to managing the running configuration, you also need to distinguish between legacy and current command packages. **ifconfig** is part of the legacy net-tools package. Use of these commands is deprecated on most modern Linux distributions. `ifconfig` can still safely be used to report the network interface configuration, however.

```
lamp@lamp:~$ ifconfig
eth0: flags=4163<UP,BROADCAST,RUNNING,MULTICAST>  mtu 1500
        inet 172.16.0.201  netmask 255.255.255.0  broadcast 172.16.0.255
        inet6 fe80::215:5dff:fe00:6517  prefixlen 64  scopeid 0x20<link>
        ether 00:15:5d:00:65:17  txqueuelen 1000  (Ethernet)
        RX packets 4042  bytes 589111 (589.1 KB)
        RX errors 0  dropped 0  overruns 0  frame 0
        TX packets 7788  bytes 2885069 (2.8 MB)
        TX errors 0  dropped 0 overruns 0  carrier 0  collisions 0

lo: flags=73<UP,LOOPBACK,RUNNING>  mtu 65536
        inet 127.0.0.1  netmask 255.0.0.0
        inet6 ::1  prefixlen 128  scopeid 0x10<host>
        loop  txqueuelen 1000  (Local Loopback)
        RX packets 5244  bytes 413133 (413.1 KB)
        RX errors 0  dropped 0  overruns 0  frame 0
        TX packets 5244  bytes 413133 (413.1 KB)
        TX errors 0  dropped 0 overruns 0  carrier 0  collisions 0
```

ifconfig output.

net-tools has been replaced by the iproute2 package. These tools can interface properly with modern network configuration manager packages. As part of the iproute2 package, the **ip** command has options for managing routes as well as the local interface configuration. The basic reporting functionality of `ifconfig` (show the current address configuration) is performed by running `ip addr`; to report a single interface only, use `ip addr show dev eth0`. The `ip link` command shows the status of interfaces, while `ip -s link` reports interface statistics.

```
lamp@lamp:~$ ip a
1: lo: <LOOPBACK,UP,LOWER_UP> mtu 65536 qdisc noqueue state UNKNOWN group default qlen 1000
    link/loopback 00:00:00:00:00:00 brd 00:00:00:00:00:00
    inet 127.0.0.1/8 scope host lo
       valid_lft forever preferred_lft forever
    inet6 ::1/128 scope host
       valid_lft forever preferred_lft forever
2: eth0: <BROADCAST,MULTICAST,UP,LOWER_UP> mtu 1500 qdisc mq state UP group default qlen 1000
    link/ether 00:15:5d:00:65:17 brd ff:ff:ff:ff:ff:ff
    inet 172.16.0.201/24 brd 172.16.0.255 scope global dynamic eth0
       valid_lft 6026sec preferred_lft 6026sec
    inet6 fe80::215:5dff:fe00:6517/64 scope link
       valid_lft forever preferred_lft forever
```

ip a command output.

The `ip link set eth0 up|down` command is used to enable or disable an interface, while `ip addr add|delete` can be used to modify the IP address configuration. These changes are not persistent and apply only to the running configuration, unless run as part of a startup script.

ARP Cache Utility

The Address Resolution Protocol (ARP) is used by hosts to determine which MAC address is associated with an IP address on the local network. ARP queries are sent as broadcasts. ARP broadcasts can generate considerable traffic on a network, which can reduce performance. To optimize this process, the results of an ARP broadcast are cached in an ARP table. If the entry is used within the timeout period, the entry is held in the cache for a few minutes before it is deleted.

The **arp** utility can be used to perform functions related to the ARP table cache. You would use this to diagnose a suspected problem with local addressing and packet delivery.

- `arp -a` (or `arp -g`) shows the ARP cache contents. You can use this with `IPAddress` to view the ARP cache for the specified interface only. The ARP cache will not necessarily contain the MAC addresses of every host on the local segment. There will be no cache entry if there has not been a recent exchange of frames.

- `arp -s IPAddress MACAddress` adds an entry to the ARP cache. Under Windows, `MACAddress` needs to be entered with hyphens between each hex byte.

- `arp -d *` deletes all entries in the ARP cache; it can also be used with IPAddress to delete a single entry.

```
PS C:\Windows\system32> arp -a

Interface: 10.1.24.101 --- 0x9
  Internet Address        Physical Address      Type
  10.1.24.254             00-15-5d-00-65-10     dynamic
  10.1.24.255             ff-ff-ff-ff-ff-ff     static
  224.0.0.22              01-00-5e-00-00-16     static
  224.0.0.251             01-00-5e-00-00-fb     static
  224.0.0.252             01-00-5e-00-00-fc     static
  239.255.255.250         01-00-5e-7f-ff-fa     static
  255.255.255.255         ff-ff-ff-ff-ff-ff     static
```

Output from the arp command showing network (IP) addresses mapped to physical (MAC) addresses. Host interfaces are learned (dynamic), while broadcast and multicast interfaces are configured statically. (Screenshot used with permission from Microsoft.)

In Linux, the `ip neigh` command shows entries in the local ARP cache (replacing the old `arp` command).

Internet Control Message Protocol and ping

The **Internet Control Message Protocol (ICMP)** is used to report errors and send messages about the delivery of a packet. ICMP messages are generated under error conditions in most types of unicast traffic, but not for broadcast or multicast packets.

ICMP can also be used to test and troubleshoot connectivity issues on IP networks. The **ping** utility sends a configurable number and size of ICMP request packets to a destination host. `ping` is implemented on both Windows and Linux hosts. `ping` can be used to perform a basic connectivity test that is not dependent on the target host running any higher-level applications or services.

Basic ping Usage

A basic connectivity test is performed by running `ping IPAddress`, where *IPAddress* is an IPv4 or IPv6 address.

If the probe is successful (as in the first attempts shown in the screen capture), the output shows the message "Reply from IPAddress" and the time it takes for the server's response to arrive. The millisecond measures of Round Trip Time (RTT) can be used to diagnose latency problems on a link.

```
PS C:\Windows\system32> ping 127.0.0.1 -n 1

Pinging 127.0.0.1 with 32 bytes of data:
Reply from 127.0.0.1: bytes=32 time<1ms TTL=128

Ping statistics for 127.0.0.1:
    Packets: Sent = 1, Received = 1, Lost = 0 (0% loss),
Approximate round trip times in milli-seconds:
    Minimum = 0ms, Maximum = 0ms, Average = 0ms
PS C:\Windows\system32> ping 10.1.24.101 -n 1

Pinging 10.1.24.101 with 32 bytes of data:
Reply from 10.1.24.101: bytes=32 time<1ms TTL=128

Ping statistics for 10.1.24.101:
    Packets: Sent = 1, Received = 1, Lost = 0 (0% loss),
Approximate round trip times in milli-seconds:
    Minimum = 0ms, Maximum = 0ms, Average = 0ms
PS C:\Windows\system32> ping 10.1.24.254 -n 1

Pinging 10.1.24.254 with 32 bytes of data:
Reply from 10.1.24.254: bytes=32 time<1ms TTL=64

Ping statistics for 10.1.24.254:
    Packets: Sent = 1, Received = 1, Lost = 0 (0% loss),
Approximate round trip times in milli-seconds:
    Minimum = 0ms, Maximum = 0ms, Average = 0ms
PS C:\Windows\system32> ping 203.0.113.33 -n 1

Pinging 203.0.113.33 with 32 bytes of data:
Reply from 203.0.113.33: bytes=32 time=2ms TTL=60

Ping statistics for 203.0.113.33:
    Packets: Sent = 1, Received = 1, Lost = 0 (0% loss),
Approximate round trip times in milli-seconds:
    Minimum = 2ms, Maximum = 2ms, Average = 2ms
```

Using ping in Windows. (Screenshot used with permission from Microsoft.)

The Time to Live (TTL) IP header field is reduced by one every time a packet is forwarded by a router (referred to as a hop). The TTL output field in the ping command shows the value of the counter when the packet arrived at its destination.

To work out the number of hops it took, you need to know the initial value. Different operating systems and OS versions use different default values. For example, if you ping a remote host from a Windows 10 host and the TTL value in the output is 52, then you know the packet took 12 hops (64-52) to reach its destination.

ping Error Messaging

If ping probes are unsuccessful, one of two messages are commonly received:

- **Destination host unreachable**—There is no routing information (that is, the local computer does not know how to get to that IP address). This might be caused by some sort of configuration error on the local host, such as an incorrect default gateway, by a loss of connectivity with a router, or by a routing configuration error.

- **No reply (Request timed out.)**—The host is unavailable or cannot route a reply to your computer. Requests time out when the TTL is reduced to 0 because the packet is looping (because of a corrupted routing table), when congestion causes delays, or when a host does not respond.

ping Switches

ping can be used with several switches. You can use a host name or fully qualified domain name rather than an IP address to test name resolution. When pinging by name, -4 or -6 force the tool to query the IPv4 host record or IPv6 host record respectively. Also, -t continues to ping the host until interrupted (by pressing `Ctrl+C`).

ping has different syntax when used under Linux. By default, the command executes until manually halted, unless run with the number of packets set by the -c switch.

Review Activity:

Test IP Configuration

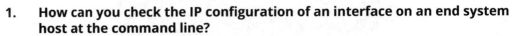

Answer the following questions:

1. **How can you check the IP configuration of an interface on an end system host at the command line?**

   ip config's

2. **What output would you expect when running the command ip neigh?**

   Linx local ARP

3. **True or False? The arp utility will always show another host's MAC address if that host is on the same subnet.**

   ARP Purges frea.

4. **Output from a ping command reports some values in milliseconds. What does this measure?**

   TTL

5. **True or False? Receiving an echo reply message indicates that the link between two hosts is operational.**

Topic 6B
Troubleshoot IP Networks

EXAM OBJECTIVES COVERED
5.5 Given a scenario, troubleshoot general networking issues.

While some support scenarios require a top-to-bottom or bottom-to-top approach, in practical terms a lot of troubleshooting activity starts with the network layer. Connectivity tests and configuration information can identify issues within this layer or inform your decision of whether to move up or down layers to pinpoint the cause of a problem.

Hardware Failure and Network Interface Issues

When you are using the CompTIA Network+ troubleshooting model, it is wise to rule out physical hardware failure and Data Link layer issues before diagnosing a Network layer or service issue. Failures at the Network layer are more common, but if you can isolate a connectivity problem to a particular network segment, the cause may lie in a hardware failure rather than a configuration issue.

Power Issues

Like any computer system, networks require stable power to operate properly. Power anomalies, such as surges and spikes, can damage devices, brownouts (very brief power loss) can cause systems to lockup or reboot, while power failures (blackouts) will down everything, including the lights. Enterprise sites have systems to protect against these issues. Uninterruptible power supplies (UPSs) can keep servers, switches, and routers running for a few minutes. This provides time to either switch in a secondary power source (a generator) or shut down the system gracefully, hopefully avoiding data loss. Most power problems will have to be escalated to an electrician or to the power company, depending on where the fault lies.

Hardware Failure Issues

If power is not the issue, consider other components that might have experienced hardware failure, including host network adapters, switch/router/modem appliances, and the cabling between them. You can test for specific cabling faults and bad ports using cable and loopback testers and certifiers. Complete hardware failure is relatively uncommon, so if you can rule out power and cabling problems, then for a network adapter, verify that the driver is working correctly. The easiest thing to do is to replace the driver (in Windows®, use Device Manager to do this). For a network appliance, use status LEDs to confirm operation and check that things like plug-in cards and modules are seated correctly. You should also consider overheating as a potential cause of hardware issues. Make sure there is good airflow around the intake and outlet vents. Check that fans and internal components are not clogged with dust and that systems are not exposed to direct sunlight.

At the data link layer, most wired hosts connect to the network via a switch. If you suspect a device like a switch, analyze the topology of your network. You should be able to view those users who are suffering the problem, identify which part of the network is affected, and identify the problem bridging or switching device.

When you have narrowed the problem to a device, you must determine what the nature of the problem is. It is always worth resetting the switch to see if that resolves the problem. Often, restarting network devices can clear any errors.

Interface Status Issues

If you can isolate the issue to a single host and then rule out cable and transceiver issues at the physical layer, bear in mind that the data link configuration might not be working. Use the LED status indicators and switch's command line utility to check the interface status. If the line and protocol status is not up/up, check whether autonegotiation of speed and duplex settings is configured and whether it is failing. If the speed setting (10, 100, or 1000 Mbps) is mismatched between the host and the switch port, the link will fail.

Interface status commands will also report whether any collisions are being generated. Collisions might occur if the duplex setting on the switch port and host is mismatched or if a legacy hub device or host NIC is connected to a switch. If neither of these conditions apply, check for a faulty host NIC or driver.

IP Configuration Issues

If you can rule out a problem at the Physical and Data Link layers, the next thing to check is basic addressing and protocol configuration. If a host cannot perform neighbor discovery to contact any other nodes on the local network, first use ipconfig (Windows) or ip or ifconfig (Linux) to verify the host configuration.

Incorrect IP Address

Each end system host must have the same subnet mask as its neighbors and an IP address that produces a valid, unique host address within that subnet. A neighbor in this sense is another host in the same layer 2 broadcast domain. For example, if the subnet is 192.168.1.0/24, consider the following host address configurations:

- Host A: IP: 192.168.1.10, Mask: 255.255.255.0

- Host B: IP: 192.168.1.11, Mask: 255.255.255.0

- Host C: IP: 192.168.0.21, Mask: 255.255.255.0

Host A and Host B have valid configurations, but Host C has an address in a different subnet (192.168.0.0 compared to 192.168.1.0). Hosts A and B will try to use the default gateway to forward packets to Host C. Host C is unlikely to be able to communicate on the network at all.

When you encounter nondefault masks, it can be slightly more difficult to identify valid host ranges. For example, if the subnet address is 198.51.100.16/28, consider the following host address configurations:

- Host A: IP: 198.51.100.10, Mask: 255.255.255.240

- Host B: IP: 198.51.100.11, Mask: 255.255.255.240

- Host C: IP: 198.51.100.21, Mask: 255.255.255.240

The network prefix boundary lies within the last octet, so you cannot rely on the first three octets alone. Again, host C is in a different subnet.

Also, remember that the network address and broadcast address cannot be used as a host address.

Incorrect Subnet Mask

Another issue that might arise if a netmask is incorrect, is that the host can receive communications, but misroutes its replies, thinking that the hosts communicating with it are on a different subnet. The replies may still get through, although they may go via the default gateway (router), rather than directly.

- Host A: IP: 192.168.1.10, Mask: 255.255.255.0

- Host B: IP: 192.168.1.11, Mask: 255.255.255.0

- Host C: IP: 192.168.1.21, Mask: 255.255.255.240

Because it is using a longer prefix than it should, Host C will think it needs to route to a different subnet to communicate with hosts A and B. This will cause packets to go via the router, placing unnecessary load on it.

The other scenario for an incorrect mask is where the mask is shorter than it should be:

- Host A: IP: 192.168.1.10, Mask: 255.255.255.0

- Host B: IP: 192.168.1.11, Mask: 255.255.255.0

- Host C: IP: 192.168.1.21, Mask: 255.255.0.0

- Host D: IP: 192.168.0.10, Mask: 255.255.255.0

In this case, the problem will not be obvious if hosts A, B, and C are all on the same local network, as they will be able to use ARP messaging and receive replies. However, host C will not be able to contact host D, as it thinks that host D is on the same local network, whereas in fact it needs to route messages for 192.168.0.0/24 via the default gateway.

 In this scenario, the router might send ICMP redirect status messages to host C.

Duplicate IP and MAC Address Issues

Two systems could end up with the same IP address because of a configuration error; perhaps both addresses were statically assigned, or one was assigned an address that was part of a DHCP scope. If Windows detects a duplicate IP address, it will display a warning and disable IP. Linux® does not typically check for duplicate IP addresses. If there are two systems with duplicate IPs, a sort of race condition will determine which receives traffic. Obviously, this is not a good way for the network to be configured, and you should identify and fix the machines. To do this, obtain the MAC addresses of both interfaces using `ping` and then `arp -a` to examine the ARP cache table. On Linux, you can use the `arping` tool (`arping -D`) to report duplicate replies. Once identified, configure each host to use a unique address.

A duplicate MAC address will cause a problem similar to a duplicate IP address. Both hosts will contend to respond to ARP queries, and communications could be split between them or reach only one of the hosts. Duplicate MAC addresses are unlikely to arise unless the network uses locally administered addressing.

Issues with MAC addressing can be a sign that someone is attempting to perform a spoofing attack. Spoofing attacks are discussed later in the course.

To diagnose MAC address issues, use the `arp` utility to verify the MAC addresses recorded for each host and `ipconfig` or `ip neigh` to check the MAC address assigned to the interface. Also check the MAC address and ARP tables on any switches and routers involved in the communications path. You can use a protocol analyzer to examine ARP traffic and identify which IP hosts are attempting to claim the same MAC address.

Problem Isolation

If the address configuration on the local host seems to be correct, you can complete a series of connectivity tests using ping to determine the likely location and scope of a fault.

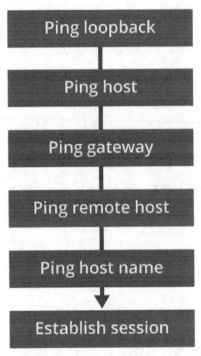

A general ping sequence for identifying connectivity issues.

1. Ping the loopback address (`ping 127.0.0.1`) to verify TCP/IP is installed and loaded correctly. If this fails, reinstall the network protocol stack.

2. Ping the IP address of the local host to verify it was added correctly and to verify that the network adapter is functioning properly. If you cannot ping your own address, there might have been a configuration error, or the network adapter or adapter driver could be faulty.

3. Ping the IP address of the default gateway to verify it is up and running and that you can communicate with another host on the local network.

4. Ping the IP address of other hosts on the same subnet to test for local configuration or link problems.

   If a local host cannot be pinged and the error is destination unreachable, then verify the IP configuration does not contain an incorrect IP address or netmask. If these are correct but pings still time out, suspect either a security issue (such as a switch port security issue) or a problem at the data link or physical layer.

5. Ping the IP address of a remote host to verify you can communicate through the router. If a remote IP address cannot be contacted, check the default gateway parameter on the local host to rule out an incorrect gateway issue. If the gateway is configured correctly and you can ping the router, you need to start investigating the routing infrastructure.

 When performing tests using ping, always be aware that ICMP could be blocked by a firewall or other security software, especially when pinging remote hosts.

Incorrect DNS Issues

If you can successfully perform all connectivity tests by IP address but cannot ping by host name, then this suggests a name resolution problem. Many services use host names and domain names to make them easier to reconfigure and easier for people to access. The Domain Name System (DNS) is used to map these names to IP addresses. When a host receives a client request to access a name and it does not have the IP mapping cached, it asks a DNS server configured as a resolver to perform the lookup and return the IP address. As name resolution is a critical service, most hosts are configured with primary and secondary DNS servers for redundancy. The server addresses are entered as IP addresses. On most workstation hosts, these addresses are likely to be autoconfigured via DHCP.

In Windows, you can view the DNS servers using `ipconfig /all`. In Linux, the DNS server addresses are recorded in `/etc/resolv.conf`. Typically, a package such as NetworkManager or systemd-networkd would add the entries. Entries added directly will be overwritten at reboot.

If a host cannot resolve names, check that the correct DNS server addresses have been configured and that you can ping them. If there are configuration errors, either correct them (if the interface is statically configured) or investigate the automatic addressing server. If there are connectivity errors, check the network path between the host and its DNS servers.

Multicast Flooding Issues

Multicast is a one-to-many type of transmission designed for more efficient delivery of packets. Rather than a transmitter sending separate unicast packets to each receiver, a copy of the same packet is delivered to each receiver that has joined the relevant multicast group. Multicast groups are established at layer 3 by protocols such as Internet Group Management Protocol (IGMP).

At layer 2, if a switch is not multicast-aware, it will treat multicast transmissions as broadcasts and flood them across all ports in the broadcast domain. This can consume a lot of bandwidth and slow down the network. This problem becomes particularly acute if the switch floods multicast traffic to virtual LANs (VLANs) that do not need to receive it. To combat this, IGMP snooping can be enabled as a global option on a switch and as a per-VLAN option. IGMP snooping means the switch reads IGMP messages and can determine if the host on an access port or one or more hosts in a VLAN have joined a multicast group. Multicast traffic is filtered from ports and VLANs that have no hosts participating in the multicast group.

Review Activity:

Troubleshoot IP Networks

Answer the following questions:

1. Users on a floor served by a single switch cannot get a network connection. What is the best first step?

2. A workstation cannot connect to a server application on a remote network. What is the first test you could perform to establish whether the workstation's link is OK?

3. A technician is troubleshooting a network and has asked your advice. He is trying to ping 192.168.16.192. The network has been subnetted with the custom mask 255.255.255.224. Why might this return a "Destination host unreachable" message?

4. Two client hosts have intermittent connectivity issues when accessing a server service on another subnet. No other client hosts exhibit this problem. What configuration problem might you suspect?

5. You have pinged the router for the local subnet and confirmed that there is a valid link. The local host cannot access remote hosts, however. No other users are experiencing problems. What do you think is the cause?

6. A Windows client workstation cannot access a help desk application server by its name support.515support.com. The service can be accessed using its IP address. What two command line tools should you use to identify possible causes of this issue?

Topic 6C

Explain IPv6 Addressing Schemes

EXAM OBJECTIVES COVERED
1.4 Given a scenario, configure a subnet and use appropriate IP addressing schemes.
2.3 Given a scenario, configure and deploy common Ethernet switching features.
(ND protocol only)

The previous topics focused on IP version 4 (IPv4), which is still the mainstream version of the protocol. In this topic, you will learn to explain IP version 6 (IPv6) addressing. As a network professional, you should be aware of the limitations of IPv4 and the increasing adoption of IPv6. You need to understand the characteristics of IPv6, as well as how it can interoperate with existing IPv4 implementations.

IPv4 versus IPv6

In IPv4, the addressing scheme is based on a 32-bit binary number. 32 bits can express 2^{32} unique addresses (in excess of four billion). However, the way in which addresses have been allocated has been inefficient, leading to waste of available addresses. Inefficiencies in the addressing scheme and unceasing demand for more addresses mean that the available IPv4 address supply is exhausted.

IP version 6 (IPv6) provides a long-term solution to this problem of address space exhaustion. Its 128-bit addressing scheme has space for 340 undecillion unique addresses. Even though only a small part of the scheme can currently be allocated to hosts, there is still enough address space within that allocation for every person on the planet to own approximately 4,000 addresses. As well as coping with the growth in ordinary company networks and Internet access subscribers, IPv6 is designed to meet the demands of billions of personal and embedded devices with Internet connectivity.

This blog explains why we have jumped from IPv4 to IPv6: colocationamerica.com/blog/ipv4-ipv6-what-happened-to-ipv5.htm.

An IPv6 packet consists of two or three elements: the main header, which is a fixed length (unlike in IPv4), one or more optional extension headers, and the payload. As with an IPv4 header, there are fields for the source and destination addresses and the version (0110 or 0x06 for IPv6). Some of the other header fields are as follows:

Field	Explanation
Traffic Class	Describes the packet's priority.
Flow Label	Used for quality of service (QoS) management, such as for real-time streams. This is set to 0 for packets not part of any delivery sequence or structure.
Payload Length	Indicates the length of the packet payload, up to a maximum of 64 KB; if the payload is bigger than that, this field is 0 and a special Jumbo Payload (4 GB) option is established.
Next Header	Used to describe what the next extension header (if any) is, or where the actual payload begins.
Hop Limit	Replaces the TTL field in IPv4 but performs the same function.

Extension headers replace the Options field in IPv4. There are several predefined extension headers to cover functions such as fragmentation and reassembly, security (IPSec), source routing, and so on.

IPv6 Address Format

An IPv6 address contains eight 16-bit numbers (double-byte or double-octet), with each double-byte number expressed as 4 hex digits. For example, consider the following binary address:

```
0010 0000 0000 0001 : 0000 1101 1011 1000 : 0000
0000 0000 0000 : 0000 0000 0000 0000 : 0000 1010
1011 1100 : 0000 0000 0000 0000 : 1101 1110 1111
0000 : 0001 0010 0011 0100
```

This binary value can be represented in hex notation as:

```
2001:0db8:0000:0000:0abc:0000:def0:1234
```

Using **canonical notation**, the hex notation can be compressed further. Where a double byte contains leading 0s, they can be ignored. In addition, one contiguous series of 0s can be replaced by a double colon place marker. Thus, the prior address would become:

```
2001:db8::abc:0:def0:1234
```

You can only use double colon compression once in a given address. For example, `2001:db8::abc::def0:1234` is not valid as it is unclear which of the following two addresses is represented:

```
2001:db8:0000:0abc:0000:0000:def0:1234
```

```
2001:db8:0000:0000:0abc:0000:def0:1234
```

Where IPv6 addresses are used as part of a URL (web address), because both formats use colon delimiters to mean different things, the IPv6 address must be contained within brackets. For example:

```
https://[2001:db8::abc:0:def0:1234]/index.htm
```

IPv6 Network Prefixes

An IPv6 address is divided into two parts: the first 64 bits are used as a network ID, while the second 64 bits designate a specific interface. Unlike in IPv4, the interface address (or host ID portion) is always the same 64-bit length.

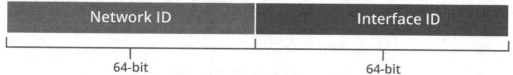

Network ID	Interface ID
64-bit	64-bit

In IPv6, the interface identifier is always the last 64 bits. The first 64 bits are used for network addressing.

Network addresses are written using classless notation, where /nn is the length of the network prefix in bits. Within the 64-bit network ID, as with IPv4 netmasks, the length of any given network prefix is used to determine whether two addresses belong to the same IP network. For example, if the prefix is /48, then if the first 48 bits of an IPv6 address were the same as another address, the two would belong to the same IP network. This means that a given organization's network can be represented by a global routing prefix 48 bits long, and they then have 16 bits left in the network ID to subnet their network. For example,

    2001:db8:3c4d::/48

would represent a network address, while:

    2001:db8:3c4d:0001::/64

would represent a subnet within that network address.

Like IPv4, IPv6 can use unicast, multicast, and anycast addressing. Unlike IPv4, there is no broadcast addressing.

IPv6 Unicast Addressing

As with IPv4, an IPv6 unicast address identifies a single network interface. IPv6 unicast addressing is scoped; a scope is a region of the network. Global scopes provide the equivalent of public addressing schemes in IPv4, while link local schemes provide private addressing.

IPv6 Global Addressing

Globally scoped unicast addresses are routable over the Internet and are the equivalent of public IPv4 addresses. The parts of a global address are:

- The first 3 bits (001) indicate that the address is within the global scope. Most of the IPv6 address space is unused. The scope for globally unique unicast addressing occupies just 1/8th of the total address space. In hex, globally scoped unicast addresses will start with a 2 (0010) or 3 (0011).

- The next 45 bits are allocated in a hierarchical manner to regional registries and from them to ISPs and end users.

- The next 16 bits identify site-specific subnet addresses.

- The final 64 bits are the interface ID.

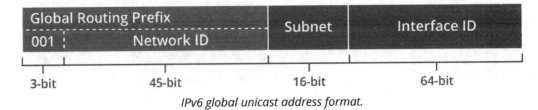

IPv6 global unicast address format.

Interface ID/EUI-64

The 64-bit interface ID can be determined by using two techniques.

One is by using the interface's MAC address. This is known as a MAC-derived address or interface identifier. As a MAC address is currently 48 bits (6 bytes), a (relatively) simple translation mechanism allows driver software to create a 64-bit interface ID (an EUI-64) from these 48 bits.

Two changes occur to derive the EUI-64 interface ID from an interface's MAC address. First, the digits fffe are added in the middle of the MAC address. Second, the first 8 bits, or 2 hex digits, are converted to binary, and the 7th bit (or U/L bit) is flipped (from 0 to 1 or 1 to 0). For example, the MAC address 00608c123abc would become the EUI-64 address 02608cfffe123abc, which (when expressed in double bytes) becomes 0260:8cff:fe12:3abc, or (without the leading 0) 260:8cff:fe12:3abc.

In the second technique, referred to as privacy extensions, the client device uses a pseudorandom number for the interface ID. This is known as a temporary interface ID or token. There is some concern that using interface identifiers would allow a host to be identified and closely monitored when connecting to the Internet, and using a token mitigates this to some degree.

IPv6 Link Local Addressing

Link local addresses span a single subnet (they are not forwarded by routers). Nodes on the same link are referred to as neighbors. The link local range is fe80::/10. Link local addresses start with a leading fe80, with the next 54 bits set to 0, and the last 64 bits are the interface ID.

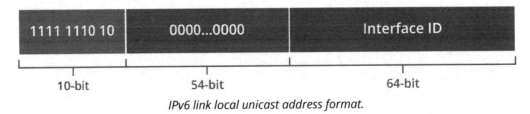

IPv6 link local unicast address format.

The equivalent in IPv4 is Automatic Private IP Addressing (APIPA) and its 169.254.0.0 addresses. However, unlike IPv4, an IPv6 host is always configured with link local addresses (one for each link), even if it also has a globally unique address.

A link local address is also appended with a **zone index** (or scope id) of the form %1 (Windows) or %eth0 (Linux). This is used to define the source of the address and make it unique to a particular link. For example, a given host may have links to a loopback address, Ethernet, and a VPN. Each of these links may use the same link local address, so each is assigned a zone ID to make it unique. Zone indices are generated by the host system, so where two hosts communicate, they may be referring to the link using different zone IDs.

While it is relatively uncommon for an interface to have more than one IPv4 address, in IPv6 it is typical for an interface to have multiple addresses.

IPv6 Interface Autoconfiguration and Testing

In IPv6, an interface must always be configured with a link local address. One or more routable addresses can be assigned to the interface in addition to the link local address. As with IPv4, you can either assign a routable IPv6 address statically or use an automatic addressing scheme. Static address configuration would generally be reserved to routers and possibly some types of servers.

Neighbor Discovery Protocol and Router Advertisements

The **Neighbor Discovery (ND) protocol** performs some of the functions on an IPv6 network that ARP and ICMP perform under IPv4. The main functions of ND are:

- **Address autoconfiguration**—Enables a host to configure IPv6 addresses for its interfaces automatically and detect whether an address is already in use on the local network, by using neighbor solicitation (NS) and neighbor advertisement (NA) messages.

- **Prefix discovery**—Enables a host to discover the known network prefixes that have been allocated to the local segment. This facilitates next-hop determination (whether a packet should be addressed to a local host or a router). Prefix discovery uses router solicitation (RS) and **router advertisement (RA)** messages. An RA contains information about the network prefix(es) served by the router, information about autoconfiguration options, plus information about link parameters, such as the MTU and hop limit. Routers send RAs periodically and in response to a router solicitation initiated by the host.

- **Local address resolution**—Allows a host to discover other nodes and routers on the local network (neighbors). This process also uses neighbor solicitation (NS) and neighbor advertisement (NA) messages.

- **Redirection**—Enables a router to inform a host of a better route to a particular destination.

Stateless Address Autoconfiguration

IPv4 has a system for generating link local addresses, but these are not routable outside the local network. Consequently, IPv4 depends heavily on the Dynamic Host Configuration Protocol (DHCP) for address autoconfiguration. IPv6 uses a more flexible system of address autoconfiguration called **stateless address autoconfiguration (SLAAC)**:

- The host generates a link local address and tests that it is unique by using the Neighbor Discovery (ND) protocol.

- The host listens for a router advertisement (RA) or transmits a router solicitation (RS) using ND protocol messaging. The router can either provide a network prefix, direct the host to a DHCPv6 server to perform stateful autoconfiguration, or perform some combination of stateless and stateful configuration.

ICMPv6

IPv6 uses an updated version of ICMP. The key new features are:

- **Error messaging**—ICMPv6 supports the same sort of destination unreachable and time exceeded messaging as ICMPv4. One change is the introduction of a Packet Too Big class of error. Under IPv6, routers are no longer responsible for packet fragmentation and reassembly, so the host must ensure that they fit in the MTUs of the various links used.

- **Informational messaging**—ICMPv6 supports ICMPv4 functions, such as echo and redirect, plus a whole new class of messages designed to support ND and MLD, such as router and neighbor advertisements and solicitations.

IPv6 Multicast Addressing

A multicast address is used to send a packet from a single source to multiple network interfaces. Unlike IPv4, IPv6 routers must support multicast. The parts of a multicast address are subdivided as follows:

- The first 8 bits indicate that the address is within the multicast scope (1111 1111 or ff).

- The next 4 bits are used to flag types of multicast if necessary; otherwise, they are set to 0.

- The next 4 bits determine the scope; for example, 1 is node-local (to all interfaces on the same node) and 2 is link local.

- The final 112 bits define multicast groups within that scope.

The Multicast Listener Discovery (MLD) protocol allows nodes to join a multicast group and discover whether members of a group are present on a local subnet.

Broadcast addresses are not implemented in IPv6. Instead, hosts use an appropriate multicast address for a given situation. The well-known multicast addresses are ones reserved for these types of broadcast functionality. They allow an interface to transmit to all interfaces or routers on the same node or local link.

In IPv4, IP address resolution to a specific hardware interface is performed using ARP. ARP is chatty and requires every node to process its messages, whether they are relevant to the node or not. IPv6 replaces ARP with the Neighbor Discovery (ND) protocol.

Each unicast address for an interface is configured with a corresponding solicited-node multicast address. It has the prefix ff02::1:ff plus the last 24 bits of the unicast address. The solicited-node address is used by ND to perform address resolution. It greatly reduces the number of hosts that are likely to receive ND messages (down to one in most cases) and is therefore much more efficient than the old ARP broadcast mechanism.

IPv4 and IPv6 Transition Mechanisms

A network is likely to have to run both IPv4 and IPv6 in some or all segments and for connectivity with internetworks. This interoperability can be implemented using dual stack hosts or by a tunneling mechanism.

Dual Stack

Dual stack hosts and routers can run both IPv4 and IPv6 simultaneously and communicate with devices configured with either type of address. Most modern desktop and server operating systems implement dual stack IP. Most modern dual stack systems will try to initiate communications using IPv6 by default.

 Most services are addressed using names rather than IP addresses. This means that the preference for IPv6 over IPv4 or the availability of either addressing method depends on the Domain Name Server (DNS) records for the network.

```
PS C:\Windows\system32> ipconfig /all

Windows IP Configuration

    Host Name . . . . . . . . . . . . : PC10
    Primary Dns Suffix  . . . . . . . : corp.515support.com
    Node Type . . . . . . . . . . . . : Mixed
    IP Routing Enabled. . . . . . . . : No
    WINS Proxy Enabled. . . . . . . . : No
    DNS Suffix Search List. . . . . . : corp.515support.com

Ethernet adapter Ethernet:

    Connection-specific DNS Suffix  . : corp.515support.com
    Description . . . . . . . . . . . : Microsoft Hyper-V Network Adapter
    Physical Address. . . . . . . . . : 00-15-5D-00-65-31
    DHCP Enabled. . . . . . . . . . . : Yes
    Autoconfiguration Enabled . . . . : Yes
    IPv6 Address. . . . . . . . . . . : fdf0:2413:6d1c:30:997b:634e:5b90:7e(Preferred)
    Link-local IPv6 Address . . . . . : fe80::997b:634e:5b90:7e%9(Preferred)
    IPv4 Address. . . . . . . . . . . : 10.1.24.101(Preferred)
    Subnet Mask . . . . . . . . . . . : 255.255.255.0
    Lease Obtained. . . . . . . . . . : Wednesday, August 4, 2021 12:11:31 AM
    Lease Expires . . . . . . . . . . : Thursday, August 12, 2021 12:11:30 AM
    Default Gateway . . . . . . . . . : fe80::215:5dff:fe00:6510%9
                                        10.1.24.254
    DHCP Server . . . . . . . . . . . : 10.1.16.1
    DHCPv6 IAID . . . . . . . . . . . : 67114333
    DHCPv6 Client DUID. . . . . . . . : 00-01-00-01-27-E6-CC-0C-00-15-5D-00-65-31
    DNS Servers . . . . . . . . . . . : 10.1.16.1
    NetBIOS over Tcpip. . . . . . . . : Enabled
PS C:\Windows\system32> _
```

Dual stack IP in Windows. (Screenshot used with permission from Microsoft.)

Tunneling

As an alternative to dual stack, **tunneling** can be used to deliver IPv6 packets across an IPv4 network. Tunneling means that IPv6 packets are inserted into IPv4 packets and routed over the IPv4 network to their destination. Routing decisions are based on the IPv4 address until the packets approach their destinations, at which point the IPv6 packets are stripped from their IPv4 carrier packets and forwarded according to IPv6 routing rules. This carries a high protocol overhead and is not nearly as efficient as operating dual stack hosts.

In 6to4 automatic tunneling, no host configuration is necessary to enable the tunnel. 6to4 addresses use the prefix 2002::/16. 6to4 has been widely replaced by an enhanced protocol called IPv6 Rapid Deployment (6RD). With 6RD, the 2002::/16 prefix is replaced by an ISP-managed prefix and there are various other performance improvements.

Microsoft provides support for tunneling by Windows hosts using its Teredo protocol. Teredo tunnels IPv6 packets as IPv4-based UDP messages over port 3544. Teredo requires compatible clients and servers. The open-source Miredo package implements the Teredo for UNIX/Linux operating systems.

Another option for tunneling is Generic Routing Encapsulation (GRE). GRE allows a wide variety of Network layer protocols to be encapsulated inside virtual point-to-point links. This protocol has the advantage that because it was originally designed for IPv4, it is considered a mature mechanism and can carry both v4 and v6 packets over an IPv4 network.

Common IPv6 Address Prefixes

Use the following table to help you recognize some of the commonly used classes of IPv6 address by prefix notation or leading hex digits.

Type	Prefix	Leading Hex Characters
Global unicast	2000::/3	2 3
Link local unicast	fe80::/10	fe80
Multicast	ff00::/8	ff
Multicast (link local)	ff02::/16	ff02::1 (all nodes) ff02::2 (all routers) ff02::1:2 (DHCP)
Solicited-node	ff02::1:ff00:0/104	ff02::1:ff
Unspecified	::/128	0::0
Loopback	::1/128	::1
Documentation/Examples	2001:db8::/32	2001:db8

Globally unique unicast addresses are also widely referred to as /48s.

The 0000::/8 block (that is, IPv6 addresses where the first bits are 0000 0000) is reserved for special functions. Within this block, there are two special addresses defined:

- **Unspecified address (0:0:0:0:0:0:0:0)**—A host that has not obtained a valid address. This is often expressed as ::

- **Loopback address (0:0:0:0:0:0:0:1)**—Used for testing (for the host to send a packet to itself). This is often expressed as ::1

Review Activity:

IPv6 Addressing Schemes

Answer the following questions:

1. Which of the following IPv6 addresses is a valid unicast host address?

2. What is an EUI-64, and how might it be used by IPv6?

3. In IPv6, how is the loopback address best expressed?

4. In IPv6, how can a host obtain a routable IPv6 address without requiring manual configuration?

5. True or false? 6to4 is a dual stack method of transitioning from IPv4 to IPv6.

Lesson 6

Summary

You should be able to configure and troubleshoot host addressing and use an appropriate IPv6 addressing scheme.

Guidelines for Supporting IP Addressing Schemes

Follow these guidelines to support IPv4 and IPv6 networks:

- Use netsh or PowerShell to configure IP address properties in Windows. The ipconfig tool can be used to quickly report the adapter configuration.

- Use ip or the legacy ifconfig command to report adapter configuring in Linux.

- Use the arp and ping utilities to troubleshoot issues with local addressing and connectivity.

- Use methodical troubleshooting techniques to diagnose common problems:

  - Determine the scope of a problem to identify power/hardware issues with adapters and intermediate systems.

  - View the local configuration and cache to identify address configuration issues, such as mismatched speed/duplex, incorrect IP, incorrect mask, incorrect gateway, or duplicate IP/MAC address.

  - Ping loopback, local, and then remote to determine connectivity and problem scope.

- Ensure good understanding of IPv6 addressing concepts to facilitate network design and support:

  - The use of 128-bit IPv6 addresses and with network prefixes and 64-bit interface identifiers.

  - The use of local and global unicast plus multicast addressing schemes.

  - The role of Neighbor Discovery and router advertisements in address autoconfiguration.

  - Dual stack and tunneling mechanisms to transition from IPv4 to IPv6 networks.

Lesson 7

Configuring and Troubleshooting Routers

LESSON INTRODUCTION

Now that you are aware of the basic concepts of IP addressing and forwarding, you can start identifying ways that paths between networks are implemented. Routers work at layer 3 to aggregate information about neighboring networks and forward packets along an appropriate path to their final destination.

While configuring routing infrastructure is often a senior job role, you should understand basic concepts and be able to apply them to solve common issues.

Lesson Objectives

In this lesson, you will:

- Compare and contrast routing concepts.

- Compare and contrast dynamic routing concepts.

- Install and troubleshoot routers.

Topic 7A

Compare and Contrast Routing Concepts

EXAM OBJECTIVES COVERED
2.2 Compare and contrast routing technologies and bandwidth management concepts.

As a network professional, you should understand the way routers make forwarding decisions and how you can implement them so that you can support internetworks of all sizes and types. In this topic, you will examine routing tables and how they are used to select a forwarding path.

Routing Tables and Path Selection

Most end system workstation and server computers are configured with a single network adapter connected to only one network. Although potentially capable of routing, they are not equipped with the necessary interfaces and knowledge of the location of other networks. A router is a multihomed intermediate system with links and network topology information to facilitate forwarding packets between subnets or around an internetwork.

Information about the location of other IP networks and hosts is stored in the **routing table**. Each entry in the routing table represents an available route to a destination network or host. The following main parameters define a routing entry:

- **Protocol**—The source of the route.

- **Destination**—Routes can be defined to specific hosts but are more generally directed to network IDs. The most specific destination prefix (the longest mask) will be selected as the forwarding path if there is more than one match.

- **Interface**—The local interface to use to forward a packet along the chosen route. This might be represented as the IP address of the interface or as a layer 2 interface ID.

- **Gateway/next hop**—The IP address of the next router along the path to the destination.

```
vyos@vyos:~$ show ip route
Codes: K - kernel route, C - connected, S - static, R - RIP,
       O - OSPF, I - IS-IS, B - BGP, E - EIGRP, N - NHRP,
       T - Table, v - VNC, V - VNC-Direct, A - Babel, D - SHARP,
       F - PBR, f - OpenFabric,
       > - selected route, * - FIB route, q - queued route, r - rejected route

C>* 10.0.0.2/32 is directly connected, lo, 00:06:52
S>* 10.0.1.0/24 [1/0] via 10.0.2.254, eth0, 00:02:26
C>* 10.0.2.0/24 is directly connected, eth0, 00:02:26
C>* 10.0.3.0/24 is directly connected, eth1, 00:06:51
S>* 10.0.4.0/24 [1/0] via 10.0.3.254, eth1, 00:06:49
```

Routing table on a VyOS router showing connected and static route entries.

Static and Default Routes

Routing table entries fall into four general categories:

- Direct network routes, for subnets to which the router is directly attached.

- Remote network routes, for subnets and IP networks that are not directly attached.

- Host routes, for routes to a specific IP address. A host route has a /32 network prefix.

- Default routes, which are used when an exact match for a network or host route is not found.

Directly Connected Routes

The IP network or subnet for each active router interface is automatically added to the routing table. These are known as **directly connected routes**.

Static Routes

A **static route** is manually added to the routing table and only changes if edited by the administrator. Configuring static routing entries can be useful in some circumstances, but it can be problematic if the routing topology changes often, as each route on each affected router needs to be updated manually.

 Static routes can be configured either as non-persistent or persistent/permanent. A non-persistent route is removed from the routing table if the router is rebooted. A non-persistent route might be added as a troubleshooting action, for instance. If a static route is not reachable, it will be disabled.

Default Route

A **default route** is a special type of static route that identifies the next hop router for a destination that cannot be matched by another routing table entry. The destination address 0.0.0.0/0 (IPv4) or ::/0 (IPv6) is used to represent the default route. The default route is also described as the gateway of last resort. Most end systems are configured with a default route (pointing to the default gateway). This may also be the simplest way for an edge router to forward traffic to an ISP's routers.

Routing Table Example

As examples of directly connected, static, and default route entries that might appear in a routing table, consider the following example of three routers connected in a series:

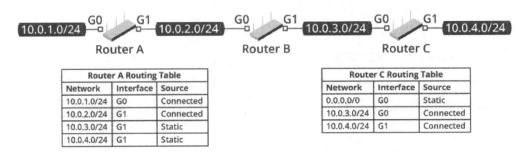

Router B Routing Table		
Network	Interface	Source
10.0.1.0/24	G0	Static
10.0.2.0/24	G0	Connected
10.0.3.0/24	G1	Connected
10.0.4.0/24	G1	Static

Router A Routing Table		
Network	Interface	Source
10.0.1.0/24	G0	Connected
10.0.2.0/24	G1	Connected
10.0.3.0/24	G1	Static
10.0.4.0/24	G1	Static

Router C Routing Table		
Network	Interface	Source
0.0.0.0/0	G0	Static
10.0.3.0/24	G0	Connected
10.0.4.0/24	G1	Connected

Routing tables for three routers connected in series. (Images © 123RF.com.)

First, consider the routing table of router A:

- The router is directly connected to networks 10.0.1.0/24 (via interface G0) and 10.0.2.0/24 (via interface G1).

- The router has been configured with static routes to 10.0.3.0/24 and 10.0.4.0/24, both of which are reachable via interface G1.

Router B has been configured in the same way, but here the networks 10.0.2.0/24 and 10.0.3.0/24 are directly connected and the paths to 10.0.1.0/24 and 10.0.4.0/24 are configured as static entries.

Router C has been configured differently. It is directly connected to 10.0.3.0/24 and 10.0.4.0/24, but the only static route configured is for 0.0.0.0/0. This is a default route. While the router has no specific knowledge of networks 10.0.1.0/24 and 10.0.2.0/24, it will forward packets for these destinations over its G0 interface.

Packet Forwarding

When a router receives a packet, it reads the destination address in the packet and looks up a matching destination network IP address and prefix in its routing table. If there is a match, the router will forward the packet out of one of its interfaces by encapsulating the packet in a new frame:

- If the packet can be delivered to a directly connected network via an Ethernet interface, the router uses ARP (IPv4) or Neighbor Discovery (ND in IPv6) to determine the interface address of the destination host.

- If the packet can be forwarded via a gateway over an Ethernet interface, it inserts the next hop router's MAC address into the new frame.

- If the packet can be forwarded via a gateway over another type of interface (leased line or DSL, for instance), the router encapsulates the packet in an appropriate frame type.

- If the destination address cannot be matched to a route entry, the packet is either forwarded via the default route or dropped (and the source host is notified that it was undeliverable).

Hop Count

If the packet is forwarded via a gateway, this process is repeated at each router to deliver the packet through the internetwork. Each router along the path counts as one **hop**. For example, in the network shown in the figure, host A takes 1 hop to communicate with LOCAL_SRV via a directly connected interface on the LAN router. Note that the switches do not count as hops. Host B takes multiple hops (9) to communicate with REMOTE_SRV, with traffic routed via two ISP networks. Also, observe the alternative routes that could be taken. Do any have a lower hop count?

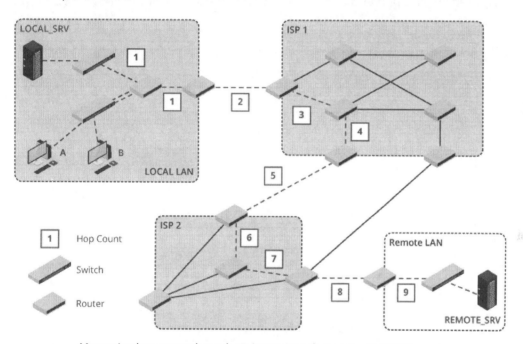

Measuring hop count through an internetwork. (Images © 123RF.com.)

Time To Live

At each router, the **Time to Live (TTL)** IP header field is decreased by at least 1. This could be greater if the router is congested. The TTL is nominally the number of seconds a packet can stay on the network before being discarded. While TTL is defined as a unit of time (seconds), in practice, it is interpreted as a maximum hop count. When the TTL is 0, the packet is discarded. This prevents badly addressed packets from permanently circulating the network.

Fragmentation

IP provides best-effort delivery of an unreliable and connectionless nature. Delivery is not guaranteed, and a packet might be lost, delivered out of sequence, duplicated, or delayed. It is possible that due to limitations in the underlying network, IP may fragment the packet into more manageable pieces to fit within the Maximum Transmission Unit (MTU) of the Data Link protocol frame.

In IPv4, the ID, Flags, and Fragment Offset IP header fields are used to record the sequence in which the packets were sent and to indicate whether the IP datagram has been split between multiple frames for transport over the underlying Data Link protocol. For example, the MTU of an Ethernet frame is usually 1500 bytes. An IP datagram larger than 1500 bytes would have to be fragmented across more than one Ethernet frame. A datagram passing over an internetwork might have to be encapsulated in different Data Link frame types, each with different MTUs.

Most systems try to avoid IP **fragmentation**. IPv6 does not allow routers to perform fragmentation. Instead, the host performs path MTU discovery to work out the MTU supported by each hop and crafts IP datagrams that will fit the smallest MTU.

Review Activity:

Routing Concepts

Answer the following questions:

1. **What is a directly connected route?**

2. **Which of the parameters in the following routing table entry represents the gateway?**

   ```
   R 192.168.1.0/24 [120/1] via 198.51.100.254,
   GigabitEthernet0/1
   ```

3. **What type of routing table entry is shown below?**

   ```
   S* 0.0.0.0/0 [1/0] via 192.0.2.1
   ```

4. **True or False? A router will not forward a packet when the TTL field is 0.**

Topic 7B

Compare and Contrast Dynamic Routing Concepts

EXAM OBJECTIVES COVERED
1.4 Given a scenario, configure a subnet and use appropriate IP addressing schemes.
2.2 Compare and contrast routing technologies and bandwidth management concepts.

Complex networks need to exchange routing information rapidly to prevent outages, making static routing updates impractical in most cases. This issue is solved by implementing dynamic routing protocols. In this topic, you will compare these protocols to understand the features that make them more or less appropriate for different networks. You will also identify advanced addressing schemes that maximize utilization of scarce IPv4 address space.

Dynamic Routing Protocols

A **dynamic routing** protocol uses an algorithm and metrics to build and maintain a routing information base. This database stores information about the networks to which the router is connected and where there are multiple paths, prioritizes one over the rest. This information can be shared with the router's neighbors. A learned route is one that was communicated to a router by another router. A router can add learned routes from one or more routing protocols to its IP routing table.

Topology and Metrics

The algorithms used for path selection can be categorized according to the topology and metrics that they use to build and update a routing information base and prioritize optimal (or least-cost) paths. Most algorithms are classed as either **distance vector** or as **link state**. Some protocols use a hybrid of different methods to perform path selection more efficiently.

For each protocol that it runs, the router maintains a routing information base of routes discovered by that protocol. These databases are separate to the IP routing table used to determine the forwarding path. The routing protocol's database might contain more than one route to the same destination prefix. In this case, a metric is calculated to determine which path will be selected for use in the IP routing table. The path with the lowest cost metric is preferred.

The type of algorithm determines which factors are used to calculate the metric. For example, distance vector protocols use the number of hops to the destination as the metric. The route with the fewest hops is the least-cost path and will be selected for use.

Convergence

Convergence is the process whereby routers running dynamic routing algorithms agree on the network topology. Routers must be capable of adapting to changes such as newly added networks, router or router interface failures, link failures, and so on. Routers must be able to communicate changes to other routers quickly to avoid black holes and loops. A black hole means that a packet is discarded without notification back to the source; a loop causes a packet to be forwarded around the network until its TTL expires.

A network where all the routers share the same topology is described as steady state. The time taken to reach steady state is a measure of a routing protocol's convergence performance.

 A flapping interface is one that frequently changes from online to offline and offline to online. Similarly, route flapping refers to a router changing the properties of a route it is advertising quickly and often. Flapping can cause serious convergence problems.

Interior versus Exterior Gateway Protocols

As well as the algorithm used to determine the network topology, routing protocols can be classified according to the way they deal with administrative boundaries. A network under the administrative control of a single owner is referred to as an **autonomous system (AS)**. An **Interior Gateway Protocol (IGP)** is one that identifies routes within an AS.

An **Exterior Gateway Protocol (EGP)** is one that can advertise routes between autonomous systems. An EGP includes a field to communicate the network's autonomous system ID and allows network owners to determine whether they can use paths through another organization's network.

Some of the most popular protocols are listed in the following table.

Protocol	Type	Class	Transport
Routing Information Protocol (RIP)	Distance Vector	IGP	UDP (port 520 or 521)
Enhanced Interior Gateway Routing Protocol (EIGRP)	Distance Vector/ Hybrid	IGP	Native IP (88)
Open Shortest Path First (OSPF)	Link State	IGP	Native IP (89)
Border Gateway Protocol (BGP)	Path Vector	EGP	TCP (port 179)

Another factor used to compare routing protocols or protocol versions is whether they support classless addressing. While all modern protocols use classless addressing, you should understand that legacy classful protocols do not use subnet masks or network prefixes. They determine an IPv4network ID based on the value of the first three bits of the address.

Finally, some older protocol versions support IPv4 only. If IPv6 routing is required, you must select a dynamic routing protocol version that supports it. Most routers now operate dual stack routing of both IPv4 and IPv6. Each IP version has a separate routing table.

Routing Information Protocol

The **Routing Information Protocol (RIP)** is a distance vector routing protocol. RIP only considers a single piece of information about the network topology—the next hop router to reach a given network or subnet (vector). It considers only one metric to select the optimal path to a given destination network—the one with the lowest hop count (distance).

RIP sends regular updates (typically every 30 seconds) of its entire routing database to neighboring routers. It can also send triggered updates whenever changes occur. When a router receives an update from a neighbor, it adds unknown routes to its own routing table, increases the hop count by 1, and identifies the originator of the update as the next hop to the specified networks.

In the following figure, RIP has been used to propagate route information between three routers connected in a chain. Router A learns about networks 10.0.3.0/24 and 10.0.4.0/24 from Router B. It adds 1 to the hop count metric of these routes. Router B learns about 10.0.1.0/24 from Router A and about 10.0.4.0/24 from Router C. Router A and Router C do not exchange any information directly. The distance vector process by which Router A learns about Router C's networks is often referred to as "routing by rumor."

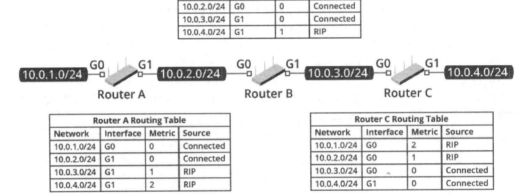

Routers connected in series exchanging distance vector path updates.

The following example illustrates a mesh topology where there are multiple paths between networks. Router A has two possible paths to network 10.0.3.0/24, which it learns from Router B and Router C. It can forward a packet out of its G1 interface over network 10.0.2.0/24, which will take one hop to reach the destination. It could also forward the packet out of G2 and reach the destination via Router C and then Router B. This takes two hops and so is not used as the preferred route.

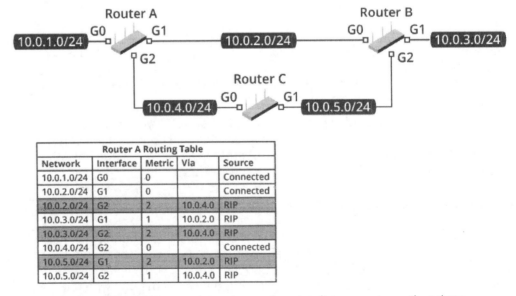

Routers connected in a mesh topology exchanging distance vector path updates.

If Router A's G1 link goes down, those entries will be removed from the routing table and the alternative routes via 10.0.4.0/24 will be selected:

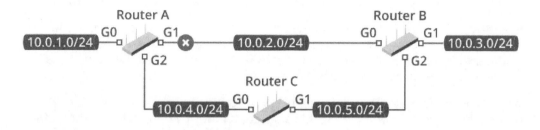

Router A Routing Table				
Network	Interface	Metric	Via	Source
10.0.1.0/24	G0	0		Connected
10.0.2.0/24	G1	0		Connected
10.0.2.0/24	G2	2	10.0.4.0	RIP
10.0.3.0/24	G1	1	10.0.2.0	RIP
10.0.3.0/24	G2	2	10.0.4.0	RIP
10.0.4.0/24	G2	0		Connected
10.0.5.0/24	G1	2	10.0.2.0	RIP
10.0.5.0/24	G2	1	10.0.4.0	RIP

Routers connected in a mesh topology exchanging distance vector path updates.

To help prevent looping, the maximum hop count allowed is 15. Consequently, this limits the maximum size of a RIP network, since networks that have a hop count of 16 or higher are unreachable.

RIP Versions

There are three versions of RIP:

- RIPv1 is a classful protocol and uses inefficient broadcasts to communicate updates over UDP port 520.

- RIPv2 supports classless addressing and uses more efficient multicast transmissions over UDP port 520. It also supports authentication.

- RIPng (next generation) is a version of the protocol designed for IPv6. RIPng uses UDP port 521.

The simplicity of RIP makes it suited to small networks with limited failover routes. Distance vector algorithms require that routers periodically propagate their entire routing table to their immediate neighbors. This is not scalable to environments with large numbers of networks. Distance vector algorithms provide for slower convergence than link state algorithms. For more complex networks with redundant paths, other dynamic routing protocols should be considered.

Enhanced Interior Gateway Routing Protocol

The Interior Gateway Routing Protocol (IGRP) was developed by Cisco to provide a routing protocol for routing within a domain or autonomous system. Limitations in IGRP, such as lack of support for classless addressing, led to the development of **Enhanced IGRP (EIGRP)**. There are versions for IPv4 and IPv6.

EIGRP is usually classed as an advanced distance vector or hybrid routing protocol. Like RIP, EIGRP is a distance vector protocol because it relies on neighboring routers to report paths to remote networks. Unlike RIP, which is based on a simple hop count metric, EIGRP uses a metric composed of administrator weighted elements. The two default elements are bandwidth and delay:

- **Bandwidth**—Applies a cost based on the lowest bandwidth link in the path.

- **Delay**—Applies a cost based on the time it takes for a packet to traverse the link. This metric is most important if the route is used to carry time-sensitive data, such as voice or video. Delay is calculated as the cumulative value for all outgoing interfaces in the path.

Where RIP sends periodic updates of its entire routing information base, EIGRP sends a full update when it first establishes contact with a neighbor and thereafter only sends updates when there is a topology change. This is more efficient and less disruptive to large networks, giving it the best convergence performance in many scenarios. EIGRP does use regular hello messaging to confirm connectivity with its neighbors. Unlike RIP, EIGRP maintains a topology table alongside its routing information base. The topology table is used to prevent loops while also supporting a greater number of maximum hops than RIP (nominally up to 255). In this respect, EIGRP has some similarities with link state routing protocols.

Unlike RIP, EIGRP is a native IP protocol, which means that it is encapsulated directly in IP datagrams, rather than using TCP or UDP. It is tagged with the protocol number 88 in the Protocol field of the IP header. Updates are transmitted using multicast addressing.

Open Shortest Path First

A distance vector algorithm relies on directly connected neighbors for information about remote networks. By contrast, a link state algorithm allows a router to store the complete network topology and assess the least-cost paths from this topology database.

Open Shortest Path First (OSPF) is the most widely adopted link state protocol. It is suited to large organizations with multiple redundant paths between networks. It has better convergence performance than RIP. It was designed from the outset to support classless addressing.

Where RIP and EIGRP are flat routing systems, OSPF is hierarchical. Networks and their connected hosts and routers within an autonomous system are grouped into OSPF areas. Routers within a given area share the same topological database of the networks they serve. Routers that can connect to multiple areas are known as area border routers. A backbone (always called Area 0) is created by the collection of border routers. This backbone is only visible to the border routers and invisible to the routers within a specific area.

In a given area, routers exchange OSPF hello messages, both as a form of a keep-alive packet and in order to acquire neighbors with which to exchange routing information. Neighbors share Link State Advertisement (LSA) updates to build a consistent link state database (LSDB) that represents the network topology of the area. The router applies an algorithm called shortest path first (SPF) to analyze the LSDB and add least-cost, loop free routes to its routing table. This use of a topology table of the whole network to select routes is the key difference between link state and distance vector algorithms.

The small, frequent updates used by OSPF lead to more rapid convergence and more efficiently support larger networks. The use of areas to subdivide the network minimizes the amount of routing traffic that must be passed around the network as a whole, further improving convergence performance. However, link state algorithms can be more expensive to implement because they require more CPU and memory resource.

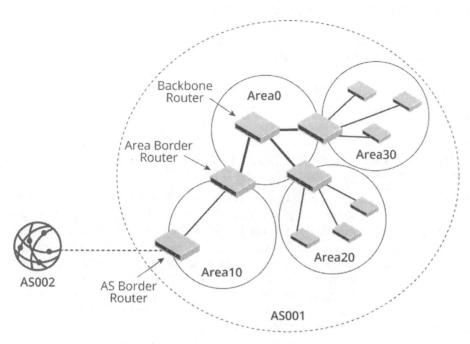

Typical OSPF topology. (Images © 123RF.com.)

Messages are sent as multicasts using OSPF's own datagram format. This is tagged as protocol number 89 in the IP datagram's Protocol field. There are various packet types and mechanisms to ensure sequencing and reliable delivery and to check for errors. OSPF also supports plaintext or cryptographic authentication.

Border Gateway Protocol

The **Border Gateway Protocol (BGP)** is designed to be used between routing domains in a mesh internetwork and as such is used as the routing protocol on the Internet, primarily between ISPs.

All the protocols discussed so far have been classed as interior gateway protocols (IGPs) used for communications between routers within a single routing domain, referred to an autonomous system (AS). Autonomous system numbers (ASN) are allocated to ISPs by IANA via the various regional registries. BGP is a type of exterior gateway protocol (in fact, it replaced a protocol named EGP) for communications between routers in separate autonomous systems. When BGP is used within an AS, it is referred to as Interior BGP (IBGP), and when implemented between autonomous systems, it is referred to as Exterior BGP (EBGP).

An AS is designed to hide the complexity of private networks from the public Internet. If all Internet locations had to be propagated to all Internet routers, the routing tables would become too large to process. Edge routers for each AS exchange only as much network-reachability information as is required to access other autonomous systems (the AS path), rather than networks and hosts within each AS. BGP prioritizes stability and can be slow to converge.

BGP works with classless network prefixes called Network Layer Reachability Information (NLRI). Path selection is based on multiple metrics, including hop count, weight, local preference, origin, and community. BGP is not a pure distance vector algorithm. In fact, BGP is more usually classed as a p ath vector routing protocol.

BGP works over TCP on port 179.

Administrative Distance

If a router has multiple entries to similar networks in its routing table, it must determine which route to prefer. The first determining factor is that longer prefixes are preferred over shorter ones. This is referred to as longest prefix match. For example, a routing table contains the following two entries:

```
198.51.100.0/24  g0
198.51.100.0/28  g1
```

If the router receives a packet for 198.51.100.1, the packet will be routed via g1, as that has the longer and more specific prefix.

Each routing protocol supported by the router can add a single route for any given destination prefix to the routing table. This means that there might be more than one route with an identical length prefix in the routing table. Each routing protocol uses its metric to determine the least-cost path. However, as routing protocols use different methods to calculate the metric, it cannot be used to compare routes from different protocols in the overall IP routing table. Instead, an **administrative distance (AD)** value is used to express the relative trustworthiness of the protocol supplying the route. Default AD values are coded into the router but can be adjusted by the administrator if necessary.

Source	AD
Local interface/Directly connected	0
Static route	1
BGP	20
EIGRP	90
OSPF	110
RIP	120
Unknown	255

This means, for example, that given identical prefix lengths, a static route will be preferred to anything other than directly connected networks and that a route discovered by OSPF would be preferred to one reported by RIP. The value of 255 for unknown routes means that they will not be used.

Conversely, a static route with a high AD could be defined to function as a backup if a learned route update fails. In normal circumstances, the router will prefer the learned route because it has a lower AD.

Classless Inter-Domain Routing

Classless addressing was designed to solve two major problems of the classful addressing scheme as more and more networks joined the internet through the early 1990s. The first was that network addresses, specifically, Class B addresses, were becoming very scarce and the second was near exponential growth in Internet routing tables. **Classless Inter-Domain Routing (CIDR)** uses bits normally assigned to the network ID to mask the complexity of the subnet and host addressing scheme within that network. CIDR is also sometimes described as supernetting.

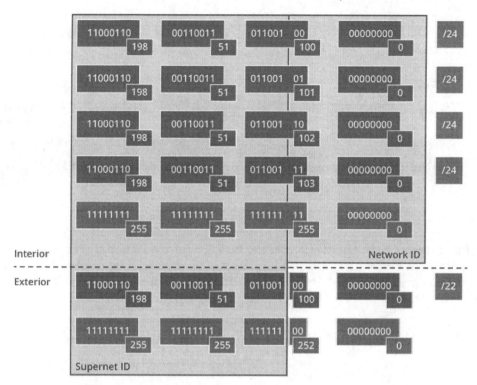

Using CIDR/supernetting to summarize four /24 networks as one /22 network.

For example, rather than allocate a Class B (or /16) network address to a company, several contiguous Class C (or /24) addresses could be assigned. Four /24 network addresses gives 1,016 hosts. However, this would mean complicated routing with many entries in the routing tables to represent four IP networks at the same location. Using CIDR collapses these routing entries into one single entry. If the network addresses assigned to a company were 198.51.101.0 through to 198.51.103.0 and you wanted to view this as one network, you need to allocate two bits from the network address to summarize the four networks. This makes the supernet p refix /22 or the subnet mask 255.255.252.0.

The ANDing process is still used to determine whether to route. If the ANDed result reveals the same network ID as the destination address, then it is the same network. In this next example, the first IP addresses belong to the supernet, but the second is on a different company's network:

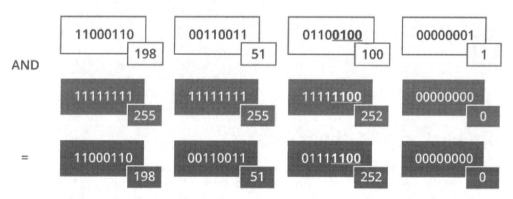

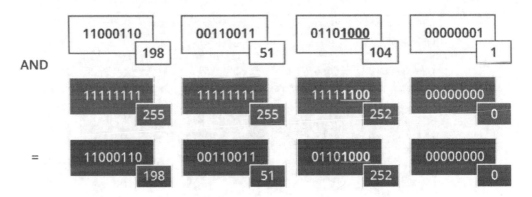

Comparing network prefixes.

Routers external to the network just use this /22 prefix, so the complexity of the LAN subnets is hidden and doesn't need to clog up their routing tables. The LAN's internal routers use the /24 prefix or even multiple prefixes to create subnets of different sizes.

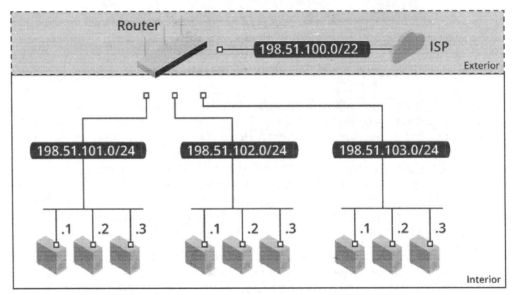

CIDR public and private route advertisements. (Images © 123RF.com.)

 Remember that both subnetting and supernetting require the use of a classless routing protocol (one that does not determine the network mask based on the first octet in the IP address). Dynamic routing protocols that support classless addressing include RIPv2, EIGRP, OSPF, and BGPv4.

Variable Length Subnet Masks

The IPv4 address space is close to being exhausted, making it difficult for ISPs to allocate public addresses to the companies that want them. To mitigate this, more efficient methods of allocating IP addresses must be used. Supernetting simplifies the information Internet routers need to locate IP networks. A complementary classless addressing technique, called **variable length subnet masking (VLSM)**, allows a network designer to allocate ranges of IP addresses to subnets that match the predicted need for numbers of subnets and hosts per subnet more closely.

Without VLSM, you have to allocate subnetted ranges of addresses that are the same size and use the same subnet mask throughout the network. This typically means that some subnets have many wasted IP addresses or additional routing interfaces must be in   stalled to connect several smaller subnets together within a single building or department.

VLSM allows different length netmasks to be used within the same IP network, allowing more flexibility in the design process.

For this example, consider a company with three sites, each with differing network sizes and IP address requirements. There are also subnets representing point-to-point WAN links between the routers.

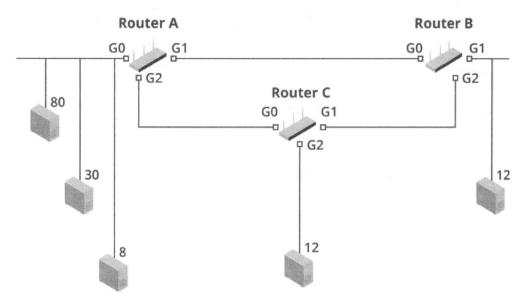

VLSM requirements for host addresses. (Images © 123RF.com.)

VLSM design usually proceeds by identifying the subnets with the most hosts and organizing the scheme in descending order. As with any subnet calculations, it helps to remember that each power of 2 is double the previous one:

2^2	2^3	2^4	2^5	2^6	2^7	2^8
4	8	16	32	64	128	256

1. In the example, the largest requirement is for 80 hosts. 2^6 has a maximum of 64 values, which is not enough, so the nearest match in the table is 2^7. This tells us that we need 7 bits for host addressing. This actually allows for 126 host addresses once the network and broadcast addresses have been accounted for (2^7-2). Using 7 bits makes the prefix /25 (32 minus 7).

2. The next requirement is technically met by a 5-bit host address space, but as this allows for exactly 30 addresses, there would be no room for growth. Using 6 bits might be safer, but for this scenario, we will choose the closest match and adopt the /27 prefix.

3. The next three requirements are for 8, 12, and 12 hosts. These all require 4 bits, which gives up to 14 usab   le addresses.

4. The routers use point-to-point links, so no more than two addresses will ever be required. This can be met by selecting a /30 prefix.

VLSM Design

The final VLSM design is summarized in the following table:

Office/Subnet	Required Number of IP Addresses	Mask Bits	Actual Number of IP Addresses	Prefix
Main Office 1 (Router A)	80	7	126	/25
Main Office 2 (Router A)	30	5	30	/27
Main Office 3 (Router A)	8	4	14	/28
Branch Office (Router B)	12	4	14	/28
Branch Office (Router C)	12	4	14	/28
Router A – Router B	2	2	2	/30
Router A – Router C	2	2	2	/30
Router B – Router C	2	2	2	/30

All subnets except for Main Office 2 have room for growth.

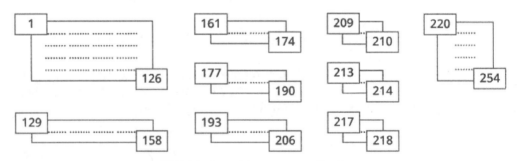

VLSM design address space utilization.

In fact, if you analyze the final design, you will find that there are 36 unused addresses at the end of the range. Consequently, there would have been space to use a /26 prefix for the group of 30 hosts.

The actual IP address ranges generated by the VLSM design are shown in this table.

Office	Subnet	Subnet Mask	Useable Host Address Range	Broadcast Address
Main Office 1 (Router A)	198.51.100.0/25	255.255.255.128	1—126	127
Main Office 2 (Router A)	198.51.100.128/27	255.255.255.224	129—158	159
Main Office 3 (Router A)	198.51.100.160/28	255.255.255.240	161—174	175
Branch Office (Router B)	198.51.100.176/28	255.255.255.240	177—190	191
Branch Office (Router C)	198.51.100.192/28	255.255.255.240	193—206	207
Router A – Router B	198.51.100.208/30	255.255.255.252	209—210	211
Router A – Router C	198.51.100.212/30	255.255.255.252	213—214	215
Router B – Router C	198.51.100.216/30	255.255.255.252	217—218	219

The VLSM network topology can be summarized by this diagram:

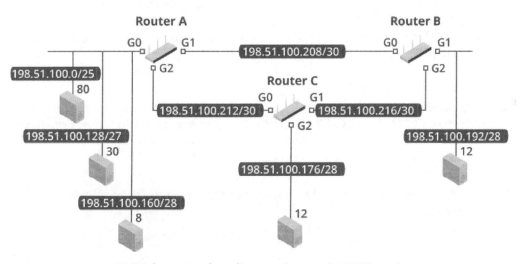

VLSM design topology diagram. (Images © 123RF.com.)

Review Activity:

Dynamic Routing Concepts

Answer the following questions:

1. Which factors are used by default in EIGRP to identify the least-cost path?

2. What is an ASN and how does it assist route aggregation?

3. Of the routing protocols listed in the CompTIA Network+ syllabus, which has the highest default value AD and does that make it more or less trusted than other protocols?

4. An IP network comprises hundreds of subnets deployed to offices in multiple geographical locations. Of the routing protocols listed in the CompTIA Network+ syllabus, which is best suited to this scale of network and why?

5. A company has eight networks, using the subnet addresses 192.168.0.0/24, 192.168.1.0/24 ... 192.168.7.0/24. What network prefix and subnet mask can be used to summarize a supernet route to these networks?

6. True or False? VLSM means using more than one mask to subnet an IP network.

Review Activity:

Design VLSM Subnets

In this activity, you will be designing an IP subnetting plan for an organization using VLSM. This division of the company must use the 172.30.0.0/16 network address range and subnet this down to develop an address scheme for the network displayed in the topology diagram. You should be as efficient as possible when designing your VLSM ranges, as additional branch offices may be added in the future.

Using the above scenario, answer the following questions:

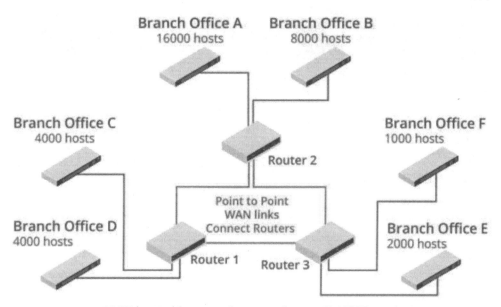

VLSM host address requirements. (Images © 123RF.com.)

1. **How large will each of the subnets that join the three routers together need to be?**

2. **Which is the largest subnet in the topology? What is the minimum number of bits that will be needed for that number of hosts? How many IP addresses will that subnet provide? What would be the VLSM and address range for the largest subnet?**

3. **What is the next largest subnet in the design? How many host bits will be needed for that subnet? How many IP addresses will that subnet provide and what is the VLSM?**

4. **Work out the remaining subnets, remembering to ensure that subnet ranges do not overlap, but equally that you do not waste IP addresses. Complete the table.**

Office/Subnet	Required Number of IP Addresses	VLSM Subnet ID	Actual Number of IP Addresses
Branch A	16,000	172.30.0.0/18	16,382
Branch B	8,000	172.30.64.0/19	8,190
Branch C	4,000		
Branch D	4,000		
Branch E	2,000		
Branch F	1,000		
Router 1 – Router 2	2		
Router 2 – Router 3	2		
Router 1 – Router 3	2		

Office/Subnet	Required Number of IP Addresses	VLSM Subnet ID	Actual Number of IP Addresses
Branch A	16,000	172.30.0.0/18	16,382
Branch B	8,000	172.30.64.0/19	8,190
Branch C	4,000	172.30.96.0/20	4,094
Branch D	4,000	172.30.112.0/20	4,094
Branch E	2,000	172.30.128.0/21	2,046
Branch F	1,000	172.30.136.0/22	1,022
Router 1 – Router 2	2	172.30.140.0/30	2
Router 2 – Router 3	2	172.30.140.4/30	2
Router 1 – Router 3	2	172.30.140.8/30	2

Topic 7C

Install and Troubleshoot Routers

EXAM OBJECTIVES COVERED
1.4 Given a scenario, configure a subnet and use appropriate IP addressing schemes.
(Subinterfaces only)
2.1 Compare and contrast various devices, their features, and their appropriate placement on the network.
5.3 Given a scenario, use the appropriate network software tools and commands.
5.5 Given a scenario, troubleshoot general networking issues.

As well as understanding the different types of routing algorithms, you must be able to install routing devices to an appropriate place in the network. This topic will help you to install and configure routers, and to use command-line tools to test the routing infrastructure.

Edge Routers

Routers serve both to link physically remote networks and subdivide autonomous IP networks into multiple subnets. Router placement is primarily driven by the IP networks and subnets that have been created:

- Hosts with addresses in the same subnet or IP network must not be separated by a router.

- Conversely, hosts with addresses in different subnets or IP networks must be separated by a router.

Edge routers, placed at the network perimeter, are typified by distinguishing external (Internet-facing) and internal interfaces. These routers can perform framing to repackage data from the private LAN frame format to the WAN Internet access frame format. The customer's router is referred to as the customer edge (CE), while the service provider's router is referred to as the provider edge (PE).

Edge routers designed to work with DSL or cable broadband access methods are called small office/home office (SOHO) routers. Router with similar integrated functionality are often deployed by enterprises for branch office connectivity.

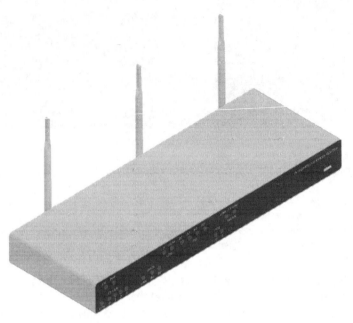

An integrated services router. This type of device combines DSL Internet access with Ethernet switch, Wi-Fi, and VoIP for a "one box" solution for remote sites and branch offices. (Image © 123RF.com.)

Routers designed to service medium to large networks are complex and expensive appliances. They feature specialized processors to handle the routing and forwarding processes, and memory to buffer data. Most routers of this class will also support plug-in cards for WAN interfaces. Another important feature is support for different methods of configuring site-to-site virtual private networks (VPNs).

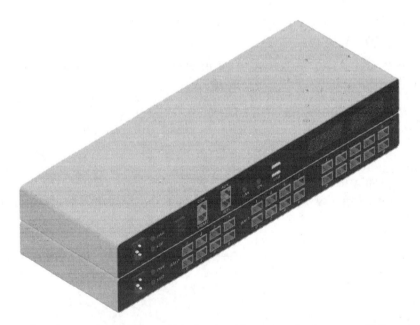

An advanced services router. This type of device provides network edge connectivity over Carrier Ethernet networks. (Image © 123RF.com.)

Internal Routers

An internal router has no public interfaces. Internal routers are positioned to implement whatever network topology is required. The figure shows a simplified example of a typical network configuration. An edge router/firewall provides access to the Internet. Traffic between the local subnets is controlled by a separate internal router.

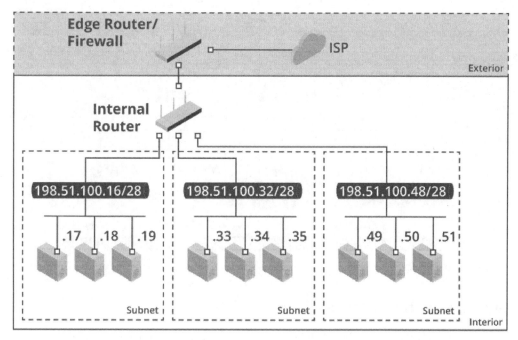

Network placement of edge and internal routers. (Images © 123RF.com.)

A network may also use a more complex topology, such as division into OSPF areas.

Subinterfaces

Many networks are segmented using the virtual LAN (VLAN) feature of managed switches. Traffic between VLANs must be routed. In this scenario, it is possible to use a router with a single interface (a one-armed router or router on a stick) connected to a trunk port on the switch. The trunk port carries all the VLAN-to-VLAN traffic that must be routed. The router's physical interface is configured with multiple **subinterfaces** or virtual interfaces. Each subinterface is configured with a specific VLAN ID. The subinterface receives traffic from a given VLAN and then routes it to the subinterface serving the destination VLAN.

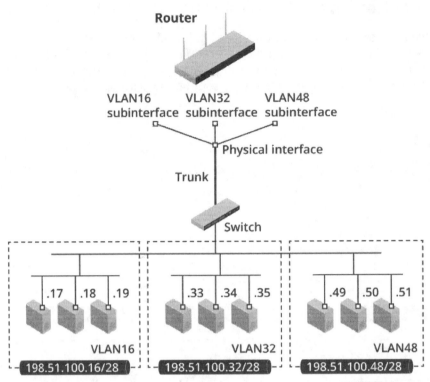

Router on a Stick topology with subinterfaces serving each VLAN/subnet. (Images © 123RF.com.)

Layer 3 Capable Switches

Passing traffic between a router appliance and the switch over a trunk link is relatively inefficient and does not scale well to tens of VLANs. Consequently, enterprise networks usually deploy layer 3 switches at the core of their networks. A **layer 3 capable switch** is one that is optimized for routing between VLANs. It can use static and dynamic routing to identify which VLAN an IP address should be forwarded to. A layer 3 switch can maintain a mapping table of IP addresses to MAC addresses so that when a path is established, it can use low-latency hardware-based forwarding. However, layer 3 switches do not typically have WAN interfaces and so are not usually used for routing at the network edge.

Router Configuration

As a router appliance does not have a screen or keyboard, it is configured locally either via a serial connection known as a console port or (more usually) remotely over the network by using a protocol such as Secure Shell (SSH). SSH can be used to communicate with the router via the IP address of any configured interface. However, as any given physical interface could suffer a hardware fault or be temporarily unavailable for various reasons, it is considered best practice to create a virtual interface, known as a loopback interface, in the router's operating system and assign it an IP address for use in remotely managing the router. This is a way of giving the router an internal IP address, not connected to any physical network, that is therefore not reliant on a specific network link being available.

```
vyos@vyos:~$ conf
[edit]
vyos@vyos# set protocols rip interface eth0
[edit]
vyos@vyos# set protocols rip interface eth1
[edit]
vyos@vyos# set protocols rip redistribute connected
[edit]
vyos@vyos# commit && save && exit
Saving configuration to '/config/config.boot'...
Done
exit
vyos@vyos:~$ show ip rip
Codes: R - RIP, C - connected, S - Static, O - OSPF, B - BGP
Sub-codes:
       (n) - normal, (s) - static, (d) - default, (r) - redistribute,
       (i) - interface

     Network            Next Hop         Metric From            Tag Time
R(n) 10.0.0.1/32        10.0.2.254            2 10.0.2.254         0 02:57
C(r) 10.0.0.2/32        0.0.0.0              1 self               0
R(n) 10.0.1.0/24        10.0.2.254            2 10.0.2.254         0 02:57
C(i) 10.0.2.0/24        0.0.0.0              1 self               0
C(i) 10.0.3.0/24        0.0.0.0              1 self               0
```

Configuring RIP on a VyOS-based software router. The host can be configured at a local terminal or from a remote computer over Secure Shell (SSH).

Having placed the router at an appropriate point in the network, connected its cabling, and established a management session, the principal configuration tasks are as follows:

- Apply an IP configuration to each interface.

- Configure one or more routing protocols and/or static routes so that the router can serve its function.

The `show route`, `show ip route`, `show ipv6 route`, or similar command will output the active routing table. As well as destination, gateway, AD/ metric, and interface, the output will show the source of the route, identified as a letter code (C = connected, S = static, R = RIP, B = BGP, D = EIGRP, O = OSPF, and so on).

route

The **route** command is used to view and modify the routing table of end system Windows and Linux hosts.

Apart from loopback addresses and the local subnet, the routing table for an end system generally contains a single entry for the default route. The default route is represented as the destination 0.0.0.0/0. Any traffic that is not addressed to the local subnet is sent over this default route.

In Windows, to show the routing table, run `route print`.

```
PS C:\Windows\system32> route print
===========================================================================
Interface List
  9...00 15 5d 00 65 31 ......Microsoft Hyper-V Network Adapter
  1...........................Software Loopback Interface 1
===========================================================================

IPv4 Route Table
===========================================================================
Active Routes:
Network Destination        Netmask          Gateway       Interface  Metric
          0.0.0.0          0.0.0.0      10.1.24.254    10.1.24.101     15
        10.1.24.0    255.255.255.0         On-link     10.1.24.101    271
      10.1.24.101  255.255.255.255         On-link     10.1.24.101    271
      10.1.24.255  255.255.255.255         On-link     10.1.24.101    271
        127.0.0.0        255.0.0.0         On-link       127.0.0.1    331
        127.0.0.1  255.255.255.255         On-link       127.0.0.1    331
  127.255.255.255  255.255.255.255         On-link       127.0.0.1    331
        224.0.0.0        240.0.0.0         On-link       127.0.0.1    331
        224.0.0.0        240.0.0.0         On-link     10.1.24.101    271
  255.255.255.255  255.255.255.255         On-link       127.0.0.1    331
  255.255.255.255  255.255.255.255         On-link     10.1.24.101    271
===========================================================================
Persistent Routes:
  None

IPv6 Route Table
===========================================================================
Active Routes:
 If Metric Network Destination      Gateway
  9     31 ::/0                      fe80::215:5dff:fe00:6510
  1    331 ::1/128                   On-link
  9     31 fdf0:2413:6d1c:30::/64    On-link
  9    271 fdf0:2413:6d1c:30:997b:634e:5b90:7e/128
                                     On-link
```

IPv4 and IPv6 routing tables for a Windows host. For IPv4, the host uses 10.1.0.254 as its default gateway. The IPv6 configuration has no route from the local network. (Screenshot used with permission from Microsoft.)

To add a route, the syntax for the Windows version of the tool is:

```
route [-f -p] add DestinationIP mask Netmask
GatewayIP metric MetricValue if Interface
```

The variables in the syntax are defined as:

- DestinationIP is a network or host address.

- Netmask is the subnet mask for DestinationIP.

- GatewayIP is the router to use to contact the network or host.

- MetricValue is the cost of the route.

- Interface is the adapter the host should use (used if the host is multihomed).

For example:

```
route add 192.168.3.0 mask 255.255.255.0 192.168.5.1
metric 2
```

Routes added in this manner are nonpersistent by default. This means that they are stored in memory and will be discarded if the machine is restarted. A route can be permanently configured (stored in the registry) using the -p switch. The tool also allows for routes to be deleted (`route delete`) and modified (`route change`).

The Linux version of `route` performs the same function, but the syntax is different. The routing table is shown by entering route with no parameters. The `change` parameter is not supported, and the command cannot be used to add persistent routes. A nonpersistent route can be added using the following general syntax:

```
route add -net 192.168.3.0 netmask 255.255.255.0
metric 2 dev eth0
```

```
lamp@lamp:~$ route
Kernel IP routing table
Destination     Gateway         Genmask         Flags Metric Ref    Use Iface
default         172.16.0.254    0.0.0.0         UG    100    0        0 eth0
172.16.0.0      0.0.0.0         255.255.255.0   U     0      0        0 eth0
172.16.0.254    0.0.0.0         255.255.255.255 UH    100    0        0 eth0
```

Output of Linux route command.

 The iproute2 suite of tools is designed to replace deprecated legacy command-line tools in Linux. You can use `ip route show` *and* `ip route add` *to achieve the same ends.*

tracert and traceroute

The **traceroute** tool allows you to test the whole path between two nodes with a view to isolating the node or link that is causing the problem.

traceroute

`traceroute` is supported on Linux and router OSes (such as Cisco IOS). `traceroute` uses UDP probe messages by default. The command issues a UDP probe for port 32767 with a TTL of 1. The first hop should reduce this to zero and respond with an ICMP Time Exceeded message. The command then increments the TTL by one and sends a second probe, which should reach the second hop router. This process is repeated until the end node is reached, which should reply with an ICMP Port Unreachable response.

The output shows the number of hops, the IP address of the ingress interface of the router or host (that is, the interface from which the router receives the probe), and the time taken to respond to each probe in milliseconds (ms). If no acknowledgment is received within the timeout period, an asterisk is shown against the probe. Note that while this could indicate that the router interface is not responding, it could also be that the router is configured to drop packets with expired TTLs silently.

`traceroute` can be configured to send ICMP Echo Request probes rather than UDP by using `traceroute -I`. The `traceroute -6` or `traceroute6` commands are used for IPv6 networks.

tracert

On a Windows system, the same function is performed using the `tracert` command. `tracert` uses ICMP Echo Request probes by default. The command issues an Echo Request probe with a TTL of 1. The first hop should reduce this to zero and respond with a Time Exceeded response. `tracert` then increments the TTL by one each time to discover the full path.

```
PS C:\Windows\system32> tracert 203.0.113.33

Tracing route to 203.0.113.33 over a maximum of 30 hops

  1    <1 ms    <1 ms    <1 ms   10.1.24.254
  2    <1 ms    <1 ms    <1 ms   10.1.128.253
  3     1 ms      *        1 ms   198.51.100.30
  4     1 ms     1 ms     1 ms   198.51.100.253
  5     2 ms     2 ms     1 ms   203.0.113.33

Trace complete.
```

Using tracert in Windows to plot the path from a host in the UK to CompTIA's web server.
(Screenshot used with permission from Microsoft.)

`tracert` can be used with several switches, which must precede the target IP address or host.

You can use the `-d` switch to suppress name resolution, `-h` to specify the maximum number of hops (the default is 30), and `-w` to specify a timeout in ms (the default is 4000). If, after increasing the value, destinations are then reachable, you probably have a bandwidth issue to resolve. When used with host names (rather than IP addresses), `tracert` can be forced to use IPv6 instead of IPv4 by adding the `-6` switch.

`tracert -6 www.microsoft.com`

Missing Route Issues

If you can ping a host's default gateway, but you cannot ping some or all hosts on remote networks, then you should suspect a routing issue. In many cases, this will be because a router has gone offline and there is no alternative path to the network. You should also be prepared to consider configuration issues too.

If you suspect a problem with router configuration and the network topology, use `traceroute` to try to identify where the network path is failing and the `route` or `show route` commands to investigate the routing tables of intermediate systems at that point in the path.

When inspecting a routing table, you can use `show ip route w.x.y.z` to check for the presence of a route to a specific IP network. A **missing route** may arise because a required static routing entry has not been entered or has been entered incorrectly. Missing routes may also arise because a router fails to communicate with its neighbors and so does not receive routing protocol updates. Performing a device configuration review means checking that the running configuration matches the documented baseline.

You might start troubleshooting this by pinging the router nodes that are neighbors of the system with the issue to check basic connectivity. If there is a network path and the neighbors are up, you would investigate the protocol configuration (perhaps there is an authentication issue or incorrect parameter).

Routing Loop Issues

A **routing loop** occurs when two routers use one another as the path to a network. Packets caught in a routing loop circle around until the TTL expires. One symptom of a potential routing loop is for routers to generate ICMP Time Exceeded error messages.

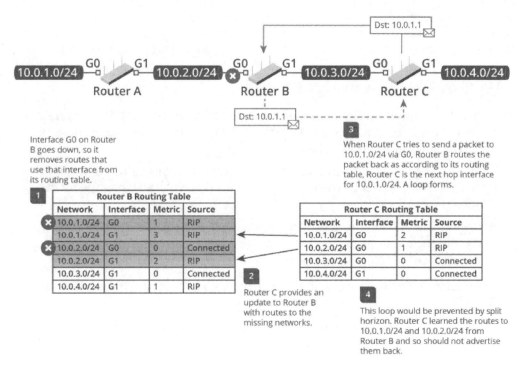

A routing loop created between routers B and C. (Images © 123RF.com.)

Routing protocols use various mechanisms to prevent loops. For example, distance vector protocols use the following mechanisms:

- **Maximum hop count**—If the cost exceeds a certain value (16 in RIP), the network is deemed unreachable. A poison route is one advertised with a hop count of 16. This can provide an explicit failure notice to other routers.

- **Holddown timer**—If a node declares a network unreachable, its neighbors start a holddown timer. Any updates about that route received from other nodes are discarded for the duration of the timer. This is designed to ensure that all nodes have converged information about an unreachable network.

- **Split horizon**—Prevents a routing update from being copied back to the source. In the example above, this would prevent router C from sending an update about a route to router A via router B to router B.

Link state protocols try to ensure that each node has a consistent view of the network through continual, timely updates flooded to all nodes in the routing domain. A loop in a link state routing domain typically indicates that updates are not being propagated correctly.

You can use `traceroute` to diagnose a routing loop by looking for IP addresses that appear multiple times in the output.

Asymmetrical Routing Issues

Asymmetrical routing refers to a topology where the return path is different to the forward path. This is common where there are load balancers and where routing takes place over multiple redundant paths across the Internet or other complex internetwork. Asymmetric routing is problematic where the return path is much higher latency than the forward path or where the difference between the paths causes stateful firewall or network address translation (NAT) devices to filter or drop communications. These types of devices should not be placed in the middle of a network where the forward and return paths could diverge. Problematic asymmetric routing could be caused by incorrectly configured static or dynamic routes. You should use traceroute from both sender and receiver to compare the per-hop latency to identify where the routing topology is misconfigured.

Low Optical Link Budget Issues

As well as the routing configuration, you should also consider physical and data link issues when troubleshooting WAN and datacenter routing. One such issue is poor connectivity across fiber optic links.

An **optical link budget**, or loss budget, is the amount of loss suffered by all components along a fiber transmission path. This is calculated using the following parameters:

- **Attenuation**—This is the loss over the length of the cable, based on fiber type and the wavelength used. Single mode has a loss of up to 0.4 dB/km, while multimode can be from 0.8 dB/km to 3 dB/km.

- **Connectors**—Each connector in the path incurs a loss, usually assumed to be 0.75 dB.

- **Splices**—Additional splices in the cable are budgeted at around 1 dB for mechanical and 0.3 dB for fusion.

Typically, an estimated loss budget is calculated when planning the link. The link is tested at deployment using an optical time domain reflectometer (OTDR) to derive an actual value. Differences between these values may reveal an installation fault or some unexpected source of signal loss.

 FOA have a loss budget calculator at thefoa.org/tech/ref/Loss_Budget/Loss_Budget.htm.

The loss budget must be less than the power budget. The power budget is calculated from the transceiver transmit (Tx) power and receiver (Rx) sensitivity, which are both typically measured in dB per milliwatt or dBm. For example, if Tx is -8 dBm and Rx is -15 dBm, then the power budget is 7 dB.

 dBm measures signal strength against a reference value, where 0 dBm is 1 milliwatt. A negative dBm is typical of Ethernet transceivers, which output less than 1 mw.

If the loss budget is 5 dB, the margin between the power budget and loss budget will be 2 dB. Margin is a safety factor to account for suboptimal installation conditions (such as bends or stress), aging, repair of accidental damage (additional splices), and performance under different thermal conditions (extreme temperatures can cause loss).

If the margin between the transmitter power and link budget is low, the link is less likely to achieve the expected bandwidth. There may be opportunities to improve performance with better or fewer splices, or it may be necessary to use an amplifier to boost the signal. Most outdoor plant would be designed with a margin of at least 5 dB. In a datacenter where conditions are less variable a lower margin might be acceptable.

Review Activity:

Router Installation and Troubleshooting

Answer the following questions:

1. **A router must forward traffic received over a single physical interface connected to a switch trunk port to the appropriate virtual LAN (VLAN). What feature must be configured on the router?**

2. **True or false? Layer 3 capable switches are interchangeable with routers.**

3. **True or false? Any occurrence of an asterisk in traceroute output indicates that there is no connectivity the destination along that path.**

4. **Your network monitor is recording high numbers of ICMP Time Exceeded notifications. What type of routing issue does this typically indicate?**

5. **A campus to datacenter fiber optic link has been laid over 15 km of single mode fiber with one fusion splice along this run. The termination at each end requires two connectors. You need to evaluate a proposal to use 10GBASE-LR transceiver modules for the router. The module specification quotes Tx power of –8.2 dBm and Rx sensitivity of –14.4 dBm. Assuming attenuation of 0.4 dB/km, 0.75 dB loss per connector, and 0.3 dB loss per splice, do these modules work within the expected loss budget?**

Review Activity:

Design a Branch Office Internetwork

Helpful Help is a charitable organization that operates out of numerous small offices spread all over the country. Each office has a team of 10–20 people who currently use a network of PCs and Apple Macs running various applications. Each office is connected back to a main site, which has a connection to the Internet via an ISP. Staff at each local office uses the link for web access and to access an online email service. Each office has a 192.168.x.0/24 subnet allocated to it. The East region is shown in the graphic.

Using the above scenario, answer the following questions:

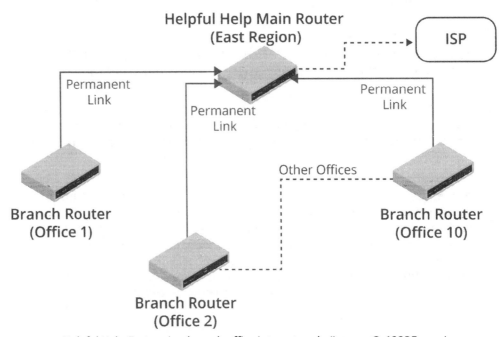

Helpful Help East region branch office internetwork. (Images © 123RF.com.)

1. **Given the current scenario of the charity, how would the routers at each local office be configured?**

Presently, each local office has several PSTN (landline) telephones. The plan is to replace these with a unified communications system for VoIP, conferencing, and messaging/information. This will require devices in each local office to be able to contact devices in other offices for direct media streaming. It is also anticipated that additional links may be added between branch offices where larger numbers of users are situated due to the increased bandwidth required by the new applications at this site. Here is the revised diagram:

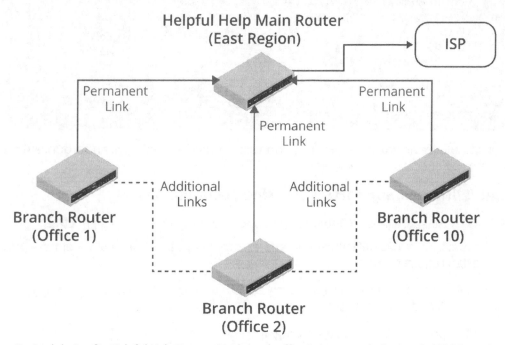

Revised design for Helpful Help East region branch office internetwork. (Image © 123RF.com.)

2. **With this new infrastructure in place, what changes would need to be made to the router's configuration?**

3. **Which protocol would be best here?**

If the new system works well in the East region (the smallest), the plan is to roll out the system to the three other regions (North, South, and West). This will involve connecting the main routers for each region together, plus some additional links for redundancy. The other regions use different IP numbering systems and some use VLSM.

4. **Considering the potential changes a successful pilot in the East region might bring about in the whole organization, would your router configuration options change?**

5. **What might you do to manage the much larger number of IP subnets?**

Lesson 7

Summary

You should be able to compare and contrast routing technologies and troubleshoot common general routing issues.

Guidelines for Supporting Routing Technologies

Follow these guidelines to deploy and support routing technologies effectively:

- Assess how static, default, and dynamic routing updates can best meet network design requirements:

  - Distance vector versus link state versus hybrid convergence performance in small and large networks.

  - Support for classless addressing and IPv6.

- Assess how features of classless addressing such as supernetting and VLSM allow for better routing design and address space utilization.

- Create device configuration documentation when deploying edge and internal routers to facilitate support and troubleshooting.

- Develop understanding of routing tables and forwarding decisions to assist with network design and troubleshooting:

  - How routing protocols use metrics to determine the least-cost route.

  - How the destination prefix length and route source administrative distance affects forwarding.

  - Next hop and time to live attributes of network paths.

- Use the route tool to investigate host routing tables.

- Use traceroute/tracert to test routing.

Lesson 8

Explaining Network Topologies and Types

LESSON INTRODUCTION

The cabling, switching, and routing functions of the first three layers in the OSI model can be deployed in many ways to implement networks of varying sizes and with different purposes. Being able to summarize these network types and topologies and the different network appliance models that support them will help you to build networks that meet customer goals for performance and security.

Lesson Objectives

In this lesson, you will:

- Explain network types and characteristics.

- Explain tiered switching architecture.

- Explain virtual LANs.

Topic 8A

Explain Network Types and Characteristics

EXAM OBJECTIVES COVERED
1.2 Explain the characteristics of network topologies and network types.

Network types and topologies determine the scale and flow of data through a network at layers 1, 2, and 3. Getting to know the different topologies is essential to designing or troubleshooting a network. No matter what your specific role in network implementation and management, you will need to understand the characteristics of the network topology you are working with and identify how the topology affects network performance and troubleshooting.

Client-Server versus Peer-to-Peer Networks

A network comprises nodes and links. Intermediate system nodes perform a forwarding function, while end system nodes are those that send and receive data traffic. End system nodes can be classified as either clients or servers:

- A server makes network applications and resources available to other hosts.

- A client consumes the services provided by servers.

A **client-server** network is one where some nodes, such as PCs, laptops, and smartphones, act mostly as clients. The servers are more powerful computers. Application services and resources are centrally provisioned, managed, and secured.

A **peer-to-peer** network is one where each end system acts as both client and server. This is a decentralized model where provision, management, and security of services and data is distributed around the network.

Business and enterprise networks are typically client-server, while residential networks are more often peer-to-peer (or workgroup). However, note that in a client-server network, often, nodes will function as both clients and servers at the same time. For example, a computer hosting a web application acts as a server to browser clients but is itself a client of database services running on other server computers. It is the centrally administered nature of the network that really defines it as client-server.

Network Types

A network type refers primarily to its size and scope. The size of a network can be measured as the number of nodes, while the scope refers to the area over which nodes sharing the same network address are distributed.

Local Area Networks

A local area network (LAN) describes a network type that is confined to a single geographical location. In a LAN, all nodes and segments are directly connected with cables or short-range wireless technologies. It does not require a leased telecommunication system to function. Most of the network infrastructure in a LAN would be directly owned and managed by a single organization. Some typical examples of LANs include:

- **Home/residential networks**—with an Internet router and a few computers, plus mobile devices, gaming consoles, and printers.

- **Small office/home office (SOHO) networks**—A business-oriented network possibly using a centralized server in addition to client devices and printers, but often still using a single Internet router/switch/access point to provide connectivity.

- **Small and medium-sized enterprise (SME) networks**—A network supporting dozens of users. Such networks would use structured cabling and multiple switches and routers to provide connectivity.

- **Enterprise LANs**—A larger network with hundreds or thousands of servers and clients. Such networks would require multiple enterprise-class switch and router appliances to maintain performance levels. The term **campus area network (CAN)** is sometimes used for a LAN that spans multiple nearby buildings.

- **Datacenters**—A network that hosts only servers and storage, not end user client devices.

The term **wireless local area network (WLAN)** is used for LANs based on Wi-Fi. Open (public) WLANs are often referred to as hotspots.

Wide Area Networks

A wide area network (WAN) is a network of networks, connected by long-distance links. A typical enterprise WAN would connect a main office site with multiple branch office sites, possibly in different countries. A WAN could link two or more large LANs or could be used for remote workers connecting to an enterprise network via a public network such as the Internet. WANs are likely to use leased network devices and links, operated and managed by a service provider.

The term **metropolitan area network (MAN)** is sometimes used for something a bit smaller than a WAN: a city-wide network encompassing multiple buildings.

Personal Area Networks

The terms **personal area network (PAN)** and wireless PAN (WPAN) have gained some currency over the last few years. They refer to the fact that a person might establish close-range network links between a variety of devices, such as smartphones, tablets, headsets, and printers. As digital and network functionality continues to be embedded in more and more everyday objects, appliances (the Internet of Things), and clothing, the use of PANs will only grow.

Network Topology

Where the type defines the network scope, the topology describes the physical or logical structure of the network in terms of nodes and links.

The physical network topology describes the placement of nodes and how they are connected by the network media. For example, in one network, nodes might be directly connected via a single cable; in another network, each node might connect to a switch via separate cables. These two networks have different physical topologies.

The logical topology describes the flow of data through the network. For example, given the different physical network topologies described previously, if in each case the nodes can send messages to one another, the logical topology is the same. The different physical implementations (directly connected via a cable versus connected to the same switch) achieve the same logical layout.

In the simplest type of topology, a single link is established between two nodes. This is called a **point-to-point** link. Because only two devices share the connection, they are guaranteed a level of bandwidth.

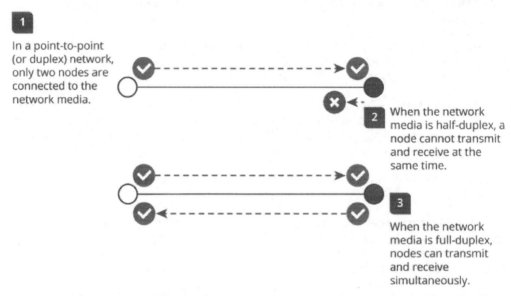

1 — In a point-to-point (or duplex) network, only two nodes are connected to the network media.

2 — When the network media is half-duplex, a node cannot transmit and receive at the same time.

3 — When the network media is full-duplex, nodes can transmit and receive simultaneously.

Physical point-to-point topologies using different media types for half-duplex and duplex communications.

A point-to-point link can be a physical or logical topology. For example, on a WAN, two routers might be physically linked via multiple intermediate networks and physical devices but still share a logical point-to-point link, where each can address only the other router. With either a physical or logical topology, it is the 1:1 relationship that defines a point-to-point link.

Star Topology

In a **star topology**, each endpoint node is connected to a central forwarding node, such as a hub, switch, or router. The central node mediates communications between the endpoints. The star topology is the most widely used physical topology. For example, a typical SOHO network is based around a single Internet router appliance that clients can connect to with a cable or wirelessly. The star topology is easy to reconfigure and easy to troubleshoot because all data goes through a central point, which can be used to monitor and manage the network. Faults are automatically isolated to the media, node (network card), or the hub, switch, or router at the center of the star.

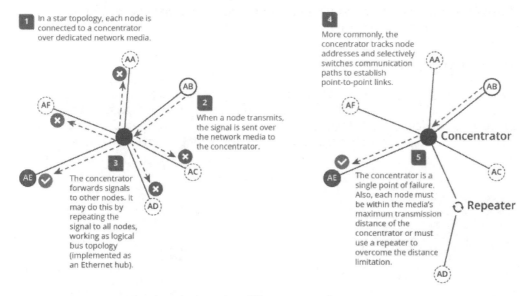

Star topologies using different types of concentrator.

You may also encounter the **hub-and-spoke** topology. This is the same layout as a star topology. The hub-and-spoke terminology is used when speaking about WANs with remote sites.

Mesh Topology

A **mesh topology** is commonly used in WANs, especially public networks like the Internet. In theory, a mesh network requires that each device has a point-to-point link with every other device on the network (fully connected). This approach is normally impractical, however. The number of links required by a full mesh is expressed as $n(n-1)/2$, where n is the number of nodes. For example, a network of just four nodes would require six links, while a network of 40 nodes would need 780 links! Consequently, a hybrid approach is often used, with only the most important devices interconnected in the mesh, perhaps with extra links for fault tolerance and redundancy. In this case, the topology is referred to as a partial mesh.

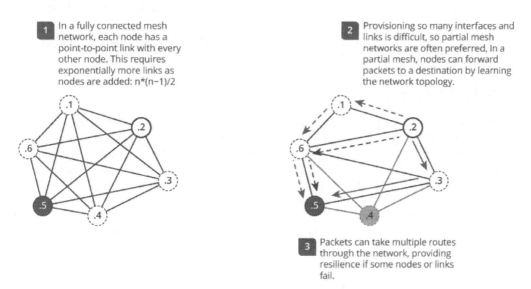

Fully connected and partial mesh topology examples.

Mesh networks provide excellent redundancy, because other routes, via intermediary devices, are available between locations if a link failure occurs.

Ring Topology

In a physical **ring topology**, each node is wired to its neighbor in a closed loop. A node receives a transmission from its upstream neighbor and passes it to its downstream neighbor until the transmission reaches its intended destination. Each node can regenerate the transmission, improving the potential range of the network.

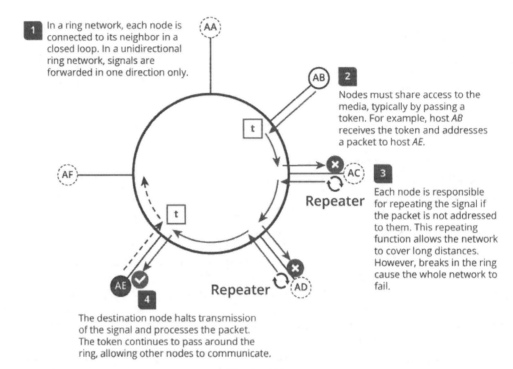

1 In a ring network, each node is connected to its neighbor in a closed loop. In a unidirectional ring network, signals are forwarded in one direction only.

2 Nodes must share access to the media, typically by passing a token. For example, host *AB* receives the token and addresses a packet to host *AE*.

3 Each node is responsible for repeating the signal if the packet is not addressed to them. This repeating function allows the network to cover long distances. However, breaks in the ring cause the whole network to fail.

4 The destination node halts transmission of the signal and processes the packet. The token continues to pass around the ring, allowing other nodes to communicate.

Ring topology.

The physical ring topology is no longer used on LANs, but it does remain a feature of many WANs. Two ring systems (dual counter-rotating rings) can be used to provide fault tolerance. These dual rings allow the system to continue to operate if there is a break in one ring.

Bus Topology

A physical **bus topology** with more than two nodes is a shared access topology, meaning that all nodes share the bandwidth of the media. Only one node can be active at any one time, so the nodes must contend to put signals on the media. All nodes attach directly to a single cable segment via cable taps. A signal travels down the bus in both directions from the source and is received by all nodes connected to the segment. The bus is terminated at both ends of the cable to absorb the signal when it has passed all connected devices.

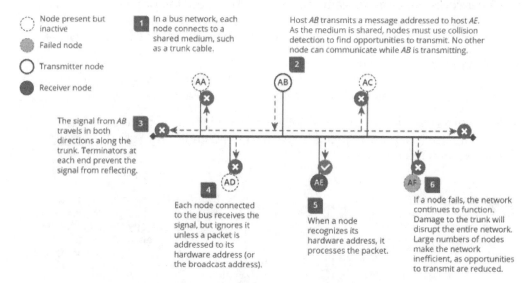

Physical bus topology. (Images © 123RF.com.)

This type of physical bus topology is the basis of the earliest Ethernet networks but is no longer in widespread use. Bus networks are comparatively difficult to reconfigure (adding or removing nodes can disrupt the whole network), impose limitations on the maximum number of nodes on a segment of cable, and are difficult to troubleshoot (a cable fault could be anywhere on the segment of cable). Perhaps most importantly, a fault anywhere in the cable means that all nodes are unable to communicate.

 A bus network does allow cables to be connected using a device called a repeater. Two lengths of cable joined by a repeater is considered one length of cable for the purpose of the bus topology. A repeater is a passive device and is not considered a network node in the way that a switch or router would.

A logical bus topology is one in which nodes receive the data transmitted all at the same time, regardless of the physical wiring layout of the network. Because the transmission medium is shared, only one node can transmit at a time. Nodes within the same logical bus segment are in the same collision domain. When Ethernet is deployed with a legacy hub appliance, this can be described as a physical star-logical bus topology.

Hybrid Topology

A **hybrid topology** is anything that uses a mixture of point-to-point, star, mesh, ring, and bus physical and/or logical topologies. As noted, an Ethernet hub establishes a logical bus topology, but the physical topology is a star. Another common legacy topology is the star-wired ring, where nodes in the ring are wired to a central multistation access unit (MAU) rather than to its neighbors. The MAU implements the logical ring and handles token passing.

On modern networks, hybrid topologies are often used to implement redundancy and fault tolerance or to connect sites in WANs:

* **Hierarchical star**—corporate networks are often designed in a hierarchy, also known as a tree topology. This can be combined with a star topology to implement each node in the overall tree. The links between nodes in the tree are referred to as backbones or trunks because they aggregate and distribute traffic from multiple different areas of the network.

- **Hierarchical star-mesh**—Alternatively, nodes at the top of the hierarchy can be configured in a partial or full mesh for redundancy. Switches lower in the hierarchy establish star topologies that connect end systems to the network.

- **Star of stars**—A WAN might be configured as a hub-and-spoke between a central office and branch offices, with each site implementing a star topology to connect end systems. This is also referred to as a snowflake topology.

- **Star with ring**—Alternatively, a ring topology might be used to connect geographically separate sites, with each site implementing a star topology to connect end systems.

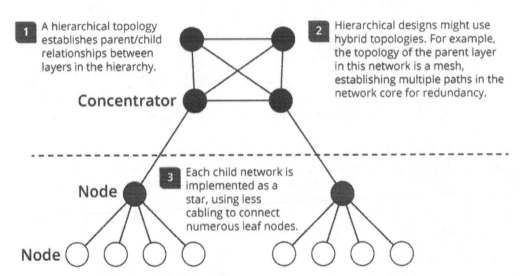

1 A hierarchical topology establishes parent/child relationships between layers in the hierarchy.

2 Hierarchical designs might use hybrid topologies. For example, the topology of the parent layer in this network is a mesh, establishing multiple paths in the network core for redundancy.

3 Each child network is implemented as a star, using less cabling to connect numerous leaf nodes.

Hierarchical hybrid topology example where a mesh network distributes traffic between multiple star networks.

Review Activity:

Network Types and Characteristics

Answer the following questions:

1. **What network infrastructure implementation links multiple buildings within the same city?**

2. **What term is used to describe a topology in which two nodes share a single link?**

3. **You need operations to continue if one link fails. How many links does it take to connect three sites?**

4. **What types of devices are connected in a PAN?**

Topic 8B

Explain Tiered Switching Architecture

EXAM OBJECTIVES COVERED
1.7 Explain basic corporate and datacenter network architecture.
2.3 Given a scenario, configure and deploy common Ethernet switching features. (STP only)
5.5 Given a scenario, troubleshoot general networking issues.

Ethernet, switching, and IP routing are the principal technologies used to implement cabled local networks. There are many types and sizes of network, however, and many different ways of designing cabling and forwarding to suit the requirements of large and small organizations and budgets. While you might not be responsible for network design at this stage of your career, it is important that you be able to identify the components and advantages of tiered network hierarchies.

Three-Tiered Network Hierarchy

A hierarchical model breaks down a large and complex network design into smaller sections based on the functions performed. Each function can be assessed by network designers to identify the most efficient hardware and software to use to implement it.

As a practical example of this type of model, many corporate office networks follow Cisco's design principles for a **three-tiered hierarchy**: access, distribution, and core.

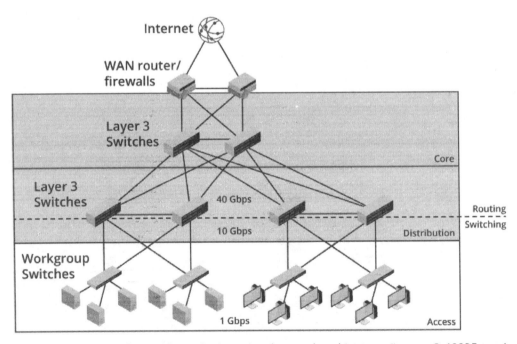

Core, distribution, and access layers in three-tiered network architecture. (Images © 123RF.com.)

Access/Edge Layer

The **access or edge layer** allows end-user devices, such as computers, printers, and smartphones to connect to the network. The access layer is implemented for each site using structured cabling and wall ports for wired access and access points for wireless access. Both are ultimately connected to workgroup switches. Switches deployed to serve the access layer might also be referred to as LAN switches or data switches. End systems connect to switches in the access/edge layer in a star topology. There are no direct links between the access switches.

Distribution/Aggregation Layer

The **distribution or aggregation layer** provides fault-tolerant interconnections between different access blocks and either the core or other distribution blocks. Each access switch has full or partial mesh links to each router or layer 3 switch in its distribution layer block. The distribution layer is often used to implement traffic policies, such as routing boundaries, filtering, or quality of service (QoS).

The layer 3 capable switches used to implement the distribution/aggregation layer have different capabilities to the layer 2 only workgroup switches used in the access tier. Rather than 1 Gbps access ports and 10 Gbps uplink ports, as would be typical of a workgroup switch, basic interfaces on an aggregation switch would be 10 Gbps and uplink/backbone ports would be 40 Gbps (or possibly 40 Gbps/100 Gbps). Layer 3 switches work on the principle of "route once, switch many," which means that once a route is discovered, it is cached with the destination MAC address and subsequent communications are switched without invoking the routing lookup. While a router uses a generic processor and firmware to process incoming packets, a layer 3 switch uses an **application-specific integrated circuit (ASIC)**. This can have an impact on the relative performance of the two types of devices. Layer 3 switches can be far faster, but they are not always as flexible. Layer 3 switches cannot usually perform WAN routing and work with interior routing protocols only. Often layer 3 switches support Ethernet only.

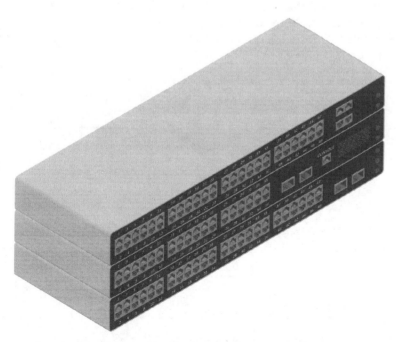

An example of a core/distribution switch. (Image © 123RF.com.)

Core Layer

The **core layer** provides a highly available network backbone. Devices such as client and server computers should not be attached directly to the core. Its purpose should be kept simple: provide redundant traffic paths for data to continue to flow around the access and distribution layers of the network. Routers or layer 3 switches in the core layer establish a full mesh topology with switches in distribution layer blocks.

 In a two tier or collapsed core model, the core must be implemented as a full mesh. This is impractical if there are large numbers of core switches.

Spanning Tree Protocol

The three-tiered network model makes use of mesh or partial mesh topologies to implement redundant links. Multiple paths are part of good network design as they increase resilience; if one link fails, then the network can remain operational by forwarding frames over a different path. However, as a layer 2 protocol, Ethernet has no concept of time to live, so layer 2 broadcast traffic could continue to loop through a network with multiple paths indefinitely.

The **spanning tree protocol (STP)** is a means for the bridges or switches to organize themselves into a hierarchy. The switch at the top of the hierarchy is the root. The switch with the lowest ID, comprising a priority value and the MAC address, will be selected as the root.

Each switch then determines the shortest path to the root bridge by exchanging information with other switches. This STP information is packaged as bridge protocol data unit (BPDU) multicast frames. A port that forwards "up" to the root, possibly via intermediate switches, is identified as a root port. Ports that can forward traffic "down" through the network with the least cost are identified as designated ports. A port that would create a loop is identified as a blocking or non-designated port. Subsequently, bridges exchange Topology Change Notifications if devices are added or removed, enabling them to change the status of forwarding/ blocked ports appropriately.

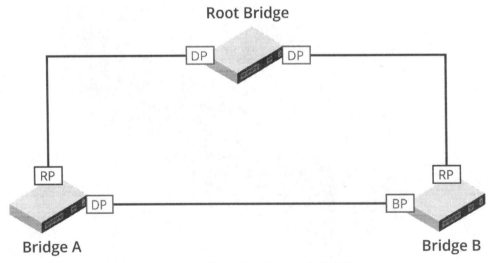

Spanning tree configuration. (Images © 123RF.com.)

This image shows the minimum configuration necessary to prevent loops in a network with three bridges or switches. The root bridge has two designated ports (DP) connected to Bridge A and Bridge B. Bridges A and B both have root ports (RP) connected back to the interfaces on the root bridge. Bridges A and B also have a connection directly to one another. On Bridge A, this interface is active and traffic for Bridge B can be forwarded directly over it. On Bridge B, the interface is blocked (BP) to prevent a loop, and traffic for Bridge A must be forwarded via the root bridge.

Spanning Tree Protocol Configuration

If a switch supports STP (not all do), it should operate by default without configuration. An administrator can (and should) set the priority value to make the choice of one switch as root over another more likely. The root will usually be part of a high-bandwidth backbone or core switch group; performance will suffer if a switch on a low-bandwidth segment becomes root.

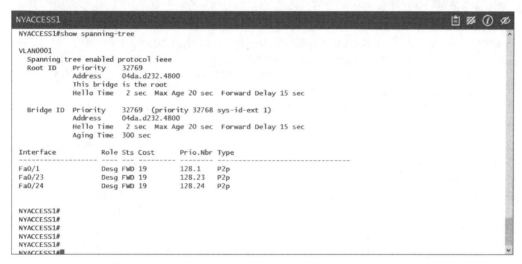

```
NYACCESS1
NYACCESS1#show spanning-tree

VLAN0001
  Spanning tree enabled protocol ieee
  Root ID    Priority    32769
             Address     04da.d232.4800
             This bridge is the root
             Hello Time   2 sec  Max Age 20 sec  Forward Delay 15 sec

  Bridge ID  Priority    32769  (priority 32768 sys-id-ext 1)
             Address     04da.d232.4800
             Hello Time   2 sec  Max Age 20 sec  Forward Delay 15 sec
             Aging Time  300 sec

Interface        Role Sts Cost      Prio.Nbr Type
---------------- ---- --- --------- -------- ------------------------------
Fa0/1            Desg FWD 19        128.1    P2p
Fa0/23           Desg FWD 19        128.23   P2p
Fa0/24           Desg FWD 19        128.24   P2p


NYACCESS1#
NYACCESS1#
NYACCESS1#
NYACCESS1#
NYACCESS1#
NYACCESS1#
```

Viewing spanning tree configuration on a Cisco switch. (Image © and Courtesy of Cisco Systems, Inc. Unauthorized use not permitted.)

The following table shows the different states that a port can be in.

State	Forwards Frames?	Learns MACs?	Notes
Blocking	No	No	Drops all frames other than BPDUs.
Listening	No	No	Port is listening for BPDUs to detect loops.
Learning	No	Yes	The port discovers the topology of the network and builds the MAC address table.
Forwarding	Yes	Yes	The port works as normal.
Disabled	No	No	The port has been disabled by the administrator.

When all ports on all switches are in forwarding or blocking states, the network is converged. When the network is not converged, no communications can take place. Under the original 802.1D standard, this made the network unavailable for extended periods—tens of seconds—during configuration changes. STP is now more likely to be implemented as 802.1D-2004/802.1w or Rapid STP (RSTP). The rapid version creates outages of a few seconds or less. In RSTP, the blocking, listening, and disabled states are aggregated into a discarding state.

Switching Loop and Broadcast Storm Issues

A **switching loop** is where flooded frames circulate the network perpetually. Because switches flood broadcasts, such as ARP or DHCP requests, out all ports, these frames will go down one link to the next switch, which will send the broadcast back up the redundant link, and back to the originating switch. As this repeats, the switches start to see source MAC addresses associated with multiple ports and so clear the MAC address table mapping, which causes them to start flooding unicast traffic too.

Without intervention, this loop will continue indefinitely, causing a **broadcast storm**. A broadcast storm will cause network utilization to go to near maximum capacity, and the CPU utilization of the switches to jump to 80 percent or more. This makes the switched segment effectively unusable until the broadcast storm stops. A broadcast storm may quickly consume all link bandwidth and crash network appliances.

If there is a loop, spanning tree should shut down the port. This will isolate the problem to a segment of the network. Inspect physical ports that correspond to the disabled interfaces for looped connections. At the patch panel, this could mean a patch cable that connects two ports on the same switch. On the office floor, it could mean a patch cable between two wall ports. Check the switch for log events related to MAC address flapping.

If a broadcast storm occurs on a network where STP is already enabled, you should investigate the following potential causes:

- Verify compatible versions of STP are enabled on all switches.

- Verify the physical configuration of segments that use legacy equipment, such as Ethernet hubs.

- Investigate networking devices in the user environment and verify that they are not connected as part of a loop. Typical sources of problems include unmanaged desktop switches and VoIP handsets.

Review Activity:

Tiered Switching Architecture

Answer the following questions:

1. **Which two topologies are used in the three-tier hierarchical model?**

2. **Spanning tree has been deployed without the administrator setting a priority value. Which of the following switches will be selected as the root?**
   - **Switch A with base MAC f062.81ff.0001 and a 10 Gbps uplink**
   - **Switch B with base MAC f062.81ff.0002 and a 40 Gbps uplink**
   - **Switch C with base MAC f062.81ff.0003 and a 40 Gbps uplink**

3. **In what STP-configured state(s) are all ports when a network running STP is converged?**

4. **True or false? A broadcast storm can only be resolved by investing interface configurations.**

Topic 8C

Explain Virtual LANs

EXAM OBJECTIVES COVERED
2.3 Given a scenario, configure and deploy common Ethernet switching features.

Most networks make use of virtual LANs (VLANs), both to improve network security and network performance, so they are an important concept for you to understand. In this topic, you will identify the benefits of network segmentation and the characteristics and functions of VLANs.

Virtual LAN IDs and Membership

At the data link and network layers, a segment is a group of hosts in the same broadcast domain. At the network layer, this group is identified as either an IP network or as a subnet within an IP network. At the data link layer, a broadcast domain can be established by connecting the hosts to the same unmanaged switches. This hardware-based approach is inflexible, however, so managed switches allow the configuration of virtual LANs (VLANs) to isolate ports to separate broadcast domains.

If a VLAN were to contain multiple IP networks or subnets, nodes would receive broadcast traffic for all the subnets. This would be a very complex configuration, however. Normally, the network would be designed with a 1:1 mapping between VLANs and subnets.

Implementing VLANs can reduce broadcast traffic when a network has expanded beyond a certain number of hosts or users. As well as reducing the impact of broadcast traffic, from a security point of view, each VLAN can represent a separate zone. VLANs are also used to separate nodes based on traffic type and the need for Quality of Service. For example, it is commonplace to put all VoIP handsets on a voice VLAN to minimize interference coming from nodes that are sending email or downloading large files on the same network. The switches and routers can then be configured to give the VoIP VLAN priority over ordinary data VLANs.

The VLAN with ID 1 is referred to as the default VLAN. Unless configured differently, all ports on a switch default to being in VLAN 1.

The simplest means of assigning a node to a VLAN is by configuring the port interface on the switch with a VLAN ID in the range 2 to 4,094. For example, from the switch management interface, ports 1 through 10 could be configured as a VLAN with the ID 10 and ports 11 through 20 could be assigned to VLAN 20. Host A connected to port 2 would be in VLAN 10, and host B connected to port 12 would be in VLAN 20. Host A and Host B would not be able to communicate directly, even though they are connected to the same switch. Each VLAN is typically configured with its own subnet address and IP address range. Communications between VLANs must go through an IP router or layer 3 capable switch.

```
interface swp5
  bridge-access 100

interface swp6
  bridge-access 100

interface swp7
  bridge-access 100

interface swp8
  bridge-access 100

interface swp9
  bridge-access 200

interface swp10
  bridge-access 200

interface swp11
  bridge-access 200

interface swp12
  bridge-access 200

interface bridge
  bridge-ports swp5 swp6 swp7 swp8 swp9 swp10 swp11 swp12
  bridge-vids 10 100 200
  bridge-vlan-aware yes
```

Cumulus VX switch output showing switch ports swp 5-8 configured in VLAN 100 and ports 9-12 in VLAN 200. (Screenshot courtesy of Nvidia.)

This type of port-based assignment is described as a static VLAN. Nodes or hosts can also be assigned to dynamic VLANs using some feature of the host, such as its MAC address or authentication credentials supplied by the user.

Trunking and IEEE 802.1Q

On a large network, a single switch will not provide enough ports for all the hosts that need to be connected to the network. This means that multiple switches must be interconnected to build the network fabric. Multiple switches may also be deployed to provide redundant links. The interconnections between switches are referred to as **trunks**. One of the ports on each switch would be configured as a trunk port for this purpose.

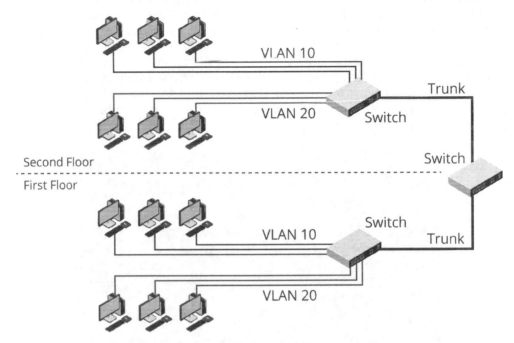

VLAN trunk link. (Images © 123RF.com.)

When frames designated for different VLANs are transported across a trunk, the VLAN ID (VID) of each frame must be preserved for the receiving switch to forward it correctly. VIDs are normally defined by the IEEE **802.1Q** standard. Under 802.1Q, per-VLAN traffic is identified by a tag inserted in the Ethernet frame between the Source Address and EtherType fields. The tag contains information about the VID (from 1 to 4,094) and priority (used for QoS functions). The EtherType value is set to identify the frame as 802.1Q.

Construction of an 802.1Q (VLAN tagged) Ethernet frame.

Tagged and Untagged Ports

If a switch port will only ever participate in a single VLAN, that port can be configured as untagged. This is also referred to as an access port or host port. An untagged/access port uses the following **port tagging** logic:

- If a frame is addressed to a port in the same VLAN on the same switch, no tag needs to be added to the frame.

- If the frame needs to be transported over a trunk link, the switch adds the relevant 802.1Q tag to identify the VLAN, and then forwards the frame over the trunk port.

- If the switch receives an 802.1Q tagged frame on an access port, it strips the tag before forwarding it.

Conversely, a tagged port will normally be one that is operating as a trunk; that is, capable of transporting traffic addressed to multiple VLANs using the 802.1Q frame format. A trunk might be used to connect switches or to connect a switch to a router. In some circumstances, a host attached to a port might need to be configured to use multiple VLANs and would need to be attached to a trunk port, rather than an access port. Consider a virtualization host with multiple guest operating systems. The virtual servers might need to be configured to use different VLANs.

Voice VLANs

Voice over IP (VoIP) transmits voice traffic as data packets, rather than over circuit-based transmission lines. The bandwidth and latency requirements of voice traffic mean that it is often necessary to prioritize it over other types of data packets. This can be accomplished using a dedicated VLAN for voice traffic. However, in many cases, VoIP has been implemented into network infrastructures that were originally designed for just desktop and laptop computers, with limited numbers of physical network access ports.

To accommodate the lack of dedicated wall ports for handsets, most VoIP endpoints incorporate an embedded switch with just two external ports. The handset is connected via its uplink port to the wall port and via the structured cabling to an access switch. The PC or laptop is connected to the handset via the other port. The handset forwards data traffic from the PC to the access switch as untagged frames. The handset sends voice traffic over the same physical link but uses 802.1Q tagged frames.

Normally, for a switch interface to process tagged frames, it would have to be configured as a trunk port. This adds a lot of configuration complexity, so most switches now support the concept of a **voice or auxiliary VLAN** to distinguish the PC and VoIP traffic without having to configure a trunk. In the following example, the interface configuration assigns traffic from the PC to VLAN 100 and the voice traffic to VLAN 101:

```
interface GigabitEthernet0/0
switchport mode access
switchport access vlan 100
switchport voice vlan 101
```

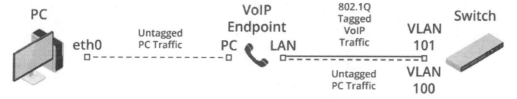

Sharing a single physical wall port between a PC and VoIP handset. The handset and switch interface configuration allow VoIP traffic to be assigned to a different VLAN than the PC's data traffic. (Images © 123RF.com.)

The switch will only accept tagged frames that match the configured voice VLAN ID. To avoid having to configure this manually, the voice VLAN ID and other configuration parameters can be communicated to the handset using a protocol such as Cisco Discovery Protocol (CDP).

Review Activity:

Virtual LANs

Answer the following question:

1. **At which layer of the OSI model do VLANs establish network segments?**

2. **True or false? A VLAN is a single broadcast domain.**

3. **Which values can be used to assign a port to a specific VLAN?**

4. **What type of frames are carried over tagged ports?**

5. **True or false? When configuring a voice VLAN, the voice VLAN ID must be lower than the access VLAN ID.**

Lesson 8

Summary

You should be able to explain network types, scopes, and characteristics and how topologies such as three-tiered switching and VLANs can make corporate networks more manageable.

Guidelines for Supporting Network Topologies and Types

While you might not be responsible for network design at this state in your career, it helps to understand design principles to provide support for existing networks.

- Identify zones within complex networks, such as PANs or WLANs within a LAN or CAN and the perimeter network between the private local network and public WANs/MANs.

- Determine whether to implement a core and distribution layer or a single collapsed core layer, based on network size and projected requirements for future expansion.

- Determine bandwidth requirements within the core/distribution layer (typically 10 Gbps+) and provision appropriate switch modules, transceivers, and cabling (typically fiber optic).

- Provision redundant trunk links within the core and between the core and distribution layer.

- Determine bandwidth requirements for the access layer (typically 1 Gbps) and provision appropriate workgroup/LAN switches based on media type.

- Enable spanning tree to prevent loops around redundant circuits and ensure the selection of a root bridge within the core or distribution layer as appropriate.

- Provision redundant trunk links between distribution layer switch blocks and access layer switches.

- Connect client devices (PCs, VoIP endpoints, and printers) and non-datacenter servers to access layer switches.

Follow these general guidelines for implementing VLANs:

- Determine the organizational principles that will guide VLAN assignment. There are no rules to govern what these principles should be, but some commonly followed practices include:

  - Assign devices to VLANs by type (wired workstations, VoIP endpoints, wireless clients, printers, servers, and SAN). This should be governed by the performance and security requirements of each device type.

  - Use VLANs for distinct security zones, such as management traffic, guest network access, and Internet/WAN edge.

  - Aim for 250 as the maximum number of hosts in a single VLAN (/24 subnet). Use VLANs for separate building floors to minimize traffic that must pass over a trunk.

- Consider using VLANs to represent departmental boundaries and functions, but don't create VLANs just for the sake of it. Physical location will generally override function, as moving more traffic over trunk links will affect performance.

- Design IP subnets for each VLAN and design a VLAN numbering system.

- Map the logical topology to the physical switch topology and identify trunk links. Tag the interfaces that will participate in trunk links with the VLANs they are permitted to carry.

- Configure other interfaces as untagged/access ports within the appropriate VLAN.

- Ensure that hosts in each VLAN can obtain leases from DHCP servers, route to other network segments (as permitted), and contact DNS servers.

Lesson 9
Explaining Transport Layer Protocols

LESSON INTRODUCTION

Layers 1 through 3 of the OSI model are concerned with addressing and packet forwarding and delivery. This basic connectivity is established for the purpose of transporting application data. In this lesson, you will learn to describe how protocols at layer 4 provision the transport services that network applications depend upon.

Lesson Objectives

In this lesson, you will:

- Compare and contrast transport protocols.

- Use appropriate tools to scan network ports.

Topic 9A

Compare and Contrast Transport Protocols

EXAM OBJECTIVES COVERED
1.1 Compare and contrast the Open Systems Interconnection (OSI) model layers and encapsulation concepts.
1.5 Explain common ports and protocols, their application, and encrypted alternatives.

You have seen how IP provides addressing and delivery at layer 3 of the OSI model. At layer 4, the TCP/IP protocol suite also defines how different applications on separate hosts establish connections and track communications. Understanding how application protocols use ports to establish connections is critical to being able to configure and support network services.

Transport Layer Ports and Connections

At layer 3, IP provides addressing and routing functionality for internetworks. Protocols at the Transport layer (layer 4) are concerned with delivery of multiplexed application data.

A TCP/IP host may be running multiple services or communicating with multiple servers, clients, or peers in parallel. This means that incoming packets must be directed to the appropriate service or application. To facilitate this, each application is assigned a unique identification number called a **port**. A host can operate multiple ports simultaneously.

Port numbers 0 through 1,023 are preassigned by the Internet Assigned Numbers Authority (IANA) to "well-known" server applications. These port assignments are documented at iana.org/assignments/service-names-port-numbers/service-names-port-numbers.xhtml. Other server applications have been registered in the port range 1,024 through 49,151.

The remaining ports (up to 65,535) are designated for private or dynamic use. As well as the server application needing a port, each client application must assign its own port number to track its requests. Client ports are also referred to as ephemeral ports or source ports.

OS implementations of TCP/IP have not always conformed to these recommendations. For example, earlier versions of Windows and UNIX/Linux used 1,024—5,000 for client ports. Modern Linux kernels often use 32,768–60,999.

The port number is used in conjunction with the source IP address to form a **socket**. Each socket is bound to a software process. Only one process can operate a socket at any one time. A connection is formed when a client socket requests a service from the server socket. A connection is uniquely identified by the combination of server port and IP address and client port and IP address. A server socket can therefore support multiple connections from a number of client sockets.

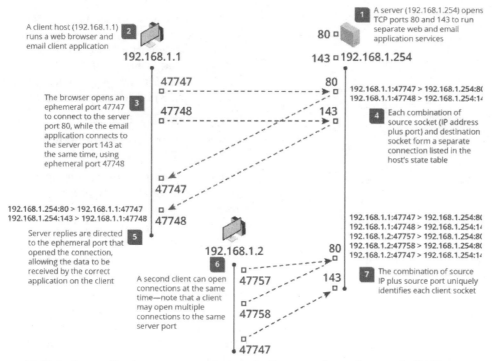

Multiplexing application ports as sockets at the Transport layer. (Images © 123RF.com.)

Transmission Control Protocol

The **Transmission Control Protocol (TCP)** works at the Transport layer to provide connection-oriented, guaranteed communication using acknowledgements to ensure that delivery has occurred. If packets are missing, they can be retransmitted. TCP can be used for unicast transmission only.

TCP takes data from the Application layer as a stream of bytes and divides it up into segments, each of which is given a header. The TCP segments become the payload of the underlying IP datagrams. The use of sequencing, acknowledgments, and retransmissions means that TCP requires numerous header fields to maintain state information. The main fields in the header of a TCP segment are:

Field	Explanation
Source port	TCP port of sending host.
Destination port	TCP port of destination host.
Sequence number	The ID number of the current segment (the sequence number of the last byte in the segment). This allows the receiver to rebuild the message correctly and deal with out-of-order packets.

(continued)

Field	Explanation
Ack number	The sequence number of the next segment expected from the other host (that is, the sequence number of the last segment received +1). Packets might be out-of-order because they are delayed, but they could also be lost completely or arrive in a damaged state. In the first case, the lack of acknowledgement results in the retransmission of data and, in the second case, a Negative Acknowledgement (NAK or NACK) forces retransmission.
Data length	Length of the TCP segment.
Flags	Type of content in the segment (ACK, SYN, FIN, and so on).
Window	The amount of data the host is willing to receive before sending another acknowledgement. TCP's flow control mechanism means that if it is getting overwhelmed with traffic, one side can tell the other to slow the sending rate.
Checksum	Ensures validity of the segment. The checksum is calculated on the value of not only the TCP header and payload but also part of the IP header, notably the source and destination addresses. Consequently, the mechanism for calculating the checksum is different for IPv6 (128-bit addresses) than for IPv4 (32-bit addresses).
Urgent Pointer	If urgent data is being sent, this specifies the end of that data in the segment.
Options	Allows further connection parameters to be configured. The most important of these is the Maximum Segment Size. This allows the host to specify how large the segments it receives should be, minimizing fragmentation as they are transported over data link frames.

TCP Handshake and Teardown

A TCP connection is typically established to transfer a single file, so a client session for something like a web page (HTTP) might involve multiple TCP connections being opened with the server. These connections are managed using handshake transactions, which make use of a number of **TCP flags.**

TCP Three-Way Handshake

A connection is established using a three-way handshake:

No.	Time	Source	Destination	Protocol	Length	Info
1	0.0..	10.1.0.101	10.1.0.2	TCP	66	1624 → 80 [SYN] Seq=0 Win=65535 Len=0 MSS=1460 WS=25(
2	0.0..	10.1.0.2	10.1.0.101	TCP	66	80 → 1624 [SYN, ACK] Seq=0 Ack=1 Win=8192 Len=0 MSS=:
3	0.0..	10.1.0.101	10.1.0.2	TCP	54	1624 → 80 [ACK] Seq=1 Ack=1 Win=262144 Len=0
4	0.0..	10.1.0.101	10.1.0.2	HTTP	433	GET / HTTP/1.1
5	0.0..	10.1.0.2	10.1.0.101	TCP	54	80 → 1624 [ACK] Seq=1 Ack=380 Win=2102272 Len=0
6	0.2..	10.1.0.2	10.1.0.101	TCP	1514	80 → 1624 [ACK] Seq=1 Ack=380 Win=2102272 Len=1460 ['

```
> Internet Protocol Version 4, Src: 10.1.0.101, Dst: 10.1.0.2
∨ Transmission Control Protocol, Src Port: 1624, Dst Port: 80, Seq: 1, Ack: 1, Len: 0
      Source Port: 1624
      Destination Port: 80
      [Stream index: 0]
      [TCP Segment Len: 0]
      Sequence number: 1    (relative sequence number)
      [Next sequence number: 1    (relative sequence number)]
      Acknowledgment number: 1    (relative ack number)
      0101 .... = Header Length: 20 bytes (5)
   > Flags: 0x010 (ACK)
      Window size value: 1024
      [Calculated window size: 262144]
      [Window size scaling factor: 256]
```

```
0000  00 15 5d 01 ca 76 00 15  5d 01 ca 77 08 00 45 00    ··]··v·· ]··w··E·
0010  00 28 16 49 40 00 80 06  00 00 0a 01 00 65 0a 01    ·(·I@··· ·····e··
0020  00 02 06 58 00 50 61 ff  66 ce 99 26 04 92 50 10    ···X·Pa· f··&··P·
0030  04 00 14 83 00 00                                   ······
```

Observing the 3-way handshake with the Wireshark protocol analyzer.
(Screenshot courtesy of Wireshark.)

1. The client sends a segment with the TCP flag SYN set to the server with a randomly generated sequence number. The client enters the SYN-SENT state.

2. The server, currently in the LISTEN state (assuming it is online), responds with a SYN/ACK segment, containing its own randomly generated sequence number. The server enters the SYN-RECEIVED state.

3. The client responds with an ACK segment. The client assumes the connection is ESTABLISHED.

4. The server opens a connection with the client and enters the ESTABLISHED state.

 Servers can (usually) support thousands or even millions of TCP connections simultaneously.

The sending machine expects regular acknowledgments for segments it sends and, if a period elapses without an acknowledgment, it assumes the information did not arrive and automatically resends it. This overhead makes the system relatively slow. Connection-oriented transmission is suitable when reliability and data integrity are important.

TCP Connection Teardown

There are also functions for resetting a connection and (in some implementations) keeping a connection alive if no actual data is being transmitted (hosts are configured to timeout unused connections). To close a connection, also referred to as teardown, the following basic steps are performed:

1. The client sends a FIN segment to the server and enters the FIN-WAIT1 state.

2. The server responds with an ACK segment and enters the CLOSE-WAIT state.

3. The client receives the ACK segment and enters the FIN-WAIT2 state. The server sends its own FIN segment to the client and goes to the LAST-ACK state.

4. The client responds with an ACK and enters the TIME-WAIT state. After a defined period, the client closes its connection.

5. The server closes the connection when it receives the ACK from the client.

Some implementations may use one less step by combining the FIN and ACK responses into a single segment operation.

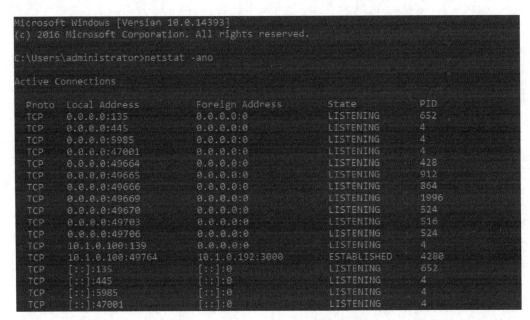

Observing TCP connections with the netstat tool. (Screenshot used with permission from Microsoft.)

A host can also end a session abruptly using a reset (RST) segment. This would not be typical behavior and might need to be investigated. A server or security appliance might refuse connections using RST, a client or server application might be faulty, or there could be some sort of suspicious scanning activity ongoing.

User Datagram Protocol

The **User Datagram Protocol (UDP)** also works at the Transport layer, but unlike TCP, it is a connectionless, nonguaranteed method of communication with no acknowledgments or flow control. There is no guarantee regarding the delivery of messages or mechanism for retransmitting lost or damaged packets. When an application uses UDP, it must specify reliability mechanisms in the application layer headers or software logic, if this is required.

UDP is suitable for applications that send small amounts of data in each packet and do not require acknowledgement of receipt. It is used by Application layer protocols that need to send multicast or broadcast traffic. It may also be used for applications that transfer time-sensitive data but do not require complete reliability, such as voice or video. Using small packets means that if a few are lost or arrive out of order, they only manifest as minor glitches in playback quality. The reduced overhead means that overall delivery is faster.

This table shows the structure of a UDP datagram.

Field	Explanation
Source port	UDP port of sending host.
Destination port	UDP port of destination host.
Sequence number	The ID number of the current segment (the sequence number of the last byte in the segment). This allows the receiver to rebuild the message correctly and deal with out-of-order packets.
Message length	Size of the UDP packet.
Flags	Type of content in the segment (ACK, SYN, FIN, and so on).
Checksum	Ensures validity of the packet

The header size is 8 bytes, compared to 20 bytes (or more) for TCP.

Common TCP and UDP Ports

The following table lists some of the well-known and registered port numbers.

Port Number	Transport Protocol	Service or Application	Description
20	TCP	ftp-data	File Transfer Protocol—Data
21	TCP	ftp	File Transfer Protocol—Control
22	TCP	ssh/sftp	Secure Shell/FTP over SSH
23	TCP	telnet	Telnet
25	TCP	smtp	Simple Mail Transfer Protocol
53	TCP/UDP	domain	Domain Name System
67	UDP	bootps	BOOTP/DHCP Server
68	UDP	bootpc	BOOTP/DHCP Client
69	UDP	tftp	Trivial File Transfer Protocol
80	TCP	http	HTTP
110	TCP	pop	Post Office Protocol
123	UDP	ntp/sntp	Network Time Protocol/Simple NTP

(continued)

Port Number	Transport Protocol	Service or Application	Description
143	TCP	imap	Internet Message Access Protocol
161	UDP	snmp	Simple Network Management Protocol
162	UDP	snmp-trap	Simple Network Management Protocol Trap
389	TCP/UDP	ldap	Lightweight Directory Access Protocol
443	TCP	https	HTTP-Secure (Secure Sockets Layer (SSL)/Transport Layer Security (TLS)
445	TCP	smb	Server Message Block over TCP/IP
514	UDP	syslog	Syslog
546	UDP	dhcpv6-client	DHCPv6 Client
547	TCP	dhcpv6-server	DHCPv6 Server
587	TCP	smtps	SMTP-Secure
636	TCP	ldaps	LDAP-Secure
993	TCP	imaps	IMAP-Secure
995	TCP	pop3s	POP3-Secure
1433	TCP	sql-server	MS Structured Query Language (SQL) Server
1521	TCP	sqlnet	Oracle SQL*Net
3306	TCP	mysql	MySQL/MariaDB
3389	TCP	rdp	Remote Desktop Protocol
5004	UDP	rtp	Real-Time Protocol
5005	UDP	rtcp	Real-Time Control Protocol
5060	TCP/UDP	sip	Session Initiation Protocol
5061	TCP/UDP	sips	SIP-Secure

Review Activity:

Transport Protocols

Answer the following questions:

1. How many port numbers are required to establish a connection at the Transport layer?

2. What is the purpose of the window field in a TCP segment?

3. What are the sizes of TCP and UDP headers?

4. True or False? User Datagram Protocol (UDP), like TCP, uses flow control in the sending of data packets.

5. What port and protocol does TFTP use at the Transport layer?

Topic 9B

Use Appropriate Tools to Scan Network Ports

EXAM OBJECTIVES COVERED
5.3 Given a scenario, use the appropriate network software tools and commands.

One of the critical tasks for network administrators is to identify and analyze the traffic passing over network links. This information is used to troubleshoot network services, and to verify the security of the network.

IP Scanners

One of the management tasks facing a network administrator is to verify exactly what is connected to the network and what is being communicated over it. This is usually described as network visibility. Visibility is necessary to confirm that servers and clients are in the correct VLANs or subnets and to try to identify rogue or unauthorized machines. An **IP scanner** is a tool that performs host discovery and can establish the overall logical topology of the network in terms of subnets and routers.

IP scanning can be performed using lightweight standalone open source or commercial tools, such as Nmap, AngryIP, or PRTG. Enterprise network management suites will also be able to perform IP scanning and combine that with asset or inventory information about each host. This functionality is often referred to as IP Address Management (IPAM). Suites that integrate with DHCP and DNS servers can be referred to as DHCP, DNS, and IPAM (DDI). Windows Server is bundled with a DDI product. Other notable vendors and solutions include ManageEngine, Infoblox, SolarWinds, Bluecat, and Men & Mice.

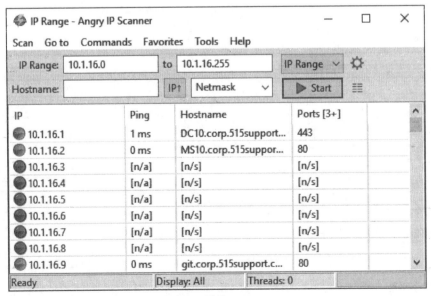

Angry IP Scanner.

Host discovery is a basic type of IP scanning that only attempts to determine whether an IP address is "up." There are many different host discovery techniques. Some are best at discovering large numbers of legitimate hosts quickly; others are optimized for identifying rogue hosts that are attempting to remain hidden. The most basic techniques use the ping, arp, and traceroute tools. Some suites use Simple Network Management Protocol (SNMP) queries, which can also report more detailed information about interface statistics, while as noted above, enterprise suites can query local DHCP and DNS servers for information. Security-oriented scanners can use specially crafted probes to locate hosts that might be configured not to respond to pings.

Nmap

The **Nmap Security Scanner** (nmap.org) is widely used for IP scanning, both as an auditing and as a penetration testing tool. The tool is open-source software with packages for most versions of Windows, Linux, and macOS®. It can be operated with a command line or via a GUI (Zenmap).

The basic syntax of an Nmap command is to give the IP subnet (or IP address) to scan. When used without switches like this, the default behavior of Nmap is to ping and send a TCP ACK packet to ports 80 and 443 to determine whether a host is present. On a local network segment, Nmap will also perform ARP and Neighbor Discovery (ND) sweeps. If a host is detected, Nmap performs a port scan against that host to determine which services it is running. This OS fingerprinting can be time consuming on a large IP scope. If you want to perform only host discovery, you can use Nmap with the `-sn` switch to suppress the port scan. The tool can also work out hop counts by specifying the `--traceroute` switch.

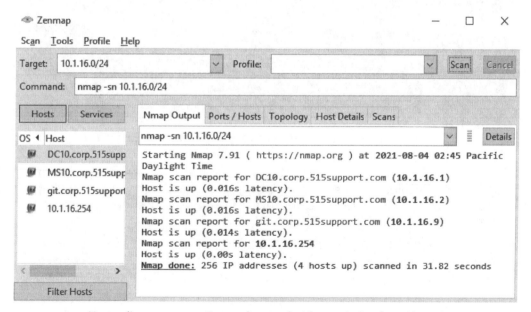

Nmap discovery scan. (Screenshot used with permission from Nmap.)

A variety of options are available for custom scans to try to detect stealthy hosts (nmap.org/book/host-discovery-techniques.html).

netstat

As well as discovering hosts, one other visibility challenge is to establish what services a host is running. The **netstat** command allows you to check the state of ports on the local host. You can use `netstat` to check for service misconfigurations, such as a host running a web or FTP server that a user installed without authorization. You may also be able to identify suspicious remote connections to services on the local host or from the host to remote IP addresses.

On Windows®, used without switches, the command outputs active TCP connections, showing the local and foreign addresses and ports. Using the `-a` switch displays all open ports, including both active TCP and UDP connections and ports in the listening state.

On Linux®, running `netstat` without switches shows active connections of any type. If you want to show different connection types, you can use the switches for Internet connections for TCP (`-t`) and UDP (`-u`), raw connections (`-w`), and UNIX® sockets/local server ports (`-x`). Using the `-a` switch includes ports in the listening state in the output. `-l` shows only ports in the listening state, omitting established connections.

For example, the following command shows listening and established Internet connections (TCP and UDP) only: `netstat -tua`

```
lamp@lamp:~$ netstat -tua
Active Internet connections (servers and established)
Proto Recv-Q Send-Q Local Address           Foreign Address         State
tcp        0      0 0.0.0.0:5000            0.0.0.0:*               LISTEN
tcp        0      0 localhost:mysql         0.0.0.0:*               LISTEN
tcp        0      0 localhost:domain        0.0.0.0:*               LISTEN
tcp        0      0 0.0.0.0:ssh             0.0.0.0:*               LISTEN
tcp        0      0 localhost:33060         0.0.0.0:*               LISTEN
tcp        0      1 172.16.0.201:52492      172.16.0.254:domain     SYN_SENT
tcp6       0      0 [::]:http               [::]:*                  LISTEN
tcp6       0      0 [::]:ssh                [::]:*                  LISTEN
udp        0      0 172.16.0.201:43367      172.16.0.254:domain     ESTABLISHED
udp        0      0 172.16.0.201:42410      172.16.0.254:domain     ESTABLISHED
udp        0      0 172.16.0.201:47084      172.16.0.254:domain     ESTABLISHED
udp        0      0 localhost:domain        0.0.0.0:*
udp        0      0 172.16.0.201:bootpc     0.0.0.0:*
```

Linux netstat output showing active and listening TCP and UDP connections.

On both Windows and Linux, `-n` displays ports and addresses in numerical format. Skipping name resolution speeds up each query. On Linux, using `-4` or `-6` filters sockets by IPv4 or IPv6 addresses respectively. In Windows, use the `-p` switch with the protocol type (`TCP`, `TCPv6`, `UDP`, or `UDPv6`).

Another common task is to identify which software process is bound to a socket. On Windows, `-o` shows the Process ID (PID) number that has opened the port, while `-b` shows the process name. In Linux, use `-p` to show the PID and process name.

`netstat -s` reports per protocol statistics, such as packets received, errors, discards, unknown requests, port requests, failed connections, and so on. The tool will report Ethernet statistics using `-e` (Windows) or `-I` (Linux). `netstat -r` displays the routing table.

```
lamp@lamp:~$ netstat -i
Kernel Interface table
Iface      MTU    RX-OK RX-ERR RX-DRP RX-OVR    TX-OK TX-ERR TX-DRP TX-OVR Flg
eth0      1500     4069      0      0 0          8134      0      0      0 BMRU
lo       65536     5322      0      0 0          5322      0      0      0 LRU
```

Linux netstat interface statistics showing receive and transmit packets numbers plus errors and dropped packets.

`netstat` can also be set to run continuously. In Windows, run `netstat nn`, where *nn* is the refresh interval in seconds (press `Ctrl+C` to stop); in Linux, run `netstat -c`.

 The Linux `netstat` command is part of the deprecated net-tools package. The preferred package iproute2 contains a number of different commands to replace netstat functionality. Most of the port scanning functions are performed by `ss`, while interface statistics are reported by `nstat`.

Remote Port Scanners

Where `netstat` reports on the status of local ports, a remote **port scanner** performs the probes from another machine, or even a machine on another network.

Many of the tools used for host discovery can also perform remote port scanning. As with host discovery, there are many different techniques for performing port scans. Some techniques are designed for covert use (to try to avoid detection of the scanning activity by the target) and some are designed to probe beyond security barriers, such as firewalls.

As examples, the following represent some of the main types of scanning that Nmap can perform:

- TCP SYN (`-sS`)—This is a fast technique (also referred to as half-open scanning) as the scanning host requests a connection without acknowledging it. The target's response to the scan's SYN packet identifies the port state.

- TCP connect (`-sT`)—A half-open scan requires Nmap to have privileged access to the network driver so that it can craft packets. If privileged access is not available, Nmap must use the OS to attempt a full TCP connection. This type of scan is less stealthy.

- UDP scans (`-sU`)—Scan UDP ports. As these do not use ACKs, Nmap needs to wait for a response or timeout to determine the port state, so UDP scanning can take a long time. A UDP scan can be combined with a TCP scan.

- Port range (`-p`)—By default, Nmap scans 1,000 commonly used ports. Use the `-p` argument to specify a port range. You can also use `--top-ports n`, where *n* is the number of commonly used ports to scan. The frequency statistics for determining how commonly a port is used are stored in the nmap-services configuration file.

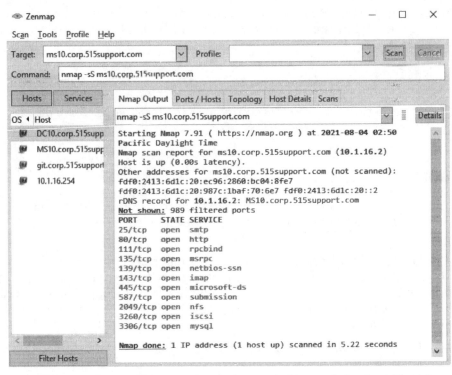

Half-open scanning with Nmap. (Screenshot used with permission from Nmap.)

When services are discovered, you can use Nmap with the ‑sV or ‑A switch to probe a host more intensively to discover the software or software version operating each port. The process of identifying an OS or software application from its responses to probes is called fingerprinting.

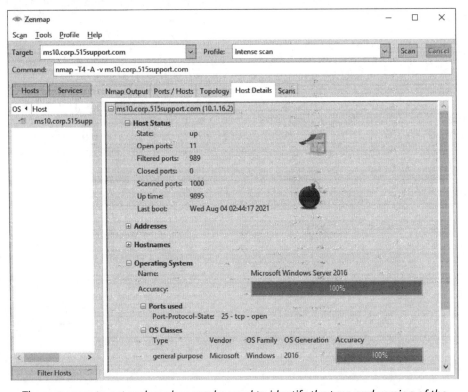

The responses to network probes can be used to identify the type and version of the host operating system. (Screenshot used with permission from Nmap.)

Protocol Analyzers

A **protocol analyzer** works in conjunction with a packet capture or sniffer tool. You can either analyze a live capture to analyze frames as they are read by a sniffer or open a saved capture (.pcap) file. Most protocol analyzer tools bundle a sniffer component with the analyzer in the same software package.

One function of a protocol analyzer is to parse each frame in a stream of traffic to reveal its header fields and payload contents in a readable format. This is referred to as packet analysis. Analyzing protocol data at the frame or packet level will help to identify protocol or service misconfigurations. As a live stream or capture file can contain hundreds or thousands of frames, you can use display filters to show only particular frame or sequence of frames. Another useful option is to use the **Follow TCP Stream** context command to reconstruct the packet contents for a TCP session.

Another function of a protocol analyzer is to perform traffic analysis. Rather than reading each frame individually, you use the tool to monitor statistics related to communications flows, such as bandwidth consumed by each protocol or each host, identifying the most active network hosts, monitoring link utilization and reliability, and so on. In Wireshark, you can use the **Statistics** menu to access traffic analysis tools.

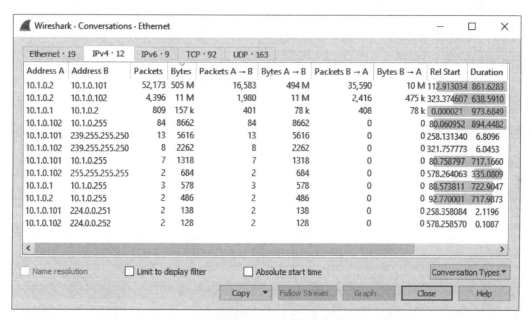

Using the Conversations option from Wireshark's Statistics tools.
(Screenshot courtesy of Wireshark.)

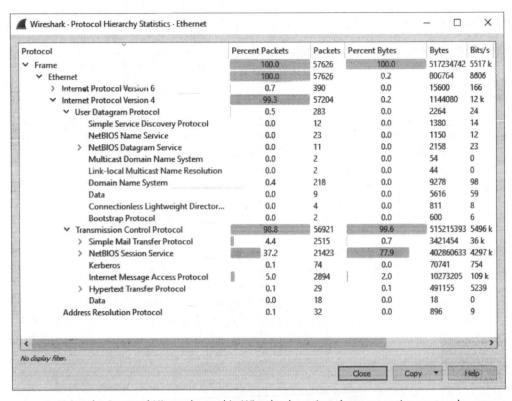

Protocol	Percent Packets	Packets	Percent Bytes	Bytes	Bits/s
⌄ Frame	100.0	57626	100.0	517234742	5517 k
⌄ Ethernet	100.0	57626	0.2	806764	8806
> Internet Protocol Version 6	0.7	390	0.0	15600	166
⌄ Internet Protocol Version 4	99.3	57204	0.2	1144080	12 k
⌄ User Datagram Protocol	0.5	283	0.0	2264	24
Simple Service Discovery Protocol	0.0	12	0.0	1380	14
NetBIOS Name Service	0.0	23	0.0	1150	12
> NetBIOS Datagram Service	0.0	11	0.0	2158	23
Multicast Domain Name System	0.0	2	0.0	54	0
Link-local Multicast Name Resolution	0.0	2	0.0	44	0
Domain Name System	0.4	218	0.0	9278	98
Data	0.0	9	0.0	5616	59
Connectionless Lightweight Director...	0.0	4	0.0	811	8
Bootstrap Protocol	0.0	2	0.0	600	6
⌄ Transmission Control Protocol	98.8	56921	99.6	515215393	5496 k
> Simple Mail Transfer Protocol	4.4	2515	0.7	3421454	36 k
> NetBIOS Session Service	37.2	21423	77.9	402860633	4297 k
Kerberos	0.1	74	0.0	70741	754
Internet Message Access Protocol	5.0	2894	2.0	10273205	109 k
> Hypertext Transfer Protocol	0.1	29	0.1	491155	5239
Data	0.0	18	0.0	18	0
Address Resolution Protocol	0.1	32	0.0	896	9

Using the Protocol Hierarchy tool in Wireshark to view the most active protocols on a network link. This sort of report can be used to baseline network activity. (Screenshot courtesy of Wireshark.)

Review Activity:

Port Scanning

Answer the following questions:

1. What type of scanning tool outputs a "Host is up" status report.

2. You are auditing the service configuration of a Linux server. Which command can you use to check the PID associated with a TCP port, even if there are no active connections?

3. A technician has identified an undocumented host using an IP address in a range set aside as unallocated. The technician is going to run a fingerprinting scan. What type of information could this yield about the host?

4. You need to analyze the information saved in a .pcap file. What type of command-line tool or other utility is best suited to this task?

Lesson 9

Summary

You should be able to compare and contrast appropriate uses of TCP and UDP and select appropriate tools to support and troubleshoot Transport layer issues.

Guidelines for Supporting Transport Layer Protocols

Follow these guidelines to make effective use of transport protocols:

- Identify required ports for each host and record this information in configuration management documentation. Ensure that only legitimate applications and services can bind to a server port.

- Understand the use of handshakes and acknowledgements to support and troubleshoot reliable transport mechanisms using TCP.

- Understand that applications may use UDP for unreliable unicast, multicast, or broadcast transmissions to minimize protocol overheads.

- Deploy IP and port scanners to gain visibility into hosts attached to the network and protocol traffic passing over it.

- Deploy packet capture and protocol analyzer software to gain visibility into individual packets and per-per-host or per-protocol statistics.

Lesson 10

Explaining Network Services

LESSON INTRODUCTION

You have identified the Physical, Data Link, Network, and Transport layer technologies and protocols that underpin basic connectivity. The TCP/IP protocol suite also includes application protocols that implement network services.

This lesson focuses on application protocols that perform low-level network operations tasks, such as providing dynamic address or name resolution services. You should understand the functions of the network services protocols and the ports that they rely upon to operate.

Lesson Objectives

In this lesson, you will:

- Explain the use of network addressing services.

- Explain the use of name resolution services.

- Configure DNS services.

Topic 10A

Explain the Use of Network Addressing Services

EXAM OBJECTIVES COVERED
1.5 Explain common ports and protocols, their application, and encrypted alternatives. (DHCP only)
1.6 Explain the use and purpose of network services.

Every host interface needs an IP configuration to communicate on a TCP/IP network. An administrator can manually assign these IP addresses, or the assignment can be done automatically without manual intervention. By understanding the different methods available to you for assigning IP addresses, you can choose the method that best suits different networks and hosts.

Dynamic Host Configuration Protocol

The **Dynamic Host Configuration Protocol (DHCP)** provides an automatic method for allocating an IP address, subnet mask, and optional parameters, such as the default gateway and DNS server addresses, when a host joins the network. All the major operating systems provide support for DHCP clients and servers. DHCP servers are also embedded in many SOHO routers and modems.

A host is configured to use DHCP by specifying in the TCP/IP configuration that it should automatically obtain an IP address.

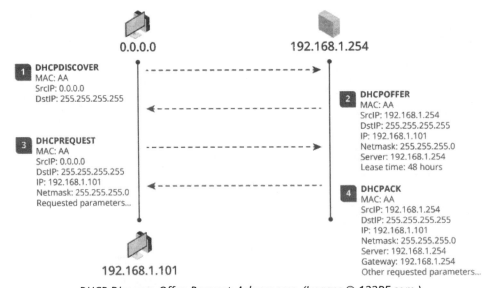

DHCP Discover, Offer, Request, Ack process. (Images © 123RF.com.)

When a DHCP client initializes, it broadcasts a DHCPDISCOVER packet to find a DHCP server. All communications are sent using UDP, with the server listening on port 67 and the client on port 68.

Presuming it has an IP address available, the DHCP server responds to the client with a DHCPOFFER packet, containing the address and other configuration information.

While the client doesn't have an IP address yet, the DHCPOFFER is usually delivered as unicast because the server knows the client's MAC address. Some hosts cannot receive unicast without an IP address. They should set a broadcast bit in the DHCPDISCOVER packet.

The client may choose to accept the offer using a DHCPREQUEST packet—also broadcast onto the network.

Assuming the offer is still available, the server will respond with a DHCPACK packet. The client broadcasts an ARP message to check that the address is unused. If so, it will start to use the address and options; if not, it declines the address and requests a new one.

The IP address is leased by the server for a limited period only. A client can attempt to renew or rebind the lease before it expires. If the lease cannot be renewed, the client must release the IP address and start the discovery process again.

Sometimes, the DHCP lease process is called the DORA process: Discover, Offer, Request, and Ack(nowledge).

DHCP Server Configuration

DHCP is normally deployed as a service of a network operating system or through an appliance such as a switch or router. A DHCP server must be allocated a static IP address and configured with a range (or pool) of IP addresses and subnet masks plus option values to allocate.

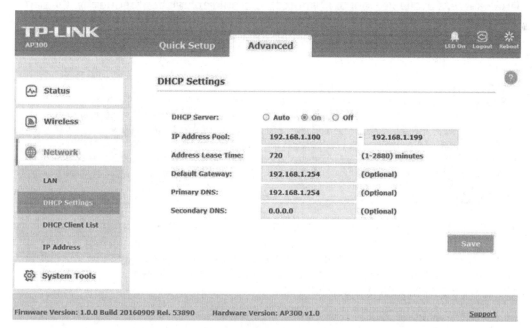

Configuring DHCP on a TP-LINK wireless access point. (Screenshot courtesy of TP-Link Technologies Co., Ltd.)

A range of addresses and options configured for a single subnet is referred to as a **scope**. To define a scope, you must provide a start and end IP address along with a subnet mask. The server maintains a one-to-one mapping of scopes to subnets. That is, no scope can cover more than one subnet and no subnet can contain more than one scope.

The multifunction device shown only supports a single scope. The DHCP server must be placed in the same subnet as its clients. More advanced DHCP servers might be configured to manage multiple scopes. Where a server provides IP configuration for multiple subnets/scopes, it must choose the pool to service each request based on the subnet from which the request originated.

There is no mechanism for a client to choose between multiple servers. Therefore, if multiple DHCP servers are deployed—for fault tolerance, for instance—they must be configured with nonoverlapping or split scopes. DHCP for multiple subnets is usually handled by configuring relay agents to forward requests to a central DHCP server.

DHCP Options Configuration

Along with an address scope, you also need to define other parameters, such as lease time and options.

DHCP Lease Time and Available Leases

The client can renew the lease when at least half the lease's period has elapsed (T1 timer) so that it keeps the same IP addressing information. If the original DHCP server does not respond to the request to renew the lease, the client attempts to rebind the same lease configuration with any available DHCP server. By default, this happens after 87.5% of the lease duration is up (T2 timer). If this fails, the client releases the IP address and continues to broadcast to discover a server.

A long lease time means the client does not have to renew the lease often, but the DHCP server's available pool of IP addresses is not replenished frequently. Where IP addresses are in short supply, a short lease period enables the DHCP server to allocate addresses previously assigned to hosts that are now not active on the network.

A Windows client can be forced to release a lease by issuing a command such as ipconfig. In Linux, the utility dhclient is often used for this task, though modern distributions might use NetworkManager or systemd-networkd. A Windows host that fails to obtain a lease will revert to an automatic IP address (APIPA) or link-local configuration and select an address in the 169.254.0.0/16 range. Linux might use link-local addressing, set the address to unknown (0.0.0.0), or leave the interface unconfigured.

DHCP Options

When the DHCP server offers a configuration to a client, at a minimum it must supply an IP address and subnet mask. Typically, it will also supply other IP-related settings, known as DHCP options. Each option is identified by a tag byte or decimal value between 0 and 255 (though neither 0 nor 255 can be used as option values). Some widely used options include:

- The default gateway (IP address of the router).

- The IP address(es) of DNS servers that can act as resolvers for name queries.

- The DNS suffix (domain name) to be used by the client.

- Other useful server options, such as time synchronization (NTP), file transfer (TFTP), or VoIP proxy.

A set of default (global) options can be configured on a server-wide basis. Default options can be overridden by setting scope-specific options.

DHCP Reservations and Exclusions

One disadvantage of the standard dynamic assignment method is that it does not guarantee that any given client will retain the same IP address over time. There are some cases where it would be advantageous for certain hosts, such as network printers or wireless access points, to retain their IP addresses.

One solution is to configure static assignments, using IP addresses outside the DHCP scope. Alternatively, statically assigned addresses can be assigned from a specially configured exclusion range, if this is supported by the server. While these solutions are functional, they lose the advantages of centralized configuration management.

An alternative approach is to create a **reservation**. A reservation is a mapping of a MAC address or interface ID to a specific IP address within the DHCP server's address pool. When the DHCP server receives a request from the given interface, it always provides the same IP address. This is also referred to as static or fixed address assignment. An automatically allocated reservation refers to an address that is leased permanently to a client. This is distinct from static allocation as the administrator does not predetermine which specific IP address will be leased.

DHCP Relay and IP Helper

Normally, routers do not forward broadcast traffic. This means that each broadcast domain must be served by its own DHCP server. On a large network with multiple subnets, this would mean provisioning and configuring many DHCP servers. To avoid this scenario, a **DHCP relay** agent can be configured to provide forwarding of DHCP traffic between subnets. Routers that can provide this type of forwarding are described as RFC 1542 compliant.

The DHCP relay intercepts broadcast DHCP frames, applies a unicast address for the appropriate DHCP server, and forwards them over the interface for the subnet containing the server. The DHCP server can identify the original IP subnet from the packet and offer a lease from the appropriate scope. The DHCP relay also performs the reverse process of directing responses from the server to the appropriate client subnet.

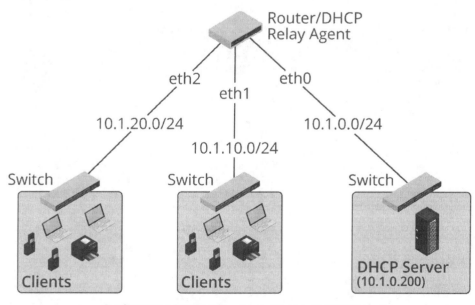

Configuring a DHCP relay agent. (Images © 123RF.com)

This **IP helper** functionality can be configured on routers to allow set types of broadcast traffic (including DHCP) to be forwarded to an interface. The IP helper function supports the function of the DHCP relay agent. For example, in the diagram, hosts in the 10.1.20.0/24 and 10.1.10.0/24 subnets need to use a DHCP server for autoconfiguration, but the DHCP server is located in a different subnet. The router is configured as a DHCP relay agent, using the following commands to enable forwarding of DHCP broadcasts on the interfaces serving the client subnets:

```
interface eth1
ip helper-address 10.1.0.200
interface eth2
ip helper-address 10.1.0.200
```

UDP forwarding is a more general application of the same principle. As well as DHCP, it is used for the Network Time Protocol (NTP) and other broadcast-based applications.

DHCPv6 Server Configuration

IPv6's Stateless Address Autoconfiguration (SLAAC) process can locate routers (default gateways) and generate a host address with a suitable network prefix automatically. In this context, the role of a DHCP server in IPv6 is different. DHCPv6 is often just used to provide additional option settings, rather than leases for host IP addresses. The format of messages is different, but the process of DHCP server discovery and address leasing (if offered) is fundamentally the same. As IPv6 does not support broadcast, clients use the multicast address ff02::1:2 to discover a DHCP server. DHCPv6 uses ports 546 (clients) and 547 (servers), rather than ports 68 and 67 as in DHCPv4.

In stateless mode, a client obtains a network prefix from a Router Advertisement and uses it with the appropriate interface ID. The router can also set a combination of flags to tell the client that a DHCP server is available. If so configured, the client solicits a DHCPv6 server using the multicast address ff02::1:2 and requests additional configuration information.

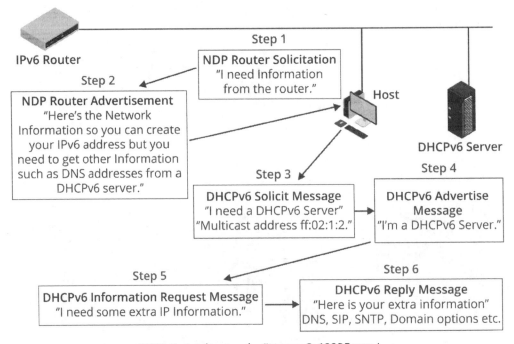

DHCPv6 stateless mode. (Images © 123RF.com.)

By contrast, stateful mode means that a host can also obtain a routable IP address from a DHCPv6 scope, plus any other options (like with DHCP for IPv4).

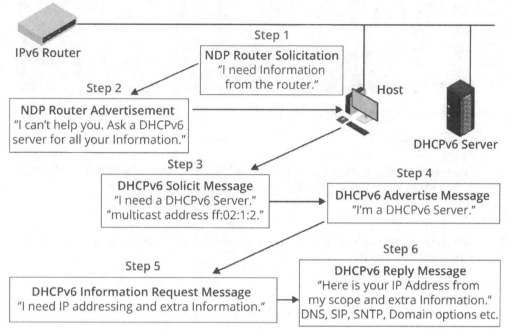

DHCPv6 stateful mode. (Images © 123RF.com.)

Configuring the scope requires you to define the network prefix and then any IP addresses that are to be excluded from being offered. All other addresses that are not explicitly excluded can be offered. The host must still listen for a router advertisement to obtain the network prefix and configure a default gateway. There is no mechanism in DHCPv6 for setting the default route.

Review Activity:

Network Addressing Services

Answer the following questions:

1. True or False? If a client accepts a DHCPOFFER, the DHCPREQUEST packet is broadcast on the network.

2. When configuring multiple DHCP servers for redundancy, what should you take care to do?

3. True or False? DHCP options can be configured on a per-scope basis.

4. What address is used to contact a DHCPv6 server?

5. In a stateless environment, what sort of information does DHCPv6 provide?

Topic 10B

Explain the Use of Name Resolution Services

EXAM OBJECTIVES COVERED
1.5 Explain common ports and protocols, their application, and encrypted alternatives. (DNS only)
1.6 Explain the use and purpose of network services.

Each host that has an IP address assigned to it can also have a descriptive name. This makes it easier for human users to identify and access it on the network and for application services to be configured with an addressing scheme that allows for changes in the underlying network. Almost all networks depend on this name resolution functionality to operate smoothly and securely, so it is important to understand how it works. In this topic, you will identify methods for host name resolution for TCP/IP networks.

Host Names and Fully Qualified Domain Names

The Internet Protocol uses a binary IP address to locate a host on an internetwork. The dotted decimal (IPv4) or hex (IPv6) representation of this IP address is used for configuration purposes, but it is not easy for people to remember. For this reason, a "friendly" name is also typically assigned to each host. There are two types of names: host names and Fully Qualified Domain Names (FQDNs).

A **host name** is assigned to a computer by the administrator, usually when the OS is installed. The host name needs to be unique on the local network.

To avoid the possibility of duplicate host names on the Internet, a **fully qualified domain name (FQDN)** is used to provide a unique identity for the host belonging to a particular network. An example of an FQDN might be `nut.widget.example.` An FQDN is made up of the host name and a domain suffix. In the example, the host name is `nut` and the domain suffix is `widget.example.` This domain suffix consists of the domain name `widget` within the top-level domain (TLD) `.example.` A domain suffix could also contain subdomains between the host and domain name. The trailing dot or period represents the root of the hierarchy.

When you are configuring name records, an FQDN must include the trailing period to represent the root, but this can be omitted in most other use cases.

A domain name must be registered with a registrar to ensure that it is unique within a top-level domain. Once a domain name has been registered, it cannot be used by another organization. The same domain name may be registered within different top-level domains, however—`widget.example.` and `widget.example.uk.` are distinct domains, for instance.

Numerous hosts may exist within a single domain. For example: `nut`, `bolt`, and `washer` might all be hosts within the `widget.example.` domain. Given that, FQDNs must follow certain rules:

- The host name must be unique within the domain.

- The total length of an FQDN cannot exceed 253 characters, with each label (part of the name defined by a period) no more than 63 characters (excluding the periods).

- A DNS label should use letter, digit, and hyphen characters only. A label should not start with a hyphen. Punctuation characters such as the period (.) or forward slash (/) should not be used.

- DNS labels are not case-sensitive.

Additionally, Internet registries may have their own restrictions.

Domain Name System

The **Domain Name System (DNS)** is a global hierarchy of distributed name server databases that contain information on domains and hosts within those domains. At the top of the DNS hierarchy is the root, which is represented by the null label, consisting of just a period (.). There are 13 root level servers (A to M).

Immediately below the root lie the top-level domains (TLDs). There are several types of top-level domains, but the most prevalent are generic (such as .com, .org, .net, .info, .biz), sponsored (such as .gov, .edu), and country code (such as .uk, .ca, .de). DNS is operated by ICANN (icann.org), which also manages the generic TLDs. Country codes are generally managed by an organization appointed by the relevant government.

Information about a domain is found by tracing records from the root down through the hierarchy. The root DNS servers have complete information about the top-level domain servers. In turn, these servers have information relating to servers for the second level domains. No name server has complete information about all domains. Records within the DNS tell them where an authoritative name server for the missing information is found.

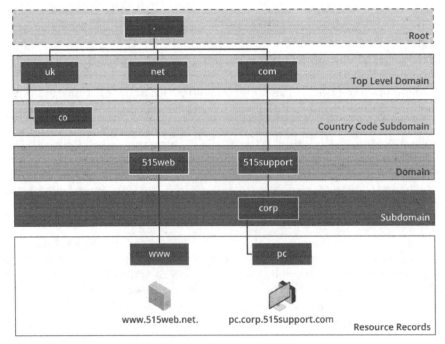

DNS hierarchy. (Images © 123RF.com.)

An FQDN reflects this hierarchy, from most specific on the left (the host's resource record with its name:IP address mapping) to least specific on the right (the TLD followed by the root). For example: `pc.corp.515support.com`.

Name Resolution Using DNS

The signal for the name resolution process to commence occurs when a user presents an FQDN (often within a web address) to an application program, such as a web browser. The client application, referred to as a stub resolver, checks its local cache for the mapping. If no mapping is found, it forwards the query to its local name server. The IP addresses of one or more name servers that can act as resolvers are usually set in the TCP/IP configuration. The resolution process then takes place as follows:

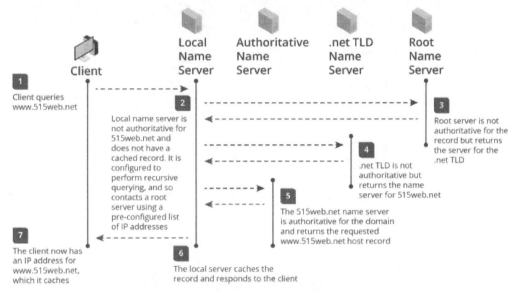

DNS name resolution process. (Images © 123RF.com.)

Most queries between name servers are performed as **iterative lookups**. This means that a name server responds to a query with either the requested record or the address of a name server at a lower level in the hierarchy that is authoritative for the namespace. It makes no effort to try to make additional queries to locate information that it does not have. In the figure, at steps 4 and 5, the root server and .net name server simply pass the querying server the address of an authoritative name server. They do not take on the task of resolving the original query for www.515web.net.

A **recursive lookup** means that if the queried server is not authoritative, it does take on the task of querying other name servers until it finds the requested record or times out. The name servers listed in a client's TCP/IP configuration accept recursive queries. This is the type of querying performed by the corp.515support. com name server.

A DNS server may be configured to only perform recursive querying (a resolver), or it may perform both recursive querying and maintain zone records, or it may only maintain zone records. Usually the roles are split, especially if the servers are open to the Internet. Most Internet-accessible DNS servers disable recursive queries. Recursive resolvers are typically only accessible by authorized clients—subscribers within an ISP's network or clients on a private LAN, for instance.

Resource Record Types

A DNS zone will contain numerous **resource records**. These records allow a DNS name server to resolve queries for names and services hosted in the domain into IP addresses. Resource records can be created and updated manually (statically), or they can be generated dynamically from information received from client and server computers on the network.

The Start of Authority (SOA) record identifies the primary **authoritative name server** that maintains complete resource records for the zone. The primary name server can be used to modify resource records. The SOA also includes contact information for the zone and a serial number for version control.

Configuring a Start of Authority record in Windows DNS.
(Screenshot courtesy of Microsoft.)

Name Server (NS) records identify authoritative DNS name servers for the zone. As well as the primary name server, most zones are configured with secondary name servers for redundancy and load balancing. Secondary name servers hold read-only copies of resource records but can still be authoritative for the zone.

```
;
; BIND data file for 515support.com
;
       604800
@     IN    SOA    ns1.515support.com. hostmaster.515support.com. (
                   2012080402         ; Serial
                        3600          ; Refresh
                        1800          ; Retry
                      604800          ; Expire
                       86400 )        ; Negative Cache TTL
)
      IN    NS     ns1.515support.com.
      IN    A      203.0.113.33
      IN    MX 10  mail.515support.com.
ns1   IN    A      203.0.113.33
www   IN    A      198.51.100.29
mail  IN    A      198.51.100.29
dvwa  IN    CNAME  www
```

Resourcerecords configured on a BIND DNS server.

Host Address and Canonical Name Records

An address (A) record is used to resolve a host name to an IPv4 address. An AAAA record resolves a host name to an IPv6 address.

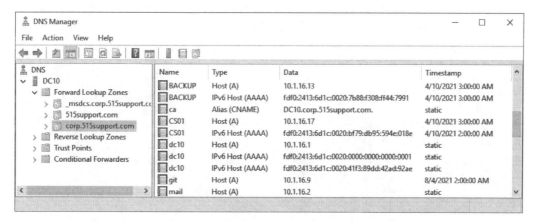

Both types of host records (A and AAAA) plus a CNAME record in Windows Server DNS. (Screenshot courtesy of Microsoft.)

DNS uses the UDP transport protocol over port 53 by default, and UDP has a maximum packet size of 512 bytes. Due to the much larger address sizes of IPv6, AAAA records can exceed this size. This can result in UDP packets being fragmented into several smaller packets. This can result in these packets being blocked by firewalls if they are not configured to expect them. Network administrators should check that their DNS servers can accept these transmissions and that intermediary components are not blocking them.

A Canonical Name (CNAME) (or alias) record is used to configure an alias for an existing address record (A or AAAA). For example, the IP address of a web server with the host record `lamp` could also be resolved by the alias www. CNAME records are also often used to make DNS administration easier. For example, an alias can be redirected to a completely different host temporarily during system maintenance.

Multiple different named resource records can refer to the same IP address (and vice versa in the case of load balancing).

There is nothing to stop an administrator configuring multiple address records to point different host names to the same IP address. Using CNAME records is usually considered better practice, however. It is also possible to configure multiple A or AAAA records with the same host name but different IP addresses. This is usually done as a basic load balancing technique, referred to as round robin DNS.

Mail Exchange, Service, and Text Records

A Mail Exchange (MX) record is used to identify an email server for the domain. In a typical network, multiple servers are installed to provide redundancy, and each one will be represented with an MX record. Each server record is given a preference value with the lowest numbered entry preferred. The host identified in an MX record must have an associated A or AAAA record. An MX record must not point to a CNAME record.

While most DNS records are used to resolve a name into an IP address, a Service (SRV) record contains the service name and port on which a particular application is hosted. SRV records are often used to locate VoIP or media servers. SRV records are also an essential part of the infrastructure supporting Microsoft's Active Directory; they are used by clients to locate domain controllers, for instance. As with MX, SRV records can be configured with a priority value.

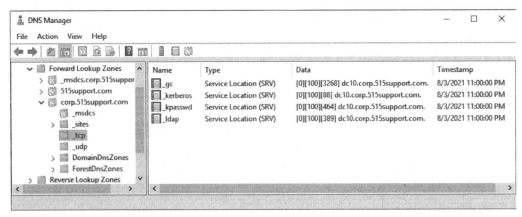

SRV records in Windows Server DNS. (Screenshot courtesy of Microsoft.)

A TXT record is used to store any free-form text that may be needed to support other network services. A single domain name may have many TXT records, but most commonly they are used as part of Sender Policy Framework (SPF) and DomainKeys Identified Mail (DKIM). An SPF record is used to list the IP addresses or names of servers that are permitted to send email from a particular domain and is used to combat the sending of spam. DKIM records are used to decide whether you should allow received email from a given source, preventing spam and mail spoofing. DKIM can use encrypted signatures to prove that a message really originated from the domain it claims.

Pointer Records

A DNS server may have two types of zones: forward lookup and reverse lookup. Forward lookup zones contain the resource records listed previously. For example, given a name record, a forward lookup returns an IP address; an MX record returns a host record associated with the domain's mail services. Conversely, a **reverse DNS** query returns the host name associated with a given IP address. This information is stored in a reverse lookup zone as a pointer (PTR) record.

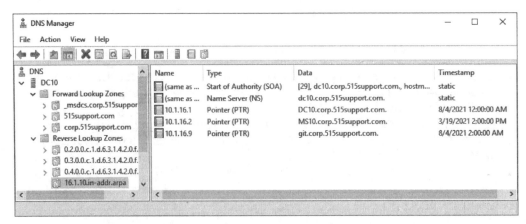

Reverse lookup zone and pointer records in Windows Server DNS.
(Screenshot courtesy of Microsoft.)

Reverse DNS querying uses a special domain named by the first three octets of IP addresses in the zone in reverse order and appended with `in-addr.arpa`. The name server is configured with a reverse lookup zone . This zone contains PTR records consisting of the final octet of each host record. For example, the reverse lookup for a host record containing the IP address 198.51.100.1 is:

```
1.100.51.198.in-addr.arpa
```

IPv6 uses the ip6.arpa domain; each of the 32 hex characters in the IPv6 address is expressed in reverse order as a subdomain. For example, the IPv6 address:

```
2001:0db8:0000:0000:0bcd:abcd:ef12:1234
```

is represented by the following pointer record:

```
4.3.2.1.2.1.f.e.d.c.b.a.d.c.b.0.0.0.0.0.0.0.0.0.8.
b.d.0.1.0.0.2.ip6.arpa
```

Reverse lookup zones are not mandatory and are often omitted from DNS servers, as they can be used by hackers to sequentially work through a range of IP addresses to discover useful or interesting device names, which can then be targeted by other hacking mechanisms.

Review Activity:

Name Resolution Services

Answer the following questions:

1.   **What type of DNS record resolves a host name to an IPv6 address?**

2.   **What use is a PTR DNS record?**

3.   **What types of DNS records have priority or preference values?**

4.   **What type of DNS record is used to prove the valid origin of email?**

Topic 10C

Configure DNS Services

EXAM OBJECTIVES COVERED
1.6 Explain the use and purpose of network services.
5.3 Given a scenario, use the appropriate network software tools and commands.

The name resolution process performed by DNS servers is a critical service for almost all types of networks. As a network technician, you will often be involved in configuring name servers.

DNS Server Configuration

DNS is essential to the function of the Internet. Windows Active Directory® and most Linux networks also require a DNS service to be running and correctly configured. It is important to realize that there are different kinds of DNS servers however, fulfilling different roles in network architecture.

DNS Server Types

A DNS server is usually configured to listen for queries on UDP port 53. Some DNS servers are also configured to allow connections over TCP port 53, as this allows larger record transfers (over 512 bytes). Larger transfers might be required if IPv6 is deployed on the network or if the DNS servers are using a security protocol (DNSSEC).

DNS name servers maintain the DNS namespace in zones. A single zone namespace might host records for multiple domains. A single name server might be configured to manage multiple zones. A name server can maintain primary and/or secondary zones:

- Primary means that the zone records held on the server are editable. A zone can be hosted by multiple primary servers for redundancy. As the zone records are editable on all primaries, changes must be carefully replicated and synchronized. It is critically important to update the serial number for each change.

- Secondary means that the server holds a read-only copy of the zone. This is maintained through a process of replication known as a **zone transfer** from a primary name server. A secondary zone would typically be provided on two or more separate servers to provide fault tolerance and load balancing. Again, the serial number is a critical part of the zone transfer process.

The noninclusive terms "master" to mean primary and "slave" to mean secondary are used in some DNS server versions. This type of terminology is deprecated in the latest versions.

A name server that holds complete records for a domain can be defined as authoritative. This means that a record in the zone identifies the server as a name server for that namespace. Both primary and secondary name servers are authoritative.

Servers that don't maintain a zone (primary or secondary) are referred to as cache-only servers. A non-authoritative answer from a server is one that derives from a cached record, rather than directly from the zone records.

DNS Caching

Each resource record can be configured with a default **time to live (TTL)** value, measured in seconds. This value instructs resolvers how long a query result can be kept in cache. Setting a low TTL allows records to be updated more quickly but increases load on the server and latency on client connections to services. Some common TTL values include 300 (5 minutes), 3,600 (1 hour), 86,400 (1 day), and 604,800 (1 week).

DNS caching is performed by both servers and client computers. In fact, each application on a client computer might be configured to manage its own DNS cache. For example, separate web browser applications typically maintain their own caches rather than relying on a shared OS cache.

If there is a change to a resource record, server and client caching means that the updated record can be relatively slow to propagate around the Internet. These changes need to be managed carefully to avoid causing outages. Planning for a record change involves reducing the TTL in the period before the change, waiting for this change to propagate before updating the record, and then reverting to the original TTL value when the update has safely propagated.

Internal versus External DNS

As well as making sure that resource records for the managed domain(s) are accurate, administrators should ensure that DNS services are highly available and secure, to prevent DNS spoofing, where an attacker is able to supply false name resolutions to clients.

A company will use primary and secondary name servers to maintain authoritative zone records for the domains that it manages. Internal DNS zones refer to the domains used on the private network only. These name records should only be available to internal clients. For example, a company might run a Windows Active Directory network using the domain name `corp.515support.com`. The zone records for the subdomain `corp.515support.com` would be served from internal name servers. This would allow a client PC (`pc1.corp.515support.com`) to contact a local application server (`crm.corp.515support.com`). The name servers hosting these internal subdomain records must not be accessible from the Internet.

External DNS zones refer to records that Internet clients must be able to access. For example, the company might run web and email services on the domain `515support.com`. In order for Internet hosts to use a web server at `www.515support.com` or send email to an `@515support.com` address, the zone records for 515support.com must be hosted on a name server that is accessible over the Internet.

Companies must also provide name resolution services to support their internal clients contacting other domains. The function of a resolver is to perform recursive queries in response to requests from client systems (stub resolvers). If a name server is not authoritative for the requested domain, it can either perform a recursive query to locate an authoritative name server or it can forward the request to another name server. A recursive resolver must be configured with a root hints file so that it can query the whole DNS hierarchy from the root servers down. DNS servers should allow recursive queries only from authorized internal clients. It is also a good idea to separate the DNS servers used to host zone records from ones used to service client requests for nonauthoritative domains.

It is possible for the same DNS server instance to perform in both name server and resolver roles, but more typically these functions are separated to different servers for security reasons.

As an alternative to recursion (or to supplement it), name servers can be configured to resolve queries via forwarding. A forwarder transmits a client query to another DNS server and routes the replies it gets back to the client. A conditional forwarder performs this task for certain domains only. For example, you might configure a DNS server that is authoritative for the local private network (internal DNS), but that forwards any requests for Internet domains to an external DNS resolver run by your ISP.

nslookup

Name resolution troubleshooting typically involves testing multiple clients and servers. The use of caching and the distributed nature of the system means that configuration errors can occur in several different places.

You might start investigating a name resolution issue by verifying the name configured on a host. In Windows, you can use the command `ipconfig / all` to display the FQDN of the local host. In Linux, you can use the command `hostname --fqdn`.

In a Windows environment, you can troubleshoot DNS name resolution with the **nslookup** command:

```
nslookup -Option Host DNSServer
```

Host can be either a host name, domain name, FQDN, or IP address. *DNSServer* is the IP address of a server used to resolve the query; the default DNS server is used if this argument is omitted. *Option* specifies an nslookup subcommand. For example, the following command queries Google's public DNS server (8.8.8.8) for information about 515support.com's mail records:

```
nslookup -type=mx 515support.com 8.8.8.8
```

If `nslookup` is run without any arguments (or by specifying the server only with `nslookup -DNSServer`, the tool is started in interactive mode. You can perform specific query types and output the result to a text file for analysis.

```
C:\Users\Admin>nslookup -type=mx comptia.org 8.8.8.8
Server:  dns.google
Address:  8.8.8.8

Non-authoritative answer:
comptia.org     MX preference = 10, mail exchanger = comptia-org.mail.protection.outlook.com

C:\Users\Admin>nslookup -type=ns comptia.org 8.8.8.8
Server:  dns.google
Address:  8.8.8.8

Non-authoritative answer:
comptia.org     nameserver = ns2.comptia.org
comptia.org     nameserver = ns1.comptia.org

C:\Users\Admin>nslookup -type=mx comptia.org ns1.comptia.org
Server:  UnKnown
Address:  209.117.62.56

comptia.org     MX preference = 10, mail exchanger = comptia-org.mail.protection.outlook.com

C:\Users\Admin>
```

The first two nslookup commands identify comptia.org's MX and primary name server records using Google's public DNS resolver (8.8.8.8). Note that the answers are nonauthoritative. The third command queries CompTIA's name server for the MX record. This answer is authoritative. (Screenshot courtesy of Microsoft.)

The Windows PowerShell environment provides a more sophisticated scripted environment that you can use to issue cmdlets to test DNS name resolution (and change DNS settings as well, if required). PowerShell® provides a cmdlet called Resolve-DnsName, which allows a more flexible method of testing name resolution than nslookup, as it allows testing of the different methods of name resolution (HOSTS file, DNS cache, and DNS server).

dig

Domain Information Groper (dig) is a command-line tool for querying DNS servers that ships with the BIND DNS server software published by the Internet Systems Consortium (ISC) (isc.org/downloads/bind).

`dig` can be run pointing at a specific DNS server; otherwise, it will use the default resolver. Without any specific settings, it queries the DNS root zone. A simple query uses the syntax: `dig host`. This will search for the address record for the host, domain, or FQDN or PTR record for an IP address.

The following command example directs the resolve request to the specific DNS server identified after the @ symbol. This can be an FQDN or IP address.

`dig @ns1.isp.example host`

Other examples of `dig` are to display all the resource records about a domain or just specific ones such as Mail Exchange:

`dig @ns1.isp.example host all`

`dig @ns1.isp.example host MX`

`dig` often generates a lot of information, so it is possible to add parameters to the end of the command like `+nocomments` or `+nostats`, which will reduce the output.

```
root@LX20D:  $ dig +nocmd +noedns +noquestion 515support.com MX
;; Got answer:
;; ->>HEADER<<- opcode: QUERY, status: NOERROR, id: 12449
;; flags: qr rd ra; QUERY: 1, ANSWER: 1, AUTHORITY: 0, ADDITIONAL: 0

;; ANSWER SECTION:
515support.com.          6968      IN       MX       10 mail.515support.com.

;; Query time: 0 msec
;; SERVER: 127.0.0.53#53(127.0.0.53)
;; WHEN: Wed Aug 04 10:08:20 BST 2021
;; MSG SIZE  rcvd: 53

root@LX20D:  $ dig +nocmd +noedns +noquestion mail.515support.com
;; Got answer:
;; ->>HEADER<<- opcode: QUERY, status: NOERROR, id: 57840
;; flags: qr rd ra; QUERY: 1, ANSWER: 1, AUTHORITY: 0, ADDITIONAL: 0

;; ANSWER SECTION:
mail.515support.com.     7029      IN       A        198.51.100.29

;; Query time: 0 msec
;; SERVER: 127.0.0.53#53(127.0.0.53)
;; WHEN: Wed Aug 04 10:08:32 BST 2021
;; MSG SIZE  rcvd: 53
```

Using dig to locate MX and A records.

You can install dig on Windows by downloading the BIND DNS server package and installing it using the tools-only option.

Review Activity:

DNS Services

Answer the following questions:

1. **When you configure name server addresses as part of a host's IP settings, do you need to specify servers that perform iterative queries only or ones that accept recursive queries?**

2. **What type of DNS service would you configure on the LAN to use a public DNS server to resolve queries for external domains?**

3. **What is the function of the following command?**

    ```
    nslookup - 8.8.8.8
    ```

4. **What is the function of a dig subcommand such as +nostats?**

Lesson 10

Summary

You should be able to explain the uses and purposes of the network services protocols DHCP and DNS.

Guidelines for Supporting Network Services

Follow these guidelines to make effective use of network addressing services:

- Configure secure DHCP and DNS servers and ensure that all network hosts can contact them, using DHCP relay where appropriate.

- Ensure DHCP servers are configured with accurate IP, default gateway, and DNS server parameters for the scopes/subnets that they serve.

- Configure reservations or static assignments for hosts that need to be allocated a consistent IP address.

- If the address pool is limited, use short lease times to prevent address exhaustion.

- Set up primary and secondary name servers to host records for your LAN. These name services should be accessible only by authorized clients.

- Configure the appropriate host, MX, and service records for the forward lookup zone on the primary server.

- Optionally, configure a reverse lookup zone to allow clients to resolve IP addresses to host names.

- Configure the secondary server to obtain up-to-date records periodically through a zone transfer with the primary server.

- To resolve client Internet queries, set up a forwarder to pass queries to trusted resolvers on the Internet, such as your ISP's DNS server or trusted public services such as those from Google or Quad9.

- For external DNS, consider using a third-party provider, ideally with a cloud service, to ensure high availability. Without public DNS, your customers will not be able to browse your websites or send you email.

- Set up a process for checking that your external DNS records are accurate and working correctly.

Lesson 11
Explaining Network Applications

LESSON INTRODUCTION

Where DHCP and DNS support basic network operations, other application protocols provide platforms for user-level services, such as websites, databases, file/printer sharing, email, and voice/video calling.

You must be able to identify the ports used by these services and their performance and security requirements so that you can assist with product deployments and upgrades and perform basic troubleshooting.

In this lesson, you will identify common network applications and service platforms.

Lesson Objectives

In this lesson, you will:

- Explain the use of web, file/print, and database services.

- Explain the use of email and voice services.

Topic 11A

Explain the Use of Web, File/Print, and Database Services

EXAM OBJECTIVES COVERED

1.5 Explain common ports and protocols, their application, and encrypted alternatives.
2.1 Compare and contrast various devices, their features, and their appropriate placement on the network. (Printer only)
5.3 Given a scenario, use the appropriate network software tools and commands. (TFTP server only)

So far, you have studied lower-layer services that enable basic connectivity between nodes. Above these are the services that provide useful functions to users, such as web browsing, file/print sharing, and databases. The services that form part of the TCP/IP protocol suite are mostly client-server protocols and applications. Client-server applications are based around a centralized server that stores information and waits for requests from clients. You need a good understanding of how these protocols are used so that you can support them on your networks.

HyperText Transfer Protocol

Websites and web applications are perhaps the most useful and ubiquitous of network services. Web technology can be deployed for a huge range of functions and applications, in no way limited to the static pages of information that characterized the first websites. The foundation of web technology is the **HyperText Transfer Protocol (HTTP)**. HTTP enables clients (typically web browsers) to request resources from an HTTP server. A client connects to the HTTP server using an appropriate TCP port (TCP/80, by default) and submits a request for a resource, using a uniform resource locator (URL). The server acknowledges the request and either responds with the data or with an error message.

HTTP Headers and Payload

The response and request formats are defined in the HTTP header. The HTTP payload is usually used to serve HyperText Markup Language (HTML) web pages, which are plain text files with coded tags describing how the page should be formatted. A web browser can interpret the tags and display the text and other resources associated with the page, such as binary picture or sound files linked to the HTML page.

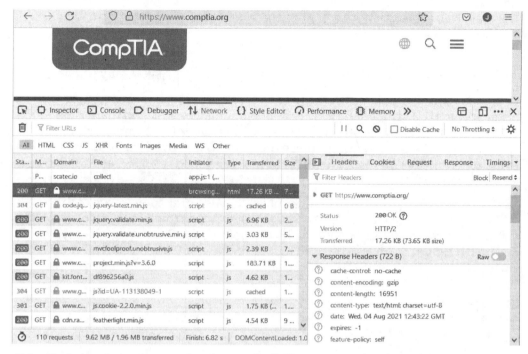

Using Firefox's web developer tools to inspect the HTTP requests and response headers involved in serving a typical modern web page. (Screenshot courtesy of Mozilla Foundation.)

HTTP also features a forms mechanism (POST) that enables a user to submit data from the client to the server. HTTP is nominally a stateless protocol; this means that the server is not required to preserve information about the client during a session. However, the basic functionality of HTTP servers is also often extended by support for scripting and programmable features (web applications). Servers can also set text file cookies to preserve session information. These coding features, plus integration with databases, increase flexibility and interactivity, but also increase the attack surface and expose more vulnerabilities.

 Many argue that HTTP is a stateful protocol. Version 2 of HTTP adds more state-preserving features (blog.zamicol.com/2017/05/is-http2-stateful-protocol-application.html).

Web Servers

Most organizations have an online presence, represented by a website. In order to run a website, it must be hosted on an HTTP server connected to the Internet. Larger organizations or SMEs with the relevant expertise may host websites themselves, but more typically, an organization will lease a server or space on a server from an ISP. The following types of hosting packages are common:

- **Dedicated server**—The ISP allocates your own private server computer. This type of service is usually unmanaged (or management comes at additional cost).

- **Virtual Private Server (VPS)**—The ISP allocates you a virtual machine (VM) on a physical server. This is isolated from other customer instances by the hypervisor.

- **Cloud hosting**—Your website is run on a cloud over several hardware computers, allowing more scalability if demand patterns change.

- **Shared hosting**—Your website is hosted within a private directory on a shared server. Performance can be severely affected by other sites hosted on the server, because all the sites are competing for the same resources.

The main web server platforms are Apache®, Microsoft Internet Information Server (IIS), and nginx.

Secure Sockets Layer/Transport Layer Security

One of the critical problems for the provision of early websites was the lack of security in HTTP. Under HTTP, all data is sent unencrypted, and there is no authentication of client or server. **Secure Sockets Layer (SSL)** was developed by Netscape in the 1990s to address these problems. SSL proved very popular with the industry. **Transport Layer Security (TLS)** was developed from SSL and ratified as a standard by the IETF.

SSL/TLS works as a layer between the Application and Transport layers of the TCP/IP stack, or, in OSI terms, at the Session layer. It's normally used to encrypt TCP connections. When it is used with the HTTP application, it is referred to as HTTP Secure (HTTPS). TLS can also be used to secure other TCP application protocols, such as FTP, POP3/IMAP, SMTP, and LDAP.

 TLS can also be used with UDP, referred to as Datagram Transport Layer Security (DTLS), most often in virtual private networking (VPN) solutions.

To implement HTTPS, the web server is installed with a digital certificate issued by some trusted certificate authority (CA). The certificate uses encrypted data to prove the identity of the server, assuming that the client also trusts the CA. The certificate is a wrapper for a public/private encryption key pair. The private key is kept a secret known only to the server; the public key is given to clients via the digital certificate.

The server and client use the key pair in the digital certificate and a chosen cipher suite within the SSL/TLS protocol to set up an encrypted tunnel. Even though someone else might know the public key, they cannot decrypt the contents of the tunnel without obtaining the server's private key. This means that the communications cannot be read or changed by a third party.

Encrypted traffic between the client and server is sent over TCP port 443 (by default), rather than the open and unencrypted port 80. A web browser will open a secure session to a server providing this service by using a URL starting with https:// and it will also show a padlock icon in the address bar to indicate that the connection is secure. A website can be configured to require a secure session and reject or redirect plain HTTP requests.

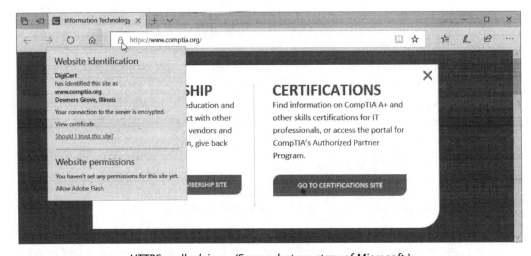

HTTPS padlock icon. (Screenshot courtesy of Microsoft.)

File Transfer Protocol

It is often necessary to transfer files to and from appliances or servers from a remote host. Many methods of remote file access use some form of the **File Transfer Protocol (FTP)**. While HTTPS-based web services and web applications can now offer file downloads to end users, FTP is still often used to perform administrative upload/download of files to and from servers and appliances. For these uses, it is important to secure the FTP session.

Active versus Passive FTP

An FTP client connects to TCP port 21 on an FTP server and opens a chosen dynamic client port number (n). The TCP port 21 control port is used to transfer commands and status information, but not for data transfer. Data transfer can operate in one of two modes: active or passive. In active mode, the client sends a PORT command specifying its chosen data connection port number (typically n+1), and the server opens the data connection between the chosen client port and TCP port 20 on the server.

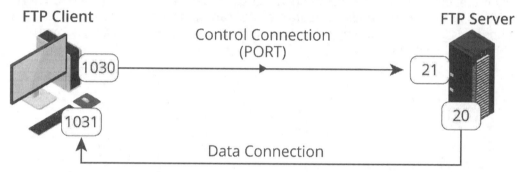

FTP in active mode. (Images © 123RF.com.)

In passive mode, the client opens a data port (again, typically n+1) and sends the PASV command to the server's control port. The server then opens a random high port number and sends it to the client using the PORT command. The client then initiates the connection between the two ports.

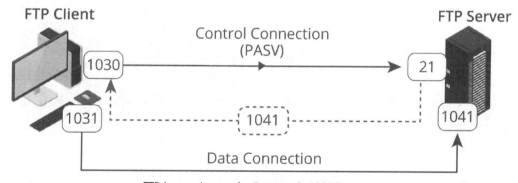

FTP in passive mode. (Images © 123RF.com.)

Active FTP poses a configuration problem for some firewalls, as the server is initiating the inbound connection, but there is no way of predicting which port number will be utilized. However, not all FTP servers and clients can operate in passive mode. If this is the case, check that firewalls installed between the client and server can support active FTP (stateful inspection firewalls).

 Another problem is that the control connection can remain idle when the data connection is in use, meaning that the connection can be "timed out" by the firewall (or other routing device).

Trivial File Transfer Protocol

The **Trivial File Transfer Protocol (TFTP)** is a connectionless protocol running over UDP port 69. Consequently, TFTP does not provide the guaranteed delivery offered by FTP and is only suitable for transferring small files. Also, it only supports reading (`GET`) and writing (`PUT`) files, not directory browsing, file deletion, or any of the other features of FTP. A TFTP server is most commonly used by legacy network appliances (switches, routers, diskless workstations, and printers) to download configuration files. It can also be used as a backup and restore method for configuration files. However, TFTP has no security mechanisms and appliances are no longer as resource constrained as they were in the early days of networking. Consequently, secure protocols are now preferred for these functions.

Secure File Transfer Protocol

Secure FTP (SFTP) addresses the privacy and integrity issues of FTP by encrypting the authentication and data transfer between client and server. In SFTP, a secure link is created between the client and server using Secure Shell (SSH) over TCP port 22. Ordinary FTP commands and data transfer can then be sent over the secure link without risk of eavesdropping. This solution requires an SSH server that supports SFTP plus SFTP client software.

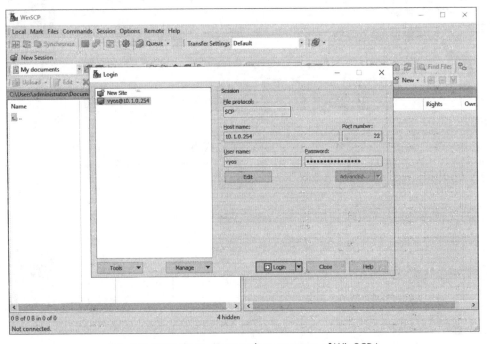

WinSCP SFTP client. (Screenshot courtesy of WinSCP.)

Another means of securing FTP is to use the connection security protocol SSL/TLS. There are two means of configuring FTP over TLS:

- **Explicit TLS (FTPES)**—Use the `AUTH TLS` command to upgrade an unsecure connection established over port 21 to a secure one. This protects authentication credentials. The data connection for the actual file transfers can also be encrypted (using the `PROT` command).

- **Implicit TLS (FTPS)**—Negotiate an SSL/TLS tunnel before the exchange of any FTP commands. This mode uses the secure port 990 for the control connection.

FTPS is tricky to configure when there are firewalls between the client and server. Consequently, FTPES is usually the preferred method.

File and Print Services

File and print services allow network clients to share access to disk and printer resources.

Server Message Block

On a Windows® network, the File/Print Sharing Service is provided by the **Server Message Block (SMB)** protocol. SMB allows a host to share its directories/files and printers to make them available for other machines to use. Support for SMB in UNIX- or Linux-based machines and network attached storage (NAS) appliances is provided by using the Samba software suite (samba.org/samba/what_is_samba.html), which allows a Windows client to access a Linux host as though it were a Windows file or print server.

On legacy networks, SMB ran as part of an older network services protocol called NetBIOS on TCP port 139. If no legacy client support is required, however, SMB is more typically run directly over TCP port 445. SMB should be restricted to use only on local networks. It is important that any traffic on the NetBIOS port ranges (137-139) and port 445 be blocked by a perimeter firewall.

SMB version 3 supports message encryption, which can be enabled on a file server or on a per-share basis. An encrypted share can only be accessed by an SMB 3.0 or higher client.

 SMB has gone through several updates, with SMB3 as the current version. SMB1 has very serious security vulnerabilities and is now disabled by default on current Windows versions (docs.microsoft.com/en-us/windows-server/storage/file-server/troubleshoot/detect-enable-and-disable-smbv1-v2-v3).

Remote Print Protocols

A **printer** can be connected to the network using a cabled or wireless link and configured with an IP address and FQDN. Hosts need to be able to connect to the printer, configure options and print settings, send print jobs, and receive status messaging, such as out of paper errors. These functions are implemented using a remote print protocol to communicate between the print monitor process running on the host and the print device:

- **Port 9100**—This can be referred to as the standard TCP/IP port, AppSocket, or JetDirect. This port just establishes a TCP connection to transfer raw Page Description Language (PDL) print job data and Printer Job Language (PJL) configuration and management data. The two most common PDLs are PostScript (PS) and Printer Command Language (PCL). Most printers support bidirectional status messaging to inform the host's print monitor about error conditions, such as out of paper or paper jam.

- **Internet Printing Protocol (IPP)**—This is an adapted form of HTTP that uses TCP port 631 and can be implemented as a secure protocol (IPPS). It provides better support for status messaging than port 9100.

- **Web Services for Devices (WSD)/AirPrint**—These technologies allow a print device to advertise service capabilities over the network and for Windows and MacOS/iOS hosts respectively to add the device using plug-and-play and manage it using bidirectional status messaging. They also allow for secure connections to the print device.

- **Printer sharing**—This means that a host connects to the printer (using a local or network connection) and then shares the printer object with other hosts using SMB. Print jobs and status messaging are sent via the host that shared the printer.

Database Services

A database provisions information in a format that can be read and updated through some type of query language. There are two main types of databases. Relational databases store information In tables with rows (records) and columns (fields). Relationships between data fields in different tables is created using key fields that uniquely identify each record. Relational databases are operated using **structured query language (SQL)**. SQL defines commands such as SELECT to retrieve information or UPDATE to change it.

SQL has been implemented in relational database management system (RDBMS) platforms by several different vendors. As well as providing an implementation of SQL, an RDBMS provides management tools and often a GUI to use to operate the database. A remote access protocol allows a client to connect to the database server over the network and allows replication traffic to move between database servers. Replication is a means of synchronizing the data held on each server. Each RDBMS uses a different TCP port to distinguish it as an application service:

- Oracle's remote data access protocol SQL*Net uses TCP/1521.

- Microsoft SQL Server uses TCP/1433.

- The open-source MySQL platform uses TCP/3306. The MariaDB platform forked from MySQL uses the same port.

- The open-source PostgreSQL platform uses TCP/5432.

 These are the principal ports. An RDBMS is likely to use other TCP or UDP ports for additional functions.

By default, these ports are unsecure. However, the RDBMS server can be installed with a certificate and configured to enable TLS transport encryption. The connection is still made over the same port. Either the server or the client can be configured to require encryption and drop the connection if a valid security profile is not available. Optionally, the client can also be installed with a certificate and the server configured to refuse connections from clients without a valid certificate.

The other type of database is referred to as NoSQL or "not only SQL." Rather than highly structured relational tables, NoSQL data can use a variety of formats, such as key-value pairs or wide columns (where rows do not have to have the same set of fields). NoSQL databases are typically accessed using an application programming interface (API) over HTTPS.

 All the RDBMS platforms also provide support for NoSQL datastores. There are also dedicated NoSQL platforms, such as MongoDB, Amazon's DynamoDB, and CouchDB.

Review Activity:

Use of Web, File/Print, and Database Services

Answer the following questions:

1. **True or false? An HTML web page is sent as the response to a client in an HTTP header field.**

2. **What must be installed on a server to use secure (HTTPS) connections?**

3. **What distinguishes TFTP from FTP?**

4. **You need to configure clients to be able to communicate with print devices in a remote subnet. Which port number must you allow on a network firewall to enable the standard TCP/IP port?**

5. **You are configuring a firewall to allow a Linux web server to communicate with a database server over port TCP/3306. Assuming it has been left configured with the default port, what type of database is being used?**

Topic 11B

Explain the Use of Email and Voice Services

EXAM OBJECTIVES COVERED
1.5 Explain common ports and protocols, their application, and encrypted alternatives.
2.1 Compare and contrast various devices, their features, and their appropriate placement on the network.

The use of messaging, voice, and video services is now common in homes and in many workplaces. These real-time applications bring their own challenges for network architecture, and you need to understand these performance demands to build networks that can support them.

Simple Mail Transfer Protocol

Electronic mail enables a person to compose a message and send it to another user on their own network (intranet) or anywhere in the world via the Internet. Email uses separate mail transfer and mailbox access protocols:

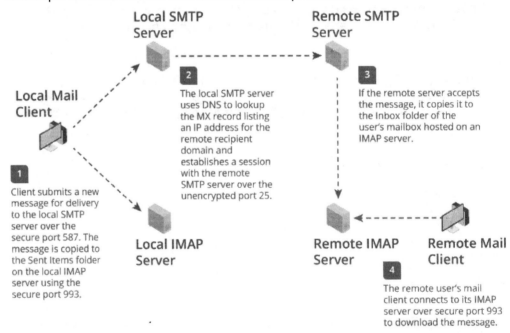

Operation of delivery and mailbox email protocols. (Images © 123RF.com.)

The **Simple Mail Transfer Protocol (SMTP)** specifies how email is delivered from one system to another. The SMTP server of the sender discovers the IP address of the recipient SMTP server by using the domain name part of the recipient's email address. The SMTP servers for the domain are registered in DNS using Mail Exchange (MX) and host (A/AAAA) records.

SMTP does not queue messages indefinitely. If there is a communication problem, the SMTP server retries at regular intervals before timing out and returning a non-delivery report (NDR) to the sender. The NDR will contain an error code indicating the reason the item could not be delivered. SMTP provides no mechanism for persistent storage of messages.

SMTP communications can be secured using the TLS version of the protocol (SMTPS). This works much like HTTPS with a certificate on the SMTP server and a negotiation between client and server about which cipher suites to use. There are two ways for SMTP to use TLS:

- **STARTTLS**—This is a command that upgrades an existing unsecure connection to use TLS. This is also referred to as explicit TLS or opportunistic TLS.

- **SMTPS**—This establishes the secure connection before any SMTP commands (HELO, for instance) are exchanged. This is also referred to as implicit TLS.

The STARTTLS method is generally more widely implemented than SMTPS. Typical SMTP configurations use the following ports and secure services:

- **Port 25**—Used for message relay between SMTP servers, or message transfer agents (MTAs). If security is required and supported by both servers, the STARTTLS command can be used to set up the secure connection.

- **Port 587**—Used by mail clients or message submission agents (MSAs) to submit messages for delivery by an SMTP server. Servers configured to support port 587 should use STARTTLS and require authentication before message submission.

 Mail clients can use port 25 to submit messages to the server for delivery, but this is not best practice. Use of port 25 is typically reserved for relay between servers.

Mailbox Access Protocols

SMTP is useful only to deliver mail to hosts that are permanently available. When a message is received by an SMTP server, it delivers the message to a mailbox server. This could be a separate machine or a separate process running on the same server. A mailbox access protocol allows the user's client email software to operate the mailbox.

Post Office Protocol

The **Post Office Protocol (POP)** is an early example of a mailbox access protocol. POP is often referred to as POP3 because the active version of the protocol is version 3. A POP client application, such as Microsoft Outlook® or Mozilla Thunderbird®, establishes a connection to the POP server on TCP port 110. The user is authenticated (by username and password), and the contents of his or her mailbox are downloaded for processing on the local PC. Generally speaking, the messages are deleted from the mailbox server when they are downloaded, though some clients have the option to leave messages on the server.

```
GNU nano 2.2.2          File: /etc/dovecot/dovecot.conf          Modified

protocols = imap imaps
#protocols = none

# A space separated list of IP or host addresses where to listen in for
# connections. "*" listens in all IPv4 interfaces. "[::]" listens in all IPv6
# interfaces. Use "*, [::]" for listening both IPv4 and IPv6.
#
# If you want to specify ports for each service, you will need to configure
# these settings inside the protocol imap/pop3/managesieve { ... } section,
# so you can specify different ports for IMAP/POP3/MANAGESIEVE. For example:
   protocol imap {
     listen = *:143
     ssl_listen = *:943
   }
#   protocol pop3 {
     listen = *:10100
#
#    ..
#   }
#   protocol managesieve {
     listen = *:12000
#
#    ..
#   }
#listen = *

# Disable LOGIN command and all other plaintext authentications unless
                       [ Read 1280 lines ]
^G Get Help    ^O WriteOut    ^R Read File    ^Y Prev Page    ^K Cut Text    ^C Cur Pos
^X Exit        ^J Justify     ^W Where Is     ^V Next Page    ^U UnCut Text  ^T To Spell
```

Configuring mailbox access protocols on a server. (Screenshot courtesy of Mozilla Foundation.)

Like other TCP application protocols, POP transfers all information as cleartext. This means anyone able to monitor the session would be able to obtain the user's credentials and snoop on messages. POP can be secured by using TLS encryption. The default TCP port for secure POP (POP3S) is port 995.

Internet Message Access Protocol

POP has some significant limitations, some of which are addressed by the **Internet Message Access Protocol (IMAP)**. Like POP, IMAP is a mail retrieval protocol, but with mailbox management features lacking in POP. POP is primarily designed for dial-up access; the client contacts the server to download its messages, and then disconnects. IMAP supports permanent connections to a server and connecting multiple clients to the same mailbox simultaneously. It also allows a client to manage the mailbox on the server (to organize messages in folders and to control when they are deleted, for instance) and to create multiple mailboxes.

A client connects to an IMAP server over TCP port 143, but this port is unsecure. Connection security can be established using a TLS. The default port for IMAPS is TCP/993.

 In a Windows environment, the proprietary Messaging Application Programming Interface (MAPI) protocol is typically used to access Microsoft Exchange mailboxes. MAPI uses HTTPS as a secure transport protocol.

Voice and Video Services

Voice over IP (VoIP), web conferencing, and video teleconferencing (VTC) solutions have become standard methods for the provision of business and social communications. Many networks are upgrading from legacy voice services to IP-based protocols and products.

Private Branch Exchange

Legacy voice services use the public switched telephone network (PSTN). A residential telephone installation would be serviced by a simple box providing a one- or two-line analog interface to the local exchange. This analog interface is also referred to as the **plain old telephone service (POTS)**. Each line provides a single channel for an incoming or outgoing call. A typical business requires tens or hundreds of lines for voice communications, let alone capacity for data communications. Historically, this requirement would have been facilitated by a digital trunk line, also referred to as a Time Division Multiplexing (TDM) circuit. A TDM can multiplex separate voice and data channels for transmission over a single cable.

A **private branch exchange (PBX)** is an automated switchboard providing a single connection point for an organization's voice lines. A TDM-based PBX connects to the telecommunications carrier over a digital trunk line, which will support multiple channels (inward and outward calls). The PBX allows for the configuration of the internal phone system to direct and route calls to local extensions, and provides other telephony features such as call waiting, music on hold, and voice mail.

VoIP-Enabled PBX

TDM-based PBXes are being replaced by hybrid and fully IP/VoIP PBXes. For internal calls and conferences, a VoIP PBX establishes connections between local VoIP endpoints with data transmitted over the local Ethernet network. A VoIP PBX can also route incoming and outgoing calls from and to external networks. This might involve calls between internal and external VoIP endpoints, or with voice telephone network callers and receivers. A VoIP PBX will also support features such as music on hold and voice mail.

A TDM PBX is supplied as vendor-specific hardware. A VoIP PBX can be implemented as software running on a Windows or Linux server. Examples of software-based solutions include 3CX ([3cx.com](3cx.com)) and Asterisk (asterisk.org). There are also hardware solutions, where the VoIP PBX runs on a router, such as Cisco Unified Communications Manager (cisco.com/c/en/us/products/unified-communications/unified-communications-manager-callmanager/index.html).

A VoIP PBX would normally be placed at the network edge and be protected by a firewall. Internal clients connect to the PBX over Ethernet data cabling and switching infrastructure, using Internet Protocol (IP) at the Network layer for addressing. The VoIP PBX uses the organization's Internet link to connect to a VoIP service provider, which facilitates inward and outward dialing to voice-based telephone networks.

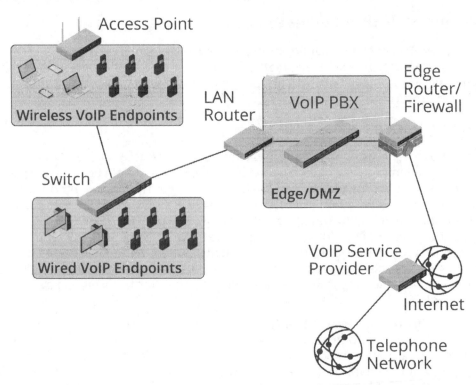

A VoIP PBX facilitates internal IP calls and calls to and from external VoIP networks and the landline and cellular telephone networks. (Images © 123RF.com)

VoIP Protocols

Voice and video services can be challenging to support because they require response times measured in milliseconds (ms). Delayed responses will result in poor call or video quality. This type of data can be one-way, as is the case with media streaming, or two-way, as is the case with VoIP and VTC.

The protocols designed to support real-time services cover one or more of the following functions:

- **Session control**—Used to establish, manage, and disestablish communications sessions. They handle tasks such as user discovery (locating a user on the network), availability advertising (whether a user is prepared to receive calls), negotiating session parameters (such as use of audio/video), and session management and termination.

- **Data transport**—Handles the delivery of the actual video or voice information.

- **Quality of Service (QoS)**—Provides information about the connection to a QoS system, which in turn ensures that voice or video communications are free from problems, such as dropped packets, delay, or jitter.

Session Initiation Protocol

The **Session Initiation Protocol (SIP)** is one of the most widely used session control protocols. SIP endpoints are the end-user devices (also known as user agents), such as IP-enabled handsets or client and server web conference software. Each device, conference, or telephony user is assigned a unique SIP address known as a SIP Uniform Resource Indicator (URI). Examples of SIP URIs include:

```
sip:jaime@515support.com

sip:2622136227@515support.com

sip:jaime@2622136227

meet:sip:organizer@515support.com;ms-app=conf;ms-
conf-id=subg42
```

 There is also a tel: URI scheme allowing SIP endpoints to dial a landline or cell phone. A tel: URI can either use the global (E.164) format (such as tel:+1-866-8358020) or a local format (for internal extensions).

SIP typically runs over UDP or TCP ports 5060 (unsecured) and 5061 (SIP-TLS). SIP has its own reliability and retransmission mechanisms and can thus be seen to benefit most from the lower overhead and reduced latency and jitter of UDP. Some enterprise SIP products use TCP anyway.

Real-Time Transport Protocol and RTP Control Protocol

While SIP provides session management, the actual delivery of real-time data uses different protocols. The principal one is Real-time Transport Protocol (RTP). RTP enables the delivery of a stream of media data via UDP, while implementing some of the reliability features usually associated with TCP communications. RTP works closely with the RTP Control Protocol (RTCP). Each RTP stream uses a corresponding RTCP session to monitor the quality of the connection and to provide reports to the endpoints. These reports can then be used by the applications to modify codec parameters or by the network stacks to tune Quality of Service (QoS) parameters.

VoIP Phones

A VoIP/SIP endpoint can be implemented as software running on a computer or smartphone or as a dedicated hardware handset. **VoIP phones** use VLAN tagging to ensure that the SIP control and RTP media protocols can be segregated from normal data traffic. In a typical voice VLAN configuration, the LAN port on the handset is connected to the wall port, while the PC is connected to the PC port on the handset. The two devices share the same physical link, but data traffic is distinguished from voice traffic by configuring separate VLAN IDs.

Handsets can use Power over Ethernet (PoE), if available, to avoid the need for separate power cabling or batteries. There are also wireless handsets that work over 802.11 Wi-Fi networks.

Connection security for VoIP works in a similar manner to HTTPS. To initiate the call, the secure version of SIP (SIPS) uses digital certificates to authenticate the endpoints and establish an SSL/TLS tunnel. The secure connection established by SIPS can also be used to generate a master key to use with the secure versions of the transport and control protocols.

When you are installing a new handset, you should also test that the connection works and that the link provides sufficient call quality. Most service providers have test numbers to verify basic connectivity and perform an echo test call, which replays a message you record so that you can confirm voice quality.

Voice Gateways

SIP endpoints can establish communications directly in a peer-to-peer architecture, but it is more typical to use intermediary servers, directory servers, and VoIP gateways. There can also be requirements for on-premises integration between data and voice networks and equipment. A **voice gateway** is a means of translating between a VoIP system and legacy voice equipment and networks, such as POTS lines and handsets. There are many types of VoIP gateways, serving different functions. For example, a company may use VoIP internally, but connect to the telephone network via a gateway. To facilitate this, you could use a hybrid or hardware-based VoIP PBX with a plug-in or integrated VoIP gateway, or you could use a separate gateway appliance. There are analog and digital types to match the type of incoming landline. An analog version of this type of gateway is also called a Foreign Exchange Office (FXO) gateway.

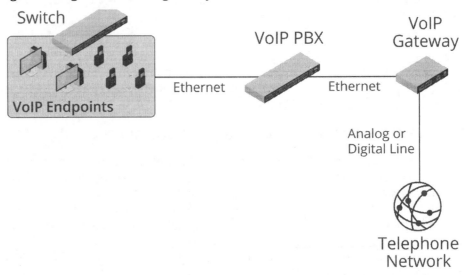

VoIP gateway connecting a local network using VoIP calling to the ordinary telephone network. (Images © 123RF.com)

A VoIP gateway can also be deployed to allow a legacy analog or digital internal phone system to use a VoIP service provider to place calls. In this type of setup, low rate local and national calls might be placed directly, while international calls that would attract high charges if placed directly are routed via the VoIP service provider.

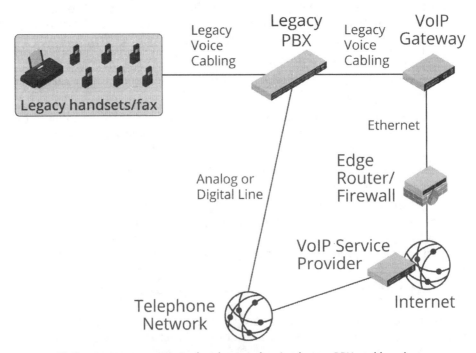

VoIP gateway connecting a local network using legacy PBX and handsets to a VoIP service provider. (Images © 123RF.com)

Finally, a VoIP gateway or adapter can be used to connect POTS handsets and fax machines to a VoIP PBX. This type of device is also called a Foreign Exchange Subscriber (FXS) gateway.

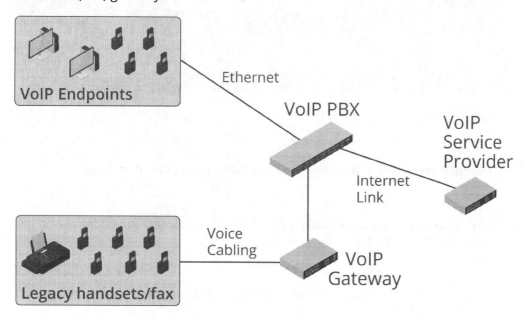

VoIP gateway connecting legacy handsets to a VoIP PBX. (Images © 123RF.com)

Review Activity:

Use of Email and Voice Services

Answer the following questions:

1. **What happens if a message sent via SMTP cannot be delivered?**

2. **What protocol would enable a client to manage mail subfolders on a remote mail server?**

3. **True or False? SIP enables the location of user agents via a specially formatted URI.**

4. **Which component in a VoIP network allows calls to be placed to and from the voice telephone or public switched telephone network (PSTN)?**

Lesson 11

Summary

You should be able to explain the characteristics of common application ports and protocols, especially in terms of security/encryption requirements.

Guidelines for Supporting Network Applications

Follow these guidelines to support network applications effectively:

- Deploy web servers to intranets as required. Public websites can be deployed to a perimeter network, but most organizations use some type of hosted or cloud service.

- Configure web servers with a valid certificate issued by a locally trusted or public certificate authority (CA) to enable HTTPS over TCP/443.

- Enable secure FTP on web servers, file servers, and appliances as a means of transferring files securely. FTP can be secured using SSH (SFTP) or TLS (FTPES or FTPS).

- Ensure that unencrypted local file and printer sharing services such as SMB are used only on trusted local networks. Block the SMB ports (TCP/UDP/137-139 and TCP/445) at the network perimeter. Ensure that legacy versions of the protocol are disabled.

- Deploy database services for access by application servers, rather than being directly accessible to client workstations and devices. Use access control lists to block access to RDBMS ports TCP/1521 (Oracle SQL*Net), TCP/1433 (MS SQL), TCP/3306 (MySQL/MariaDB), or TCP/5432 (PostgreSQL).

- Deploy SMTP servers to the network edge to transfer email messages to and from external recipients over TCP/25. Use TCP/587 and TLS to allow mail clients to submit messages for delivery securely. POP3 or IMAP mailbox servers should be deployed as secure version (TCP/995 and TCP/993 respectively).

- Deploy VoIP/hybrid PBX with voice gateways to local and perimeter networks to support legacy and packetized telephony devices. Configure VoIP endpoints to use secure SIP (TCP/5061) for session control and RTP/RTCP for data transfer.

Lesson 12
Ensuring Network Availability

LESSON INTRODUCTION

So far in this course, you have learned about all the different network media and topologies plus the application protocols that go toward building network connectivity and services. In this lesson, you will investigate some tools and management methods that will help you determine your network's baseline and optimize your network's performance.

Lesson Objectives

In this lesson, you will:

- Explain the use of network management services.

- Use event management to ensure network availability.

- Use performance metrics to ensure network availability.

Topic 12A

Explain the Use of Network Management Services

EXAM OBJECTIVES COVERED
1.5 Explain common ports and protocols, their application, and encrypted alternatives.
1.6 Explain the use and purpose of network services.
5.3 Given a scenario, use the appropriate network software tools and commands.

A remote management tool allows you to configure servers and devices over the network. Having to perform configuration and troubleshooting activity at a local console would be incredibly time-consuming. Efficient network administration depends upon remote access tools. It is imperative to configure these tools securely, however.

Secure Shell Servers and Terminal Emulators

The name "terminal" comes from the early days of computing where configuration was performed by a teletype (TTY) device. The TTY is the terminal or endpoint for communication between the computer and the user. The TTY handles text input and output between the user and the shell, or command environment. Where the terminal accepts input and displays output, the shell performs the actual processing.

A **terminal emulator** is any kind of software that replicates this TTY input/output function. A given terminal emulator application might support connections to multiple types of shell. A remote terminal emulator allows you to connect to the shell of a different host over the network.

Secure Shell (SSH) is the principal means of obtaining secure remote access to UNIX and Linux servers and to most types of network appliances (switches, routers, and firewalls). As well as terminal emulation, SSH can be used as the secure file transfer protocol (SFTP). There are numerous commercial and open source SSH servers and terminal emulation clients available for all the major NOS platforms (UNIX®, Linux®, Windows®, and macOS®). The most widely used is OpenSSH (openssh.com). An SSH server listens on TCP port 22 by default.

SSH Host Key

An SSH server is identified by a public/private key pair, referred to as the host key. A mapping of host names to public keys can be kept manually by each SSH client, or there are various enterprise software products designed for SSH key management.

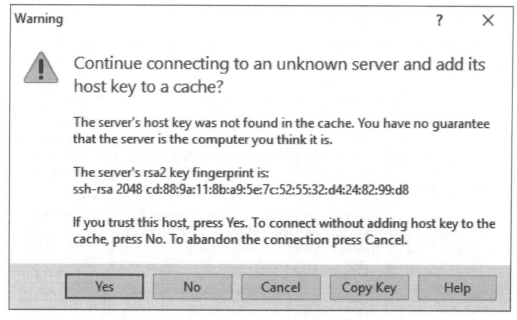

Confirming the SSH server's host key using the PuTTY SSH client. (Screenshot courtesy of PuTTY.)

The host key must be changed if any compromise of the host is suspected. If an attacker has obtained the private key of a server or appliance, they can masquerade as that server or appliance and perform a spoofing attack, usually with a view to obtaining other network credentials. You might also change the key to use a longer bit strength.

SSH Client Authentication

The server's host key is used to set up a secure channel to use for the client to submit authentication credentials. SSH allows various methods for the client to authenticate to the SSH server. Each of these methods can be enabled or disabled as required on the server:

- **Username/password**—The client submits credentials that are verified by the SSH server either against a local user database or using a network authentication server.

- **Public key authentication**—Each remote user's public key is added to a list of keys authorized for each local account on the SSH server.

- **Kerberos**—The client submits the Kerberos credentials (a Ticket Granting Ticket) obtained when the user logged onto the workstation to the server using the Generic Security Services Application Program Interface (GSSAPI). The SSH server contacts the Ticket Granting Service (in a Windows environment, this will be a domain controller) to validate the credential.

Managing valid client public keys is a critical security task. Many recent attacks on web servers have exploited poor key management. If a user's private key is compromised, delete the public key from the appliance then regenerate the key pair on the user's (remediated) client device and copy the public key to the SSH server. Always delete public keys if the user's access permissions have been revoked.

Secure Shell Commands

SSH features a rich command set, fully documented at the OpenSSH website (openssh.com/manual.html). Some of the most important commands are:

- `sshd`—Start the SSH Daemon (server). Parameters such as the host's certificate file, port to listen on, and logging options can be set via switches or in a configuration file.

- `ssh-keygen`—Create a key pair to use to access servers. The private key must be stored securely on your local computer. The public key must be copied to the server. You can use the `ssh-copy-id` command to do this, or you can copy the file manually.

- `ssh-agent`—Configure a service to use to store the keys used to access multiple hosts. The agent stores the private key for each public key securely and reduces the number of times use of a private key has to be confirmed with a passphrase. This provides a single sign-on (SSO) mechanism for multiple SSH servers. The `ssh-add` command is used to add a key to the agent.

- `ssh Host`—Use the SSH client to connect to the server running at *Host*. *Host* can be an FQDN or IP address. You can also create a client configuration file.

- `ssh Username@Host`—Use the SSH client to connect to the server running at *Host* with a different *Username*.

- `ssh Host "Command or Script"`—Use the SSH client to execute a command or script on the remote server running at *Host* without starting a shell.

- `scp Username@Host:RemoteFile /Local/Destination`—A file transfer client with remote copy/rcp-like command interface.

- `sftp`—A file transfer client with FTP-like command interface.

Telnet

Telnet is both a protocol and a terminal emulation software tool that transmits shell commands and output between a client and the remote host. In order to support Telnet access, the remote computer must run a service known as the Telnet Daemon. The Telnet Daemon listens on TCP port 23 by default.

A Telnet interface can be password protected but the password and other communications are not encrypted and therefore could be vulnerable to packet sniffing and replay. Historically, Telnet provided a simple means to configure switch and router equipment, but only secure access methods should be used for these tasks now. Ensure that the Telnet service is uninstalled or disabled, and block access to port 23.

```
mail.classroom.local - PuTTY
220 mail.classroom.local ESMTP
helo localhost
250 Hello.
mail from:<administrator@web.local>
250 OK
rcpt to:<administrator@classroom.local>
250 OK
data
354 OK, send.
from: Tech Support <administratator@web.local>
to: Hostmaster <administrator@classroom.local>
subject: Virus infection
mime-version: 1.0;
content-type: text/html;

<html>
<body>
<p>Viruses have been detected on your hosted server. Visit the <a href="http://w
www.notagoodidea.net">Hosting Services Portal</a> and enter your password to sca
n and remove them.</p>
</body>
</html>
.
250 Queued (199.078 seconds)
```

PuTTY Telnet client. (Screenshot courtesy of PuTTY.)

Remote Desktop Protocol

Telnet and SSH provide terminal emulation for command-line shells. This is sufficient for most administrative tasks, but where users want to connect to a desktop, they usually prefer to work with a graphical interface. A GUI remote administration tool sends screen and audio data from the remote host to the client and transfers mouse and keyboard input from the client to the remote host. **Remote Desktop Protocol (RDP)** is Microsoft's protocol for operating remote GUI connections to a Windows machine. RDP uses TCP port 3389. The administrator can specify permissions to connect to the server via RDP and can configure encryption on the connection.

RDP is mainly used for the remote administration of a Windows server or client, but another function is to publish software applications on a server, rather than installing them locally on each client (application virtualization).

 RDP clients are available for other operating systems, including Linux, macOS, iOS, and Android so you can connect to a Windows desktop remotely using a non-Windows device. There are also open-source RDP server products, such as xrdp (xrdp.org).

Network Time Protocol

Many applications on networks are time-dependent and time-critical, such as authentication and security mechanisms, scheduling applications, and backup software. The **Network Time Protocol (NTP)** enables the synchronization of these time-dependent applications. NTP works over UDP on port 123.

Top-level NTP servers (stratum 1) obtain the Coordinated Universal Time (UTC) via a direct physical link to an accurate clock source, such as an atomic clock accessed over the General Positioning System (GPS). An NTP server that synchronizes its time with a stratum 1 server over a network is operating at stratum 2. Each stratum level represents a step away from the accurate clock source over a network link. These lower stratum servers act as clients of the stratum 1 servers and as servers or time sources to lower stratum NTP servers or client hosts. Most switches and routers can be configured to act as time servers to local client hosts and this function is also typically performed by network directory servers. It is best to configure each of these devices with multiple reference time sources (at least three) and to establish them as peers to allow the NTP algorithm to detect drifting or obviously incorrect time values.

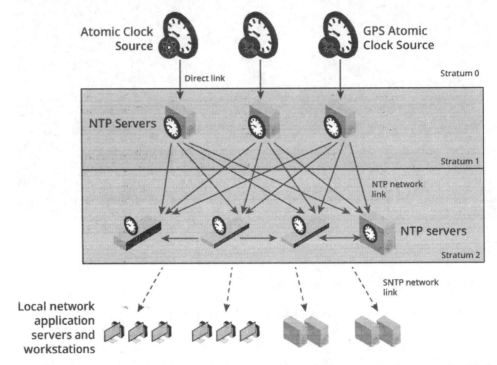

Stratum 1 NTP servers are directly connected to an accurate clock source. Each stratum level below one represents a network hop away from that accurate time source. (Images © 123RF.com.)

Client hosts (application servers and workstations) usually obtain the time by using a modified form of the protocol called Simple NTP (SNTP). SNTP works over the same port as NTP. A host that supports only SNTP cannot act as a time source for other hosts. In Windows, the Time Service can be configured by using the w32tm command. In Linux, the ntp package can be configured via /etc/ntp.conf.

If a server or host is configured with the incorrect time, it may not be able to access network services. Authentication, and other security mechanisms will often fail if the time is not synchronized on both communicating devices. In this situation, errors are likely to be generic failed or invalid token type messages. Always try to rule out time synchronization as an issue early in the troubleshooting process.

 If a local stratum 1 server cannot be implemented on the local network, the time source can be configured using one or more public NTP server pools, such as time.google.com, time.windows.com, time.apple.com, time.nist.gov, or pool.ntp.org.

Review Activity:

Network Management Services

Answer the following questions:

1. **True or false? SSH must be configured with two key pairs to operate; one on the server and one on the client.**

2. **What remote management service is associated with TCP port 23?**

3. **Which port is used by the Network Time Protocol (NTP)?**

4. **What is SNTP?**

Topic 12B

Use Event Management to Ensure Network Availability

EXAM OBJECTIVES COVERED
1.5 Explain common ports and protocols, their application, and encrypted alternatives.
3.1 Given a scenario, use the appropriate statistics and sensors to ensure network availability.

Managing network performance is an essential task for network technicians. By proactively monitoring network device status and event logs, you can provide reliable services to your users.

Performance Metrics, Bottlenecks, and Baselines

Network monitoring tools fulfill a wide range of functions. As input, they can capture and analyze traffic, monitor interface and device metrics, and consolidate log data. As output, they can alert you to events, help you define baselines, analyze traffic patterns and congestion, determine upgrade and forecast needs, and generate reports for management.

Performance Metrics

When you are monitoring a network host or intermediate system, several **performance metrics** can tell you whether the host is operating normally:

- **Bandwidth/throughput**—This is the rated speed of all the interfaces available to the device, measured in Mbps or Gbps. For wired Ethernet links, this will not usually vary, but the bandwidth of WAN and wireless links can change over time.

- **CPU and memory**—Devices such as switches and routers perform a lot of processing. If CPU and/or system memory utilization (measured as a percentage) is very high, an upgrade might be required. High CPU utilization can also indicate a problem with network traffic.

- **Storage**—Some network devices require persistent storage (typically, one or more flash drives) to keep configuration information and logs. Storage is measured in MB or GB. If the device runs out of storage space, it could cause serious errors. Servers also depend on fast input/output (I/O) to run applications efficiently.

Bottlenecks

A **bottleneck** is a point of poor performance that reduces the productivity of the whole network. A bottleneck may occur because a device is underpowered or faulty. It may also occur because of user or application behavior. To identify the cause of a bottleneck, you need to identify where and when on the network overutilization or excessive errors occur. If the problem is continual, it is likely to be device-related; if the problem only occurs at certain times, it is more likely to be user- or application-related.

Performance Baselines

A **performance baseline** establishes the resource utilization metrics at a point in time, such as when the system was first installed. This provides a comparison to measure system responsiveness later. For example, if a company is expanding a remote office that is connected to the corporate office with an ISP's basic tier package, the baseline can help determine if there is enough reserve bandwidth to handle the extra user load, or if the basic package needs to be upgraded to support higher bandwidths.

Reviewing baselines is the process of evaluating whether a baseline is still fit for purpose or whether a new baseline should be established. Changes to the system usually require a new baseline to be taken.

Environmental Monitoring

As distinct from performance monitors, an environmental **sensor** is used to detect factors that could threaten the integrity or availability of an appliance or its function.

Servers and appliances are fitted with internal sensors to monitor conditions within the device chassis. These can report problems such as excessive temperatures within the device chassis, fan speeds, component failure, and chassis intrusion to a monitoring system.

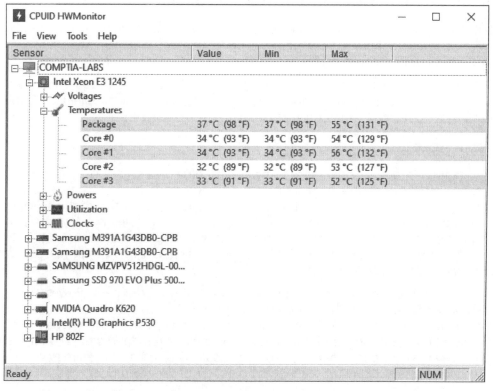

CPUID's HWMONITOR app can report temperatures from sensors installed on PC components. (Screenshot used by permission of CPUID.)

Sensors can also be installed to measure ambient environmental conditions for a network rack or enclosure or within a server room or equipment closet. The following environmental factors need monitoring:

- **Temperature**—High temperature will make it difficult for device and rack cooling systems to dissipate heat effectively. This increases the risk of overheating of components within device chassis and consequent faults.

- **Humidity**—More water vapor in the air risks condensation forming within a device chassis, leading to corrosion and short circuit faults. Conversely, very low humidity increases risks of static charges building up and damaging components.

- **Electrical**—Computer systems need stable power supply, free from outages (blackouts), voltage dips (brownouts), and voltage spikes and surges. Sensors built into power distribution systems and backup battery systems can report deviations from a normal power supply.

- **Flooding**—There may be natural or person-made flood risks from nearby water courses and reservoirs or risks from leaking plumbing or fire suppression systems. Electrical systems need to be shut down immediately in the presence of any significant amount of water.

Simple Network Management Protocol

Stand-alone devices may have a web console to use for performance and environmental monitoring. Local access is not scalable to managing tens or hundreds of devices, however.

The **Simple Network Management Protocol (SNMP)** is a widely used framework for remote management and monitoring of servers and network appliances. SNMP consists of agents and a monitoring system.

SNMP Agents

The agent is a process (software or firmware) running on a switch, router, server, or other SNMP-compatible network device. This agent maintains a database called a Management Information Base (MIB) that holds statistics relating to the activity of the device, such as the number of frames per second handled by a switch. Each parameter stored in a MIB is referred to by a numeric Object Identifier (OID). OIDs are stored within a tree structure. Part of the tree is generic to SNMP, while part can be defined by the device vendor.

An agent is configured with the community name of the computers allowed to manage the agent and the IP address or host name of the server running the management system. The community name acts as a rudimentary type of password. An agent can pass information only to management systems configured with the same community name. There are usually two community names; one for read-only access and one for read-write access (or privileged mode).

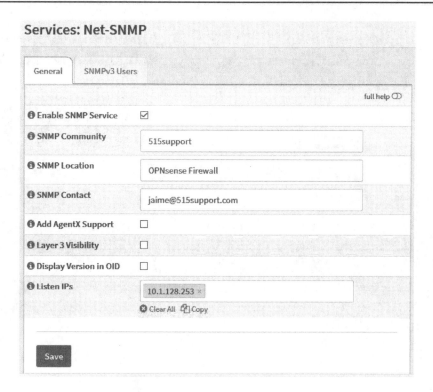

Configuring an SNMP agent on an OPNsense security appliance. (Screenshot courtesy of OPNsense.)

SNMP Monitor

An SNMP monitor is management software that provides a location from which you can oversee network activity. The monitor polls agents at regular intervals for information from their MIBs and displays the information for review. It also displays any trap operations as alerts for the network administrator to assess and act upon as necessary. The monitor can retrieve information from a device in two main ways:

- **Get**—The software queries the agent for a single OID. This command is used by the monitor to perform regular polling (obtaining information from devices at defined intervals).

- **Trap**—The agent informs the monitor of a notable event (port failure, for instance). The threshold for triggering traps can be set for each value.

The monitor can be used to change certain variables using the Set command. It can also walk an MIB subtree by using multiple Get and Get Next commands. This is used to discover the complete layout of an MIB. Device queries take place over UDP port 161; traps are communicated over UDP port 162.

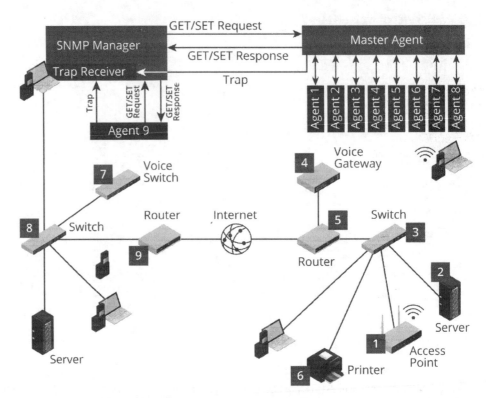

SNMP collects information from network devices for diagnostic purposes. (Images © 123RF.com)

Network Device Logs

Network device logs are one of the most valuable sources of performance, troubleshooting, and security auditing information. A single logged event consists of metadata, such as the date and time, category, and event ID, plus a description and contents of error or informational output. For example, you can use a system log to troubleshoot an IP conflict by looking for TCP/IP events or to determine when and why a system was shut down.

While the specifics of what and where events are logged can vary widely from platform to platform, it is possible to discern some general log types, including system, security, application, and performance or traffic.

System and Application Logs

A system log records startup events plus subsequent changes to the configuration at an OS level. This will certainly include kernel processes and drivers but could also include core services.

By contrast, an application log records data for a single specific service, such as DNS, HTTP, or an RDBMS. Note that a complex application could write to multiple log files, however. For example, the Apache web server logs errors to one file and access attempts to another.

Audit Logs

An audit log records use of authentication and authorization privileges. It will generally record success/fail type events. An audit log might also be described as an access log or security log. Audit logging might be performed at an OS level and at a per-application level.

Firewall: Log Files: Live View

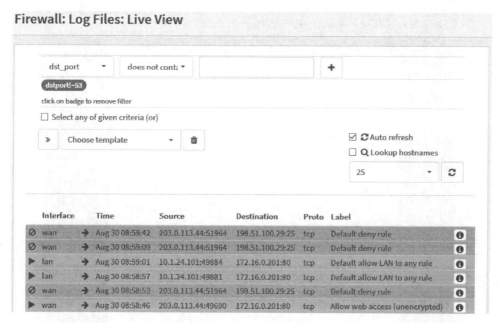

Viewing audit logs on an OPNsense security appliance. (Screenshot courtesy of OPNsense.)

Audit logs typically associate an action with a particular user. This is one of the reasons that it is critical that users not share logon details. If a user account is compromised, there is no means of tying events in the log to the actual attacker.

Performance/Traffic Logs

Performance and traffic logs record statistics for compute, storage, and network resources over a defined period.

Log Collectors and Syslog

A log collector aggregates event messages from numerous devices to a single storage location. As well as aggregating logs, the system can be configured to run one or more status and alerting dashboards.

Syslog is an example of a protocol and supporting software that facilitates log collection. It has become a de facto standard for logging events from distributed systems. For example, syslog messages can be generated by Cisco® routers and switches, as well as UNIX or Linux servers and workstations. A syslog collector usually listens on UDP port 514.

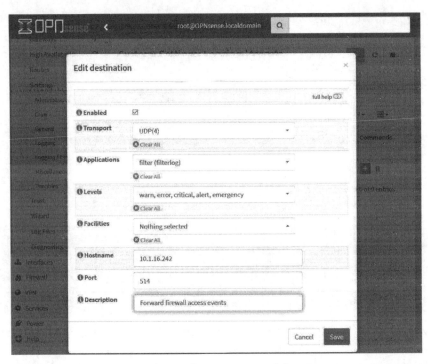

Configuring an OPNsense security appliance to transmit logs to a remote syslog server.
(Screenshot courtesy of OPNsense.)

As well as a protocol for forwarding messages to a remote log collector, Syslog provides an open format for event data. A syslog message comprises a PRI code, a header containing a timestamp and host name, and a message part. The PRI code is calculated from the facility and a severity level. The message part contains a tag showing the source process plus content. The format of the content is application dependent. It might use space- or comma-delimited fields or name/value pairs, such as JavaScript Object Notation (JSON) data.

Event Management

Devices can generate thousands of events per hour. A system for prioritizing them between ones that require immediate or long-term response is vital. Most logging systems categorize each event. For example, in Windows, system and application events are defined as Informational, Warning, or Critical, while audit events are categorized as Success or Fail.

Syslog severity levels are as follows:

Code	Level	Interpretation
0	Emergency	The system is unusable (kernel panic)
1	Alert	A fault requiring immediate remediation has occurred
2	Critical	A fault that will require immediate remediation is likely to develop
3	Error	A nonurgent fault has developed
4	Warning	A nonurgent fault is likely to develop

Code	Level	Interpretation
5	Notice	A state that could potentially lead to an error condition has developed
6	Informational	A normal but reportable event has occurred
7	Debug	Verbose status conditions used during development and testing

The **logging level** configured on each host determines the maximum level at which events are recorded or forwarded. For example, if the logging level for remote forwarding is set to 4, events that are level 5, 6, or 7 are *not* forwarded.

An automated event management system can be configured to generate some sort of alert when certain event types of a given severity are encountered. Alerts can also be generated by setting thresholds for performance counters. Examples include packet loss, link bandwidth drops, number of sessions established, delay/jitter in real-time applications, and so on. Most network monitors also support heartbeat tests so that you can receive an alert if a device or server stops responding to probes.

Setting alerts is a matter of balance. On the one hand, you do not want performance to deteriorate to the point that it affects user activity; on the other hand, you do not want to be overwhelmed by alerts.

You can also make a distinction between alerts and notifications. An alert means that the system has matched some sort of pattern or filter that should be recorded and highlighted. A notification means that the system sends a message to advertise the occurrence of the alert. A low priority alert may simply be displayed in the system dashboard. A high priority alert might use some sort of active notification messaging, such as emailing a system administrator, sending a text message (SMS) to a phone, or triggering a physical alarm signal.

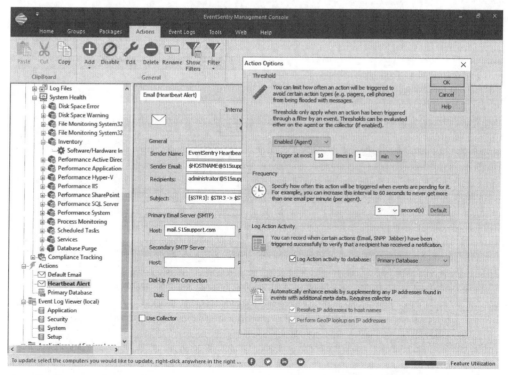

Configuring alert and notification settings in EventSentry SIEM. (Screenshot courtesy of NETIKUS.NET Ltd.)

There should be some process for acknowledging and dismissing alerts as they are raised. A serious alert may need to be processed as an incident and assigned a job ticket for formal investigation. If an alert is a false positive, it can be dismissed. If the management system or dashboard is allowed to become cluttered with old alerts, it is much more difficult to identify new alerts and gauge the overall status of the network.

Log Reviews

Monitoring involves viewing traffic, protocols, and events in real time. Network and log reviewing, or analysis involves later inspection and interpretation of captured data to determine what the data shows was happening on the network during the capture. Monitoring is aligned with incident response; analysis is aligned with investigating the cause of incidents or preventing incidents in the first place. It is important to perform performance analysis and log review continually. Referring to the logs only after a major incident is missing the opportunity to identify threats and vulnerabilities or performance problems early and to respond proactively.

Not all performance incidents will be revealed by a single event. One of the features of log analysis and reporting software should be to identify trends. A trend is difficult to spot by examining each event in a log file. Instead, you need software to chart the incidence of types of events and show how the number or frequency of those events changes over time.

Plotting data as a graph is particularly helpful as it is easier to spot trends or spikes or troughs in a visualization of events, rather than the raw data. Most performance monitors can plot metrics in a graph.

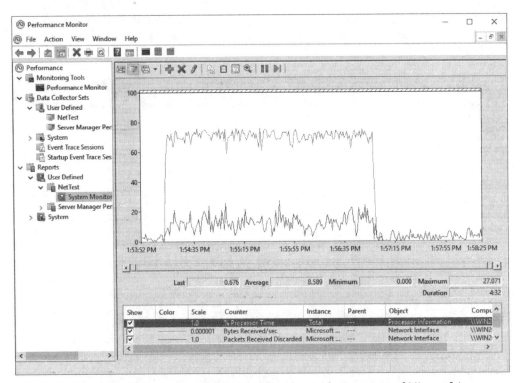

Data retrieved from a performance log file. (Screenshot courtesy of Microsoft.)

Review Activity:

Ensure Network Availability with Event Management

Answer the following questions:

1. You have a plan for monitoring switches and routers that accommodates network metrics (bandwidth, latency, and jitter) plus chassis temperature and intrusion. What other performance metric should be monitored?

2. How does an SNMP agent report an event to the management system?

3. What sort of log would you inspect if you wanted to track web server access attempts?

4. A technician has recommended changing the syslog logging level from its current value of 3 to 6. Will this cause more or fewer events to be forwarded?

5. What would be the purpose of configuring thresholds in network monitoring software?

Topic 12C

Use Performance Metrics to Ensure Network Availability

EXAM OBJECTIVES COVERED
2.2 Compare and contrast routing technologies and bandwidth management concepts.
3.1 Given a scenario, use the appropriate statistics and sensors to ensure network availability.
5.3 Given a scenario, use the appropriate network software tools and commands.

Modern networks have demanding performance requirements that can only be evaluated and met by assessing a range of performance metrics. Understanding these metrics and how to record and measure them will help you to optimize a network to perform at its peak level.

Network Metrics

Quality of Service (QoS) protocols and appliances are designed to support real-time services. Applications such as voice and video that carry real-time data have different network requirements to the sort of data represented by file transfer. With "ordinary" data, it might be beneficial to transfer a file as quickly as possible, but the sequence in which the packets are delivered and the variable intervals between packets arriving do not materially affect the application. This type of data transfer is described as bursty.

While streaming video applications can have a high bandwidth requirement in terms of the sheer amount of data to be transferred, bandwidth on modern networks is typically less of a problem than packet loss, latency, and jitter.

Bandwidth

Bandwidth is the amount of information that can be transmitted, measured in bits per second (bps), or some multiple thereof. When monitoring, you need to distinguish between the nominal data link/Ethernet bit rate, the throughput of a link at Layer 3, and the goodput available to an application.

Bandwidth for audio depends on the sampling frequency (Hertz) and bit depth of each sample. For example, telecommunications links are based on 64 Kbps channels. This was derived through the following calculation:

- The voice frequency range is 4000 Hz. This must be sampled at twice the rate to ensure an accurate representation of the original analog waveform.

- The sample size is 1 byte (or 8 bits). Therefore, 8 KHz x 8 bits = 64 Kbps.

For VoIP, bandwidth requirements for voice calling can vary, but allowing 100 Kbps per call upstream and downstream should be sufficient in most cases.

Bandwidth required for video is determined by image resolution (number of pixels), color depth, and the frame rate, measured in frames per second (fps).

Latency and Jitter

Problems with the timing and sequence of packet delivery are defined as latency and jitter. **Latency** is the time it takes for a transmission to reach the recipient, measured in milliseconds (ms). **Jitter** is defined as being a variation in the delay. Jitter manifests itself as an inconsistent rate of packet delivery. Jitter is also measured in milliseconds, using an algorithm to calculate the value from a sample of transit times.

Latency and jitter are not significant problems when data transfer is bursty, but real-time applications are much more sensitive to their effects because they manifest as echo, delay, and video slow down. If packets are delayed, arrive out of sequence, or are lost, then the receiving host must buffer received packets until the delayed packets are received. If packet loss or delay is so excessive that the buffer is exhausted, then noticeable audio or video problems (artifacts) are experienced by users.

You can test the latency of a link using tools such as ping, pathping, and mtr. You can also use mtr to calculate jitter. When assessing latency, you need to consider the Round Trip Time (RTT). VoIP is generally expected to require an RTT of less than 300 ms. Jitter should be 30 ms or less. The link should also not exhibit more than 1 percent packet loss.

Bandwidth Management

Latency and jitter on the Internet are difficult to control because of the number of different parties that are involved (both caller networks plus any ISP transit networks). On a local network, delay is typically caused by congestion. This means that the network infrastructure is not capable of meeting the demands of peak load.

You can either provision higher bandwidth links and/or faster switches and routers, or you can use some sort of bandwidth management mechanism. For example, if you are running VoIP over your network and someone decides to copy a 40 GB file down from a server, the file transfer has the potential to wreak havoc with VoIP call quality. Without QoS, switches and routers forward traffic based on best effort or first-in, first-out, meaning that frames or packets are forwarded in the order in which they arrive. A QoS system identifies the packets or traffic streams belonging to a specific application, such as VoIP, and prioritizes them over other applications, such as file transfer.

Differentiated Services

The **Differentiated Services (DiffServ)** framework classifies each packet passing through a device. Router policies can then be defined to use the packet classification to prioritize delivery. DiffServ is an IP (layer 3) service tagging mechanism. It uses the Type of Service field in the IPv4 header (Traffic Class in IPv6). The field is populated with a 6-byte DiffServ Code Point (DSCP) by either the sending host or by the router. Packets with the same DSCP and destination are referred to as Behavior Aggregates and allocated the same Per Hop Behavior (PHB) at each DiffServ-compatible router.

DiffServ traffic classes are typically grouped into three types:

- Best Effort.

- Assured Forwarding (which is broken down into sub-levels).

- Expedited Forwarding (which has the highest priority).

IEEE 802.1p

While DiffServ works at layer 3, IEEE **802.1p** can be used at Layer 2 (independently or in conjunction with DiffServ) to classify and prioritize traffic passing over a switch or wireless access point. 802.1p defines a tagging mechanism within the 802.1Q VLAN field (it also often referred to as 802.1Q/p). The 3-bit priority field is set to a value between 0 and 7. Most vendors map DSCP values to 802.1p ones. For example, 7 and 6 can be reserved for network control (such as routing table updates), 5 and 4 map to expedited forwarding levels for 2-way communications, 3 and 2 map to assured forwarding for streaming multimedia, and 1 and 0 for "ordinary" best-effort delivery.

As well as invoking the priority tag, VLAN infrastructure is often used for traffic management on local networks. For example, voice traffic might be allocated to a different VLAN than data traffic.

Traffic Shaping

Quality of Service (QoS) is distinct from Class of Service (CoS). CoS mechanisms such as DiffServ and 802.1p just categorize protocols into groups that require different service levels and provide a tagging mechanism to identify a frame or packet's class. QoS allows fine-grained control over traffic parameters. For example, if a network link is congested, there is nothing that DiffServ and 802.1p can do about it, but a protocol such as Multiprotocol Label Switching (MPLS) with QoS functionality can reserve the required bandwidth and pre-determine statistics such as acceptable packet loss and maximum latency and jitter when setting up the link.

In terms of QoS, network functions are commonly divided into three planes:

- **Control plane**—makes decisions about how traffic should be prioritized and where it should be switched.

- **Data plane**—handles the actual switching of traffic.

- **Management plane**—monitors traffic conditions.

Protocols, appliances, and software that can apply these three functions can be described as traffic shapers or bandwidth shapers. **Traffic shapers** delay certain packet types—based on their content—to ensure that other packets have a higher priority. This can help to ensure that latency is reduced for critical applications.

Simpler devices, performing traffic policing, do not offer the enhanced traffic management functions of a shaper. For example, typical traffic policing devices will simply fail to deliver packets once the configured traffic threshold has been reached (this is often referred to as tail drop). Consequently, there will be times when packets are being lost, while other times when the network is relatively idle, and the bandwidth is being under-utilized. A traffic shaper will store packets until there is free bandwidth available. Hopefully, this leads to consistent usage of the bandwidth and few lost packets.

It is essential that the selected device is capable of handling high traffic volumes. As these devices have a limited buffer, there will be situations when the buffer overflows. Devices can either drop packets and in essence provide traffic policing, or else they must implement a dropping algorithm. Random Early Detection (RED) is one of several algorithms that can be implemented to help manage traffic overflow on the shaper.

Traffic Analysis Tools

Effective bandwidth management or traffic shaping policies depend on detailed information about network traffic flows. Network analysis tools will help you to report on traffic conditions.

Throughput Testers

One fairly simple way to measure network throughput is to transfer a large file between two appropriate hosts. Appropriate in this sense means an appropriate subnet and representative of servers and workstations that you want to measure. It is also important to choose a representative time. There is not much point in measuring the throughput when the network is carrying no other traffic.

To determine your network throughput using this method, simply divide the file size by the amount of time taken to copy the file. For example, if you transfer a 1 GB file in half an hour, the throughput can be calculated as follows:

- 1 gigabyte is 10243 bytes (1,073,741,824 bytes or 8,589,934,592 bits).

- 8,589,934,592 bits in 1,800 seconds is 4,772,186 bits per second or 4.55 Mbps.

This method derives a value that is different from the nominal data rate. Because two hosts are transferring the files between one another, it is the Application layers that handle the file transfer. The intervening layers on both hosts add complexity (headers) and introduce inaccuracy, such as corrupt frames that have to be retransmitted.

Several software utilities, such as **iperf** (iperf.fr), Ttcp (linux.die.net/man/1/ttcp), and bwping (bwping.sourceforge.io), can be used to measure network throughput. An instance of the tool is configured on two network hosts and the tools measure the throughput achieved between the sender and the listener.

```
longmon10:                $ iperf3 -c 172.16.0.201 -u -b100M -t 30 -i 10
Connecting to host 172.16.0.201, port 5201
[  5] local 10.1.16.242 port 35889 connected to 172.16.0.201 port 5201
[ ID] Interval           Transfer      Bitrate         Total Datagrams
[  5]   0.00-10.00  sec   119 MBytes   100 Mbits/sec   86319
[  5]  10.00-20.00  sec   119 MBytes   100 Mbits/sec   86325
[  5]  20.00-30.00  sec   119 MBytes   100 Mbits/sec   86326
- - - - - - - - - - - - - - - - - - - - - - - - -
[ ID] Interval           Transfer      Bitrate         Jitter    Lost/Total Datag
rams
[  5]   0.00-30.00  sec   358 MBytes   100 Mbits/sec   0.000 ms  0/258970 (0%)  s
ender
[  5]   0.00-30.00  sec   358 MBytes   100 Mbits/sec   0.016 ms  0/258970 (0%)  r
eceiver

iperf Done.
```

iperf3 transfer report showing bitrate, jitter, and packet loss.
(Screenshot courtesy of iperf.)

Top Talkers/Listeners

Top talkers are interfaces generating the most outgoing traffic (in terms of bandwidth), while top listeners are the interfaces receiving the most incoming traffic. Identifying these hosts and the routes they are using is useful in identifying and eliminating performance bottlenecks. Most network analyzer software comes with filters or built-in reporting to identify top talkers or top listeners.

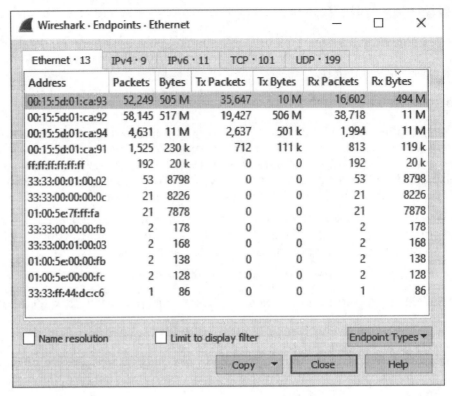

The Endpoints report in Wireshark can be used to identify top talkers and top listeners.
(Screenshot courtesy of Wireshark.)

Bandwidth Speed Testers

In addition to testing performance on a local network, you may also want to test Internet links using some type of **bandwidth speed tester**. There are many Internet tools available for checking performance. The two main classes are:

- **Broadband speed checkers**—These test how fast the local broadband link to the Internet is. They are mostly designed for SOHO use. The tool will test downlink and uplink speeds, test latency using ping, and can usually compare the results with neighboring properties and other users of the same ISP.

- **Website performance checkers**—These query a nominated website to work out how quickly pages load. One of the advantages of an online tool is that you can test your site's response times from the perspective of customers in different countries.

NetFlow

A packet analyzer can be used to measure network traffic statistics but trying to record each frame imposes a heavy processing overhead on the network tap or mirror port. Collecting just the packet metadata, rather than the whole packet payload, reduces the bandwidth required by the sniffer. Technologies such as Cisco's **NetFlow** (cisco.com/c/en/us/products/ios-nx-os-software/ios-netflow/index.html) gather traffic metadata only and report it to a structured database. These technologies can also use sampling to further reduce processing demands. NetFlow has been redeveloped as the IP Flow Information Export (IPFIX) IETF standard (tools.ietf.org/html/rfc7011).

Using NetFlow involves deploying three types of components:

- A NetFlow exporter is configured on network appliances (switches, routers, and firewalls). Each flow is defined on an exporter. A traffic flow is defined by packets that share the same characteristics, such as IP source and destination addresses and protocol type. These five bits of information are referred to as a 5-tuple. A 7-tuple flow adds the input interface and IP type of service data. Each exporter caches data for newly seen flows and sets a timer to determine flow expiration. When a flow expires or becomes inactive, the exporter transmits the data to a collector.

- A NetFlow collector aggregates flows from multiple exporters. A large network can generate huge volumes of flow traffic and data records, so the collector needs a high bandwidth network link and substantial storage capacity. The exporter and collector must support compatible versions of NetFlow and/or IPFIX. The most widely deployed versions of NetFlow are v5 and v9.

- A NetFlow analyzer reports and interprets information by querying the collector and can be configured to generate alerts and notifications. In practical terms, the collector and analyzer components are often implemented as a single product.

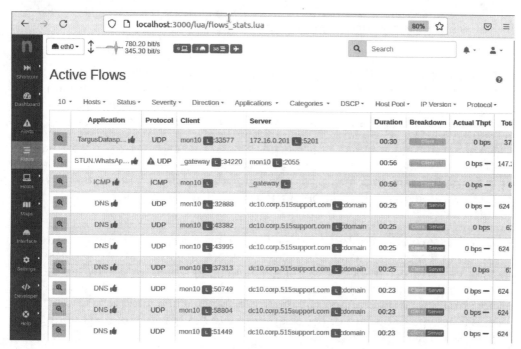

ntopng community edition being used to monitor NetFlow traffic data.
(Screenshot used courtesy of ntop.)

Interface Monitoring Metrics

You can collect data and configure alerts for **interface statistics**, whether on a network adapter or switch or router port.

- **Link state**—Measures whether an interface is working (up) or not (down). You would configure an alert if an interface goes down so that it can be investigated immediately. You may also want to track the uptime or downtime percentage so that you can assess a link's reliability over time.

- **Resets**—The number of times an interface has restarted over the counter period. Interfaces may be reset manually or could restart automatically if traffic volume is very high, or a large number of errors are experienced. Anything but occasional resets should be closely monitored and investigated. An interface that continually resets is described as flapping.

- **Speed**—This is the rated speed of the interface, measured in Mbps or Gbps. For wired Ethernet links this will not usually vary, but the bandwidth of WAN and wireless links may change over time. For Ethernet links, the interface speed should be the same on both the host and switch ports.

- **Duplex**—Most Ethernet interfaces operate in full duplex mode. If an interface is operating in half duplex mode, there is likely to be some sort of problem, unless you are supporting a legacy device.

- **Utilization**—The data transferred over a period. This can either be measured as the amount of data traffic both sent and received (measured in bits or bytes per second or a multiple thereof) or calculated as a percentage of the available bandwidth.

You also need to differentiate between average utilization and peak utilization. If average utilization is around 80%, it may appear that there is sufficient bandwidth. However, if peak utilization often spikes to 100%, then that will manifest as delay and packet loss and may require that you upgrade the link. Monitoring the queue length can help to determine whether the link is a bottleneck.

- **Per-protocol utilization**—Packet or byte counts for a specific protocol. It is often useful to monitor both packet counts and bandwidth consumption. High packet counts will incur processing load on the CPU and system memory resources of the appliance, even if the size of each packet is quite small.

- **Error rate**—The number of packets per second that cause errors. Errors may occur as a result of interference or poor link quality causing data corruption in frames. In general terms, error rates should be under 1 percent; high error rates may indicate a driver problem, if a network media problem can be ruled out.

- **Discards/drops**—An interface may discard incoming and/or outgoing frames for several reasons, including checksum errors, mismatched MTUs, packets that are too small (runts) or too large (giants), high load, or permissions— the sender is not on the interface's access control list (ACL) or there is some sort of VLAN configuration problem, for instance. Each interface is likely to class the type of discard or drop separately to assist with troubleshooting the precise cause.

Some vendors may use the term discard for frames that are rejected because of errors or security policies and drop for frames that are lost due to high load, but often the terms are used interchangeably.

- **Retransmissions**—Errors and discards/drops mean that frames of data are lost during transmission between two devices. As a result, the communication will be incomplete, and the data will, therefore, have to be retransmitted to ensure application data integrity. If you observe high levels of retransmissions (as a percentage of overall traffic), you must analyze and troubleshoot the specific cause of the underlying packet loss, which could involve multiple aspects of network configuration and connectivity.

Troubleshooting Interface Errors

As well as monitoring for traffic bottlenecks and other performance issues, **interface errors** might indicate a misconfiguration problem at the data link layer or interference at the physical layer.

Cyclic Redundancy Check Errors

A cyclic redundancy check (CRC) is calculated by an interface when it sends a frame. A CRC value is calculated from the frame contents to derive a 32-bit value. This is added to the header as the frame check sequence. The receiving interface uses the same calculation. If it derives a different value, the frame is rejected. The number of CRC errors can be monitored per interface.

CRC errors are usually caused by interference. This interference might be due to poor quality cable or termination, attenuation, mismatches between optical transceivers or cable types, or due to some external factor.

Encapsulation Errors

Encapsulation is the frame format expected on the interface. Encapsulation errors will prevent transmission and reception. If you check the interface status, the physical link will be listed as up, but the line protocol will be listed as down. This type of error can arise in several circumstances:

- **Ethernet frame type**—Ethernet can use a variety of frame types. The most common is Ethernet II, but if a host is configured to use a different type, such as SNAP, then errors will be reported on the link.

- **Ethernet trunks**—When a trunk link is established between two switches, it will very commonly use the Ethernet 802.1Q frame format. 802.1Q specifies an extra frame header to carry a VLAN ID and type of service data. If one switch interface is using 802.1Q but the other is not, this may be reported as an encapsulation error.

- **WAN framing**—Router interfaces to provider networks can use a variety of frame formats. Often these are simple serial protocols, such as High-level Data Link Control (HDLC) or Point-to-Point Protocol (PPP). Alternatively, the interface may use encapsulated Ethernet over Asynchronous Transfer Mode (ATM) or Virtual Private LAN Service (VPLS) or an older protocol, such as Frame Relay. The interface on the Customer Edge (CE) router must be configured for the same framing type as the Provider Edge (PE) router.

Runt Frame Errors

A runt is a frame that is smaller than the minimum size (64 bytes for Ethernet). A runt frame is usually caused by a collision. In a switched environment, collisions should only be experienced on an interface connected to a legacy hub device and there is a duplex mismatch in the interface configuration (or possibly on a misconfigured link to a virtualization platform). If runts are generated in other conditions, suspect a driver issue on the transmitting host.

Giant Frame Errors

A giant is a frame that is larger than the maximum permissible size (1518 bytes for Ethernet II). There are two likely causes of giant frames:

- **Ethernet trunks**—As above, if one switch interface is configured for 802.1Q framing, but the other is not, the frames will appear too large to the receiver, as 802.1Q adds 4 bytes to the header, making the maximum frame size 1522 bytes.

 An Ethernet frame that is slightly larger (up to 1600 bytes) is often referred to as a baby giant.

- **Jumbo frames**—A host might be configured to use jumbo frames, but the switch interface is not configured to receive them. This type of issue often occurs when configuring storage area networks (SANs) or links between SANs and data networks.

Review Activity:

Ensure Network Availability with Performance Metrics

Answer the following questions:

1. How is jitter mitigated by a VoIP application?

2. How many different traffic classes can be defined by 802.1Q/p?

3. How does a traffic shaper benefit real-time data applications?

4. What is a top listener in terms of network monitoring?

5. You suspect that a network application is generating faulty packets. What interface metric(s) might help you to diagnose the problem?

Lesson 12

Summary

You should be use remote management interfaces and appropriate statistics and sensors to ensure network availability.

Guidelines for Ensuring Network Availability

Setting up a management and monitoring system for a network can be a complex process, involving the evaluation and testing of different products. Follow these guidelines to make effective use of network management and monitoring tools:

- Select a log collection system that will provide the best compatibility with the endpoints used on your network, plus the reporting and management features that you require.

- Configure accounts with the rights to monitor endpoints, and (optionally) perform remote management and deployment of agent-based tools.

- Configure endpoints to provide information to the log collector. This could involve one or more different methods, such as:

  - Configure SNMP traps.

  - Configure remote logging to the using syslog or a similar protocol.

  - Configure NetFlow/IPFIX exporters.

  - Deploy agents to the endpoints to perform log and performance counter collection and measurement.

- Identify metrics to use to monitor network interfaces, device health and performance, plus network traffic levels.

- Record baseline measurements for the selected metrics.

- Set up filters to alert and notify administrators when key thresholds are exceeded or when hosts fail heartbeat tests.

- Set up a process for responding to alerts, making use of secure remote access tools such as SSH to manage configurations effectively.

- Set up a process for reviewing logs and diagnosing trends. Use this analysis to plan deployment of traffic marking (DiffServ/802.1p) and traffic shaping/bandwidth management solutions.

Lesson 13

Explaining Common Security Concepts

LESSON INTRODUCTION

You have identified the basic components and concepts for deploying and monitoring a network, but a network implementation is not complete without security mechanisms. In this lesson, you will describe basic concepts related to network security. As a networking professional, it is part of your responsibility to understand these fundamental concepts so that you can support network security controls.

Lesson Objectives

In this lesson, you will:

- Explain common security concepts.

- Explain authentication methods.

Topic 13A

Explain Common Security Concepts

EXAM OBJECTIVES COVERED
4.1 Explain common security concepts.

In this topic, you will describe basic concepts related to network security assessments. It's important to have a solid foundation and awareness of the industry terminology used when you are discussing network security.

Security Concepts

Establishing computer and network security means developing processes and controls that protect data assets and ensure business continuity by making network systems and hosts resilient to different kinds of attack.

The Confidentiality, Integrity, and Availability (CIA) Triad

One of the foundational principles of computer security is that the systems used to store, transmit, and process data must demonstrate three properties, often referred to as the **CIA Triad**:

- Confidentiality means that certain information should only be known to certain people.

- Integrity means that the data is stored and transferred as intended and that any modification is authorized.

- Availability means that information is accessible to those authorized to view or modify it.

Vulnerability, Threat, and Risk

To perform assessment and monitoring, security teams must identify ways in which their systems could be attacked. These assessments involve vulnerabilities, threats, and risk:

- **Vulnerability**—A weakness that could be accidentally triggered or intentionally exploited to cause a security breach.

- **Threat**— The potential for someone or something to exploit a vulnerability and breach security. A threat may be intentional or unintentional. The person or thing that poses the threat is called a threat actor or threat agent. The path or tool used by a malicious threat actor can be referred to as the attack vector.

- **Risk**—The likelihood and impact (or consequence) of a threat actor exercising a vulnerability.

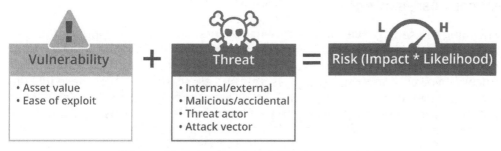

Relationship between vulnerability, threat, and risk.

Security Risk Assessments

Many tools and techniques are available to ensure that network systems demonstrate three properties of the CIA triad. Selection and deployment of these tools is guided by security policies. Security policies ensure that an organization has evaluated the risks it faces and has put security controls in place to mitigate those risks. Making a system more secure is also referred to as hardening. Different security policies should cover every aspect of an organization's use of computer and network technologies, from procurement and change control to acceptable use.

Risk management is a process for identifying, assessing, and mitigating vulnerabilities and threats to the essential functions that a business must perform to serve its customers. Risk management is complex and treated very differently in companies and institutions of different sizes, and with different regulatory and compliance requirements. Most companies will institute enterprise risk management (ERM) policies and procedures, based on published frameworks.

Risk assessment is a subset of risk management where the company's systems and procedures are evaluated for risk factors. Separate assessments can be devised to perform an initial evaluation and ongoing monitoring of threats, vulnerabilities, and security posture.

Posture Assessment

There are many different ways of thinking about how IT services should be governed to fulfill overall business needs. Some organizations have developed IT service frameworks to provide best practice guides to implementing IT and cybersecurity. These frameworks can shape company policies and provide checklists of procedures, activities, and technologies that should ideally be in place.

Collectively, these procedures, activities, and tools can be referred to as security controls. A security control is something designed to give a system or data asset the properties of confidentiality, integrity, availability, and non-repudiation.

In theory, security controls or countermeasures could be introduced to address every risk factor. The difficulty is that security controls can be expensive, so you must balance the cost of the control with the cost associated with the risk. It is not possible to eliminate risk; rather, the aim is to mitigate risk factors to the point where the organization is exposed only to a level of risk that it can afford. The overall status of risk management is referred to as risk posture. Risk posture shows which risk response options can be identified and prioritized. **Posture assessment** is often performed with reference to an IT or security framework. The framework can be used to assess the organization's maturity level in its use of security policies and controls.

Process Assessment

Mitigating risk can involve a large amount of expenditure so it is important to focus efforts. Effective risk management must focus on mission essential functions that could cause the whole business to fail if they are not performed. Part of this process Involves identifying critical systems and assets that support these functions. A **mission essential function (MEF)** is one that cannot be deferred. This means that the organization must be able to perform the function as close to continually as possible, and if there is any service disruption, the mission essential functions must be restored first.

Business impact analysis (BIA) is the process of assessing what losses might occur for a range of threat scenarios. For instance, if a denial of service (DoS) attack suspends an e-commerce portal for five hours, the business impact analysis will be able to quantify the losses from orders not made and customers moving permanently to other suppliers based on historic data. The likelihood of a DoS attack can be assessed on an annualized basis to determine annualized impact, in terms of costs. You then have the information required to assess whether a security control, such as load balancing or managed attack mitigation, is worth the investment.

Where BIA identifies risks, business continuity planning (BCP) identifies controls and processes that enable an organization to maintain critical workflows in the face of some adverse event.

Vulnerability and Exploit Types

Vulnerabilities can exist because of misconfigurations or poor practice, but many people understand the term to mean faults in software specifically. A software vulnerability is a design flaw that can cause the application security system to be circumvented or that will cause the application to crash. The most serious vulnerabilities allow the attacker to execute arbitrary code on the system, which could allow the installation of malware or allow the threat actor to disable or weaken a secure configuration. Typically, applications such as web servers, web browsers, web browser plug-ins, email clients, and databases are targeted.

An **exploit** is the specific code or method of using a vulnerability to gain control of a system or damage it in some way. Typically, software vulnerabilities can be exploited only in quite specific circumstances, but because of the complexity of modern software and the speed with which new versions must be released to market, almost no software is free from vulnerabilities.

Zero-Day Vulnerabilities and Exploits

Most software vulnerabilities are discovered by software and security researchers, who notify the vendor to give them time to patch the vulnerability before releasing details to the wider public. A vulnerability that is exploited before the developer knows about it or can release a patch is called a **zero-day**. These can be extremely destructive, as it can take the vendor a lot of time to develop a patch, leaving systems vulnerable for days, weeks, or even years.

 The term zero-day is usually applied to the vulnerability itself but can also refer to an attack or malware that exploits it.

Unpatched and Legacy Systems

While an exploit for a zero-day vulnerability can be extremely destructive, they are relatively rare events. A greater threat is the large number of unpatched or legacy systems in use. An unpatched system is one that its owner has not updated with

OS and application patches; a legacy system is one where the software vendor no longer provides support or fixes for problems.

 This issue does not just affect PCs. Network appliances can also be vulnerable to exploits. The risks to embedded systems have become more obvious over the last few years, and the risks posed by unpatched mobile devices and the Internet of Things is likely to grow.

Vulnerability Assessment

A **vulnerability assessment** is an evaluation of a system's security and ability to meet compliance requirements based on the configuration state of the system. Essentially, the vulnerability assessment determines if the current configuration matches the ideal configuration (the baseline). Vulnerability assessments might involve manual inspection of security controls but are more often accomplished through automated vulnerability scanners.

Common Vulnerabilities and Exposures

Common Vulnerabilities and Exposures (CVE) is a dictionary of vulnerabilities in published operating systems and applications software (cve.mitre.org). Automated vulnerability scanning software makes use of this dictionary to develop tests to discover vulnerabilities on live systems. There are several elements that make up a vulnerability's entry in the CVE:

- An identifier in the format: CVE-YYYY-####, where YYYY is the year the vulnerability was discovered, and #### is at least four digits that indicate the order in which the vulnerability was discovered.

- A brief description of the vulnerability.

- A reference list of URLs that supply more information on the vulnerability.

- The date the vulnerability entry was created.

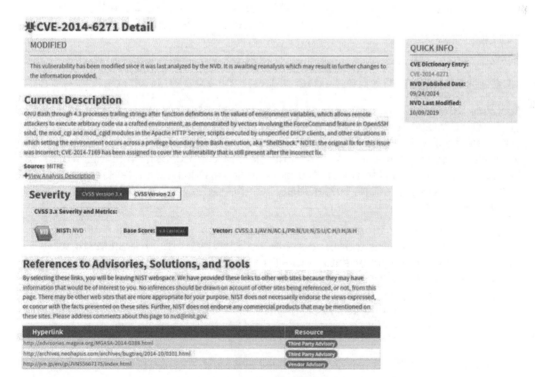

Example of a CVE.

Threat Types and Assessment

Exploits for vulnerabilities are either developed by threat actors or exposed by unintentional weaknesses in procedures. Threat assessment is the process of identifying threat sources and profiling the types and capabilities of threat actors.

External versus Internal Threats

An external threat actor or agent is one that has no account or authorized access to the target system. A malicious external threat must infiltrate the security system using malware and/or social engineering. Note that an external actor may perpetrate an attack remotely or on-premises (by breaking into the company's headquarters, for instance). It is the threat actor that is defined as external, rather than the attack method.

Conversely, an internal (or insider) threat actor is one that has been granted permissions on the system. This typically means an employee, but insider threat can also arise from contractors and business partners.

Threat Research

Threat research is a counterintelligence gathering effort in which security companies and researchers attempt to discover the tactics, techniques, and procedures (TTPs) of threat actors.

The outputs from the primary research undertaken by security solutions providers and academics can take three main forms:

- **Behavioral threat research**—narrative commentary describing examples of attacks and TTPs gathered through primary research sources.

- **Reputational threat intelligence**—lists of IP addresses and domains associated with malicious behavior, plus signatures of known file-based malware.

- **Threat data**—computer data that can correlate events observed on a customer's own networks and logs with known TTP and threat actor indicators.

Security Information and Event Management

Security Information and Event Management (SIEM) is a security control designed to integrate vulnerability and threat assessment efforts through automated collection, aggregation, and analysis of log data. The core function of a SIEM tool is to aggregate logs from multiple sources. In addition to logs from Windows and Linux-based hosts, this could include switches, routers, firewalls, intrusion detection sensors, vulnerability scanners, malware scanners, and databases.

The second critical function of SIEM (and the principal factor distinguishing it from basic log management) is that of correlation. This means that the SIEM software can link individual events or data points (observables) into a meaningful indicator of risk, or indicator of compromise (IOC). Correlation can then be used to drive an alerting system. Finally, SIEM can provide a long-term retention function and be used to demonstrate regulatory compliance.

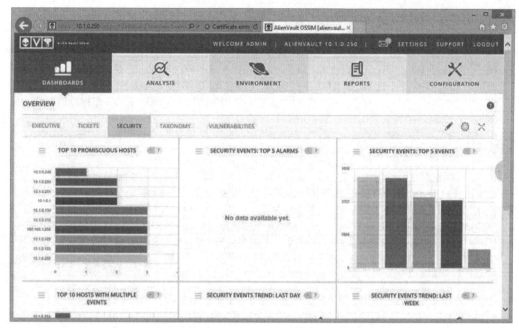

OSSIM SIEM dashboard. Configurable dashboards provide the high-level status view of network security metrics. (Screenshot used with permission from AT&T Cybersecurity.)

Penetration Testing

Where vulnerability testing uses mostly automated scanning tools and is a largely passive, or non-intrusive assessment activity, **penetration testing** aims to model how exposed the organization is to vulnerabilities that could be exploited by threat actors.

A penetration test—often shortened to pen test—uses authorized hacking techniques to discover exploitable weaknesses in the target's security systems. Pen testing is also referred to as ethical hacking.

The key difference from passive vulnerability scanning is that an attempt is made to actively test security controls and exploit any vulnerabilities discovered. Pen testing is an intrusive assessment technique. For example, a vulnerability scan may reveal that an SQL Server has not been patched to safeguard against a known exploit. A penetration test would attempt to use the exploit to perform code injection and compromise the server. This provides active testing of security controls. Even though the potential for the exploit exists, in practice the permissions on the server might prevent an attacker from using it. This would not be identified by a vulnerability scan but should be proven or not proven to be the case by penetration testing.

Privileged Access Management

A privileged account is one that can make significant configuration changes to a host, such as installing software or disabling a firewall or other security system. Privileged accounts also have rights to log on network appliances and application servers.

Privileged access management (PAM) refers to policies, procedures, and technical controls to prevent the malicious abuse of privileged accounts by internal threat actors and to mitigate risks from weak configuration control over privileges. These controls identify and document privileged accounts, giving visibility into their use, and manage the credentials used to access them.

Some other general principles of PAM include least privilege, role-based access, and zero trust:

- **Least privilege** means that a user is granted sufficient rights to perform his or her job and no more. This mitigates risk if the account should be compromised and fall under the control of a threat actor. Authorization creep refers to a situation where a user acquires more and more rights, either directly or by being added to security groups and roles. Least privilege should be ensured by closely analyzing business workflows to assess what privileges are required and by performing regular account audits.

- **Role-based access** means that a set of organizational roles are defined, and subjects allocated to those roles. Under this system, the right to modify roles is reserved to a system owner. Therefore, the system is nondiscretionary, as each subject account has no right to modify the ACL of a resource, even though they may be able to change the resource in other ways. Users are said to gain rights implicitly (through being assigned to a role) rather than explicitly (being assigned the right directly).

- **Zero trust** is based on the idea that perimeter security is unlikely to be completely robust. On a modern network, there are just too many opportunities for traffic to escape monitoring/filtering by perimeter devices. Zero trust uses systems such as continuous authentication and conditional access to mitigate privilege escalation and account compromise by threat actors. Another zero-trust technique is to apply microsegmentation. Microsegmentation is a security process that is capable of applying policies to a single node, as though it was in a zone of its own.

Vendor Assessment

High-profile breaches have led to a greater appreciation of the importance of the supply chain in vulnerability management. A product, or even a service, may have components created and maintained by a long chain of different companies. Each company in the chain depends on its suppliers or vendors performing due diligence on their vendors. A weak link in the chain could cause impacts on service availability and performance, or in the worst cases lead to data breaches.

Vendor management is a process for selecting supplier companies and evaluating the risks inherent in relying on a third-party product or service. When it comes to data and cybersecurity, you must understand that risks cannot be wholly transferred to the vendor. If a data storage vendor suffers a data breach, you may be able to claim costs from them, but your company will still be held liable in terms of legal penalties and damage to reputation. If your webstore suffers frequent outages because of failures at a hosting provider, it is your company's reputation that will suffer and your company that will lose orders because customers look elsewhere.

A vendor may supply documentation and certification to prove that it has implemented a security policy robustly. You might be able to see evidence of security capabilities, such as a history of effective vulnerability management and product support. Larger companies will usually ask vendors to complete a detailed audit process to ensure that they meet the required standards.

Review Activity:

Common Security Concepts

Answer the following questions:

1. **What type of assessment is most likely to measure security policies and controls against a standard framework?**

2. **True or false? An automated vulnerability scanner can be used to detect zero-days.**

3. **What type of assessment tool is configured with details of CVEs?**

4. **515web IT staff discovered an entry when reviewing their audit logs showing that a junior employee from the sales department had logged into the network at 3:00 a.m. Further review of the audit logs show that he had changed his timecard on the HR server. Which security factor was breached, and did the attack exploit a software vulnerability or a configuration vulnerability?**

5. **What type of security audit performs active testing of security controls?**

Topic 13B

Explain Authentication Methods

EXAM OBJECTIVES COVERED
1.5 Explain common ports and protocols, their application, and encrypted alternatives.
4.1 Explain common security concepts.

In this topic, you will identify network authentication methods. Strong authentication is the first line of defense to secure network resources. As a network professional, to effectively manage authentication on your network, you will need to understand these different systems and what each one can provide for your organization.

Authentication Methods and Access Controls

An access control system is the set of technical security controls that govern how subjects are permitted to interact with objects. Subjects in this sense are users, devices, or software processes, or anything else that can request and be granted access to a resource. Objects are the resources; these could be networks, servers, databases, files, and so on.

In computer security, the basis of access control is usually an **access control list (ACL)**. This is a list of subjects and the rights or permissions they have been granted on the object.

An **identity and access management (IAM)** system to mediate use of objects by subjects is usually described in terms of four main processes:

- **Identification**—Creating an account or ID that identifies the user, device, or process on the network.

- **Authentication**—Proving that a subject is who or what it claims to be when it attempts to access the resource.

- **Authorization**—Determining what rights subjects should have on each resource and enforcing those rights.

- **Accounting**—Tracking authorized usage of a resource or use of rights by a subject and alerting when unauthorized use is detected or attempted.

Multifactor and Two-Factor Authentication

An account defines a subject on the computer or network system. Assuming that an account has been created securely (the identity of the account holder has been verified), authentication verifies that only the account holder is able to use the account, and that the system may be used only by account holders. Authentication is performed when the account holder submits credentials to the system to request access. These are compared to the credentials stored on the system. If they match, the account is authenticated.

The type of data used to create a credential is called an authentication factor. Authentication factors fall into the following categories:

- **Knowledge factor**—something you know (such as a password).

- **Ownership factor**—something you have (such as a smart card).

- **Human or biometric factor**—something you are (such as a fingerprint).

- **Behavioral factor**—something you do (such as making a signature).

- **Location factor**—somewhere you are (such as using a mobile device with location services).

An authentication technology or mechanism is considered strong if it combines the use of more than one authentication data type (**multifactor**). Single-factor authentication systems can quite easily be compromised: a password could be written down or shared, or compromised by a social engineering attack, a smart card could be lost or stolen, and a biometric system could be subject to high error rates.

Two-factor authentication combines something like a smart card or biometric mechanism with a knowledge factor, such as a password or personal identity number (PIN). Three-factor authentication combines three of the possible technologies. An example of this would be a smart card with an integrated fingerprint reader. This means that to authenticate, the user must possess the card, the user's fingerprint must match the template stored on the card, and the user must input a PIN.

 Multifactor authentication requires a combination of different technologies. For example, requiring a PIN along with date of birth may be stronger than entering a PIN alone, but it is not multifactor.

Local Authentication and Single Sign-on

One of the most important features of an operating system is the authentication provider. The **local authentication** provider is the software architecture and code that underpins the mechanism by which the user is authenticated before starting a shell. This is usually described as a login (Linux) or a logon or sign-in (Microsoft). Knowledge-based authentication, using a password or PIN, is the default authentication provider for most operating systems.

Knowledge-based authentication relies on cryptographic **hashes**. A cryptographic hash is a function that converts any string to a unique, fixed-length code. The function should ensure that the code cannot be converted back into the plaintext string.

```
[s]tatus [p]ause [b]ypass [c]heckpoint [q]uit => s

Session..........: hashcat
Status...........: Running
Hash.Type........: NetNTLMv2
Hash.Target......: ADMINISTRATOR::515support:2f8cbd19fd1bfac9:881c5503...000000
Time.Started.....: Mon Jan  6 11:25:16 2020 (1 min, 38 secs)
Time.Estimated...: Sat Jan 11 07:49:57 2020 (4 days, 20 hours)
Guess.Mask.......: ?1?1?1?1?1?1?1?1 [8]
Guess.Charset....: -1 pPaAsSwWoOrRdD0123456789$, -2 Undefined, -3 Undefined, -4
Undefined
Guess.Queue......: 1/1 (100.00%)
Speed.#1.........:    364.1 kH/s (11.09ms) @ Accel:128 Loops:32 Thr:1 Vec:8
Recovered........: 0/1 (0.00%) Digests, 0/1 (0.00%) Salts
Progress.........: 34233472/152587890625 (0.02%)
Rejected.........: 0/34233472 (0.00%)
Restore.Point....: 2176/9765625 (0.02%)
Restore.Sub.#1...: Salt:0 Amplifier:1824-1856 Iteration:0-32
Candidates.#1....: $87r8678 -> dSDoRS12
```

Password credentials are stored as cryptographic hashes (such as the Hash.Target value shown in the screenshot) that cannot normally be converted back to plaintext strings. The hashcat utility attempts to recover passwords by matching hashes through dictionary or brute force methods.

A password is not usually transmitted or stored in a credential database as a plaintext because of the risk of compromise. Instead, the password is stored as a cryptographic hash. When a user enters a password to log in, an authenticator converts what is typed into a hash and transmits that to an authority. The authority compares the submitted hash to the one in the database and authenticates the subject only if they match.

Windows Authentication

Windows authentication involves a complex architecture of components (docs. microsoft.com/en-us/windows-server/security/windows-authentication/credentials-processes-in-windows-authentication), but the following three scenarios are typical:

- **Windows local sign-in**—the Local Security Authority (LSA) compares the submitted credential to a hash stored in the Security Accounts Manager (SAM) database, which is part of the registry. This is also referred to as interactive logon.

- **Windows network sign-in**—the LSA can pass the credentials for authentication to a network service. The preferred system for network authentication is based on Kerberos, but legacy network applications might use NT LAN Manager (NTLM) authentication.

- **Remote sign-in**—if the user's device is not connected to the local network, authentication can take place over some type of virtual private network (VPN) or web portal.

Linux Authentication

In Linux, local user account names are stored in /etc/passwd. When a user logs in to a local interactive shell, the password is checked against a hash stored in /etc/shadow. Interactive login over a network is typically accomplished using Secure Shell (SSH). With SSH, the user can be authenticated using cryptographic keys instead of a password.

A pluggable authentication module (PAM) is a package for enabling different authentication providers, such as smart card login (tecmint.com/configure-pam-in-centos-ubuntu-linux). The PAM framework can also be used to implement authentication to network servers.

Single Sign-On

A **single sign-on (SSO)** system allows the user to authenticate once to a local device and be authorized to access compatible application servers without having to enter credentials again. In Windows, SSO is provided by the Kerberos framework.

Kerberos

Kerberos provides SSO authentication to Active Directory®, as well as compatibility with other, non-Windows operating systems. Kerberos was named after the three-headed guard dog of Hades (Cerberus) because it consists of three parts. Clients request services from a server, which both rely on an intermediary—a Key Distribution Center (KDC)—to vouch for their identity.

There are two services that make up a KDC: the Authentication Service and the Ticket Granting Service.

The Authentication Service is responsible for authenticating user logon requests. More generally, users and services can be authenticated; these are collectively referred to as principals. For example, when you sit at a Windows domain workstation and log on to the domain (Kerberos documentation refers to realms rather than domains, which is Microsoft's terminology), the first step of logon is to authenticate with a KDC server (implemented as a domain controller).

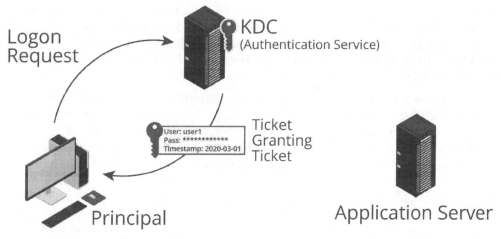

Logon Request

KDC
(Authentication Service)

User: user1
Pass: ************
Timestamp: 2020-03-01

Ticket Granting Ticket

Principal

Application Server

Kerberos Authentication Service. (Images © 123RF.com.)

When authenticated, the KDC server presents the user with a Ticket Granting Ticket. To access resources within the domain, the client requests a Service Ticket (a token that grants access to a target application server) by supplying the Ticket Granting Ticket to the Ticket Granting Service (TGS).

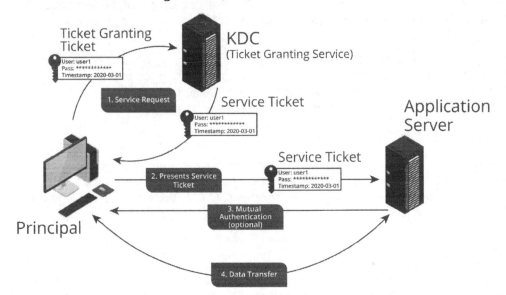

Kerberos Ticket Granting Service. (Images © 123RF.com.)

Digital Certificates and PKI

A protocol such as Kerberos can also be used with smart cards. A smart card is programmed with an encryption key pair and a **digital certificate**, issued by the authenticating domain. Digital certificates are also used to authenticate server machines when using Transport Layer Security (TLS). A certificate can be installed on a web server or email server to validate its identity and establish a secure transmission channel.

Digital certificates depend on the concept of public key cryptography. Public key cryptography, also referred to as asymmetric encryption, solves the problem of distributing encryption keys when you want to communicate securely with others, authenticate a message that you send to others, or authenticate yourself to an access control system. With asymmetric encryption, you generate a key pair. The private key in the pair remains a secret that only you know. The public key can be transmitted to other subjects. The private key cannot be derived from the public key. The key pair can be used in the following ways:

- When you want others to send you confidential messages, you give them your public key to use to encrypt the message. The message can then only be decrypted by your private key, which you keep known only to yourself. Due to the way asymmetric encryption works, the public key cannot be used to decrypt a message, even though it was used to encrypt it in the first place.

 As encryption using a public key is relatively slow; rather than encrypting the whole message using a public key, more typically, the public key is used to encrypt a symmetric encryption key for use in a single session and exchange it securely. The symmetric session key is then used to encrypt the actual message. A symmetric key can perform both encryption and decryption.

- When you want to authenticate yourself to others, you create a signature and sign it by encrypting the signature with your private key. You give others your public key to use to decrypt the signature. As only you know the private key, everyone can be assured that only you could have created the signature.

The basic problem with public key cryptography lies in proving the identity of the owner of a public key. The system is vulnerable to an on-path attack where a threat actor substitutes your public key for their own. **Public key infrastructure (PKI)** aims to prove that the owners of public keys are who they say they are. Under PKI, anyone issuing public keys should obtain a digital certificate. The validity of the certificate is guaranteed by a certificate authority (CA). A digital certificate is essentially a wrapper for a subject's (or end entity's) public key. As well as the public key, it contains information about the subject and the certificate's issuer or guarantor. The certificate is digitally signed to prove that it was issued to the subject by a particular CA.

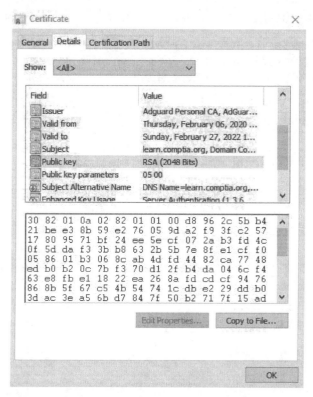

Digital certificate details. (Screenshot used with permission from Microsoft.)

Extensible Authentication Protocol and IEEE 802.1X

Smart-card authentication is used for Kerberos authentication where the computer is attached to the local network and the user is logging on to Windows. This type of multifactor authentication may also be required in other contexts:

- When the user is accessing a wireless network and needs to authenticate with the network database.

- When a device is connecting to a network via a switch and network policies require the user to be authenticated before the device is allowed to communicate.

- When the user is connecting to the network over a public network via a virtual private network (VPN).

In these scenarios, the **Extensible Authentication Protocol (EAP)** provides a framework for deploying multiple types of authentication protocols and technologies. EAP allows lots of different authentication methods, but many of them use a digital certificate on the server and/or client machines. These certificates allow the machines to establish a trust relationship and create a secure tunnel to transmit the user credential or to perform smart card authentication without a user password.

Where EAP implements a particular authentication factor and mechanism, the **IEEE 802.1X Port-based Network Access Control (NAC)** protocol provides the means of using an EAP method when a device connects to an Ethernet switch port, wireless access point, or VPN gateway. 802.1X uses authentication, authorization, and accounting (AAA) architecture. AAA uses the following components:

- **Supplicant**—the device requesting access, such as a user's PC or laptop.

- **Network access server (NAS) or network access point (NAP)**—edge network appliances, such as switches, access points, and VPN gateways. These are also referred to as AAA clients or authenticators.

- **AAA server**—the authentication server, positioned within the local network. There are two main types of AAA server: RADIUS and TACACS+.

With AAA, the NAS devices do not have to store any authentication credentials. They forward this data between the AAA server and the supplicant.

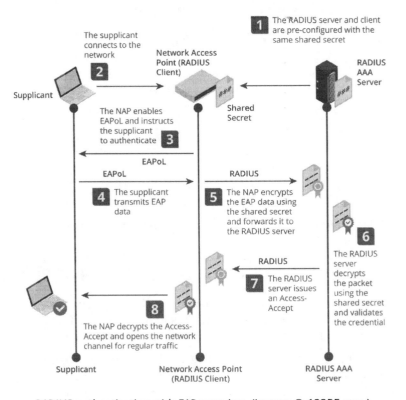

RADIUS authentication with EAP overview. (Images © 123RF.com.)

RADIUS and TACACS+

Remote Authentication Dial-in User Service (RADIUS) is very widely used for client device access over switches, wireless networks, and VPNs. There are several RADIUS server and client products. Microsoft has the Network Policy Server (NPS) for Windows platforms, and there are open-source implementations for UNIX and Linux, such as FreeRADIUS, as well as third-party commercial products, such as Cisco's Secure Access Control Server, OSC Radiator, and Juniper Networks Steel-Belted RADIUS.

RADIUS typically uses UDP ports 1812 and 1813. Each RADIUS client must be configured with the IP address of the RADIUS server plus the same shared secret.

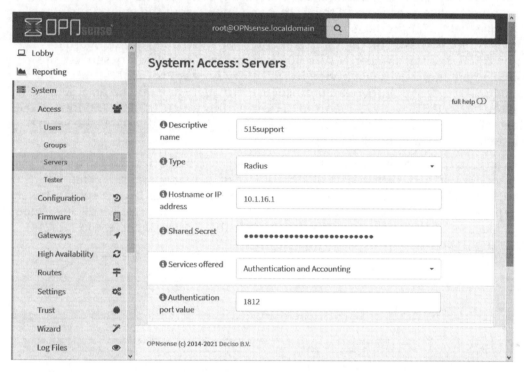

Configuring an OPNSense security appliance as a RADIUS client. The OPNSense appliance is working as a virtual private network (VPN) access server. It uses the RADIUS server at 10.1.16.1 to authenticate VPN users. The client must be configured with the same shared secret as the server. (Screenshot used with permission from OPNSense.)

Terminal Access Controller Access Control System (TACACS+) is a similar protocol to RADIUS but designed to be more flexible and reliable. TACACS+ was developed by Cisco but is also supported on many of the other third-party and open-source RADIUS server implementations. Where RADIUS is often used for network access control over end user devices, TACACS+ is often used in authenticating administrative access to routers and switches. It uses TCP over port 49 and the reliable delivery offered by TCP makes it easier to detect when a server is down.

Also, authentication, authorization, and accounting functions are discrete. Many device management tasks require reauthentication (similar to having to reenter a password for sudo or UAC) and per-command authorizations and privileges for users, groups, and roles. TACACS+ supports this workflow better than RADIUS.

Lightweight Directory Access Protocol

Directory services are the principal means of providing privilege management and authorization on an enterprise network.

When an authenticated user logs on to the network, the server security service generates an access key for the user. This contains the username and group memberships of the authenticated user. Whenever the user attempts to access a resource, his or her access key is provided as identification. The server's security service matches username and group memberships from the access key with entries in the access list, and from this, it calculates the user's access privileges.

All this information is stored in a directory. A directory is like a database, where an object is like a record, and things that you know about the object (attributes) are like fields. For products from different vendors to be interoperable, most directories are based on the same standard. The main directory standard is the X.500 series of standards. As X.500 is complex, most directory services are implementations of the **Lightweight Directory Access Protocol (LDAP)**. LDAP is not a directory standard, but a protocol used to query and update an X.500-like directory. LDAP is widely supported in current directory products (Windows Active Directory®, NetIQ eDirectory, or the open source OpenLDAP). LDAP messaging uses TCP and UDP port 389 by default.

In an X.500, each object has a unique identifier called a distinguished name. A distinguished name is made up of attribute=value pairs, separated by commas. The most specific attribute is listed first, and successive attributes become progressively broader. This most specific attribute is also referred to as the relative distinguished name, as it uniquely identifies the object within the context of successive (parent) attribute values.

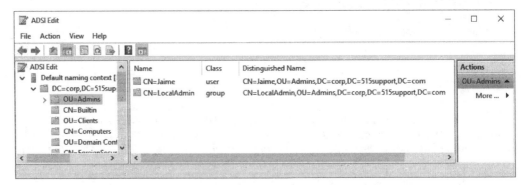

Browsing objects in an Active Directory LDAP schema. (Screenshot used with permission from Microsoft.)

The types of attributes, what information they contain, and the way object types are defined through attributes (some of which may be required and some optional) is described by the directory schema. For example, the distinguished name of a web server operated by Widget in London might be:

```
CN=WIDGETWEB, OU=Marketing, O=Widget, L=London,
ST=London, C=UK, DC=widget, DC=example
```

LDAP Secure

Like many TCP/IP protocols, LDAP provides no security, and all transmissions are in plaintext, making it vulnerable to sniffing and spoofing attacks. Also, a server that does not require clients to authenticate is vulnerable to overloading by denial of service attacks. Authentication, referred to as binding to the server, can be implemented in the following ways:

- **No authentication**—Anonymous access is granted to the directory.

- **Simple bind**—the client must supply its distinguished name (DN) and password, but these are passed as plaintext.

- **Simple Authentication and Security Layer (SASL)**—the client and server negotiate the use of a supported authentication mechanism, such as Kerberos. The STARTTLS command can be used to require encryption (sealing) and message integrity (signing). This is the preferred mechanism for Microsoft's Active Directory (AD) implementation of LDAP.

- **LDAP Secure (LDAPS)**—the server is installed with a digital certificate, which it uses to set up a secure tunnel for the user credential exchange. LDAPS uses port 636.

If secure access is required, anonymous and simple authentication access methods should be disabled on the server.

Generally, two levels of access will need to be granted on the directory: read-only access (query) and read/write access (update). This is implemented using an access control policy, but the precise mechanism is vendor-specific and not specified by the LDAP standards documentation.

Unless it is hosting a public service, the LDAP directory server should also only be accessible from the private network. This means that LDAP ports (389 over TCP and UDP) should be blocked by a firewall from access over the public interface.

Review Activity:

Authentication Methods

Answer the following questions:

1. **What element is missing from the following list, and what is its purpose?**
   - **Identification**
   - **Authentification**
   - **Accounting**

2. **What is the purpose of SSO?**

3. **True or false? A subject's private key is embedded in the digital certificate that represents its digital identity?**

4. **What is a RADIUS client, and how should it be configured?**

5. **Where would EAPoL be configured?**

Lesson 13

Summary

You should be able to explain common security concepts relating to threats, vulnerabilities, risk, and authentication.

Guidelines for Supporting Common Security Concepts

Follow these guidelines to support security assessments and authentication technologies:

- Establish security policies and deploy security controls that address the CIA triad.

- Deploy assessment and monitoring processes and tools to evaluate vulnerabilities, threats, and risk:

  - Overall risk and posture assessment for mission essential functions (MEF) to produce business impact analysis, business continuity plans, and security policies, such as privileged access management and vendor assessment.

  - Vulnerability assessment to analyze systems for misconfigurations and missing patches.

  - Threat assessment to develop awareness of tactics, techniques, and procedures (TTPs) and obtain threat data feeds for automated detection via SIEM.

- Consider the need to perform or commission penetration testing to gain a more informed perspective on the effectiveness of security controls.

- Deploy a directory server as a database of network users and resources.

- To implement EAP/AAA, deploy a RADIUS or TACACS+ server to the internal network with a static IP address, shared secret, and accepted authentication methods. Configure network access devices (AAA clients) with the IP of the server and same shared secret.

Lesson 14

Supporting and Troubleshooting Secure Networks

LESSON INTRODUCTION

Each day, the number and complexity of threats against systems integrity and data security increases. In response, there are more and more security controls available to automate the detection and prevention of these threats. Because you are a networking professional, your organization and users will be looking to you to deploy these security appliances, without compromising network availability and performance.

Lesson Objectives

In this lesson, you will:

- Compare and contrast security appliances.

- Troubleshoot service and security issues.

Topic 14A

Compare and Contrast Security Appliances

EXAM OBJECTIVES COVERED
1.4 Given a scenario, configure a subnet and use appropriate IP addressing schemes.
2.1 Compare and contrast various devices, their features, and their appropriate placement on the network.
4.1 Explain common security concepts.

Security appliances such as firewalls, proxy servers, and intrusion detection/ prevention systems enforce access controls to ensure authorized use of the network. They perform a filtering function to analyze the properties of connection requests and then allow, deny, and/or log them as appropriate. While you may not be installing and configuring these devices at this stage in your career, it is important that you understand their use on the network.

Network Segmentation Enforcement

Effective placement of security appliances depends on segmenting the network into clearly defined areas. At layers two and three, **network segmentation enforcement** is applied using a combination of virtual LANs and subnets. Each segment is a separate broadcast domain. Any traffic between segments must be routed. In security terms, the main unit of a logically segmented network is a zone. A zone is an area of the network where the security configuration is the same for all hosts within it. Network traffic between zones should be strictly controlled using a security device—typically a firewall.

These zones would typically be configured to protect the integrity and confidentiality of different asset groups within the organization. For example, servers storing financial records can be their own VLAN, and marketing servers could be another VLAN. If something like a remote access Trojan were introduced in one VLAN, it should not be able to spread to other VLANs without also being able to pass through the firewall protecting each zone.

One important distinction between different security zones is whether a host is Internet-facing. An Internet-facing host accepts inbound connections from the Internet. Internet-facing hosts are placed in the perimeter network zone. The basic principle of a perimeter network zone is that traffic cannot pass through it directly. A perimeter network enables external clients to access data on private systems, such as web servers, without compromising the security of the internal network.

If communication is required between hosts on either side of the perimeter network, a host within it can be configured to act as a proxy. For example, if a host on the local network requests a connection with a web server on the Internet, a proxy in the network perimeter takes the request and checks it. If the request is valid, it retransmits it to the destination. External hosts have no idea about what (if anything) is behind the perimeter.

Servers that provide public access services should be placed in a perimeter network. These would typically include web servers, mail and other communications servers, proxy servers, and remote access servers. The hosts in the perimeter are not fully trusted by the internal network because of the possibility that they could be compromised from the Internet. They are referred to as bastion hosts.

Screened Subnets

To configure a perimeter network, two different security configurations must be enabled: one on the external interface and one on the internal interface.

A **screened subnet** uses two firewalls placed on either side of the perimeter network zone. The edge firewall restricts traffic on the external/public interface and allows permitted traffic to the hosts in the perimeter zone subnet. The edge firewall can be referred to as the screening firewall or router. The internal firewall filters communications between hosts in the perimeter and hosts on the LAN. This firewall is often described as the choke firewall. A choke point is a purposefully narrow gateway that facilitates better access control and easier monitoring.

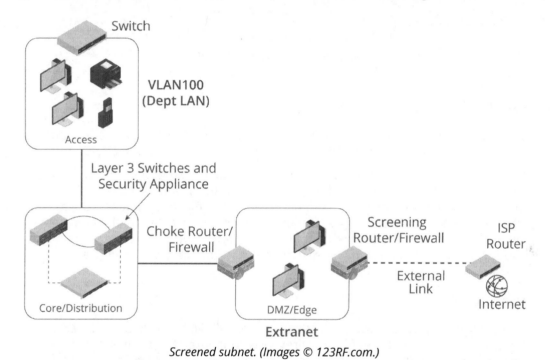

Screened subnet. (Images © 123RF.com.)

 The screened subnet topology was formerly referred to as a demilitarized zone (DMZ). The DMZ terminology is now deprecated.

A perimeter network can also be established using one router/firewall appliance with three network interfaces, referred to as triple homed. One interface is the public one, another is the perimeter subnet, and the third connects to the LAN. Routing and filtering rules determine what forwarding is allowed between these interfaces. This can achieve the same sort of configuration as a screened subnet.

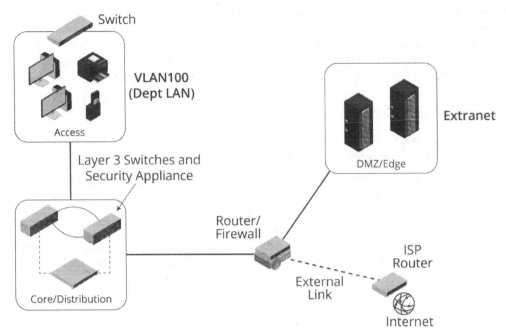

Triple-homed firewall. (Images © 123RF.com.)

Firewall Uses and Types

The basic function of a **firewall** is traffic filtering. The firewall processes traffic according to rules; traffic that does not conform to a rule that allows it access is blocked.

There are many types of firewalls and many ways of implementing a firewall. One distinction can be made between firewalls that protect a whole network (one that is placed inline in the network and inspects all traffic that passes through) and firewalls that protect a single host only (one that is installed on the host and inspects only that traffic addressed to that host). A further distinction can be made about what parts of a packet a particular firewall technology can inspect and operate on.

Packet Filtering Firewalls

Packet filtering describes the earliest type of firewall. All firewalls can still perform this basic function. A packet filtering firewall is configured by specifying rules in a network access control list (ACL). Each rule defines a specific type of data packet and the appropriate action to take when a packet matches the rule. An action can be either to deny (block or drop the packet, and optionally log an event) or to accept (let the packet pass through the firewall). A packet filtering firewall works at Layer 3 of the OSI model to inspect the headers of IP packets. This means that rules can be based on the information found in those headers:

- **IP filtering**—Accepting or denying traffic based on its source and/or destination IP address.

- Protocol ID/type (TCP, UDP, ICMP, routing protocols, and so on).

- **Port filtering/security**—Accepting or denying a packet based on source and destination port numbers (TCP or UDP application type).

Port numbers are contained in TCP or UDP headers (layer 4), rather than the IP datagram header, but packet filtering firewalls are still almost always described as working at layer 3. They can inspect only port numbers and not any other layer 4 header information.

ACLs might be designed to control only inbound traffic or both inbound and outbound traffic. This is also often referred to as "ingress" and "egress" traffic or filtering. Controlling outbound traffic is useful because it can block applications that have not been authorized to run on the network and defeat malware, such as backdoors. Ingress and egress traffic is filtered using separate ACLs.

A packet filtering firewall is stateless. This means that it does not preserve information about the connection between two hosts. Each packet is analyzed independently with no record of previously processed packets. This type of filtering requires the least processing effort, but it can be vulnerable to attacks that are spread over a sequence of packets. A stateless firewall can also introduce problems in traffic flow, especially when some sort of load balancing is being used or when clients or servers need to make use of dynamically assigned ports.

Stateful Inspection Firewalls

A circuit-level stateful inspection firewall addresses these problems by maintaining stateful information about the session established between two hosts (including malicious attempts to start a bogus session). Information about each session is stored in a dynamically updated state table. A stateful firewall operates at Layer 5 (Session) of the OSI model. When a packet arrives, the firewall checks it to confirm whether it belongs to an existing connection. If it does not, it applies the ordinary packet filtering rules to determine whether to allow it. Once the connection has been allowed, the firewall allows traffic to pass unmonitored, in order to conserve processing effort.

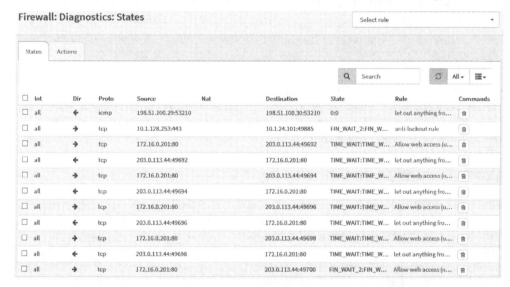

State table in the OPNsense firewall appliance. (Screenshot used with permission from OPNsense.)

Firewall Selection and Placement

You should consider how a firewall is implemented (as hardware or software, for instance) to cover a given placement or use on the network. Some types of firewalls are better suited for placement at network or segment borders; others are designed to protect individual hosts. The selection of a network firewall model will largely depend on the volume of traffic it has to process. A single firewall can represent a network bottleneck if it is not able to handle the required traffic volume.

An appliance firewall is a stand-alone hardware firewall that performs only the function of a firewall. The functions of the firewall are implemented on the appliance firmware. This is also a type of network-based firewall and monitors all traffic passing into and out of a network segment. This type of appliance could be implemented with routed interfaces or as a layer 2/virtual wire "transparent" firewall.

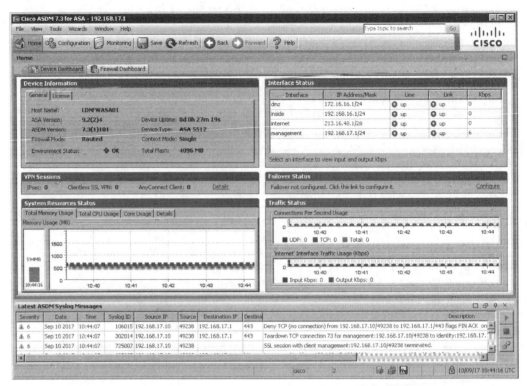

Cisco ASA (Adaptive Security Appliance) ASDM (Adaptive Security Device Manager) interface.
(Image © and Courtesy of Cisco Systems, Inc. Unauthorized use not permitted.)

A router firewall is similar, except that the functionality is built into the router firmware. Most SOHO Internet router/modems have this type of firewall functionality, though they are typically limited to supporting a single subnet within the home network. An enterprise-class router firewall would be able to support far more sessions than a SOHO one. Additionally, some Layer 3 switches can perform packet filtering.

Proxy Servers

The basic function of a network firewall is to inspect packets and determine whether to block them or allow them to pass. By contrast, a **proxy server** forwards requests and responses on behalf of its clients. Rather than inspecting traffic as it passes through, the proxy deconstructs each packet, performs analysis, then rebuilds the packet and forwards it on, providing it conforms to the rules. This type of device is placed in a perimeter network.

Forward Proxies

A forwarding proxy server provides for protocol-specific outbound traffic. For example, you might deploy a web proxy that enables client hosts to connect to websites and secure websites on the Internet. A proxy server must understand the application it is servicing. A web proxy must be able to parse and modify HTTP and HTTPS commands (and potentially HTML, too). Some proxy servers are application-specific; others are multipurpose. A multipurpose proxy is one configured with filters for multiple protocol types, such as HTTP, FTP, and SMTP.

The main benefit of a proxy server is that clients connect to a specified point within the perimeter network for web access. This provides for a degree of traffic management and security. In addition, most web proxy servers provide caching engines, whereby frequently requested web pages are retained on the proxy, negating the need to refetch those pages for subsequent requests.

Proxy servers can generally be classed as non-transparent or transparent. A nontransparent server means that the client must be configured with the proxy server address and port number to use it. The port on which the proxy server accepts client connections is often configured as port 8080. A transparent (or "forced" or "intercepting") proxy intercepts client traffic without the client having to be reconfigured. A transparent proxy must be implemented on a switch or router or other inline network appliance.

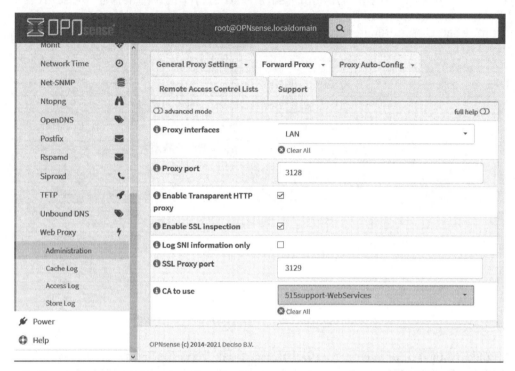

Configuring transparent proxy settings for the proxy server running on the OPNsense security appliance. (Screenshot used with permission from OPNsense.)

Reverse Proxies

A reverse proxy server provides for protocol-specific inbound traffic. For security purposes, it is inadvisable to place application servers, such as messaging and VoIP servers, in the perimeter network, where they are directly exposed to the Internet. Instead, you can deploy a reverse proxy and configure it to listen for client requests from a public network (the Internet) and create the appropriate request to the internal server on the corporate network.

Reverse proxies can publish applications from the corporate network to the Internet in this way. In addition, some reverse proxy servers can handle the encryption/decryption and authentication issues that arise when remote users attempt to connect to corporate servers, reducing the overhead on those servers. Typical applications for reverse proxy servers include publishing a web server, publishing messaging or conferencing applications, and enabling POP/IMAP mail retrieval.

Network Address Translation

Network Address Translation (NAT) was devised as a way of freeing up scarce IP addresses for hosts needing Internet access. NAT is a service translating between a private (or local) addressing scheme used by hosts on the LAN and a public (or global) addressing scheme used by an Internet-facing device. NAT is configured on a border device, such as a router, proxy server, or firewall. NAT is not a security mechanism; security is provided by the router/firewall's ACL.

In a basic NAT static configuration, a simple 1:1 mapping is made between the private (inside local) network address and the public (inside global) address. If the destination network is using NAT, it is described as having outside global and outside local addressing schemes.

Basic NAT is useful in scenarios where an inbound connection to a host must be supported. For example, you might position a web server behind a firewall running NAT. The firewall performs 1:1 address translation on the web server's IP address. This means that external hosts do not know the true IP address of the web server, but they can communicate with it successfully.

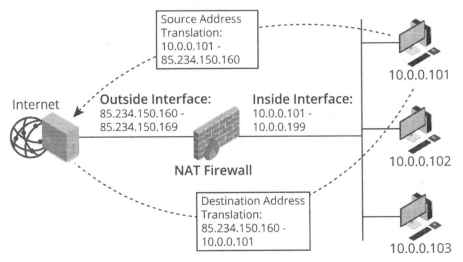

Network Address Translation (NAT). (Images © 123RF.com.)

A single static mapping is not very useful in most scenarios. Under dynamic NAT, the NAT device exposes a pool of public IP addresses. To support inbound and outbound connections between the private network and the Internet, the NAT service builds a table of public to private address mappings. Each new session creates a new public-private address binding in the table. When the session is ended or times out, the binding is released for use by another host.

Defining NAT rules in Cisco Adaptive Security Appliance (ASA). (Screenshot used with permission from Cisco.)

Port Address Translation

Basic NAT supports multiple simultaneous connections but is still limited by the number of available public IP addresses. Smaller companies may only be allocated a single or small block of addresses by their ISPs. In such cases, a means for multiple private IP addresses to be mapped onto a single public address would be useful. This function is provided by **Port Address Translation (PAT)**. This can be referred to as Network Address Port Translation (NAPT) or NAT overloading or one-to-many NAT.

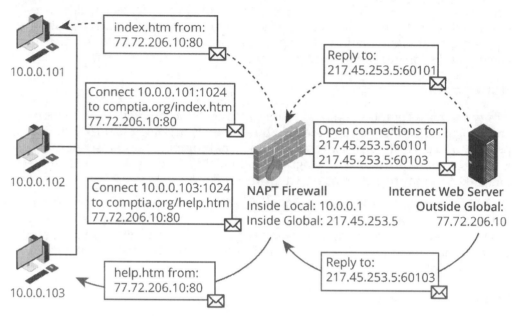

Port Address Translation (PAT). (Images ©123RF.com.)

PAT works by allocating each new connection an ephemeral TCP or UDP port. For example, say two hosts (10.0.0.101 and 10.0.0.102) initiate a web connection at the same time. The PAT service creates two new port mappings for these requests (10.0.0.101:61101 and 10.0.0.102:61102) in its state table. It then substitutes the private IP for the public IP and forwards the requests to the public Internet. It performs a reverse mapping on any traffic returned using those ports, inserting the original IP address and port number, and forwarding the packets to the internal hosts.

Defense in Depth

Firewalls, screened subnets, and proxy servers try to establish a secure barrier at the network edge. This is referred to as perimeter security. The proliferation of mobile devices with wireless or cellular data access and cloud services, plus the better recognition of insider threat and vulnerabilities to malware, has eroded confidence in a solely perimeter-based security model. Network security design must address the concept of **defense in depth**. This refers to placing security controls throughout the network, so that all access attempts are authenticated, authorized, and audited. Some examples of security controls that provide defense in depth additional to network segmentation and screened subnets include Network Access Control, honeypots, separation of duties, and intrusion detection.

Network Access Control

Network Access Control (NAC) is a system for authenticating endpoints at the point they connect to the network. NAC uses 802.1X port security mechanisms, EAP, and AAA model of supplicants, network access device AAA clients, and AAA servers. NAC enables devices to be authenticated when they connect to switch ports, wireless networks, or virtual private network (VPN) remote access servers.

Basic NAC solutions can authenticate a client on the basis of machine certificates and/or user passwords. More sophisticated solutions can enforce a health policy. A health policy means that the client must submit an attestation report. This secure report proves that the client is running an authorized OS and has up-to-date patches and security scanner configuration.

Honeypots

A **honeypot** is a computer system set up to attract attackers, with the intention of analyzing attack strategies and tools, to provide early warning of attack attempts, or possibly as a decoy to divert attention from actual computer systems. Another use is to detect internal fraud, snooping, and malpractice. A honeynet is an entire decoy network. This may be set up as an actual network or simulated using an emulator.

On a production network, a honeypot is more likely to be located in a protected but untrusted area between the Internet and the private network or on a closely monitored and filtered segment within the private network itself. This provides early warning and evidence of whether a threat actor has been able to penetrate to a given security zone.

Separation of Duties

Separation of duties is a means of establishing checks and balances against the possibility that critical systems or procedures can be compromised by insider threats. Duties and responsibilities should be divided among individuals to prevent ethical conflicts or abuse of powers.

Intrusion Detection and Prevention Systems

An **intrusion detection system (IDS)** performs real-time analysis of either network traffic or system and application logs. Where a firewall applies rules from an ACL, an IDS is configured with signature patterns. Each pattern represents a known type of malicious activity. If a pattern is matched in a traffic stream, the IDS raises an alert. Like antivirus software, the IDS must be kept up to date with the latest signature patterns. An IDS is often also configured with automated threat data, such as lists of IP addresses and domains that are associated with threat actors.

Like a packet analyzer, an IDS must be configured with a sniffer to read frames from a mirrored port or TAP. Placement of the sniffer must be carefully considered to meet security goals. Typically, an IDS is positioned behind a firewall. The aim is to detect suspicious traffic that the firewall has not blocked, providing defense in depth. This type of passive sensor does not slow down traffic and is undetectable by the attacker (it does not have an IP address on the monitored network segment).

Configuration file for the Snort IDS.

Compared to the passive logging/alerting functionality of an IDS, an **intrusion prevention system (IPS)** can provide an active response to any network threats that it matches. One typical preventive measure is to end the session by sending a TCP reset packet to the attacking host. Another option is for the sensor to apply a temporary filter on the firewall to block the attacker's IP address (shunning). Other advanced measures include throttling bandwidth to attacking hosts, applying complex firewall filters, and even modifying suspect packets to render them harmless. Finally, the appliance may be able to run a script or third-party program to perform some other action not supported by the IPS software itself.

IPS functionality is now very commonly built into firewall appliances and proxy servers. An IPS-enable firewall is inline with the network, meaning that all traffic passes through it (also making them a single point-of-failure if there is no fault tolerance mechanism). This obviously means that they need to be able to cope with high bandwidths and process each packet very quickly to avoid slowing down the network.

 Network IDS/IPS can be combined with host-based IDS/IPS. These run as agents on end systems to monitor application processes, data files, and log files for suspicious activity. Advanced IDS/IPS suites analyze information from multiple sensors to identify suspicious traffic flows and host activity.

Review Activity:

Security Appliances

Answer the following questions:

1. What type of security configuration uses edge and choke firewalls?

2. What parameters in packet headers can a layer 3 firewall ruleset use?

3. Why would you deploy a reverse proxy?

4. What type of security control uses an attestation report?

5. How does placement of an IDS sensor assist with a defense in depth policy?

Topic 14B

Troubleshoot Service and Security Issues

EXAM OBJECTIVES COVERED
5.5 Given a scenario, troubleshoot general networking issues.

Issues at the application or services layer can be the most complex to diagnose and troubleshoot. Both complex configuration options and security issues can be factors in service-related problems. In this topic, you will work through some common scenarios to identify typical symptoms and causes of problems with network security and services.

DHCP Issues

The Dynamic Host Configuration Protocol (DHCP) provides IP addressing autoconfiguration to hosts without static IP parameters. If a Windows client fails to obtain a DHCP lease, it defaults to using an address in the Automatic Private IP Addressing (APIPA) range of 169.254.0.0/16. It will be limited to communication with other APIPA hosts on the same network segment (broadcast domain). Linux hosts will use the 169.254.0.0/16 range if they have Zeroconf support, leave the IP address set to 0.0.0.0, or disable IPv4 on the interface.

APIPA is Microsoft terminology. Standards documentation refers to this address range as IPv4 Link-local (IPV4LL).

DHCP Server and Scope Exhaustion Issues

Possible reasons for a client to fail to obtain a lease include:

- The DHCP server is offline. If your DHCP servers go offline, users will continue to connect to the network for a period and thereafter start to lose contact with network services and servers as they come to try to renew a lease.

- No more addresses available (DHCP scope exhaustion). Create a new scope with enough addresses or reduce the lease period. Remember that IP Address Management (IPAM) software suites can be used to track address usage across a complex DHCP infrastructure.

- The router between the client and DHCP server doesn't support BOOTP forwarding. Either install RFC 1542-compliant routers or add another type of DHCP relay agent to each subnet or VLAN.

If you reconfigure your DHCP servers and their scopes, the clients will gradually get reconfigured. You will need to ensure that you plan for the fact that not all clients' IP configurations will be updated when the server scopes are edited and could be left with an expired IP, default gateway, or DNS server address. You could do this by lowering the lease duration in advance of changes, forcing all clients to renew, or running parallel settings for a period.

Rogue DHCP Server Issues

Clients have no means of preferring a DHCP server. If two DHCP servers are running on the same subnet, clients could end up with an incorrect IP configuration because they have obtained a lease from a rogue server. A rogue DHCP server may be deployed accidentally (forgetting to disable a DHCP server in an access point or router, for instance) or may be used by a malicious attacker to subvert the network. An attacker would normally use a rogue server to change the default gateway and/ or DNS resolver addresses for the subnet and route communications via his or her machine (an on-path attack).

Name Resolution Issues

When you perform a successful connectivity test by IP address, the next step may be to try pinging by name, thus testing name resolution.

Name Resolution Methods

To troubleshoot name resolution, you should establish exactly how the process works on that specific host. A host can use a variety of methods to resolve a name or FQDN to an IP address. In very general terms, these will be as follows:

1. Check local cache. One complication here is that there are different types of cache and separate caches for individual applications, such as web browsers. On Windows, you can use `ipconfig /displaydns` and `ipconfig / flushdns` to monitor and clear the system cache.

2. Check HOSTS. The HOSTS file is a static list of host name to IP address mappings. The default location under Windows is `%SystemRoot%\ system32\drivers\etc\`, while under Linux it is usually placed in the `/etc` directory. In most cases, HOSTS should not contain any entries (other than the loopback address). Any static entries in HOSTS could be the cause of a name resolution issue. The file can also be used for troubleshooting.

3. Query DNS. A host uses the name servers defined in its IP configuration to resolve queries.

 Any text preceded by the # symbol in a HOSTS file is a comment and will not be processed.

 While we are focusing on name resolution via DNS here, note that a host can use multiple methods, especially on Windows workgroup networks. Link Local Multicast Name Resolution (LLMNR) and multicastDNS (mDNS) are modified forms of DNS that allow clients to perform name resolution on a local link without needing a server.

DNS Configuration Issues

Linux and Windows systems usually rely on DNS server infrastructure for name resolution and service discovery. In the absence of DNS servers, network client machines will be unable to log on or connect to services or servers.

If your hosts are experiencing DNS issues, symptoms will include the inability to connect to a server by name, despite it being accessible by IP address. To verify a name resolution problem, edit the HOSTS file and place the correct name and IP address record in the file for the test host. When you ping, if that is successful, it suggests a name resolution problem.

If a single client is unable to resolve names, the issue is likely to lie with the client configuration.

- The client has been configured either with no DNS server address or the wrong DNS server address. Reconfigure the DNS server address.

- The client has the incorrect DNS suffix. Verify the DNS domain in which the client is supposed to be and verify the host's configuration matches.

Bear in mind that in both of these situations, DHCP might be configuring these settings incorrectly. Therefore, check the server options or scope options configuration on the DHCP server as well.

If multiple clients are affected, the issue is likely to lie with the server service (or the way a subnet accesses the server service). Check that the server configured as a DNS resolver is online and available (that you can ping the server from the client).

If some DNS queries work from the client and others don't, then the problem is more complex. Use the `nslookup` or `dig` utilities to check what records are returned by the resolver. If trying to connect to an Internet resource, compare these records to those returned by public resolvers (such as Google's servers at 8.8.8.8). Consider whether clients have cached a record that has been changed recently. Reconfiguration of DNS records should be planned and implemented carefully to avoid caching problems.

VLAN Assignment Issues

When you partition a network into separate VLANs, as each VLAN is a discrete broadcast domain, you must ensure that services, such as DHCP and DNS, are properly available to all VLANs. Otherwise, users will complain that "the Internet is down," when it transpires that there is no local DNS server available to handle their name resolution requests.

If devices are not in the same VLAN and must communicate, ensure that routing has been configured to enable VLAN-to-VLAN communications. You may also need to configure services such as DHCP relay to allow hosts to contact a DHCP server. Also, if a device is placed in a designated VLAN, its IP configuration must be appropriate in terms of IP address, subnet mask, default gateway, and DNS servers.

Another issue is that a host has been placed in an incorrect VLAN. Make sure all devices are placed into the appropriate VLAN as per the configuration baseline. VLAN assignments can be configured manually, and the administrator may have made a mistake, so check the interface configuration for switch port. VLAN assignments can also be configured automatically, using parameters such as the host MAC address or authentication credentials, and this process may have failed, or the database used to map the dynamic data to a VLAN ID might be misconfigured.

Unresponsive Service and Network Performance Issues

If you can rule out connectivity problems with a local client or subnet, the issue may be with an application server, rather than the client. Such unresponsive service issues will usually manifest with multiple clients being unable to connect. There can be any number of underlying causes, but consider some of the following:

- The application or OS hosting the service has crashed (or there is a hardware or power problem).

- The server hosting the service is overloaded (high CPU/memory/disk I/O utilization/disk space utilization). Try throttling client connections until the server resources can be upgraded.

- There is congestion in the network, either at the client or server end (or both). Use ping or traceroute to check the latency experienced over the link and compare to a network performance baseline. Again, throttling connections or bandwidth may help to ease the congestion until higher bandwidth links can be provisioned.

- A broadcast storm is causing loss of network bandwidth. Switching loops cause broadcast and unknown unicast frames to circulate the network perpetually, as each switch repeatedly floods each frame. A broadcast storm may quickly consume all link bandwidth and crash network appliances (check for excessive CPU utilization on switches and hosts). The Spanning Tree Protocol (STP) is supposed to prevent such loops, but this can fail if STP communications between switches do not work correctly, either because of a fault in cabling or a port/ transceiver or because of a misconfiguration.

- Network congestion may also be a sign that the service is being subject to a Denial of Service (DoS) attack. Look for unusual access patterns (for example, use GeoIP to graph source IP addresses by country and compare to baseline access patterns).

If users on a LAN cannot connect to an external service, such as a cloud application, you can use a site such as isitdownrightnow.com to test whether the issue is local to your network or a problem with the service provider site.

Be proactive in monitoring service availability so that you can resolve problems before they affect large numbers of clients.

Misconfigured Firewall and ACL Issues

One type of firewall, ACL, or content filter misconfiguration causes blocked services, ports, or addresses that are supposed to be allowed through. This will cause an application or protocol to fail to function correctly. For example, the firewall might be blocking TCP or UDP ports that are supposed to be open, or it might be allowing the ports but denying access to an IP network or host address that is supposed to be able to connect. Also consider that advanced firewalls are capable of applying additional filtering criteria, such as evaluating process/service executable names/ locations or authorizations based on user accounts or group memberships.

A deny type of error will usually be easy to identify, as users will report incidents connected with the failure of the data traffic. With such incidents, firewall configuration will always be a likely cause, so will be high on the list to investigate. Diagnosis can be confirmed by trying to establish the connection from both inside and outside the firewall. If it connects from outside the firewall but not from inside, this will confirm the firewall to be the cause of the issue.

Another potential issue is where there are both network-based and host-based firewall settings to navigate in the communication path. There could be a host firewall running on the client, on the server, or on both. To diagnose an issue with a host firewall, attempt the connection with the host firewall disabled. If the connection attempt succeeds, then the network firewall ACL is allowing the packets, but the host firewall is configured to block them. If the connection attempt fails, investigate the network firewall ACL first. You can also inspect the firewall's log files to discover what rules have been applied to block traffic at a particular time.

The other possible outcome of a badly configured firewall is that packets may be allowed through that should be blocked. This is a more serious outcome, because the result is to open the system to security vulnerabilities. It is also not necessarily so easily detected, as it does not typically cause anything to stop functioning. As no incidents usually arise from this outcome (except in the case that a vulnerability is exploited), it is not a scenario that is subject to troubleshooting. Rather, it underlines the need for regular firewall audits and thorough change control processes to deal with firewall change requests.

Untrusted Certificate Issues

If the digital certificate presented by a subject (server or user) is not trusted by the client application (such as a browser), the client will notify the user. The most common reason for a certificate not to be trusted is that the certificate issuer is not trusted. For example, say Widget's web server receives a certificate signed by MyCA. Unless MyCA's own certificate is stored in the browser's trusted root store, the client application will not trust the Widget server. The user can usually choose to ignore this warning and add an exception, but this should be done only if the cause of the lack of a trust relationship is understood.

If you trust the issuer, you can add their certificate to the client device's root certificate store. In Windows, you can use the certmgr.msc console to manage user certificates and the certlm.msc console to manage machine certificates. You also use these consoles to manage certificates used by the computer or its user accounts.

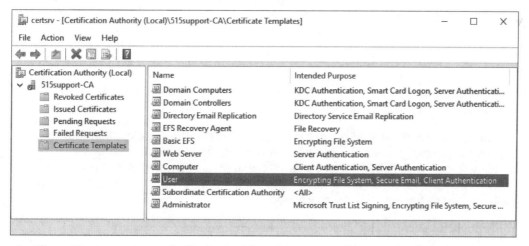

Certificate Management console. The Trusted Root CA contains all Microsoft and enterprise trusts, plus the third-party CA trusts. (Screenshot used with permission from Microsoft.)

One complication here is that different applications may have different stores of trusted certificates. For example, there is a Windows certificate store, but the Firefox® browser does not trust it by default and maintains its own certificate stores. The various Linux distributions store trusted root certificates in several different locations.

Frequently, certificates are untrusted because they are self-signed (the certificate holder is both the issuer and the subject of the certificate). This is often the case with the certificates used to protect the web management interfaces of consumer-grade appliances and server applications. You might be able to replace the default certificate with one trusted by the enterprise.

Some other causes of untrusted certificates are:

- The certificate's subject name does not match the URL. This is usually a configuration error on the part of the web server manager, but it could indicate malicious activity. You should confirm the certificate's common name and access the website by using that URL.

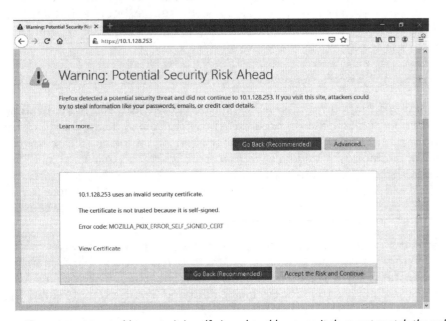

This certificate is not trusted because it is self-signed and because it does not match the subject name (because the host is being accessed via an IP address instead of an FQDN). (Screenshot courtesy of Mozilla Foundation.)

- The certificate is not being used for its stated purpose. For example, a certificate issued to sign email is being used on a web server. In this circumstance, you should not add an exception. The service owner or subject should obtain a correctly formatted certificate.

- The certificate is expired or revoked. Again, unless there are explainable circumstances, you should not allow an exception. If you are managing a legacy appliance (a SOHO router or NAS drive, for instance), it is likely that the certificate installed on it will have expired. If you know that the appliance has not been tampered with, you can proceed.

- Time is not correctly synchronized between the server and client.

 Browsers and email applications usually display informative error messages. In other contexts, such as EAP authentication, it might not be so obvious that the certificate is the cause of the failure or why the certificate is being rejected. Inspect the logs recording the connection for clues.

Other Common Issues

When it comes to application layer troubleshooting, you will usually need to use references that are specific to the environment or app to solve problems. Some other generic issues you may encounter include time synchronization, mobile devices, and licensing.

NTP Issues

Most network services, and especially authentication and authorization mechanisms, depend upon each host using a synchronized time source. Inaccurate time sources also affect the reliability and usability of log data, which can have implications for regulatory compliance.

Time synchronization is usually accomplished via the Network Time Protocol (NTP). Clients must be able to access a time source over port UDP 123. In a Windows environment, the time source for clients will usually be a domain controller. The domain controller can either use a hardware GPS-based time source or rely on Internet servers, depending on the level accuracy required. In Windows, the `w32tm /query /configuration` command can be used to check the current configuration.

BYOD Challenges

Bring Your Own Device (BYOD) is a smartphone/tablet provisioning model that allows users to select a personal device to use to interact with corporate network services and cloud apps. Allowing user selection of devices introduces numerous compatibility, support, and security challenges:

- **Compatibility/support**—The wide range of devices, mobile OS versions, and vendor support for patches make the job of ensuring that each device can connect to corporate network apps and data resources highly complex.

- **Security**—This device variety also causes security issues, especially in terms of unpatched devices. Another issue is that the device is not fully under the administrative control of the IT department. An insider threat actor could install apps that might pose a risk to corporate data or misuse the device to exfiltrate data.

Some of the impact of these issues can be mitigated through the use of enterprise mobility management (EMM) suites and corporate workspaces. EMM (or mobile device management) is a type of network access control solution that registers devices as they connect to the network. It can then enforce security policies while the device is connected. These might restrict use of device functions or personal apps. A corporate workspace is an app that is segmented from the rest of the device and allow more centralized control over corporate data. Users must also agree to acceptable use policies, which might prohibit installing nonstore apps and rooting/jailbreaking a device and keeping the device up to date with patches. Users will also usually have to submit to inspection of the device to protect corporate data.

Licensed Feature Issues

Licensing for servers and network appliances can be complex and it is easy to make configuration errors. When faced with an unexpected problem, it is often worth considering whether a licensing or feature activation issue could be the cause. On a switch or router, license failures could restrict the number of ports available, the number of routes allowed in the routing table, or the availability of routing protocols. Security and management features may have been configured under a trial or evaluation period and suddenly stop working when that grace period ends.

The starting point for troubleshooting license issues will be the log. This should show whether an evaluation/trial period has just expired or when a seat/instance count has been exceeded. Verify that the appliance has the correct licenses or activation keys installed. If relevant, ensure that the appliance can connect to its licensing or activation server.

Review Activity:

Service and Security Issues

Answer the following questions:

1. You are planning to reconfigure static and DHCP-assigned IP addresses across the network during scheduled downtime. What preliminary step should you take to minimize connectivity issues when the network is reopened?

2. If a network adapter is using the address 169.254.1.10 on a host connected to the LAN, what would you suspect?

3. Following maintenance on network switches, users in one department cannot access the company's internal web and email servers. You can demonstrate basic connectivity between the hosts and the servers by IP address. What might the problem be?

4. You are troubleshooting a connectivity problem with a network application server. Certain clients cannot connect to the service port. How could you rule out a network or remote client host firewall as the cause of the problem?

Review Activity:

Scenarios in Service and Security Issues

You are staffing the network help desk and dealing with support requests as they arrive. Your network uses four access switches to support four subnets. One subnet contains network servers (authentication, directory services, DNS, and DHCP) and another contains Line of Business (LoB) application servers, for sales and order processing. There are two client subnets, serving different floors in the building.

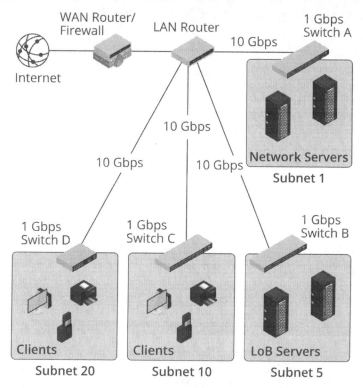

Using the above scenario and network diagram, answer the following questions:

1. **You receive a call from the user of host A who has always been able to connect to the LoB application servers, but today she is unable to connect. You verbally check with other users and discover that none of the hosts on subnet 20 can connect, but that users in subnet 10 report no problems. What tests should you perform to narrow down the cause of the problem?**

2.   You send a junior technician to the equipment room to fix the problem. Sometime later, another user from subnet 20 calls complaining that he cannot connect to the Internet. What questions should you ask to begin troubleshooting?

3.   You asked a junior technician to step in because your manager had asked you to deploy a wireless access point on the network to support a sales event due to start the next day. There will be lots of guests, and your manager wants them all to have Internet access. You did not have much time, so you simply added the access point to the switch supporting subnet 10. The next day arrives, and sometime after the sales event starts, multiple employees in subnet 10 report that when they attempt to connect to the network, they get a message that the Windows network has limited connectivity. What might be the cause and what test should you use to confirm the issue?

Lesson 14

Summary

You should be able to compare and contrast features and placement of security appliances and to troubleshoot service and security issues.

Guidelines for Supporting and Troubleshooting Secure Networks

Follow these guidelines to support use of security appliances and service/security troubleshooting procedures:

- Identify requirements for different types of security appliances, based on the following factors:

  - Using firewalls or proxy servers to establish perimeter security in a screened subnet topology.

  - Using firewalls to protect internal zones or individual hosts.

  - Using network access control, honeypots, separation of duties and intrusion detection/prevention for defense in depth.

- Identify suitable types of firewall or proxy appliance based on load and filtering requirements.

- Use network address translation and port address translation to implement Internet addressing for hosts configured in IPv4 private address ranges.

- Consider the impact of segmentation and VLANs on DHCP and DNS servers.

- Use monitoring to detect service and performance issues.

- Use configuration documentation to troubleshoot untrusted certificate and firewall/ACL misconfiguration issues.

- Be prepared to assess the impact of time synchronization, BYOD, and feature licensing on common support issues.

Lesson 15

Deploying and Troubleshooting Wireless Networks

LESSON INTRODUCTION

Unbounded or wireless media technologies have distinct advantages for businesses over bounded media. They can be easier to install to existing premises and they support the device mobility that users require from laptop or smartphone-based access to networks. Wireless technology implementations offer various advantages, but you need to understand their limitations and security issues to support them properly in your network environments.

Lesson Objectives

In this lesson, you will:

- Summarize wireless standards.

- Install wireless networks.

- Troubleshoot wireless networks.

- Configure and troubleshoot wireless security.

Topic 15A

Summarize Wireless Standards

EXAM OBJECTIVES COVERED
2.4 Given a scenario, install and configure the appropriate wireless standards and technologies.

Wireless connectivity is a core feature of most network environments today because they support users need for mobility using different devices. To support a wireless network, you must be able to summarize the features of Wi-Fi and cellular standards.

IEEE 802.11 Wireless Standards

Most wireless LANs (WLANs) are based on the IEEE **802.11 standards**, better known by its brand name Wi-Fi. 802.11 standards define the physical layer media by which data is encoded into a radio carrier signal by using a modulation scheme. The properties of radio waves include amplitude (the height of peaks and troughs), frequency (the number of peaks per unit of time), and phase (the angle of a wave at a point in time). Modulation changes one or more of those properties to encode a signal. As well as modulation schemes, Wi-Fi standards use different carrier methods to provide sufficient resistance to interference from noise and other radio sources.

A wireless radio transmitting and receiving within a particular range of frequencies with the same modulation scheme is a half-duplex shared access medium (a physical bus). 802.11 uses **Carrier Sense Multiple Access with Collision Avoidance (CSMA/CA)** to cope with contention. Under CSMA/CA, when a station receives a frame, it performs error checking. If the frame is intact, the station responds with an acknowledgment (ACK). If the ACK is not received, the transmitting station resends the frame until timing out. 802.11 also defines a Virtual Carrier Sense flow control mechanism to further reduce the incidence of collisions. A station broadcasts a Request to Send (RTS) with the source and destination and the time required to transmit. The receiving station responds with a Clear To Send (CTS) and all other stations in range do not attempt to transmit within that period.

The original 802.11 Wi-Fi standard worked only at 1 Mbps, but like the 802.3 Ethernet standard, it has been revised many times, with each iteration specifying different signaling and transmission mechanisms. Products conforming to the various standards can be certified by the Wi-Fi Alliance (wi-fi.org).

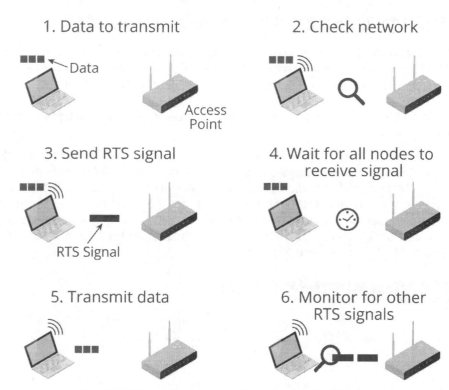

1. Data to transmit

Data

Access Point

2. Check network

3. Send RTS signal

RTS Signal

4. Wait for all nodes to receive signal

5. Transmit data

6. Monitor for other RTS signals

The CSMA/CA media access method. (Images © 123RF.com.)

IEEE 802.11a and 5 GHz Channel Bandwidth

Every wireless device operates on a specific radio frequency range within an overall **frequency band**. The specific frequency range is referred to as a **channel**. It is important to understand the difference between the two frequency bands used by the IEEE 802.11 standards:

- 2.4 GHz is better at propagating through solid surfaces, making it ideal for providing the longest signal range. However, the 2.4 GHz band does not support a high number of individual channels and is often congested, both with other Wi-Fi networks and other types of wireless technology, such as Bluetooth®. Consequently, with the 2.4 GHz band, there is increased risk of interference, and the maximum achievable data rates are typically lower than with 5 GHz.

- 5 GHz is less effective at penetrating solid surfaces and so does not support the maximum ranges achieved with 2.4 GHz standards, but the band supports more individual channels and suffers less from congestion and interference, meaning it supports higher data rates at shorter ranges.

The IEEE 802.11a standard specifies use of the 5 GHz frequency band and a multiplexed carrier scheme called Orthogonal Frequency Division Multiplexing (OFDM). 802.11a has a nominal data rate of 54 Mbps.

The 5 GHz band is subdivided into 23 non-overlapping channels, each of which is 20 MHz wide. Initially, there were 11 channels, but the subsequent 802.11h standard added another 12. 802.11h also adds the Dynamic Frequency Selection (DFS) method to prevent access points (APs) working in the 5 GHz band from interfering with radar and satellite signals. The exact use of channels can be subject to different regulation in different countries. Regulatory impacts also include a strict limit on power output, constraining the range of Wi-Fi devices.

IEEE 802.11b/g and 2.4 GHz Channel Bandwidth

The 802.11b standard uses the 2.4 GHz frequency band and was released in parallel with 802.11a. It standardized the use of the carrier method Direct Sequence Spread Spectrum (DSSS), along with Complementary Code Keying (CCK) signal encoding. While in some ways DSSS was an inferior technology to OFDM—with a nominal data rate of just 11 Mbps—802.11b products were quicker to market and became better established than 802.11a.

The 2.4 GHz band is subdivided into up to 14 channels, spaced at 5 MHz intervals from 2412 MHz up to 2484 MHz. Because the spacing is only 5 MHz and Wi-Fi needs ~20 MHz channel bandwidth, 802.11b channels overlap quite considerably. This means that co-channel interference is a real possibility unless widely spaced channels are chosen (1, 6, and 11, for instance). Also, in the Americas, regulations permit the use of channels 1-11 only, while in Europe channels 1-13 are permitted, and in Japan all 14 channels are permitted.

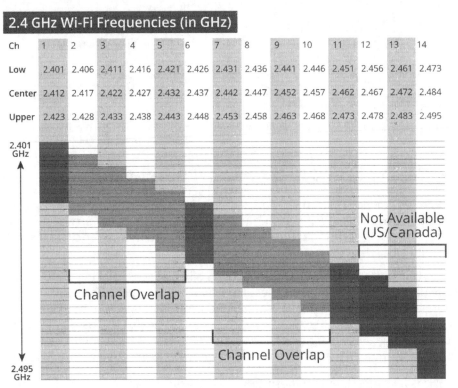

Channel overlap in the 2.4 GHz band.

The 802.11g standard offered a relatively straightforward upgrade path from 802.11b. Like 802.11a, 802.11g uses OFDM, but in the 2.4 GHz band used by 802.11b and with the same channel layout. This made it straightforward for vendors to offer 802.11g devices that could offer backwards support for legacy 802.11b clients. 802.11g has a nominal data rate of 54 Mbps. When in 802.11b compatibility mode, it drops back to using DSSS.

IEEE 802.11n, MIMO, and Channel Bonding

The 802.11n standard increases bandwidth by multiplexing the signals from 2 to 4 separate antennas (a radio chain) using a collection of technologies generally referred to as **Multiple Input Multiple Output (MIMO)**. The configuration of an 802.11n radio chain is identified by AxB:C notation, where A is the number of transmit antennas, B is the number of receive antennas, and C is the number of simultaneous transmit and receive streams. The maximum possible is 4x4:4, but common configurations are 2x2:2 or 3x3:2. For example, a 4x4:4 access point could allocate two streams carrying different data to a 2x2:2 client, increasing bandwidth. This is referred to as spatial multiplexing.

Having more transmit and receive antennas can also be used to improve signal reliability, rather than boosting bandwidth. If the same data stream is sent by two or three transmit antennas, the receiver can combine them to derive a stronger signal and increase range at a given data rate. Similarly, multiple receive antennas can derive a stronger signal, even if there is only one transmit stream. This is referred to as spatial diversity. For example, 2x2:2 and 2x3:2 radio chains have the same throughput, but the 2x3:2 chain could make more use of spatial diversity to increase range.

802.11n products can also use channels in the 2.4 GHz band or the 5 GHz band. 802.11n also allows two adjacent 20 MHz channels to be combined into a single 40 MHz channel, referred to as **channel bonding**. Due to the restricted bandwidth of 2.4 GHz, on a network with multiple APs, channel bonding is a practical option only in the 5 GHz band. The 5 GHz band has a larger frequency range (up to 500 MHz in the USA), so it can provide up to 23 nonoverlapping channels. However, those channels are not necessarily contiguous, which slightly reduces the options for bonded channels.

	U-NII-1				U-NII-2				U-NII-2 Extended											U-NII-3			
20 MHz	36	40	44	48	52	56	60	64	100	104	108	112	116	120	124	128	132	136	140	149	153	157	161
40 MHz	38		46		54		62		102		110		118		126		134			151		159	
80 MHz	42				58				106				122							155			
160 MHz	50								114														

Dynamic Frequency Selection (DFS) Range

Bonded channel options in the 5 GHz Unlicensed National Information Infrastructure (U-NII) sub-bands. Channels within the DFS range may be disabled if the site is near a radar transmitter.

Cheaper client adapters may support only the 2.4 GHz band. An access point (AP) or adapter that can support both is referred to as dual band. A dual band AP can support both 2.4 GHz and 5 GHz bands simultaneously. This allows legacy clients to be allocated to the 2.4 GHz band.

The data rate for 802.11n is 72 Mbps per stream. Assuming the maximum number of four spatial streams and optimum conditions, the nominal data rate could be as high as 600 Mbps for a 40 MHz bonded channel. 802.11n can work in High Throughput (HT)/greenfield mode for maximum performance or HT mixed mode for compatibility with older standards (801.11a-ht, 802.11b-ht, and 802.11g-ht). Mixed mode reduces overall WLAN performance, as it involves the transmission of legacy identification and collision avoidance frames (HT protection) but not to the extent that 802.11n devices are reduced to, for example, 802.11g data rates. Operating in greenfield mode is likely to cause substantial interference if there are legacy WLANs operating nearby on the same channel(s). There is also a legacy (non-HT) mode, in which 802.11n's HT mechanisms are disabled completely. You might use this mode if you have an 802.11n-capable access point but don't have any 802.11n client devices.

In recent years, Wi-Fi standards have been renamed with simpler digit numbers. 802.11n is now officially designated as Wi-Fi 4.

Wi-Fi 5 and Wi-Fi 6

The Wi-Fi 5 (or 802.11ac) and Wi-Fi 6 (802.11ax) standards continue the development of Wi-Fi technologies to increase bandwidth and support modern networks.

Wi-Fi 5 (802.11ac)

Wi-Fi 5 is designed to work only in the 5 GHz band. The 2.4 GHz band can be used for legacy standards (802.11g/n) in mixed mode. The aim for Wi-Fi 5 is to get throughput like that of Gigabit Ethernet or better. It supports more channel bonding (up to 80 or 160 MHz channels), up to 8 spatial streams, rather than 4, and denser modulation (at close ranges). The way Wi-Fi 5 uses the radio spectrum is designated as very high throughput (VHT).

As with 802.11n, only enterprise-class equipment is equipped with enough antennas to make use of three streams or more, and no devices were ever produced with more than 4x4:4 streams. Wi-Fi 5 access points are marketed using AC values, such as AC5300. The 5300 value represents 1000 Mbps over a 40 MHz 2.4 GHz band channel and two 2,167 Mbps streams over 80 MHz 5 GHz band channels.

Wi-Fi 6 (802.11ax)

Wi-Fi 6 uses more complex modulation and signal encoding to improve the amount of data sent per packet by about 40%. As with Wi-Fi 6, products are branded using the combined throughput. For example, AX6000 allows 1,148 Mbps on the 2.4 GHz radio and 4,804 over 5 GHz.

The way Wi-Fi 6 uses the radio spectrum is designated as high efficiency (HE) to reflect these improvements. The aim for Wi-Fi 6 is to approximate 10G connection speeds (AX11000). These data rates can only be achieved through use of a new 6 GHz frequency band.

Wi-Fi 6 reinstates operation in the 2.4 GHz band, mostly to support Internet of Things (IoT) device connectivity. In Wi-Fi 6, the OFDM with multiple access (OFDMA) modulation scheme allows sub-carriers or tones to be allocated in groups of different sizes, referred to as resource units (RUs), each of which can communicate in parallel. Where small RUs are used, this reduces throughput but provides more opportunities for a larger number of devices to transmit. The effect is to reduce latency where numerous small data packets are being transmitted. This technology provides better support for IoT devices. Stations that require more bandwidth can be assigned larger RUs. RUs can also be assigned based on class of service parameters, such as prioritizing voice over IP (VoIP) traffic. It also allows an access point to support legacy (Wi-Fi 4/5 stations) efficiently.

Multiuser MIMO

In basic 802.11 operation modes, bandwidth is shared between all stations because of the CSMA/CA contention protocol. An AP can communicate with only one station at a time; multiple station requests go into a queue. Wi-Fi 5 and Wi-Fi 6 products address this problem using beamforming or **Multiuser MIMO (MU-MIMO)**.

Downlink MU-MIMO (DL MU-MIMO) allows the AP to use its multiple antennas to process a spatial stream of signals in one direction separately to other streams. This means that groups of stations on a different alignment can connect simultaneously and also obtain more bandwidth. For example, if four stations are positioned north, south, east, and west of a 4x4:4 AP, the AP should be able to allow each of them to connect at close to the maximum speed. If another station is added to the north, those two northern stations will share the available bandwidth along that beam path. Both stations and AP must support MU-MIMO. Where Wi-Fi 5 supports up to four stations communicating in parallel over 5 GHz only, Wi-Fi 6 can support up to eight in 2.4 GHz, 5 GHz, and 6 GHz bands, giving it better performance in congested areas.

With DL MU-MIMO, only the AP can initiate beamforming, so it is only available on the downlink from AP to station (not station to AP). Wi-Fi 6 supports uplink MU-MIMO (UL MU-MIMO), allowing stations to initiate beamforming with the access point.

For both Wi-Fi 5 and Wi-Fi 6, improvements are released to market in waves. For example, UL MU-MIMO was released in wave 2 Wi-Fi 6 products, which also added support for the 6 GHz frequency band.

MU-MIMO and OFDMA are different but complementary technologies. MU-MIMO makes use of spatial streams, where OFDMA makes flexible use of subcarriers within a channel. Both can work together to increase parallelism (supporting communication with more devices simultaneously).

2G and 3G Cellular Technologies

Where Wi-Fi is typically operated as private infrastructure, **cellular radio** is operated by telecommunications providers. A cellular radio establishes a connection using the nearest available cell or base station. Each base station has an effective range of up to 5 miles (8 km). The base station links the device to global telecommunications networks. Cellular radio works in the 850 and 1900 MHz frequency bands (mostly in the Americas) and the 900 and 1800 MHz bands (rest of the world).

Cellular digital communications standards are described as belonging to a generation. For 2G, there were two competing formats, established in different markets:

- **Global System for Mobile Communication (GSM)**-based phones using Time Division Multiple Access (TDMA). With TDMA, each subscriber gets access to the radio channel by being allocated a time slot. GSM allows subscribers to use a subscriber identity module (SIM) card to use an unlocked handset with their chosen network provider. GSM is adopted internationally and by AT&T and T-Mobile in the United States.

- TIA/EIA IS-95 (cdmaOne)-based handsets, using **Code Division Multiple Access (CDMA)**. CDMA means that each subscriber uses a code to key the modulation of their signal and this "key" is used by the receiver to extract the subscriber's traffic from the radio channel. With CDMA, the handset is managed by the provider, not the SIM. CDMA adoption is largely restricted to the telecom providers Sprint and Verizon.

In both cases, the cell network was built primarily to support voice calls, so 2G data access was provided on top, using Circuit Switched Data (CSD). CSD is somewhat similar to a dial-up modem, though no analog transmissions are involved. CSD requires a data connection to be established to the base station (incurring call charges) and is only capable of around 14.4 Kbps at best.

The transition from 2G to 3G saw various packet-switched technologies deployed to mobiles:

- General Packet Radio Services/Enhanced Data Rates for GSM Evolution (GPRS/EDGE) is a precursor to 3G (2.5G), with GPRS offering up to about 48 Kbps and EDGE about 3-4 times that. Unlike CSD, GPRS and EDGE allow "always on" data connections, with usage billed by bandwidth consumption rather than connection time.

- Evolved High Speed Packet Access (HSPA+) is a 3G standard developed via several iterations from the Universal Mobile Telecommunications System (UMTS) used on GSM networks. HSPA+ nominally supports download speeds up to 168 Mbps and upload speeds up to 34 Mbps. HSPA+-based services are often marketed as 4G if the nominal data rate is better than about 20 Mbps.

 Note that with HSPA, the TDMA channel access technology has been abandoned and a type of CDMA used.

- CDMA2000/Evolution Data Optimized (EV-DO) are the main 3G standards deployed by CDMA network providers. EV-DO can support a 3.1 Mbps downlink and 1.8 Mbps uplink.

4G and 5G Cellular Technologies

The replacements for 3G networks have seen convergence on a single set of worldwide standards.

4G/Long Term Evolution

Long Term Evolution (LTE) is a converged 4G standard supported by both the GSM and CDMA network providers. LTE devices must have a SIM card issued by the network provider installed. LTE has a maximum downlink of 150 Mbps in theory, but no provider networks can deliver that sort of speed at the time of writing, with around 20 Mbps far more typical of real-word performance.

 LTE uses neither TDMA nor CDMA but Orthogonal Frequency Division Multiple Access (OFDMA), which is also used by Wi-Fi 6.

LTE Advanced (LTE-A) is intended to provide a 300 Mbps downlink, but again this aspiration is not matched by real-world performance. Current typical performance for LTE-A is up to 90 Mbps.

5G

According to the original specification, a 4G service was supposed to deliver 1 Gbps for stationary or slow-moving users (including pedestrians) and 100 Mbps for access from a fast-moving vehicle. Those data rates are now the minimum hoped-for standards for 5G. As with 4G, real-world speeds are nowhere near the hoped-for minimums, ranging from about 50 Mbps to 300 Mbps at time of writing.

5G uses different spectrum bands from low (sub-6 GHz) to medium/high (20-60 GHz). Low bands have greater range and penetrating power; high bands, also referred to as millimeter wave (mmWave) require close range (a few hundred feet) and cannot penetrate walls or windows. Consequently, design and rollout of 5G services is relatively complex. Rather than a single large antenna serving a large wireless cell, 5G involves installing hundreds of smaller antennas to form an array that can take advantage of multipath and beamforming to overcome the propagation limitations of the spectrum. This is also referred to as massive MIMO. As well as faster mobile speeds, 5G is expected to provide fixed-wireless broadband solutions for homes and businesses, and to support IoT networks.

Review Activity:

Wireless Standards

Answer the following questions:

1. **What mechanism does RTS/CTS support?**

2. **Which IEEE WLAN standards specify a data transfer rate of up to 54 Mbps?**

3. **What options may be available for an 802.11n network that are not supported under 802.11g?**

4. **True or False? Stations with 802.11ac capable adapters must be assigned to the 5 GHz frequency band.**

5. **Which frequency band is less likely to suffer from co-channel interference?**

6. **What standard(s) are intended to support 4G mobile wireless services?**

Topic 15B

Install Wireless Networks

EXAM OBJECTIVES COVERED
2.1 Compare and contrast various devices, their features, and their appropriate placement on the network.
2.4 Given a scenario, install and configure the appropriate wireless standards and technologies.

Designing a wireless network to meet requirements to support multiple types of devices can be a complex task. Planning the installation using survey tools can ensure that range and interference issues are accounted for at the outset, and do not become support issues later on.

Infrastructure Topology and Wireless Access Points

Wireless network devices are referred to as stations (STA), similar to a node on a wired network. Most wireless networks are deployed in an infrastructure topology. In an infrastructure topology, each station is configured to connect through a base station or **access point (AP)**, forming a logical star topology. The AP mediates communications between client devices and can also provide a bridge to a cabled network segment. In 802.11 documentation, this is referred to as an infrastructure Basic Service Set (BSS). The MAC address of the AP is used as the **Basic Service Set Identifier (BSSID)**. More than one BSS can be grouped together in an Extended Service Set (ESS).

Access point. (Image © 123RF.com.)

Each client station requires a wireless adapter compatible with the standard(s) supported by the AP.

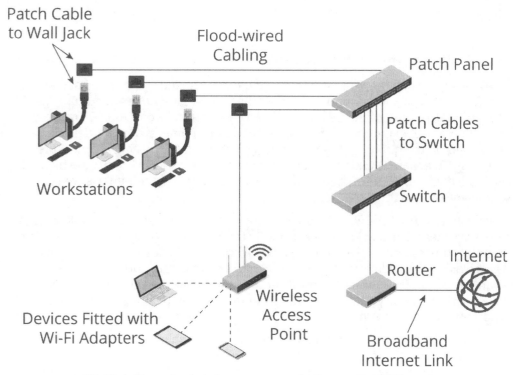

WLAN configuration in infrastructure mode. (Images © 123RF.com.)

Wireless Site Design

Clients are configured to join a WLAN through the network name or **Service Set Identifier (SSID)**. An SSID can be up to 32 bytes in length and for maximum compatibility should only use ASCII letters and digits plus the hyphen and underscore characters. In infrastructure mode, when multiple APs connected to the same distribution system are grouped into an ESS, this is more properly called the **Extended SSID (ESSID)**. This just means that all the APs are configured with the same SSID and security information. The area served by a single AP is referred to as a basic service area (BSA) or wireless cell. The area in which stations can roam between access points to stay connected to the same ESSID is referred to as an extended service area (ESA).

SSID Broadcast and Beacon Frame

A WLAN is typically configured to advertise its presence by broadcasting the SSID. This allows a user to connect to a named network. If SSID broadcast is suppressed, the user must configure the connection to the network manually. A beacon is a special management frame broadcast by the AP to advertise the WLAN. The beacon frame contains the SSID (unless broadcast is disabled), supported data rates and signaling, plus encryption/authentication requirements. The interval at which the beacon is broadcast (measured in milliseconds) can be modified. The default is usually 100 ms. Increasing the interval reduces the overhead of broadcasting the frame but delays joining the network and can hamper roaming between APs.

Even if SSID broadcast is suppressed, it is fairly easy for a network sniffer to detect it as clients still use it when connecting with the AP.

Speed and Distance Requirements

A device supporting the Wi-Fi standard should have an indoor range of at least 30 m (100 feet). 2.4 GHz radios support better ranges than 5 GHz ones and 802.11n and later standards improve range compared to earlier standards. Outdoor range can be double or treble indoor range. Each station determines an appropriate data rate based on the quality of the signal using a mechanism called Dynamic Rate Switching/Selection (DRS). If the signal is strong, the station will select the highest available data rate (determined by the 802.11 standard); if the signal is weak, the station will reduce the data rate.

Radio signals pass through solid objects, such as ordinary brick or drywall walls, but can be weakened or blocked by particularly thick walls or those of dense concrete or metal construction. Other radio-based devices can also cause interference as can devices as various as fluorescent lighting, microwave ovens, cordless phones, and (in an industrial environment), power motors and heavy machinery. Bluetooth uses the 2.4 GHz frequency range but a different modulation technique, so interference is possible but not common.

Consequently, a complex set of factors need to be taken into consideration when you are planning a wireless network. A site survey is a critical planning tool to ensure that the WLAN delivers acceptable data rates to the supported number of devices in all the physical locations expected.

Site Surveys and Heat Maps

A **site survey** is performed first by examining the blueprints or floor plan of the premises to understand the layout and to identify features that might produce radio frequency interference (RFI). This can be backed up by a visual inspection that may reveal things that are not shown on the blueprints, such as thick metal shelving surrounding a room that needs to have WLAN access. Each AP mounting point needs a network port and power jack, so it will help to obtain plans that show the locations of available ports.

A switch that supports Power over Ethernet (PoE) can be used to power a PoE-compatible AP.

The next step is to create a new plan on which you will mark the WLAN cells and associated APs and booster antennas. The idea here to is to place APs close enough together to avoid "dead zones"—areas where connectivity is difficult or data transfer rates are below an acceptable tolerance level—but far enough apart that one AP does not interfere with another or that one AP is overutilized and a nearby one underutilized.

Position an AP in the first planned location, then use a laptop with a wireless adapter and a wireless survey tool, such as Cisco Aironet, Metageek inSSIDer, or Ekahau Site Survey, to record signal strength and supported data rate at various points in the intended basic service area (BSA). Many tools can show the signal strength within a particular channel obtained in different locations graphically using a **heat map**. The heat map would show areas with a strong signal in greens and yellows with warning oranges and reds where signal strength drops off. This step is then repeated for each planned location. Neighboring APs should be configured with non-overlapping channels to avoid interfering with one another. It may also be necessary to adjust the transmit power of an AP to size its BSA appropriately.

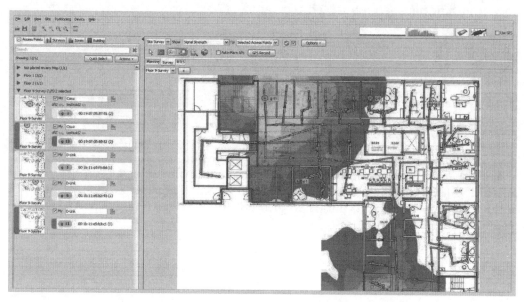

Heat map generated by Ekahau Site Survey. (Image © Ekahau Inc.)

Wireless Roaming and Bridging

Clients can **roam** within an extended service area (ESA). An ESA is created by installing APs with the same SSID and security configuration connected by a wired network, or Distribution System (DS). The access points are configured with different channels so that where BSAs overlap, there is no interference. When the client detects that it is no longer receiving a good signal, it checks for another signal with the same SSID on other channels or on a different frequency band, and if there is a stronger signal, it disassociates from the current AP. The station can then reassociate with the new AP. Depending on the roaming infrastructure and security type, the station may have to reauthenticate, or if 802.11r fast roaming is supported, it may be able to use its existing authentication status to generate security properties for the new association.

Roaming is supposed to be seamless, but in practice reestablishing the connection can often cause time-out problems for applications. To improve mobility, there needs to be a balance between determining what constitutes a "good" signal and the frequency with which a client tries to associate with different APs. Many adapters support a roaming "aggressiveness" setting that can be configured to prevent a Wi-Fi adapter "flapping" between two APs or (conversely) to prevent a client remaining associated with a more distant AP when it could achieve better bandwidth through one closer to it.

You can also configure multiple access points to cover areas where it is not possible to run cabling. This is referred to as a wireless distribution system (WDS). You must set the APs to use the same channel, SSID, and security parameters. The APs are configured in WDS/repeater mode. One AP is configured as a base station, while the others are configured as remote stations. The base station can be connected to a cabled segment. The remote stations must not be connected to cabled segments. The remote stations can accept connections from wireless stations and forward all traffic to the base station.

Another use for WDS is to bridge two separate cabled segments. When WDS is configured in bridge mode, the APs will not support wireless clients; they simply forward traffic between the cabled segments.

WDSs support and implementation can vary between manufacturers. If you are implementing WDS, it is usually best to use APs from the same vendor.

Wireless LAN Controllers

An enterprise network might require the use of tens or hundreds of access points. If APs are individually managed, this can lead to configuration errors on specific APs and can make it difficult to gain an overall view of the wireless deployment, including which clients are connected to which APs and which clients or APs are producing the most traffic.

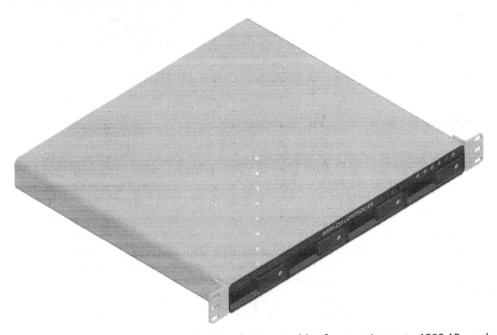

A wireless controller, an enterprise-level appliance capable of supporting up to 1500 APs and 20,000 clients. (Image © 123RF.com.)

Rather than configure each device individually, enterprise wireless solutions such as those manufactured by Cisco, Ruckus, or Ubiquiti allow for centralized management and monitoring of the APs on the network. This may be achieved through use of a dedicated hardware device called a **wireless LAN controller**. Alternatively, some implementations use a software application to centralize the management function, which can be run on a server or workstation.

An AP whose firmware contains enough processing logic to be able to function autonomously and handle clients without the use of a wireless controller is known as a **fat AP**, while one that requires a wireless controller in order to function is known as a **thin AP**. Cisco wireless controller usually communicate with the APs by using the Lightweight Access Point Protocol (LWAPP). LWAPP allows an AP configured to work in lightweight mode to download an appropriate SSID, standards mode, channel, and security configuration. Alternatives to LWAPP include the derivative Control And Provisioning of Wireless Access Points (CAPWAP) protocol or a proprietary protocol.

As well as autoconfiguring the appliances, a wireless controller can aggregate client traffic and provide a central switching and routing point between the WLAN and wired LAN. It can also assign clients to separate VLANs. Automated VLAN pooling ensures that the total number of stations per VLAN is kept within specified limits, reducing excessive broadcast traffic. Another function is to supply power to wired access points, using Power over Ethernet (PoE).

Ad Hoc and Mesh Topologies

While most corporate and many SOHO networks are configured in infrastructure mode, there are also wireless topologies that allow stations to establish peer-to-peer links.

Ad Hoc Topology

In an ad hoc topology, the wireless adapter allows connections to and from other devices. In 802.11 documentation, this is referred to as an **Independent Basic Service Set (IBSS)**. This topology does not require an access point. All the stations within an ad hoc network must be within range of one another. An ad hoc network might suit a small workgroup of devices, or connectivity to a single device, such as a shared printer, but it is not scalable to large network implementations.

 IBSS is not supported by the updated WDI driver model in the latest versions of Windows (docs.microsoft.com/en-us/windows-hardware/drivers/network/wdi-features-not-carried-over-in-wdi).

Mesh Topology

The 802.11s standard defines a Wireless Mesh Network (WMN). There are also various proprietary mesh protocols and products. Unlike an ad hoc network, nodes in a WMN (called mesh stations) are capable of discovering one another and peering, forming a Mesh Basic Service Set (MBSS). The mesh stations can perform path discovery and forwarding between peers using a routing protocol, such as the Hybrid Wireless Mesh Protocol (HWMP).

These features make a mesh topology more scalable than an ad hoc topology because the stations do not need to be within direct radio range of one another—a transmission can be relayed by intermediate stations. Mesh topologies are becoming increasingly popular and are the foundation of most Internet of Things (IoT) networks.

Review Activity:

Wireless Network Installation

Answer the following questions:

1. **What value is used as the BSSID?**

2. **True or False? Suppressing transmission of the WLAN beacon improves security.**

3. **What is a heat map?**

4. **True or false? To support client roaming within an extended service area, each access point must be configured with the same SSID, security parameters, and Wi-Fi channel.**

5. **What type of AP requires a wireless controller?**

6. **What are the advantages of deploying a wireless mesh topology over an IBSS?**

Topic 15C
Troubleshoot Wireless Networks

EXAM OBJECTIVES COVERED
2.4 Given a scenario, install and configure the appropriate wireless standards and technologies.
5.3 Given a scenario, use the appropriate network software tools and commands.
5.4 Given a scenario, troubleshoot common wireless connectivity issues.

Some environments and performance demands can complicate wireless network deployment. A variety of tools and techniques are available to assess Wi-Fi performance and ensure a highly available network for all users.

Wireless Performance Assessment

Wireless issues can be broadly divided into issues with signal strength or interference (like cabling issues in a wired LAN) and configuration issues. This topic focuses on issues that affect signal strength and performance, but always check that the security and authentication parameters are correctly configured before assuming you have a Physical layer connectivity problem. Configuration issues are discussed in the next topic.

As with cabled networks, you should distinguish between speed and throughput when measuring and assessing wireless performance against the specifications and limitations of a particular Wi-Fi standard:

- Speed is the data rate established at the physical and data link layers. The nominal link speed is determined by standards support (Wi-Fi 5 or Wi-Fi 6, for instance), use of bonded channels, and optimizations, such as MU-MIMO. If the sender and receiver are far apart or subject to interference, a lower rate will be negotiated to make the link more reliable.

- Throughput is the amount of data that can be transferred at the network layer, discarding overhead from layers 1 and 2. Often the term goodput is used to describe data transfer achieved at the application layer (accounting for overhead from header fields and packet loss/retransmissions).

As with cabling, attenuation refers to the weakening of the signal as the distance between the devices increases. This can be described more precisely as **radio frequency (RF) attenuation** or free space path loss. As the distance from the antenna increases, the strength of the signal decreases in accordance with the inverse-square rule. For example, doubling the distance decreases the signal strength by a factor of four. Meanwhile, interference sources collectively overlay a competing background signal, referred to as noise. These factors impose distance limitations on how far a client can be from an access point.

Attenuation and signal strength are measured in decibels. Signal strength is represented as the ratio of a measurement to 1 milliwatt (mw), where 1 mW is equal to 0 dBm. dB and dBm units can be combined to analyze losses and gains in signal strength along a communications path. For example, if you transmit a radio signal at 1 mW and use an antenna to boost the signal, the effective power is:

$$0 \text{ dBm} + 3 \text{ dB} = 2 \text{ mW} = \sim 3 \text{ dBm}$$

Conversely, dB loss due to attenuation or noise means loss of power/signal strength:

```
3 dBm - 1 dB = 2 dBm = ~1.58 mW
```

Because 0 dBm is 1 mW, a negative value for dBm represents a fraction of a milliwatt. For example, -30 dBm is 0.001 mW; -60 dBm is 0.000001 mW. Wi-Fi devices are all constrained by regulations governing spectrum use and output only small amounts of power.

Signal Strength

The **Received Signal Strength Indicator (RSSI)** is the strength of the signal from the transmitter at the client end. When you are measuring RSSI, dBm will be a negative value (a fraction of a milliwatt) with values closer to zero representing better performance. A value around -65 dBm represents a good signal, while anything over -80 dBm is likely to suffer packet loss or be dropped. The RSSI must exceed the minimum receiver sensitivity.

Depending on the vendor, RSSI might be measured directly in dBm or might be an index value related to a scale of dBm measurements. RSSI indices can be measured as 0-60, 0-127, or as 0-255. On a client, this index is displayed as a number of bars of signal strength on the adapter icon.

The comparative strength of the data signal to the background noise is called the Signal-To-Noise Ratio (SNR). Noise is also measured in dBm, but here values closer to zero are less welcome as they represent higher noise levels. For example, if signal is -65 dBm and noise is -90 dBm, the SNR is the difference between the two values, expressed in dB (25 dB). If noise is -80 dBm, the SNR is 15 dB and the connection will be much, much worse.

RSSI and SNR can be measured by using a **Wi-Fi analyzer**. This type of software can be installed to a laptop or smartphone. It will record statistics for the AP that the client is currently associated with and detect any other access points in the vicinity.

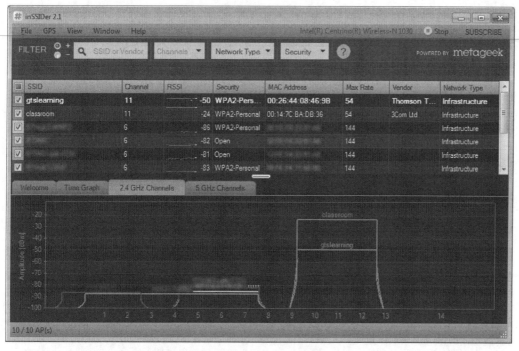

Surveying Wi-Fi networks using inSSIDer. The chart shows which channels are active and the signal strength of different networks in each channel. (Screenshot used with permission from MetaGeek.)

Antenna Types

The **antenna type** determines the propagation pattern or shape of the radio waves transmitted. Most wireless devices have simple omnidirectional vertical rod-type antennas, which receive and send signals in all directions more-or-less equally. Access points with omnidirectional antennas should ideally be ceiling mounted for best coverage, unless the ceiling is particularly high. The propagation pattern is shaped like a torus (donut), rather than a sphere, and radiates more powerfully in the horizontal plane than it does in the vertical plane. Locating the antenna above head height will minimize interference from obstructing furniture by allowing line-of-sight to most connecting devices but positioning it too high (above around 25 ft) will reduce signal strength, especially for stations directly below the antenna. You can obtain APs with downtilt omnidirectional antennas for use on high ceilings.

To extend the signal to a particular area, you can use an antenna focused in a single direction (unidirectional). Both the sender and receiver must use directional antennas, or one will be able to receive signals but not send responses. Unidirectional antenna types include the Yagi (a bar with fins) and parabolic (dish or grid) form factors. Unidirectional antennas are useful for point-to-point wireless bridge connections. The increase in signal strength obtained by focusing the signal is referred to as the gain and is measured in dBi (decibel isotropic). The amount of directionality, referred to as the beamwidth, is measured in degrees. A pair of 10-degree antennas are very highly directional and will require more exact alignment than a pair of 90 degree antennas.

A variety of generic antenna types: from left to right, a vertical rod antenna, a Yagi antenna, a parabolic/dish antenna, and a parabolic grid antenna.

Polarization refers to the orientation of the wave propagating from the antenna. If you imagine a rod-type antenna, when the rod is pointed up relative to the floor, the wave is horizontally polarized; if you orient the rod parallel to the floor, the wave is vertically polarized. To maximize signal strength, the transmission and reception antennas should normally use the same polarization. This is particularly important when deploying unidirectional antennas for a point-to-point link. Some antennas are dual-polarized, meaning that they can be installed in either orientation. Dual-polarized antennas are also the best way to support mobile devices, as these can be held by their user in a variety of orientations.

Insufficient Wireless Coverage Issues

Insufficient wireless coverage refers to spots within a building with no or weak Wi-Fi signal. If a sufficient signal strength cannot be obtained and sources of interference cannot be mitigated, the only solution to is to install an additional device to cover the gap. If you cannot extend the distribution system (cabled network) to support an additional access point, you will need to configure a wireless bridge or use a range extender.

Antenna Placement

Incorrect antenna placement could cause or exacerbate attenuation and interference problems. Use a site survey and heat map to determine the optimum position for APs and (if available) the direction in which to point adjustable antennas. Also, using an incorrect antenna type may adversely affect the signal strength at any given point. A unidirectional antenna is only suitable for point-to-point connections, not for general client access. The internal antennas built into APs may also be optimized to transmit and receive in some directions more than others. For example, an AP designed for ceiling mounting may produce a stronger signal in a cone directed downwards from its central axis, whereas the signal from a similar AP designed for wall installation is more likely to be angled outwards. Consult the documentation for your specific model of AP or use site survey software to produce a heat map.

Remember that some client devices might support a standard such as 802.11n, but only have a single band 2.4 GHz radio. They will not be able to join a 5 GHz network.

Antenna Cable Attenuation

Another source of attenuation is where the antenna is connected at some distance from the access point via coax cabling. Signal loss along this cable is referred to as **antenna cable attenuation**. LMR/HDF/CFD 200 cable has attenuation of about 0.6 dB/m (decibels per meter), while 400 cable improves that to about 0.22 dB/m. Connector loss is usually calculated as 0.15 dB.

If a device has removable antennas, check that these are screwed in firmly. A loose or disconnected antenna may reduce the range of the device or prevent connectivity altogether.

Effective Isotropic Radiated Power/Power Settings

The power at which an access point transmits is configurable. **Effective Isotropic Radiated Power (EIRP)** is calculated as the sum of transmit power, antenna cable/connector loss, and antenna gain. For example, if you are configuring a point-to-point link with a directional antenna, you might derive the following value for EIRP:

```
15 dBm (Transmit Power) - 1 dB (Cable Loss) + 6 dBi
(Gain) = 20 dBm (100 mW)
```

The EIRP for each radio is reported through the access point or controller management software. EIRP must not exceed regulatory limits. Power limits are different for the 2.4 GHz and 5 GHz bands and for point-to-multipoint versus point-to-point operation modes.

Increasing transmit power is not usually an effective solution to improving wireless coverage. While an AP might have an EIRP of around 23 dBm, smartphone devices are more likely to be around 10 to 14 dBm. If the client detects a strong signal, it will set a high data rate. However, because the EIRP of the client radio is much lower, it fails to transmit a strong signal back to the AP. Because it is trying to use a high data rate, this results in excessive packet errors.

As a general rule of thumb, AP power should be 2/3rds of the weakest client power. For example, if the weakest client can output 14 dBm, the AP should transmit at 9 to 10 dBm.

Channel Utilization and Overlap Issues

Channel overlap refers to interference issues resulting from multiple access points that are all in range of one another and are configured to use similar wavelengths. There are two main types of channel interference:

- **Co-channel interference (CCI)**—This can be more accurately described as contention. When multiple access points use the same channel, opportunities to transmit are reduced. The wireless devices must use CSMA/CA to find opportunities to transmit. CCI can be measured as a percentage referred to as channel utilization. Channel utilization can be measured from the access point or using a Wi-Fi analyzer. As a design goal, a channel should exhibit no more than 50% utilization.

- **Adjacent channel interference (ACI)**—This occurs when access points are configured to use different but overlapping channels, such as 1 and 3 in the 2.4 GHz band. ACI slows down the CSMA/CA process and raises noise levels.

One of the design goals for a multi-AP site is to create clean cells so that clients can select an AP with the strongest signal easily and the WLAN operates with a minimum of co-channel interference. At least 25 MHz spacing should be allowed to avoid channel overlap. In practice, therefore, no more than three nearby APs using the 2.4 GHz band can have non-overlapping channels. This could be implemented, for example, by selecting channel 1 for AP1, channel 6 for AP2, and channel 11 for AP3. When you are using the 5 GHz band for 802.11a or Wi-Fi 4/5/6, more non-overlapping channels are available.

In a complex environment, it may be necessary to adjust the power level used by an AP on a given channel. Using the maximum available power on an AP can result in it interfering with other "cells" and to situations where a client can "hear" the AP but cannot "talk" to it because it lacks sufficient power.

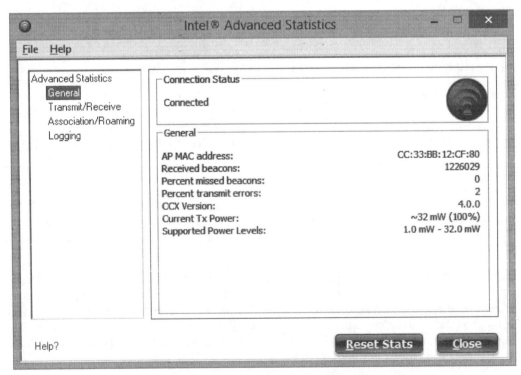

Checking power levels on a wireless station using Intel's PROSet Wi-Fi configuration utility. (Screenshot courtesy of Intel Corp.)

In order to enable seamless roaming for mobile clients, the cells served by each AP need to overlap to some extent in order to support roaming. This is one of the trickiest elements of site design to get right, as client behaviors and capabilities for roaming can vary widely. If there is a bring your own device (BYOD) policy in place, these support issues are even more greatly magnified.

Issues with roaming can be identified by analyzing access point association times for client devices. A WLAN controller will be able to track client mobility, showing each access point and the time that the client associated with it. If a large number of clients flap between two access points repeatedly, the site design might need to be investigated to solve the roaming issue.

Overcapacity Issues

Overcapacity (or device saturation) occurs when too many client devices connect to the same AP. The maximum number of clients that an AP can support varies, depending on the Wi-Fi standard used and the type of network traffic generated. For example, web browsing will typically place a lighter load on the network than local client-server traffic or is likely at least to move any bottleneck further upstream to the WAN, rather than the wireless network. While individual circumstances must be considered, a maximum of 30 clients per AP is generally accepted as a rule of thumb. In designing the network, enough APs should be provided in appropriate locations to support the expected client density at this ratio. APs can usually be configured to enforce a maximum number of connections, so that additional clients will connect to the next nearest AP. Even with a relatively low number of clients, the wireless network can suffer from bandwidth saturation. Since wireless is a broadcast medium, the available bandwidth is shared between all clients. Thus, if one client is a bandwidth hog, others may find it difficult to maintain a reliable connection.

In an enterprise Wi-Fi solution, a controller will normally provide reporting tools to diagnose bandwidth issues and to report on which clients are consuming the most bandwidth. It could also report on wireless channel utilization and configure APs and clients to reassign channels dynamically to reduce overutilization. If a traffic shaper is deployed, it may work automatically to throttle bandwidth to overactive nodes.

Interference Issues

If a device is within the supported range but the signal is weak or you cannot get a connection, there is likely to be interference. Apart from channel interference described earlier, there are several other sources of interference to consider:

- **Reflection/bounce (multipath interference)**—Mirrors or shiny surfaces cause signals to reflect, meaning that a variable delay is introduced. This causes packets to be lost and consequently the data rate to drop.

 The Wi-Fi 4/5/6 standards actually use bounce (multipath) as a means of optimizing throughput and range via MIMO.

- **Refraction**—Glass or water can cause radio waves to bend and take a different path to the receiver. This can also cause the data rate to drop.

- **Absorption**—This refers to the degree to which walls and windows will reduce signal strength (some of the radio wave's energy is lost as heat when passing through construction materials). An internal wall might "cost" 3 to 15 dB, depending on the material used (concrete being the most effective absorber). The 2.4 GHz frequency has better penetration than the 5 GHz one, given the same power output. To minimize absorption from office furniture (and people), use ceiling-mounted APs.

- **Electromagnetic interference (EMI)**—Interference from a powerful radio or electromagnetic source working in the same frequency band, such as a Bluetooth device, cordless phone, or microwave oven.

EMI can be detected by using a **spectrum analyzer**. Unlike a Wi-Fi analyzer, a spectrum analyzer must use a special radio receiver—Wi-Fi adapters filter out anything that isn't a Wi-Fi signal. They are usually supplied as handheld units with a directional antenna, so that the exact location of the interference can be pinpointed. A 6 dB change in the level of a particular source represents a halving or doubling of the distance between the analyzer and the source of the RF source.

Also consider that signal problems could be a result of someone trying to attack the network by jamming the legitimate AP and making clients connect to a rogue AP.

Review Activity:

Wireless Network Troubleshooting

Answer the following questions:

1. **You are planning WLAN for an office building with an attached warehouse. Where would you recommend placing Wi-Fi antennas for the best coverage in an office full of cubicles as well as in the warehouse?**

2. **The lobby area of your office building has undergone a renovation, the centerpiece of which is a large aquarium in the middle of the room, separating a visitor seating and greeting area from the reception desks, where the AP facilitating guest Internet access is located. Since the renovation, many guests have been unable to connect to Wi-Fi from the seating area. Could the aquarium really be the cause, and what solution could you recommend?**

3. **What is the difference between a Wi-Fi analyzer and a spectrum analyzer?**

4. **Users in the corner of an office building cannot get good Wi-Fi reception. Your office manager doesn't want to use his budget to purchase a new AP. He's noticed that the power level control on the AP is set to 3 out of 5 and wants to know why turning up the power isn't the best solution?**

Topic 15D

Configure and Troubleshoot Wireless Security

EXAM OBJECTIVES COVERED
2.4 Given a scenario, install and configure the appropriate wireless standards and technologies.
5.4 Given a scenario, troubleshoot common wireless connectivity issues.

Wireless connections are popular with users but also pose considerable risk to the whole network unless they are properly secured with access controls. In this topic, you will identify different wireless security methods and their configuration requirements and troubleshoot common issues with wireless settings.

Wi-Fi Encryption Standards

As well as the site design, a wireless network must be configured with security settings. Without encryption, anyone within range can intercept and read packets passing over the wireless network. The choice of which security settings to apply is determined by device support for the various Wi-Fi encryption standards, by the type of authentication infrastructure, and by the purpose of the WLAN. The encryption standard determines the cryptographic protocols that are supported, the means of generating the encryption key, and available methods for authenticating wireless stations when they try to join (or associate with) the network.

The first version of **Wi-Fi Protected Access (WPA)** was designed to fix critical vulnerabilities in the earlier wired equivalent privacy (WEP) standard. Like WEP, version 1 of WPA uses the RC4 stream cipher to encrypt traffic but adds a mechanism called the Temporal Key Integrity Protocol (TKIP) to try to mitigate the various attacks against WEP that had been developed.

Neither WEP nor the original WPA version are considered secure enough for continued use. They can be exploited by various types of replay attack that aim to recover the encryption key. WPA2 uses the Advanced Encryption Standard (AES) cipher deployed within the Counter Mode with Cipher Block Chaining Message Authentication Code Protocol (CCMP). AES replaces RC4 and CCMP replaces TKIP. CCMP provides authenticated encryption, which is designed to make replay attacks harder.

Weaknesses have also been found in WPA2, however, which has led to its intended replacement by WPA3.

Configuring a TP-LINK SOHO access point with wireless encryption and authentication settings. In this example, the 2.4 GHz band allows legacy connections with WPA2-Personal security, while the 5 GHz network is for 802.11ax (Wi-Fi 6) capable devices using WPA3-SAE authentication. (Screenshot used with permission from TP-Link Technologies.)

Personal Authentication

In order to secure a network, you need to be able to confirm that only valid users are connecting to it. Wi-Fi authentication comes in three types: personal, open, and enterprise. Within the personal authentication category, there are two methods: pre-shared key authentication (PSK) and simultaneous authentication of equals (SAE).

WPA2 Pre-Shared Key Authentication

In WPA2, **pre-shared key (PSK)** authentication uses a passphrase to generate the key that is used to encrypt communications. It is also referred to as group authentication because a group of users share the same secret. When the access point is set to WPA2-PSK mode, the administrator configures a passphrase of between 8 and 63 characters. This is converted to a type of hash value, referred to as the pairwise master key (PMK). The same secret must be configured on the access point and on each node that joins the network. The PMK is used as part of WPA2's 4-way handshake to derive various session keys.

All types of Wi-Fi PSK authentication have been shown to be vulnerable to attacks that attempt to recover the passphrase. At a minimum, the passphrase must be at least 14 characters long to try to mitigate risks from cracking.

WPA3 Personal Authentication

While WPA3 still uses a passphrase to authenticate stations in personal mode, it changes the method by which this secret is used to agree session keys. The scheme used is also referred to as Password Authenticated Key Exchange (PAKE). In WPA3, the **Simultaneous Authentication of Equals (SAE)** protocol replaces the 4-way handshake, which has been found to be vulnerable to various attacks.

The configuration interfaces for access points can use different labels for these methods. You might see WPA2-Personal and WPA3-SAE rather than WPA2-PSK and WPA3-Personal, for example. Additionally, an access point can be configured for WPA3 only or with support for legacy WPA2 (WPA3-Personal Transition mode).

Enterprise/IEEE 802.1X Authentication

The main problems with personal modes of authentication are that distribution of the key or passphrase cannot be secured properly, and that users may choose unsecure phrases. Personal authentication also fails to provide accounting, as all users share the same credential.

As an alternative to personal authentication, WPA's **enterprise authentication** method implements IEEE 802.1X to use an Extensible Authentication Protocol (EAP) mechanism to authenticate against a network directory. 802.1X defines the use of EAP over Wireless (EAPoW) to allow an access point to forward authentication data without allowing any other type of network access. It is configured by selecting WPA2-Enterprise or WPA3-Enterprise as the security method on the access point.

With enterprise authentication, when a wireless station requests an association, the AP enables the channel for EAPoW traffic only. It passes the credentials of the supplicant to an AAA (RADIUS or TACACS+) server on the wired network for validation. When the supplicant has been authenticated, the AAA server transmits a master key (MK) to the supplicant. The supplicant and authentication server then derive the same pairwise master key (PMK) from the MK. The AAA server transmits the PMK to the access point. The wireless station and access point use the PMK to derive session keys, using either the WPA2 four-way handshake or WPA3 SAE methods.

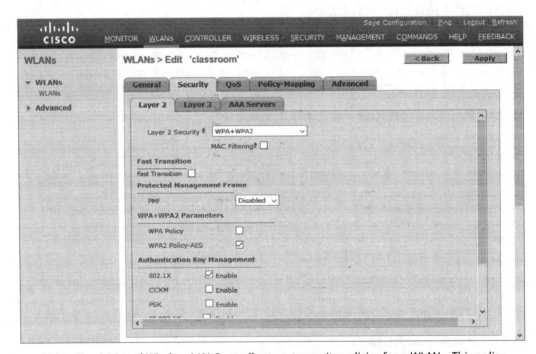

Using Cisco's Virtual Wireless LAN Controller to set security policies for a WLAN—This policy enforces use of WPA2 and the use of 802.1X (Enterprise) authentication. (Image © and Courtesy of Cisco Systems, Inc. Unauthorized use not permitted.)

Wi-Fi Security Configuration Issues

While signal loss and interference are factors that always need considering, if there is a basic connectivity problem, then you will probably want to investigate the configuration of the client and/or AP first.

Wrong SSID and Incorrect Passphrase Issues

If SSID broadcast is suppressed, a station can still connect to a WLAN by entering the network name manually. If this is the case, check that the clients are configured with the correct SSID/ESSID. Remember that this value is case sensitive. Technically, an SSID can contain spaces and special characters, but this can cause problems so is best avoided. Check that the authentication settings are the same on all devices. If a passphrase is used, make sure it is entered correctly. On the AP, ensure the authentication type is not set to open, unless the intention is to provide unrestricted public access.

It is possible that two APs are operating with the same SSID. If authentication is required, the connection with the wrong SSID will fail. If there is no authentication (open network), then the host will connect but take care, as this may be an attempt to snoop on the host's traffic using a rogue AP. Also, if a user is joining a WLAN for the first time, it may be the case that there are SSIDs from overlapping WLANs with very similar default names and the user may be confused about which name to choose.

Encryption Protocol Mismatch Issues

If the user is definitely supplying the correct key or credentials, check that the client can support the encryption and authentication standards configured on the AP—a driver update or OS patch may be required. An encryption protocol mismatch will cause the connection to fail, even if the correct credentials are supplied.

Client Disassociation Issues

In the normal course of operations, an access point and client use management frames to control connections. The access point normally broadcasts a beacon frame to advertise service capabilities. Clients can choose to first authenticate and then associate to an access point when they move into range of the beacon. The client or access point can use **disassociation** and/or deauthentication frames to notify the other party that it has ended a connection. A legitimate client might disassociate but not deauthenticate because it is roaming between wireless access points in an extended service area. A client might "flap" between two access points, causing numerous disassociations and reassociations. Investigate the access point or controller event log to identify the cause of disassociations.

If clients are disassociated unexpectedly and there is no roaming, interference, or driver issue, you should consider the possibility of a malicious attack. A disassociation attack exploits the lack of encryption in management frame traffic to send spoofed frames. One type of disassociation attack injects management frames that spoof the MAC address of a single victim station in a disassociation notification, causing it to be disconnected from the network. Another variant of the attack broadcasts spoofed frames to disconnect all stations. Frames can be spoofed to send either disassociation or deauthentication notifications.

Disassociation/deauthentication attacks may be used to perform a denial of service attack against the wireless infrastructure or to exploit disconnected stations to try to force reconnection to a rogue WAP. Disassociation/deauthentication attacks might also be used in conjunction with a replay attack aimed at recovering the network key.

Open Authentication and Captive Portal Issues

Configuring an access point for **open authentication** means that the client is not required to authenticate. This mode would be used on a public AP or "hotspot". In WPA/WPA2, this also means that data sent over the link is unencrypted. Open authentication may be combined with a secondary authentication mechanism managed via a browser. When the client associates with the open hotspot and launches the browser, the client is redirected to a **captive portal** or splash page. This will allow the client to authenticate to the hotspot provider's network (over HTTPS, so the login is secure). The portal may also be designed to enforce terms and conditions and/or take payment to access the Wi-Fi service.

Most captive portal issues arise because the redirect does not work. The captive portal should use HTTPS. Most modern browsers will block redirection to sites that do not use TLS. This means that the captive portal also needs to be installed with a digital certificate issued by a certification authority (CA) that is trusted by the client browser.

When using open wireless, users must ensure they send confidential web data only over HTTPS connections and only use email, VoIP, IM, and file transfer services with SSL/TLS enabled. Another option is for the user to join a virtual private network (VPN). The user would associate with the open hotspot then start the VPN connection. This creates an encrypted "tunnel" between the user's computer and the VPN server. This allows the user to browse the web or connect to email services without anyone eavesdropping on the open Wi-Fi network being able to intercept those communications. The VPN could be provided by the user's company or they could use a third-party VPN service provider. Of course, if using a third party, the user needs to be able to trust them implicitly. The VPN must use certificate-based tunneling to set up the "inner" authentication method.

Review Activity:

Wireless Security Configuration and Troubleshooting

Answer the following questions:

1. What is the main difference between WPA and WPA2?

2. What configuration information is required on an access point to authenticate users joining the wireless network against a network authentication server?

3. Widget Corporation has provided wireless access for its employees using several APs located in different parts of the building. Employees connect to the network using 802.11g-compatible network cards. On Thursday afternoon, several users report that they cannot log on to the network. What troubleshooting step would you take first?

4. Why might an attacker launch a disassociation attack against an access point?

5. Your company has a lobby area where guest access is provided so that visitors can get Internet access. The open guest WLAN is currently connected to the production network. The only protection against visitors and hackers getting into the organization's data is file and directory rights. What steps should be taken to provide guest access and better protect the organization's data?

Lesson 15

Summary

You should be able to install and configure appropriate wireless standards and technologies.

Guidelines for Deploying and Troubleshooting Wireless Networks

Follow these guidelines to deploy and troubleshoot wireless networks:

- Create a list of requirements for your network so that you can work toward meeting them. These requirements may include how many users need to connect, the physical area it will need to cover, external connections, and more.

- Consider the devices you will need and any compatibility requirements they have, in terms of Wi-Fi standards support, such as 802.11a, b, g or Wi-Fi 4 (n), 5 (ac), 6 (ax).

- Obtain a scale drawing of the building and a Wi-Fi analyzer to use to perform a site survey and generate heat maps of signal strength and channel utilization.

- Determine the range of the AP for the wireless technology you have chosen. This will help you to better determine how many APs you will need to ensure adequate coverage for the space.

- Balance the number of users who will have access to the AP, and ensure that the AP can cover all employees in the range of the AP. More employees in a given area means more APs.

- Tour the area in the range of the AP, and check to see if there are any devices that will interfere with the wireless network. This can include devices such as microwave ovens, Bluetooth-enabled devices, or an existing wireless network— whether from a community network, a neighboring building, or another floor of your company's building. These devices or networks can possibly interfere with your new implementation.

- Ensure that there are no obstacles in the path of the AP, such as doors, closed windows, walls, and furniture, that the wireless signal will need to pass through on its way to a client. If there are too many obstacles in the path, adjust the placement of your AP accordingly.

- Install the APs. The specific steps for installing the AP will vary by vendor, but the common steps may include:

  - Connecting the AP to the cabled network (distribution system) via a switch.

  - Setting the SSID/ESSID and an 802.11 beacon.

  - Configuring frequency bands and channel layout within each frequency band.

  - Adjusting transmit power to reduce channel overlap.

  - Configuring the appropriate encryption and authentication schemes, such as WPA2/3 personal versus WPA2/3 enterprise. If appropriate, configure RADIUS or TACACS+ support for enterprise authentication.

- Test to ensure that the installation is appropriately sized, secure, and operational. Make sure these tests are done under real-world conditions so that you have an accurate test.

- Perform period site surveys to check RSSI at key locations and compare it to previous performance levels from previous site surveys.

- Document the steps and establish a baseline for future installations.

Lesson 16
Comparing WAN Links and Remote Access Methods

LESSON INTRODUCTION

Most local networks require some sort of external connection, whether to the global Internet or within an enterprise WAN. These long-distance communications are typically facilitated by service provider links. Supporting WAN and Internet access effectively is an essential competency to learn.

In this lesson, you will identify the characteristics of WAN service provider offers and components of remote access network implementations.

Lesson Objectives

In this lesson, you will:

- Explain WAN provider links.

- Compare and contrast remote access methods.

Topic 16A

Explain WAN Provider Links

EXAM OBJECTIVES COVERED
1.2 Explain the characteristics of network topologies and network types.
2.1 Compare and contrast various devices, their features, and their appropriate placement on the network.

Understanding the various WAN connectivity devices and methods will help you support Internet connectivity and the configuration of enterprise WANs. You will need to understand the capabilities of and limitations of WAN provider links to choose the one best suited for your network.

Wide Area Networks and the OSI Model

Wide area network (WAN) technologies support data communications over greater distances than LANs. The term enterprise WAN is used to describe a WAN that is used and controlled by a single organization. However, even though an enterprise may control its WAN, it rarely owns all the infrastructure that supports it. Long distance communications usually involve the use of public networks. Public networks are owned by telecommunications (telco) companies and provide WAN services to businesses and households. Organizations often choose to use public networks, as the cost is far less than implementing a private solution. Service providers often have rights of access to locations that are not available to other organizations, such as under roads.

As with a LAN, the WAN Physical layer describes the media type and interface specifications. Where the provider link is a copper cable, some type of modem is usually used, rather than a switch. A modem performs modulation of outgoing signals and demodulation of incoming data, working only at the physical layer of the OSI model. Modulation means transforming an electromagnetic wave to represent information, such as using the amplitude (height) of the wave to represent bits. Legacy modems perform digital to analog modulation for transmission over voice lines. An analog (or dial-up) modem only supports low bandwidths (up to 56 Kbps). Digital modems perform a different type of modulation to transform digital signals received as Ethernet frames for transmission over the WAN media. Digital modem types include data service units (DSUs) for leased lines, digital subscriber line (DSL) modems, cable modems, and satellite modems.

At the data link layer, WANs often use simpler protocols to Ethernet LANs as the links are more likely to be point-to-point and do not need much complexity. That said, Ethernet is increasingly being deployed for end-to-end connectivity over WANs.

At the network layer, the customer and provider site are addressed using IP. A customer edge (CE) router connects to a provider edge (PE) via the underlying link layer interface. The provider allocates public IPv4/IPv6 addresses or address ranges to the customer.

WAN Provider Links

Establishing a WAN provider link means terminating the access provider's cabling at some point in your premises, and then attaching modem and routing equipment to that line. The service-related entry point at which the access provider's network terminates is called the **demarcation point** (or demarc for short) or minimum point of entry (MPOE). The demarc point represents the end of the telco's responsibility for maintaining that part of the cabling. Any cable problems arising from the other side of the demarc point are the responsibility of the customer.

Modems and routers or other access equipment that are provided or leased by the customer and installed at their site are referred to as customer premises equipment (CPE). Some providers may take on responsibility for faults that arise in CPE, depending on the contract and installation circumstances.

The demarc and CPE should be installed to a secure location within the premises, with access controls to restrict the area to authorized staff. This location is referred to as entrance facilities in TIA/EIA structured cabling standards.

T-Carrier and Leased Line Provider Links

The **T-carrier** system was developed by the telecommunications provider Bell Labs to allow multiple calls to be placed on a single cable. T-carrier enabled voice traffic to be digitized for transport around the core of the telecommunications network. It also enabled other types of digital data to be transported and could be provisioned directly to subscribers as a leased line. T-carrier is based on Time Division Multiplexing (TDM). The protocol assigns each circuit (or channel) a time slot. Each 64 Kbps channel provides enough bandwidth for a digitized voice call.

A single 64 Kbps channel is known as a DS0 or narrowband link. For leased line data services, however, the foundation level of T-carrier is the DS1 or T1 digital signal circuit. This service comprises 24 channels multiplexed into a single 1.544 Mbps full duplex digital connection that can be used for voice and/or data. The T1 lines themselves can be multiplexed to provide even more bandwidth.

A T1 line from the service provider is terminated at the demarc on a **smartjack** or Network Interface Unit (NIU). The smartjack has an RJ-48C or RJ-48X interface on the customer side that is used to connect to the customer's **Channel Service Unit/ Data Service Unit (CSU/DSU)**. The cabling from the smartjack to the CSU/DSU can use an ordinary RJ-45 patch cord (up to 3 meters/10 feet in length), but a shielded two-pair 22 AWG cable with connectors wired for RJ-48 is required for any distance longer than that.

The RJ-48X jack has a shorting bar to provide loopback on the connection if the equipment on the customer side is unplugged. This allows the service provider to test the line remotely.

The DSU encodes the signal from Data Terminal Equipment (DTE)—that is, the company's private branch exchange (PBX) internal telecoms system and/or an IP router—to a serial digital signal transmitted over copper wiring. The DSU part functions as a digital modem, while the CSU is used to perform diagnostic tests on the line. The devices can be supplied separately, but more typically they are combined as a single WAN interface card that can be plugged into a compatible router or PBX.

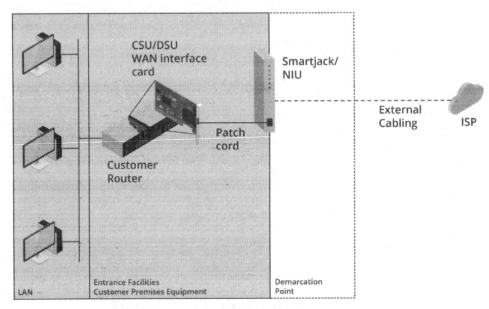

WAN termination equipment. (Images © 123RF.com.)

At the data link layer, T1 leased lines typically use either High-level Data Link Control (HDLC) or Point-to-Point Protocol (PPP).

Digital Subscriber Line Provider Links

Digital subscriber line (DSL) is a technology for transferring data over voice-grade telephone lines, often referred to as the local loop. DSL uses the frequencies above those used by the human voice as a full duplex communications channel.

DSL Modems

A DSL modem is installed as CPE, typically as a multifunction "wireless router," where the RJ-11 WAN port connects to the provider's phone jack over a short length of ribbon cable. DSL modems can also be supplied as separate appliances or plug-in cards for routers. A standalone DSL modem is connected to the phone line via an RJ-11 port and to the local network's router (or a single computer on the local network) via an RJ-45 Ethernet port.

RJ-11 DSL (left) and RJ-45 LAN (right) ports on a DSL modem. (Image © 123RF.com.)

A filter (splitter) must be installed on each phone point to prevent noise from affecting either voice calls or the DSL link. These can either be installed at the demarc point by the telco engineer or self-installed on each phone point by the customer.

The main drawback of DSL is that, as a copper-wire technology, it suffers from attenuation. The maximum range of a DSL modem is typically about 3 miles (5 km), but the longer the connection, the greater the deterioration in data rate. Domestic cabling may also be relatively poor quality and pass through "noisy" environments.

DSL Types

There are various types or flavors of DSL. These are standardized by the ITU in a series of G. recommendations.

- Symmetrical DSL (SDSL) is so-called because it provides the same downlink and uplink bandwidth. There are various types of symmetric DSL service. SDSL services tend to be provided as business packages, rather than to residential customers.

- Asymmetrical DSL (ADSL) (G.992) is a consumer version of DSL that provides a fast downlink but a slow uplink. There are various iterations of ADSL, with the latest (ADSL2+) offering downlink rates up to about 24 Mbps and uplink rates up to 3.3 Mbps. Service providers may impose usage restrictions to limit the amount of data downloaded per month. Actual speed may be affected by the quality of the cabling in the consumer's premises and between the premises and the exchange, and by the number of users connected to the same DSLAM (contention).

Fiber to the Curb

The major obstacle to providing WAN access that can approach LAN performance is bandwidth in the last mile, where the copper wiring infrastructure is generally not good. The projects to update this wiring to use fiber optic links are referred to by the umbrella term Fiber to the X (FTTx).

The most expensive solution is Fiber to the Premises (FTTP) or its residential variant Fiber to the Home (FTTH). The essential point about both these implementations is that the fiber link is terminated at the demarc. Other solutions can variously be described as Fiber to the Node (FTTN) or Fiber to the Curb (FTTC). These retain some sort of copper wiring to the demarc while extending the fiber link to a communications cabinet servicing multiple subscribers. The service providers with their roots in telephone networks use Very high-speed DSL (VDSL) to support FTTC. VDSL (G.993) achieves higher bit rates than other DSL types at the expense of range. It allows for both symmetric and asymmetric modes. Over 300 m (1000 feet), an asymmetric link supports 52 Mbps downstream and 6 Mbps upstream, while a symmetric link supports 26 Mbps in both directions. VDSL2 specifies a very short range (100 m/300 feet) rate of 100 Mbps (bi-directional).

The modem type must match the service. An ADSL-only modem cannot be used to access a VDSL service, for instance.

Cable Provider Links

A cable Internet connection is usually available along with Cable Access TV (CATV). These networks are sometimes described as hybrid fiber coax (HFC) because they combine a fiber optic core network with coax links to CPE, but are more simply just described as cable broadband.

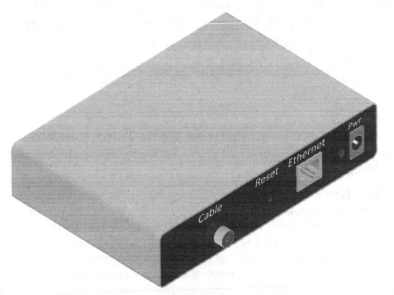

A cable modem—The RJ-45 port connects to the local network, while the coax port connects to the service provider network. (Image © 123RF.com.)

Installation of a **cable modem** follows the same general principles as for a DSL modem. The cable modem is interfaced to a computer or router through an Ethernet or USB adapter and with the access provider's network by a short segment of coax. More coax then links all the premises in a street with a Cable Modem Termination System (CMTS), which routes data traffic via the fiber backbone to the ISP's Point of Presence (PoP) and from there to the Internet. Cable based on the Data Over Cable Service Interface Specification (DOCSIS) supports downlink speeds of up to 38 Mbps (North America) or 50 Mbps (Europe) and uplinks of up to 27 Mbps. DOCSIS version 3 allows the use of multiplexed channels to achieve higher bandwidth.

Metro-optical Provider Links

Carrier Ethernet provisions point-to-point or point-to-multipoint Ethernet leased lines over wide area networks. Carrier Ethernet may also be also referred to as a **metro-optical** provider link. The term Metro Ethernet refers to Carrier Ethernet where the geographic scope is limited to a single city. Standards for Carrier Ethernet are developed by the MEF (mef.net). Carrier Ethernet can use different types of physical connectivity. Some examples include:

- **Ethernet over Fiber**—Uses the IEEE 802.3 10GBASE-LR and 10GBASE-ER specifications.

- **Ethernet over Copper**—Uses DSL variants such as single-pair high-speed DSL (SHDSL) and VDSL to overcome the usual distance limitations of copper Ethernet. This does not support anything like the same speeds as LAN Ethernet (more typically 2-10 Mbps), but multiple pairs can be aggregated for higher bandwidth.

On top of the physical connectivity method, there are multiple service categories for Carrier Ethernet. Two of these are E-line and E-LAN:

- **E-line**—Establishes a point-to-point link between two sites. Multiple E-lines can be configured on a single Metro Ethernet interface, with each E-line representing a separate VLAN.

- **E-LAN**—Establishes a mesh topology between multiple sites.

These services can be used by the customer to join multiple sites together or as a way of connecting their enterprise network to the Internet. From the customer's perspective, Carrier Ethernet has many advantages. The fact that Carrier Ethernet is easily scalable affords businesses the flexibility to match the service to their changing demands. Also, the fact that the same Ethernet protocol and framing is used on the LAN and connectivity into the public network space can make the configuration of routers, Layer 3 switches, and firewalls simpler.

Full fiber connections are also being provisioned to residential and small business customers, though availability can often be limited to a few metropolitan areas. Rather than dedicated leased lines, these services are deployed as a **passive optical network (PON)**. Packages are offered in tiers from 100 Mbps up to 1 Gbps.

In a PON, a single fiber cable is run from the nearest exchange to an optical line terminal (OLT) located in the street. This link uses dense wavelength division multiplexing (DWDM) to support a ratio of backhaul cable to subscribers of 1:64 or 1:128. From the OLT, splitters direct each subscriber's wavelength frequency over a shorter length of fiber to an optical network unit (ONU) or optical network terminal (ONT) installed at the demarc. The ONU/ONT converts the optical signal to an electrical one. The ONU/ONT is connected to the customer's router using a copper wire patch cord.

Microwave Satellite

Satellite systems provide far bigger areas of coverage than can be achieved by using other technologies. The microwave dishes are aligned to orbital satellites that can either relay signals between sites directly or via another satellite. The widespread use of satellite television receivers allows for domestic Internet connectivity services over satellite connections. Satellite services for business are also expanding, especially in rural areas where DSL or cable services are unlikely to be available.

Satellite connections experience quite severe latency problems as the signal must travel over thousands of miles more than terrestrial connections, introducing a delay of four to five times what might be expected over a land link. For example, if you know that accessing a site in the US from Europe takes 200 ms over a land (undersea) link, accessing the same site over a satellite link could involve a 900 ms delay. This is an issue for real-time applications, such as videoconferencing, VoIP, and multiplayer gaming.

To create a satellite Internet connection, the ISP installs a satellite dish, referred to as a very small aperture terminal (VSAT), at the customer's premises and aligns it with the orbital satellite. The size of a VSAT ranges from 1.2 to 2.4 meters in diameter. The satellites are in geostationary orbit over the equator, so in the northern hemisphere the dish will be pointing south. The antenna is connected via coaxial cabling to a Digital Video Broadcast Satellite (DVB-S) modem.

Review Activity:

Explain WAN Provider Links

Answer the following questions:

1. What component of a structured cabling system protects the demarc against tampering?

2. What type of cable can be used to connect a CSU/DSU to a smartjack, assuming a maximum link distance of 1m (3 feet)?

3. You are connecting a SOHO network to a VDSL service using a separate VDSL modem. What cables do you require and how should they be connected?

4. You need to cable a service that terminates at an optical network unit (ONU) to the customer router. What type of cable is required?

5. Assuming that sufficient bandwidth can be provided, what factor limits the usefulness of a microwave satellite Internet link?

Topic 16B

Compare and Contrast Remote Access Methods

EXAM OBJECTIVES COVERED

1.5 Explain common ports and protocols, their application, and encrypted alternatives.
2.1 Compare and contrast various devices, their features, and their appropriate placement on the network. (VPN headend only)
4.4 Compare and contrast remote access methods and security implications.

With today's mobile workforce, most networks have to support connections by remote employees, contractors, and customers to their network resources. These remote connections often make use of untrusted public networks, such as the Internet. To counter the security risks associated with public networks, organizations implement a virtual private network (VPN) over the public network to ensure secure communications. Consequently, understanding how to implement secure remote access VPN protocols will be a major part of your job as a network professional.

Remote Network Access Authentication and Authorization

Remote network access means that the user's device does not make a direct cabled or wireless connection to the network. The connection occurs over or through an intermediate network, usually a public WAN. Historically, remote network access might have used analog modems connecting over the telephone system. These days, most remote access is implemented as a virtual private network (VPN), running over the Internet.

Given that, administering remote access involves essentially the same tasks as administering the local network. Only authorized users who have successfully authenticated should be allowed access to local network resources and communication channels. Additional complexity comes about because it can be more difficult to ensure the security of remote workstations and servers and there is greater opportunity for remote logins to be exploited.

The creation of a remote access server (RAS) should be accompanied by documentation describing the uses of the service, security risks and countermeasures, and authorized users of the service. There should also be authorization to run the service from the network manager. The remote access policy should then implement the measures identified through compiling the documentation. Typical policy restrictions would be:

- Restricting access to defined users or groups.

- Restricting access to defined times of day or particular days of the week.

- Restricting privileges on the local network (ideally, remote users would only be permitted access to a clearly defined part of the network).

- Logging and auditing access logons and attempted logons.

In addition to this, a management plan should ensure that RASs and other hardware are kept up to date with the latest software or firmware updates. Administrative access to the devices should also be secured, using strong authentication.

Tunneling and Encapsulation Protocols

Most modern remote network access solutions use Internet access infrastructure and setup a secure tunnel for private communications through the Internet. This is referred to as a **virtual private network (VPN)**. Most business and residential sites have Internet connectivity, so this solution is very efficient in terms of cost. The main concerns are providing security for the transmissions that pass through the public network and preventing unauthorized users from making use of the VPN connection.

Point-to-Point Protocol

VPNs depend on tunneling protocols. Tunneling is used when the source and destination hosts are on the same logical network but connected via different physical networks. The **Point-to-Point Protocol (PPP)** is an encapsulation protocol that works at the Data Link layer (layer 2). PPP is used to encapsulate IP packets for transmission over serial digital lines. PPP has no security mechanisms, so must be used with other protocols to provision a secure tunnel.

Generic Routing Encapsulation

Where PPP works at layer 2, **Generic Routing Encapsulation (GRE)** works at layer 3. A GRE packet can itself encapsulate an IP packet (or most other network layer protocol types) as its payload. The "outer" GRE packet is assigned protocol number 47 and has its own IP source and header address fields. The GRE packet is then itself encapsulated in a layer 2 frame for transmission to the next hop router. Each intermediate router inspects only the outer GRE header to determine the forwarding destination. At the final destination, the receiving router de-encapsulates the GRE packet to extract the inner IP payload and forwards that inner packet to its destination. GRE does not have any mechanisms for authenticating users or devices and so is often used with other protocols in a VPN solution.

IP Security

Internet Protocol Security (IPSec) also operates at the network layer (layer 3) of the OSI model to encrypt packets passing over any network. IPSec is often used with other protocols to provide connection security, but is increasingly used as a native VPN protocol.

Transport Layer Security

Transport Layer Security (TLS) over TCP or datagram TLS (DTLS) over UDP can be used to encapsulate frames or IP packets. The main drawback is that as TLS already operates at the session layer, the headers from the inner and outer packets add up to a significant overhead.

Client-to-Site Virtual Private Networks

A VPN can be implemented in several topologies. In a client-to-site or remote access topology, the VPN client connects over the public network to a VPN gateway (a VPN-enabled router) positioned on the edge of the local network (typically the VPN access server will be in a screened subnet). Client-to-site is the "telecommuter" model, allowing home-workers and employees working in the field to connect to the corporate network.

Client-to-site VPNs can be configured using a number of protocols. An SSL/TLS VPN solution uses certificates to establish the secure tunnel. One example is Microsoft's Secure Socket Tunneling Protocol (SSTP). Cisco's Layer 2 Tunneling Protocol (L2TP) is also widely used, in conjunction with IPSec. All these solutions require client software to operate. Most VPN solutions use EAP and AAA/RADIUS architecture to authenticate client devices and users.

 Microsoft's Point-to-Point Tunneling Protocol (PPTP) was once very widely used but has too many security flaws to be deployed safely.

When a client connected to a remote access VPN tries to access other sites on the Internet, there are two ways to manage the connection:

- **Split tunnel**—the client accesses the Internet directly using its "native" IP configuration and DNS servers.

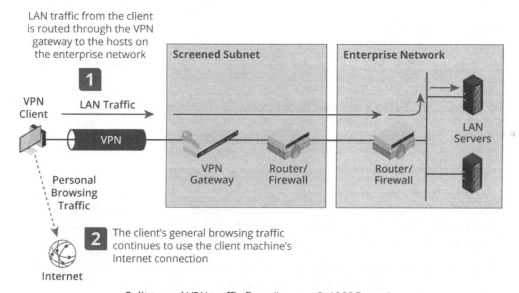

Split tunnel VPN traffic flow. (Images © 123RF.com.)

- **Full tunnel**—Internet access is mediated by the corporate network, which will alter the client's IP address and DNS servers and may use a proxy.

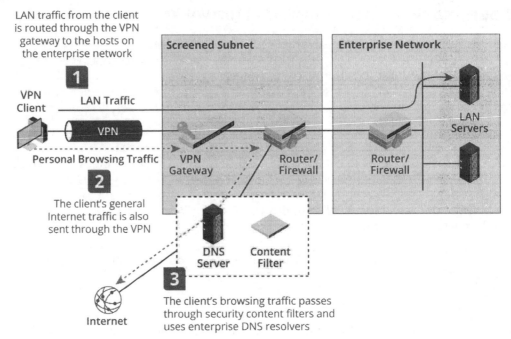

Full tunnel VPN traffic flow. (Images © 123RF.com.)

Full tunnel offers better security, but the network address translations and DNS operations required may cause problems with some websites, especially cloud services. It also means more data is channeled over the link and the connection can exhibit higher latency.

Remote Host Access and Remote Desktop Gateways

A remote access VPN refers to extending local network access over an intermediate public network, so that a remote computer is effectively joined to the local network. Remote access can also refer to remote host access, where a user operates a computer or configures a network appliance without having to use a local terminal. This type of remote host access can be implemented within a local network or over a public network. It can be used for a variety of purposes:

- Remote configuration of network appliances. Most of these appliances are headless (they do not have a video monitor or input devices) and remote connections are the only practical configuration option. This type of connection it typically implemented using Secure Shell (SSH).

- Remote desktop connections either allow an administrator to configure a server or a user to operate a computer remotely. Where remote desktop protocols provide GUI access, other protocols can be used for terminal-only access.

- Remote desktop gateways allow user access to networked apps. A gateway can also be used to connect a user to a virtual desktop, where a client OS and applications software is provisioned as a virtual appliance. Alternatively, a remote desktop gateway is a means of implementing a clientless VPN.

Remote Desktop Protocol and Virtual Network Computing

Microsoft's Remote Desktop Protocol (RDP) can be used to access a physical machine on a one-to-one basis. Alternatively, the site can operate a remote desktop gateway that facilitates access to virtual desktops or individual apps running on the network servers (docs.microsoft.com/en-us/windows-server/remote/remote-desktop-services/welcome-to-rds). Similar services are provided by Citrix's products (citrix.com/products).

There are several popular alternatives to Remote Desktop. Most support remote access to platforms other than Windows (macOS and iOS, Linux, Chrome OS, and Android for instance). Examples include TeamViewer (teamviewer.com/en) and **Virtual Network Computing (VNC)**, which is implemented by several different providers (notably realvnc.com/en).

Clientless VPNs

Traditionally, remote desktop products and client-to-site VPNs require a client app that implements the protocols and authentication methods supported by the remote desktop/VPN gateway. The canvas element introduced in HTML5 allows a browser to draw and update a desktop with relatively little lag. It can also handle audio. This allows ordinary browser software to connect to a remote desktop or VPN. This is referred to as an **HTML5 VPN or clientless VPN** (guacamole. apache.org). This solution also uses a protocol called WebSockets, which enables bidirectional messages to be sent between the server and client without requiring the overhead of separate HTTP requests.

Site-to-Site Virtual Private Networks

A VPN can also be deployed in a site-to-site model to connect two or more private networks. Where remote access VPN connections are typically initiated by the client, a site-to-site VPN is configured to operate automatically. The gateways exchange security information using whichever protocol the VPN is based on. This establishes a trust relationship between the gateways and sets up a secure connection through which to tunnel data. Hosts at each site do not need to be configured with any information about the VPN. The routing infrastructure at each site determines whether to deliver traffic locally or send it over the VPN tunnel. This is also referred to as compulsory tunneling. Compulsory tunnels can be in place permanently (static), or they can be put in place based on the data or client type (dynamic).

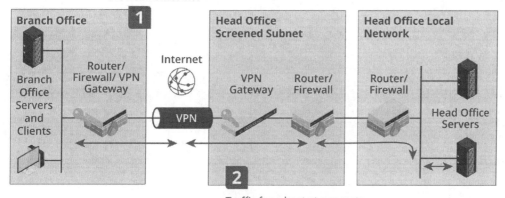

Site-to-site VPN. (Images © 123rf.com.)

 VPNs are not always established over the public Internet. A WAN service provider can implement VPNs via its network. The provider can use VLAN-like technology to isolate a customer's data from other traffic. This is a common model for site-to-site VPNs.

While VPNs are being covered here as part of remote access, they can be just as usefully deployed on local networks as a type of network segmentation. For example, the department for product development might need to provide secure communications with the marketing department.

Hub and Spoke VPNs and VPN Headends

A site-to-site VPN that involves more than two sites connects the remote sites (or spokes) to a headquarters site (hub) by using static tunnels configured between the hub and each spoke. This is referred to as a hub and spoke topology. The VPN router installed in the central office or hub needs to be a powerful machine capable of aggregating high traffic volumes. This VPN router is also referred to as a **VPN headend**. VPN headends would normally be installed in groups for load balancing and fault tolerance. A VPN headend must be able to scale to meet changing demand levels. The VPN routers installed at the spokes, are referred to as branch office routers.

A **dynamic multipoint VPN (DMVPN)** allows VPNs to be set up dynamically according to traffic requirements and demand. The original concept was developed by Cisco but has been adopted by other vendors and now runs on diverse router platforms. DMVPN allows for the use of a dynamic mesh topology between multiple remote sites, effectively setting up direct VPNs, rather than the remote sites having to route traffic via the hub. Each site can communicate with all other spokes directly no matter where they are located.

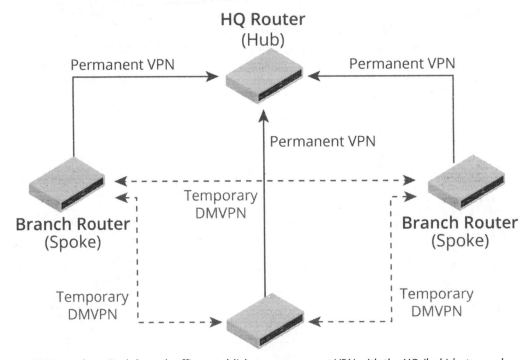

DMVPN topology. Each branch office establishes a permanent VPN with the HQ (hub) but can also create spoke-to-spoke VPNs dynamically. (Images © 123RF.com.)

To configure a DMVPN, each remote site's router is still connected to the hub router using an IPSec tunnel. As a large percentage of a remote site's traffic is likely to be with the main HQ, this ensures this normal traffic is dealt with efficiently. If two remote sites (spokes) wish to communicate with one another, the spoke instigating the link informs the hub. The hub will provide the connection details for the other spoke facilitating a dynamic IPSec tunnel to be created directly between the two spokes. This process invokes the use of the Next Hop Router Protocol (NHRP) to identify destination addresses and the GRE tunneling. GRE encapsulates the encrypted IPSec packets. The two remote sites use the physical communications links between the two locations but all traffic flows over the temporary, encrypted VPN tunnel setup between them. DMVPN will then decide how long this temporary VPN remains in place based on timers and traffic flows.

In this way, DMVPN allows remote sites to connect with each other over the public WAN or Internet, such as when using video conferencing, but doesn't require a static VPN connection between sites. This on-demand deployment of IPSec VPNs is more efficient. Routing policies can be used to select the most reliable path between the remote sites, which potentially reduces the chance of latency and jitter affecting any voice/video services running over the VPN.

Internet Protocol Security

Internet Protocol Security (IPSec) can be used to secure IPv4 and/or IPv6 communications on local networks and as a remote access protocol.

Each host that uses IPSec must be assigned a policy. An IPSec policy sets the authentication mechanism and also the protocols and mode for the connection. Hosts must be able to match at least one matching security method for a connection to be established. There are two core protocols in IPSec, which can be applied singly or together, depending on the policy.

Authentication Header

The **Authentication Header (AH)** protocol performs a cryptographic hash on the whole packet, including the IP header, plus a shared secret key (known only to the communicating hosts), and adds this secret in its header as an Integrity Check Value (ICV). The recipient performs the same function on the packet and key and should derive the same value to confirm that the packet has not been modified. The payload is not encrypted so this protocol does not provide confidentiality. Also, the inclusion of IP header fields in the ICV means that the check will fail across NAT gateways, where the IP address is rewritten. Consequently, AH is not often used.

IPSec datagram using AH—The integrity of the payload and IP header is ensured by the Integrity Check Value (ICV), but the payload is not encrypted.

Encapsulating Security Payload

Encapsulating Security Payload (ESP) provides confidentiality and/or authentication and integrity. It can be used to encrypt the packet rather than simply calculating a hash. ESP attaches three fields to the packet: a header, a trailer (providing padding for the cryptographic function), and an Integrity Check Value. Unlike AH, ESP excludes the IP header when calculating the ICV.

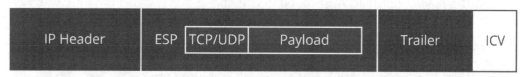

IPSec datagram using ESP—The TCP header and payload from the original packet is encapsulated within ESP and encrypted to provide confidentiality.

With ESP, algorithms for both confidentiality (symmetric cipher) and authentication/ integrity (hash function) are usually applied together. It is possible to use one or the other, however.

 The principles underlying IPSec are the same for IPv4 and IPv6, but the header formats are different. IPSec makes use of extension headers in IPv6 while in IPv4, ESP and AH are allocated new IP protocol numbers (50 and 51), and either modify the original IP header or encapsulate the original packet, depending on whether transport or tunnel mode is used.

IKE and IPSec Modes

IPSec's encryption and hashing functions depend on a shared secret. The secret must be communicated to both hosts and the hosts must confirm one another's identity (mutual authentication). The **Internet Key Exchange (IKE)** protocol handles authentication and key exchange, referred to as Security Associations (SA).

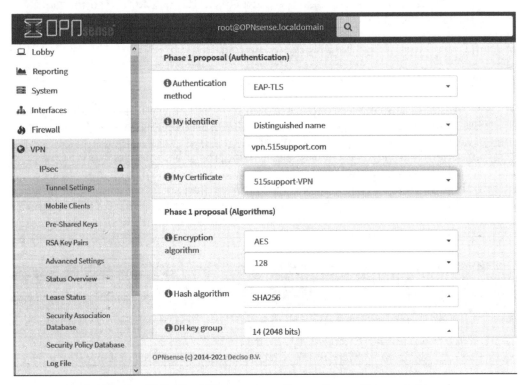

Configuring IKE in the OPNsense security appliance. (Screenshot used with permission from OPNsense.)

IPSec can be used in two modes:

- **Transport mode**—this mode is used to secure communications between hosts on a private network (an end-to-end implementation). When ESP is applied in transport mode, the IP header for each packet is not encrypted, just the payload data. If AH is used in transport mode, it can provide integrity for the IP header.

- **Tunnel mode**—this mode is used for communications between VPN gateways across an unsecure network (creating a VPN). This is also referred to as a router implementation. With ESP, the whole IP packet (header and payload) is encrypted and encapsulated as a datagram with a new IP header. AH has no real use case in tunnel mode, as confidentiality will usually be required.

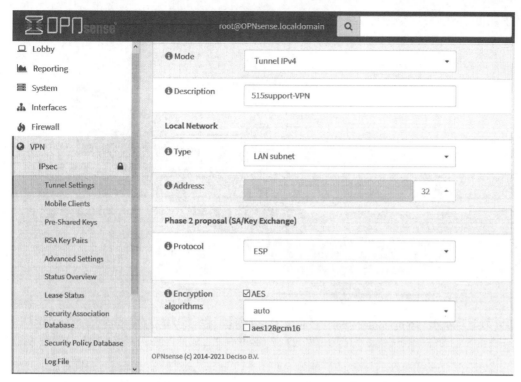

Configuring an IPSec tunnel in the OPNsense security appliance.
(Screenshot used with permission from OPNsense.)

Out-of-Band Management Methods

Some network appliances, such as unmanaged switches, do not offer any configuration options or interface. You just have to plug them in, and they operate automatically. Managed switches and appliances, such as routers, firewalls, switches, and access points, support more complex functions and can be configured and monitored over several interfaces. The functions of a managed appliance can be accessed via one of the device's management interfaces. An appliance may support the following interfaces:

- **Console Port**—This requires connecting a device running terminal emulator software (a laptop, for instance) to the device via a separate physical interface using a special console (or rollover) cable. The terminal emulator can then be used to start a command line interface (CLI).

- **AUX port**—This port is designed to connect to an analog modem and provide remote access over a dial-up link. Once the AUX port is enabled and configured, the modem can be connected to it by using an RS-232 serial cable, a specially wired RJ-45 rollover cable and terminal adapter (RJ-45 to DB9), or a management cable (RJ-45 to DB9). Configure the modem with appropriate serial link settings (refer to the vendor guide), connect it to an appropriate telephone line, and allocate an extension number. A remote host can connect to the appliance CLI by using a terminal emulation program such as HyperTerminal or PuTTY.

- **Management port**—This means configuring a virtual network interface and IP address on the device to use for management functions and connecting to it via one of the normal Ethernet ports. The port must be enabled for this function (some appliances come with a dedicated management port). Using Telnet (unsecure) or Secure Shell (SSH) to connect to a CLI remotely over the management interface in this way is referred to as a virtual terminal.

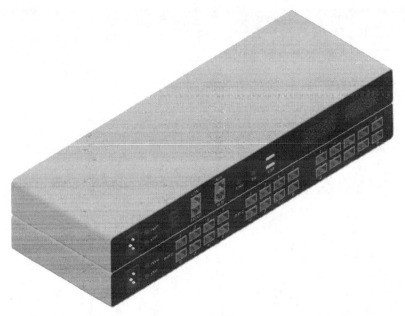

USB and RJ-45 type console ports plus AUX and other management interfaces on a router.
(Image © 123RF.com.)

Management methods can be described as either in-band or **out-of-band (OOB)**. An in-band management link is one that shares traffic with other communications on the "production" network. The console port is a physically out-of-band management method; the link is limited to the attached device. When you are using a browser-based management interface or a virtual terminal, the link can be made out-of-band by connecting the port used for management access to physically separate network infrastructure. Obviously, this is costly to implement, but out-of-band management is more secure and means that access to the device is preserved when there are problems affecting the production network.

With an in-band connection, better security can be implemented by using a VLAN to isolate management traffic. This makes it harder for potential eavesdroppers to view or modify traffic passing over the management interface. This sort of virtual OOB does still mean that access could be compromised by a system-wide network failure, however.

 Use a secure connection protocol (HTTPS rather than HTTP, or SSH rather than Telnet) for the management interface. This applies to OOB too, but it is critical for in-band management.

Review Activity:

Remote Access Methods

Answer the following questions:

1. **What step can you take to prevent unauthorized use of a remote access server?**

2. **What type of client-to-site VPN ensures that any traffic from the remote node can be monitored from the corporate network while the machine is joined to the VPN?**

3. **What replaces the VPN client in a clientless remote access solution?**

4. **What difference does DMVPN make to a hub and spoke VPN topology?**

5. **What IPSec mode would you use for data confidentiality on a private network?**

6. **What is a virtual terminal?**

Lesson 16

Summary

You should be able to explain WAN provider links and compare and contrast remote access methods and security implications.

Guidelines for Supporting WAN Links and Remote Access Methods

Follow these guidelines to support WAN links and remote access methods:

- Evaluate available types of WAN provider, including leased line, DSL, cable, Carrier Ethernet, FTTx, and satellite, to select a service that matches reliability and bandwidth requirements.

- Provision Layer 1/2 WAN connectivity at the demarc/entrance facilities by connecting an appropriate type of digital modem to the service provider smartjack or network terminal. If the digital modem is not provisioned as a WAN interface card, connect it to a router to establish connectivity at Layer 3.

- Develop a remote access policy to ensure only authorized users can connect and ensure that the network is not compromised by remote clients with weak security configurations.

- Support client-to-site VPNs and/or remote desktop services by selecting a protocol supported by client devices and installing the remote access server to the network edge by using a secure firewall configuration to prevent compromise.

- Support site-to-site VPNs in hub and spoke topologies using protocols such as IPSec and GRE.

- Support remote access to critical network infrastructure using out-of-band links.

Lesson 17

Explaining Organizational and Physical Security Concepts

LESSON INTRODUCTION

The cabling, switches, routers, security appliances, servers, and clients that make up a local network must all be located within a site. Managing a site so that the network is highly available and secure involves creating policies and best practices, supported by documentation. This might seem less immediately rewarding than getting a new application or server up-and-running, but these kinds of operational procedures are just as important to well-managed networks.

Site management can also involve the management of unfamiliar technologies, such as physical access controls, embedded systems, and Internet of Things (IoT) devices. As a network technician, you will be expected to be aware of the unique challenges posed by incorporating these systems within sites and networks.

Lesson Objectives

In this lesson, you will:

- Explain organizational documentation and policies.

- Explain physical security methods.

- Compare and contrast Internet of Things devices.

Topic 17A

Explain Organizational Documentation and Policies

 EXAM OBJECTIVES COVERED
3.2 Explain the purpose of organizational documents and policies.

In this topic, you will learn to explain how configuration management documentation, diagrams, written policies, and best practices are used to manage and troubleshoot networks.

Operating Plans and Procedures

Running an efficient network is not just about installing cabling and network devices. The administration of the network in terms of documentation and management is a critical task.

Configuration Management

Configuration management means identifying and documenting all the infrastructure and devices installed at a site. ITIL® is a popular documentation of good and best practice activities and processes for delivering IT services. Under ITIL, configuration management is implemented using the following elements:

- Service assets are things, processes, or people that contribute to the delivery of an IT service. Each asset must be identified by some sort of label.

- A Configuration Item (CI) is an asset that requires specific management procedures for it to be used to deliver the service. CIs are defined by their attributes.

- A baseline documents the approved or authorized state of a CI. This allows auditing processes to detect unexpected or unauthorized change. A baseline can be a **configuration baseline** (the ACL applied to a firewall, for instance) or a performance baseline (such as the throughput achieved by the firewall).

- A Configuration Management System (CMS) is the tools and databases that collect, store, manage, update, and present information about CIs. A small network might capture this information in spreadsheets and diagrams; there are dedicated applications for enterprise CMS.

Change Management

A documented **change management** process minimizes the risk of unscheduled downtime by implementing changes in a planned and controlled way. The need to change is often described either as reactive, where the change is forced on the organization, or as proactive, where the need for change is initiated internally. Changes can also be categorized according to their potential impact and level of risk (major, significant, minor, or normal, for instance).

In a formal change management process, the need or reasons for change and the procedure for implementing the change is captured in a Request for Change (RFC) document and submitted for approval. The RFC will then be considered at the appropriate level and affected stakeholders will be notified. Major or significant changes might be managed as a separate project and require approval through a Change Advisory Board (CAB).

Standard Operating Procedures

Configuration changes should be made only when there is a valid job ticket authorizing the change. This means that the activity of all network personnel, whether it be installing new devices or troubleshooting, is recorded in job logs. In a fully documented environment, each task will be governed by a **standard operating procedure (SOP)**. A SOP sets out the principal goals and considerations, such as budget, security, or customer contact standards, for performing a task and identifies lines of responsibility and authorization for performing it. A SOP may also contain detailed steps for completing a task in an approved way, or these steps may be presented as work instructions.

System Life Cycle Plans and Procedures

It is crucial for an organization to have an inventory of its tangible and intangible assets. In terms of network management, assets are network appliances (routers, switches, threat management devices, access points), servers, workstations, and passive network infrastructure (cabling and cross-connects).

Audit Reports

An **audit report** focuses on identifying and recording assets. There are many software suites and associated hardware solutions available to assist with audit tracking and managing inventory. An asset management database can be configured to store as much or as little information as is deemed necessary, though typical data would be type, model, serial number, asset ID, location, user(s), value, and service information. For each asset record, there should also be a copy of or link to the appropriate vendor documentation. This includes both an invoice and warranty/support contract and support and troubleshooting guidance.

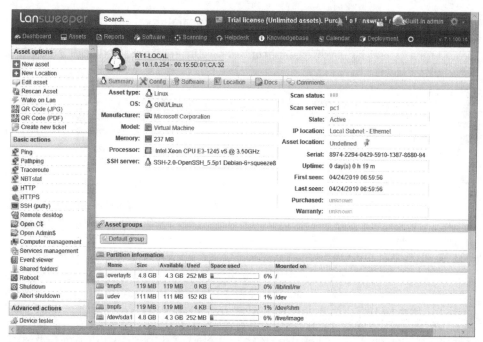

A product such as Lansweeper assists inventory management by scanning network hosts and compiling an asset information database automatically. (Screenshot used with permission from Lansweeper.)

Assessment Reports

Where an audit report focuses on identifying and documenting assets, an assessment report evaluates the configuration and deployment of those assets, such as deviation from baseline configuration or performance. The report will make recommendations where the network is not meeting goals for performance or security. Audit and assessment reports are often contracted to third parties and might be driven by regulatory or compliance demands.

System Life Cycle

One of the functions of auditing and assessment is to manage **system life cycle**. A system life cycle roadmap refers to the controlled acquisition, deployment, use, and decommissioning of assets. An audit and assessment report can identify assets that are no longer fully supported by the vendor or that otherwise no longer meet performance or security requirements.

Physical Network Diagrams

Asset and configuration item (CI) documentation makes significant use of diagrams. A diagram is the best way to capture the complex relationships between network elements. It is important not to try to include too much information as this tends to make the diagram too complex to be useful. Consequently, a large number of diagram types are used in network management. One basic distinction is between physical and logical network diagrams. Within the class of physical network diagrams, the following types are commonly used.

Floor Plan

A **floor plan** is a detailed diagram of wiring and port locations. For example, you might use floor plans to document wall port locations and cable runs in an office. Physically accurate floor plans are hard to design and are likely to require the help of an architect or graphics professional.

Wiring Diagram

A **wiring diagram** (or pin-out) shows detailed information about the termination of twisted pairs in an RJ-45 or RJ-48C jack or Insulation Displacement Connector (IDC). You might also use a wiring diagram to document how fiber-optic strands are terminated.

You should document the wiring diagrams used to terminate twisted pairs. Ethernet is wired by T568A or T568B, and the same standard should be used consistently throughout the network.

Distribution Frame

A port location diagram identifies how wall ports located in work areas are connected back to ports in a distribution frame or patch panel and then from the patch panel ports to the switch ports. Within a structured cabling system, there are two types of distribution frame:

- **Main Distribution Frame (MDF)**—The location for distribution/core level internal switching. The MDF will terminate trunk links from multiple Intermediate Distribution Frames (IDFs). The MDF also serves as the location for termination of external (WAN) circuits. You should ensure that WAN links to the Internet or to remote offices from the MDF are clearly labeled and that key information such as IP addresses and bandwidth is documented. The WAN provider will assign a circuit ID, and you will need to quote this if raising any sort of support issue.

- **Intermediate Distribution Frame (IDF)**—In a large network, one or more IDFs provides termination for access layer switches that serve a given area, such as a single office floor. Each IDF has a trunk link to the MDF. Make sure that these are clearly labeled and distinct from access ports.

In addition to having a diagram, it can be very useful to take a photo of the current configuration by using a digital camera or smartphone. This provides an additional visual reference for troubleshooting and identifying unauthorized changes.

In order for a physical diagram of cabling and assets to make any sense, there must be a system of labeling in place for identifying these assets. A typical type of port naming convention is for alphanumeric identifiers for the campus (for multicampus networks), building (for campus networks), telecommunications space, and port. For example, CB01-01A-D01 could refer to a cable terminating at Main Campus Building (CB01), telecommunications space A on floor 1 (01A), data port 1 (D01). Structured cable and patch cords should be labeled at both ends to fully identify the circuit.

Site Survey Report

A wireless site survey report overlays a floor plan with graphics showing signal strength and channel utilization at different points in the building.

Rack Diagrams

A **rack** system is a specially configured steel shelving system for patch panels, switches and routers, and server devices. Racks are standard widths and can fit appliances using standard height multiples of 1.75" called units (U). For example, a basic switch might be 1U while a server might be 4U (7") in height.

A rack diagram records the position of each appliance in the rack. You can obtain stencils that represent vendor equipment from their websites or a collection such as visiocafe.com. You can record key configuration information for each item using labels. As well as service tags and port IDs and links, you should identify which power outlets on the uninterruptible power supply (UPS) connect to which appliance power supply units (PSU)s.

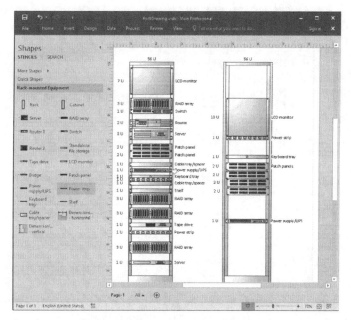

Designing rack layout in Microsoft Visio. (Screenshot used with permission from Microsoft.)

Logical versus Physical Network Diagrams

In contrast to diagrams such as floor plans that are drawn to an accurate scale, a schematic is a simplified or abstracted representation of a system. In terms of the physical network topology, a schematic diagram can show the general placement of equipment and telecommunications rooms, plus device and port IDs, without trying to capture the exact position or relative size of any one element. Schematics can also be used to represent the logical structure of the network in terms of zones and subnets.

When you make network schematics, resist the urge to represent too much in a single diagram. For example, create separate diagrams for the PHY, Data Link, and Logical (IP) layers. Some of the information appropriate to show at each layer includes:

- **PHY (Physical layer)**—Asset IDs and cable links. You can use color-coding or line styles to represent the cable type (make sure the diagram has an accompanying legend to explain your scheme).

- **Data Link (Layer 2)**—Shows interconnections between switches and routers, with asset IDs (or the management IP of the appliance), interface IDs, and link-layer protocol and bandwidth. You could use line thickness to represent bandwidth, but for clarity it is a good idea to use labels as well.

- **Logical (IP/Layer 3)**—IP addresses of router interfaces (plus any other static IP assignments) and firewalls, plus links showing the IP network ID and netmask, VLAN ID (if used), and DHCP scopes.

- **Application**—Server instances and TCP/UDP ports in use. You might also include configuration information and performance baselines (CPU, memory, storage, and network utilization) at this level.

Schematics can either be drawn manually using a tool such as Microsoft® Visio® or compiled automatically from network mapping software.

Schematics can use either representative icons or pictures or drawings of actual product models. As far as icons go, the ones created by Cisco are recognized as standards. These are freely available (without alteration) from Cisco's website (cisco.com/c/en/us/about/brand-center/network-topology-icons.html). Some of the more commonly used devices are shown here:

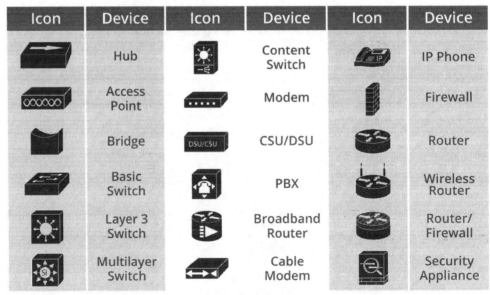

Icon	Device	Icon	Device	Icon	Device
	Hub		Content Switch		IP Phone
	Access Point		Modem		Firewall
	Bridge		CSU/DSU		Router
	Basic Switch		PBX		Wireless Router
	Layer 3 Switch		Broadband Router		Router/ Firewall
	Multilayer Switch		Cable Modem		Security Appliance

Common Cisco network icons. (Images © and Courtesy of Cisco Systems, Inc. Unauthorized use not permitted.)

Security Response Plans and Procedures

Security response plans and procedures establish what to do when certain types of events occur. These plans attempt to anticipate adverse events so that impacts can be minimized.

Incident Response Plan

An **incident response plan** sets out the procedures, tools, methods of communication, and guidelines for dealing with security incidents. An incident is where security is breached or there is an attempted breach. Incident response is one of the most difficult areas of security to plan for and implement because its aims can be incompatible:

1. The immediate aim is usually to protect confidential data or minimize impacts from its loss and re-establish a secure working system.

2. It may also be important to preserve evidence of the incident with the aim of prosecuting the perpetrators. Forensic evidence collection can interfere with re-establishing availability, however.

3. Follow-up or lessons learned analysis will attempt to prevent reoccurrence of similar incidents.

The actions of first responders immediately following detection of an incident can have a critical impact on these aims, so an effective policy and well-trained incident response professionals are crucial. Incident response is also likely to require coordinated action and authorization from several different departments or managers, which adds further levels of complexity.

Disaster Recovery Plan

Where incident response is focused on individual security policy violations, a **disaster recovery plan (DRP)** addresses large-scale incidents. These will typically be incidents that threaten the performance or security of a whole site. A DRP should accomplish the following:

*   Identify scenarios for natural and non-natural disasters and options for protecting systems.

*   Identify tasks, resources, and responsibilities for responding to a disaster. Disaster recovery focuses on tasks such as switching services to failover systems or sites and restoring systems and data from backups.

*   Train staff in the disaster planning procedures and how to react well to adverse events.

Business Continuity Plan

Where disaster recovery focuses on plans for specific scenarios, a **business continuity plan (BCP)** or continuity of operations plan (COOP) is a collection of processes and resources that enable an organization to maintain normal business operations in the face of some adverse event. Continuity planning activity focuses on the functions performed by a business or other organization:

*   Business impact analysis (BIA) identifies mission essential and primary business functions and the risks that would arise if the organization cannot fulfil them.

*   IT contingency planning (ITCP) or IT service continuity planning (ITSCP) ensures that these functions are supported by resilient IT systems, working to identify and mitigate all single points of failure from a process or function.

Hardening and Security Policies

Security policy establishes a duty for each employee to ensure the confidentiality, integrity, and availability of any data assets or processing systems that they use as part of their job. This overall security policy will be supplemented by numerous operational policies to govern specific areas of activity or configuration.

Human Resources (HR) is the department given the task of recruiting and managing the organization's most valuable and critical resource: people. One function of HR is to communicate security policies to employees, including any updates to the policies. Another function is to enforce disciplinary measures (perhaps in conjunction with departmental managers).

Onboarding

Onboarding is the process of welcoming a new employee to the organization. Similar principles apply to taking on new suppliers or contractors. Some of the tasks that most affect security during the onboarding process are as follows:

- **Background check**—This process essentially determines that a person is who they say they are and are not concealing criminal activity, bankruptcy, or connections that would make them unsuitable or risky. Employees working in high confidentiality environments or with access to high value transactions will obviously need to be subjected to a greater degree of scrutiny.

- **Identity and access management (IAM)**—Create an account for the user to access the computer system, assign the appropriate privileges, and ensure the account credentials are known only to the valid user.

- **Asset allocation**—Provision computers or mobile devices for the user or agree on the use of BYOD devices.

- **Training/policies**—Schedule appropriate security awareness and role-relevant training and certification.

Offboarding

Offboarding is the process of ensuring that an employee leaves a company gracefully. In terms of security, there are several processes that must be completed:

- **IAM**—Disable the user account and privileges. Ensure that any information assets created or managed by the employee but owned by the company are accessible (in terms of encryption keys or password-protected files).

- **Retrieving company assets**—Secure mobile devices, keys, smart cards, USB media, and so on. The employee will need to confirm (and in some cases prove) that they have not retained copies of any information assets.

- **Returning personal assets**—Employee-owned devices need to be wiped of corporate data and applications. The employee may also be allowed to retain some information assets (such as personal emails or contact information), depending on the policies in force.

The departure of some types of employees should trigger additional processes to resecure network systems. Examples include employees with detailed knowledge of security systems and procedures and access to shared or generic account credentials. These credentials must be changed immediately.

Usage Policies

Usage policies set out rules for how users should interact with network systems and data.

Password Policy

A **password policy** instructs users on best practice in choosing and maintaining a network access credential. Password protection policies mitigate against the risk of attackers being able to compromise an account and use it to launch other attacks on the network. For example, users must be instructed not to write down passwords, store them in unsecure files, or share them with other users. The credential management policy also needs to alert users to different types of social engineering and phishing attacks.

System-enforced policies can help to enforce credential management principles by stipulating requirements for user-selected passwords. The following rules enforce password complexity and make them difficult to guess or compromise:

- **Length**—The longer a password, the stronger it is. A typical strong network password should be 12 to 16 characters. A longer password or passphrase might be used for mission critical systems or devices where logon is infrequent.

- **Complexity**—Varying the characters in the password makes it more resistant to dictionary-based attacks.

- **Aging and history**—Requiring that the password be changed periodically and preventing the reuse of previously selected passwords.

 You should also note that recent guidance issued by NIST (nvlpubs.nist.gov/nistpubs/ SpecialPublications/NIST.SP.800-63b.pdf) deprecates some of the "traditional" elements of password policy, such as complexity and aging.

Acceptable Use Policies

An **acceptable use policy (AUP)** sets out the permitted uses of a product or service. It might also state explicitly prohibited uses. Such a policy might be used in different contexts. For example, an AUP could be enforced by a business to govern how employees use equipment and services, such as telephone or Internet access, provided to them at work. Another example might be an ISP enforcing a fair use policy governing usage of its Internet access services.

BYOD Policies

A mobile deployment model describes the way employees are provided with smartphone or tablet devices and applications. Some companies issue employees with corporate-owned and controlled devices and insist that only these are used to process company data. Other companies might operate a bring your own device (BYOD) policy. BYOD means that the mobile is owned by the employee and can be used on the corporate network so long as it meets a minimum specification required by the company (in terms of OS version and functionality). The employee will have to agree on the installation of corporate apps and to some level of oversight and auditing. Very often, BYOD devices are registered with enterprise management software and configured with sandboxed corporate workspaces and apps.

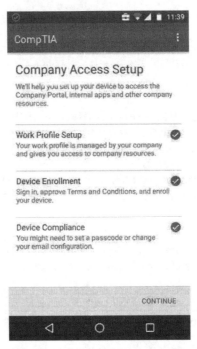

Enterprise management software can be used to segment corporate data from personal data on BYOD devices. (Screenshot used with permission from Google.)

Data Loss Prevention

The theft or loss of confidential and/or personal information is referred to as a data breach. Data breach can expose an organization to huge reputational and financial costs. Consequently, data handling is an area of activity that should be tightly managed by both policies and technical controls.

Data loss prevention (DLP) products scan content in structured formats (such as a database with a formal access control model) or unstructured formats, such as email or word processing documents. DLP products use some sort of dictionary database or algorithm (regular expression matching) to identify confidential or personal/sensitive data. The transfer of content to removable media or by email or to social networking or cloud storage services can then be blocked if it does not conform to a predefined policy.

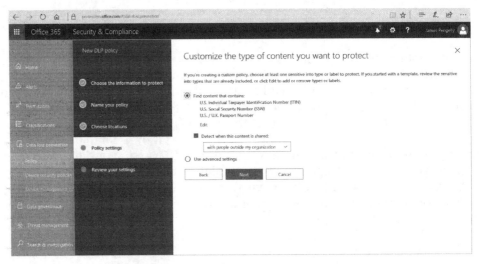

Creating a data loss prevention policy in Office 365. (Screenshot used with permission from Microsoft.)

Remote Access Policies

Where employees are assigned the right to connect to the corporate network from a remote location using a VPN, their use of remote access privileges must be governed by technical and policy controls. Some of the issues that must be mitigated include the following:

- **Malware protection**—The computer may not be accessible to network systems used to update and enforce malware protection. This may have to be left to the end-user. If a worm or Trojan is installed, network security may be compromised.

- **Security information**—Authentication information may be stored on the client (saving a password, for instance), making the network vulnerable if the computer is stolen.

- **Data transfer**—Files copied to the client may no longer be properly secured, raising the potential that confidential information could be stolen along with the device.

- **Local privileges**—The user of a remote computer might be configured with administrative privileges but have no understanding of how such privileges can be exploited or misused. They might install unauthorized software on the machine or make it more vulnerable to malware by browsing the web using their administrative account.

- **Weak authentication**—Relying on a username and password combination is simply not secure enough in a remote access scenario. Two-factor authentication using smart cards or biometric recognition in addition to a PIN or password should be enforced. If this is not an option, a strong password policy must be enforced, and users made aware of the very real risks of writing down or sharing their password.

- **Untrusted networks**—The user might configure weak authentication on a home wireless network or use a public access point, raising the risk of snooping attacks.

The principal solution to remote access security problems is to educate remote users about security risks and their responsibilities. Enforcement can be provided by having remote devices audited periodically to ensure that antivirus, firewall, and OS/browser/application patches are being kept up to date and to check that unlicensed software has not been installed. It is also wise to limit what remote users can access on the local network and to severely restrict the rights of remote computer accounts. The principle of least privilege should be applied.

Common Agreements

Agreements are used between a company and its employees and between companies to enforce performance and security objectives.

Service Level Agreement Requirements

A **service level agreement (SLA)** is a contractual agreement setting out the detailed terms under which an ongoing service is provided. This can be a legally binding formal contract between supplier and customer businesses or a less formal agreement, such as an SLA agreed between internal departments. SLA requirements define aspects of the service, such as scope, performance characteristics, and responsibilities that are agreed upon between the service provider and the customer.

Depending on the nature of your organization's business, you may be responsible for maintaining SLA requirements agreed with your customers, use SLAs to guarantee service standards from your suppliers, or both.

Non-Disclosure Agreement

A **non-disclosure agreement (NDA)** is the legal basis for protecting information assets. It defines what uses of sensitive data are permitted, what storage and distribution restrictions must be enforced, and what penalties breaches of the agreement will incur. A contract of employment is highly likely to contain NDA clauses. NDAs are also used between companies and contractors and between two companies.

Memorandum of Understanding

A **memorandum of understanding (MOU)** is a preliminary or exploratory agreement to express an intent to work together. MOUs are usually intended to be relatively informal and not to act as binding contracts. MOUs almost always have clauses stating that the parties shall respect confidentiality, however.

Review Activity:

Organizational Documentation and Policies

Answer the following questions:

1. What types of baselines are useful when you are performing configuration management?

2. What type of security control provisions resources and procedures to cope with incidents that cause major service outages?

3. How is the person who first receives notification of a potential security incident designated?

4. What configuration request would be implemented by IT services during employee onboarding?

Topic 17B

Explain Physical Security Methods

EXAM OBJECTIVES COVERED
4.5 Explain the importance of physical security.

In this topic, you will examine ways to enhance the physical security of a network site. For a network to be secure, access to the building and certain areas must be controlled. An understanding of procedures and hardware that improve the physical security of site premises will help reduce the risk of intrusion.

Badges and Site Secure Entry Systems

Prevention-type physical controls are ones that stop an intruder from gaining unauthorized access, if they work effectively. Where an area is controlled by being enclosed by walls or fencing, access is channeled through defined points of entry, such as doors and gates. These entry points can be protected by types of electronic lock.

Access Control Hardware

Various types of access control hardware or electronic locks can be deployed to enable users to authenticate quickly at access points:

- **Badge reader**—A photographic ID badge showing name and access level is one of the cornerstones of building security. A smart badge comes with an integrated chip and data interface that stores the user's key pair and digital certificate. The user presents the card and enters a PIN and then the card uses its cryptographic keys to authenticate securely via the entry point's badge reader. A smart badge is either contact based, meaning that it must be physically inserted into a reader, or contactless, meaning that data is transferred using a tiny antenna embedded in the card. The ISO has published various ID card standards to promote interoperability, including ones for smart cards (ISO 7816 for contact and ISO 14443 for contactless types).

- **Biometric**—An electronic lock may also be integrated with a biometric scanner. A biometric device is activated by human physical features, such as a fingerprint, voice, retina, or signature. Each user's biometric is recorded as a template and stored on an authentication server. To gain access, the user's biometric is scanned again by a fingerprint reader or iris/retina scanner and compared to the template scan.

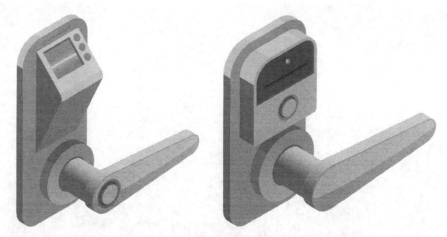

Two types of electronic lock with biometric reader (left) and badge/card reader (right). (Images © 123RF.com.)

Access Control Vestibule

The main problem with a simple door or gate as an entry mechanism is that it cannot accurately record who has entered or left an area. More than one person may pass through the gateway at the same time; a user may hold a door open for the next person; an unauthorized user may "tailgate" behind an authorized user. This risk may be mitigated by installing a turnstile (a type of gateway that only allows one person through at a time). The other option is to add some sort of surveillance on the gateway. Where security is critical and cost is no object, an access control vestibule, or mantrap, could be employed. An **access control vestibule** is where one gateway leads to an enclosed space protected by another barrier.

Physical Security for Server Systems

The access control hardware measures that can be deployed to prevent unauthorized entry to sites, buildings, and floors or zones within a building can also be used to manage access to IT assets.

Locking Racks

Installing equipment within secure cabinets or enclosures provides mitigation against insider attack and attacks that have broken through the perimeter security mechanisms. These can be supplied with key-operated or electronic locks. It is also possible to provision lockable brackets and drawers to protect or isolate individual elements within a rack.

Some datacenters may contain racks with equipment owned by different companies (colocation). These racks can be installed inside cages so that technicians can only physically access the racks housing their own company's servers and appliances.

Colocation cages. (Image © Chris Dag and shared with CC BY 2.0 flickr.com/photos/chrisdag/ 865711871.)

Locking Cabinets

Lockable cabinets or safes can provide secure storage for individual items, such as media with cryptographic keys or shared password lists.

Smart Lockers

A smart locker is a cabinet that supports unlocking via a smart card/badge or biometric. Lockers may also have built-in monitoring and surveillance that can alert an administrator when an item is added ore removed.

Detection-Based Devices

Detection-based controls provide an important additional layer of defense in the event that prevention-based controls fail to work. For example, surveillance is another layer of security designed to improve the resilience of perimeter gateways. Effective surveillance mechanisms ensure that attempts to penetrate a barricade are detected. Surveillance may be focused on perimeter areas or within security zones themselves. Surveillance can be performed by security guards or via video. Camera-based surveillance is a cheaper means of monitoring than maintaining separate guards at each gateway or zone.

Cameras

A security camera is either fixed or can be operated using Pan-Tilt-Zoom (PTZ) controls. Different cameras suit different purposes. If you want to record the image of every person entering through an access control vestibule, a fixed, narrow focal length camera positioned on the doorway will be perfectly adequate. If you want to survey a large room and pick out individual faces, a camera with PTZ is required.

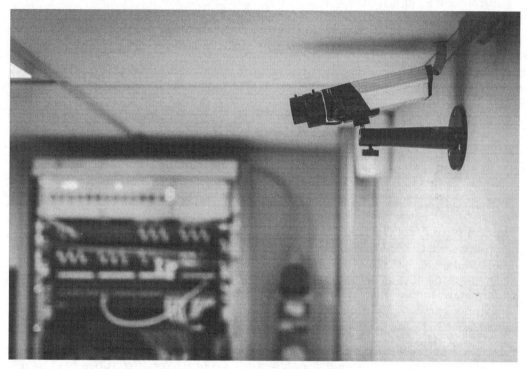

Pan-tilt-zoom CCTV installed to monitor a server room. (Image by Dario Lo Presti © 123RF.com.)

The cameras in a Closed-Circuit Television (CCTV) network are typically connected to a multiplexer using coaxial cabling. The multiplexer can then display images from the cameras on one or more screens, allow the operator to control camera functions, and record the images to tape or hard drive. Newer camera systems may be linked in an IP network, using regular data cabling. Small IP cameras can use Power over Ethernet (PoE), avoiding the need to provision a separate power circuit.

Asset Tags

An asset tag shows the ID of a device or component and links it to an inventory management database. **Radio Frequency ID (RFID)** asset tracking tags allow electronic surveillance of managed assets. The tags can be detected at entry/exit points to prevent theft. A battery-powered component might be in the tag, or the tag might be passive and read and scanned by a powered device. The tags are entered into a tracking database, which also usually has a map of the coverage area so that a particular asset can be located.

Alarms and Tamper Detection

Alarms provide a detection-based security mechanism, though an audible alarm can also be an effective deterrent by causing the attacker to abandon the intrusion attempt. There are two main types:

- **Circuit**—A circuit-based alarm sounds when the circuit is opened or closed, depending on the type of alarm. This could be caused by a door or window opening or by a fence being cut. A closed-circuit alarm is more secure because an open circuit alarm can be defeated by cutting the circuit. This type of system can be used for tamper detection.

- **Motion detection**—A motion-based alarm is linked to a detector triggered by any movement within a relatively large area, such as a room. The sensors in these detectors are either microwave radio reflection (similar to radar) or passive infrared (PIR), which detect moving heat sources.

As well as protecting building areas, alarms can be installed on rack systems and appliance chassis. For example, a chassis intrusion alarm can alert an administrator if a server case is opened.

Another potential threat is that an attacker could splice a tap into network data cable. A physically secure cabled network is referred to as a Protected Distribution System (PDS). A hardened PDS is one where all cabling is routed through sealed metal conduit and subject to periodic visual inspection. Lower grade options are to use different materials for the conduit (plastic, for instance). Tamper detection alarm systems can be implemented within the cable conduit.

Asset Disposal

Physical security controls also need to take account of the disposal phase of the system life cycle. When a server or appliance is disposed of by resale, gift, or recycling, there is a risk that software licenses could be misused or that configuration information valuable to an attacker could be leaked. These risks can be mitigated by ensuring that the built-in **factory reset** routine is invoked to wipe any custom configuration settings or modifications when decommissioning a server, switch, router, firewall, or printer.

A factory reset may leave **data remnants**, however. Data remnant removal is critical because an organization's confidential data or personal/sensitive data held could be compromised.

Data remnant removal refers to ensuring that no data is recoverable from hard disk drives (HDDs), flash devices or solid state drives (SSDs), tape media, CD and DVD ROMs before they are disposed of or put to a different use. Paper documents must also be disposed of securely. Data remnants can be dealt with either by destroying the media or by sanitizing it (removing the confidential information but leaving the media intact for reuse).

Methods of destroying media include incineration, pulverization, and degaussing (for magnetic media such as hard drives).

Media **sanitization** refers to erasing data from HDD, SSD, and tape media before they are disposed of or put to a different use. The standard method of sanitizing an HDD is called overwriting. This can be performed using the drive's firmware tools or a utility program. The basic type of overwriting is called zero filling, which just sets each bit to zero. Single- pass zero filling can leave patterns that can be read with specialist tools. A more secure method is to overwrite the content with one pass of all zeros, then a pass of all ones, and then one or more additional passes in a pseudorandom pattern.

Secure Erase

Since 2001, the SATA and Serial Attached SCSI (SAS) specifications have included a **Secure Erase (SE)** command. This command can be invoked using a drive/array utility or the hdparm Linux utility. On HDDs, this performs a single pass of zero-filling.

For SSDs and hybrid drives and some USB thumb drives and flash memory cards, overwriting methods are not reliable, because the device uses wear-leveling routines in the drive controller to communicate which locations are available for use to any software process accessing the device. On SSDs, the SE command marks all blocks as empty. A block is the smallest unit on flash media that can be given an erase command. The drive firmware's automatic garbage collectors then perform the actual erase of each block over time. If this process is not completed (and there is no progress indicator), there is a risk of remnant recovery, though this requires removing the chips from the device to analyze them in specialist hardware.

Instant Secure Erase

HDDs and SSDs that are self-encrypting drives (SEDs) support another option, invoking a SANITIZE command set in SATA and SAS standards from 2012 to perform a crypto erase. Drive vendors implement this as **Instant Secure Erase (ISE)**. With an SED, all data on the drive is encrypted using a media encryption key. When the erase command is issued, the MEK is erased, rendering the data unrecoverable.

Employee Training

Employee training is another type of prevention-based security control. Untrained users represent a serious vulnerability because they are susceptible to social engineering and malware attacks and may be careless when handling sensitive or confidential data or allowing access to premises.

Train users in secure behavior. (Image by dotshock © 123RF.com.)

Appropriate security awareness training needs to be delivered to employees at all levels, including end users, technical staff, and executives. Some of the general topics that need to be covered include the following:

- Overview of the organization's security policies and the penalties for non-compliance.

- Incident identification and reporting procedures.

- Site security procedures, restrictions, and advice, including safety drills, escorting guests, use of secure areas, and use of personal devices.

- Data handling, including document confidentiality, PII, backup, encryption, and so on.

- Password and account management plus security features of PCs and mobile devices.

- Awareness of social engineering and malware threats, including phishing, website exploits, and spam plus alerting methods for new threats.

- Secure use of software such as browsers and email clients plus appropriate use of Internet access, including social networking sites.

There should also be a system for identifying staff performing security-sensitive roles and grading the level of training and education required (between beginner, intermediate, and advanced, for instance). Note that in defining such training programs you need to focus on job roles, rather than job titles, as employees may perform different roles and have different security training, education, or awareness requirements in each role.

Review Activity:

Physical Security Methods

Answer the following questions:

1. Some of the businesses near 515support have recently had break-ins where some equipment was stolen. As news of these events spread, it generated some concern within the organization that their physical security measures should be reviewed and possibly enhanced. There is currently a security guard on duty during business hours, video monitoring of the front and back doors, and employees use plastic badges with their name and photo to enter the building. Access beyond the lobby area requires swiping a badge to enter the rest of the building. What, if anything, would you recommend adding or improving for their physical security?

2. What technology could be used to provision security cameras without having to provide a separate circuit for electrical power?

3. Following a security incident, the lessons learned report recommends upgrading premises entry control to prevent tailgating. What type of prevention control will provide the most effective solution?

4. What is a PDS, and what type of security control does it provide?

5. What technology provides data security assurance during the asset disposal phase of system life cycle?

Topic 17C

Compare and Contrast Internet of Things Devices

 EXAM OBJECTIVES COVERED
2.1 Compare and contrast various devices, their features, and their appropriate placement on the network.

Many people and businesses are deploying Internet of Things (IoT) devices in their homes and offices, and some businesses depend on the underlying embedded systems technology for manufacturing and inventory control. In this topic, you will examine how these technologies can be integrated securely with or alongside corporate data networks.

Internet of Things

The term **Internet of Things (IoT)** is used to describe the global network of personal devices, home appliances, home control systems, vehicles, and other items that have been equipped with sensors, software, and network connectivity. These features allow these types of objects to communicate and pass data between themselves and other traditional systems like computer servers. This is often referred to as Machine to Machine (M2M) communication.

Consumer-grade Smart Devices

Smart devices are used to implement home automation systems. An IoT smart device network will generally use the following types of components:

- **Hub/control system**—IoT devices usually require a communications hub to facilitate wireless networking. There must also be a control system, as most IoT devices are headless, meaning they have no user control interface. A headless hub could be implemented as a smart speaker operated by voice control or use smartphone/PC app for configuration.

- **Smart devices**—IoT endpoints implement the function, such as a smart lightbulb, refrigerator, thermostat/heating control, or doorbell/video entry phone that you can operate remotely. These devices are capable of compute, storage, and network functions that are all potentially vulnerable to exploits. Most smart devices use a Linux or Android kernel. Because they're effectively running mini-computers, smart devices are vulnerable to some of the standard attacks associated with web applications and network functions. Integrated peripherals such as cameras or microphones could be compromised to facilitate surveillance.

Physical Access Control Systems and Smart Buildings

A **physical access control system (PACS)** is a network of monitored locks, intruder alarms, and video surveillance cameras. A building automation system (BAS) or smart building for offices and datacenters can include PACS, but also network-based configuration and monitoring of heating, ventilation, and air conditioning (HVAC), fire control, power and lighting, and elevators and escalators. These subsystems are implemented by programmable logic controllers (PLCs) and various types of sensors that measure temperature, air pressure, humidity, room occupancy, and so on.

Industrial Control Systems/Supervisory Control and Data Acquisition

Internet of Things and other embedded systems are used within many sectors of industry, including energy generation and distribution, mining and refining raw materials, fabrication and manufacturing, and logistics (moving and delivering components and goods).

Industrial systems have different priorities to IT systems. Often, hazardous electromechanical components are involved, so safety is the overriding priority. Industrial processes also prioritize availability and integrity over confidentiality—reversing the CIA triad as the AIC triad.

Workflow and Process Automation Systems

An **industrial control system (ICS)** provides mechanisms for workflow and process automation. An ICS controls machinery used in critical infrastructure, like power suppliers, water suppliers, health services, telecommunications, and national security services. An ICS that manages process automation within a single site is usually referred to as a distributed control system (DCS).

An ICS comprises plant devices and equipment with embedded PLCs. The PLCs are linked by a cabled network to actuators that operate valves, motors, circuit breakers, and other mechanical components, plus sensors that monitor some local state, such as temperature. Output and configuration of a PLC is performed by one or more human-machine interfaces (HMIs). An HMI might be a local control panel or software running on a computing host. PLCs are connected within a control loop, and the whole process automation system can be governed by a control server. Another important concept is the data historian, which is a database of all the information generated by the control loop.

Supervisory Control and Data Acquisition

A **supervisory control and data acquisition (SCADA)** system takes the place of a control server in large-scale, multiple-site ICSs. SCADA typically run as software on ordinary computers, gathering data from and managing plant devices and equipment with embedded PLCs, referred to as field devices. SCADA typically use WAN communications, such as cellular or satellite, to link the SCADA server to field devices.

IoT Networks

Each device in an IoT network is identified with some form of unique serial number or code embedded within its own operating or control system and can interoperate within the existing Internet infrastructure, either directly or via an intermediary. As these devices tend to be small and often either unpowered or dependent on battery power, the standard Ethernet, cellular, and Wi-Fi networking products that connect computers are not always suitable for use. Other networking standards and products have been developed to facilitate IoT networks.

Operational Technology Networks

A cabled network for industrial applications is referred to as an **operational technology (OT)** network. These typically use either serial data protocols or industrial Ethernet. Industrial Ethernet is optimized for real-time, deterministic transfers. Such networks might use vendor-developed data link and networking protocols, as well as specialist application protocols.

Cellular Networks

A cellular network for IoT enables long-distance communication over the same system that supports mobile and smartphones. This is also called baseband radio, after the baseband processor that performs the function of a cellular modem. There are several baseband radio technologies:

- **Narrowband-IoT (NB-IoT)**—this refers to a low-power version of the Long Term Evolution (LTE) or 4G cellular standard. The signal occupies less bandwidth than regular cellular. This means that data rates are limited (20-100 kbps), but most sensors need to send small packets with low latency, rather than making large data transfers. Narrowband also has greater penetrating power, making it more suitable for use in inaccessible locations, such as tunnels or deep within buildings, where ordinary cellular connectivity would be impossible.

- **LTE Machine Type Communication (LTE-M)**—this is another low-power system but supports higher bandwidth (up to about 1 Mbps).

Z-Wave and Zigbee

Z-Wave is a wireless communications protocol used primarily for home automation. The Z-Wave Alliance operates a certification program for devices and software. Z-Wave creates a mesh network topology. Devices can be configured to work as repeaters to extend the network but there is a limit of four "hops" between a controller device and an endpoint. Z-Wave has been registered in most countries worldwide and uses radio frequencies in the high 800 to low 900 MHz range. It is designed to run for long periods (years) on battery power.

Zigbee has similar uses to Z-Wave and is an open-source competitor technology to it. The Zigbee Alliance operates certification programs for its various technologies and standards. Zigbee uses the 2.4 GHz frequency band. This higher frequency allows more data bandwidth at the expense of range compared to Z-Wave and the greater risk of interference from other 2.4 GHz radio communications. Zigbee supports more overall devices within a single mesh network (65,000 compared to 232 for Z-Wave), and there is no hop limit for communication between devices.

Placement and Security

Placement issues for embedded and IoT systems are best considered by dividing them into three principal groups: consumer-grade devices, smart building technology, and industrial systems.

Consumer-Grade Smart Devices

While the network of individual devices might use Z-Wave or Zigbee, the hub for home automation plus larger appliances are usually connected directly to the local Wi-Fi network. Consumer-grade smart devices and home automation products can be poorly documented and patch management/security response processes of vendors can be inadequate. When they are designed for residential use, IoT devices can suffer from weak defaults. They may be configured to "work" with a minimum of configuration effort. There may be recommended steps to secure the device that the customer never takes.

In a corporate workspace, the main risk from smart device placement is that of shadow IT, where employees deploy a network-enabled device without going through a change and configuration management process. A vulnerability in the device would put it at risk of being exploited as an access point to the network. These devices also pose a risk for remote working, where the employee joins the corporate VPN using a home wireless network that is likely to contain numerous undocumented vulnerabilities and configuration weaknesses.

These risks can be mitigated by regular audits and through employee security awareness training.

Smart Buildings

By contrast with consumer-grade components, there should be less scope for compromise in the entry mechanisms and climate/lighting control components of a properly designed smart building system. Management and monitoring of the system should be performed over isolated network segments. Configuration management and change control processes should ensure that no weak configurations are introduced and that vendor advisories are tracked for any known vulnerabilities or exploits so that these can be patched or mitigated.

ICS/SCADA

While an ICS or SCADA is typically implemented as a dedicated OT or wireless WAN network, there may be points where these networks are linked to a corporate data network. Historically, these vulnerable links and bridging hosts have been exploited by threat actors. There are risks both to embedded systems from the data network and to corporate data assets and systems from the embedded network. Links between OT and IT networks must be monitored and subject to access controls.

Review Activity:

Internet of Things Devices

Answer the following questions:

1. What type of network topology is used by IoT technologies such as Z-Wave and Zigbee?

2. What is a principal requirement of IoT networking technologies?

3. A technician is configuring a PC with software to manage and monitor a network of field devices. What type of host is being configured and what factors should govern its connection to a corporate data network?

Lesson 17

Summary

You should be able to explain the purpose and importance of organizational documents and policies and physical security and to compare and contrast IoT and embedded systems networked devices.

Guidelines for Supporting Organizational and Site Security

Follow these guidelines to support site security:

- Establish a configuration management and change management system so that there is a full inventory of assets and configuration items, documented using diagrams where appropriate. Use audit and assessment reports to update documentation and manage system life cycles.

- Establish security response plans and procedures for incident response, disaster recovery, and business continuity.

- Develop an overall security policy and then determine the number and type of subpolicies and agreement types that must be created, such as onboarding/offboarding, AUPs, BYOD, password management, remote access, employee training, SLA, NDA, MoU, and so on.

- Review use of access control hardware and surveillance methods to ensure that sites and server/equipment rooms are protected by prevention and detection security controls.

- Enforce policies and procedures for ensuring a configuration wipe and remnant removal when disposing of assets.

- Enforce policies and procedures for ensuring secure use of IoT devices and industrial control systems, especially in terms of patch/security management and connections to data networks.

Lesson 18

Explaining Disaster Recovery and High Availability Concepts

LESSON INTRODUCTION

Even with effective management procedures and premises security controls, disasters can overwhelm a site and threaten the core functions that a business must perform. Planning for disasters and designing systems for high availability is critical to supporting these mission essential functions. As an entry-level technician or administrator, you should be able to explain the importance of these concepts and identify the tools and techniques used to implement them.

Lesson Objectives

In this lesson, you will:

- Explain disaster recovery concepts.

- Explain high availability concepts.

Topic 18A

Explain Disaster Recovery Concepts

 EXAM OBJECTIVES COVERED
3.3 Explain high availability and disaster recovery concepts and summarize which is the best solution.

While you have considered troubleshooting scenarios in which a single host loses network connectivity or where a fault in a switch, router, or DHCP/DNS service creates problems for a network segment, you also need to consider problems with network availability across an entire site. The plans used to minimize the risk of site-wide problems are referred to as business continuity, while the plans used to mitigate these issues if they do occur are called disaster recovery. At this stage in your career, it is important that you understand the concepts underpinning these plans, so that you can assist with business continuity and disaster recovery operations.

High Availability

One of the key properties of a resilient system is availability. Availability is the percentage of time that the system is online, measured over a certain period, typically one year. The corollary of availability is downtime; that is, the percentage or amount of time during which the system is unavailable.

High availability is a characteristic of a system that can guarantee a certain level of availability. The **Maximum Tolerable Downtime (MTD)** metric states the requirement for a business function. Downtime is calculated from the sum of scheduled service intervals (Agreed Service Time) plus unplanned outages over the period. High availability might be implemented as 24x7 (24 hours per day, 7 days per week) or 24x365 (24 hours per day, 365 days per year). For a critical system, availability will be described as two-nines (99%) up to five- or six-nines (99.9999%).

Availability	Annual MTD (hh:mm:ss)
99.9999%	00:00:32
99.999%	00:05:15
99.99%	00:52:34
99.9%	08:45:36
99%	87:36:00

A system where there is almost no scheduled downtime and outages are extremely rare is also referred to as continuous availability. This sort of availability is required when there is not just a commercial imperative, but a danger of injury or loss of life associated with systems failure. Examples include networks supporting medical devices, air traffic control systems and communications satellites, as well as emerging technologies such as networked autonomous vehicles and new smart city applications, from smart law enforcement systems to smart traffic signaling systems.

The MTD metric sets the upper limit on the amount of recovery time that system and asset owners have to resume operations. Additional metrics can be used to govern recovery operations:

- **Recovery time objective (RTO)** is the period following a disaster that an individual IT system may remain offline. This represents the maximum amount of time allowed to identify that there is a problem and then perform recovery (restore from backup or switch in an alternative system, for instance).

- **Work Recovery Time (WRT)**. Following systems recovery, there may be additional work to reintegrate different systems, restore data from backups, test overall functionality, and brief system users on any changes or different working practices so that the business function is again fully supported.

  RTO+WRT must not exceed MTD!

- **Recovery Point Objective (RPO)** is the amount of data loss that a system can sustain, measured in time units. That is, if a database is destroyed by a virus, an RPO of 24 hours means that the data can be recovered from a backup copy to a point not more than 24 hours before the database was infected.

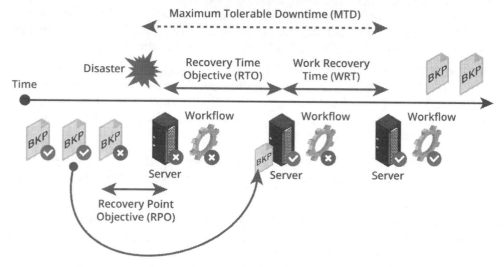

Metrics governing mission essential functions. (Images © 123RF.com.)

Fault Tolerance and Redundancy

A fault is usually defined as an event that causes a service to become unavailable. Each IT system will be supported by assets, such as servers, disk arrays, switches, routers, and so on. Each asset is susceptible to faults. Key Performance Indicators (KPIs) can be used to determine the reliability of each asset and assess whether goals for MTD, RTO, and RPO can be met. Some of the main KPIs relating to component reliability are as follows:

- **Mean Time Between Failures (MTBF)** represents the expected lifetime of a product. The calculation for MTBF is the total operational time divided by the number of failures. For example, if you have 10 appliances that run for 50 hours and two of them fail, the MTBF is 250 hours/failure (10*50)/2.

- **Mean Time to Failure (MTTF)** expresses a similar metric for non-repairable components. For example, a hard drive may be described with an MTTF, while a server, which could be repaired by replacing the hard drive, would be described with an MTBF. The calculation for MTTF is the total operational time divided by the number of devices. For example, say two drives were installed in the server in a RAID array. One had failed after 10 years, but had never been replaced, and the second failed after 14 years, bringing down the array and the server. The MTTF of the drives is (10+14)/2 = 12 years.

MTTF/MTBF can be used to determine the amount of asset redundancy a system should have. A redundant system can failover to another asset if there is a fault and continue to operate normally. It can also be used to work out how likely failures are to occur.

- **Mean Time to Repair (MTTR)** is a measure of the time taken to correct a fault so that the system is restored to full operation. This can also be described as mean time to replace or recover. MTTR is calculated as the total number of hours of unplanned maintenance divided by the number of failure incidents. This average value can be used to estimate whether a recovery time objective (RTO) is achievable.

A system that can experience failures in individual components and sub-systems and continue to provide the same (or nearly the same) level of service is said to be fault tolerant. Fault tolerance is often achieved by provisioning redundancy for critical components to eliminate single points of failure. A redundant or failover component is one that is not essential to the normal function of a system but that allows the system to recover from the failure of another component. Examples of devices and solutions that provide fault tolerance include the following:

- **Redundant spares**—Components such as power supplies, network cards, drives (RAID), and cooling fans provide protection against hardware failures. A fully redundant server configuration is configured with multiple components for each function (power, networking, and storage). A faulty component will then automatically failover to the working one.

- **Network links**—If there are multiple paths between switches and routers, these devices can automatically failover to a working path if a cable or network port is damaged.

- **Uninterruptible power supplies (UPSs) and standby power supplies**— Provide power protection in the event of complete power failure (blackout) and other types of building power issues.

- **Backup strategies**—Provide protection for data.

- **Cluster services**—A means of ensuring that the total failure of a server does not disrupt services generally.

Recovery Sites

Within the scope of business continuity planning, disaster recovery plans (DRPs) describe the specific procedures to follow to recover a system or site to a working state. A disaster could be anything from a loss of power or failure of a minor component to manmade or natural disasters, such as fires, earthquakes, or acts of terrorism.

Providing redundant devices and spares or network links allows the spare devices to be swapped in if existing systems fail. Enterprise-level networks often also provide for spare sites. A spare site is another location that can provide the same (or similar) level of service. A disaster or systems failure at one site will cause services to failover to the alternate processing site. Disaster recovery planning must demonstrate how this will happen, what checks need to be made to ensure that failover has occurred successfully (without loss of transactional data or service availability), and how to revert to the primary site once functionality is restored there.

Site resiliency is described as hot, warm, or cold:

- A **hot site** can failover almost immediately. It generally means that the site is already within the organization's ownership and is ready to deploy. For example, a hot site could consist of a building with operational computer equipment that is kept updated with a live data set.

- A **warm site** could be similar, but with the requirement that the latest data set will need to be loaded.

- A **cold site** takes longer to set up. A cold site may be an empty building with a lease agreement in place to install whatever equipment is required when necessary.

Clearly, providing redundancy on this scale can be very expensive. Sites are often leased from service providers. However, in the event of a nationwide emergency, demand for the services is likely to exceed supply! Another option is for businesses to enter into reciprocal arrangements to provide mutual support. This is cost effective but complex to plan and set up.

For many companies, the most cost-effective solution is to move processing and data storage to a cloud site. A cloud operator should be able to maintain hot site redundancy so that a disaster in one geographic area will not disrupt service, because the cloud will be supported by a datacenter in a different region.

Facilities and Infrastructure Support

The reliability of an individual site does not solely depend on the IT systems. A site must be provisioned with reliable power and climate conditions.

Heating, Ventilation, Air Conditioning

Environmental controls mitigate the loss of availability through mechanical issues with equipment, such as overheating. Building control systems maintain an optimum working environment for different parts of the building. The acronym **HVAC (Heating, Ventilation, Air Conditioning)** is often used to describe these services. An HVAC uses temperature sensors and moisture detection sensors (to measure humidity).

Fire Suppression

Health and safety legislation dictates what mechanisms an organization must put in place to detect and suppress fires. Some basic elements of fire safety include:

- Well-marked fire exits and an emergency evacuation procedure that is tested and practiced regularly.

- Building design that does not allow fire to spread quickly, by separating different areas with fire-resistant walls and doors.

- Automatic smoke or fire detection systems, as well as alarms that can be operated manually.

Fire suppression systems work on the basis of the fire triangle. The fire triangle works on the principle that a fire requires heat, oxygen, and fuel to ignite and burn. Removing any one of those elements provides fire suppression (and prevention). In the United States (and most other countries), fires are divided by class under the NFPA (National Fire Protection Association) system, according to the combustible material that fuels the fire. Portable fire extinguishers come in several different types, with each type being designed for fighting a particular class of fire. Notably, Class C extinguishers use gas-based extinguishing and can be used where the risk of electric shock makes other types unsuitable.

Premises may also be fitted with an overhead sprinkler system. Wet-pipe sprinklers work automatically, are triggered by heat, and discharge water. Wet-pipe systems constantly hold water at high pressure, so there is some risk of burst pipes and accidental triggering, as well as the damage that would be caused in the event of an actual fire. There are several alternatives to wet-pipe systems that can minimize damage that may be caused by water flooding the room.

Power Management

All types of network nodes require a stable power supply to operate. Electrical events, such as voltage spikes or surges, can crash computers and network appliances, while loss of power from brownouts or blackouts will cause equipment to fail. A brownout is where the voltage drops briefly, while a blackout is a complete loss of power lasting seconds or more. Power management means deploying systems to ensure that equipment is protected against these events and that network operations can either continue uninterrupted or be recovered quickly.

Power Distribution Units

The circuits supplying grid power to a rack, network closet, or server room must meet the load capacity of all the installed equipment (plus room for growth). Consequently, circuits to a server room will typically be higher capacity than domestic or office circuits (30 or 60 amps as opposed to 13 amps, for instance). These circuits may be run through a **power distribution unit (PDU)**. A PDU has circuitry to "clean" the power signal, provides protection against spikes, surges, and brownouts, and can integrate with an uninterruptible power supply (UPS).

On a smaller scale, PDUs are also available as "strip" sockets that can take a higher load than a typical 13 amp rated strip. Such sockets are rack mounted and can be oriented horizontally or vertically to allow for different cabling and layout options. PDUs also often support remote power monitoring functions, such as reporting load and status, switching power to a socket on and off, or switching sockets on in a particular sequence.

Battery Backups and Uninterruptible Power Supplies

If there is loss of power, system operation can be sustained for a few minutes or hours (depending on load) using battery backup. Battery backup can be provisioned at the component level for disk drive and RAID array cache. The battery protects any read or write operations cached at the time of power loss.

At the system level, an **uninterruptible power supply (UPS)** will provide a temporary power source in the event of a blackout. UPS runtime may range from a few minutes for a desktop-rated model to hours for an enterprise system. In its simplest form, a UPS comprises a bank of batteries and their charging circuit plus an inverter to generate AC voltage from the DC voltage supplied by the batteries. Different UPS models support different power outputs and form factors—from desktop to rack mounted depending on your needs.

Generators

The runtime allowed by a UPS should be sufficient to failover to an alternative power source, such as a standby **generator**. If there is no secondary power source, a UPS will at least allow the administrator to shut down the server or appliance properly—users can save files, and the OS can complete the proper shut down routines.

A backup power generator can provide power to the whole building, often for several days. Most generators use diesel, propane, or natural gas as a fuel source. A UPS is always required to protect against any interruption to computer services. A backup generator cannot be brought online fast enough to respond to a power failure.

Datacenters are also investing in renewable power sources, such as solar, wind, geothermal, hydrogen fuel cells, and hydro. The ability to use renewable power is a strong factor in determining the best site for new datacenters. Large-scale battery solutions, such as Tesla's Powerpack (tesla.com/powerpack), may be able to provide an alternative to backup power generators. There are also emerging technologies to use all the battery resources of a datacenter as a microgrid for power storage (scientificamerican.com/article/how-big-batteries-at-data-centers-could-replace-power-plants).

Network Device Backup Management

All business continuity and disaster recovery planning procedures make use of backups. The execution and frequency of backups must be carefully planned and guided by policies. In network management, backup policies are less focused on the data stored on servers and more on swiftly restoring faulty switches, routers, firewalls, and load balancers.

Each device should have a documented baseline configuration. The deployment process should be capable of applying this configuration to a replacement device or when restoring a faulty device.

One complication here is that most network appliances have a startup or persistent configuration and a running configuration. In most cases, these should be the same. It is possible that a configuration oversight left a valid running configuration that was never saved as the startup configuration. Regular audits and other configuration management procedures should be used to detect and remediate running configs that differ from the saved config.

Most devices will also support a version history of previous configurations enabling a change to be rolled back if it causes problems.

An appliance may also support two backup modes:

- **State/bare metal**—A snapshot-type image of the whole system. This can be re-deployed to any device of the same make and model as a system restore.

- **Configuration file**—A copy of the configuration data in a structured format, such as extensible markup language (XML). This file can be used in a two-stage restore where the OS or firmware image is applied first (or a new appliance provisioned) and then the configuration is restored by importing the backup file.

A network appliance may also hold state information that has not been written to a log and that will not be captured by a backup of the configuration file only. State information includes data such as the MAC tables in switches or the NAT table in a firewall. Advanced firewalls may contain additional data such as malware/intrusion detection signatures. Some devices might log state data to an internal database that can be backed up periodically. In other cases, if this information needs to be preserved, the appliance should be configured to log state data to a remote server, using a protocol such as syslog.

Review Activity:

Disaster Recovery Concepts

Answer the following questions:

1. Which metric is used to determine frequency of data backups?

2. A server group installed with storage devices from Vendor A experiences two failures across 20 devices over a period of 5 years. A server group using storage devices from Vendor B experiences one failure across 12 devices over the same period. Which metric is being tracked and which vendor's metric is superior?

3. 515web have experienced three web server outages in the last five years. These outages all occurred in separate years and caused one hour, three hour, and one hour downtime incidents. Assuming the company uses the same value for MTD and RTO, did the company meet the RTO of two hours specified in the SLA agreed annually with its customers?

4. What type of failover site generally requires only data to be restored before it can resume processing?

5. What rack-mountable device can provide line filtering and power monitoring features?

Topic 18B

Explain High Availability Concepts

EXAM OBJECTIVES COVERED
1.4 Given a scenario, configure a subnet and use appropriate IP addressing schemes. (Virtual IP only)
2.1 Compare and contrast various devices, their features, and their appropriate placement on the network. (Load Balancer only)
3.3 Explain high availability and disaster recovery concepts and summarize which is the best solution.

A network link is often a critical single point of failure. Routers and switches can provide multiple paths through a network to prevent overdependence on single critical nodes. A load balancer can switch client traffic to alternative processing nodes, reducing bottlenecks and allowing for failover services in the event of a host or network route going down. In this topic, you will learn to explain the technologies used to provision highly available networks.

Multipathing

Multipathing means that a network node has more than one physical link to another node. Multipathing is a default feature of full and partial mesh internetworks, where routers can select alternative paths through the network if a link is not available. Multipathing can be used anywhere that link redundancy is required. Two common additional scenarios are connections to storage area networks (SANs) and Internet access via an Internet Service Provider (ISP):

- **SAN multipathing**—In a SAN, a server uses shared storage accessed over a network link. Multipathing means that the server has at least two SAN controllers each with a dedicated link to the storage network.

- **Multiple ISPs**—If an organization depends on a single ISP for Internet access, that circuit represents a critical single point of failure. Even if there are multiple circuits to the same ISP, problems within that ISP's routing or DNS infrastructure could result in complete loss of connectivity. Contracting with multiple ISPs and using routing policies to forward traffic over multiple external circuits provides fault tolerance and load balancing. You need to ensure that the ISPs are operating separate infrastructure and not using peering arrangements.

This fault tolerance is reduced if both ISP's links use the same entrance facility. A physical disaster event such as an earthquake or construction damage is likely to affect both sets of cables. **Diverse paths** refers to provisioning links over separate cable conduits that are physically distant from one another. Another option is to provision cellular links as a backup, although even if 5G technologies are available, this is likely to reduce link bandwidth substantially, and even then, it could be that the 5G backhaul uses some of the same fiber infrastructure as the cabled circuit.

Link Aggregation/NIC Teaming

Link aggregation means combining two or more separate cabled links between a host and a switch into a single logical channel. From the host end, this can also be called **NIC teaming**; at the switch end, it can be called port aggregation and is referred to by Cisco as an EtherChannel. The term bonding is also widely substituted for aggregation. For example, a single network adapter and cable segment might support 1 Gbps; bonding this with another adapter and cable segment gives a link of 2 Gbps. Link aggregation can also be used in an uplink between two switches or between a switch and a router or between two routers.

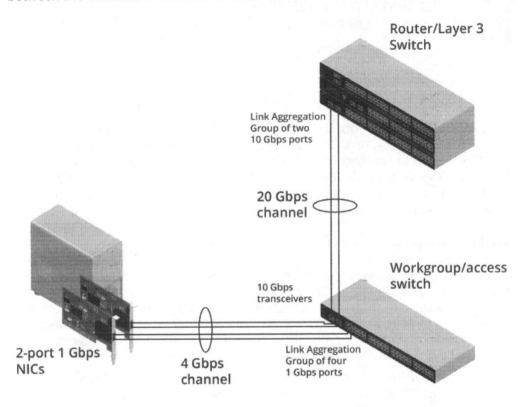

A server node uses NIC teaming to create a 4 Gbps channel link from four 1 Gbps ports to a workgroup switch, while the workgroup switch bonds its uplink transceivers to create a 20 Gbps channel to a router.

Link aggregation can also provide redundancy; if one link is broken, the connection is still maintained by the other. It is also often cost-effective; a four-port Gigabit Ethernet card might not match the bandwidth of a 10 GbE port but will cost less.

 This configuration is fully redundant only if the business function does not depend on the full speed of the bonded link. If one port fails, and the link drops to 1 Gbps, but that bandwidth is insufficient, there is not full redundancy.

Link aggregation is typically implemented using the IEEE 802.3ad/802.1ax standard. 802.3ad bonded interfaces are described as a Link Aggregation Group (LAG). 802.3ad also defines the Link Aggregation Control Protocol (LACP), which can be used to detect configuration errors and recover from the failure of one of the physical links.

Load Balancers

Where NIC teaming allows load balancing at the component level, a **load balancer** can be deployed as a hardware appliance or software instance to distribute client requests across server nodes in a farm or pool. You can use a load balancer in any situation where you have multiple servers providing the same function. Examples include web servers, front-end email servers, and web conferencing, A/V conferencing, or streaming media servers. The load balancer is placed in front of the server network and distributes requests from the client network or Internet to the application servers. The service address is advertised to clients as a virtual server. This is used to provision services that can scale from light to heavy loads, provision fault tolerant services, and to provide mitigation against distributed denial of service (DDoS) attacks.

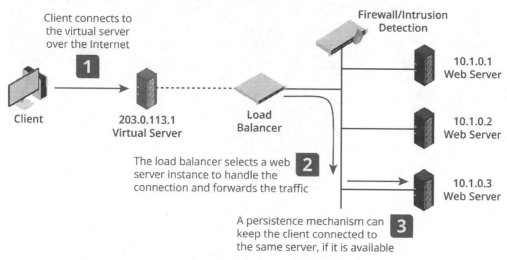

Topology of basic load balancing architecture. (Images © 123RF.com.)

There are two main types of load balancers:

- **Layer 4 switch**—Basic load balancers make forwarding decisions on IP address and TCP/UDP header values, working at the transport layer of the OSI model.

- **Layer 7 switch (content switch)**—As web applications have become more complex, modern load balancers need to be able to make forwarding decisions based on application-level data, such as a request for a particular URL or data types like video or audio streaming. This requires more complex logic, but the processing power of modern appliances is sufficient to deal with this.

We are used to associating switches with Layer 2 (Ethernet), but appliances can perform switch-like forwarding at Layer 3, Layer 4, and Layer 7. These are collectively referred to as multilayer switches.

Redundant Hardware/Clusters

Where a load balancer distributes traffic between independent processing nodes, **clustering** allows multiple redundant processing nodes that share data with one another to accept connections. If one of the nodes in the cluster stops working, connections can failover to a working node. To clients, the cluster appears to be a single server.

Virtual IP

For example, you might want to provision two load balancer appliances so that if one fails, the other can still handle client connections. Unlike load balancing with a single appliance, the public IP used to access the service is shared between the two instances in the cluster. This is referred to as a **virtual IP** or shared or floating address. The instances are configured with a private connection, on which each is identified by its "real" IP address. This connection runs some type of redundancy protocol, such as Common Address Redundancy Protocol (CARP), that enables the active node to "own" the virtual IP and respond to connections. The redundancy protocol also implements a heartbeat mechanism to allow failover to the passive node if the active one should suffer a fault.

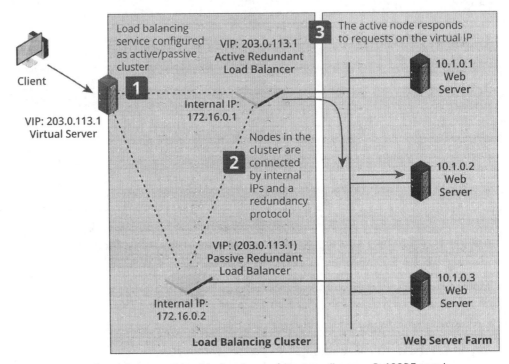

Topology of clustered load balancing architecture. (Images © 123RF.com.)

The same sort of topology can be used to deploy routers and firewalls for high availability and load sharing.

Active-Passive and Active-Active Clustering

In the previous example, if one node is active, the other is passive. This is referred to as active-passive clustering. The major advantage of active/passive configurations is that performance is not adversely affected during failover. However, the hardware and operating system costs are higher because of the unused capacity.

An active-active cluster means that both nodes are processing connections concurrently. This allows the administrator to use the maximum capacity from the available hardware while all nodes are functional. In the event of a failover the workload of the failed node is immediately and transparently shifted onto the remaining node. At this time, the workload on the remaining nodes is higher and performance is degraded.

 In a standard active-passive configuration, each active node must be matched by a passive node. There are N+1 and N+M configurations that provision fewer passive nodes than active nodes, to reduce costs.

First Hop Redundancy

In a full or partial mesh network topology, alternate routes can be found to bypass failed routers or faulty connections. However, end systems are typically served by a single router configured as the default gateway. While it is possible to configure hosts with multiple default gateways for fault tolerance, this does not work well in practice, as it requires a greater degree of complexity in the hosts' routing algorithms than is typically implemented on an end system host.

To address this problem, various types of **first hop redundancy protocol (FHRP)** have been developed.

Hot Standby Router Protocol

The proprietary Hot Standby Router Protocol (HSRP) developed by Cisco allows multiple physical routers to serve as a single default gateway for a subnet. To do this, each router must have an interface connected to the subnet, with its own unique MAC address and IP address. In addition, they also need to be configured to share a common virtual IP address and a common MAC address. The group of routers configured in this way is known as a standby group. They communicate among themselves using IP multicasts and choose an active router based on priorities configured by an administrator. The active router responds to any traffic sent to the virtual IP address. Of the remaining routers in the standby group, the router with the next highest priority is chosen as the standby router. The standby router monitors the status of the active router and takes over the role if the active router becomes unavailable, also triggering the selection of a new standby router from the remaining routers in the group.

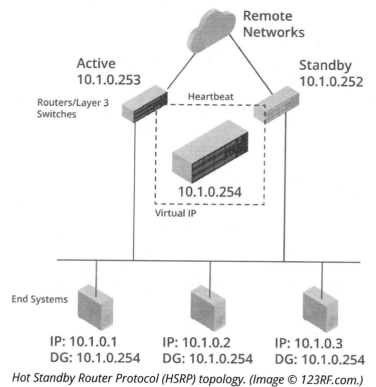

Hot Standby Router Protocol (HSRP) topology. (Image © 123RF.com.)

 Cisco also have the Gateway Load Balancing Protocol (GLBP) which allows for an active/ active load balanced configuration.

Virtual Router Redundancy Protocol

The open standard protocol Virtual Router Redundancy Protocol (VRRP) is similar to HSRP, the differences mainly being in terminology and packet formats. In VRRP, the active router is known as the master, and all other routers in the group are known as backup routers. There is no specific standby router; instead, all backup routers monitor the status of the master, and in the event of a failure, a new master router is selected from the available backup routers based on priority.

One advantage of VRRP over HSRP is that it does not require each router interface to be assigned a unique IP address. It is possible to configure VRRP routers to use only the virtual IP address. This can be useful on subnets where address space utilization is high.

Review Activity:

High Availability Concepts

Answer the following questions:

1. **Why might contracting with multiple ISPs still fail to provide highly available Internet access infrastructure?**

2. **True or false? Link aggregation can only be configured between intermediate systems, such as switch-to-switch or switch-to-router.**

3. **You are configuring a load balanced web application. Which IP address should be configured as a host record in DNS to advertise the application?**

4. **What is the purpose of HSRP and VRRP?**

Lesson 18

Summary

You should be able to explain high availability and disaster recovery concepts and summarize which is the best solution.

Guidelines for Supporting Disaster Recovery and High Availability

Follow these guidelines to support high availability site design and disaster recovery procedures:

- Use business impact analysis to determine mission essential functions and the reliability characteristics of the IT assets that underpin them, using MTD, RTO, RPO, MTBF/MTTF, and MTTR metrics.

- Use disaster recovery planning to assess risks and develop response procedures and resources, incorporating backup and restore procedures for both data and network systems.

- Provision power and data redundancy at component, network link, and system levels to mitigate single points of failure. Consider the use of load balancers and clusters to provision highly redundant services.

- Ensure facilities support for climate control, fire suppression, and power reliability, using PDUs, UPS, and standby generators.

- Provision site redundancy at hot, warm, or cold levels based on risk, MTD, and cost factors.

Lesson 19

Applying Network Hardening Techniques

LESSON INTRODUCTION

There are many ways in which networks can be attacked and just as many ways for making networks more secure. You will need a basic understanding of the security risks, and security methods and tools, in order to protect your network. In this lesson, you will learn to compare and contrast common types of attacks and to apply network hardening techniques.

Lesson Objectives

In this lesson, you will:

- Compare and contrast types of attacks

- Apply network hardening techniques.

Topic 19A

Compare and Contrast Types of Attacks

 EXAM OBJECTIVES COVERED
4.2 Compare and contrast common types of attacks.

Effective network security design requires an understanding of how threat actors can compromise defenses. Threat research produces analysis of common types of attacks, or threat actor tactics, techniques, and procedures (TTPs). You should be able to compare and contrast common types of attacks to participate effectively in incident response and to harden systems against intrusion.

General Attack Types

A network can be attacked by many kinds of intruders or adversaries for many different reasons. The goals of most types of adversaries will be to steal (exfiltrate) information from the network, to misuse network services (for fraud, for instance), or to compromise the availability of the network. Insider threat-type attacks may be launched with privileged access to the network, while external threats must find some way of accessing the network, perhaps by installing malware on a host system.

Footprinting and Fingerprinting Attacks

Footprinting and fingerprinting are **enumeration** or information gathering attacks. Footprinting allows a threat actor to discover the topology and general configuration of the network and security systems. Footprinting can be done by social engineering attacks—persuading users to give information or locating information that has been thrown out as trash, for instance. Port scanning specifically aims to enumerate the TCP or UDP application ports on which a host will accept connections.

Fingerprinting allows a threat actor to identify device and OS types and versions. When a host running a particular operating system responds to a port scan, the syntax of the response might identify the specific operating system. This fact is also true of application servers, such as web servers, FTP servers, and mail servers. The responses these servers make often include headers or banners that can reveal a great deal of information about the server. A threat actor can use this information to probe for known vulnerabilities.

Spoofing Attacks

The term **spoofing** covers a wide range of different attacks. Spoofing can include any type of attack where the attacker disguises his or her identity, or in which the source of network information is forged to appear legitimate. Social engineering and techniques such as phishing and pharming, where the attacker sets up a false website in imitation of a real one, are types of spoofing attacks. It is also possible to abuse the way a protocol works or how network packets are constructed to inject false or modified data onto a network. The ARP and DNS protocols are often used as vectors for this type of attack.

Denial of Service Attacks

A **denial of service (DoS)** attack causes a service at a given host to fail or to become unavailable to legitimate users. Resource exhaustion DoS attacks focus on overloading a service by using up CPU, system RAM, disk space, or network bandwidth. It is also possible for DoS attacks to exploit design failures or other vulnerabilities in application software. A physical DoS attack might involve cutting telephone lines or network cabling or switching off the power to a server. DoS attacks may be motivated by the malicious desire to cause trouble. They may also be part of a wider attack, such as the precursor to a spoofing or data exfiltration attack. DoS can assist these attacks by diverting attention and resources away from the real target. For example, a blinding attack attempts to overload a logging or alerting system with events.

On-path Attacks

An **on-path** attack is a specific type of spoofing attack where a threat actor compromises the connection between two hosts and transparently intercepts and relays all communications between them. The threat actor might also have the opportunity to modify the traffic before relaying it.

 On-path attacks are also known by the term "Man-in-the-Middle (MitM)." Such terms are non-inclusive and/or use inappropriate or vague metaphors and are deprecated in the latest CompTIA exam objectives documents.

MAC Spoofing and IP Spoofing

A host can arbitrarily select any MAC and/or IP address and attempt to use it on the network. A threat actor might exploit this to spoof the value of a valid MAC or IP address to try to circumvent an access control list or impersonate a legitimate server. For this type of attack to succeed, the threat actor must normally disable the legitimate host or there will be duplicate addresses on the network, which will have unpredictable results.

IP spoofing is also used in most denial of service (DoS) attacks to mask the origin of the attack and make it harder for the target system to block packets from the attacking system. In this type of spoofing, the threat actor does not care about not receiving return traffic.

ARP Spoofing

ARP spoofing, or ARP cache poisoning, is a common means of perpetrating an on-path attack. It works by broadcasting unsolicited ARP reply packets, also known as gratuitous ARP replies, with a source address that spoofs a legitimate host or router interface. Because ARP has no security, all devices in the same broadcast domain as the rogue host trust this communication and update their MAC:IP address cache table with the spoofed address. Because the threat actor broadcasts endless ARP replies, it overwhelms the legitimate interface.

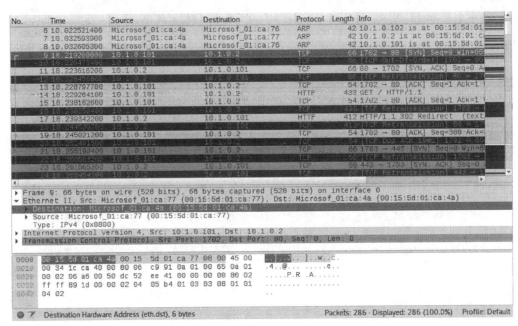

Observing ARP poisoning in a Wireshark packet capture. (Screenshot courtesy of Wireshark.)

The usual target will be the subnet's default gateway. If the attack is successful, all traffic destined for remote networks will be sent to the attacker. The threat actor can then perform an on-path attack to monitor the communications and continue to forward them to the router to avoid detection. The attacker could also modify the packets before forwarding them. ARP poisoning could also perform a DoS attack by not forwarding the packets.

ARP poisoning can be difficult to detect without closely monitoring network traffic. However, attempts at ARP poisoning are likely to cause sporadic communications difficulties, such as an unreachable default gateway. In such cases, performing network captures and examining ARP packets may reveal the poison packets, as will examining local ARP caches for multiple IP addresses mapping to the same MAC address.

 While IPv6 does not use ARP, it is also vulnerable to layer 2 spoofing if the unencrypted Neighbor Discovery (ND) protocol is used.

Rogue DHCP

An on-path attack can also be launched by running a rogue DHCP server. DHCP communications cannot be authenticated, so a host will generally trust the first offer packet that it receives. The threat actor can exploit this to set his or her machine as the subnet's default gateway or DNS resolver.

DNS Poisoning Attacks

DNS poisoning is an attack that compromises the name resolution process. Typically, the attacker will replace the valid IP address for a trusted website, such as mybank.example, with the attacker's IP address. The attacker can then intercept all the packets directed to mybank.example and bounce them to the real site, leaving the victim unaware of what is happening (referred to as pharming). Alternatively, DNS spoofing could be used for a DoS attack by directing all traffic for a particular FQDN to an invalid IP address (a black hole).

One way to attack DNS is to corrupt the client's name resolution process. This can be accomplished by changing the servers used for resolving queries, intercepting and modifying DNS traffic, or polluting the client's name cache (by modifying the HOSTS file, for instance). DNS server cache poisoning (or pollution) is another redirection attack, but instead of trying to subvert the name service used by the client, it aims to corrupt the records held by the DNS server itself.

```
HOSTNAME     www.web.local      yes      Hostname to hijack
INTERFACE                       no       The name of the interface
NEWADDR      192.168.2.192      yes      New address for hostname
RECONS       192.168.2.254      yes      The nameserver used for reconnaissance
RHOST        192.168.1.1        yes      The target address
SNAPLEN      65535              yes      The number of bytes to capture
SRCADDR      Real               yes      The source address to use for sending t
he queries (Accepted: Real, Random)
SRCPORT      0                  yes      The target server's source query port (
0 for automatic)
TIMEOUT      500                yes      The number of seconds to wait for new d
ata
TTL          46348              yes      The TTL for the malicious host entry
XIDS         0                  yes      The number of XIDs to try for each quer
y (0 for automatic)

msf auxiliary(bailiwicked_host) > run

[-] Failure: This hostname is already in the target cache: www.web.local
[-]       Cache entry expires on 2017-09-17 09:08:17 -0700... sleeping.
^C[-] Auxiliary interrupted by the console user
[*] Auxiliary module execution completed
msf auxiliary(bailiwicked_host) > set hostname updates.web.local
hostname => updates.web.local
msf auxiliary(bailiwicked_host) > run

[*] Targeting nameserver 192.168.1.1 for injection of updates.web.local. as 192.
168.2.192
[*] Querying recon nameserver for web.local.'s nameservers...
[*]   Got an NS record: web.local.            604800  IN      NS      ns.web.lo
cal.
[*]   Querying recon nameserver for address of ns.web.local....
[*]     Got an A record: ns.web.local.        604800  IN      A       192.168.
1.1
[*]     Checking Authoritativeness: Querying 192.168.1.1 for web.local....
[*]     ns.web.local. is authoritative for web.local., adding to list of nameser
vers to spoof as
[*] Calculating the number of spoofed replies to send per query...
[*]   race calc: 100 queries | min/max/avg time: 0.0/0.0/0.0 | min/max/avg repli
es: 0/1/0
[*] The server did not reply, giving up.
[*] Auxiliary module execution completed
msf auxiliary(bailiwicked_host) > █
```

Attempting to poison a DNS server cache—This attack has failed.

VLAN Hopping Attacks

VLAN hopping is an attack designed to send traffic to a VLAN other than the one the host system is in. This exploits the native VLAN feature of 802.1Q. Native VLANs are designed to provide compatibility with non-VLAN capable switches. The attacker, using a device placed in the native VLAN, crafts a frame with two VLAN tag headers. The first trunk switch to inspect the frame strips the first header, and the frame gets forwarded to the target VLAN. Such an attack can only send packets one way but could be used to perform a DoS attack against a host on a different VLAN. Double tagging can be mitigated by ensuring that the native VLAN uses a different ID to any user accessible VLAN.

A VLAN hopping attack can also be launched by attaching a device that spoofs the operation of a switch to the network and negotiating the creation of a trunk port. As a trunk port, the attacker's device will receive all inter-VLAN traffic. This attack can be mitigated by ensuring that ports allowed to be used as trunks are pre-determined in the switch configuration and that access ports are not allowed to auto-configure as trunk ports.

Wireless Network Attacks

Wireless networks can open several avenues for a threat actor to gain unauthorized network access.

Rogue Access Points

A **rogue access point** is one that has been installed on the network without authorization, whether with malicious intent or not. A malicious user can set up such an AP with something as basic as a smartphone with tethering capabilities, and a non-malicious user could enable such an AP by accident. If connected to a LAN without security, an unauthorized AP creates a backdoor through which to attack the network.

Evil Twins

A rogue AP masquerading as a legitimate one is called an **evil twin**. An evil twin might advertise a similar network name (SSID) to the legitimate one. For example, an evil twin might be configured with the network name "compeny" where the legitimate network name is "company." Alternatively, the evil twin might spoof the SSID and BSSID (MAC address) of an authorized access point and then the attacker might use some DoS technique to overcome the legitimate AP. After a successful DoS attack, the users will be forced to disconnect from the network and then manually attempt to reconnect. At that point, with many users busy and trying to get back to work, some or all may associate with the evil twin AP and submit the network passphrase or their credentials for authentication.

However it is configured, when a user connects to an evil twin, it might be able to harvest authentication information and, if it is able to provide wider network or Internet access, execute an on-path attack to snoop on connections established with servers or websites.

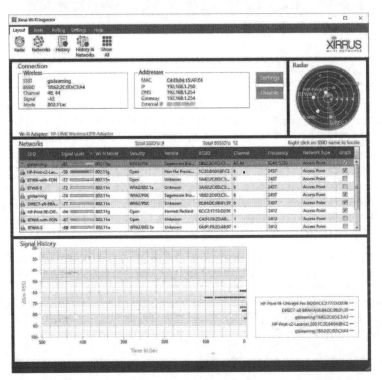

Surveying Wi-Fi networks using Xirrus Wi-Fi Inspector (xirrus.com)—Note the presence of print devices configured with open authentication (no security) and a smart TV appliance (requiring authentication). (Screenshot used with permission from Xirrus.)

One solution to the risk of rogue access points is to use EAP-TLS security so that the authentication server and clients perform mutual authentication. There are also various scanners and monitoring systems that can detect rogue APs, referred to as a wireless intrusion detection system (WIDS) or wireless intrusion prevention system (WIPS).

Deauthentication Attacks

The use of an evil twin may be coupled with a **deauthentication attack**. This sends a stream of spoofed management frames to cause a client to deauthenticate from an AP. This might allow the attacker to interpose the evil twin, sniff information about the authentication process, or perform a denial of service (DoS) attack against the wireless infrastructure. These attacks work against both WEP and WPA. The attacks can be mitigated if the wireless infrastructure supports Management Frame Protection (MFP/802.11w). Both the AP and clients must be configured to support MFP.

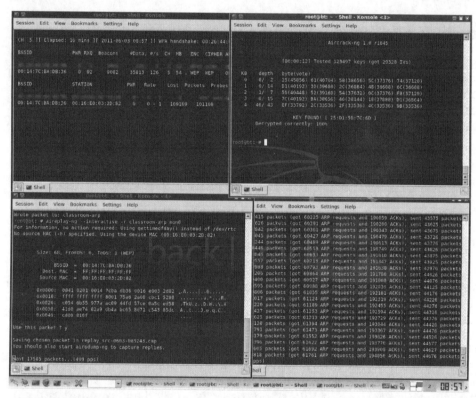

Aireplay sniffs ARP packets to harvest IVs while Airodump saves them to a capture, which Aircrack can analyze to identify the correct encryption key.

Distributed DoS Attacks and Botnets

A **distributed DoS (DDoS)** attack is launched simultaneously by multiple hosts. Some types of DDoS attack simply aim to consume network bandwidth, denying it to legitimate hosts. Others cause resource exhaustion on the hosts processing requests, consuming CPU cycles and memory. This delays processing of legitimate traffic and could potentially crash the host system completely. For example, a SYN flood attack works by withholding the client's ACK packet during TCP's three-way handshake. The client's IP address is spoofed, meaning that an invalid or random IP is entered so the server's SYN/ACK packet is misdirected. A server can maintain a queue of pending connections. When it does not receive an ACK packet from the client, it resends the SYN/ACK packet a set number of times before "timing out" and giving up on the connection. The problem is that a server may only be able to manage a limited number of pending connections, which the DoS attack quickly fills up. This means that the server is unable to respond to genuine traffic.

Distributed Reflection DoS/Amplification Attacks

A more powerful TCP SYN flood attack is a type of distributed reflection DoS (DRDoS) or amplification attack. In this attack, the adversary spoofs the victim's IP address and attempts to open connections with multiple servers. Those servers direct their SYN/ACK responses to the victim server. This rapidly consumes the victim's available bandwidth.

The same sort of technique can be used to bombard a victim network with responses to bogus DNS queries. One of the advantages of this technique is that while the request is small, the response to a DNS query can be made to include a lot of information, so this is a very effective way of overwhelming the bandwidth of the victim network with much more limited resources on the attacker's network. The Network Time Protocol (NTP) can be abused in a similar way.

Botnets

A **botnet** is a group of compromised hosts that can be used to launch DDoS and DRDoS attacks. A threat actor will first compromise one or two machines to use as handlers or herders. The handlers are used to compromise hundreds or thousands or millions of zombie hosts with DoS tools (the bots). To compromise a host, the attacker must install malware that opens a backdoor remote connection. The attacker can then use the malware to install bots and trigger the zombies to launch the attack at the same time. The network established between the handlers and the bots is called a **command and control (C&C or C2)** network.

 Any type of Internet-enabled device is vulnerable to compromise. This includes web-enabled cameras, SOHO routers, and smart TVs and other appliances. This is referred to as an Internet of Things (IoT) botnet.

Malware and Ransomware Attacks

Many of the intrusion attempts perpetrated against computer networks depend on the use of malicious software, or **malware**. Malware can be defined simply as software that does something bad, from the perspective of the system owner. There are many types of malware, but they are not classified in a rigorous way, so some definitions overlap or are blurred. Some malware classifications, such as Trojan, virus, and worm, focus on the vector used by the malware. The vector is the method by which the malware executes on a computer and potentially spreads to other network hosts. Another complicating factor with malware classification is the degree to which its installation is expected or tolerated by the user. The following categories describe some types of malware according to vector:

- **Viruses and worms**—These represent some of the first types of malware and spread without any authorization from the user by being concealed within the executable code of another process.

- **Trojan**—Malware concealed within an installer package for software that appears to be legitimate. This type of malware does not seek any type of consent for installation and is actively designed to operate secretly.

- **Potentially unwanted programs (PUPs)/Potentially unwanted applications (PUAs)**—Software installed alongside a package selected by the user or perhaps bundled with a new computer system. Unlike a Trojan, the presence of a PUP is not automatically regarded as malicious. It may have been installed without active consent or consent from a purposefully confusing license agreement. This type of software is sometimes described as grayware rather than malware.

Other classifications are based on the payload delivered by the malware. The payload is an action performed by the malware other than simply replicating or persisting on a host. Examples of payload classifications include spyware, rootkit, remote access Trojan (RAT) or backdoor, and ransomware.

Ransomware is a type of malware that tries to extort money from the victim. One class of ransomware will display threatening messages, such as requiring Windows to be reactivated or suggesting that the computer has been locked by the police because it was used to view child pornography or for terrorism. This may block access to the computer by installing a different shell program or browser window that is difficult to close, but this sort of attack is usually relatively simple to fix.

The crypto-malware class of ransomware attempts to encrypt data files on any fixed, removable, and network drives. If the attack is successful, the user will be unable to access the files without obtaining the private encryption key, which is held by the attacker. If successful, this sort of attack is extremely difficult to mitigate, unless the user has up to date backups of the encrypted files. One example of this is Cryptolocker, a Trojan that searches for files to encrypt and then prompts the victim to pay a sum of money before a certain countdown time, after which the malware destroys the key that allows the decryption.

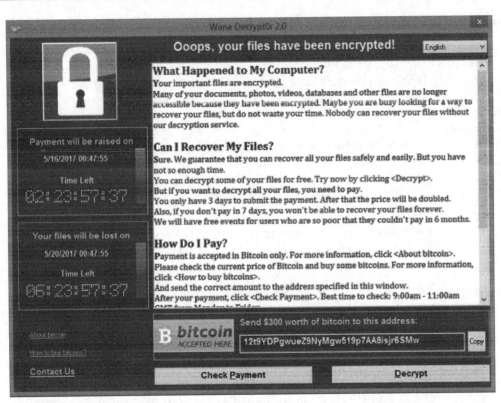

WannaCry ransomware. Wikimedia Public Domain image. (Image by Wikimedia Commons.)

Password Attacks

On-path and malware attacks can be difficult to perpetrate. Many network intrusions occur because a threat actor is able to obtain credentials to access the network. Also, when a threat actor gains some sort of access via an on-path or malware attack, they are likely to attempt to escalate privileges to gain access to other targets on the network by harvesting credentials for administrative accounts.

Passwords or password hashes can be captured by obtaining a password file or by sniffing the network. If the protocol uses cleartext credentials, then the threat actor can simply read the cleartext password from the captured frames.

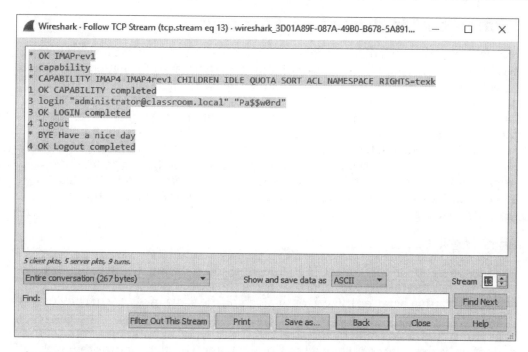

```
Wireshark · Follow TCP Stream (tcp.stream eq 13) · wireshark_3D01A89F-087A-49B0-B678-5A891...   —   □   ×

* OK IMAPrev1
1 capability
* CAPABILITY IMAP4 IMAP4rev1 CHILDREN IDLE QUOTA SORT ACL NAMESPACE RIGHTS=texk
1 OK CAPABILITY completed
3 login "administrator@classroom.local" "Pa$$w0rd"
3 OK LOGIN completed
4 logout
* BYE Have a nice day
4 OK Logout completed
```

5 client pkts, 5 server pkts, 9 turns.

Entire conversation (267 bytes)   Show and save data as ASCII   Stream 13

Find: Find Next

Filter Out This Stream   Print   Save as...   Back   Close   Help

If authentication credentials are transmitted in cleartext, such as the unencrypted version of the IMAP mailbox access protocol, it is a simple matter for the credentials to be intercepted via packet sniffing. (Screenshot courtesy of Wireshark.)

A password might be sent in an encoded form, such as Base64, which is simply an ASCII representation of binary data. This is not the same as encryption. The password value can easily be derived from the Base64 string.

In most cases, a password is stored and transmitted securely by making a cryptographic hash of the string entered by the user. A cryptographic hash algorithm, such as Secure Hash Algorithm (SHA) or Message Digest v5 (MD5), produces a fixed length string from a variable length string. This means that, in theory, no one except the user (not even the system administrator) knows the password, because the plaintext should not be recoverable from the hash.

Password cracking software uses various methods to work out the plaintext password string from a cryptographic hash:

- **Dictionary**—The software matches the hash to those produced by ordinary words found in a dictionary. This could also include information such as user and company names, pet names, or any other data that people might naively use as passwords.

- **Brute force**—The software tries to match the hash against one of every possible combination it could be. If the password is short (under eight characters) and non-complex (using only letters, for instance), a password might be cracked in minutes. Longer and more complex passwords increase the amount of time the attack takes to run.

A threat actor might obtain password hashes from a protocol such as SMB with no encryption configured. The risks posed by cracking software mean that it is more secure to use end-to-end encryption, such as IPSec or Transport Layer Security (TLS). This means that all payload data is encrypted, and a network sniffer cannot even recover the password hashes.

Human and Environmental Attacks

Threat actors can use a diverse range of techniques to compromise a security system. A prerequisite of many types of attacks is to obtain information about the network and security system. **Social engineering** (or hacking the human) refers to a collection of techniques and tricks designed to make victims reveal confidential information. Impersonation (pretending to be someone else) is one of the basic social engineering techniques. The classic impersonation attack is for the threat actor to phone into a department pretending to be calling from IT support, claim they have to adjust something on the user's system remotely, and get the user·to reveal their password. For this attack to succeed, the approach must be persuasive and establish trust. Social engineering might also use intimidation or hoaxes as a means of eliciting information.

Phishing Attacks

Phishing is a combination of social engineering and spoofing. It persuades or tricks the target into interacting with a malicious resource disguised as a trusted one, traditionally using email as the vector. A phishing message might try to convince the user to perform some action, such as installing disguised malware or allowing a remote access connection by the attacker. Other types of phishing campaign use a spoof website set up to imitate a bank or e-commerce site or some other web resource that should be trusted by the target. The attacker then emails users of the genuine website informing them that their account must be updated or with some sort of hoax alert or alarm, supplying a disguised link that actually leads to the spoofed site. When the user authenticates with the spoofed site, their logon credentials are captured.

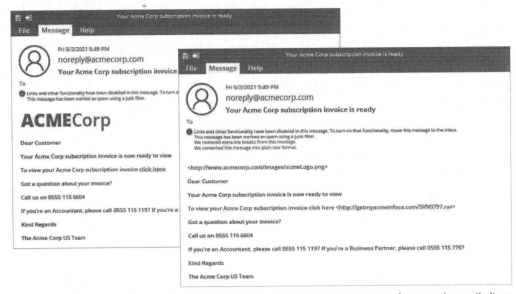

Example phishing email—On the right, you can see the message in its true form as the mail client has stripped out the formatting (shown on the left) designed to disguise the nature of the links.

Shoulder Surfing

A threat actor can learn a password or PIN (or other secure information) by watching the user type it. This is referred to as a **shoulder surfing** attack. Despite the name, the attacker may not have to be in close proximity to the target—they could use high-powered binoculars or CCTV to directly observe the target remotely.

Tailgating and Piggybacking

Tailgating is a means of entering a secure area without authorization by following closely behind the person that has been allowed to open the door or checkpoint. **Piggybacking** is a similar situation but means that the attacker enters a secure area with an employee's permission. For instance, an attacker might impersonate a member of the cleaning crew and request that an employee hold the door open while they bring in a cleaning cart or mop bucket. Another technique is to persuade someone to hold a door open, using an excuse, such as "I've forgotten my badge (or key)." Alternatively, piggybacking may be a means of an insider threat actor to allow access to someone without recording it in the building's entry log.

Review Activity:

Types of Attacks

Answer the following questions:

1. Response time on the website that hosts the online version of your product catalog is getting slower and slower. Customers are complaining that they cannot browse the catalog items or search for products. What type of attack do you suspect?

2. The network administrator at your organization analyzes a network trace capture file and discovers that packets have been intercepted and retransmitted to both a sender and a receiver during an active session. What class of attack has been detected?

3. True or false? To perpetrate an ARP spoofing attack, the threat actor spoofs the IP address of a legitimate host, typically the subnet's default gateway.

4. A threat actor forces clients to disconnect from a legitimate access point to try to force them to reconnect to an access point controlled by the attacker using the same network name. What two attack types are being used?

5. Analysis of outgoing traffic shows connections by IP cameras to unidentifiable domain names. What type of traffic has been detected?

6. Employees have received emails prompting them to register for a new benefit package. The link in the mail resolves to a malicious IP address. What type of attack is being performed?

Topic 19B
Apply Network Hardening Techniques

EXAM OBJECTIVES COVERED
4.3 Given a scenario, apply network hardening techniques.

Endpoint and switch port security is an important network security control, providing defense in depth by preventing the attachment of unauthorized devices. If you are configuring policies to ensure only authorized devices connect to the network, you also need policies for ensuring that those devices are in a secure configuration and fully patched against vulnerabilities. As a network technician, one of your roles will be ensuring that network hosts are put in a secure configuration before being granted access.

Device and Service Hardening

As part of a defense in depth strategy, you need to think about making each host and network infrastructure device secure against tampering or abuse. It can be tempting to think of network devices such as switches and routers as self-contained. In fact, these devices often run quite complex firmware and host numerous services to enable remote management and configuration. Deploying systems in a secure configuration is known as device **hardening**. Some of the policies that will make up a secure configuration involve the following:

- **Change default passwords/credentials**—Devices such as wireless access points, switches, and routers sometimes ship with a default management password such as password, admin, or the device vendor's name. These should be changed on installation.

- **Enforce password complexity/length requirements**—Passwords for network infrastructure must be highly resistant to guessing and cracking attacks:

  - **Length**—No passwords should be less than eight characters. However, as critical infrastructure, passwords for network appliances should be 14+ characters.

  - **Complexity**—Requiring multiple character classes (mixing letters, case, digits, and symbols) is deprecated by NIST's latest guidance, but is still a requirement in many local password policies.

  - **Avoiding common passwords**—The number of successful attacks against web servers and company networks has led to huge databases of credentials being posted online. Analysis of these databases shows how many users—even administrative users—rely on trivially simple passwords, such as 123456 or password. These password database dumps give attackers a useful dictionary to work with when trying to crack credentials. Any password that could be matched to a dictionary term is completely unsecure and must not be used.

- **Configure role-based access**—The default administrator, superuser, or root account has unrestricted access to the device. If the credentials for this account are shared, the risk of compromise is greatly magnified. Role-based access means that a limited set of permissions are configured for different administrative groups, such as separating permissions for configuring the system to those for configuring logging and auditing. This separation of duties reduces impacts from the compromise of any single account.

- **Disable unneeded network services**—Any services or protocols that are not used should be disabled. This reduces the attack surface of a network appliance or OS. Attack surface means the range of things that an attacker could possibly exploit in order to compromise the device. It is particularly important to disable unused administration interfaces.

- **Disable unsecure protocols**—Sniffing attacks can be mitigated by encrypting the channel over which communications takes place. This means that even if the eavesdropper can listen to the message, he or she cannot understand it without obtaining the encryption key. It is important to understand which protocols are unsecure in terms of using unencrypted channels. This is particularly important when using a channel to authenticate. Unsecure protocols should be deprecated, and secure protocols used instead. For example, the original versions of SNMP are unencrypted. To implement secure SNMP, either configure SNMPv3, which supports encryption, or use an encapsulation protocol such as IPSec to encrypt SNMP traffic.

Endpoint Security and Switchport Protection

Endpoint security is a set of security procedures and technologies designed to restrict network access at a device level. Endpoint security contrasts with the focus on perimeter security established by topologies such as screened subnets and technologies such as firewalls. Endpoint security is designed not to replace perimeter security but to supplement it, creating defense in depth.

Disable Unneeded Switch Ports

Access to the physical switch ports and switch hardware should be restricted to authorized staff, using a secure server/equipment room and/or lockable hardware cabinets. To prevent the attachment of unauthorized client devices, a switch port can be disabled using the management software or isolated to a VLAN with no route to the network (a black hole VLAN). On a Cisco switch, these configuration settings will generally be applied using some version of a `switchport` command or sub-command. As another option, the patch cable can be physically removed from the port. Completely disabling ports in this way can introduce a lot of administrative overhead and scope for error. Also, it doesn't provide complete protection, as an attacker could unplug a device from an enabled port and connect their own laptop. Consequently, more sophisticated methods of ensuring port security have been developed.

MAC Filtering and Dynamic ARP Inspection

Configuring **MAC filtering** on a switch means defining which MAC addresses are permitted to connect to a particular port. This can be done by creating a list of valid MAC addresses or by specifying a limit to the number of permitted addresses. For example, if port security is enabled with a maximum of two MAC addresses, the switch will record the first two MACs to connect to that port but then drop any traffic from machines with different network adapter IDs that try to connect.

A malicious host may use a spoofed MAC address to try to perform ARP cache poisoning against other hosts on the network and perpetrate an on-path attack. A switch port security feature such as dynamic ARP inspection (DAI) prevents a host attached to an untrusted port from flooding the segment with gratuitous ARP replies. ARP inspection maintains a trusted database of IP:ARP mappings. It also ensures that ARP packets are validly constructed and use valid IP addresses.

```
NYCORE1>
NYCORE1#
*Mar  1 00:02:27.991: %SYS-5-CONFIG_I: Configured from console by console
*Mar  1 00:02:46.287: %LINEPROTO-5-UPDOWN: Line protocol on Interface Vlan1, changed state to up
NYCORE1#configure terminal
Enter configuration commands, one per line.  End with CNTL/Z.
NYCORE1(config)#ip arp inspection vlan 1,999
NYCORE1(config)#
*Mar  1 00:07:20.561: %SW_DAI-4-DHCP_SNOOPING_DENY: 1 Invalid ARPs (Req) on Fa1/0/23, vlan 1.([0023.04S
0.0000/192.168.16.21/00:07:20 UTC Mon Mar 1 1993])▊
```

Configuring ARP inspection and DHCP snooping on a Cisco switch. (Image © and Courtesy of Cisco Systems, Inc. Unauthorized use not permitted.)

DHCP Snooping

Configuring **DHCP snooping** causes the switch to inspect DHCP traffic arriving on access ports to ensure that a host is not trying to spoof its MAC address. It can also be used to prevent rogue DHCP servers from operating on the network. With DHCP snooping, only DHCP offers from ports configured as trusted are allowed.

Neighbor Discovery Inspection and Router Advertisement Guard

Neighbor Discovery (ND) Inspection and **Router Advertisement (RA) Guard** perform similar functions to DAI and DHCP snooping for IPv6 networks. Most hosts have IPv6 enabled by default and disabling it can often cause unexpected problems. Consequently, these switch protections should be enabled to mitigate spoofing and on-path attacks over IPv6.

Port Security/IEEE 802.1X Port-Based Network Access Control

MAC limiting and filtering and ARP inspection provide some protection against attacks, but they are not a means of ensuring only valid hosts are connecting to the network. **Port security** refers to the IEEE 802.1X standard's Port-Based Network Access Control (PNAC) mechanism. PNAC means that the switch performs some sort of authentication of the attached device before activating the port.

Under 802.1X, the device requesting access is the supplicant. The switch, referred to as the authenticator, enables the Extensible Authentication Protocol over LAN (EAPoL) protocol only and waits for the device to supply authentication data. The authenticator passes this data to an authenticating server, typically a RADIUS server, which checks the credentials and grants or denies access. If access is granted, the switch will configure the port to use the appropriate VLAN and enable it for ordinary network traffic. Unauthenticated hosts may be denied any type of access or be placed in a guest VLAN with only limited access to the rest of the network.

VLAN and PVLAN Best Practices

The virtual LAN (VLAN) feature of managed Ethernet switches is typically deployed to enforce segmentation policies. A VLAN isolates Layer 2 broadcast traffic to switch ports that are configured with the same VLAN ID. Each VLAN ID is typically mapped to a subnet and any traffic forwarding between VLANs must be performed by a router (or Layer 3 switch).

Private VLANs

A **private VLAN (PVLAN)** applies an additional layer of segmentation by restricting the ability of hosts within a VLAN to communicate directly with one another. This might be used by a hosting company to prevent web servers operated by different customers being able to communicate. Isolating these server instances using PVLANs is simpler than creating multiple VLANs and subnets. Similarly, ISPs use PVLANs to isolate subscriber traffic.

When configuring a PVLAN, the "host" VLAN is referred to as the primary VLAN. The following types of PVLAN ports can be configured within the primary VLAN:

- **Promiscuous port**—Can communicate with all ports in all domains within the PVLAN. This is normally the port through which routed and/or DHCP traffic is sent.

- **Isolated port**—Can communicate with the promiscuous port only. This creates a subdomain of a single host only. The PVLAN can contain multiple isolated ports, but each is in its own subdomain.

- **Community port**—Can communicate with the promiscuous port and with other ports in the same community. This creates a subdomain that can contain multiple hosts.

Default VLAN and Native VLAN

The VLAN with ID 1 is referred to as the **default VLAN**. This cannot be changed. However, unless configured differently, all ports on a switch default to being in VLAN 1. When you are implementing VLANs, you should avoid sending user data traffic over the default VLAN. It should remain unused or used only for inter-switch protocol traffic, where necessary. For example, spanning tree traffic would be permitted to run over the default VLAN. Make sure that unused ports are not assigned to VLAN 1.

A **native VLAN** is one into which any untagged traffic is put when receiving frames over a trunk port. When a switch receives an untagged frame over a trunk, it assigns the frame to the native VLAN. Untagged traffic might derive from legacy devices such as hubs or older switches that do not support 802.1Q encapsulated frames. The native VLAN is initially set with the same VID as the default VLAN (VID 1). You can and should change this, however, to make the native VID any suitable ID. This should not be the same as any VLAN used for any other data traffic. The same native VLAN ID (VID) should be configured for the trunk port on both switches.

Firewall Rules and ACL Configuration

Firewall access control lists (ACLs) are configured on the principle of least access. This is the same as the principle of least privilege; only allow the minimum amount of traffic required for the operation of valid network services and no more. The rules in a firewall's ACL are processed top-to-bottom. If traffic matches a rule that allows the packet, then it is allowed to pass. Consequently, the most specific rules are placed at the top. The final default rule is typically to block any traffic that has not matched a rule. This is called an **implicit deny**. If the firewall does not have a default implicit deny rule, an **explicit deny** all rule can be added manually to the end of the ACL.

Sample firewall ruleset configured on OPNsense. This ruleset blocks all traffic from bogon networks and private IP address ranges, but it allows ICMP traffic directed at a firewall interface, HTTP traffic from any source, and SMTP traffic from known networks, defined as the MAILHOSTS alias. (Screenshot used with permission from OPNsense.)

Each rule can specify whether to block or allow traffic based on parameters, often referred to as tuples. If you think of each rule being like a row in a database, the tuples are the columns. For example, in the screenshot, the tuples include Protocol, Source (address), (Source) Port, Destination (address), (Destination) Port, and so on.

As an example of ACL configuration, **iptables** is a command line utility provided by many Linux distributions that allows administrators to edit the rules enforced by the Linux kernel firewall. Iptables works with the firewall chains, which apply to the different types of traffic passing through the system. The three main chains are:

- **INPUT**—Affecting incoming connections. For example, if a user attempts to SSH into the Linux server, iptables will attempt to match the source IP address and destination port to a rule in the input chain.

- **OUTPUT**—For outgoing connections. For example, if you try to ping an FQDN such as comptia.org, iptables will check its output chain to see what the rules are regarding ping and comptia.org (or the IP address that comptia.org resolves to) before deciding to allow or deny the connection attempt.

- **FORWARD**—Used for connections that are passing through the host, rather than being delivered locally. This chain would be used when configuring the host as a network firewall.

Rules can be assigned to these chains, or new chains can be created and then linked to the standard system chains to affect traffic flow. To view the current status of the iptables and the volume of traffic using the chains, use the command:

```
iptables -L -v
```

To change the firewall rules, commands such as those that follow would be used.

These examples allow one IP address from a specific subnet to connect and block all others from the same subnet.

```
iptables -A INPUT -s 10.1.0.1 -j ACCEPT
iptables -A INPUT -s 10.1.0.0/24 -j DROP
```

When you set least access rules (if both INPUT and OUTPUT default policy is set to deny all), you must set both INPUT and OUTPUT rules to allow most types of client/server traffic. For example, to allow a host to operate as an SSH server, configure the following rules:

```
iptables -A INPUT -p tcp --dport 22 -s 10.1.0.0/24
-m state --
state NEW,ESTABLISHED -j ACCEPT
iptables -A OUTPUT -p tcp --sport 22 -d 10.1.0.0/24
-m state --
state ESTABLISHED -j ACCEPT
```

These commands use the stateful nature of the firewall to differentiate between new and established connections. The first rule allows hosts in the 10.1.0.0/24 net to initiate connections with the SSH server on the local host over port 22. The second rule allows the server to respond to existing connections established by hosts in the same subnet.

Control Plane Policing

The quality of service (QoS) stack distinguishes three operational layers: control, data, and management. A network appliance uses minimal resources to process ordinary data traffic, which is often processed by dedicated hardware (one or more ASIC chips) and does not require the general purpose CPU. Conversely, control and management traffic requires software-based processing and is "punted" to the CPU's pipeline, requiring memory resource and processor time. The control plane comprises traffic that keeps the network itself operational, including routing updates, ARP traffic, STP notifications, NTP updates, QoS classification and link reservation requests, and so on. The management plane comprises traffic that allows remote administration and monitoring of network appliances, such as SSH, SNMP, NetFlow, and syslog. Management traffic is typically directed to the appliance's loopback address.

The network must always allow sufficient bandwidth and CPU/memory resource for control and management traffic. If this traffic is blocked, the ability of the network to function is disrupted. Worm malware or malicious reconnaissance tools may attempt to masquerade as high-priority traffic of multiple different types. This places unusually high demands on the routers and switches that process control plane traffic, effecting a DoS attack on the other functions they have to perform. This is also described as a route processor (RP) attack (though note that it can be performed against both routers and switches). Route processing can also be threatened by accidental misconfigurations.

A **control plane policing** policy is designed to mitigate the risk from route processor vulnerabilities. Such a policy can use ACLs to allow or deny control traffic from certain sources and apply rate-limiting if a source threatens to overwhelm the route processor.

Wireless Security

The following features can be enabled to provision secure wireless network access.

- **Preshared keys (PSKs)**—Group authentication allows stations to connect to the network using a shared passphrase, which is used to generate a preshared key (PSK). The passphrase should be sufficient length (14+ characters) to ensure a strong key.

- **Extensible Authentication Protocol**—An access point can implement a similar port security mechanism to switches. This is configured on the access point by selecting enterprise authentication. This allows users to authenticate to the wireless network against a RADIUS server using their regular network credential. EAP also allows for device authentication using digital certificates.

- **Captive portal**—A guest network might be configured to perform authentication by redirecting stations to a secure web page. The user must authenticate to the page and meet other administrator-set requirements, such as accepting a use policy, before the station is authorized to use the network.

- **MAC filtering**—As with a switch, an access point can be configured with an accept or deny list of known MAC addresses.

- **Geofencing**—Can be used to ensure that the station is within a valid geographic area to access the network, such as ensuring the device is within a building rather than trying to access the WLAN from a car park or other external location.

- **Antenna placement and power levels**—Site designs and surveys facilitate robust wireless coverage when all expected areas receive a strong signal. Power levels and channel selection should be tuned so that access points do not interfere with one another or broadcast a signal that stations can "hear" but cannot reply to. The presence of an unusually strong transmitter (30 dBm+) might indicate the presence of an evil twin rogue access point.

- **Wireless client isolation**—Clients connected to a WLAN are normally within the same broadcast domain and can communicate with one another. An access point can be configured to prevent this so that stations can only communicate via its gateway. Peer-to-peer traffic is dropped by the AP.

- **Guest network isolation**—A guest network can have separate security and forwarding policies applied to it than the network that permits access to the corporate LAN. Typically, a guest network is permitted access to the Internet but not to local servers. Most SOHO routers come with a preconfigured guest network. Within an enterprise, a guest network would be implemented using a separate VLAN.

IoT Access Considerations

Internet of Things (IoT) devices might be present in dedicated embedded systems and smart building networks and/or as individual smart devices installed in employee workplaces. Unmanaged access to these devices can pose a security risk so management and audit procedures must detect and secure them:

- Perform regular audits to prevent "shadow IT" uncontrolled deployment of smart devices and appliances. This can be assisted through scanning software that specializes in identification of IoT devices, giving visibility into their deployment. Also, educate users about the risks from IoT devices and the necessity of complying with security and IT policies.

- Ensure that administrative interfaces are secured, and that device configuration and management is assigned to appropriate organizational roles.

- Include all IoT devices in patch and vulnerability management audits.

- Isolate management and monitoring traffic for embedded systems to minimize access to and from the corporate data network.

- Audit supplier security policies and procedures regularly, especially where there are external monitoring or management channels.

Patch and Firmware Management

Each type of OS and applications software has vulnerabilities that present opportunities for would-be attackers. As soon as a vulnerability is identified in a supported product, the vendor will (or should) try to correct it. At the same time, attackers will try to exploit it. There can never be a single comprehensive list of vulnerabilities for each OS and app, so you must stay up to date with the system security advisories posted on vendor websites and in other security reference sources. Patch management refers to the procedures put in place to manage the installation of updates for hardware (firmware) and software.

The firmware on a device such as a router/firewall may be a very sophisticated piece of software. It is quite common for such software to have known vulnerabilities, so it is vital to use a secure version. Updating firmware is known as flashing the chip. This is generally done via a vendor-supplied setup program. It is important to make a backup of the system configuration (especially for a firewall) before performing a firmware update or upgrade.

A host OS, such as Windows, can apply patches individually. An appliance OS, such as Cisco IOS, must be patched to a particular version number by applying a new software image. To address a particular vulnerability, you could use a tool such as the IOS Software Checker (tools.cisco.com/security/center/softwarechecker.x) to identify the "first fix" version of IOS for that security advisory. This does mean that other changes could be introduced, so careful testing and impact assessment is required.

Once you have completed environment and compatibility checks and backed up the existing configuration, the basic upgrade process is to copy the new system image to the appliance's flash memory. This can be done over a network using Trivial File Transfer Protocol (TFTP) or remote file copy or by using a removable flash memory card. Once the image update is in place, you run a command sequence to replace the old image and load the new one at startup.

Most software and firmware version changes and updates are upward, toward newer versions. Downgrading (or rollback) refers to reverting to a previous version of the software or firmware. This might be necessary to fix a problem caused by a recently upgraded or updated device or software. In some circumstances downgrading might not be possible. A network appliance might not support downgrading to an earlier firmware version, for instance, or an OS might have to be reinstalled completely. When applying a patch or upgrade, it is common practice to make a configuration backup, in case settings must be reapplied after the update. When downgrading, a configuration backup might not work because it may involve settings not included in the earlier version.

Review Activity:

Network Hardening Techniques

Answer the following questions:

1. The network administrator configures a switch with custom privilege levels and assigns commands to each. What type of best practice network hardening will this configuration support?

2. A technician configures a switch with an IP address and shared secret of a network authentication server. What type of best practice network hardening is being performed?

3. What switch configuration feature could you use to prevent web servers in the same subnet from communicating with one another?

4. What is the default rule on a firewall?

5. Network hosts are flooding a switch's SSH port with malicious traffic. The switch applies a rate-limiting mechanism to drop the traffic. What best practice network hardening control is being used?

6. How would a router appliance be patched to protect against a specific vulnerability described in a security advisory?

Lesson 19

Summary

You should be able to compare and contrast common types of attacks and apply network hardening techniques.

Guidelines for Applying Network Hardening Techniques

Follow these guidelines to support network hardening techniques:

- Use role-based training to develop awareness of common attacks such as footprinting/fingerprinting, spoofing, DoS/DDoS, on-path, DNS poisoning, VLAN hopping, ARP spoofing, rogue DHCP, rogue/evil twin AP, malware, password, and social engineering.

- Change default device credentials on installation and ensure that accounts are secured with strong passwords. Configure fine-grained permissions to support role-based access and enforcement of least privilege management practices.

- Use only secure channels for administration traffic or any other protocol where credentials need to be submitted.

- Configure services according to the device's baseline and disable any services which are not required. Consider setting up alerting mechanisms to detect service configuration changes.

- Ensure that only the necessary IP ports (TCP and UDP ports) to run permitted services are open and that access to a port is controlled by a firewall ACL if appropriate.

- Use switch port protection, port authentication, wireless security, IoT device management, and control plane policing to prevent the attachment of rogue devices and DoS attacks against critical infrastructure.

- Ensure segmentation of security zones using VLANs and PVLANs. Ensure that trunks carrying inter-VLAN traffic are correctly configured to mitigate against hopping attacks.

- Use vulnerability and patch assessment and scanning to ensure that all types of hosts (servers, clients, appliances, and IoT devices) are fully patched.

Lesson 20

Summarizing Cloud and Datacenter Architecture

LESSON INTRODUCTION

As the Internet becomes more robust and capable of matching the performance of local networks, many services are being moved from on-premises servers to cloud providers. Even where services are kept on-site, the different requirements and design principles of datacenters are essential competencies for network technicians at all levels.

This lesson completes the Network+ course by summarizing the software-driven virtualization, automation, and orchestration functionality that underpins cloud services.

Lesson Objectives

In this lesson, you will:

- Summarize cloud concepts.

- Explain virtualization and storage area network technologies.

- Explain datacenter network architecture.

Topic 20A

Summarize Cloud Concepts

 EXAM OBJECTIVES COVERED
1.8 Summarize cloud concepts and connectivity options.

Cloud services allow companies to outsource computing power and network/application infrastructure. Cloud computing encompasses different implementations and services. If you plan to use a cloud service, you need to know what the choices are and the advantages and disadvantages. Having a solid grasp of these choices will enable you to better manage and implement these technologies in your environment.

Cloud Scalability and Elasticity

From the consumer point of view, cloud computing is a service that provides on-demand resources—server instances, file storage, databases, or applications—over a network, typically the Internet. The service is a cloud because the end user is not aware of or responsible for any details of the procurement, implementation, or management of the infrastructure that underpins those resources. The end user is interested in and pays for only the services provided by the cloud.

From the provider point of view, provisioning a cloud is like provisioning any other type of large-scale datacenter. Cloud computing almost always uses one or more methods of virtualization to ensure that resources are quickly and easily provisioned to the client who requires them.

Among other benefits, the cloud provides scalability and elasticity:

- **Scalability** means that the costs involved in supplying the service to more users are linear. For example, if the number of users doubles in a scalable system, the costs to maintain the same level of service would also double (or less than double). If costs more than double, the system is less scalable. Scalability can be achieved by adding nodes (horizontal/scaling out) or by adding resources to each node (vertical/scaling up).

- **Elasticity** refers to the system's ability to handle changes on demand in real time. A system with high elasticity will not experience loss of service or performance if demand suddenly doubles (or triples, or quadruples). Conversely, it may be important for the system to be able to reduce costs when demand is low.

In order to meet scalability and elasticity requirements, cloud providers must be able to provision and deprovision resources automatically. This is achieved through resource pooling and virtualization. Resource pooling means that the hardware making up the cloud provider's datacenter is not dedicated or reserved to a single customer account. The layers of virtualization used in the cloud architecture allow the provider to provision more CPU, memory, disk, or network resource using management software, rather than (for instance) having to go to the datacenter floor, unplug a server, add a memory module, and reboot.

Cloud Deployment Models

In most cases, the cloud—that is, the hardware and/or software hosting the service—will be offsite relative to the organization's users. The cloud users will typically require an Internet link to access the cloud services. There can be different ownership and access arrangements for clouds, however. These **cloud deployment models** can be broadly categorized as follows:

- **Public (or multitenant)**—a service offered over the Internet by cloud service providers (CSPs) to cloud consumers, often referred to as tenants. With this model, businesses can offer subscriptions or pay-as-you-go financing, while at the same time providing lower-tier services free of charge. As a shared resource, there are risks regarding performance and security. Multicloud architectures are where the consumer organization uses services from more than one CSP.

- **Hosted Private**—Hosted by a third party for the exclusive use of the organization. This is more secure and can guarantee a better level of performance, but it is correspondingly more expensive.

- **Private**—Cloud infrastructure that is completely private to and owned by the organization. In this case, there is likely to be one business unit dedicated to managing the cloud while other business units make use of it. With private cloud computing, organizations can exercise greater control over the privacy and security of their services. This type of delivery method is geared more toward banking and governmental services that require strict access control in their operations.

  This type of cloud could be on-premises or offsite relative to the other business units. An onsite link can obviously deliver better performance and is less likely to be subject to outages (loss of an Internet link, for instance). On the other hand, a dedicated offsite facility may provide better shared access for multiple users in different locations.

- **Community**—This is where several organizations share the costs of either a hosted private or fully private cloud. This is usually done in order to pool resources for a common concern, like standardization and security policies.

- **Hybrid**—A cloud computing solution that implements some sort of hybrid public/private/community/hosted/onsite/offsite solution. For example, a travel organization may run a sales website for most of the year using a private cloud but "break out" the solution to a public cloud at times when much higher utilization is forecast. As another example, a hybrid deployment may be used to provide some functions via a public cloud, but keep sensitive or regulated infrastructure, applications, and data on-premises.

Flexibility is a key advantage of cloud computing, but the implications for data risk must be well understood when you are moving data between private and public storage environments.

Cloud Service Models

As well as the deployment model—public, private, hybrid, or community—cloud services are often differentiated on the level of complexity and preconfiguration provided. These models are referred to as Something/Anything/Everything as a Service (XaaS). Some of the most common XaaS models are infrastructure, software, platforms, and desktops.

Infrastructure as a Service

Infrastructure as a Service (IaaS) is a means of provisioning IT resources such as servers, load balancers, and storage area network (SAN) components quickly. Rather than purchase these components and the Internet links they require, you rent them on an as-needed basis from the service provider's datacenter. Examples include Amazon Elastic Compute Cloud (aws.amazon.com/ec2), Microsoft® Azure® Virtual Machines (azure.microsoft.com/services/virtual-machines), and OpenStack® (openstack.org).

Software as a Service

Software as a Service (SaaS) is a different model of provisioning software applications. Rather than purchasing software licenses for a given number of seats, a business would access software hosted on a supplier's servers on a pay-as-you-go or lease arrangement (on-demand). Virtual infrastructure allows developers to provision on-demand applications much more quickly than previously. The applications can be developed and tested in the cloud without the need to test and deploy on client computers. Examples include Microsoft Office 365® (support.office.com), Salesforce® (salesforce.com), and Google Workspace™ (workspace.google.com).

Platform as a Service

Platform as a Service (PaaS) provides resources somewhere between SaaS and IaaS. A typical PaaS solution would deploy servers and storage network infrastructure (as per IaaS) but also provide a multi-tier web application/database platform on top. This platform could be based on Oracle® or MS SQL or PHP and MySQL™. Examples include Oracle Database (cloud.oracle.com/paas), Microsoft Azure SQL Database (azure.microsoft.com/services/sql-database), and Google App Engine™ (cloud.google.com/appengine).

As distinct from SaaS though, this platform would not be configured to actually do anything. Your own developers would have to create the software (the CRM or e-commerce application) that runs using the platform. The service provider would be responsible for the integrity and availability of the platform components, but you would be responsible for the security of the application you created on the platform.

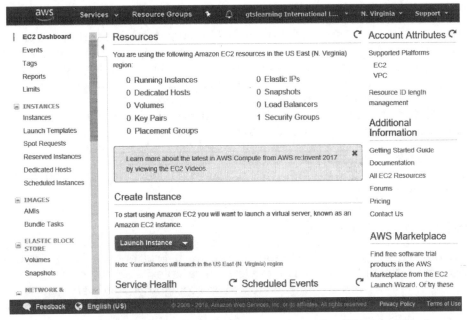

Dashboard for Amazon Web Services Elastic Compute Cloud (EC2) IaaS/PaaS. (Screenshot courtesy of Amazon.)

Desktop as a Service

Desktop as a Service (DaaS) is a means of provisioning virtual desktop infrastructure (VDI) as a cloud service. VDI allows a client browser to operate an OS desktop plus software apps. This removes the need for an organization to deploy and maintain client PCs and software installs.

Cloud Connectivity Options

Cloud connectivity is the mechanism by which clients connect to the cloud service. Connectivity with cloud-based services is always going to involve some tradeoffs but should consider price, bandwidth, latency (delay), and availability. In practical terms, there are a few options for connecting an organization's staff with cloud-based services.

Internet/Virtual Private Network

The simplest way of interfacing with a cloud service is to use the provider's website or application programming interface (API) over the Internet. This type of connection can also be implemented as a virtual private network (VPN), if this is supported by the cloud service provider. The VPN method has the advantages of being cost-effective and straightforward to set up wherever there is Internet connectivity, which is ideal for organizations that have a fragmented or distributed network structure. However, any connection running over the public Internet can suffer from poor performance due to latency and bandwidth throttling, so this would not normally be a solution for a mission critical or high-volume application.

Private-Direct Connection/Colocation

Colocation within a datacenter offers a higher bandwidth solution by providing a direct or private link. The customer establishes infrastructure within a datacenter supported by the cloud provider or provisions a direct link from his or her enterprise network to the datacenter, possibly using private connections configured within a service provider's network. The datacenter installs a cross-connect cable or VLAN between the customer and the cloud provider, establishing a low latency, high bandwidth secure link. This solution is preferred for organizations which have a more centralized operation where the connection to the cloud can be from the main HQ and the company's own enterprise network is used to allow branch locations access.

Infrastructure as Code

The use of cloud technologies encourages the use of scripted approaches to provisioning, rather than installing operating systems and apps and making configuration changes or installing patches manually. An approach to infrastructure management where automation and orchestration fully replace manual configuration is referred to as **infrastructure as code (IaC)**.

One of the goals of IaC is to eliminate snowflake systems. A snowflake is a configuration or build that is different from any other. The lack of consistency—or drift—in the platform environment leads to security issues, such as patches that have not been installed, and stability issues, such as scripts that fail to run because of some small configuration difference.

Automation

Automation using scripting means that each configuration or build task is performed by a block of code. The script will take standard arguments as data, so there is less scope for uncertainty over configuration choices leading to errors. There are two principal types of automation tool:

- Imperative tools require the precise steps to follow to achieve the desired configuration as input. This approach is most similar to automation through traditional scripting languages such as Bash and PowerShell.

- Declarative tools take the desired configuration as input and leave detail of how that configuration should be achieved to the implementation platform.

Orchestration

Where automation focuses on making a single, discrete task easily repeatable, **orchestration** performs a sequence of automated tasks. For example, you might orchestrate adding a new VM to a load-balanced cluster. This end-to-end process might include provisioning the VM, configuring it with an app and network settings, adding the new VM to the load-balanced cluster, and reconfiguring the load-balancing weight distribution given the new cluster configuration. In doing this, the orchestrated steps would have to run numerous automated scripts or API service calls.

For orchestration to work properly, automated steps must occur in the right sequence, taking dependencies into account; it must provide the right security credentials at every step along the way; and it must have the rights and permissions to perform the defined tasks. Orchestration can automate processes that are complex, requiring dozens or hundreds of manual steps.

Automation and orchestration platforms connect to and provide administration, management, and orchestration for many popular cloud platforms and services. One of the advantages of using a third-party orchestration platform is protection from vendor lock in. If you wish to migrate from one cloud provider to another, or wish to move to a multicloud environment, automated workflows can often be adapted for use on new platforms. Industry leaders in this space include Chef (chef. io), Puppet (puppet.com), Ansible (ansible.com), and Kubernetes (kubernetes.io).

Cloud Security Implications

One of the risks of using a cloud-based solution is that potentially confidential or commercially secret data may be transferred over links that extend beyond the enterprise's infrastructure and direct control. As such, it is imperative to identify precisely which risks you are transferring; to identify which responsibilities the service provider is undertaking, and which remain with you. This should be set out in a service level agreement (SLA) as a **cloud responsibility matrix**. This division of responsibility is referred to by Amazon as security of the cloud versus security in the cloud (aws.amazon.com/compliance/shared-responsibility-model).

For example, in a SaaS solution, the provider may be responsible for the confidentiality, integrity, and availability of the software. They would be responsible for configuring a fault tolerant, clustered server service; for firewalling the servers and creating proper authentication, authorization, and accounting procedures; for scanning for intrusions and monitoring network logs; applying OS and software patches; and so on. You may or may not be responsible for some or all of the software management functions, such as ensuring that administrators and users practice good password management, configuring system privileges, making backups of data, and so on. Where critical tasks are the responsibility of the service provider, you should try to ensure that there is a reporting mechanism to show that these tasks are being completed, that their disaster recovery plans are effective, and so on.

Another provision is that your company is likely to remain directly liable for serious security breaches. If customer data is stolen, for instance, or if your hosted website is hacked and used to distribute malware, the legal and regulatory "buck" still stops with you. You might be able to sue the service provider for damages, but your company would still be the point of investigation. You may also need to consider the legal implications of using a cloud provider if its servers are in a different country.

You must also consider the risk of insider threat, where the insiders are administrators working for the service provider. Without effective security mechanisms, such as separation of duties, it is possible that they would be able to gain privileged access to your data. Consequently, the service provider must be able to demonstrate to your satisfaction that they are prevented from doing so. There is also the risk that your data is in proximity to other, unknown virtual servers and that some sort of attack could be launched on your data from another virtual server.

Review Activity:

Cloud Concepts

Answer the following questions:

1. A cloud service provider is reviewing performance metrics. On a graph, increases and decreases in customer request volumes are closely tracked by CPU and RAM provisioning levels. What characteristic of cloud platforms does this demonstrate?

   elasticity

2. 515accounting uses colocation to host its servers in datacenters across multiple geographic regions. It configures the servers to run a software as a service (SaaS) app for use by its employees. What type of deployment model is this?

   Private

3. What type of cloud solution would be used to implement a SAN?

   iaas

4. What are the main options for implementing connections to a cloud service provider?

   internet / VPN   & private
   direct link

5. A technician writes a configuration file that specifies the creation of an Ubuntu Server VM with a 2 GHz CPU, 16 GB RAM, and a mass storage disk provisioned from a high-speed resource. What type of cloud concept or model is being used?

   Automation

Topic 20B

Explain Virtualization and Storage Area Network Technologies

EXAM OBJECTIVES COVERED
1.2 Explain the characteristics of network topologies and network types.
1.7 Explain basic corporate and datacenter network architecture.

Virtualization technology is now a mainstream feature of networks and is critical to the operation of cloud services. There are different types of virtualization and several methods of networking with virtualized components. It is important to understand them if you want to implement virtualization in your environment.

In this topic, you will also learn to describe the technologies underpinning storage area networks (SANs). When planning a network storage solution, you need to understand the strengths of each type to ensure you select the solution that best fits your needs.

Hypervisor Types

In a virtualization host, the **hypervisor**—or virtual machine monitor (VMM)—manages the virtual environment and facilitates interaction with the computer hardware and network. One basic distinction that can be made between virtual platforms is between host and bare metal methods of interacting with the host hardware. In a guest OS (or host-based) system, the hypervisor application (known as a Type II hypervisor) is itself installed onto a host operating system. Examples of host-based hypervisors include VMware Workstation™, Oracle® Virtual Box, and Parallels® Workstation. The hypervisor software must support the host OS.

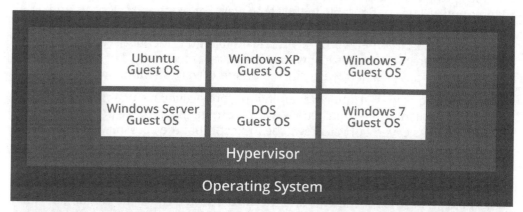

Guest OS virtualization (Type II hypervisor). The hypervisor is an application running within a native OS, and guest OSes are installed within the hypervisor.

A bare metal virtual platform means that a Type I hypervisor is installed directly onto the computer and manages access to the host hardware without going through a host OS. Examples include VMware ESXi® Server, Microsoft's Hyper-V®, and Citrix's XEN Server. The hardware needs to support only the base system requirements for the hypervisor plus resources for the type and number of guest OSes that will be installed.

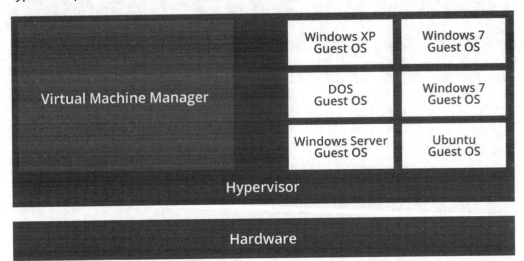

Type I bare metal hypervisor. The hypervisor is installed directly on the host hardware along with a management application, then VMs are installed within the hypervisor.

Virtual NICs and Switches

Where multiple VMs are running on a single platform, virtualization provides a means for these VMs to communicate with each other and with other computers on the network (both physical and virtual) by using standard networking protocols. The guest OS running in each virtual machine is presented with an emulation of a standard hardware platform. Among the hardware devices emulated will be one or more network adapters. The number of adapters and their connectivity can be configured via the hypervisor.

Within the VM, the virtual NIC (vNIC) will look exactly like an ordinary network adapter and will be configurable in the same way. For example, protocols and services can be bound to it, it has a MAC address, and it can be assigned IPv4 and/ or IPv6 addresses. In other words, a virtual NIC functions identically to a physical NIC for data transmission; it is just wholly software-based instead of being a combination of physical hardware, firmware, and driver software.

Typically, a hypervisor will implement network connectivity by means of one or more virtual switches (or vSwitch in VMware's terminology). These perform the same function as Layer 2 physical switches, except that they are implemented in software instead of hardware. Connectivity between the virtual network adapters in the guest VMs and the virtual switches is configured via the hypervisor. This is analogous to connecting patch cables between real computers and real switches.

In this networking model, the VMs and the virtual switch can all be contained within a single hardware platform, so no actual network traffic is generated; instead, data is moved from buffers in one VM to another. It is also possible to configure connectivity with a virtual switch that bridges the virtual and physical networks via the host computer's physical NIC. For example, in Microsoft's Hyper-V virtualization platform, three types of virtual switches can be created:

- **External**—Binds to the host's NIC to allow the VM to communicate on the physical network.

- **Internal**—Creates a bridge that is usable only by VMs on the host and the host itself. This type of switch does not permit access to the wider physical network.

- **Private**—Creates a switch that is usable only by the VMs. They cannot use the switch to communicate with the host.

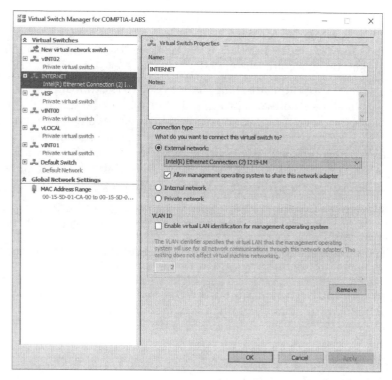

Configuring a virtual switch in Microsoft's Hyper-V hypervisor. The external switch allows the VM to use the physical network via the host's NIC. The private switches have no external access. (Screenshot used with permission from Microsoft.)

 When the VMs are permitted to interact with a "real" network, the host must support a high bandwidth, high availability network link. Any failure of the physical link will affect multiple VMs.

Virtual switches can be as simple or complex as the hypervisor software makes them. For example, they can be used to implement VLANs or be configured to perform port mirroring. In a more advanced network, such as VMware's vSphere, you could also have virtual switches that can connect guests running on multiple hosts and configure advanced switching, such as QoS and traffic shaping.

Network Function Virtualization

When a VM is joined to a virtual switch, the MAC address for its virtual NIC is configured via the hypervisor. The VM must be configured with an appropriate IP address for the subnet it is in. If the VM needs a link to other networks, it must be assigned a default gateway. You might also want to configure security for the network link, such as implementing a firewall. None of the requirements of a virtual network are different than physical networks.

You can configure the VM's IP parameters statically, or you can use DHCP. You could provision a DHCP server as a VM on the virtual network, or the VM could use the physical network's DHCP server. With some types of virtual switches that bridge VMs to the physical network, the hypervisor can implement a DHCP and/or network address translation (NAT) service to VMs.

You must also provision DNS and time synchronization services for the virtual network.

Any guest Linux or Windows Server VM can be configured as a router for a VM network. Similarly, either OS (or third-party software installed under the guest VM) could be used to implement a firewall. The VMs have the same functionality as software installed on real computers.

It is also possible to provision virtual appliances. With a virtual appliance, the vendor either develops a software product that emulates the functions of an existing dedicated hardware appliance (router, firewall, load balancer, or malware/ intrusion detection, for instance) or creates software that implements that kind of functionality in a new product. These virtual appliances might be developed against a standard architecture, such as ETSI's **Network Function Virtualization (NFV)**. NFV divides the provisioning of these appliances into three domains:

- **Virtual Network Function (VNF)**—Specifies and deploys instances of each virtual appliance. VNFs are designed to run as VMs on standard CPU platforms.

- **NFV infrastructure**—Controls the allocation of compute (CPU and memory) plus storage and networking resources to each VNF.

- **Management and orchestration (MANO)**—Positions VNFs within workflows to perform the forwarding and filtering tasks they are designed for.

Storage Area Networks

A **storage area network (SAN)** provisions access to storage devices at block level. Each read or write operation addresses the actual location of data on the media (Block I/O). A SAN is isolated from the main network. It is only accessed by servers, not by client PCs and laptops. SAN clients are servers running databases or applications that require access to shared storage.

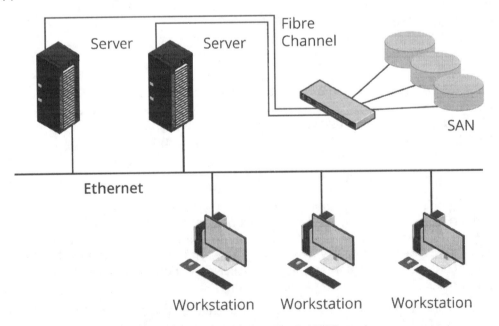

Storage area network. (Images © 123RF.com.)

A SAN can integrate different types of storage technology—RAID arrays and tape libraries, for instance. It can contain a mixture of high-speed and low-cost devices, allowing for tiered storage to support different types of file access requirements without having to overprovision high-cost, fast drives.

SAN Connection Types

A SAN can be implemented using a variety of technologies, but the most popular are high bandwidth Fibre Channel and Fibre Channel over Ethernet fiber optic networks.

Fibre Channel

Fibre Channel is defined in the T11 ANSI standard. The British spelling "fibre" is deliberately chosen to distinguish the standard from fiber optic cabling, which it often uses but on which it does not rely. A SAN based on a Fibre Channel (FC) Switched Fabric (FC-SW) involves three main types of components:

- **Initiator**—This is a client device of the SAN, such as a file or database server installed with a fibre channel host bus adapter (HBA).

- **Target**—The network port for a storage device. Typical devices include single drives, RAID drive arrays, tape drives, and tape libraries. Space on the storage devices is divided into logical volumes, each identified by a 64-bit logical unit number (LUN). The initiator will use SCSI, Serial Attached SCSI (SAS), SATA, or NVMe commands to operate the storage devices in the network, depending on which interface they support. Most devices have multiple ports for load balancing and fault tolerance.

  The initiators and targets are identified by 64-bit WorldWide Names (WWN), similar to network adapter MAC addresses. Collectively, initiators and targets are referred to as nodes. Nodes can be allocated their own WWN, referred to as a WWNN (WorldWide Node Name). Also, each port on a node can have its own WorldWide Port Name (WWPN).

- **FC switch**—This provides the interconnections between initiators and targets (a fabric). The switch topology and interconnections would be designed to provide multiple paths between initiators and targets, allowing for fault tolerance and load balancing. High performance FC switches are often referred to as directors.

Fibre Channel can use rates from 1GFC (1 Gbps) up to 128GFC. Using fiber optic cabling, an FC fabric can be up to 10 km (6 miles) in length using single mode cable or 500 m (1640 ft) using multimode cable.

Fibre Channel over Ethernet

Provisioning separate Fibre Channel adapters and cabling is expensive. As its name suggests, **Fibre Channel over Ethernet (FCoE)** is a means of delivering Fibre Channel packets over Ethernet cabling and switches. FCoE requires special 10/40/100G adapters that combine the function of NIC and HBA, referred to as converged network adapters (CNAs). FCoE uses a special frame type, identified by the EtherType value 0x8096. The protocol maps WWNs onto MAC addresses.

 FCoE does not quite run over standard Ethernet. It requires QoS mechanisms to ensure flow control and guaranteed delivery. FCoE compliant products are referred to as lossless Ethernet, Datacenter Ethernet, or Converged Enhanced Ethernet.

iSCSI

Internet Small Computer System Interface (iSCSI) is an IP tunneling protocol that enables the transfer of SCSI data over an IP-based network. iSCSI works with ordinary Ethernet network adapters and switches.

```
/> ls
o- / ...................................................................... [...]
  o- backstores .......................................................... [...]
  | o- block ................................................. [Storage Objects: 1]
  | | o- md0 ...................................... [/dev/md/md0 (10.0GiB) write-thru activated]
  | |   o- alua ................................................ [ALUA Groups: 1]
  | |     o- default_tg_pt_gp ................... [ALUA state: Active/optimized]
  | o- fileio ................................................ [Storage Objects: 0]
  | o- pscsi ................................................. [Storage Objects: 0]
  | o- ramdisk ............................................... [Storage Objects: 0]
  o- iscsi ..................................................... [Targets: 1]
  | o- iqn.2021-03.com.515support.smb10-iscsi:server ................ [TPGs: 1]
  |   o- tpg1 ................................ [no-gen-acls, auth per-acl]
  |     o- acls .................................................... [ACLs: 1]
  |     | o- iqn.2021-03.com.515support.ms10-iscsi:client ... [1-way auth, Mapped LUNs: 1]
  |     |   o- mapped_lun0 ............................... [lun0 block/md0 (rw)]
  |     o- luns .................................................... [LUNs: 1]
  |     | o- lun0 ........................ [block/md0 (/dev/md/md0) (default_tg_pt_gp)]
  |     o- portals ................................................. [Portals: 1]
  |       o- 0.0.0.0:3260 ............................................. [OK]
  o- loopback .................................................. [Targets: 0]
  o- vhost ..................................................... [Targets: 0]
/>
```

Configuring a Linux host as an iSCSI target.

iSCSI can be used to link SANs but is also seen as an alternative to Fibre Channel itself, as it does not require FC-specific switches or adapters. iSCSI initiator and target functions are supported by both Windows Server and Linux operating systems.

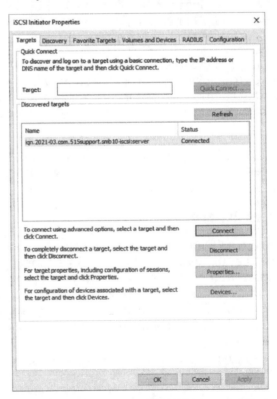

Connecting to an iSCSI target using an iSCSI initiator in Windows Server. (Screenshot used with permission from Microsoft.)

Review Activity:

Virtualization and Storage Area Network Technologies

Answer the following questions:

1. A technician boots a server from USB media and installs a virtualization product. What type of hypervisor is being used?

   Bare metal (I)

2. If a VM is connected to a bridged virtual switch, what sort of network access does it have?

   Internal

3. A technician deploys a standard Linux virtual machine and then installs and configures an open switching OS to run on it. Which virtual network concept is being deployed?

   Guest (II) OS

4. What role does an initiator play in a SAN and what hardware must be installed on it?

   HbA

5. What protocol can be used to implement a SAN without provisioning dedicated storage networking adapters and switches?

Topic 20C

Explain Datacenter Network Architecture

EXAM OBJECTIVES COVERED
1.2 Explain the characteristics of network topologies and network types.
1.7 Explain basic corporate and datacenter network architecture.

Datacenters play a critical part in both on-premises and cloud networks. Understanding the different topology and automation requirements of these networks will be critical for pursuing a successful career in networking.

Datacenter Network Design

A datacenter is a site that is dedicated to provisioning server resources. The datacenter hosts network services (such as authentication, addressing, and name resolution), application servers, and storage area networks (SANs). Most datacenters are housed in purpose-built facilities, but some of the concepts also apply to server rooms.

A datacenter has dedicated networking, power, climate control, and physical access control features all designed to provide a highly available environment for running critical applications. Unlike a corporate network, a datacenter contains no client PCs, other than hardened secure administrative workstations (SAWs) used solely to manage servers.

Historically, datacenters were designed to use the same three-tiered architecture as an enterprise campus network, with core, distribution, and access layer switches. The changing way that applications are designed as services making use of virtualization and on-demand instances has changed the nature of network traffic flows. These changes are reflected in different topology designs in the datacenter.

Traffic Flows

Traffic that goes to and from a datacenter is referred to as north-south. This traffic represents clients outside the datacenter making requests and receiving responses. Corporate network traffic flows are also typically north-south. A client device is located on a workgroup switch connected to a router, while the server is connected to a separate switch or VLAN. Traffic from the client to the server passes "north" from the client's switch to the router and then back "south" to the server's switch.

In datacenters that support cloud and other Internet services, most traffic is actually between servers within the datacenter. This is referred to as **east-west traffic**. Consider a client uploading a photograph as part of a social media post. The image file might be checked by an analysis server for policy violations (indecent or copyright images, for instance), a search/indexing service would be updated with the image metadata, the image would be replicated to servers that provision content delivery networks (CDNs), the image would be copied to backup servers, and so on. A single request to the cloud tends to cascade to multiple requests and transfers within the cloud.

Overlay Networks

The preponderance of east-west traffic complicates security design. If each of these cascading transactions were to pass through a firewall or other security appliance, it would create a severe bottleneck. These requirements are driving the creation of virtualized security appliances that can monitor traffic as it passes between servers (blogs.cisco.com/security/trends-in-data-center-security-part-1-traffic-trends). At the same time, security implementations are moving towards zero trust architectures. Zero trust implies a highly segmented network where each link between two servers must be authenticated and authorized.

An **overlay network** is used to implement this type of point-to-point logical link between two nodes or two networks. The overlay network abstracts the complexity of the underlying physical topology. An overlay network uses encapsulation protocols and software defined networking to create a logical tunnel between two nodes or networks. When used inside the datacenter, overlay networks are typically implemented using virtual extensible LANs (VXLANs).

Software Defined Networking

Cloud services require the rapid provisioning and deprovisioning of server instances and networks using automation and orchestration, plus the use of overlay networks to establish point-to-point links quickly and reliably. This means that these components must be fully accessible to scripting—representing the ideal of infrastructure as code. **Software defined networking (SDN)** is a model for how these processes can be used to provision and deprovision networks.

SDN Architecture

In the SDN model defined by IETF (datatracker.ietf.org/doc/html/rfc7426), network functions are divided into three layers. The top and bottom layers are application and infrastructure:

- **Application layer**—Applies the business logic to make decisions about how traffic should be prioritized and secured and where it should be switched. This layer defines policies such as segmentation, ACLs, and traffic prioritization and policing/shaping.

- **Infrastructure layer**—Devices (physical or virtual) that handle the actual forwarding (switching and routing) of traffic and imposition of ACLs and other policy configurations for security.

The principal innovation of SDN is to insert a control layer between the application layer and infrastructure layer. The functions of the control plane are implemented by a virtual device referred to as the SDN controller. Each layer exposes an application programming interface (API) that can be automated by scripts that call functions in the layer above or below. The interface between SDN applications and the SDN controller is described as the service interface or as the "northbound" API, while that between the SDN controller and infrastructure devices is the "southbound" API.

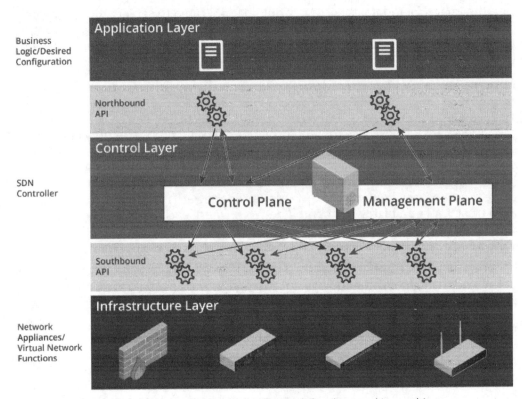

Layers and components in a typical software defined networking architecture.
(Images © 123RF.com.)

Management Plane

In IETF's SDN model, there are separate forwarding (data) and operational planes at the infrastructure level. The operational plane implements device state, such as CPU and memory utilization. A management plane sits at the same level as the control plane to interface with the operational plane. This is used to implement monitoring of traffic conditions and network status.

Spine and Leaf Topology

The **spine and leaf topology** provides better support for east-west traffic and the use of SDN and overlay networks within datacenters. A spine and leaf topology has two layers:

- The spine layer comprises a backbone of top-tier switches. Note that while this is described as a backbone, the spine switches are not linked to one another.

- The leaf layer contains access switches. Each access switch is connected to every spine switch in a full mesh topology. The access switches never have direct connections to one another.

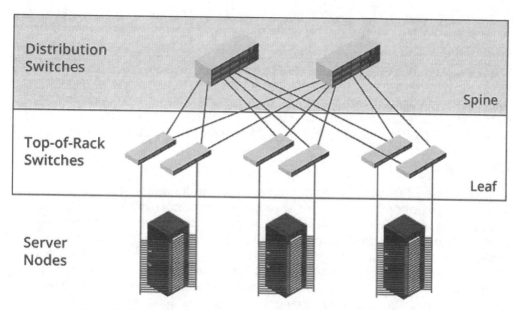

Spine and leaf topology diagram. (Image © 123RF.com.)

The spine and leaf topology has a number of advantages:

- Each server is only ever a single hop from the backbone, making network latency more predictable.

- There are multiple redundant paths between a leaf switch and the backbone, allowing for load balancing and failover.

- As there are no direct connections between spine switches in the backbone or between leaf switches, the network is loop free and does not need to run spanning tree. Instead, each leaf switch runs a protocol called Equal Cost Multipathing (ECMP) to distribute traffic between the links to the spine switches.

- Servers are connected to multiple leaf switches for multipath redundancy, using a first hop gateway protocol to determine the active path.

The leaf layer access switches are implemented as **top-of-rack (ToR)** switch models. These are switch models designed to provide high-speed connectivity to a rack of server appliances and support higher bandwidths than ordinary workgroup switches. For example, where a workgroup switch might have 1 Gbps access ports and a 10 Gbps uplink port, top-of-rack switches have 10 Gbps access ports and 40/100 Gbps uplink ports.

Datacenter Access Types

As well as the internal design and configuration of the datacenter, you also need to consider the changing way that datacenter services are accessed. An on-premises datacenter is one that is located at the same site as the corporate client network that it serves. This type of datacenter would be accessed over Ethernet links, but would be placed in a separate network zone with ACLs to filter access by client systems.

Branch Office Datacenter Access

Many corporate networks are traditionally based on a hub and spoke design, where services are concentrated in a main office, or hub, but access is distributed around multiple branch offices in geographically separate locations. Branch offices may be limited in terms of low bandwidth, high latency links. This can mean having to install servers to branch locations and replicate data between them and the head office or corporate network.

The Generic Routing Encapsulation (GRE) protocol encapsulates data from layer 2 (Ethernet) or layer 3 (IP) for tunneling over any suitable transport network. Multipoint GRE (mGRE) is a version of the protocol that supports point-to-multipoint links, such as the hub and spoke dynamic multipoint VPN. This protocol is widely used to connect branch offices to an on-premises datacenter located at the head office.

Colocation

An on-premises datacenter does not have any site redundancy and is also likely to suffer from poor performance when accessed by remote offices in different countries. Establishing on-premises datacenter services for multiple geographic locations is expensive. One option is to use public cloud services where your applications and data are installed to third-party servers. This is cost-effective, but also associated with a number of risks. **Colocation** means that a company's private servers and network appliances are installed to a datacenter that is shared by multiple tenants. The colocation provider manages the datacenter environment; the company's servers are installed to dedicated rack space on the datacenter floor. The rack or space within a rack is locked so that only authorized keyholders can gain physical access to the server equipment.

Multiprotocol Label Switching

VPN solutions based on mGRE/DMVPN that use the public Internet as the transport network can suffer from unpredictable performance levels. Most WAN providers offer **Multiprotocol Label Switching (MPLS)** as a means of establishing private links with guaranteed service levels. MPLS can operate as an overlay network to configure point-to-point or point-to-multipoint links between nodes regardless of the underlying physical and data link topologies.

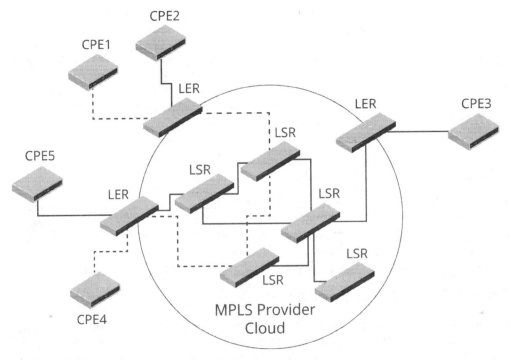

MPLS topology. (Images © 123RF.com.)

For example, in this diagram, the CPE router at site 1 wants to communicate with site 4. The router is attached to the service provider's MPLS cloud via a Label Edge Router (LER). This router inserts or "pushes" a label or "shim" header into each packet sent from CPE1, and then forwards it to an LSR. Each LSR examines the shim and determines the Label Switched Path (LSP) for the packet, based on the type of data, network congestion, and any other traffic engineering parameters determined by the service provider. It uses the label, rather than the Layer 3 header, to forward the packet to its neighbor. In this way, costly routing table lookups are avoided. The shim is removed (or "popped") by the egress LER and delivered to CPE4.

MPLS allows WAN providers to offer various solutions for enterprise networking requirements. A basic use of MPLS is to create site-to-site VPNs to interconnect LANs or connect a branch office to a datacenter. The traffic passing over an MPLS VPN is isolated from any other customer or public traffic. Different sites can use any access method available (DSL, cellular, leased line, or Ethernet), and the sites can use point-to-point or multipoint topologies as required. The MPLS provider can apply traffic shaping policies to communications between enterprise LANs and the datacenter to guarantee a service level and provide link redundancy, making the connection much more reliable than one over the open Internet would be.

Software-defined WAN

The hub and branch office design with on-premises datacenters has a number of performance and reliability drawbacks. Shifting services to one or more dedicated datacenters in the cloud or using colocation mitigates some of these issues. Service availability and integrity is separated from site accessibility considerations. In this model access to the datacenter from the corporate network, branch offices, and remote/teleworker locations can be facilitated through a **software-defined WAN (SD-WAN)**. SD-WAN replaces hub and spoke type designs with more efficient, but still secure, connectivity to corporate clouds with less of the expense associated with provisioning an MPLS service to each remote location.

In a branch office topology, access to the datacenter or the cloud would be routed and authorized via the hub office. An SD-WAN is a type of overlay network that provisions a corporate WAN across multiple locations and can facilitate secure access to the cloud directly from a branch office or other remote location. It uses automation and orchestration to provision links dynamically based on application requirements and network congestion, using IPSec to ensure that traffic is tunneled through the underlying transport networks securely. An SD-WAN solution should also apply microsegmentation and zero trust security policies to ensure that all requests and responses are authenticated and authorized.

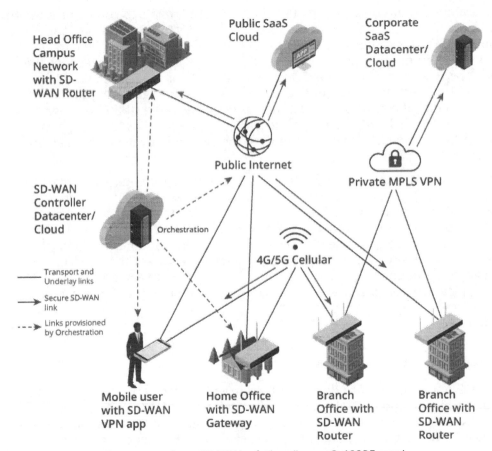

Components in an SD-WAN solution. (Image © 123RF.com.)

The SD-WAN is managed by a controller and management software located in a corporate datacenter or public cloud. Each site has a SD-WAN capable router, gateway, or VPN app. The SDN controller orchestrates connections to networks and clouds enrolled in the SD-WAN. It uses any available IP underlay network, such as broadband Internet, 4G/5G cellular, or private MPLS VPNs to provision the fastest or most reliable available transport to networks and clouds enrolled in the SD-WAN. The controller also ensures that each access request is authenticated and authorized.

Review Activity:

Datacenter Network Architecture

Answer the following questions:

1. A technician is configuring a firewall appliance to work with an SDN controller. What functionality on the firewall must be enabled?

2. A technician is cabling a top-of-rack switch in a spine and leaf architecture. Each server has been cabled to the switch. What cabling must the technician add to complete the design?

3. True or false? An enterprise WAN can be configured using either MPLS or SD-WAN, but the two cannot work together.

Lesson 20

Summary

You should be able to summarize cloud concepts and connectivity options and explain basic datacenter network architecture.

Guidelines for Supporting Cloud and Datacenter Architecture

Follow these guidelines to support the deployment of cloud and datacenter architecture and technologies:

- Identify apps and services that can utilize the elasticity and scalability benefits of cloud provision and determine an appropriate deployment model (such as public, private, and on-/off-premises) and service model (such as IaaS, SaaS, PaaS, or DaaS).

- Consider developing cloud-based apps using the infrastructure as code model to gain most benefit from automation, orchestration, and software defined networking.

- When implementing a private cloud/datacenter:

    - Consider a spine and leaf topology with aggregation and top-of-rack switch models to create a network fabric that best supports east-west traffic flows and use of overlay networks.

    - Identify virtualization and SAN products that can support the goals of elasticity and scalability and benefit from SDN and network function virtualization.

- When using a public cloud vendor, create a cloud responsibility matrix and perform regular risk assessments and security audits.

- Develop a WAN access strategy that provision secure and high-performing links between corporate data networks, branch offices, remote teleworkers, and on-/off-premises datacenters and clouds, making use of technologies such as mGRE, MPLS, and SD-WAN.

Appendix A

Mapping Course Content to CompTIA Certification

Achieving CompTIA Network+ certification requires candidates to pass Exam N10-008. This table describes where the exam objectives for Exam N10-008 are covered in this course.

1.0 Networking Fundamentals	
1.1 Compare and contrast the Open Systems Interconnection (OSI) model layers and encapsulation concepts.	**Covered in**
OSI Model	Lesson 1, Topic A
Layer 1 – Physical	Lesson 1, Topic A
Layer 2 – Data link	Lesson 1, Topic A
Layer 3 – Network	Lesson 1, Topic A
Layer 4 – Transport	Lesson 1, Topic A
Layer 5 – Session	Lesson 1, Topic A
Layer 6 – Presentation	Lesson 1, Topic A
Layer 7 – Application	Lesson 1, Topic A
Data encapsulation and decapsulation within the OSI model context	Lesson 1, Topic A Lesson 3, Topic B Lesson 5, Topic A Lesson 9, Topic A
Ethernet header	Lesson 3, Topic B
Internet Protocol (IP) header	Lesson 5, Topic A
Transmission Control Protocol (TCP)/User Datagram Protocol (UDP) headers	Lesson 9, Topic A
TCP flags	Lesson 9, Topic A
Payload	Lesson 1, Topic A
Maximum transmission unit (MTU)	Lesson 3, Topic B

1.2 Explain the characteristics of network topologies and network types.	Covered in
Mesh	Lesson 8, Topic A
Star/hub-and-spoke	Lesson 8, Topic A
Bus	Lesson 8, Topic A
Ring	Lesson 8, Topic A
Hybrid	Lesson 8, Topic A
Network types and characteristics	Lesson 8, Topic A Lesson 20, Topic B Lesson 20, Topic C

1.2 Explain the characteristics of network topologies and network types.	Covered in
Peer-to-peer	Lesson 8, Topic A
Client-server	Lesson 8, Topic A
Local area network (LAN)	Lesson 8, Topic A
Metropolitan area network (MAN)	Lesson 8, Topic A
Wide area network (WAN)	Lesson 8, Topic A
Wireless local area network (WLAN)	Lesson 8, Topic A
Personal area network (PAN)	Lesson 8, Topic A
Campus area network (CAN)	Lesson 8, Topic A
Storage area network (SAN)	Lesson 20, Topic B
Software-defined wide area network (SDWAN)	Lesson 20, Topic C
Multiprotocol label switching (MPLS)	Lesson 20, Topic C
Multipoint generic routing encapsulation (mGRE)	Lesson 20, Topic C
Service-related entry point	Lesson 16, Topic A
Demarcation point	Lesson 16, Topic A
Smartjack	Lesson 16, Topic A
Virtual network concepts	Lesson 20, Topic B
vSwitch	Lesson 20, Topic B
Virtual network interface card (vNIC)	Lesson 20, Topic B
Network function virtualization (NFV)	Lesson 20, Topic B
Hypervisor	Lesson 20, Topic B
Provider links	Lesson 16, Topic A
Satellite	Lesson 16, Topic A
Digital subscriber line (DSL)	Lesson 16, Topic A
Cable	Lesson 16, Topic A
Leased line	Lesson 16, Topic A
Metro-optical	Lesson 16, Topic A

1.3 Summarize the types of cables and connectors and explain which is the appropriate type for a solution.	Covered in
Copper	Lesson 2, Topic B
Twisted pair	Lesson 2, Topic B
Cat 5	Lesson 2, Topic B
Cat 5e	Lesson 2, Topic B
Cat 6	Lesson 2, Topic B
Cat 6a	Lesson 2, Topic B
Cat 7	Lesson 2, Topic B
Cat 8	Lesson 2, Topic B
Coaxial/RG-6	Lesson 2, Topic B
Twinaxial	Lesson 2, Topic B

1.3 Summarize the types of cables and connectors and explain which is the appropriate type for a solution.	Covered in
Termination standards	Lesson 2, Topic B
TIA/EIA-568A	Lesson 2, Topic B
TIA/EIA-568B	Lesson 2, Topic B
Fiber	Lesson 2, Topic C
Single-mode	Lesson 2, Topic C
Multimode	Lesson 2, Topic C
Connector types	Lesson 2, Topic B Lesson 2, Topic C Lesson 2, Topic D
Local connector (LC), straight tip (ST), subscriber connector (SC), mechanical transfer (MT), registered jack (RJ)	Lesson 2, Topic C
Angled physical contact (APC)	Lesson 2, Topic C
Ultra-physical contact (UPC)	Lesson 2, Topic C
RJ11	Lesson 2, Topic B
RJ45	Lesson 2, Topic B
F-type connector	Lesson 2, Topic B
Transceivers/media converters	Lesson 2, Topic D
Transceiver type	Lesson 2, Topic D
Small form-factor pluggable (SFP)	Lesson 2, Topic D
Enhanced form-factor pluggable (SFP+)	Lesson 2, Topic D
Quad small form-factor pluggable (QSFP)	Lesson 2, Topic D
Enhanced quad small form-factor pluggable (QSFP+)	Lesson 2, Topic D
Cable management	Lesson 2, Topic D
Patch panel/patch bay	Lesson 2, Topic D
Fiber distribution panel	Lesson 2, Topic D
Punchdown block	Lesson 2, Topic D
66	Lesson 2, Topic D
110	Lesson 2, Topic D
Krone	Lesson 2, Topic D
Bix	Lesson 2, Topic D
Ethernet standards	Lesson 2, Topic A Lesson 2, Topic C Lesson 2, Topic D
Copper	Lesson 2, Topic A
10BASE-T	Lesson 2, Topic A
100BASE-TX	Lesson 2, Topic A
1000BASE-T	Lesson 2, Topic A
10GBASE-T	Lesson 2, Topic A
40GBASE-T	Lesson 2, Topic A

1.3 Summarize the types of cables and connectors and explain which is the appropriate type for a solution.	Covered in
Fiber	Lesson 2, Topic C
	Lesson 2, Topic D
100BASE-FX	Lesson 2, Topic C
100BASE-SX	Lesson 2, Topic C
1000BASE-SX	Lesson 2, Topic C
1000BASE-LX	Lesson 2, Topic C
10GBASE-SR	Lesson 2, Topic C
10GBASE-LR	Lesson 2, Topic C
Coarse wavelength division multiplexing (CWDM)	Lesson 2, Topic D
Dense wavelength division multiplexing (DWDM)	Lesson 2, Topic D
Bidirectional wavelength division multiplexing (WDM)	Lesson 2, Topic D

1.4 Given a scenario, configure a subnet and use appropriate IP addressing schemes.	Covered in
Public vs. private	Lesson 5, Topic C
	Lesson 14, Topic A
RFC1918	Lesson 5, Topic C
Network address translation (NAT)	Lesson 14, Topic A
Port address translation (PAT)	Lesson 14, Topic A
IPv4 vs. IPv6	Lesson 5, Topic B
	Lesson 5, Topic C
	Lesson 6, Topic C
Automatic Private IP Addressing (APIPA)	Lesson 5, Topic C
Extended unique identifier (EUI-64)	Lesson 6, Topic C
Multicast	Lesson 5, Topic B
Unicast	Lesson 5, Topic B
Anycast	Lesson 5, Topic B
Broadcast	Lesson 5, Topic B
Link local	Lesson 6, Topic C
Loopback	Lesson 5, Topic C
Default gateway	Lesson 5, Topic B
IPv4 subnetting	Lesson 5, Topic C
	Lesson 7, Topic B
Classless (variable-length subnet mask)	Lesson 7, Topic B
Classful	Lesson 5, Topic C
A	Lesson 5, Topic C
B	Lesson 5, Topic C
C	Lesson 5, Topic C
D	Lesson 5, Topic C
E	Lesson 5, Topic C

1.4 Given a scenario, configure a subnet and use appropriate IP addressing schemes.	Covered in
Classless Inter-Domain Routing (CIDR) notation	Lesson 7, Topic B
IPv6 concepts	Lesson 6, Topic C
Tunneling	Lesson 6, Topic C
Dual stack	Lesson 6, Topic C
Shorthand notation	Lesson 6, Topic C
Router advertisement	Lesson 6, Topic C
Stateless address autoconfiguration (SLAAC)	Lesson 6, Topic C
Virtual IP (VIP)	Lesson 18, Topic B
Subinterfaces	Lesson 7, Topic C

1.5 Explain common ports and protocols, their application, and encrypted alternatives.		
Protocols	**Port(s)**	**Covered in**
File Transfer Protocol (FTP)	20/21	Lesson 11, Topic A
Secure Shell (SSH)	22	Lesson 12, Topic A
Secure File Transfer Protocol (SFTP)	22	Lesson 11, Topic A
Telnet	23	Lesson 12, Topic A
Simple Mail Transfer Protocol (SMTP)	25	Lesson 11, Topic B
Domain Name System (DNS)	53	Lesson 10, Topic B
Dynamic Host Configuration Protocol (DHCP)	67/68	Lesson 10, Topic A
Trivial File Transfer Protocol (TFTP)	69	Lesson 11, Topic A
Hypertext Transfer Protocol (HTTP)	80	Lesson 11, Topic A
Post Office Protocol v3 (POP3)	110	Lesson 11, Topic B
Network Time Protocol (NTP)	123	Lesson 12, Topic A
Internet Message Access Protocol (IMAP)	143	Lesson 11, Topic B
Simple Network Management Protocol (SNMP)	161/162	Lesson 12, Topic B
Lightweight Directory Access Protocol (LDAP)	389	Lesson 13, Topic B
Hypertext Transfer Protocol Secure (HTTPS) [Secure Sockets Layer (SSL)]	443	Lesson 11, Topic A
HTTPS [Transport Layer Security (TLS)]	443	Lesson 11, Topic A
Server Message Block (SMB)	445	Lesson 11, Topic A
Syslog	514	Lesson 12, Topic B
SMTP TLS	587	Lesson 11, Topic B
Lightweight Directory Access Protocol (over SSL) (LDAPS)	636	Lesson 13, Topic B
IMAP over SSL	993	Lesson 11, Topic B
POP3 over SSL	995	Lesson 11, Topic B

1.5 Explain common ports and protocols, their application, and encrypted alternatives.

Protocols	Port(s)	Covered in
Structured Query Language (SQL) Server	1433	Lesson 11, Topic A
SQLnet	1521	Lesson 11, Topic A
MySQL	3306	Lesson 11, Topic A
Remote Desktop Protocol (RDP)	3389	Lesson 12, Topic A
Session Initiation Protocol (SIP)	5060/5061	Lesson 11, Topic B
IP protocol types		Lesson 6, Topic A Lesson 9, Topic A Lesson 16, Topic B
Internet Control Message Protocol (ICMP)		Lesson 6, Topic A
TCP		Lesson 9, Topic A
UDP		Lesson 9, Topic A
Generic Routing Encapsulation (GRE)		Lesson 16, Topic B
Internet Protocol Security (IPSec)		Lesson 16, Topic B
Authentication Header (AH)/Encapsulating Security Payload (ESP)		Lesson 16, Topic B
Connectionless vs. connection-oriented		Lesson 9, Topic A

1.6 Explain the use and purpose of network services.

	Covered in
DHCP	Lesson 10, Topic A
Scope	Lesson 10, Topic A
Exclusion ranges	Lesson 10, Topic A
Reservation	Lesson 10, Topic A
Dynamic assignment	Lesson 10, Topic A
Static assignment	Lesson 10, Topic A
Lease time	Lesson 10, Topic A
Scope options	Lesson 10, Topic A
Available leases	Lesson 10, Topic A
DHCP relay	Lesson 10, Topic A
IP helper/UDP forwarding	Lesson 10, Topic A
DNS	Lesson 10, Topic B Lesson 10, Topic C
Record types	Lesson 10, Topic B
Address (A vs. AAAA)	Lesson 10, Topic B
Canonical name (CNAME)	Lesson 10, Topic B
Mail exchange (MX)	Lesson 10, Topic B
Start of authority (SOA)	Lesson 10, Topic B
Pointer (PTR)	Lesson 10, Topic B
Text (TXT)	Lesson 10, Topic B
Service (SRV)	Lesson 10, Topic B
Name server (NS)	Lesson 10, Topic B

1.6 Explain the use and purpose of network services.	Covered in
Global hierarchy	Lesson 10, Topic B
Root DNS servers	Lesson 10, Topic B
Internal vs. external	Lesson 10, Topic C
Zone transfers	Lesson 10, Topic C
Authoritative name servers	Lesson 10, Topic B
Time to live (TTL)	Lesson 10, Topic C
DNS caching	Lesson 10, Topic C
Reverse DNS/reverse lookup/forward lookup	Lesson 10, Topic B
Recursive lookup/iterative lookup	Lesson 10, Topic B
NTP	Lesson 12, Topic A
Stratum	Lesson 12, Topic A
Clients	Lesson 12, Topic A
Servers	Lesson 12, Topic A

1.7 Explain basic corporate and datacenter network architecture.	Covered in
Three-tiered	Lesson 8, Topic B
Core	Lesson 8, Topic B
Distribution/aggregation layer	Lesson 8, Topic B
Access/edge	Lesson 8, Topic B
Software-defined networking	Lesson 20, Topic C
Application layer	Lesson 20, Topic C
Control layer	Lesson 20, Topic C
Infrastructure layer	Lesson 20, Topic C
Management plane	Lesson 20, Topic C
Spine and leaf	Lesson 20, Topic C
Software-defined network	Lesson 20, Topic C
Top-of-rack switching	Lesson 20, Topic C
Backbone	Lesson 20, Topic C
Traffic flows	Lesson 20, Topic C
North-South	Lesson 20, Topic C
East-West	Lesson 20, Topic C
Branch office vs. on-premises datacenter vs. colocation	Lesson 20, Topic C
Storage area networks	Lesson 20, Topic B
Connection types	Lesson 20, Topic B
Fibre Channel over Ethernet (FCoE)	Lesson 20, Topic B
Fibre Channel	Lesson 20, Topic B
Internet Small Computer Systems Interface (iSCSI)	Lesson 20, Topic B

1.8 Summarize cloud concepts and connectivity options.	Covered in
Deployment models	Lesson 20, Topic A
Public	Lesson 20, Topic A
Private	Lesson 20, Topic A
Hybrid	Lesson 20, Topic A
Community	Lesson 20, Topic A
Service models	Lesson 20, Topic A
Software as a service (SaaS)	Lesson 20, Topic A
Infrastructure as a service (IaaS)	Lesson 20, Topic A
Platform as a service (PaaS)	Lesson 20, Topic A
Desktop as a service (DaaS)	Lesson 20, Topic A
Infrastructure as code	Lesson 20, Topic A
Automation/orchestration	Lesson 20, Topic A
Connectivity options	Lesson 20, Topic A
Virtual private network (VPN)	Lesson 20, Topic A
Private-direct connection to cloud provider	Lesson 20, Topic A
Multitenancy	Lesson 20, Topic A
Elasticity	Lesson 20, Topic A
Scalability	Lesson 20, Topic A
Security implications	Lesson 20, Topic A

2.0 Network Implementations	
2.1 Compare and contrast various devices, their features, and their appropriate placement on the network.	Covered in
Networking devices	Lesson 3, Topic A Lesson 7, Topic C Lesson 11, Topic B Lesson 14, Topic A Lesson 15, Topic B Lesson 16, Topic A Lesson 16, Topic B Lesson 18, Topic B
Layer 2 switch	Lesson 3, Topic A
Layer 3 capable switch	Lesson 7, Topic C
Router	Lesson 7, Topic C
Hub	Lesson 3, Topic A
Access point	Lesson 15, Topic B
Bridge	Lesson 3, Topic A
Wireless LAN controller	Lesson 15, Topic B
Load balancer	Lesson 18, Topic B
Proxy server	Lesson 14, Topic A
Cable modem	Lesson 16, Topic A
DSL modem	Lesson 16, Topic A

2.1 Compare and contrast various devices, their features, and their appropriate placement on the network.	Covered in
Repeater	Lesson 3, Topic A
Voice gateway	Lesson 11, Topic B
Media converter	Lesson 3, Topic A
Intrusion prevention system (IPS)/intrusion detection system (IDS) device	Lesson 14, Topic A
Firewall	Lesson 14, Topic A
VPN headend	Lesson 16, Topic B
Networked devices	Lesson 11, Topic A Lesson 18, Topic B Lesson 17, Topic C
Voice over Internet Protocol (VoIP) phone	Lesson 11, Topic B
Printer	Lesson 11, Topic A
Physical access control devices	Lesson 17, Topic C
Cameras	Lesson 17, Topic C
Heating, ventilation, and air conditioning (HVAC) sensors	Lesson 17, Topic C
Internet of Things (IoT)	Lesson 17, Topic C
Refrigerators	Lesson 17, Topic C
Smart speakers	Lesson 17, Topic C
Smart thermostats	Lesson 17, Topic C
Smart doorbells	Lesson 17, Topic C
Industrial control systems/supervisory control and data acquisition (SCADA)	Lesson 17, Topic C

2.2 Compare and contrast routing technologies and bandwidth management concepts.	Covered in
Routing	Lesson 7, Topic A Lesson 7, Topic B
Dynamic routing	Lesson 7, Topic B
Protocols [Routing Internet Protocol (RIP), Open Shortest Path First (OSPF), Enhanced Interior Gateway Routing Protocol (EIGRP), Border Gateway Protocol (BGP)]	Lesson 7, Topic B
Link state vs. distance vector vs. hybrid	Lesson 7, Topic B
Static routing	Lesson 7, Topic A
Default route	Lesson 7, Topic A
Administrative distance	Lesson 7, Topic B
Exterior vs. interior	Lesson 7, Topic B
Time to live	Lesson 7, Topic A
Bandwidth management	Lesson 12, Topic C
Traffic shaping	Lesson 12, Topic C
Quality of service (QoS)	Lesson 12, Topic C

2.3 Given a scenario, configure and deploy common Ethernet switching features.	Covered in
Data virtual local area network (VLAN)	Lesson 8, Topic C
Voice VLAN	Lesson 8, Topic C
Port configurations	Lesson 3, Topic C
Port tagging/802.1Q	Lesson 3, Topic C
Port aggregation	Lesson 3, Topic C
Link Aggregation Control Protocol (LACP)	Lesson 3, Topic C
Duplex	Lesson 3, Topic C
Speed	Lesson 3, Topic C
Flow control	Lesson 3, Topic C
Port mirroring	Lesson 3, Topic C
Port security	Lesson 3, Topic C
Jumbo frames	Lesson 3, Topic C
Auto-medium-dependent interface crossover (MDI-X)	Lesson 3, Topic C
Media access control (MAC) address tables	Lesson 3, Topic C
Power over Ethernet (PoE)/Power over Ethernet plus (PoE+)	Lesson 3, Topic C
Spanning Tree Protocol	Lesson 8, Topic B
Carrier-sense multiple access with collision detection (CSMA/CD)	Lesson 2, Topic A
Address Resolution Protocol (ARP)	Lesson 5, Topic B
Neighbor Discovery Protocol	Lesson 6, Topic C

2.4 Given a scenario, install and configure the appropriate wireless standards and technologies.	Covered in
802.11 standards	Lesson 15, Topic A
a	Lesson 15, Topic A
b	Lesson 15, Topic A
g	Lesson 15, Topic A
n (WiFi 4)	Lesson 15, Topic A
ac (WiFi 5)	Lesson 15, Topic A
ax (WiFi 6)	Lesson 15, Topic A
Frequencies and range	Lesson 15, Topic A
2.4GHz	Lesson 15, Topic A
5GHz	Lesson 15, Topic A
Channels	Lesson 15, Topic A
Regulatory impacts	Lesson 15, Topic A
Channel bonding	Lesson 15, Topic A
Service set identifier (SSID)	Lesson 15, Topic B
Basic service set	Lesson 15, Topic B
Extended service set	Lesson 15, Topic B

2.4 Given a scenario, install and configure the appropriate wireless standards and technologies.	Covered in
Independent basic service set (Ad-hoc)	Lesson 15, Topic B
Roaming	Lesson 15, Topic B
Antenna types	Lesson 15, Topic C
Omni	Lesson 15, Topic C
Directional	Lesson 15, Topic C
Encryption standards	Lesson 15, Topic D
WiFi Protected Access (WPA)/WPA2 Personal [Advanced Encryption Standard (AES)/Temporal Key Integrity Protocol (TKIP)]	Lesson 15, Topic D
WPA/WPA2 Enterprise (AES/TKIP)	Lesson 15, Topic D
Cellular technologies	Lesson 15, Topic A
Code-division multiple access (CDMA)	Lesson 15, Topic A
Global System for Mobile Communications (GSM)	Lesson 15, Topic A
Long-Term Evolution (LTE)	Lesson 15, Topic A
3G, 4G, 5G	Lesson 15, Topic A
Multiple input, multiple output (MIMO) and multi-user MIMO (MU-MIMO)	Lesson 15, Topic A

3.0 Network Operations	
3.1 Given a scenario, use the appropriate statistics and sensors to ensure network availability.	Covered in
Performance metrics/sensors	Lesson 12, Topic B
Device/chassis	Lesson 12, Topic B
Temperature	Lesson 12, Topic B
Central processing unit (CPU) usage	Lesson 12, Topic B
Memory	Lesson 12, Topic B
Network metrics	Lesson 12, Topic B
Bandwidth	Lesson 12, Topic B
Latency	Lesson 12, Topic B
Jitter	Lesson 12, Topic B
SNMP	Lesson 12, Topic B
Traps	Lesson 12, Topic B
Object identifiers (OIDs)	Lesson 12, Topic B
Management information bases (MIBs)	Lesson 12, Topic B
Network device logs	Lesson 12, Topic B
Log reviews	Lesson 12, Topic B
Traffic logs	Lesson 12, Topic B
Audit logs	Lesson 12, Topic B
Syslog	Lesson 12, Topic B
Logging levels/severity levels	Lesson 12, Topic B

3.1 Given a scenario, use the appropriate statistics and sensors to ensure network availability.	Covered in
Interface statistics/status	Lesson 12, Topic C
Link state (up/down)	Lesson 12, Topic C
Speed/duplex	Lesson 12, Topic C
Send/receive traffic	Lesson 12, Topic C
Cyclic redundancy checks (CRCs)	Lesson 12, Topic C
Protocol packet and byte counts	Lesson 12, Topic C
Interface errors or alerts	Lesson 12, Topic C
CRC errors	Lesson 12, Topic C
Giants	Lesson 12, Topic C
Runts	Lesson 12, Topic C
Encapsulation errors	Lesson 12, Topic C
Environmental factors and sensors	Lesson 12, Topic B
Temperature	Lesson 12, Topic B
Humidity	Lesson 12, Topic B
Electrical	Lesson 12, Topic B
Flooding	Lesson 12, Topic B
Baselines	Lesson 12, Topic B
NetFlow data	Lesson 12, Topic C
Uptime/downtime	Lesson 12, Topic C

3.2 Explain the purpose of organizational documents and policies.	Covered in
Plans and procedures	Lesson 17, Topic A
Change management	Lesson 17, Topic A
Incident response plan	Lesson 17, Topic A
Disaster recovery plan	Lesson 17, Topic A
Business continuity plan	Lesson 17, Topic A
System life cycle	Lesson 17, Topic A
Standard operating procedures	Lesson 17, Topic A
Hardening and security policies	Lesson 17, Topic A
Password policy	Lesson 17, Topic A
Acceptable use policy	Lesson 17, Topic A
Bring your own device (BYOD) policy	Lesson 17, Topic A
Remote access policy	Lesson 17, Topic A
Onboarding and offboarding policy	Lesson 17, Topic A
Security policy	Lesson 17, Topic A
Data loss prevention	Lesson 17, Topic A

3.2 Explain the purpose of organizational documents and policies.	Covered in
Common documentation	Lesson 17, Topic A
Physical network diagram	Lesson 17, Topic A
Floor plan	Lesson 17, Topic A
Rack diagram	Lesson 17, Topic A
Intermediate distribution frame (IDF)/main distribution frame (MDF) documentation	Lesson 17, Topic A
Logical network diagram	Lesson 17, Topic A
Wiring diagram	Lesson 17, Topic A
Site survey report	Lesson 17, Topic A
Audit and assessment report	Lesson 17, Topic A
Baseline configurations	Lesson 17, Topic A
Common agreements	Lesson 17, Topic A
Non-disclosure agreement (NDA)	Lesson 17, Topic A
Service-level agreement (SLA)	Lesson 17, Topic A
Memorandum of understanding (MOU)	Lesson 17, Topic A

3.3 Explain high availability and disaster recovery concepts and summarize which is the best solution.	Covered in
Load balancing	Lesson 18, Topic B
Multipathing	Lesson 18, Topic B
Network interface card (NIC) teaming	Lesson 18, Topic B
Redundant hardware/clusters	Lesson 18, Topic B
Switches	Lesson 18, Topic B
Routers	Lesson 18, Topic B
Firewalls	Lesson 18, Topic B
Facilities and infrastructure support	Lesson 18, Topic A
Uninterruptible power supply (UPS)	Lesson 18, Topic A
Power distribution units (PDUs)	Lesson 18, Topic A
Generator	Lesson 18, Topic A
HVAC	Lesson 18, Topic A
Fire suppression	Lesson 18, Topic A
Redundancy and high availability (HA) concepts	Lesson 18, Topic A Lesson 18, Topic B
Cold site	Lesson 18, Topic A
Warm site	Lesson 18, Topic A
Hot site	Lesson 18, Topic A
Cloud site	Lesson 18, Topic A
Active-active vs. active-passive	Lesson 18, Topic B
Multiple Internet service providers (ISPs)/diverse paths	Lesson 18, Topic B
Virtual Router Redundancy Protocol (VRRP)/First Hop Redundancy Protocol (FHRP)	Lesson 18, Topic B

3.3 Explain high availability and disaster recovery concepts and summarize which is the best solution.	Covered in
Mean time to repair (MTTR)	Lesson 18, Topic A
Mean time between failure (MTBF)	Lesson 18, Topic A
Recovery time objective (RTO)	Lesson 18, Topic A
Recovery point objective (RPO)	Lesson 18, Topic A
Network device backup/restore	Lesson 18, Topic A
State	Lesson 18, Topic A
Configuration	Lesson 18, Topic A

4.0 Network Security	
4.1 Explain common security concepts.	Covered in
Confidentiality, integrity, availability (CIA)	Lesson 13, Topic A
Threats	Lesson 13, Topic A
Internal	Lesson 13, Topic A
External	Lesson 13, Topic A
Vulnerabilities	Lesson 13, Topic A
Common vulnerabilities and exposures (CVE)	Lesson 13, Topic A
Zero-day	Lesson 13, Topic A
Exploits	Lesson 13, Topic A
Least privilege	Lesson 13, Topic A
Role-based access	Lesson 13, Topic A
Zero Trust	Lesson 13, Topic A
Defense in depth	Lesson 14, Topic A
Network segmentation enforcement	Lesson 14, Topic A
Screened subnet [previously known as demilitarized zone (DMZ)]	Lesson 14, Topic A
Separation of duties	Lesson 14, Topic A
Network access control	Lesson 14, Topic A
Honeypot	Lesson 14, Topic A
Authentication methods	Lesson 13, Topic B
Multifactor	Lesson 13, Topic B
Terminal Access Controller Access-Control System Plus (TACACS+)	Lesson 13, Topic B
Single sign-on (SSO)	Lesson 13, Topic B
Remote Authentication Dial-in User Service (RADIUS)	Lesson 13, Topic B
LDAP	Lesson 13, Topic B
Kerberos	Lesson 13, Topic B
Local authentication	Lesson 13, Topic B
802.1X	Lesson 13, Topic B
Extensible Authentication Protocol (EAP)	Lesson 13, Topic B

4.1 Explain common security concepts.	Covered in
Risk Management	Lesson 13, Topic A
Security risk assessments	Lesson 13, Topic A
Threat assessment	Lesson 13, Topic A
Vulnerability assessment	Lesson 13, Topic A
Penetration testing	Lesson 13, Topic A
Posture assessment	Lesson 13, Topic A
Business risk assessments	Lesson 13, Topic A
Process assessment	Lesson 13, Topic A
Vendor assessment	Lesson 13, Topic A
Security information and event management (SIEM)	Lesson 13, Topic A

4.2 Compare and contrast common types of attacks.	Covered in
Technology-based	Lesson 19, Topic A
Denial-of-service (DoS)/distributed denial-of-service (DDoS)	Lesson 19, Topic A
Botnet/command and control	Lesson 19, Topic A
On-path attack (previously known as man-in-the-middle attack)	Lesson 19, Topic A
DNS poisoning	Lesson 19, Topic A
VLAN hopping	Lesson 19, Topic A
ARP spoofing	Lesson 19, Topic A
Rogue DHCP	Lesson 19, Topic A
Rogue access point (AP)	Lesson 19, Topic A
Evil twin	Lesson 19, Topic A
Ransomware	Lesson 19, Topic A
Password attacks	Lesson 19, Topic A
Brute-force	Lesson 19, Topic A
Dictionary	Lesson 19, Topic A
MAC spoofing	Lesson 19, Topic A
IP spoofing	Lesson 19, Topic A
Deauthentication	Lesson 19, Topic A
Malware	Lesson 19, Topic A
Human and environmental	Lesson 19, Topic A
Social engineering	Lesson 19, Topic A
Phishing	Lesson 19, Topic A
Tailgating	Lesson 19, Topic A
Piggybacking	Lesson 19, Topic A
Shoulder surfing	Lesson 19, Topic A

4.3 Given a scenario, apply network hardening techniques.	Covered in
Best practices	Lesson 19, Topic B
Secure SNMP	Lesson 19, Topic B
Router Advertisement (RA) Guard	Lesson 19, Topic B
Port security	Lesson 19, Topic B
Dynamic ARP inspection	Lesson 19, Topic B
Control plane policing	Lesson 19, Topic B
Private VLANs	Lesson 19, Topic B
Disable unneeded switchports	Lesson 19, Topic B
Disable unneeded network services	Lesson 19, Topic B
Change default passwords	Lesson 19, Topic B
Password complexity/length	Lesson 19, Topic B
Enable DHCP snooping	Lesson 19, Topic B
Change default VLAN	Lesson 19, Topic B
Patch and firmware management	Lesson 19, Topic B
Access control list	Lesson 19, Topic B
Role-based access	Lesson 19, Topic B
Firewall rules	Lesson 19, Topic B
Explicit deny	Lesson 19, Topic B
Implicit deny	Lesson 19, Topic B
Wireless security	Lesson 19, Topic B
MAC filtering	Lesson 19, Topic B
Antenna placement	Lesson 19, Topic B
Power levels	Lesson 19, Topic B
Wireless client isolation	Lesson 19, Topic B
Guest network isolation	Lesson 19, Topic B
Preshared keys (PSKs)	Lesson 19, Topic B
EAP	Lesson 19, Topic B
Geofencing	Lesson 19, Topic B
Captive portal	Lesson 19, Topic B
IoT access considerations	Lesson 19, Topic B

4.4 Compare and contrast remote access methods and security implications.	Covered in
Site-to-site VPN	Lesson 16, Topic B
Client-to-site VPN	Lesson 16, Topic B
Clientless VPN	Lesson 16, Topic B
Split tunnel vs. full tunnel	Lesson 16, Topic B
Remote desktop connection	Lesson 16, Topic B
Remote desktop gateway	Lesson 16, Topic B
SSH	Lesson 16, Topic B

4.4 Compare and contrast remote access methods and security implications.	Covered in
Virtual network computing (VNC)	Lesson 16, Topic B
Virtual desktop	Lesson 16, Topic B
Authentication and authorization considerations	Lesson 16, Topic B
In-band vs. out-of-band management	Lesson 16, Topic B

4.5 Explain the importance of physical security.	Covered in
Detection methods	Lesson 17, Topic B
Camera	Lesson 17, Topic B
Motion detection	Lesson 17, Topic B
Asset tags	Lesson 17, Topic B
Tamper detection	Lesson 17, Topic B
Prevention methods	Lesson 17, Topic B
Employee training	Lesson 17, Topic B
Access control hardware	Lesson 17, Topic B
Badge readers	Lesson 17, Topic B
Biometrics	Lesson 17, Topic B
Locking racks	Lesson 17, Topic B
Locking cabinets	Lesson 17, Topic B
Access control vestibule (previously known as a mantrap)	Lesson 17, Topic B
Smart lockers	Lesson 17, Topic B
Asset disposal	Lesson 17, Topic B
Factory reset/wipe configuration	Lesson 17, Topic B
Sanitize devices for disposal	Lesson 17, Topic B

5.0 Network Troubleshooting	
5.1 Explain the network troubleshooting methodology.	Covered in
Identify the problem	Lesson 4, Topic A
Gather information	Lesson 4, Topic A
Question users	Lesson 4, Topic A
Identify symptoms	Lesson 4, Topic A
Determine if anything has changed	Lesson 4, Topic A
Duplicate the problem, if possible	Lesson 4, Topic A
Approach multiple problems individually	Lesson 4, Topic A
Establish a theory of probable cause	Lesson 4, Topic A
Question the obvious	Lesson 4, Topic A
Consider multiple approaches	Lesson 4, Topic A
Top-to-bottom/bottom-to-top OSI model	Lesson 4, Topic A
Divide and conquer	Lesson 4, Topic A

5.1 Explain the network troubleshooting methodology.	Covered in
Test the theory to determine the cause	Lesson 4, Topic A
If the theory is confirmed, determine the next steps to resolve the problem	Lesson 4, Topic A
If the theory is not confirmed, reestablish a new theory or escalate	Lesson 4, Topic A
Establish a plan of action to resolve the problem and identify potential effects	Lesson 4, Topic A
Implement the solution or escalate as necessary	Lesson 4, Topic A
Verify full system functionality and, if applicable, implement preventive measures	Lesson 4, Topic A
Document findings, actions, outcomes, and lessons learned	Lesson 4, Topic A

5.2 Given a scenario, troubleshoot common cable connectivity issues and select the appropriate tools.	Covered in
Specifications and limitations	Lesson 4, Topic B
Throughput	Lesson 4, Topic B
Speed	Lesson 4, Topic B
Distance	Lesson 4, Topic B
Cable considerations	Lesson 4, Topic B
Shielded and unshielded	Lesson 4, Topic B
Plenum and riser-rated	Lesson 4, Topic B
Cable application	Lesson 4, Topic B
Rollover cable/console cable	Lesson 4, Topic B
Crossover cable	Lesson 4, Topic B
Power over Ethernet	Lesson 4, Topic B
Common issues	Lesson 4, Topic B
Attenuation	Lesson 4, Topic B
Interference	Lesson 4, Topic B
Decibel (dB) loss	Lesson 4, Topic B
Incorrect pinout	Lesson 4, Topic B
Bad ports	Lesson 4, Topic B
Open/short	Lesson 4, Topic B
Light-emitting diode (LED) status indicators	Lesson 4, Topic B
Incorrect transceivers	Lesson 4, Topic B
Duplexing issues	Lesson 4, Topic B
Transmit and receive (TX/RX) reversed	Lesson 4, Topic B
Dirty optical cables	Lesson 4, Topic B
Common tools	Lesson 2, Topic D Lesson 3, Topic B Lesson 4, Topic B

5.2 Given a scenario, troubleshoot common cable connectivity issues and select the appropriate tools.

	Covered in
Cable crimper	Lesson 2, Topic D
Punchdown tool	Lesson 2, Topic D
Tone generator	Lesson 4, Topic B
Loopback adapter	Lesson 4, Topic B
Optical time-domain reflectometer (OTDR)	Lesson 4, Topic B
Multimeter	Lesson 4, Topic B
Cable tester	Lesson 4, Topic B
Wire map	Lesson 4, Topic B
Tap	Lesson 3, Topic B
Fusion splicers	Lesson 2, Topic D
Spectrum analyzers	Lesson 4, Topic B
Snips/cutters	Lesson 2, Topic D
Cable stripper	Lesson 2, Topic D
Fiber light meter	Lesson 4, Topic B

5.3 Given a scenario, use the appropriate network software tools and commands.

	Covered in
Software tools	Lesson 9, Topic B Lesson 11, Topic A Lesson 12, Topic C Lesson 15, Topic C
WiFi analyzer	Lesson 15, Topic C
Protocol analyzer/packet capture	Lesson 9, Topic B
Bandwidth speed tester	Lesson 12, Topic C
Port scanner	Lesson 9, Topic B
iperf	Lesson 12, Topic C
NetFlow analyzers	Lesson 12, Topic C
Trivial File Transfer Protocol (TFTP) server	Lesson 11, Topic A
Terminal emulator	Lesson 12, Topic A
IP scanner	Lesson 9, Topic B
Command line tool	Lesson 3, Topic B Lesson 6, Topic A Lesson 7, Topic C Lesson 9, Topic B Lesson 10, Topic C Lesson 12, Topic A
ping	Lesson 6, Topic A
ipconfig/ifconfig/ip	Lesson 6, Topic A
nslookup/dig	Lesson 10, Topic C
traceroute/tracert	Lesson 7, Topic C
arp	Lesson 6, Topic A

5.3 Given a scenario, use the appropriate network software tools and commands.	Covered in
netstat	Lesson 9, Topic B
hostname	Lesson 10, Topic C
route	Lesson 7, Topic C
telnet	Lesson 12, Topic A
tcpdump	Lesson 3, Topic B
nmap	Lesson 9, Topic B
Basic network platform commands	Lesson 3, Topic C
show interface	Lesson 3, Topic C
show config	Lesson 3, Topic C
show route	Lesson 3, Topic C

5.4 Given a scenario, troubleshoot common wireless connectivity issues.	Covered in
Specifications and limitations	Lesson 15, Topic C
Throughput	Lesson 15, Topic C
Speed	Lesson 15, Topic C
Distance	Lesson 15, Topic C
Received signal strength indication (RSSI) signal strength	Lesson 15, Topic C
Effective isotropic radiated power (EIRP)/power settings	Lesson 15, Topic C
Considerations	Lesson 15, Topic C
Antennas	Lesson 15, Topic C
Placement	Lesson 15, Topic C
Type	Lesson 15, Topic C
Polarization	Lesson 15, Topic C
Channel utilization	Lesson 15, Topic C
AP association time	Lesson 15, Topic C
Site survey	Lesson 15, Topic C
Common issues	Lesson 15, Topic C Lesson 15, Topic D
Interference	Lesson 15, Topic C
Channel overlap	Lesson 15, Topic C
Antenna cable attenuation/signal loss	Lesson 15, Topic C
RF attenuation/signal loss	Lesson 15, Topic C
Wrong SSID	Lesson 15, Topic D
Incorrect passphrase	Lesson 15, Topic D
Encryption protocol mismatch	Lesson 15, Topic D
Insufficient wireless coverage	Lesson 15, Topic C
Captive portal issues	Lesson 15, Topic D
Client disassociation issues	Lesson 15, Topic D

5.5 Given a scenario, troubleshoot general networking issues.	Covered in
Considerations	Lesson 6, Topic B Lesson 7, Topic C Lesson 14, Topic B
Device configuration review	Lesson 7, Topic C
Routing tables	Lesson 7, Topic C
Interface status	Lesson 6, Topic B
VLAN assignment	Lesson 14, Topic B
Network performance baselines	Lesson 14, Topic B
Common issues	Lesson 6, Topic B Lesson 7, Topic C Lesson 8, Topic B Lesson 14, Topic B
Collisions	Lesson 6, Topic B
Broadcast storm	Lesson 8, Topic B
Duplicate MAC address	Lesson 6, Topic B
Duplicate IP address	Lesson 6, Topic B
Multicast flooding	Lesson 6, Topic B
Asymmetrical routing	Lesson 7, Topic C
Switching loops	Lesson 8, Topic B
Routing loops	Lesson 7, Topic C
Rogue DHCP server	Lesson 14, Topic B
DHCP scope exhaustion	Lesson 14, Topic B
IP setting issues	Lesson 6, Topic B
Incorrect gateway	Lesson 6, Topic B
Incorrect subnet mask	Lesson 6, Topic B
Incorrect IP address	Lesson 6, Topic B
Incorrect DNS	Lesson 6, Topic B
Missing route	Lesson 7, Topic C
Low optical link budget	Lesson 7, Topic C
Certificate issues	Lesson 14, Topic B
Hardware failure	Lesson 6, Topic B
Host-based/network-based firewall settings	Lesson 14, Topic B
Blocked services, ports, or addresses	Lesson 14, Topic B
Incorrect VLAN	Lesson 14, Topic B
DNS issues	Lesson 14, Topic B
NTP issues	Lesson 14, Topic B
BYOD challenges	Lesson 14, Topic B
Licensed feature issues	Lesson 14, Topic B
Network performance issues	Lesson 14, Topic B

Solutions

Review Activity: OSI Model Layers

1. At which OSI layer is the concept of a port number introduced?

Transport.

2. At which layer of the OSI model is no header encapsulation applied?

Physical.

3. What component performs signal amplification to extend the maximum allowable distance for a media type?

A repeater.

4. Which OSI layer packages bits of data from the Physical layer into frames?

Data Link.

5. True or False? The Session layer is responsible for passing data to the Network layer at the lower bound and the Presentation layer at the upper bound.

False. The Session layer is between the Transport and Presentation layers.

Review Activity: SOHO Networks

1. True or false? The WAN port on a SOHO router is connected to the LAN ports by an internal switch.

False—the LAN ports and access point are connected by a switch. The WAN port is separate. Packets must be routed between the LAN and WAN segments.

2. What type of address is used by the switch to forward transmissions to the appropriate host?

A media access control (MAC) address. This is a layer 2 address. It is also referred to as a hardware or physical address.

3. True or false? The DHCP server in the SOHO router assigns an IP address to the WAN interface automatically.

False—the DHCP server in the SOHO router assigns IP addresses to the hosts on the local network. The WAN address is likely to be assigned by DHCP, but a DHCP server is managed by the access provider.

4. What function or service prevents an Internet host from accessing servers on the LAN without authorization?

The firewall.

5. How is the decimal value 12 expressed in hex?

C (this might be written 0xC for clarity). Values above 9 are expressed as letters (10 = A, 11 = B, 12 = C).

6. How is the decimal value 171 expressed in hex?

0xAB. To work this out, divide 171 by 16 (144) and write the remainder (11) as the least significant hex digit (B). Note that the quotient 10 (the integer part of the sum, where 171/16 = 10.6875) is less than 16. Convert the quotient to hex (10 = A) to derive the second hex digit and complete the conversion.

Review Activity: Ethernet Standards

1. With CSMA/CD, what will happen if a host has data to transmit and there is already data on the cable?

The host will wait for a random backoff period before attempting to transmit again.

2. Which Ethernet standard works at 100 Mbps over Cat 5 or better copper cable?

100BASE-TX.

3. Which copper Ethernet standard meets the bandwidth requirements for clients in an office network while minimizing costs?

Gigabit Ethernet. Provisioning 10 GbE would require upgrading the network adapters in most client devices, as well as potentially requiring upgraded cable installation.

4. A network designer wants to run a 10 gigabit backbone between two switches in buildings that are 75 m (246 feet) apart. What is the main consideration when selecting an appropriate copper cable?

At that distance, some type of shielded or screened cat 6A or better cable is required for the installation to be compliant with Ethernet standard 10GBASE-T.

Review Activity: Copper Cabling Types

1. What is the measurement standard for wire thickness?

American Wire Gauge (AWG).

2. What are the characteristics of S/FTP cable?

This is a twisted pair type of copper cable using a braided outer screen and foil shielding for each pair to reduce interference.

3. Which categories of U/UTP cable are certified to carry data transmission faster than 100 Mbps?

Cat 5e and Cat 6/6A. Cat 7 and Cat 8 are screened/shielded types.

4. True or False? Cat standards apply only to wiring.

False—Connectors and interconnects are also rated to cat standards.

5. 100BASE-T transmit pins are 1 and 2. What color code are the wires terminated to these pins under T568A and T568B?

Green/White (pin 1) and Green (pin 2) for T658A or Orange (pin 1)/White and Orange (pin 2) for T568B.

6. Why is plenum-rated cable used when cable is run in an area where building air is circulated?

Plenum-rated cable produces minimal amounts of smoke if burned, must be self-extinguishing, and must meet other strict fire safety standards.

7. **Which cable type consists of a single core made of solid copper surrounded by insulation, a braided metal shielding, and an outer cover?**

Coax.

Review Activity: Fiber Optic Cabling Types

1. **What type of fiber optic cable is suited for long distance links?**

Single mode fiber (SMF).

2. **Which grade or grades of fiber have a 62.5 micron core?**

OM1.

3. **Which fiber Ethernet standard is best suited to implementing backbone cabling that does not exceed 200 m (656 feet) and can achieve at least 4 Gbps throughput?**

10GBASE-SR.

4. **What maximum distance is defined in standards documentation for 1000BASE-LX running over MMF?**

550 m (1804 feet). Note that 1000BASE-LX can run over MMF or SMF. SMF has much higher range.

5. **You need to provision a fiber patch panel to terminate incoming cabling with green LC connectors. What type of ports should be provisioned on the patch panel?**

Green connector color-coding indicates angled physical contact (APC) finishing. This type of finishing is incompatible with PC or UPC ports. The patch panel must be provisioned with Lucent Connector ports with APC finishing type.

Review Activity: Ethernet Cabling

1. **Which types of distribution frame are best suited to 100 MHz or better operation?**

110, BIX, and Krone blocks.

2. **What type of distribution frame is best suited to cabling wall ports to Ethernet switches in way that best supports futures changes?**

A patch panel allows wall ports to be connected to switches via patch cords. If a switch is replaced or if a wall port needs to be connected to a different switch port, the change can be made easily by moving a patch cord.

3. **What tool is used to terminate wiring at a 110 block?**

A punchdown tool is used to connect wires via insulation displacement connectors (IDCs). You must use a suitable blade for the IDC format (110, Krone, or BIX).

4. **At what layer of the OSI model does a fiber distribution panel work?**

All types of distribution frames work at the physical layer (layer 1).

5. **You need to provision modular SFP+ transceivers to support a 10 gigabit link between two switches using an existing fiber cable. What two characteristics must you check when ordering the transceivers?**

Use an appropriate Ethernet standard and wavelength for the type and grade of fiber and link distance (10GBASE-SR versus 10GBASE-LR, for instance) and match the connector type of the existing cable (LC or SC, for instance).

6. **You have selected an SFP+ 1310 nm Tx and 1490 nm Rx transceiver to implement a BiDi link between two switches. Should you provision a second SFP+ 1310 nm Tx and 1490 nm Rx for the other switch?**

No, you need an SFP+ module with 1490 nm Tx and 1310 nm Rx.

Review Activity: Networking Devices

1. **You need to run UTP cable between two switches at opposite ends of a warehouse that is 140 m (459 feet) long. What additional device (if any) is required for the installation to be compliant with 1000BASE-TX Ethernet standard?**

The maximum link length is 100 m (328 feet) so a repeater will be needed.

2. **True or false? All the nodes shown in the following figure are in the same collision domain.**

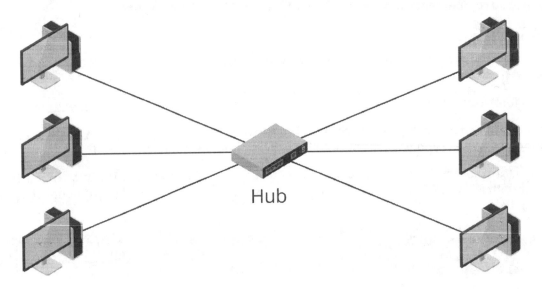

True. Hubs work at the physical layer (layer 1) and just repeat the same signal out of each port.

3. **True or False? A computer with a 10BASE-T Ethernet adapter cannot be joined to a 100BASE-T network.**

False. Fast Ethernet is backwards-compatible with 10BASE-T (and Gigabit Ethernet is backwards-compatible with Fast Ethernet).

4. **True or False? Devices can only transmit on an Ethernet network when the media is clear, and the opportunity to transmit becomes less frequent as more devices are added. Also, the probability of collisions increases. These problems can be overcome by installing a hub.**

False. The description of the problem is true, but the solution is not. This issue is resolved by using a bridge or (more likely these days) a switch.

5. **True or false? A bridge does not forward broadcast traffic.**

False. Segments on different bridge ports are in separate collision domains but the same broadcast domain.

Review Activity: Network Interfaces

1.   True or False? The CRC mechanism in Ethernet allows for the retransmission of damaged frames.

False. The CRC indicates only that a frame may be corrupt.

2.   What is an I/G bit?

Determines whether a frame is addressed to an individual node (0) or group (1). The latter is used for multicast and broadcast.

3.   What is an MTU?

Maximum transmission unit—the maximum amount of data that a frame can carry as payload.

4.   On a switched network, what configuration changes must be made to allow a host to sniff unicast traffic from all hosts connected to a switch?

The switch must be configured to mirror traffic to the sniffer's port.

5.   Write the command to use tcpdump to capture traffic from the IP address 172.16.16.254 on the interface eth0 and output the results to the file router.pcap.

```
tcpdump -i eth0 -w 'router.pcap' src host 172.16.16.254
```

Review Activity: Common Ethernet Switching Features

1.   You need to verify whether a switch port is misconfigured by checking the number of collisions being reported. What general command could you use at a CLI to report this information?

show interface

2.   True or false? A managed switch should have auto MDI/MDI-X enabled by default.

True.

3.   A technician configures a switch port with a list of approved MAC addresses. What type of feature has been enabled?

Port security.

4.   A server has a four-port gigabit Ethernet card. If a switch supports port aggregation, what bandwidth link can be achieved?

4 x 1 gigabit or 4 gigabit.

5.   What port configuration feature allows a server to smooth incoming traffic rates?

IEEE 802.3x flow control.

6.   Can you safely connect a server to a PoE+ enabled port or should you disable PoE first?

You can connect the server. PoE uses a detection mechanism to determine whether to supply power.

Review Activity: Network Troubleshooting Methodology

1. **Which step has been omitted from the following list of activities related to identifying the problem? Gather information • Duplicate the problem, if possible • Question users • Identify symptoms • Determine if anything has changed**

Approach multiple problems individually.

2. **Which three means of establishing a theory of probable cause refer to the OSI model?**

Top-to-bottom, bottom-to-top, and divide and conquer.

3. **When should you escalate a problem?**

If you cannot solve it yourself (although it won't be good for your career if you give up too easily). You might also escalate if you do not have authorization to perform the necessary changes or if the system is under some sort of warranty.

4. **Which step follows "Implement the solution or escalate as necessary" in the troubleshooting methodology?**

Verify full system functionality, and if applicable, implement preventive measures.

5. **True or False? Documentation should be created only at the end of the troubleshooting process.**

False. The last step of the methodology is to ensure that findings, actions, and outcomes are documented, but you cannot do this effectively without existing notes. Most troubleshooting takes place within a ticket system. Ideally, a documented job ticket would be opened at the start of recording the incident.

Review Activity: Common Cable Connectivity Issues

1. **What cabling faults would a wire map tester detect?**

Opens, shorts, and transpositions (reversed and crossed pairs).

2. **How would you test for excessive attenuation in a network link?**

Measure the insertion loss in dB by using a cable tester.

3. **What is the reason for making power sum crosstalk measurements when testing a link?**

Power sum crosstalk measures cable performance when all four pairs are used, as Gigabit and 10G Ethernet do.

4. **Your network uses UTP cable throughout the building. There are a few users who complain of intermittent network connectivity problems. You cannot determine a pattern for these problems that relates to network usage. You visit the users' workstations and find that they are all located close to an elevator shaft. What is a likely cause of the intermittent connectivity problems? How might you correct the problem?**

If the cabling is being run too close to the elevator equipment, when the elevator motor activates, it produces interference on the network wire. You can replace the UTP cable with screened/shielded copper wire or reposition the cables away from the elevator shaft.

5. **You have connected a computer to a network port and cannot get a link. You have tested the adapter and cable and can confirm that there are no problems. No other users are experiencing problems. The old computer also experienced no problems. What cause would you suspect, and what is a possible next step?**

Speed mismatch—Check the autonegotiate settings on the adapter and port.

Review Activity: IPv4 Addressing Schemes

1. **Convert the binary value 11110010 to decimal.**

Work out the value of the binary place positions: 128*1 + 64*1 + 32*1 + 16*1 + 8*0 + 4*0 + 2*1 + 1*0. Sum the result to derive the answer 242.

2. **Convert the decimal value 72 into binary.**

Work out the binary place positions that add up to 72: 128*0 + 64*1 + 32*0 + 16*0 + 8*1 + 4*0 + 2*0 + 1*0. Transcribe the 0s and 1s to form an octet: 01001000.

3. **What is the dotted decimal representation of an 8-bit netmask?**

An 8-bit mask means that each digit in the first octet is set to 1. Converted to dotted decimal, this becomes 255.0.0.0.

4. **What is the dotted decimal representation of an 18-bit netmask?**

The first two octets take up 16 bits. In the third octet, the first two bits are set to one. In decimal, this is 192 (128 + 64). Therefore, the full mask is 255.255.192.0.

5. **Given an 18-bit netmask, are the IP addresses 172.16.1.10 and 172.16.54.10 on the same network?**

Yes. Convert the IP addresses to binary, and you will see that the first 18 binary digits in each address are the same (10101100 00011110 00).

6. **If the network ID is 10.1.0.0/22, how many IP addresses are available for allocation to host interfaces?**

1,022. With a 22-bit mask, from the 32-bit IP address, there are 10 bits left for host addressing (32-22). 2 to the power 10 (2^{10}) is 1,024. You then need to subtract two for the network and broadcast addresses, which cannot be assigned to host interfaces.

Review Activity: IPv4 Forwarding

1. **Given the subnet mask 255.255.255.128, are the IP addresses 192.168.0.1 and 192.168.1.1 on the same network?**

No. Compare the decimal mask and dotted decimal IP addresses and note that the third octet is within the network portion but is different for each IP address. If you do convert to binary to check, remember that the subnet mask contains 25 bits. You can see that the 24th bit is different in each address. As that bit occurs within the netmask, the hosts are on different IP networks.

2. **If a packet is addressed to a remote network, what destination MAC address will the sending node use to encapsulate the IP packet in a frame?**

The MAC address of the default gateway.

3. **Assuming unmanaged switches, how many broadcast domains are present in the following figure?**

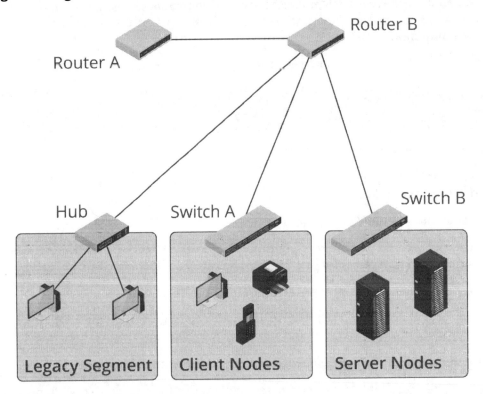

Four. Each router interface is a separate broadcast domain. One broadcast domain contains Router A and Router B, another contains the nodes on the legacy segment, and the last two are the client nodes Switch A broadcast domain and the server nodes Switch B broadcast domain.

4. **If a host is configured with the IP address 10.0.10.22 and mask 255.255.255.192, what is the broadcast address of the subnet?**

10.0.10.63. Convert the IP address to binary (00001010 00000000 00001010 00010110), then work out the number of bits in the mask (26). Change the remaining host bits (6) to 1s and convert back to dotted decimal.

5. **What type of addressing delivers a packet to a single host from a group without using unicast?**

Anycast means that a group of hosts are configured with the same IP address. When a router forwards a packet to an anycast group, it uses a prioritization algorithm and metrics to select the host that is "closest" (that will receive the packet and be able to process it the most quickly).

Review Activity: IP Networks and Subnets Configurations

1. **True or False? The IP address 172.24.0.1 is routable over the Internet.**

False. 172.16.0.0—172.31.255.255 is the Class B private address range.

2. **What is a Class D address?**

One used for multicasting.

3. **What is the significance of the address 127.0.0.1?**

This is the default loopback address for most hosts. The loopback address facilitates testing the TCP/IP implementation on a host.

4. **A host is configured with the IP address 10.0.10.22 and subnet mask 255.255.255.192. How many hosts per subnet would this addressing scheme support?**

62. Either subtract the least significant octet from 256 (256 - 192 = 64), then subtract 2 for the network and broadcast addresses, or having worked out that there are 6 host bits, calculate 2^6-2.

5. **If the IP address 10.0.10.22 were used with an /18 mask, how many subnets and hosts per subnet would be available?**

1024 subnets each with 16,382 hosts. From the default mask, 10 bits are allocated to the subnet ID and 14 remain as host bits.

Review Activity: Design an IP Subnet

At the 515support branch office, you have been asked to implement an IP network. Your network ID is currently `198.51.100.0/24`. You need to divide this in half (two subnets) to accommodate hosts on two separate floors of the building, each of which is served by managed switches. The whole network is served by a single router.

1. **To divide the network in half, what subnet mask do you need to use?**

Adding a single bit to the mask creates two subnets. The mask and network prefix will be 255.255.255.128 (/25).

2. **What are the subnet IDs for each network?**

198.51.100.0 /25 and 198.51.100.128 /25. An easy way to find the first subnet ID is to deduct the least significant octet in the mask (128 in the example) from 256, giving the answer 128.

3. **What is the broadcast address for each subnet? 198.52.100.127 and 198.51.100.255.**

You can work these out quite simply from the subnet ID that you calculated. The broadcast address for the first subnet is 1 less than the next subnet ID. The second subnet's broadcast address is the last possible address.

4. **What is the range of assignable IP addresses for each subnet?**

198.51.100.1 to 126 and 198.51.100.129 to 254. If you have each subnet ID and the broadcast ID, the host ranges are simply the values in between.

5. **Your manager has considered his original plan and realized that it does not accommodate the need for a WAN link to the head office or a separate segment for a team that works with sensitive data. What mask will you need to accommodate this new requirement, and how many hosts per subnet will it allow?**

You now need four subnets: a /28 prefix or 255.255.255.240 mask. There are only 4 bits left to work with for host addressing, though, so there are just 14 host addresses per subnet.

Review Activity: Test IP Configuration

1. **How can you check the IP configuration of an interface on an end system host at the command line?**

On Windows, run ipconfig (or netsh interface ip show config or Get-NetIPAddress). On Linux, run ifconfig or ip a.

2.   What output would you expect when running the command ip neigh?

IP:MAC address mappings held in the ARP cache of a Linux host.

3.   True or False? The arp utility will always show another host's MAC address if that host is on the same subnet.

False. While that is the function of the Address Resolution Protocol, the arp utility is used to inspect the ARP table cache, which may or may not contain the other host's address. Note that a standard means to ensure the MAC address is cached is to ping the destination address first. This is the basis of a utility called arping.

4.   Output from a ping command reports some values in milliseconds. What does this measure?

Round Trip Time (RTT) is a measure of the latency or delay between the host sending the probe and receiving a reply. ping will report minimum, maximum, and average RTT values.

5.   True or False? Receiving an echo reply message indicates that the link between two hosts is operational.

True.

Review Activity: Troubleshoot IP Networks

1.   Users on a floor served by a single switch cannot get a network connection. What is the best first step?

Check that the switch is powered on and reset it. If that does not work, check for other causes such as a poorly seated plug-in module.

2.   A workstation cannot connect to a server application on a remote network. What is the first test you could perform to establish whether the workstation's link is OK?

Ping another local system, such as the default gateway.

3.   A technician is troubleshooting a network and has asked your advice. He is trying to ping 192.168.16.192. The network has been subnetted with the custom mask 255.255.255.224. Why might this return a "Destination host unreachable" message?

The IP address resolves to the subnet network address, not a host address. Windows does not normally allow pinging the network address. Other OSs treat it as an alternative broadcast address, but most systems are configured to disallow such directed broadcasts for security reasons.

4.   Two client hosts have intermittent connectivity issues when accessing a server service on another subnet. No other client hosts exhibit this problem. What configuration problem might you suspect?

This is likely to be caused by a duplicate IP or MAC address. Replies from the server will be misdirected between the two hosts.

5.   You have pinged the router for the local subnet and confirmed that there is a valid link. The local host cannot access remote hosts, however. No other users are experiencing problems. What do you think is the cause?

The router is not configured as the default gateway for the local host. You can ping it, but the host is not using it for routing.

6.   A Windows client workstation cannot access a help desk application server by its name support.515support.com. The service can be accessed using its IP address. What two command line tools should you use to identify possible causes of this issue?

Use ipconfig to report the DNS servers that the client is trying to use and verify they are correct. Use ping to verify connectivity with the DNS servers.

Review Activity: IPv6 Addressing Schemes

1.   **Which of the following IPv6 addresses is a valid unicast host address?**

*   **fe80::218:8bff:fea7:bd37**

*   **fe80::219:d2ff::7850**

*   **ff02::219:d2ff:fea7:7850**

*   **::/128**

fe80::218:8bff:fea7:bd37

2.   **What is an EUI-64, and how might it be used by IPv6?**

Extended unique identifier (EUI) is IEEE's preferred term for a MAC address. EUI-64 is a 64-bit hardware interface ID. A 48-bit MAC address can be converted to an EUI-64 by using a simple mechanism. The EUI-64 can be used as the IPv6 interface ID, though a randomly generated token is often preferred.

3.   **In IPv6, how is the loopback address best expressed?**

::1

4.   **In IPv6, how can a host obtain a routable IPv6 address without requiring manual configuration?**

Stateless address autoconfiguration (SLAAC) allows a host to autoconfigure an interface by listening for Router Advertisements to obtain a network prefix.

5.   **True or false? 6to4 is a dual stack method of transitioning from IPv4 to IPv6.**

False. 6to4 is a method of tunneling IPv6 packets over an IPv4 network. Dual stack means that hosts and routers process both IPv4 and IPv6 traffic simultaneously.

Review Activity: Routing Concepts

1.   **What is a directly connected route?**

An IP network or subnet connected to one of the router's interfaces.

2.   **Which of the parameters in the following routing table entry represents the gateway?**

```
R 192.168.1.0/24 [120/1] via 198.51.100.254, GigabitEthernet0/1
```

198.51.100.254—the gateway is the address of the next hop router. 192.168.1.0/24 is the destination and GigabitEthernet0/1 is the interface that the packet should be forwarded out of to reach the gateway.

3.   **What type of routing table entry is shown below?**

```
S* 0.0.0.0/0 [1/0] via 192.0.2.1
```

This is a static entry for the default route. The destination 0.0.0.0/0 represents an unknown network and will be matched if there is no match to a more specific destination. 192.0.2.1 is the gateway or next hop router for the default route.

4.   **True or False? A router will not forward a packet when the TTL field is 0.**

True.

Review Activity: Dynamic Routing Concepts

1.   Which factors are used by default in EIGRP to identify the least-cost path?

The lowest bandwidth link along the path and the sum of latency along the path.

2.   What is an ASN and how does it assist route aggregation?

An Autonomous System Number (ASN) identifies a group of network prefixes under the administrative control of a single entity (such as an ISP). The AS can be advertised to other ASs through a single prefix (route aggregation), hiding the complexity of the internal network from other autonomous systems.

3.   Of the routing protocols listed in the CompTIA Network+ syllabus, which has the highest default value AD and does that make it more or less trusted than other protocols?

Routing Information Protocol (RIP) has a default administrative distance (AD) value of 120. In AD, lower values are preferred, so RIP is less trusted than other protocols.

4.   An IP network comprises hundreds of subnets deployed to offices in multiple geographical locations. Of the routing protocols listed in the CompTIA Network+ syllabus, which is best suited to this scale of network and why?

The hierarchical design of Open Shortest Path First (OSPF) means that it can divide the network into areas to represent different sites, reduce the size of routing tables, and ensure fast convergence. That said, Enhanced Interior Gateway Routing Protocol (EIGRP) can also support large networks and can have better convergence performance and so could be an equally good choice. Routing Information Protocol (RIP) is too limited to meet the requirements of a large network. Border Gateway Protocol (BGP) is not typically used on private networks as it is slower than OSPF or EIGRP and relative complex to configure.

5.   A company has eight networks, using the subnet addresses 192.168.0.0/24, 192.168.1.0/24 ... 192.168.7.0/24. What network prefix and subnet mask can be used to summarize a supernet route to these networks?

It takes 3 bits to summarize eight networks (2^3 = 8). Subtracting 3 bits from the existing network mask makes the supernet network prefix /21. The third octet of the mask will use 5 bits, which is 248 in decimal (2^5 = 248), so the full mask is 255.255.248.0.

6.   True or False? VLSM means using more than one mask to subnet an IP network.

True. By using different mask sizes, variable length subnet masking (VLSM) allows designers to match subnet sizes to requirements more precisely.

Review Activity: Design VLSM Subnets

In this activity, you will be designing an IP subnetting plan for an organization using VLSM. This division of the company must use the 172.30.0.0/16 network address range and subnet this down to develop an address scheme for the network displayed in the topology diagram. You should be as efficient as possible when designing your VLSM ranges, as additional branch offices may be added in the future.

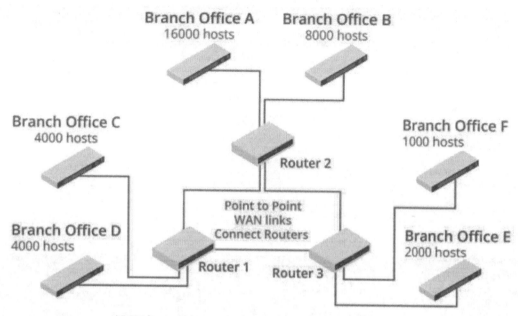

VLSM host address requirements. (Images © 123RF.com.)

1. How large will each of the subnets that join the three routers together need to be?

Large enough for just 2 IP addresses. Just 2 host bits, so /30 mask.

2. Which is the largest subnet in the topology? What is the minimum number of bits that will be needed for that number of hosts? How many IP addresses will that subnet provide? What would be the VLSM and address range for the largest subnet?

Branch A is the largest subnet with 16,000 hosts. 14 bits are needed, providing 16,382 addresses (16384 - 2). /18 will be the VLSM mask, giving an IP address range of 172.30.0.1—172.30.63.254.

3. What is the next largest subnet in the design? How many host bits will be needed for that subnet? How many IP addresses will that subnet provide and what is the VLSM?

Branch B is the next largest subnet with 8,000 hosts. 13 bits are needed, providing 8,190 addresses (8,192 - 2). /19 will be the VLSM mask, giving an IP address range of 172.30.64.1—172.30.95.254.

4. Work out the remaining subnets, remembering to ensure that subnet ranges do not overlap, but equally that you do not waste IP addresses. Complete the table.

Office/Subnet	Required Number of IP Addresses	VLSM Subnet ID	Actual Number of IP Addresses
Branch A	16,000	172.30.0.0/18	16,382
Branch B	8,000	172.30.64.0/19	8,190
Branch C	4,000		
Branch D	4,000		
Branch E	2,000		
Branch F	1,000		
Router 1 – Router 2	2		
Router 2 – Router 3	2		
Router 1 – Router 3	2		

Office/Subnet	Required Number of IP Addresses	VLSM Subnet ID	Actual Number of IP Addresses
Branch A	16,000	172.30.0.0/18	16,382
Branch B	8,000	172.30.64.0/19	8,190
Branch C	4,000	172.30.96.0/20	4,094
Branch D	4,000	172.30.112.0/20	4,094
Branch E	2,000	172.30.128.0/21	2,046
Branch F	1,000	172.30.136.0/22	1,022
Router 1 – Router 2	2	172.30.140.0/30	2
Router 2 – Router 3	2	172.30.140.4/30	2
Router 1 – Router 3	2	172.30.140.8/30	2

Review Activity: Router Installation and Troubleshooting

1. **A router must forward traffic received over a single physical interface connected to a switch trunk port to the appropriate virtual LAN (VLAN). What feature must be configured on the router?**

A subinterface for each VLAN carried over the trunk. Each subinterface must be configured with an IP address and mask for the subnet mapped to the VLAN.

2. **True or false? Layer 3 capable switches are interchangeable with routers.**

False. A layer 3 capable switch can perform fast routing and switching between subnets and virtual LANs (VLANs) on a local network. However, a layer 3 switch does not typically support WAN interface cards and so cannot be used as an edge router.

3. **True or false? Any occurrence of an asterisk in traceroute output indicates that there is no connectivity the destination along that path.**

False. Some routers along the path might not respond to probes. If there is no route to the destination, an unreachable notification will be displayed.

4. **Your network monitor is recording high numbers of ICMP Time Exceeded notifications. What type of routing issue does this typically indicate?**

This is typical of a routing loop, where packets circulate between two routers until the time to live (TTL) is exceeded.

5. **A campus to datacenter fiber optic link has been laid over 15 km of single mode fiber with one fusion splice along this run. The termination at each end requires two connectors. You need to evaluate a proposal to use 10GBASE-LR transceiver modules for the router. The module specification quotes Tx power of –8.2 dBm and Rx sensitivity of –14.4 dBm. Assuming attenuation of 0.4 dB/km, 0.75 dB loss per connector, and 0.3 dB loss per splice, do these modules work within the expected loss budget?**

The loss budget is (15 * 0.4 = 6) + (2 * 0.75 = 1.5) + (1 * 0.3 = 0.6) = 7.8 dB. The power budget is –8.2 – 14.4 dBm = 6.2 dB. Consequently, the power budget is insufficient. Note that 10GBASE-LR is rated for 10 km operation over single mode.

Review Activity: Design a Branch Office Internetwork

Helpful Help is a charitable organization that operates out of numerous small offices spread all over the country. Each office has a team of 10–20 people who currently use a network of PCs and Apple Macs running various applications. Each office is connected back to a main site, which has a connection to the Internet via an ISP. Staff at each local office uses the link for web access and to access an online email service. Each office has a 192.168.x.0/24 subnet allocated to it. The East region is shown in the graphic.

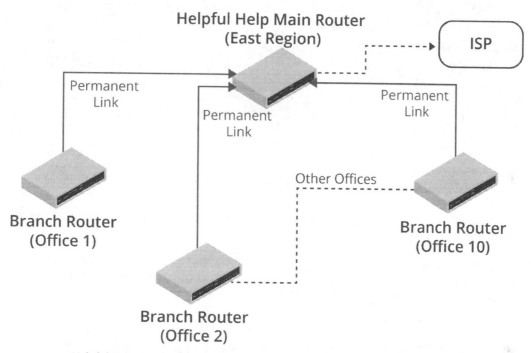

Helpful Help East region branch office internetwork. (Images © 123RF.com.)

1. **Given the current scenario of the charity, how would the routers at each local office be configured?**

As the link is only used for web browsing and online email, the local office routers would just be configured with a static route/default gateway/gateway of last resort to forward all traffic to the main site, which would forward the web traffic on.

Presently, each local office has several PSTN (landline) telephones. The plan is to replace these with a unified communications system for VoIP, conferencing, and messaging/information. This will require devices in each local office to be able to contact devices in other offices for direct media streaming. It is also anticipated that additional links may be added between branch offices where larger numbers of users are situated due to the increased bandwidth required by the new applications at this site. Here is the revised diagram:

Revised design for Helpful Help East region branch office internetwork. (Image © 123RF.com.)

2. With this new infrastructure in place, what changes would need to be made to the router's configuration?

Due to the need for offices and therefore routers to be able contact each other, additional routing table entries will be needed. This could be through more static routes, but a dynamic routing protocol would be better able to cope with any future changes to the topology.

3. Which protocol would be best here?

There are several choices. The network is relatively simple with only a few network hops, so RIPv2 could be used as it is easier to configure.

If the new system works well in the East region (the smallest), the plan is to roll out the system to the three other regions (North, South, and West). This will involve connecting the main routers for each region together, plus some additional links for redundancy. The other regions use different IP numbering systems and some use VLSM.

4. Considering the potential changes a successful pilot in the East region might bring about in the whole organization, would your router configuration options change?

Due to the potential increase in the number of routers and subnets, OSPF may be the better choice of dynamic routing protocol. This is especially true due to potential IP subnet numbering differences, including VLSM.

5. What might you do to manage the much larger number of IP subnets?

It may be worth considering different OSPF areas to manage the size of the OSPF topology tables and use route summarization to reduce the router's CPU load.

Review Activity: Network Types and Characteristics

1.   What network infrastructure implementation links multiple buildings within the same city?

Metropolitan area network (MAN).

2.   What term is used to describe a topology in which two nodes share a single link?

Point-to-point.

3.   You need operations to continue if one link fails. How many links does it take to connect three sites?

The number of links is n(n-1)/2, so with three sites, the sum is 3*2/2, which works out to three.

4.   What types of devices are connected in a PAN?

A personal area network (PAN) links devices such as laptops and smartphones and provides connectivity with peripheral devices (printers, input devices, headsets, and so on) plus wearable technology, such as fitness trackers and smart watches.

Review Activity: Tiered Switching Architecture

1.   Which two topologies are used in the three-tier hierarchical model?

This is a hybrid topology with mesh and star elements. The core layer is a mesh and the links between core and distribution and distribution and access are also a mesh or partial mesh. The access switches use a star topology to connect end systems.

2.   Spanning tree has been deployed without the administrator setting a priority value. Which of the following switches will be selected as the root?

- **Switch A with base MAC f062.81ff.0001 and a 10 Gbps uplink**

- **Switch B with base MAC f062.81ff.0002 and a 40 Gbps uplink**

- **Switch C with base MAC f062.81ff.0003 and a 40 Gbps uplink**

Switch A. The switch with the lowest value MAC address is selected if priority values are equal.

3.   In what STP-configured state(s) are all ports when a network running STP is converged?

Forwarding or blocking.

4.   True or false? A broadcast storm can only be resolved by investing interface configurations.

False. A broadcast storm could be caused by a physical layer issue, such as improper cabling.

Review Activity: Virtual LANs

1.   At which layer of the OSI model do VLANs establish network segments?

At the data link layer or layer 2.

2.   True or false? A VLAN is a single broadcast domain.

True.

3. Which values can be used to assign a port to a specific VLAN?

From 2 to 4,094. The all zeros and all ones (0 and 4,095) are reserved and VLAN ID 1 is the default for all unconfigured ports.

4. What type of frames arc carried over tagged ports?

Tagged ports typically operate as trunks to carry frames between VLANs on different switches. Frames are transported over the trunk link with an 802.1Q header to indicate the VLAN ID.

5. True or false? When configuring a voice VLAN, the voice VLAN ID must be lower than the access VLAN ID.

False. The IDs only need to be distinct and synchronized with the IDs expected by the switch.

Review Activity: Transport Protocols

1. How many port numbers are required to establish a connection at the Transport layer?

Two—a server port and a client port.

2. What is the purpose of the window field in a TCP segment?

It is used for flow control. The window indicates the amount of data that the host can receive before sending another acknowledgement.

3. What are the sizes of TCP and UDP headers?

TCP is 20 bytes (or more) while UDP is 8 bytes.

4. True or False? User Datagram Protocol (UDP), like TCP, uses flow control in the sending of data packets.

False.

5. What port and protocol does TFTP use at the Transport layer?

UDP/69.

Review Activity: Port Scanning

1. What type of scanning tool outputs a "Host is up" status report.

IP scanner. Note that while most IP scanners can also function as port scanners they are distinct types of scanning activity.

2. You are auditing the service configuration of a Linux server. Which command can you use to check the PID associated with a TCP port, even if there are no active connections?

Run netstat with the -p switch to show the process ID (PID), -a switch to show all active and listening sockets, and optionally -t to filter by TCP and -n to suppress name resolution and display output quicker: netstat -patn

3. A technician has identified an undocumented host using an IP address in a range set aside as unallocated. The technician is going to run a fingerprinting scan. What type of information could this yield about the host?

A fingerprinting scan compares specific responses to known information about hardware platforms, OS types and versions, and application/service types and versions.

4. **You need to analyze the information saved in a .pcap file. What type of command-line tool or other utility is best suited to this task?**

This type of file will contain a network packet capture. You could use a command-line protocol analyzer such as tcpdump to display the contents, but a graphical tool such as Wireshark will make analysis easier.

Review Activity: Network Addressing Services

1. **True or False? If a client accepts a DHCPOFFER, the DHCPREQUEST packet is broadcast on the network.**

True.

2. **When configuring multiple DHCP servers for redundancy, what should you take care to do?**

Configure the servers with nonoverlapping address scopes.

3. **True or False? DHCP options can be configured on a per-scope basis.**

True.

4. **What address is used to contact a DHCPv6 server?**

IPv6 does not support broadcasts, so clients use the multicast address ff:02::1:2 to discover a DHCP server.

5. **In a stateless environment, what sort of information does DHCPv6 provide?**

In a stateless environment, the host autoconfigures an address using a network prefix provided by the router (typically). DHCPv6 is then used to provide the IPv6 addresses used to access network services, such as DNS or SIP gateways.

Review Activity: Name Resolution Services

1. **What type of DNS record resolves a host name to an IPv6 address?**

AAAA.

2. **What use is a PTR DNS record?**

A pointer maps an IP address to a host name, enabling a reverse lookup. Reverse lookups are used (for example) in spam filtering to confirm that a host name is associated with a given IP address.

3. **What types of DNS records have priority or preference values?**

Typically, mail (MX) and service (SRV) records.

4. **What type of DNS record is used to prove the valid origin of email?**

Sender Policy Framework (SPF) and DomainKeys Identified Mail (DKIM) records can be used to validate the origin of email and reject spam. These are configured in DNS as text (TXT) records.

Review Activity: DNS Services

1. **When you configure name server addresses as part of a host's IP settings, do you need to specify servers that perform iterative queries only or ones that accept recursive queries?**

Recursive queries. These DNS servers are designed to assist clients with queries and are usually separate to the DNS server infrastructure designed to host authoritative name records.

2. **What type of DNS service would you configure on the LAN to use a public DNS server to resolve queries for external domains?**

A forwarder.

3. **What is the function of the following command?**

```
nslookup - 8.8.8.8
```

To start nslookup in interactive mode with the DNS server set to 8.8.8.8 (Google's public DNS server).

4. **What is the function of a dig subcommand such as +nostats?**

Control what is shown by the tool. You can use these commands to suppress certain kinds of output, such as sections of the response from the DNS server.

Review Activity: Use of Web, File/Print, and Database Services

1. **True or false? An HTML web page is sent as the response to a client in an HTTP header field.**

False. The HTML is the payload of the HTTP packet.

2. **What must be installed on a server to use secure (HTTPS) connections?**

A digital certificate and the corresponding private key.

3. **What distinguishes TFTP from FTP?**

Trivial FTP only supports GET and PUT commands—not directory browsing, file deletion, and so on. TFTP works over UDP while FTP works over TCP.

4. **You need to configure clients to be able to communicate with print devices in a remote subnet. Which port number must you allow on a network firewall to enable the standard TCP/IP port?**

TCP/9100.

5. **You are configuring a firewall to allow a Linux web server to communicate with a database server over port TCP/3306. Assuming it has been left configured with the default port, what type of database is being used?**

MySQL.

Review Activity: Use of Email and Voice Services

1. **What happens if a message sent via SMTP cannot be delivered?**

The server generates a non-delivery report (NDR) with an appropriate error code and discards the message.

2. **What protocol would enable a client to manage mail subfolders on a remote mail server?**

Internet Message Access Protocol (IMAP) or IMAP Secure (IMAPS). Post Office Protocol (POP3) allows download of mail messages but not management of the remote inbox.

3. **True or False? SIP enables the location of user agents via a specially formatted URI.**

True.

4. **Which component in a VoIP network allows calls to be placed to and from the voice telephone or public switched telephone network (PSTN)?**

This function is performed by a VoIP gateway.

Review Activity: Network Management Services

1. **True or false? SSH must be configured with two key pairs to operate; one on the server and one on the client.**

False. While the server must be configured with a key pair, the client can optionally use a key pair to authenticate, or can use another mechanism, such as a password.

2. **What remote management service is associated with TCP port 23?**

Telnet.

3. **Which port is used by the Network Time Protocol (NTP)?**

UDP/123.

4. **What is SNTP?**

Simple Network Time Protocol—A simpler protocol derived from NTP that enables workstations to obtain the correct time from time servers.

Review Activity: Ensure Network Availability with Event Management

1. **You have a plan for monitoring switches and routers that accommodates network metrics (bandwidth, latency, and jitter) plus chassis temperature and intrusion. What other performance metric should be monitored?**

Processing (CPU and memory) resource. In some circumstances, you might also want to monitor local storage capacity.

2. **How does an SNMP agent report an event to the management system?**

Via a trap.

3. **What sort of log would you inspect if you wanted to track web server access attempts?**

Audit/security/access log.

4. **A technician has recommended changing the syslog logging level from its current value of 3 to 6. Will this cause more or fewer events to be forwarded?**

Raising the level to 6 will capture less severe events (up to informational level) so more events will be forwarded.

5. **What would be the purpose of configuring thresholds in network monitoring software?**

The software could produce an alert if network performance did not meet any given metric.

Review Activity: Ensure Network Availability with Performance Metrics

1. **How is jitter mitigated by a VoIP application?**

By buffering packets.

2. **How many different traffic classes can be defined by 802.1Q/p?**

The field is 3-bit, allowing up to 8 values. In a typical schema, 7 and 6 can be reserved for network control (such as routing table updates), 5 and 4 map to expedited forwarding levels for 2-way communications, 3 and 2 map to assured forwarding for streaming multimedia, and 1 and 0 for "ordinary" best-effort delivery.

3. **How does a traffic shaper benefit real-time data applications?**

A traffic shaper can reserve bandwidth so that QoS parameters, such as maximum latency and jitter, for a real-time data application can be guaranteed.

4. **What is a top listener in terms of network monitoring?**

An interface that receives the most incoming traffic.

5. **You suspect that a network application is generating faulty packets. What interface metric(s) might help you to diagnose the problem?**

Monitoring errors and discards/drops would help to prove the cause of the problem.

Review Activity: Common Security Concepts

1. **What type of assessment is most likely to measure security policies and controls against a standard framework?**

This can be referred to as posture assessment or risk assessment.

2. **True or false? An automated vulnerability scanner can be used to detect zero-days.**

False. An automated scanner is configured with a list of known vulnerabilities to scan for. By definition, zero-day vulnerabilities are unknown to the vendor or to security practitioners. A zero-day is detected either through detailed manual research or because an exploit is discovered.

3. **What type of assessment tool is configured with details of CVEs?**

Common Vulnerabilities and Exposures (CVE) is a dictionary of vulnerabilities in published operating systems and applications software. An automated vulnerability scanner is configured with scripts to scan a host for known vulnerabilities.

4. **515web IT staff discovered an entry when reviewing their audit logs showing that a junior employee from the sales department had logged into the network at 3:00 a.m. Further review of the audit logs show that he had changed his timecard on the HR server. Which security factor was breached, and did the attack exploit a software vulnerability or a configuration vulnerability?**

The attack compromised the integrity of data stored in the network. It exploited a configuration weakness. The employee should not have had permission to alter the timecard.

5. **What type of security audit performs active testing of security controls?**

A penetration test (pen test). A vulnerability assessment is one that uses passive testing techniques.

Review Activity: Authentication Methods

1.   What element is missing from the following list, and what is its purpose?

- **Identification**

- **Authentication**

- **Accounting**

Authorization—Assigning privileges over the network object to the subject.

2.   What is the purpose of SSO?

Single Sign-on allows users to authenticate once to gain access to different resources. This reduces the number of login credential sets a user must remember.

3.   True or false? A subject's private key is embedded in the digital certificate that represents its digital identity?

False—the private key must be kept secure and not revealed to any other party. The public part of the key pair is embedded in the certificate.

4.   What is a RADIUS client, and how should it be configured?

A device or server that accepts user connections. In a RADIUS architecture, the client does not need to be able to perform authentication itself; it passes the logon request to an AAA server. The client needs to be configured with the RADIUS server address and shared secret.

5.   Where would EAPoL be configured?

On a switch interface/port. A switch that supports 802.1X port-based access control can enable a port but allow only the transfer of Extensible Authentication Protocol over LAN (EAPoL) traffic. This allows the client device and/or user to be authenticated before full network access is granted.

Review Activity: Security Appliances

1.   What type of security configuration uses edge and choke firewalls?

A screened subnet. The edge or screening firewall is the public interface while the choke firewall is the LAN interface. The screened subnet is therefore configured as a perimeter network preventing hosts on the Internet being directly connected to hosts on the LAN.

2.   What parameters in packet headers can a layer 3 firewall ruleset use?

IP source and destination address, protocol type, and port number.

3.   Why would you deploy a reverse proxy?

To publish a web application without directly exposing the servers on the internal network to the Internet.

4.   **What type of security control uses an attestation report?**

A Network Access Control (NAC) server configured to allow connections only to clients that meet a health policy, such as running an appropriate OS/OS version and being up-to-date with patches and security scanning definitions.

5.   **How does placement of an IDS sensor assist with a defense in depth policy?**

Placement behind a perimeter firewall can identify suspicious traffic that has been allowed through the firewall.

Review Activity: Service and Security Issues

1.   **You are planning to reconfigure static and DHCP-assigned IP addresses across the network during scheduled downtime. What preliminary step should you take to minimize connectivity issues when the network is reopened?**

Ensure that clients obtain a new DHCP lease, either by shortening the lease period in advance or by using a script to force clients to renew the lease at startup.

2.   **If a network adapter is using the address 169.254.1.10 on a host connected to the LAN, what would you suspect?**

That a DHCP server is offline or not contactable. The system is configured to obtain an address automatically but cannot contact a DHCP server and is using Automatic Private IP Addressing (APIPA).

3.   **Following maintenance on network switches, users in one department cannot access the company's internal web and email servers. You can demonstrate basic connectivity between the hosts and the servers by IP address. What might the problem be?**

It is likely that there is a problem with name resolution. Perhaps the network maintenance left the hosts unable to access a DNS server, possibly due to some VLAN assignment issue.

4.   **You are troubleshooting a connectivity problem with a network application server. Certain clients cannot connect to the service port. How could you rule out a network or remote client host firewall as the cause of the problem?**

Connect to or scan the service port from the same segment with no host firewall running.

Review Activity: Scenarios in Service and Security Issues

You are staffing the network help desk and dealing with support requests as they arrive. Your network uses four access switches to support four subnets. One subnet contains network servers (authentication, directory services, DNS, and DHCP) and another contains Line of Business (LoB) application servers, for sales and order processing. There are two client subnets, serving different floors in the building.

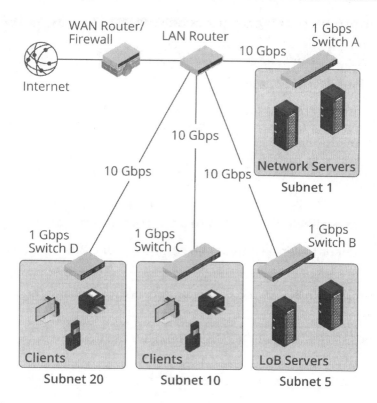

1. **You receive a call from the user of host A who has always been able to connect to the LoB application servers, but today she is unable to connect. You verbally check with other users and discover that none of the hosts on subnet 20 can connect, but that users in subnet 10 report no problems. What tests should you perform to narrow down the cause of the problem?**

You should not assume from the information gathered so far that the user can connect to the servers in subnet 10. There are two likely causes—either the link to the router from subnet 20 has failed, perhaps because of a faulty switch, or hosts in subnet 20 are no longer receiving a correct IP configuration from the network servers. To test methodically, from any host in subnet 20, ping the loopback address and then ping that host's IP address. If either of these tests fail or if the host is using APIPA, investigate communications with the network servers. If the local IP configuration on each host is good, ping the router. If this fails, suspect a problem with the switch or cabling.

2. **You send a junior technician to the equipment room to fix the problem. Sometime later, another user from subnet 20 calls complaining that he cannot connect to the Internet. What questions should you ask to begin troubleshooting?**

Again, do not assume that Internet connectivity is the only issue. The user might not have any sort of network link but has only complained about accessing the Internet because that's the particular application he was trying to use. Ask if the user can connect to one of the LoB server applications. If this fails, check whether other users are experiencing the problem and establish the scope—just the one user? All users on subnet 20? All users on both subnets?

3. **You asked a junior technician to step in because your manager had asked you to deploy a wireless access point on the network to support a sales event due to start the next day. There will be lots of guests, and your manager wants them all to have Internet access. You did not have much time, so you simply added the access point to the switch supporting subnet 10. The next day arrives, and sometime after the sales event starts, multiple employees in subnet 10 report that when they attempt to connect to the network, they get a message that the Windows network has limited connectivity. What might be the cause and what test should you use to confirm the issue?**

The most likely cause is that guest devices have exhausted the DHCP address pool for that scope. You can confirm by identifying that the hosts have autoconfigured APIPA addresses, perhaps by using ipconfig.

Review Activity: Wireless Standards

1.   What mechanism does RTS/CTS support?

Carrier sense multiple access with collision avoidance (CSMA/CA). Rather than try to detect collisions, a wireless station indicates its intent to transmit by broadcasting a Request To Send (RTS) and waits to receive a Clear To Send (CTS) before proceeding.

2.   Which IEEE WLAN standards specify a data transfer rate of up to 54 Mbps?

802.11a and 802.11g.

3.   What options may be available for an 802.11n network that are not supported under 802.11g?

Channel bonding, Multiple-Input-Multiple-Output (MIMO), and use of either 2.4 GHz or 5 GHz frequency bands.

4.   True or False? Stations with 802.11ac capable adapters must be assigned to the 5 GHz frequency band.

True—802.11ac is designed to work only in the 5 GHz frequency band, with the 2.4 GHz band used for legacy clients.

5.   Which frequency band is less likely to suffer from co-channel interference?

The 5 GHz band.

6.   What standard(s) are intended to support 4G mobile wireless services?

Long Term Evolution (LTE) and LTE Advanced (LTE-A).

Review Activity: Wireless Network Installation

1.   What value is used as the BSSID?

The MAC address of the access point.

2.   True or False? Suppressing transmission of the WLAN beacon improves security.

False—the beacon cannot be suppressed completely because clients use it when connecting with the AP. Increasing the broadcast interval reduces network overhead, but it increases the time required to find and connect to the network.

3.   What is a heat map?

Output from a site survey plotting the strength of wireless signals and channel utilization in different parts of a building.

4.   True or false? To support client roaming within an extended service area, each access point must be configured with the same SSID, security parameters, and Wi-Fi channel.

False—the SSID and security parameters must be the same, but the access points should use different channels where their coverage overlaps.

5.   What type of AP requires a wireless controller?

A lightweight or thin AP (or one working in thin mode).

6. **What are the advantages of deploying a wireless mesh topology over an IBSS?**

Stations in a wireless mesh network are capable of discovering one another, forming peering arrangements, and performing path discovery and forwarding between peers (routing). These factors make a mesh-based network more scalable than an ad hoc network or independent basic service set (IBSS).

Review Activity: Wireless Network Troubleshooting

1. **You are planning WLAN for an office building with an attached warehouse. Where would you recommend placing Wi-Fi antennas for the best coverage in an office full of cubicles as well as in the warehouse?**

Placing omnidirectional antennas on the ceiling would provide the best coverage with good line-of-sight and reduced interference between the APs and stations. Depending on the height of the warehouse ceiling, you may need to obtain APs with downtilt antennas.

2. **The lobby area of your office building has undergone a renovation, the centerpiece of which is a large aquarium in the middle of the room, separating a visitor seating and greeting area from the reception desks, where the AP facilitating guest Internet access is located. Since the renovation, many guests have been unable to connect to Wi-Fi from the seating area. Could the aquarium really be the cause, and what solution could you recommend?**

Yes, a dense body of water could cause absorption and refraction of the radio waves, weakening the signal. You could ceiling mount the AP so that signals are less affected by the body of water. You could also add a second AP at the front of the lobby area to act as a repeater. For optimum performance, both APs should be ceiling-mounted, to preserve line of sight.

3. **What is the difference between a Wi-Fi analyzer and a spectrum analyzer?**

A Wi-Fi analyzer is a software-based tool that interrogates the wireless adapter to display detailed information, based on what the Wi-Fi radio can receive. A spectrum analyzer uses dedicated radio hardware to report on frequency usage outside of Wi-Fi traffic, and so can be used more reliably to detect interference sources.

4. **Users in the corner of an office building cannot get good Wi-Fi reception. Your office manager doesn't want to use his budget to purchase a new AP. He's noticed that the power level control on the AP is set to 3 out of 5 and wants to know why turning up the power isn't the best solution?**

This might work, but you should investigate the root cause of the issue and determine whether the solution will have adverse effects. The most obvious issue is that client stations might then be able to hear the AP but not be able to speak to it. Depending on the rest of the WLAN infrastructure, increasing power on one AP may cause more co-channel interference with other cells. A better solution will be to add an access point or to configure a wireless bridge using directional antennas.

Review Activity: Wireless Security Configuration and Troubleshooting

1. **What is the main difference between WPA and WPA2?**

WPA2 supports a stronger encryption algorithm, based on the Advanced Encryption Standard (AES). AES is deployed within the Counter Mode with Cipher Block Chaining Message Authentication Code Protocol (CCMP). WPA uses the same RC4 cipher as WEP. WPA uses a mechanism called the Temporal Key Integrity Protocol (TKIP) to make it stronger than WEP, but WPA2 offers better security.

2. **What configuration information is required on an access point to authenticate users joining the wireless network against a network authentication server?**

The authentication method must be set to enterprise and the access point must be configured with the IP address and shared secret of the authentication (RADIUS or TACACS+) server.

3. **Widget Corporation has provided wireless access for its employees using several APs located in different parts of the building. Employees connect to the network using 802.11g-compatible network cards. On Thursday afternoon, several users report that they cannot log on to the network. What troubleshooting step would you take first?**

Following troubleshooting methodology, establish the scope of the problem early on the in the process. In this case, check whether the problem machines are trying to use the same AP. If the problem is apparent across multiple APs, suspect a wireless controller disabling 802.11g compatibility mode.

4. **Why might an attacker launch a disassociation attack against an access point?**

This could be a simple denial of service (DoS) attack to prevent network access, but the attacker could also be attempting to use an evil twin/rogue AP to intercept network traffic.

5. **Your company has a lobby area where guest access is provided so that visitors can get Internet access. The open guest WLAN is currently connected to the production network. The only protection against visitors and hackers getting into the organization's data is file and directory rights. What steps should be taken to provide guest access and better protect the organization's data?**

The guest WLAN should be connected to a separate network segment, isolated from the production network. Typically, this would be accomplished using a virtual LAN (VLAN) and a router/firewall to inspect and filter traffic using the Internet link. You could configure a captive portal so that users must register before accessing the WLAN. You could also change to using PSK authentication, with the passphrase obtained from the receptionists.

Review Activity: Explain WAN Provider Links

1. **What component of a structured cabling system protects the demarc against tampering?**

The demarcation point or demarc is the location where the service provider terminates cable within customer premises. In terms of the internal cable distribution components, it is identified as an entrance facility. Ideally, this should be enclosed within a secure closet with access restricted to authorized personnel only.

2. **What type of cable can be used to connect a CSU/DSU to a smartjack, assuming a maximum link distance of 1m (3 feet)?**

This connection can use an ordinary straight-through RJ-45 patch cord.

3. **You are connecting a SOHO network to a VDSL service using a separate VDSL modem. What cables do you require and how should they be connected?**

The WAN/DSL port on the modem is connected to the service provider network via a two-pair cable with RJ-11 connectors. The LAN/Ethernet port on the modem should be connected to the SOHO router via an Ethernet cable with RJ-45 connectors.

4. **You need to cable a service that terminates at an optical network unit (ONU) to the customer router. What type of cable is required?**

This connection can use an ordinary straight-through RJ-45 patch cord. The ONU converts the fiber optic signal from the service provider cable to an electrical signal for transmission over copper Ethernet.

5. **Assuming that sufficient bandwidth can be provided, what factor limits the usefulness of a microwave satellite Internet link?**

The link will be subject to high latency, which will impact real-time data services.

Review Activity: Remote Access Methods

1. **What step can you take to prevent unauthorized use of a remote access server?**

Define which user accounts have dial-in rights, consider restricting access by time of day, and configure logging and auditing of remote access logons and attempted logons.

2. **What type of client-to-site VPN ensures that any traffic from the remote node can be monitored from the corporate network while the machine is joined to the VPN?**

Full tunnel. This mode contrasts with split tunnel, where only traffic for the private network is tunneled.

3. **What replaces the VPN client in a clientless remote access solution?**

A web browser.

4. **What difference does DMVPN make to a hub and spoke VPN topology?**

A dynamic multipoint VPN (DMVPN) allows the spokes to establish a direct connection, rather than relaying all communications via the hub.

5. **What IPSec mode would you use for data confidentiality on a private network?**

Transport mode with Encapsulating Security Payload (ESP). Tunnel mode encrypts the IP header information, but this is unnecessary on a private network. Authentication Header only provides authentication and integrity validation, not confidentiality.

6. **What is a virtual terminal?**

Configuring a management IP address on a switch to connect to its command line interface over the network (rather than via a serial port).

Review Activity: Organizational Documentation and Policies

1. **What types of baselines are useful when you are performing configuration management?**

A configuration baseline records the initial setup of software or appliance. A performance baseline records the initial throughput or general performance of a network (or part of a network). These baselines allow changes in the future to be evaluated.

2. **What type of security control provisions resources and procedures to cope with incidents that cause major service outages?**

A disaster recovery plan (DRP).

3. **How is the person who first receives notification of a potential security incident designated?**

First responder.

4. **What configuration request would be implemented by IT services during employee onboarding?**

Account creation, issuance of user credentials, and allocation of permissions/roles.

Review Activity: Physical Security Methods

1. **Some of the businesses near 515support have recently had break-ins where some equipment was stolen. As news of these events spread, it generated some concern within the organization that their physical security measures should be reviewed and possibly enhanced. There is currently a security guard on duty during business hours, video monitoring of the front and back doors, and employees use plastic badges with their name and photo to enter the building. Access beyond the lobby area requires swiping a badge to enter the rest of the building. What, if anything, would you recommend adding or improving for their physical security?**

While they have a good start on physical security, they should consider installing motion detection systems for after hours; if there are additional doors, to install video monitoring on those doors; to update to using smart cards or key fobs for entrance.

2. **What technology could be used to provision security cameras without having to provide a separate circuit for electrical power?**

IP cameras could be powered over data cabling using Power over Ethernet (PoE).

3. **Following a security incident, the lessons learned report recommends upgrading premises entry control to prevent tailgating. What type of prevention control will provide the most effective solution?**

An access control vestibule, or mantrap, provisions one gateway into a monitored area and a second gateway out of it. This means that any attempt to pass through behind or with another person can easily be detected and prevented.

4. **What is a PDS, and what type of security control does it provide?**

A Protected Distribution System (PDS) is a system for hardened network cable distribution. It can work as both a preventive and a detective control. The preventive element comes from enclosing the cable in metal conduit. The detective element can be supplied by alarms that detect if the conduit has been opened or damaged.

5. **What technology provides data security assurance during the asset disposal phase of system life cycle?**

Hard drive/media sanitization, such as encryption or disk overwriting.

Review Activity: Internet of Things Devices

1. **What type of network topology is used by IoT technologies such as Z-Wave and Zigbee?**

Mesh topology.

2. **What is a principal requirement of IoT networking technologies?**

Low power consumption and low latency.

3. **A technician is configuring a PC with software to manage and monitor a network of field devices. What type of host is being configured and what factors should govern its connection to a corporate data network?**

The host is being used as part of a supervisory control and data acquisition (SCADA) system. The host might be kept completely separate from the corporate data network (air gapped). If it is connected, it should be fully segregated from other systems and subject to carefully designed access control policies.

Review Activity: Disaster Recovery Concepts

1. Which metric is used to determine frequency of data backups?

Recovery Point Objective (RPO) is the maximum amount of data loss permitted, measured in units of time (seconds, minutes, hours, or days).

2. A server group installed with storage devices from Vendor A experiences two failures across 20 devices over a period of 5 years. A server group using storage devices from Vendor B experiences one failure across 12 devices over the same period. Which metric is being tracked and which vendor's metric is superior?

The metric is Mean Time to Failure (MTTF). Note that MTTF is used for devices that cannot be repaired. Repairable system reliability is measured using Mean Time Between Failures (MTBF). Vendor A's devices have a MTTF measured at 50 years (20*5/2), while Vendor B's are 60 years (12*5/1), so Vendor B has the superior metric.

3. 515web have experienced three web server outages in the last five years. These outages all occurred in separate years and caused one hour, three hour, and one hour downtime incidents. Assuming the company uses the same value for MTD and RTO, did the company meet the RTO of two hours specified in the SLA agreed annually with its customers?

No. Recovery Time Objective (RTO) in this scenario is also equal to the maximum amount of downtime. As the service level agreement (SLA) is agreed annually, the single incident causing three hours downtime exceeded it. The mean time to repair (MTTR) is 1.66 hours, so the company is meeting its goal over a 5-year average, 515web either needs to write off the longer outage as an outlier, improve recovery procedures, or negotiate new terms for its SLAs.

4. What type of failover site generally requires only data to be restored before it can resume processing?

This is typical of a warm site.

5. What rack-mountable device can provide line filtering and power monitoring features?

A power distribution unit (PDU).

Review Activity: High Availability Concepts

1. Why might contracting with multiple ISPs still fail to provide highly available Internet access infrastructure?

The ISPs might share last mile conduit or have the same peering or transit arrangements that share the same single point of failure. For reliable failover, you need to ensure diverse paths over physically separate circuits.

2. True or false? Link aggregation can only be configured between intermediate systems, such as switch-to-switch or switch-to-router.

False. Link aggregation can be used between end systems and intermediate systems, too.

3. You are configuring a load balanced web application. Which IP address should be configured as a host record in DNS to advertise the application?

The virtual IP (VIP) address of the load balancer.

4. What is the purpose of HSRP and VRRP?

These are both first hop redundancy protocols. Hot Standby Router Protocol (HSRP) and Virtual Router Redundancy Protocol (VRRP) allow multiple physical router appliances to act as the same logical router, providing failover.

Review Activity: Types of Attacks

1. Response time on the website that hosts the online version of your product catalog is getting slower and slower. Customers are complaining that they cannot browse the catalog items or search for products. What type of attack do you suspect?

This is some type of Denial of Service (DoS) attack. Specifically, you might suspect a distributed DoS (DDoS) or distributed reflection DoS (DRDoS).

2. The network administrator at your organization analyzes a network trace capture file and discovers that packets have been intercepted and retransmitted to both a sender and a receiver during an active session. What class of attack has been detected?

On-path attack. Note that this was previously referred to as a man-in-the-middle (MitM) attack.

3. True or false? To perpetrate an ARP spoofing attack, the threat actor spoofs the IP address of a legitimate host, typically the subnet's default gateway.

True. The threat actor sends gratuitous ARP replies claiming to own the IP address of the target.

4. A threat actor forces clients to disconnect from a legitimate access point to try to force them to reconnect to an access point controlled by the attacker using the same network name. What two attack types are being used?

Disconnections are performed using a deauthentication attack, while using a rogue access point to masquerade as a legitimate one is referred to as an evil twin attack.

5. Analysis of outgoing traffic shows connections by IP cameras to unidentifiable domain names. What type of traffic has been detected?

This is command and control (C&C or C2) traffic between a handler and botnet of compromised IP camera devices, often called an Internet of Things (IoT) botnet.

6. Employees have received emails prompting them to register for a new benefit package. The link in the mail resolves to a malicious IP address. What type of attack is being performed?

This is a phishing attack that combines social engineering (techniques that convince users that a message is genuine) with a spoofed resource.

Review Activity: Network Hardening Techniques

1. The network administrator configures a switch with custom privilege levels and assigns commands to each. What type of best practice network hardening will this configuration support?

Role-based access, where different administrator and operator groups are assigned least privilege permissions.

2. A technician configures a switch with an IP address and shared secret of a network authentication server. What type of best practice network hardening is being performed?

Port security or IEEE 802.1X Port-Based Network Access Control.

3.   **What switch configuration feature could you use to prevent web servers in the same subnet from communicating with one another?**

This can be configured using a private VLAN. The servers are all placed in the same host VLAN and communicate out of the VLAN/subnet via the promiscuous port. Each server port is configured as an isolated port. The isolated ports are not able to communicate directly.

4.   **What is the default rule on a firewall?**

A system-defined rule that denies anything not permitted by the preceding rules. This is also referred to as an implicit deny rule. An explicit deny is one configured manually by the administrator.

5.   **Network hosts are flooding a switch's SSH port with malicious traffic. The switch applies a rate-limiting mechanism to drop the traffic. What best practice network hardening control is being used?**

Control plane policing. The SSH port carries management traffic. Malicious management or control traffic can be used to perform a denial of service (DoS) attack against a network appliance by overloading its general purpose CPU. A control plane policing policy protects both control and management channels against this type of attack.

6.   **How would a router appliance be patched to protect against a specific vulnerability described in a security advisory?**

This type of OS does not support patching of individual files, so the whole OS has to be replaced with a new version. Vendors keep track of which version first addresses a specific security advisory.

Review Activity: Cloud Concepts

1.   **A cloud service provider is reviewing performance metrics. On a graph, increases and decreases in customer request volumes are closely tracked by CPU and RAM provisioning levels. What characteristic of cloud platforms does this demonstrate?**

Elasticity refers to the system's ability to handle changes on demand in real time.

2.   **515accounting uses colocation to host its servers in datacenters across multiple geographic regions. It configures the servers to run a software as a service (SaaS) app for use by its employees. What type of deployment model is this?**

The cloud service is wholly operated by 515web and so this is a private deployment. The cloud is offsite relative to the corporate data network.

3.   **What type of cloud solution would be used to implement a SAN?**

This would usually be described as Infrastructure as a Service (IaaS).

4.   **What are the main options for implementing connections to a cloud service provider?**

You can use the Internet and the provider's web services (possibly over a VPN) or establish a direct connection for better security and performance. A direct connection could be established by co-locating resources in the same datacenter or provisioning a direct link to the datacenter.

5.   **A technician writes a configuration file that specifies the creation of an Ubuntu Server VM with a 2 GHz CPU, 16 GB RAM, and a mass storage disk provisioned from a high-speed resource. What type of cloud concept or model is being used?**

This is an example of declarative automation, typically deployed as part of an infrastructure as code approach to provisioning. Declarative automation means that the configuration file specifies the desired state, leaving the specific implementation to the automation platform. By contrast, imperative tools specify each step required to achieve the desired outcome.

Review Activity: Virtualization and Storage Area Network Technologies

1. **A technician boots a server from USB media and installs a virtualization product. What type of hypervisor is being used?**

A Type I hypervisor. A Type I (or bare metal) hypervisor is installed directly to the server hardware. A Type II hypervisor is installed as a software app on a server that is already running a host operating system.

2. **If a VM is connected to a bridged virtual switch, what sort of network access does it have?**

A bridged switch connects the VM to a physical network via the host's NIC.

3. **A technician deploys a standard Linux virtual machine and then installs and configures an open switching OS to run on it. Which virtual network concept is being deployed?**

Running virtual appliances on standard CPU platforms (rather than dedicated switch/router hardware) is referred to as network function virtualization (NFV). This is also a type of vSwitch. A virtual switch can be implemented either using NFV or through a built-in function of the hypervisor platform.

4. **What role does an initiator play in a SAN and what hardware must be installed on it?**

An initiator is a storage area network (SAN) client device, such as a file server or database server. The server must be installed with a host bus adapter (HBA), such as fiber channel adapter or converged Ethernet adapter.

5. **What protocol can be used to implement a SAN without provisioning dedicated storage networking adapters and switches?**

iSCSI.

Review Activity: Datacenter Network Architecture

1. **A technician is configuring a firewall appliance to work with an SDN controller. What functionality on the firewall must be enabled?**

The firewall must be able to communicate with the software defined networking (SDN) controller via an application programming interface (API). This API between the control and infrastructure layers is referred to as the southbound API.

2. **A technician is cabling a top-of-rack switch in a spine and leaf architecture. Each server has been cabled to the switch. What cabling must the technician add to complete the design?**

Cable the top-of-rack (leaf) switch to each spine (distribution) switch. The two tiers are cabled in a full mesh topology.

3. **True or false? An enterprise WAN can be configured using either MPLS or SD-WAN, but the two cannot work together.**

False. It is true that an enterprise WAN can be configured using multiprotocol label switching (MPLS). However, a software defined WAN can use any type of transport network, including MPLS, so the two can be deployed together.

Glossary

802.11 standards IEEE standards for wireless networking based on spread spectrum radio transmission in the 2.4 GHz and 5 GHz bands. The standard, known as Wi-Fi, has six main iterations: a, b, g, Wi-Fi 4 (n), Wi-Fi 5 (ac), and Wi-Fi 6 (ax). These specify different modulation techniques, supported distances, and data rates, plus special features, such as channel bonding, MIMO, and MU-MIMO.

802.1p IEEE standard defining a 3-bit (0 to 7) class of service priority field within the 802.1Q format.

802.1Q Trunking protocols enable switches to exchange data about VLAN configurations. The 802.1Q protocol is often used to tag frames destined for different VLANs across trunk links.

802.1X Standard for encapsulating EAP communications over a LAN (EAPoL) to implement port-based authentication. Also called port-based network access control, and IEEE 802.1X

acceptable use policy (AUP) Policy that governs employees' use of company equipment and Internet services. ISPs may also apply AUPs to their customers. Also called fair use policy.

access control list (ACL) Collection of access control entries (ACEs) that determines which subjects (user accounts, host IP addresses, and so on) are allowed or denied access to the object and the privileges given (read only, read/write, and so on).

access control vestibule Secure entry system with two gateways, only one of which is open at any one time. Previously known as mantrap, though this terminology is now deprecated.

access point (AP) Device that provides a connection between wireless devices and can connect to wired networks, implementing an infrastructure mode WLAN. Also called wireless access point (WAP).

access/edge layer Lowest tier in a hierarchical network topology acting as the attachment point for end systems.

ad hoc network Type of wireless network where connected devices communicate directly with each other instead of over an established medium. Also called Independent Basic Service Set (IBSS).

address resolution protocol (ARP) Broadcast mechanism by which the hardware MAC address of an interface is matched to an IP address on a local network segment.

Addressing (Network) Unique identifier for a network node, such as a MAC address, IPv4 address, or IPv6 address.

adjacent channel interference (ACI) Troubleshooting issue where access points within range of one another are configured to use different but overlapping channels, causing increased noise. Also called channel overlap.

administrative distance (AD) Metric determining the trustworthiness of routes derived from different routing protocols.

angled physical contact (APC) Fiber optic connector finishing type that uses an angled polish for the ferrule.

antenna cable attenuation Signal loss caused by an external antenna connected to an access point over cabling.

antenna type Specially arranged metal wires that can send and receive radio signals, typically implemented as either an omnidirectional or a unidirectional type.

anycast IP delivery mechanism whereby a packet is addressed to a single host from a group sharing the same address.

Application Layer OSI model layer providing support to applications requiring network services (file transfer, printing, email, databases, and so on). Also called Layer 7.

application-specific integrated circuit (ASIC) Type of processor designed to perform a specific function, such as switching.

arp command Utility to display and modify contents of host's cache of IP to MAC address mappings, as resolved by address resolution protocol (ARP) replies.

asymmetrical routing Topology where the return path is different to the forward path.

auditing Detailed and specific evaluation of a process, procedure, organization, job function, or system, in which results are gathered and reported to ensure that the target of the audit is in compliance with the organization's policies, regulations, and legal responsibilities. Also called audit report.

authentication header (AH) IPSec protocol that provides authentication for the origin of transmitted data as well as integrity and protection against replay attacks.

authoritative name server DNS server designated by a name server record for the domain that holds a complete copy of zone records.

auto MDI/MDIX Interface that can detect a connection type and configure as MDI or MDI-X as appropriate.

automatic private IP addressing (APIPA) Mechanism for Windows hosts configured to obtain an address automatically that cannot contact a DHCP server to revert to using an address from the range 169.254.x.y. This is also called a link-local address.

automation Using scripts and APIs to provision and deprovision systems without manual intervention.

autonomous system (AS) Group of network prefixes under the administrative control of a single organization used to establish routing boundaries.

badge reader Authentication mechanism that allows a user to present a smartcard to operate an entry system.

bandwidth Generally used to refer to the amount of data that can be transferred through a connection over a given period. Bandwidth more properly means the range of frequencies supported by transmission media, measured in Hertz.

bandwidth speed tester Hosted utility used to measure actual speed obtained by an Internet link to a representative server or to measure the response times of websites from different locations on the Internet.

Basic Service Set ID (BSSID) MAC address of an access point supporting a basic service area.

bidirectional wavelength division multiplexing (BWDM) System that allows bidirectional data transfer over a single fiber strand by using separate wavelengths for transmit and receive streams. Also called wavelength division multiplexing (WDM).

biometric authentication Authentication mechanism that allows a user to perform a biometric scan to operate an entry or access system. Physical characteristics stored as a digital data template can be used to authenticate a user. Typical features used include facial pattern, iris, retina, or fingerprint pattern, and signature recognition.

border gateway protocol (BGP) Path vector exterior gateway routing protocol used principally by ISPs to establish routing between autonomous systems.

botnet Group of hosts or devices that have been infected by a control program called a bot that enables attackers to exploit the hosts to mount attacks. Also referred to as a zombie.

bottleneck Troubleshooting issue where performance for a whole network or system is constrained by the performance of a single link, device, or subsystem.

bridge Intermediate system that isolates collision domains to separate segments while joining segments within the same broadcast domain.

bring your own device (BYOD) Security framework and tools to facilitate use of personally-owned devices to access corporate networks and data.

broadcast Packet or frame addressed to all hosts on a local network segment, subnet, or broadcast domain. Routers do not ordinarily forward broadcast traffic. The broadcast address of IP is one where the host bits are all set to 1; at the MAC layer it is the address ff:ff:ff:ff:ff:ff.

broadcast domain Network segment in which all nodes receive the same broadcast frames at layer 2.

broadcast storm Traffic that is recirculated and amplified by loops in a switching topology, causing network slowdowns and crashing switches.

brute force attack Type of password attack where an attacker uses an application to exhaustively try every possible alphanumeric combination to crack encrypted passwords.

bus topology A shared access media where all nodes attach directly to a single cable segment.

business continuity Collection of processes that enable an organization to maintain normal business operations in the face of some adverse event.

business impact analysis (BIA) Systematic activity that identifies organizational risks and determines their effect on ongoing, mission critical operations. Also called process assessment.

cable crimper Tool to join a network jack to the ends of network patch cable.

cable modem Cable Internet access digital modem that uses a coaxial connection to the service provider's fiber optic core network. Also called Hybrid Fiber Coax (HFC).

cable stripper Tool for stripping the cable jacket or wire insulation.

cable tester Tool that reports physical characteristics of a network link such as signal strength, noise, and crosstalk.

campus area network (CAN) Scope defining a network with direct connections between two or more buildings within the same overall area.

canonical notation Format for representing IPv6 addresses using hex double-bytes with colon delimitation and zero compression.

captive portal Web page or website to which a client is redirected before being granted full network access.

Carrier Sense Multiple Access with Collision Avoidance (CSMA/CA) Mechanism used by 802.11 Wi-Fi standards to cope with contention over the shared access media.

cat cable standards ANSI/TIA/EIA cable category designations, with higher numbers representing better support for higher data rates.

cellular radio Mobile telephony standards divided into 2G (GSM; up to about 14 Kbps), 2.5G (GPRS, HSCSD, and EDGE; up to about 48 Kbps), and 3G (WCDMA; up to about 2 Mbps).

change management Process for approving, preparing, supporting, and managing new or updated business processes or technologies.

channel Subdivision of frequency bands used by Wi-Fi products into smaller channels to allow multiple networks to operate at the same location without interfering with one another.

channel bonding Capability to aggregate one or more adjacent channels to increase bandwidth.

Channel Service Unit/Data Service Unit (CSU/DSU) Appliance or WAN interface card providing connectivity to a digital circuit. The DSU encodes the signal from Data Terminal Equipment (DTE)—a PBX or router—to a signal that can be transported over the cable. The CSU is used to perform diagnostic tests on the line.

CIA triad Three principles of security control and management: confidentiality, integrity, and availability. Also known as the information security triad. Also referred to in reverse order as the AIC triad.

classless interdomain routing (CIDR) Using network prefixes to aggregate routes to multiple network blocks ("supernetting"). This replaced the old method of assigning class-based IP addresses based on the network size.

client-server Administration paradigm where some host machines are designated as providing server and services and other machines are designated as client devices that only consume server services.

cloud deployment model Classifying the ownership and management of a cloud as public, private, community, or hybrid.

cloud responsibility matrix Documentation listing which security and management tasks are the responsibility of the cloud provider and which are the responsibility of the cloud consumer.

clustering Load balancing technique where a group of servers are configured as a unit and work together to provide network services.

co-channel interference (CCI) Troubleshooting issue where access points within range of one another are configured to use the same channel, causing increased contention.

coarse wavelength division multiplexing (CWDM) Technology for multiplexing up to 16 signal channels on a single fiber using different wavelengths.

Coaxial Cable Media type using two separate conductors that share a common axis categorized using the Radio Grade (RG) specifications.

Code Division Multiple Access (CDMA) Method of multiplexing a communications channel using a code to key the modulation of a particular signal. CDMA is associated with Sprint and Verizon cellular phone networks.

cold site Predetermined alternate location where a network can be rebuilt after a disaster.

collision domain Nodes attached to the same shared access media, such as a bus network or Ethernet hub.

colocation Deploying private servers, network appliances, and interconnects to a hosted datacenter facility shared with other customers.

command and control (C&C) Infrastructure of hosts and services with which attackers direct, distribute, and control malware over botnets. Also called C2.

Common Vulnerabilities and Exposures (CVE) Scheme for identifying vulnerabilities developed by MITRE and adopted by NIST.

configuration baseline Settings for services and policy configuration for a network appliance or for a server operating in a particular application role (web server, mail server, file/print server, and so on).

control plane policing Security methods to prevent DoS attacks against a route processor over control or management plane protocols and packets.

convergence Process whereby routers agree on routes through the network to establish the same network topology in their routing tables (steady state). The time taken to reach steady state is a measure of a routing protocol's convergence performance.

core layer Highest tier in a hierarchical network topology providing interconnections between blocks.

crossover cable Cabling where the transmit pair at one end is connected to the receive pair at the other.

crosstalk Phenomenon whereby one wire causes interference in another as a result of their close proximity.

cyclical redundancy check (CRC) Calculation of a checksum based on the contents of a frame used to detect errors.

Data Link Layer OSI model layer responsible for transferring data between nodes. Also called Layer 2.

data loss (leak) prevention (DLP) Software solution that detects and prevents sensitive information from being stored on unauthorized systems or transmitted over unauthorized networks.

data remnant Leftover information on a storage medium even after basic attempts have been made to remove that data. Also called a remnant.

datacenter Facility dedicated to the provisioning of reliable power, environmental controls, and network fabric to server computers.

deauthentication/disassociation attack Spoofing frames to disconnect a wireless station to try to obtain authentication data to crack.

decibel loss (dB loss) Loss of signal strength between a transmitter and receiver due to attenuation and interference measured in decibels. Also called insertion loss.

default gateway IP configuration parameter that identifies the address of a router on the local subnet that the host can use to contact other networks.

default route Entry in the routing table to represent the forwarding path that will be used if no other entries are matched.

default VLAN Default VLAN ID (1) for all unconfigured switch ports.

defense in depth Security strategy that positions the layers of network security as network traffic roadblocks; each layer is intended to slow an attack's progress, rather than eliminating it outright.

demarcation point Location that represents the end of the access provider's network (and therefore their responsibility for maintaining it). The demarc point is usually at the Minimum Point of Entry (MPOE). If routing equipment cannot be installed at this location, demarc extension cabling may need to be laid.

denial of service attack (DoS) Any type of physical, application, or network attack that affects the availability of a managed resource.

dense wavelength division multiplexing (DWDM) Technology for multiplexing 40 or 80 signal channels on a single fiber using different wavelengths.

desktop as a service (DaaS) Cloud service model that provisions desktop OS and applications software.

DHCP relay Configuration of a router to forward DHCP traffic where the client and server are in different subnets.

DHCP snooping Switchport protection mechanism that blocks DHCP offers from unauthorized sources.

dictionary attack Type of password attack that compares encrypted passwords against a predetermined list of possible password values.

DiffServ Header field used to indicate a priority value for a layer 3 (IP) packet to facilitate Quality of Service (QoS) or Class of Service (CoS) scheduling.

dig command Utility to query a DNS and return information about a particular domain name. Also referred to as domain information groper.

digital certificate Identification and authentication information presented in the X.509 format and issued by a Certificate Authority (CA) as a guarantee that a key pair (as identified by the public key embedded in the certificate) is valid for a particular subject (user or host).

Digital Subscriber Line (DSL) Carrier technology to implement broadband Internet access for subscribers by transferring data over voice-grade telephone lines. There are various "flavors" of DSL, notably S(ymmetric) DSL, A(symmetric)DSL, and V(ery HIgh Bit Rate)DSL.

directly connected route Entry in the routing table representing a subnet in which the router has an active interface.

disassociation Management frame handling process by which a station is disconnected from an access point.

disaster recovery plan (DRP) Documented and resourced plan showing actions and responsibilities to be used in response to critical incidents.

distance Attenuation, or degradation of a signal as it travels over media, determines the maximum distance for a particular media type at a given bit rate.

distance vector Algorithm used by routing protocols that select a forwarding path based on the next hop router with the lowest hop count to the destination network.

Distributed Denial of Service (DDoS) Attack that involves the use of infected Internet-connected computers and devices to disrupt the normal flow of traffic of a server or service by overwhelming the target with traffic.

distribution/aggregation layer Intermediate tier in a hierarchical network topology providing interconnections between the access layer and the core.

diverse paths Provisioning failover Internet access links that will not be affected by the same disaster event.

DNS caching Data store on DNS clients and servers holding results of recent queries.

DNS poisoning Attack where a threat actor injects false resource records into a client or server cache to redirect a domain name to an IP address of the attacker's choosing.

domain name system (DNS) Service that maps fully qualified domain name labels to IP addresses on most TCP/IP networks, including the Internet.

dotted decimal notation Format for expressing IPv4 addresses using four decimal values from 0 to 255 for each octet.

dual stack Host operating multiple protocols simultaneously on the same interface. Most hosts are capable of dual stack IPv4 and IPv6 operation for instance.

duplex Network link that allows interfaces to send and receive simultaneously.

dynamic host configuration protocol (DHCP) Protocol used to automatically assign IP addressing information to hosts that have not been configured manually.

Dynamic Multipoint VPN (DMVPN) Software-based mechanism that allows VPNs to be built and deleted dynamically.

dynamic route Entry in the routing table that has been learned from another router via a dynamic routing protocol. Also called a learned route.

east-west traffic Design paradigm accounting for the fact that data center traffic between servers is greater than that passing in and out (north-south).

effective isotropic radiated power (EIRP) Signal strength from a transmitter, measured as the sum of transmit power, antenna cable/connector loss, and antenna gain.

elasticity Property by which a computing environment can instantly react to both increasing and decreasing demands in workload.

electromagnetic interference (EMI) Noise that occurs when a magnetic field around one electrical circuit or device interferes with the signal being carried on an adjacent circuit. Also called interference.

Encapsulating Security Protocol (ESP) IPSec sub-protocol that enables encryption and authentication of the header and payload of a data packet.

enhanced interior gateway routing protocol (EIGRP) Advanced distance vector dynamic routing protocol using bandwidth and delay metrics to establish optimum forwarding paths.

enterprise authentication Wireless network authentication mode where the access point acts as pass-through for credentials that are verified by an AAA server.

enumeration Attack that aims to list resources on the network, host, or system as a whole to identify potential targets for further attack. Also referred to as footprinting and fingerprinting.

Ethernet Standards describing media types, access methods, data rates, and distance limitations at layers 1 and 2 of the OSI model using xBASE-y designations. Also referred to 802.3.

Ethernet header Fields in a frame used to identify source and destination MAC addresses, protocol type, and error detection.

evil twin Wireless access point that deceives users into believing that it is a legitimate network access point.

explicit deny Firewall ACL rule configured manually to block any traffic not matched by previous rules.

exploit Specific method by which malware code infects a target host, often via some vulnerability in a software process. Also called exploit technique.

Extended Service Set ID (ESSID) Network name configured on multiple access points to form an extended service area.

Extended Unique Identifier (EUI) IEEE's preferred term for a network interface's unique identifier. An EUI-48 corresponds to a MAC address while an EUI-64 is one that uses a 64-bit address space.

Extensible Authentication Protocol (EAP) Framework for negotiating authentication methods that enables systems to use hardware-based identifiers, such as fingerprint scanners or smart card readers, for authentication, and establish secure tunnels through which to submit credentials.

exterior gateway protocol (EGP) Dynamic routing protocol used to exchange information about network paths in separate autonomous systems.

F-type connector Screw down connector used with coaxial cable.

factory reset Standard routine created by manufacturer that can be invoked to restore an appliance to its shipped state, clearing any user customization, configuration, or modification.

fat AP Access point whose firmware contains enough processing logic to be able to function autonomously and handle clients without the use of a wireless controller.

fiber distribution panel Type of distribution frame with pre-wired connectors used with fiber optic cabling.

Fibre Channel (FC) High speed network communications protocol used to implement SANs.

Fibre Channel over Ethernet (FCoE) Standard allowing for a mixed use Ethernet network with both ordinary data and storage network traffic.

File Transfer Protocol (FTP) Application protocol used to transfer files between network hosts. Variants include S(ecure) FTP, FTP with SSL (FTPS and FTPES) and T(rivial)FTP. FTP utilizes ports 20 and 21.

firewall Software or hardware device that protects a system or network by blocking unwanted network traffic.

first hop redundancy protocol (FHRP) Provisioning failover routers to serve as the default gateway for a subnet. Also referred to as Virtual Router Redundancy Protocol (VRRP) and Hot Standby Router Protocol (HSRP)

floor plan Documentation detailing site premises using an accurate scale.

flow control Mechanism defined in IEEE 802.3a that allows a server to instruct a switch to pause traffic temporarily to avoid overwhelming its buffer and causing it to drop frames. Also called 802.3x.

fragmentation Mechanism for splitting a layer 3 datagram between multiple frames to fit the maximum transmission unit (MTU) of the underlying Data Link network.

frame Common term for the protocol data unit for layer 2.

frequency band Portion of the radio frequency spectrum in which wireless products operate, such as 2.4 GHz band or 5 GHz band. Also called frequencies.

full tunnel VPN configuration where all traffic is routed via the VPN gateway.

fully qualified domain name (FQDN) Unique label specified in a DNS hierarchy to identify a particular host within a subdomain within a top-level domain.

fusion splicer Tool for joining strands of fiber optic cable with minimal signal loss.

generator Standby power supply fueled by diesel or propane. In the event of a power outage, a UPS must provide transitionary power, as a backup generator cannot be cut-in fast enough. Also called a backup generator.

Generic Routing Encapsulation (GRE) Tunneling protocol allowing the transmission of encapsulated frames or packets from different types of network protocol over an IP network.

geofencing Security control that can enforce a virtual boundary based on real-world geography.

Global System for Mobile Communication (GSM) Standard for cellular radio communications and data transfer. GSM phones use a SIM card to identify the subscriber and network provider. 4G and later data standards are developed for GSM.

hardening Process of making a host or app configuration secure by reducing its attack surface, through running only necessary services, installing monitoring software to protect against malware and intrusions, and establishing a maintenance schedule to ensure the system is patched to be secure against software exploits.

hashing Function that converts an arbitrary length string input to a fixed length string output. A cryptographic hash function does this in a way that reduces the chance of collisions, where two different inputs produce the same output. Also called message digest or cryptographic hash.

heat map In a Wi-Fi site survey, a diagram showing signal strength and channel utilization at different locations.

heating, ventilation, air conditioning (HVAC) Control systems that maintain an optimum heating, cooling, and humidity level working environment for different parts of the building.

high availability (HA) Metric that defines how closely systems approach the goal of providing data availability 100 percent of the time while maintaining a high level of system performance.

honeypot Host, network, or file set up with the purpose of luring attackers away from assets of actual value and/or discovering attack strategies and weaknesses in the security configuration. Also called a honeynet or a honeyfile.

hop One link in the path from a host to a router or from router to router. Each time a packet passes through a router, its hop count (or TTL) is decreased by one.

host name Label applied to a host computer that is unique on the local network.

hot site Fully configured alternate processing site that can be brought online either instantly or very quickly after a disaster.

HTML5 VPN Using features of HTML5 to implement remote desktop/VPN connections via browser software (clientless). Also called clientless VPN.

hub Layer 1 (Physical) network device used to implement a star network topology on legacy Ethernet networks, working as a multiport repeater.

hub-and-spoke Network connectivity between multiple virtual private clouds where one virtual private cloud (VPC) acts as a hub and the other VPCs are peered with it but not with each other.

hybrid topology A network that uses a combination of physical or logical topologies. In practice most networks use hybrid topologies. For example, modern types of Ethernet are physically wired as stars but logically operate as buses.

HyperText Transfer Protocol (HTTP) Application protocol used to provide web content to browsers. HTTP uses port 80. HTTPS(ecure) provides for encrypted transfers, using SSL/TLS and port 443.

hypervisor Software or firmware that creates and manages virtual machines on the host hardware.

identity and access management (IAM) Security process that provides identification, authentication, and authorization mechanisms for users, computers, and other entities to work with organizational assets like networks, operating systems, and applications. Also referred to as identity management (IdM), and access management.

ifconfig command Deprecated Linux command tool used to gather information about the IP configuration of the network adapter or to configure the network adapter.

implicit deny Firewall ACL rule configured by default to block any traffic not matched by previous rules.

incident response plan (IRP) Procedures and guidelines covering appropriate priorities, actions, and responsibilities in the event of security incidents, divided into preparation, detection/analysis, containment, eradication/recovery, and post-incident stages.

industrial control system (ICS) Network managing embedded devices (computer systems that are designed to perform a specific, dedicated function).

Infrastructure as a Service (IaaS)
Cloud service model that provisions virtual machines and network infrastructure.

infrastructure as code (IaC)
Provisioning architecture in which deployment of resources is performed by scripted automation and orchestration.

instant secure erase (ISE) Media sanitization command built into HDDs and SSDs that are self-encrypting that works by erasing the encryption key, leaving remnants unrecoverable.

insulation displacement connector (IDC) Block used to terminate twisted pair cabling at a wall plate or patch panel available in different formats, such as 110, BIX, and Krone.

interface errors Troubleshooting issue where an interface reports packet errors due to frame corruption and other factors.

interface statistics Metrics recorded by a host or switch that enable monitoring of link state, resets, speed, duplex setting, utilization, and error rates.

interior gateway protocol (IGP) Dynamic routing protocol used to exchange path forwarding information between routers in the same autonomous system.

intermediate distribution frame (IDF) Passive wiring panel providing a central termination point for cabling. An IDF is an optional layer of distribution frame hierarchy that cross-connects "vertical" backbone cabling to an MDF to "horizontal" wiring to wall ports on each floor of a building or each building of a campus network.

internet control message protocol (ICMP) IP-level protocol for reporting errors and status information supporting the function of troubleshooting utilities such as ping.

internet group management protocol (IGMP) Layer 3 protocol that allows hosts to join and leave groups configured to receive multicast communications.

Internet Key Exchange (IKE)
Framework for creating a Security Association (SA) used with IPSec. An SA establishes that two hosts trust one another (authenticate) and agree secure protocols and cipher suites to use to exchange data.

Internet Message Access Protocol (IMAP) Application protocol providing a means for a client to access and manage email messages stored in a mailbox on a remote server. IMAP4 utilizes TCP port number 143, while the secure version IMAPS uses TCP/993.

Internet of Things (IoT) Devices that can report state and configuration data and be remotely managed over IP networks.

Internet Protocol header (IP header) Fields in a datagram used to identify source and destination IP addresses, protocol type, and other layer 3 properties.

Internet Protocol Security (IPSec) Network protocol suite used to secure data through authentication and encryption as the data travels across the network or the Internet.

Internet Service Provider (ISP) Provides Internet connectivity and web services to its customers.

Internet Small Computers Systems Interface (iSCSI) IP tunneling protocol that enables the transfer of SCSI data over an IP-based network to create a SAN.

intrusion detection system (IDS) Security appliance or software that uses passive hardware sensors to monitor traffic on a specific segment of the network. Also called a network intrusion detection system (NIDS).

intrusion prevention system (IPS) Security appliance or software that combines detection capabilities with functions that can actively block attacks.

ip command Linux command tool used to gather information about the IP configuration of the network adapter or to configure the network adapter.

IP helper Command set in a router OS to support DHCP relay and other broadcast forwarding functionality.

IP protocol type Identifier for a protocol working over the Internet Protocol, such as TCP, UDP, ICMP, GRE, EIGRP, or OSPF.

IP scanner Utility that can probe a network to detect which IP addresses are in use by hosts. Also called IP scanning.

ipconfig command Command tool used to gather information about the IP configuration of a Windows host.

iperf Utility used to measure the bandwidth achievable over a network link.

iptables command Command-line utility for configuring the netfilter firewall implemented in the Linux kernel.

iterative lookup DNS query type whereby a server responds with information from its own data store only.

jitter Variation in the time it takes for a signal to reach the recipient. Jitter manifests itself as an inconsistent rate of packet delivery. If packet loss or delay is excessive, then noticeable audio or video problems (artifacts) are experienced by users.

jumbo frame Ethernet frame with a payload larger than 1500 bytes (up to about 9000 bytes).

Kerberos Single sign-on authentication and authorization service that is based on a time-sensitive ticket-granting system.

latency The time it takes for a signal to reach the recipient. A video application can support a latency of about 80 ms, while typical latency on the Internet can reach 1000 ms at peak times. Latency is a particular problem for 2-way applications, such as VoIP (telephone) and online conferencing.

layer 3 capable switch Switch appliance capable of IP routing between virtual LAN (VLAN) subnets using hardware-optimized path selection and forwarding.

least privilege Basic principle of security stating that something should be allocated the minimum necessary rights, privileges, or information to perform its role. Also referred to as the principle of least privilege.

LED status indicator Visual indicator of the status of various devices, including PC power supplies, batteries, drive activity, and network activity. Network equipment LEDs usually show connection speed and activity.

life cycle roadmap Method to track the life cycle phases of one or more hardware, service, or software systems in your organization. Also called the system life cycle.

Lightweight Directory Access Protocol (LDAP) Network protocol used to access network directory databases, which store information about authorized users and their privileges, as well as other organizational information.

Link Aggregation Control Protocol (LACP) IEEE protocol governing the use of bonded Ethernet ports (NIC teaming). Also referred to as 802.3ad and 802.1ax.

link local IP addressing scheme used within the scope of a single broadcast domain only.

link-state Algorithm used by routing protocols that build a complete network topology to use to select optimum forwarding paths.

load balancer Type of switch, router, or software that distributes client requests between different resources, such as communications links or similarly-configured servers. This provides fault tolerance and improves throughput.

local area network (LAN) Network scope restricted to a single geographic location and owned/managed by a single organization.

local authentication OS subsystem that authenticates users when they attempt to start a shell on the host.

local connector (LC) Small form factor push-pull fiber optic connector; available in simplex and duplex versions.

logging level Threshold for storing or forwarding an event message based on its severity index or value. Also referred to as the severity level.

Long Term Evolution (LTE) Packet data communications specification providing an upgrade path for both GSM and CDMA2000 cellular networks. LTE Advanced is designed to provide 4G standard network access.

loopback adapter Used to verify the integrity of a network interface port by checking that it can receive a signal generated by itself.

loopback address IP address by which a host can address itself over any available interface.

MAC address table Data store on a switch that keeps track of the MAC addresses associated with each port. As the switch uses a type of memory called Content Addressable Memory (CAM), this is sometimes called the CAM table.

Media Access Control filtering (MAC filtering) Applying an access control list to a switch or access point so that only clients with approved MAC addresses can connect to it.

main distribution frame (MDF) Passive wiring panel providing a central termination point for cabling. A MDF distributes backbone or "vertical" wiring through a building and connections to external access provider networks.

malware Software that serves a malicious purpose, typically installed without the user's consent (or knowledge).

maximum tolerable downtime (MTD) Longest period that a process can be inoperable without causing irrevocable business failure.

maximum transmission unit (MTU) Maximum size in bytes of a frame's payload. If the payload cannot be encapsulated within a single frame at the Data Link layer, it must be fragmented.

mean time between failures (MTBF) Metric for a device or component that predicts the expected time between failures.

mean time to failure (MTTF) Metric indicating average time a device or component is expected to be in operation.

mean time to repair/replace/recover (MTTR) Metric representing average time taken for a device or component to be repaired, replaced, or otherwise recover from a failure.

mechanical transfer registered jack (MT-RJ) Small form factor duplex fiber optic connector with a snap-in design.

Media Access Control address (MAC) Hardware address that uniquely identifies each network interface at layer 2 (Data Link). A MAC address is 48 bits long with the first half representing the manufacturer's Organizationally Unique Identifier (OUI). Also called a client identifier.

media converter Layer 1 (Physical) network device that translates signals received over one media type for transmission over a different media type.

medium dependent interface/ medium dependent interface crossover (MDI/MDI-X) System that distinguishes transmit and receive pins on different interface types. The interface on an end system is MDI while that on an intermediate system is MDI-X.

memorandum of understanding (MoU) Usually a preliminary or exploratory agreement to express an intent to work together that is not legally binding and does not involve the exchange of money.

mesh topology A topology often used in WANs where each device has (in theory) a point-to-point connection with every other device (fully connected); in practice, only the more important devices are directly interconnected (partial mesh).

metro-optical City-wide fiber optic networks enabling Carrier Ethernet virtual private networks and WAN links and "full fiber" Internet access. Also called Carrier Ethernet.

metropolitan area network (MAN) A class of network that covers the area of a city (that is, no more than tens of kilometers). A MAN is larger than a LAN but smaller than a WAN but it can operate at speeds that are comparable with LANs.

microsegmentation (switching) Function of an Ethernet switch whereby collision domains are reduced to the scope of a single port only.

missing route Troubleshooting issue where a routing table does not contain a required entry due either to manual misconfiguration or failure of a dynamic routing protocol update.

mission essential function (MEF) Business or organizational activity that is too critical to be deferred for anything more than a few hours, if at all.

monitoring baseline Estimated performance or stability of a service based on historical information or vendor guidance. Also called a performance baseline.

multicast A packet addressed to a selection of hosts (in IP, those belonging to a multicast group).

multifactor authentication (MFA) Authentication scheme that requires the user to present at least two different factors as credentials, from something you know, something you have, something you are, something you do, and somewhere you are. Specifying two factors is known as 2FA.

multimeter Electrical meter capable of measuring voltage, resistance, and current. Voltage readings can be used to determine whether, for example, a power supply unit is functioning correctly. Resistance readings can be used to determine whether a fuse or network cable is functioning correctly.

multimode fiber (MMF) Fiber optic cable type using LED or vertical cavity surface emitting laser optics and graded using optical multimode types for core size and bandwidth.

multipath Overprovisioning controllers and cabling so that a host has failover connections to networks and storage media. Also called multipathing.

Multiple Input Multiple Output (MIMO) Use of multiple reception and transmission antennas to boost bandwidth via spatial multiplexing and to boost range and signal reliability via spatial diversity.

Multiprotocol Label Switching (MPLS) "Layer 2.5" network protocol used by service providers to implement WAN access links and virtual private networks with traffic engineering (congestion control), Class of Service, and Quality of Service.

multiuser MIMO (MU-MIMO) Use of spatial multiplexing to connect multiple MU-MIMO-capable stations simultaneously, providing the stations are not on the same directional path.

native VLAN VLAN ID used for any untagged frames received on a trunk port. The same ID should be used on both ends of the trunk and the ID should not be left as the default VLAN ID (1).

neighbor discovery protocol (ND) IPv6 protocol used to identify link local nodes.

Netflow Cisco-developed means of reporting network flow information to a structured database. NetFlow allows better understanding of IP traffic flows as used by different network applications and hosts.

netstat command Cross-platform command tool to show network information on a machine running TCP/IP, notably active connections and the routing table.

network access control (NAC) General term for the collected protocols, policies, and hardware that authenticate and authorize access to a network at the device level.

network address translation (NAT) Routing mechanism that conceals internal addressing schemes from the public Internet by translating between a single public address on the external side of a router and private, non-routable addresses internally.

network functions virtualization (NFV) Provisioning virtual network appliances, such as switches, routers, and firewalls, via VMs and containers.

Network Layer OSI model layer responsible for logical network addressing and forwarding. Also called Layer 3.

network mask Number of bits applied to an IP address to mask the network ID portion from the host/interface ID portion. Also referred to as a netmask or subnet mask.

Network Separation Enforcing a security zone by separating a segment of the network from access by the rest of the network. This could be accomplished using firewalls or VPNs or VLANs. A physically separate network or host (with no cabling or wireless links to other networks) is referred to as air-gapped. Also referred to as Segmentation or network segmentation enforcement.

Network Time Protocol (NTP) Application protocol allowing machines to synchronize to the same time clock that runs over UDP port 123.

NIC teaming Two or more NIC aggregated into a single channel link for fault tolerance and increased throughput. Also known as NIC bonding.

Nmap IP and port scanner used for topology, host, service, and OS discovery and enumeration.

non-disclosure agreement (NDA) Agreement that stipulates that entities will not share confidential information, knowledge, or materials with unauthorized third parties.

nslookup command Cross-platform command tool for querying DNS resource records.

offboarding Process of ensuring that all HR and other requirements are covered when an employee leaves an organization. Also called an exit interview.

on-path attack Attack where the threat actor makes an independent connection between two victims and is able to read and possibly modify traffic. Formerly called a Man-in-the-Middle (MitM) attack.

onboarding Process of bringing in a new employee, contractor, or supplier.

open authentication Wireless network authentication mode where guest (unauthenticated) access is permitted.

open shortest path first (OSPF) Dynamic routing protocol that uses a link-state algorithm and a hierarchical topology.

operational technology (OT) Communications network designed to implement an industrial control system rather than data networking.

optical link budget Assessment of allowable signal loss over a fiber optic link. Also referred to as low optical link budget.

optical mode (OM) Classification system for multimode fiber designating core size and modal bandwidth.

optical spectrum analyzer (OSA) Determines attenuation of different light wavelengths to establish suitability of fiber optic cable for long-distance applications.

optical time domain reflectometer (OTDR) Used to measure the length of a fiber optic cable run and are able to locate faults.

orchestration Automation of multiple coordinated steps in a deployment process.

Open Systems Interconnection reference model (OSI reference model) Assigns network and hardware components and functions at seven discrete layers: Physical, Data Link, Network, Transport, Session, Presentation, and Application.

out-of-band management (OOB) Accessing the administrative interface of a network appliance using a separate network from the usual data network. This could use a separate VLAN or a different kind of link, such as a dial-up modem.

overlay network Network protocols that use encapsulation to provision virtual tunnels and networks without requiring reconfiguration of the underlying transport network.

packet sniffing Recording data from frames as they pass over network media, using methods such as a mirror port or tap device.

passive optical network (PON) Technology based on DWDM to provision "near" fiber Internet access solutions (FTTx - Fiber to the Home, Fiber to the Curb, and so on).

password policy Security policy that promotes user selection of strong passwords by specifying a minimum password length, requiring complex passwords, requiring periodic password changes, and placing limits on reuse of passwords.

patch panel Type of distribution frame used with twisted pair cabling with IDCs to terminate fixed cabling on one side and modular jacks to make cross-connections to other equipment on the other. Also called a patch bay.

peer-to-peer Administration paradigm whereby any computer device may be configured to operate as both server and client.

penetration testing Test that uses active tools and security utilities to evaluate security by simulating an attack on a system. A pen test will verify that a threat exists, then will actively test and bypass security controls, and will finally exploit vulnerabilities on the system. Often abbreviated as pen test.

performance metric Measurement of a value affecting system performance, such as CPU or memory utilization.

personal area network (PAN) Close range networking (usually based on Bluetooth or NFC) allowing communications between personal devices, such as smartphones, laptops, and printers/peripheral devices.

phishing Email-based social engineering attack, in which the attacker sends email from a supposedly reputable source, such as a bank, to try to elicit private information from the victim.

physical access control system (PACS) Components and protocols that facilitate the centralized configuration and monitoring of security mechanisms within offices and data centers.

Physical Layer (PHY) Lowest layer of the OSI model providing for the transmission and receipt of data bits from node to node. This includes the network medium and mechanical and electrical specifications for using the media. Also referred to as Layer 1.

piggybacking Allowing a threat actor to enter a site or controlled location without authorization.

ping command Cross-platform command tool for testing IP packet transmission.

plain old telephone system (POTS) Parts of telephone network "local loop" that use voice-grade cabling. Analog data transfer over POTS using dial-up modems is slow (33.3Kbps).

Platform as a Service (PaaS) Cloud service model that provisions application and database services as a platform for development of apps.

Plenum Cable for use in building voids designed to be fire resistant and to produce a minimal amount of smoke if burned. Also called plenum cable.

Point to Point Protocol (PPP) Dial-up protocol working at layer 2 (Data Link) used to connect devices remotely to networks.

point-to-point A point-to-point topology is one where two nodes have a dedicated connection to one another.

polarization Orientation of the wave propagating from an antenna.

port (TCP/UDP) In TCP and UDP applications, a unique number assigned to a particular application protocol. Server ports are typically assigned well known or registered numbers while client ports use dynamic or ephemeral numbering.

port address translation (PAT) Maps private host IP addresses onto a single public IP address. Each host is tracked by assigning it a random high TCP port for communications. Also called network address port translation (NAPT) and NAT overloading.

port aggregation Combining the bandwidth of two or more switch ports into a single channel link.

port mirroring Copying ingress and/or egress communications from one or more switch ports to another port. This is used to monitor communications passing over the switch. Also called a switched port analyzer (SPAN)

port scanner Utility that can probe a host to enumerate the status of TCP and UDP ports.

port security Preventing a device attached to a switch port from communicating on the network unless it matches a given MAC address or other protection profile.

port tagging On a switch with VLANs configured, a port with an end station host connected operates in untagged mode (access port). A tagged port will normally be part of a trunk link.

Post Office Protocol (POP) Application protocol that enables a client to download email messages from a server mailbox to a client over port TCP/110 or secure port TCP/995. Also called POP3.

posture assessment Process for verifying compliance with a health policy by using host health checks.

power distribution unit (PDU) Advanced strip socket that provides filtered output voltage. A managed unit supports remote administration.

Power over Ethernet (PoE) Specification allowing power to be supplied via switch ports and ordinary data cabling to devices such as VoIP handsets and wireless access points. Devices can draw up to about 13W (or 25W for PoE+).

pre-shared key (PSK) Wireless network authentication mode where a passphrase-based mechanism is used to allow group authentication to a wireless network. The passphrase is used to derive an encryption key.

Presentation Layer OSI model layer that transforms data between the formats used by the network and applications. Also called Layer 6.

printer "Printer" is often used to mean "print device" but also refers to a term used to describe the software components of a printing solution. The printer is the object that Windows sends output to. It consists of a spool directory, a printer driver, and configuration information.

private branch exchange (PBX) Routes incoming calls to direct dial numbers and provides facilities such as voice mail, Automatic Call Distribution (ACD), and Interactive Voice Response (IVR). A PBX can also be implemented as software (virtual PBX). An IP-based PBX or hybrid PBX allows use of VoIP.

private key In asymmetric encryption, the private key is known only to the holder and is linked to, but not derivable from, a public key distributed to those with which the holder wants to communicate securely. A private key can be used to encrypt data that can be decrypted by the linked public key or vice versa.

private VLAN (PVLAN) Method of isolating hosts to prevent hosts within the same VLAN from communicating directly.

protocol analyzer Utility that can parse the header fields and payloads of protocols in captured frames for display and analysis. Also called a packet analyzer.

Protocol Data Unit (PDU) Network packet encapsulating a data payload from an upper layer protocol with header fields used at the current layer. Also referred to as Encapsulation.

proxy server Server that mediates the communications between a client and another server. It can filter and often modify communications, as well as provide caching services to improve performance. Also called a forward proxy.

public key During asymmetric encryption, this key is freely distributed and can be used to perform the reverse encryption or decryption operation of the linked private key in the pair.

public key infrastructure (PKI) Framework of certificate authorities, digital certificates, software, services, and other cryptographic components deployed for the purpose of validating subject identities.

public switched telephone network (PSTN) Global network connecting national telecommunications systems.

public versus private addressing Some IP address ranges are designated for use on private networks only.

Packets with source IP addresses in public ranges are permitted to be forwarded over the Internet. Packets with source IP addresses from private ranges should be blocked at Internet gateways or forwarded using some type of translation mechanism.

punchdown block Type of distribution frame that offers high density and available in different IDC formats, such as 110, BIX, and Krone.

punchdown tool Tool used to terminate solid twisted pair copper cable to an Insulation Displacement Connector.

quad small form factor pluggable/ enhanced quad small form factor pluggable (QSFP/QSFP+) Fiber optic transceiver module type supporting four individual duplex lanes at 1 Gbps (QSFP) or 10 Gbps (QSFP+) that can be aggregated into a single 4 Gbps or 40 Gbps channel.

quality of service (QoS) Systems that differentiate data passing over the network that can reserve bandwidth for particular applications. A system that cannot guarantee a level of available bandwidth is often described as Class of Service (CoS).

rack Storage solution for server and network equipment. Racks are designed to a standard width and height (measured in multiples of 1U or 1.75"). Racks offer better density, cooling, and security than ordinary office furniture.

radio frequency attenuation (RF attenuation) Loss of signal strength due to distance and environmental factors. Also referred to as free space path loss.

Radio Frequency ID (RFID) Means of encoding information into passive tags, which can be easily attached to devices, structures, clothing, or almost anything else.

ransomware Malware that tries to extort money from the victim by encrypting the victim's files and demanding payment.

received signal strength indicator (RSSI) Signal strength as measured at the receiver, using either decibel units or an index value.

recovery point objective (RPO) Longest period that an organization can tolerate lost data being unrecoverable.

recovery time objective (RTO) Maximum time allowed to restore a system after a failure event.

recursive lookup DNS query type whereby a server submits additional queries to other servers to obtain the requested information.

registered jack connector (RJ) Series of jack/plug types used with twisted pair cabling, such as RJ-45 and RJ-11.

Remote Authentication Dial-in User Service (RADIUS) AAA protocol used to manage remote and wireless authentication infrastructures.

Remote Desktop Protocol (RDP) Application protocol for operating remote connections to a host using a graphical interface. The protocol sends screen data from the remote host to the client and transfer mouse and keyboard input from the client to the remote host. It uses TCP port 3389.

repeater Layer 1 device that regenerates and retransmits signals to overcome media distance limitations.

reservation (DHCP) DHCP configuration that assigns either a prereserved or persistent IP address to a given host, based on its hardware address or other ID.

resource record (AAAA) Data file storing information about a DNS zone. The main records are as follows: A (maps a host name to an IPv4 address), AAAA (maps to an IPv6 address), CNAME (an alias for a host name), MX (the IP address of a mail server), and PTR (allows a host name to be identified from an IP address).

reverse DNS DNS query type to resolve an IP address to a host name.

ring topology In a ring topology, all of the computers are connected in a circle. The ring comprises a series of point-to-point links between each device. Signals pass from device to device in a single direction with the signal regenerated at each device.

risk Likelihood and impact (or consequence) of a threat actor exercising a vulnerability.

roaming WLAN configured with multiple access points in an extended service set allowing clients to remain connected to the network within an extended service area.

rogue access point Wireless access point that has been enabled on the network without authorization.

role-based access control (RBAC) Access control model where resources are protected by ACLs that are managed by administrators and that provide user permissions based on job functions.

rollover cable Cable used to connect the serial port on a host or modem to the console port on a network appliance. Also called console table.

route command Cross-platform command tools used display and manage the routing table on a Windows or Linux host.

router An intermediate system working at the Network layer capable of forwarding packets around logical networks of different layer 1 and layer 2 types.

router advertisement (RA) Packet sent by an IPv6-capable router to notify hosts about prefixes and autoconfiguration methods available on the local link.

Router Advertisement Guard (RA Guard) Switchport security feature to block router advertisement packets from unauthorized sources.

routing information protocol (RIP) Distance vector-based routing protocol that uses a hop count to determine the least-cost path to a destination network.

routing loop Troubleshooting issue where a packet is forwarded between routers in a loop until its TTL expires.

routing table Data store on an IP host used to determine the interface over which to forward a packet.

sanitization Process of thoroughly and completely removing data from a storage medium so that file remnants cannot be recovered.

scalability Property by which a computing environment is able to gracefully fulfill its ever increasing resource needs.

scope (DHCP) Range of consecutive IP addresses in the same subnet that a DHCP server can lease to clients.

screened subnet Segment isolated from the rest of a private network by one or more firewalls that accepts connections from the Internet over designated ports. Formerly referred to as a demilitarized zone (DMZ), but this usage is now deprecated.

secure erase (SE) Method of sanitizing a drive using the ATA command set.

Secure Shell (SSH) Application protocol supporting secure tunneling and remote terminal emulation and file copy. SSH runs over TCP port 22.

Secure Sockets Layer (SSL) Original, obsolete version of the security protocol now developed as TLS.

security information and event management (SIEM) Solution that provides real-time or near-real-time analysis of security alerts generated by network hardware and applications.

sensor (device/chassis) Device that can report environmental conditions such as temperature or chassis intrusion to a monitoring system.

separation of duties Security policy concept that states that duties and responsibilities should be divided among individuals to prevent ethical conflicts or abuse of powers.

Server Message Block (SMB) Application protocol used for requesting files from Windows servers and delivering them to clients. SMB allows machines to share files and printers, thus making them available for other machines to use. SMB client software is available for UNIX-based systems. Samba software allows UNIX and Linux servers or NAS appliances to run SMB services for Windows clients. Also called Common Internet File System (CIFS).

service level agreement (SLA) Agreement that sets the service requirements and expectations between a consumer and a provider.

service set identifier (SSID) Character string that identifies a particular wireless LAN (WLAN).

Session Initiation Protocol (SIP) Application protocol used to establish, disestablish, and manage VoIP and conferencing communications sessions. It handles user discovery (locating a user on the network), availability advertising (whether a user is prepared to receive calls), negotiating session parameters (such as use of audio/ video), and session management and termination.

Session Layer OSI model layer that provides services for applications that need to exchange multiple messages (dialog control). Also referred to as Layer 5.

shielded twisted pair (STP) Copper twisted pair cabling with screening and shielding elements for individual wire pairs and/or the whole cable to reduce interference. Also referred to as a screened, shielded, or foiled twisted pair.

shoulder surfing Social engineering tactic to obtain someone's password or PIN by observing him or her as he or she types it in.

show commands Set of commands in a switch OS to report configuration or interface information.

show route command Command tools used in router operating systems to list the contents of routing tables.

Simple Network Management Protocol (SNMP) Application protocol used for monitoring and managing network devices. SNMP works over UDP ports 161 and 162 by default.

Simultaneous Authentication of Equals (SAE) Personal authentication mechanism for Wi-Fi networks introduced with WPA3 to address vulnerabilities in the WPA-PSK method.

single mode fiber (SMF) Fiber optic cable type that uses laser diodes and narrow core construction to support high bandwidths over distances of over 5 km.

single sign-on (SSO) Authentication technology that enables a user to authenticate once and receive authorizations for multiple services.

site survey Documentation about a location for the purposes of building an ideal wireless infrastructure; it often contains optimum locations for wireless antenna and access point placement to provide the required coverage for clients and identifying sources of interference.

small form factor pluggable/ enhanced small form factor pluggable (SFP/SFP+) Fiber optic transceiver module type supporting duplex 1 Gbps (SFP) or 10 Gbps (SFP+) links.

small office, home office (SOHO) Typically used to refer to network devices designed for small-scale LANs.

smartjack Termination point for an access provider's cabling, also referred to as the Network Interface Unit (NIU).

Simple Mail Transfer Protocol (SMTP) Application protocol used to send mail between hosts on the Internet. Messages are sent between servers over TCP port 25 or submitted by a mail client over secure port TCP/587.

snips Electrician's scissors that are sturdy enough to cut wire and notched to assist with stripping insulation from wire.

social engineering Activity where the goal is to use deception and trickery to convince unsuspecting users to provide sensitive data or to violate security guidelines.

socket Combination of a TCP/UDP port number and IP address. A client socket can form a connection with a server socket to exchange data.

Software as a Service (SaaS) Cloud service model that provisions fully developed application services to users.

software defined networking (SDN) APIs and compatible hardware/virtual appliances allowing for programmable network appliances and systems.

software defined WAN (SD-WAN) Services that use software-defined mechanisms and routing policies to implement virtual tunnels and overlay networks over multiple types of transport network.

spanning tree protocol (STP) Protocol that prevents layer 2 network loops by dynamically blocking switch ports as needed.

spectrum analyzer Device that can detect the source of interference on a wireless network.

speed Amount of data that can be transferred over a network connection in a given amount of time, typically measured in bits or bytes per second (or some more suitable multiple thereof). Transfer rate is also described variously as data rate, bit rate, connection speed, transmission speed, or bandwidth. Transfer rates are often quoted as the peak, maximum, theoretical value; sustained, actual throughput is often considerably less.

speed (port configuration) Port setting that determines the speed of the link. The same setting must be used on the connected device and is usually autonegotiated.

spine and leaf topology Topology commonly used in datacenters comprising a top tier of aggregation switches forming a backbone for a leaf tier of top-of-rack switches.

split tunnel VPN configuration where only traffic for the private network is routed via the VPN gateway.

spoofing Attack technique where the threat actor disguises their identity or impersonates another user or resource.

standard operating procedure (SOP) Documentation of best practice and work instructions to use to perform a common administrative task.

star topology In a star network, each node is connected to a central point, typically a switch or a router. The central point mediates communications between the attached nodes. When a device such as a hub is used, the hub receives signals from a node and repeats the signal to all other connected nodes. Therefore the bandwidth is still shared between all nodes. When a device such as a switch is used, point-to-

point links are established between each node as required. The circuit established between the two nodes can use the full bandwidth capacity of the network media.

stateless address autoconfiguration (SLAAC) Mechanism used in IPv6 for hosts to assign addresses to interfaces without requiring manual intervention.

static route Entry in the routing table added manually by an administrator.

storage area network (SAN) Network dedicated to provisioning storage resources, typically consisting of storage devices and servers connected to switches via host bus adapters.

straight tip connector (ST) Bayonet-style twist-and-lock connector for fiber optic cabling.

straight-through cable Cable designed to connect an end system MDI to an intermediate system MDI-X, such as a host to a hub.

structured query language (SQL) Programming and query language common to many relational database management systems.

subinterface Configuring a router's physical interface with multiple virtual interfaces connected to separate virtual LAN (VLAN) IDs over a trunk.

subnet addressing Division of a single IP network into two or more smaller broadcast domains by using longer netmasks within the boundaries of the network. Also called a subnet mask.

subscriber connector (SC) Push/pull connector used with fiber optic cabling.

Supervisory Control and Data Acquisition (SCADA) Type of industrial control system that manages large-scale, multiple-site devices and equipment spread over geographically large areas from a host computer.

switch Intermediate system used to establish contention-free network segments at layer 2 (Data Link).

switching loop Troubleshooting issue where layer 2 frames are forwarded between switches or bridges in an endless loop.

syslog Application protocol and event logging format enabling different appliances and software applications to transmit logs or event records to a central server. Syslog works over UDP port 514 by default.

T-carrier (T1) System was developed by Bell Labs to allow multiple calls to be placed on a single cable. Each 64 Kbps channel provides enough bandwidth for a voice communication session and is known as a DS0 or a Kilostream link. Channels can be multiplexed over a leased line to provide more bandwidth (T1, T2, T3, and so on). Also called T3, E1, and DS.

T568A/T568B Twisted pair termination pinouts defined in the ANSI/TIA/EIA 568 Commercial Building Telecommunications Standards.

test access port (TAP) Hardware device inserted into a cable to copy frames for analysis.

TCP flag Field in the header of a TCP segment designating the connection state, such as SYN, ACK, or FIN.

tcpdump command Command-line packet sniffing utility.

telnet Application protocol supporting unsecure terminal emulation for remote host management. Telnet runs over TCP port 23.

Terminal Access Controller Access Control System Plus (TACACS+) AAA protocol developed by Cisco that is often used to authenticate to administrator accounts for network appliance management.

terminal emulator Software that reproduces text input and output for a given command shell or OS.

thin AP Access point that requires a wireless controller in order to function.

threat Potential for an entity to exercise a vulnerability (that is, to breach security).

three-tiered hierarchy Paradigm to simplify network design by separating switch and router functionality and placement into three tiers each with a separate role, performance requirements, and physical topology.

throughput Amount of data transfer supported by a link in typical conditions. This can be measured in various ways with different software applications. Goodput is typically used to refer to the actual "useful" data rate at the application layer (less overhead from headers and lost packets).

time domain reflectometer (TDR) Used to measure the length of a cable run and are able to locate open and short circuits, kinks/sharp bends, and other imperfections in cables that could affect performance.

time to live (DNS) (TTL) Amount of time that the record returned by a DNS query should be cached before discarding it.

time to live (IP) (TTL) Counter field in the IP header recording the number of hops a packet can make before being dropped.

tone generator Used to identify one cable within a bundle by applying an audible signal. Also called fox and hound.

top-of-rack switch (ToR) High-performance switch model designed to implement the leaf tier in a spine and leaf topology.

topology Network specification that determines the network's overall layout, signaling, and dataflow patterns.

traceroute/tracert command Diagnostic utilities that trace the route taken by a packet as it "hops" to the destination host on a remote network. tracert is the Windows implementation, while traceroute runs on Linux.

traffic shaper Appliances and/or software that enable administrators to closely monitor network traffic and to manage that network traffic. The primary function of a traffic shaper is to optimize network media throughput to get the most from the available bandwidth. Also called a bandwidth shaper.

transceiver Component in a network interface that converts data to and from the media signalling type. Modular transceivers are designed to plug into switches and routers.

transmission control protocol (TCP) Protocol in the TCP/IP suite operating at the transport layer to provide connection-oriented, guaranteed delivery of packets.

Transport Layer OSI model layer responsible for ensuring reliable data delivery. Also called Layer 4.

Transport Layer Security (TLS) Security protocol that uses certificates for authentication and encryption to protect web communications and other application protocols.

Trivial File Transfer Protocol (TFTP) Simplified form of FTP supporting only file copying. TFTP works over UDP port 69.

troubleshooting methodology Structured approach to problem solving using identification, theory of cause, testing, planning, implementation, verification, and documentation steps.

trunk Backbone link established between switches and routers to transport frames for multiple virtual LANs (VLANs).

tunneling Encapsulating data from a local protocol within another protocol's PDU to transport it to a remote network over an intermediate network. Tunneling protocols are used in many contexts, including virtual private networks (VPNs) and transport IPv6 packets over IPv4 networks.

twinaxial Media type similar to coax but with two inner conductors to improve performance.

ultra physical contact (UPC) Fiber optic connector finishing type that uses a flat polish for the ferrule.

unicast A packet addressed to a single host. If the host is not on the local subnet, the packet must be sent via one or more routers.

Uninterruptible Power Supply (UPS) Battery-powered device that supplies AC power that an electronic device can use in the event of power failure.

unshielded twisted pair Media type that uses copper conductors arranged in pairs that are twisted to reduce interference. Typically cables are 4-pair or 2-pair.

user datagram protocol (UDP) Protocol in the TCP/IP suite operating at the transport layer to provide connectionless, non-guaranteed communication.

variable length subnet masking (VSLM) Using network prefixes of different lengths within an IP network to create subnets of different sizes.

vendor management Policies and procedures to identify vulnerabilities and ensure security of the supply chain.

virtual IP Public address of a load balanced cluster that is shared by the devices implementing the cluster.

virtual local area network (VLAN) A logically separate network, created by using switching technology. Even though hosts on two VLANs may be physically connected to the same cabling, local traffic is isolated to each VLAN so they must use a router to communicate.

Virtual Network Computing (VNC) Remote access tool and protocol. VNC is the basis of macOS screen sharing.

virtual private network (VPN) Secure tunnel created between two endpoints connected via an unsecure transport network (typically the Internet).

VLAN Hopping Exploiting a misconfiguration to direct traffic to a different VLAN without authorization.

voice gateway Means of translating between a VoIP system and legacy voice equipment and networks.

Voice over Internet Protocol (VoIP) Generic name for protocols that carry voice traffic over data networks.

voice virtual local area network (voice VLAN) Feature of VoIP handsets and switches to segregate data and voice traffic while using a single network wall port to attach the handset and the computer. Also called auxiliary VLAN.

VoIP phone Handset or software client that implements a type of voice over Internet Protocol (VoIP) to allow a user to place and receive calls.

VPN headend Appliance that incorporates advanced encryption and authentication methods in order to handle a large number of VPN tunnels, often in hub and spoke site-to-site VPN topologies. Also called a VPN concentrator.

vulnerability Weakness that could be triggered accidentally or exploited intentionally to cause a security breach.

vulnerability assessment Evaluation of a system's security and ability to meet compliance requirements based on the configuration state of the system, as represented by information collected from the system. Also called vulnerability testing.

warm site Alternate processing location that is dormant or performs noncritical functions under normal conditions, but which can be rapidly converted to a key operations site if needed.

Wi-Fi analyzer Device or software that can report characteristics of a WLAN, such as signal strength and channel utilization.

Wi-Fi Protected Access (WPA) Standards for authenticating and encrypting access to Wi-Fi networks. Also called WPA2 and WPA3.

Wide Area Network (WAN) Network scope that spans a large geographical area, incorporating more than one site and often a mix of different media types and protocols plus the use of public telecommunications networks.

wire map tester Tool to verify termination/pinouts of cable.

wireless LAN controller Device that provides wireless LAN management for multiple APs.

wireless local area network (WLAN) A network using wireless radio communications based on some variant of the 802.11 standard series.

Wireshark Widely-used protocol analyzer.

wiring diagram Documentation of connector pinouts and/or cable runs.

work recovery time (WRT) In disaster recovery, time additional to the RTO of individual systems to perform reintegration and testing of a restored or upgraded system following an event.

YAML Ain't Markup Language (YAML) Language for configuration files and applications such as Netplan and Ansible.

Z-Wave Low-power wireless communications protocol used primarily for home automation. Z-Wave uses radio frequencies in the high 800 to low 900 MHz and a mesh topology.

zero trust Security design paradigm where any request (host-to-host or container-to-container) must be authenticated before being allowed.

zero-day Vulnerability in software that is unpatched by the developer or an attack that exploits such a vulnerability.

ZigBee Low-power wireless communications open source protocol used primarily for home automation. ZigBee uses radio frequencies in the 2.4 GHz band and a mesh topology.

zone index Parameter assigned by a host to distinguish ambiguous interface addresses within a link local scope.

zone transfer Mechanism by which a secondary name server obtains a read-only copy of zone records from the primary server.

Index

Page numbers with *Italics* represent charts, graphs, and diagrams.

A

AAA architecture, 310, 326, 368, 385

AAA (authentication, authorization, and accounting) architecture, 310, 326, 368, 385

AAAA records, DNS, 237, *237*, 256

absorption, 364

acceptable use policy (AUP), 403

access control, 408–409

access control list (ACL), 7, 290, 479, 481
    authentication methods, 304
    firewall, *457*, 457–458
    issues, 332–333
    packet filtering firewall configuration, 320–321

access log, 278

access or edge layer, 195

access points (APs), 350–351
    antenna, 360, 361
    ceiling-mounted, 364
    channel bonding, 345
    fat, 355
    overcapacity issues, 363
    overlap issues, 343, 362, 369
    power levels, 362, *362*
    site survey, 352
    SSID broadcast, 351
    thin, 355
    TP-LINK SOHO, configuring, *367*
    wireless, 6
    wireless LAN controllers, *354*, 354–355
    wireless roaming and bridging, 353
    wireless site design, 351

access port, 202

accounting, in IAM, 304

ACI (adjacent channel interference), 362

acknowledgment (ACK), 210, 211, 212, 217, 342, 446

ACL. *see* access control list (ACL)

ACRF (Attenuation-to-Crosstalk Ratio, Far End), 91

ACRN (Attenuation-to-Crosstalk Ration, Near End), 91

active-active clustering, 434

Active Directory, 238, 241, 242

active FTP, 251, *251*

active-passive clustering, 434

active TAP, 61

AD (administrative distance), 162, *162*

address autoconfiguration, 143

address formats
    IPv4, 98–105, *100*, *101*
    IPv6, 139–147

addressing, in network protocol, 3

address prefixes, IPv6, 146, *146*

address (A) record, 237

Address Resolution Protocol (ARP)
    cache utility, 129–130, *130*
    inspection, dynamic (DAI), 455, *455*
    IPv4, 108–109, *109*
    IPv6, 129–130
    spoofing or cache poisoning, 441–442, *442*

address scheme design, IPv4, 119–120

ad hoc topology, 355

adjacent channel interference (ACI), 362

adjacent layer interaction, 3

administrative distance (AD), 162, *162*

ADSL (Asymmetrical DSL), 379

Advanced Encryption Standard (AES), 366

AES (Advanced Encryption Standard), 366

agents, SNMP, 276, *278*

aggregation layer, 195

Agreed Service Time, 242

agreements, 405–406
    memorandum of understanding (MOU), 406
    non-disclosure agreement (NDA), 406
    service level agreement (SLA), 405–406

AH (Authentication Header), 99, 389

AIC triad, 417

Aireplay, *445*

AirPrint, 253

alarms, 411–412
    circuit-based, 411–412
    motion-based, 412

alerts, 281

algorithms, 390

alias record, 237

alien crosstalk, 91

alphanumeric identifiers, 399

Amazon
    Elastic Compute Cloud (EC2), 466, *466*
    security of the cloud *vs.* security in the cloud, 468

American National Standards Institute (ANSI), 26, 29, 41, 475

American Registry for Internet Numbers (ARIN), 15

American Standard Code for Information Interchange (ASCII), 7, 62, 351, 449

American Wire Gauge (AWG), 25–26, 31

amplification attacks, 446

amplitude, 20

analyzer, NetFlow, 289

ANDing process, 163

Angled Physical Contact (APC), 38, 39

Angry IP Scanner, *216*
anonymous access, 313
ANSI (American National Standards Institute), 26, 29, 41, 4/5
Ansible orchestration platform, 468
ANSI/TIA/EIA 568 standard, 26, *29*, 29–30, *30*, 41, 475
antennas
    5G, 348
    booster, 352
    cable attenuation, 361
    MIMO, 344–345
    MU-MIMO, 346
    placement, 361, 459
    polarization, 360
    radio chain, 344–345
    radio frequency (RF) attenuation, 358–359
    removable, loose or disconnected, 361
    types, 360, *360*
    Wi-Fi 5, 346
anycast addressing, *111*, 112
Apache, 250
APC (Angled Physical Contact), 38, 39
API (application programming interface), 254, 467, 479
APIPA (Automatic Private IP Addressing), 118, 142, 228, 329
APNIC (Asia Pacific Network Information Centre), 15
appliance OS, 460
application layer
    in Internet model, 15
    of OSI model (layer 7), 8, *8*, 13, 15, 400, 433
    in SND, 479, *480*
application logs, 278
application programming interface (API), 254, 467, 479
application servers, 440
application-specific integrated circuit (ASIC), 195
AppSocket, 253
APs. *see* access points (APs)
Area 0 (backbone), 160
ARIN (American Registry for Internet Numbers), 15

ARP. *see* Address Resolution Protocol (ARP)
arping tool, 135
artifacts, 285
AS (autonomous system), 157, 161
ASCII (American Standard Code for Information Interchange), 7, 62, 351, 449
Asia Pacific Network Information Centre (APNIC), 15
ASIC (application-specific integrated circuit), 195
ASN (autonomous system numbers), 161
assessment reports, 398
asset, 402
asset disposal, 412–413
    data remnant removal, 412
    factory reset, 412
    Instant Secure Erase (ISE), 413
    sanitization, 412
    Secure Erase (SE), 412–413
asset tags, 411
Assured Forwarding traffic class, 285
Asterisk, 259
Asymmetrical DSL (ADSL), 379
asymmetrical routing issues, 179–180
asymmetric encryption, 308, 309
Asynchronous Transfer Mode (ATM), 291
ATM (Asynchronous Transfer Mode), 291
AT&T, 347
attacks, 440–452
    disassociation/deauthentication, 369–370
    distributed DoS (DDoS), 446
    DNS poisoning, 442–443
    general, 440–441
    human and environmental, 450–451
    malware, 447
    on-path, 441–442
    password, 448–449
    ransomware, 447, *448*
    VLAN hopping, 443
    wireless network, 444–445

attack surface, 454
attack vector, 296
attenuation, 86, 90–91, 180, 358–359
Attenuation-to-Crosstalk Ratio, Far End (ACRF), 91
Attenuation-to-Crosstalk Ration, Near End (ACRN), 91
attribute=value pairs, 312
audit logs, 278, *279*
audit reports, 397
AUP (acceptable use policy), 403
authentication
    AAA, 310, 326, 368, 385
    client, SSH, 269
    factor, 305
    in IAM, 304
    methods, 304–314
        access control list (ACL), 304
        digital certificates, 308–309, *309*
        Extensible Authentication Protocol (EAP), 309–310
        identity and access management (IAM), 304
        IEEE 802.1X Port-based Network Access Control (NAC), 310
        Kerberos, *307*, 307–308, *308*
        LDAP Secure (LDAPS), 313
        Lightweight Directory Access Protocol (LDAP), 311, *311*
        local authentication, 305–307
        multifactor, 305, 310
        Public key infrastructure (PKI), 309
        Remote Authentication Dial-in User Service (RADIUS), *310*, 311
        single sign-on (SSO), 307
        Terminal Access Controller Access Control System (TACACS+), 311

three-factor, 305
two-factor, 305
mutual, 390
open, 370
personal, 367–368
plaintext, 305–306, *306*, 313
pluggable authentication module (PAM), 307
public key, 269
reauthentication, 311
remote network access, 383–384
simple bind, 313
username/password, in SSH client, 269
weak, 405
authentication, authorization, and accounting (AAA) architecture, 310, 326, 368, 385
Authentication Header (AH), 99, 389
Authentication Service, in KDC, 307
authenticator, 456
authoritative name server, 236, 241
authorization
AAA architecture, 310, 326, 368, 385
creep, 302
remote network access, 383–384
autoconfiguration
IPv4, 118
IPv6, 143–144, 230–231
stateless address autoconfiguration (SLAAC), 230–231
automatically allocated reservation, 229
automatic garbage collectors, 413
Automatic Private IP Addressing (APIPA), 118, 142, 228, 329
automation, 468
auto-MDI/MDI-X, 68, 92
auto-negotiation of speed, 68
autonomous system (AS), 157, 161
autonomous system numbers (ASN), 161

AUX port, 92, 391, *392*
availability, 296, 417, 424
see also high availability
availability, integrity, confidentiality (AIC) triad, 417
available leases, DHCP, 228
average utilization, 290
AWG (American Wire Gauge), 25–26, 31
AxB:C notation, 345
Azure SQL Database, 466
Azure Virtual Machines, 466

B

baby giant, 292
backbone (Area 0), 160
backbone cabling, 42, *42*
backdoor, 44, 446, 447
background check, 402
backoff (random period), 21
backup
battery, 428
management, network device, 429
router, 436
state/bare metal, 429
strategies, 426
badge reader, 408, *409*
badges, 408–409
bandwidth, 85, 274, 284
2.4 GHz, 343, 344, *344*
5 GHz, 343
definition, 20
EIGRP, 160
Ethernet standards, 21, 22, 23, 37
fiber optic cabling, 21, 34, 37
management, 285–286
network metrics, 284
speed testers, 288
bare metal virtual platform, 472, *472*
BAS (building automation system), 417
baseband radio, 418
base numbering systems, 15–16, *16*
Bash, 468

basic service area (BSA), 351, 353
Basic Service Set (BSS), 350
Basic Service Set Identifier (BSSID), 350
bastion hosts, 319
battery solutions, 429
baud rate, 85
BCP (business continuity plan), 298, 401
beacon, 351
beamforming, 346–347, 348
beamwidth, 360
Behavior Aggregates, 285
behavioral factor, 305
behavioral threat research, 300
Best Effort traffic class, 285
BGP (Border Gateway Protocol), *157*, 161
BIA (business impact analysis), 298, 401
bidirectional (BiDi) transceivers, 48
binary/decimal conversion, 100–101, *101*
binary digits, 15–16, *16*
BIND DNS server software, *236*, 244, *244*
binding to the server, 313
see also authentication
biometric factor, 305
biometric reader, 408, *409*
bit depth, 284
bits, 8, 286
bits per second (bps), 284
BIX distribution frame, 43
black holes, 157, 442, 454
blackouts, 133, 276, 426
blinding attack, 44
blocked ports (BP), 197
Block I/O, 474
blocks, 42–43
block tool, 45
Bluecat, 216
bonding, 69, 432
BOOTP forwarding, 329
Border Gateway Protocol (BGP), *157*, 161
botnets, 446
bottlenecks, 274, 290
bounce (multipath interference), 363

bounded media, 4
BP (blocked ports), 197
BPDU (bridge protocol data unit), 196
bps (bits per second), 284
branch office
    datacenter access, 481–482
    internetwork, designing, *182*, 182–183, *183*
    routers, 388
bridge protocol data unit (BPDU), 196
bridges/bridging, 6, *54*, 54–55, *55*, 353, 354
    access points (APs), 354
    bridge protocol data unit (BPDU), 196
    network devices, deploying, *54*, 54–55, *55*
    point-to-point wireless connections, 360
    spanning tree protocol (STP), *197*, 197–198
bring your own device (BYOD) policy, 335, 363, 403, *404*
broadband speed checkers, 288
broadcast, 109
broadcast address, 60, *60*, 109–111, *110*
broadcast domain, 55, *55*
broadcast storm, 198, 332
brownouts, 133, 276
browser error messages, 334
brute force, in password cracking, 449
BSA (basic service area), 351, 353
BSS (Basic Service Set), 350
BSSID (Basic Service Set Identifier), 350
buffer, of optical fiber, 34
building automation system (BAS), 417
burned-in addresses, 59–60
bursty data transfer, 284
business continuity, 424
business continuity plan (BCP), 298, 401
business impact analysis (BIA), 298, 401
bus topology, 190–191, *191*

bwping, 287
BYOD (bring your own device) policy, 335, 363, 403, *404*
bytes, 8, 286

C

CA (certification authority), 250, 309, 370
CAB (Change Advisory Board), 397
cable
    application issues, 91–92
    broadband, 380
    Cat standards, 26–28
    certifier, *89*, 90
    connectivity issues, 86–87
    crimper, 45
    cutting blades, 44, 45
    management, 42–44
    modem, 380, *380*
    provider links, 380
    stripper, 44
    testers, 88–89
Cable Access TV (CATV), 31, 38, 380
cabled media, 4
Cable Modem Termination System (CMTS), 380
cache-only servers, 242
cache poisoning, ARP, 441–442, *442*
caching, DNS, 242
CAM (content addressable memory), 68
cameras, 411, *411*
campus area network (CAN), 187
CAM table, 68
CAN (campus area network), 187
Canonical Name (CNAME) (or alias) record, 237, *237*
canonical notation, 140
captive portal, 370, 459
    issues, 370
CAPWAP (Control And Provisioning of Wireless Access Points), 355
CARP (Common Address Redundancy Protocol), 434
Carrier Ethernet, 380

Carrier Sense Multiple Access with Collision Avoidance (CSMA/CA), 342, *343*, 346, 362
Carrier Sense Multiple Access with Collision Detection (CSMA/CD), 21, 22, *22*, 60
Catalyst platform, 65
Cat cable standards, 26–28
    Fast Ethernet, 22–23
    Gigabit Ethernet standards, 23, *23*
    for network media, *27*, 27–28
    twisted pair copper cabling, 20, 22, 28–29
CATV (Cable Access TV), 31, 38, 380
CCI (co-channel interference), 362
CCK (Complementary Code Keying), 344
CCMP (Counter Mode with Cipher Block Chaining Message Authentication Code Protocol), 366
C&C or C2 (command and control) network, 446
CCTV (Closed-Circuit Television) network, 411, *411*
CDMA (Code Division Multiple Access), 347
CDMA2000/Evolution Data Optimized (EV-DO), 348
CDNs (content delivery networks), 479
cellular networks, 418
    2G, 347
    3G, 348
    4G, 348, 418
    5G, 348, 431
    digital communications standards, 347–348
cellular radio, 347
central node, 5
CE (customer edge) router, 171, 291, 376
certificate issues, untrusted, *333*, 333–334, *334*
certification authority (CA), 250, 309, 370
Change Advisory Board (CAB), 397

change management, 396–397

channel, 343
- bandwidth, 343, 344, *344*
- bonding, 345, *345*
- interference, 362–363
- link, 86–87
- overlap, 362
- utilization, 362–363

Channel Service Unit/ Data Service Unit (CSU/DSU), 377

character set conversion, 8

checksum
- TCP, 210
- UDP, 213

Chef orchestration platform, 468

choke firewall, 319

choke point, 319

CI (configuration item), 396, 398

CIA Triad, 296, 417

CIA (Confidentiality, Integrity, and Availability) Triad, 296, 417

CIDR (Classless Inter-Domain Routing), 162–164, *163–164*

circuit-based alarms, 411–412

Circuit Switched Data (CSD), 347

Cisco
- Adaptive Security Appliance (ASA), *322, 324*
- Adaptive Security Device Manager (ASDM), *322*
- Aironet, 353
- Discovery Protocol (CDP), 203
- DMVPN, 388
- EtherChannel, 432
- Gateway Load Balancing Protocol (GLBP), 435
- IOS, 66, 460
- Layer 2 Tunneling Protocol (L2TP), 385
- Lightweight Access Point Protocol (LWAPP), 355
- NetFlow, 288–289, *289*
- network icons, 400, *400*
- Secure Access Control Server, 311
- switches, 65, *67, 69, 70*
- TACACS+, 310, 311, 368
- three-tiered hierarchy, 194

Unified Communications Manager, 259

wireless LAN controller, 354, *368*

Citrix, 386, 472

cladding, of optical fiber, 34

Class A thru D addresses, 117, 118

classful/classless addressing, *116*, 116–117, *117*

Class I/Class II (8.1/8.2) cable, 28

Classless Inter-Domain Routing (CIDR), 162–164, *163–164*

Class of Service (CoS), 71, 286

cleartext, 258, 448, *449*

Clear To Send (CTS), 342

CLI (command line interface), 66, 391

client authentication, SSH, 269

client disassociation issues, 369–370

clientless VPNs, 387

client ports, 208

client-server network, 186

client-to-site VPNs, 385–386

Closed-Circuit Television (CCTV) network, 411, *411*

cloud concepts, 464–470
- cloud responsibility matrix, 468–469
- cloud service providers (CSPs), 465
- connectivity options, 467
- deployment models, 465
- elasticity, 464
- hosting, 249
- infrastructure as code (IaC), 467–468
- scalability, 464
- security implications, 468–469
- service models, 465–467

clustering
- active-passive/active-active, 434
- load balancing, 433–434, *434*

cluster services, 426

CMG/MMG, 30

CM/MP, 30

CMP/MMP, 30

CMR/MPR, 30

CMS (Configuration Management System), 396

CMTS (Cable Modem Termination System), 380

CNAME (Canonical Name) (or alias) record, 237, *237*

CNAs (converged network adapters), 475

Coarse Wavelength Division Multiplexing (CWDM), 48

coaxial (or coax) cable, 31, *31*

co-channel interference (CCI), 362

Code Division Multiple Access (CDMA), 347

cold site, 427

collector, NetFlow, 289

collision detection mechanism, 22

collision domains, 21–22, *22*

colocation, 409, 467, 482

colon delimiters, 140

color-coding, *25, 29, 39, 43*

command and control (C&C or C2) network, 446

command line interface (CLI), 66, 391

commands, SSH, 270

Common Address Redundancy Protocol (CARP), 434

Common Vulnerabilities and Exposures (CVE), 299, *299*

community cloud infrastructure, 465

community port, 456

company assets, retrieving, 402

Complementary Code Keying (CCK), 344

compulsory tunneling, 387, *387*

Confidentiality, Integrity, and Availability (CIA) Triad, 296, 417

configuration baseline, 396

configuration file, 429

configuration item (CI), 396, 398

configuration management, 396

Configuration Management System (CMS), 396

congestion, 285, 332

connections, transport layer, 208–209, *209*

connection teardown, TCP, 212, *212*

connectivity options, cloud, 467

connectors
    8P8C, 28
    copper cable, 31, *31*
    DB-9, 92
    for faster network applications, 27
    fiber optic cable, 35–37
    GG-45, 27, *27*
    Insulation Displacement Connector (IDC), 398
    Local Connector (LC), 36, *36*, *37*
    loss budget, 180
    Registered Jack (RJ), *28*, 28–29, *29*, *37*, *44*, *45*, *45*
    Straight Tip (ST), 35, *36*, *37*
    Subscriber Connector (SC), 36, *36*, *37*
    TERA, 27, *27*, 28
    twisted pair, 28–29

console cable, 92, *92*

console port, 92, 391, *392*

consumer-grade smart devices, 416, 419

content addressable memory (CAM), 68

content delivery networks (CDNs), 479

contention, 362

content switch (layer 7 switch), 433

continuity (open), problem of, 89

continuity of operations plan (COOP), 401

continuous availability, 424

Control And Provisioning of Wireless Access Points (CAPWAP), 355

control plane, 286

control plane policing, 458

control system, 416

Converged Enhanced Ethernet, 475

converged network adapters (CNAs), 475

convergence, 156–157

COOP (continuity of operations plan), 401

Coordinated Universal Time (UTC), 271

copper cabling, 20, 25–33
    Cat cable standards, 26–28, *27*
    coaxial cable, 31, *31*
    connectors, 31, *31*
    copper termination standards, 29–30, *30*
    plenum- and riser-rated, 30
    shielded and screened twisted pair, 26
    termination standards, 29–30, *30*
    twinaxial, 32, *32*
    twisted pair connectors, 28–29
    unshielded twisted pair, *25*, 25–26

core, of optical fiber, 34

core/distribution switch, 195, *195*

core layer, 196

correlation, 300

CoS (Class of Service), 71, 286

Counter Mode with Cipher Block Chaining Message Authentication Code Protocol (CCMP), 366

CPE (customer premises equipment), 14, 377, 378, 380, 483

CPU, 274

CPUID, *275*

crashed service, 332

CRC (cyclic redundancy check), 59, 291

crossed pair (TX/RX reverse), 90

crossover patch cord, 92

crosstalk issues, 91

crypto erase, 413

cryptographic concepts
    hashes, 305–306, *306*, 389, 449
    keys, 308–309, 408, 410
    Open Shortest Path First (OSPF), 161
    plain text, 161, 449
    Wi-Fi encryption standards, 366

Cryptolocker, 447

crypto-malware, 447

CSD (Circuit Switched Data), 347

CSMA/CA (Carrier Sense Multiple Access with Collision Avoidance), 342, *343*, 346, 362

CSMA/CD (Carrier Sense Multiple Access with Collision Detection), 21, 22, *22*, 60

CSU/DSU (Channel Service Unit/ Data Service Unit), 377

Ctrl+C, 61, 131, 219

CTS (Clear To Send), 342

customer edge (CE) router, 171, 291, 376

customer premises equipment (CPE), 14, 377, 378, 380, 483

CVE (Common Vulnerabilities and Exposures), 299, *299*

CWDM (Coarse Wavelength Division Multiplexing), 48

cyclic redundancy check (CRC), 59, 291

D

DaaS (Desktop as a Service), 467

DAC (Direct Attach Copper), 32, *32*

Daemon, SSH, 270

data
    breach, 404
    compression, 8
    exfiltration attack, 441
    historian, 417
    length, 210
    loss prevention, 404, *404*
    plane, 286
    remnant removal, 412
    service units, 376
    switches, 195
    transfer, 405
    transport protocol, 260

database services, 254

datacenter, 187, 429

Datacenter Ethernet, 475

datacenter network architecture, 478–485
    access types, 481–482

Multiprotocol Label Switching (MPLS), *482*, 482–483
  overlay networks, 479
  software defined networking (SDN), 479–480
  software-defined WAN (SD-WAN), 483–484, *484*
  spine and leaf topology, 480–481, *481*
  traffic flows, 478–479
datagram header, IPv4, 98–99, *99*
Datagram Transport Layer Security (DTLS), 250
data link (layer 2), of OSI model, 5, 5–6, *8*, 11, *11*, 85, 400
  addressing and forwarding, IPv4, *106*, 106–107
  Point-to-Point Protocol (PPP), 384
  switches, in deploying network devices, 55–56, *56*
  WAN, 376, 378
Data Link protocol frame, 154
data loss prevention (DLP), 404, *404*
Data Over Cable Service Interface Specification (DOCSIS), 380
Data Terminal Equipment (DTE), 377, *378*
dB (decibel), 86, 90, 180, 358–359
dBi (decibel isotropic), 360
dBm (decibels per milliwatt), 180, 359
DCS (distributed control system), 417
DDI (DHCP, DNS, and IPAM), 216
DDoS (distributed denial of service) attacks, 433, 446
deauthentication, 369–370
  attacks, 445
decapsulation, 3, *3*
decibel (dB), 86, 90, 180, 358–359
decibel isotropic (dBi), 360
decibels per milliwatt (dBm), 180, 359
decimal numbering, 15–16, *16*

declarative tools, 468
dedicated server, 249
default gateways, 108
  see also gateways
default routes, 151
default VLAN, 456
defense in depth, 325–326
degaussing, 412
degrees, beamwidth measured in, 360
delay, 85, 160
demarcation point (demarc), 14, 42, *42*, 377
demilitarized zone (DMZ), 319
denial of service (DoS) attacks, 332, 441
dense wavelength division multiplexing (DWDM), 48, 381
deployment models, cloud, 465
designated ports (DP), 197
Desktop as a Service (DaaS), 467
desktop switches, 66
destination (routing entry), 150
destination host unreachable, 131
destination port
  TCP, 209
  UDP, 213
detection-based devices, 410–411
device configuration review, 176, 177
device hardening, 453–454
DHCP. *see* Dynamic Host Configuration Protocol (DHCP)
DHCP, DNS, and IPAM (DDI), 216
DHCPDISCOVER packet, 226
DHCPOFFER packet, 227
DHCPv6 server, *231*, *127*, 144, 230–231
dialog, 8
dial-up modem, 92
dictionary, in password cracking, 449
Differentiated Services (DiffServ), 285
  DiffServ Code Point (DSCP), 285
  DiffServ-compatible router, 285

dig (Domain Information Groper), 244, *244*
digital certificate, 308–309, *309*
digital subscriber line (DSL), 10, 107, 376
  DSL modems, *378*, 378–379
  DSL types, 379
Digital Video Broadcast Satellite (DVB-S), 381
Direct Attach Copper (DAC), 32, *32*
direction (filter expression), 62
directional antenna, 360, *360*
directionality, 360
directly connected routes, 151
directors, 475
directory schema, 312
directory services, 312
Direct Sequence Spread Spectrum (DSSS), 344
dirty optical cables, 93
disassociation, 369–370
disaster recovery, 424–430
  availability, defined, 424
  facilities and infrastructure support, 427–428
  fault tolerance, 425–426
  high availability, *424*, 424–425
  network device backup management, 429
  plan (DRP), 401, 426
  power management, 428–429
  recovery sites, 426–427
  redundancy, 426
discards/drops, 290
dish or grid (parabolic) form factors, 360, *360*
distance specification and limitations, 85–86
distance vector, 156, *157*
distinguished name (DN), 312, 313
distributed control system (DCS), 417
distributed denial of service (DDoS) attacks, 433, 446
distributed reflection DoS (DRDoS) attacks, 446

distribution frame, 41–42, 398–399
    Intermediate Distribution Frame (IDF), 399
    Main Distribution Frame (MDF), 398
    site survey report, 399
distribution or aggregation layer, 195
Distribution System (DS), 353
diverse paths, 431
divide and conquer approach, 80
DKIM (DomainKeys Identified Mail), 238
DLP (data loss prevention), 404, *404*
DMVPN (dynamic multipoint VPN), 388–389
DMZ (demilitarized zone), 319
DN (distinguished name), 312, 313
DNS. *see* Domain Name System (DNS)
DNSSEC, 241
DOCSIS (Data Over Cable Service Interface Specification), 380
Domain Information Groper (dig), 244, *244*
DomainKeys Identified Mail (DKIM), 238
Domain Name System (DNS), 137, 145, *234*, 234–235
    AAAA records, 237, *237*, 256
    caching, 242
    Canonical Name (CNAME) (or alias) record, 237
    Domain Information Groper (dig), 244, *244*
    hierarchy, *234*
    host address, 237
    incorrect, 137
    internal *vs.* external, 242–243
    iterative lookup, 235
    Mail Exchange (MX) record, 237
    name resolution, 235, *235*, 242, 243–244, 330–331
    name servers, 241–242
    nslookup, 243, *243*

pointer (PTR) record, *238*, 238–239
    poisoning, 442–443, *443*
    recursive lookup, 235
    recursive querying, 235
    resource records, 236, *236*
    reverse lookup zones, 239
    reverse querying, 238–239
    server configuration, 241–242
    server types, 241–242
    Service (SRV) record, *238*, *238*
    services, 241–245
    suites that integrate with, 216
    Text (TXT) record, 238
    UDP transport protocol, 237
    zones, 241–242
domain suffix, 228, 233
domain widget, 233
DORA process, 227
DoS (denial of service) attacks, 332, 441
dotted decimal notation, 100, *100*
double-byte/octet, 140
downgrading, 460
downlink
    MU-MIMO (DL MU-MIMO), 346–347
    speeds, 288, 348, 379, 380
DP (designated ports), 197
DRDoS (distributed reflection DoS) attacks, 446
drop, 44, 290
DRS (Dynamic Rate Switching/Selection), 352
DS (Distribution System), 353
DS0, 377
DSL. *see* digital subscriber line (DSL)
DSSS (Direct Sequence Spread Spectrum), 344
DTE (Data Terminal Equipment), 377, *378*
DTLS (Datagram Transport Layer Security), 250
dual band AP, 345
dual-polarized antennas, 360
dual stack, 145, *145*
duplex, 290

duplex mismatch, 87
DVB-S (Digital Video Broadcast Satellite), 381
DWDM (dense wavelength division multiplexing), 48, 381
dynamic ARP inspection (DAI), 455, *455*
dynamic client port number *(n)*, 251
Dynamic Frequency Selection (DFS), 343
Dynamic Host Configuration Protocol (DHCP)
    DHCPv6 server configuration, *231*, 230–231
    IP helper, 230
    IP interface configuration in Windows, 126, 127
    IPv6 interface autoconfiguration, 143
    lease, 118
    lease time and available leases, 227, 228
    network layer functions, 12, *12*, *13*
    options configuration, 228–229
    relay, 229
    reservations and exclusions, 229
    rogue server issues, 330
    scope exhaustion, 329
    server and scope exhaustion issues, 329–330
    server configuration, 227–228
    service and security issues, 329–330
    small office/home office (SOHO) routers, 226
    snooping, 455
    suites that integrate with, 216
dynamic multipoint VPN (DMVPN), 388–389
Dynamic Rate Switching/Selection (DRS), 352
dynamic routing, 156–170
    administrative distance (AD), 162, *162*
    Border Gateway Protocol (BGP), 161

Classless Inter-Domain Routing (CIDR), 162–164, *163–164*
convergence, 156–157
dynamic routing protocols, 156–157
Enhanced IGRP (EIGRP), 159–160
Exterior Gateway Protocol (EGP), 157, *157*
Interior Gateway Protocol (IGP), 157, *157*, 159–160
Open Shortest Path First (OSPF), 160–161, *161*
protocol, 108
Routing Information Protocol (RIP), 157–159, *158*, *159*
topology and metrics, 156
variable length subnet masking (VLSM), 164–167, *165*, *166*, *167*

E

EAP (Extensible Authentication Protocol), 309–310, 368, 459
EAPoL (Extensible Authentication Protocol over LAN), 456
EAP over Wireless (EAPoW), 368
EAPoW (EAP over Wireless), 368
east-west traffic, 478–479
EBGP (Exterior BGP), 161
EC2 (Elastic Compute Cloud), 466, *466*
ECMP (Equal Cost Multipathing), 481
edge firewall, 319
edge layer, 195
edge routers, 151, 161, 171–172, *172*, 173, *173*
    see also small office/home office (SOHO) routers
Effective Isotropic Radiated Power (EIRP), 361
EGP (Exterior Gateway Protocol), 157, *157*
egress traffic or filtering, 321

EIA (Electronic Industries Alliance), 26, 27, 29, 38, 39, 41
EIGRP (Enhanced Interior Gateway Routing Protocol), 99, *157*, 159–160
EIRP (Effective Isotropic Radiated Power), 361
Ekahau Site Survey, 353, *353*
E-LAN, 381
Elastic Compute Cloud (EC2), 466, *466*
elasticity, 464
electrical, monitoring, 276
electromagnetic interference (EMI), 31, 91, *91*, 364
electromagnetic radiation, 20
Electronic Industries Alliance (EIA), 26, 27, 29, 38, 39, 41
E-line, 381
email application error messages, 334
email server, 7, 237, 308, 433, 440
EMI (electromagnetic interference), 31, 91, *91*, 364
EMM (enterprise mobility management) suites, 335
employee training, security awareness, 402, 413–141
Encapsulating Security Payload (ESP), 99, *389*, 389–390
encapsulation, 3, *3*
    errors, 291
    protocols, 384
    remote network access, 384
encoding methods, 85
encryption, 8, 13
    end-to-end, 449
    key, 447, 454, *454*
    password attacks, 449
    protocol mismatch issues, 369
    ransomware, 447
    sniffing attacks, 454
endpoint security, 454–456
    DHCP snooping, 455
    dynamic ARP inspection (DAI), 455, *455*
    MAC filtering, 454–455
    Neighbor Discovery (ND) Inspection, 455

Port Security/IEEE 802.1X PNAC, 455–456
Router Advertisement (RA) Guard, 455
switch ports, disabling unneeded, 454
endspan (or endpoint) PSE, 71
end systems, 5, 86, 92
end-to-end encryption, 449
end-to-end layer, 7
end-user devices, 260
Enhanced Interior Gateway Routing Protocol (EIGRP), 99, *157*, 159–160
enhanced quad small form-factor pluggable (QSFP+), 47
enhanced small form-factor pluggable (SFP+), 47
enterprise authentication, 368, *368*
enterprise LANs, 187
enterprise mobility management (EMM) suites, 335
enterprise networks, 10, 174, 186, 187, 216
enterprise risk management (ERM), 297
enterprise WAN, 376
entrance facilities, 42, *42*, 377
enumeration attacks, 440
environmental monitoring, 275–276
ephemeral ports, 208
Equal Cost Multipathing (ECMP), 481
ERM (enterprise risk management), 297
error checking, 59
error messages
    browsers and email applications, 334
    ICMP Time Exceeded, 179
    ICMPv6, 144
    ping, 131
error rate, 290
ESA (extended service area), 351, 353
ESP (Encapsulating Security Payload), 99, *389*, 389–390
ESSID (Extended SSID), 351
EtherChannel, 432

Ethernet
address (EA), 59
Fast, 22–23
frame, 4, 59, *59*, 291–292
Gigabit (*see* Gigabit
Ethernet)
headers, 59, *59*
over copper, 380–381
over fiber, 380
port, 12
switches, 11, *65*, 65–66, *66*
technology, 10
trunks, 291
Ethernet cabling, deploying,
41–49
cable management, 42–44
fiber distribution panels
and fusion splicing, 45–46
structured cabling system,
41–42
termination tools, 45
transceivers, 46–47
wavelength division
multiplexing, 48
wiring tools and
techniques, 44
Ethernet II, 291
Ethernet standards, 20–24, *27*
10BASE-T, 21, 22–23, *27*
10GBASE-CR, 32
10GBASE-LR, *37*, 47
10GBASE-SR, *37*, 47
10GBASE-T, *23*, *27*
10GBASE-Tv, *27*
40GBASE-CR4, 32
40GBASE-T, *23*, *27*
100BASE-FX, *37*
100BASE-SX, *37*
100BASE-TX, 22–23, *27*
1000BASE-LX, *37*
1000BASE-SX, *37*
1000BASE-T, *23*, *27*
Cat cable standards, 26–28
Gigabit Ethernet standards,
23, *23*
IEEE 802.3 Ethernet
standards, 21
media access control and
collision domains, 21–22, *22*
network data transmission,
20–21
over fiber, 37, *37*

Ethernet switching, deploying,
51–73
auto-MDI/MDIX, 68
Ethernet switching features,
deploying, 65–72
Ethernet switch types,
65–66
flow control, 71
jumbo frames, 70–71
MAC address table,
68–69, *69*
network devices, deploying,
52–57
network interfaces,
explaining, 57–64
port aggregation, 69
port mirroring, 69–70, *70*
port security, 69
power over Ethernet, 71
switch interface
configuration, 66–68
EtherTypes, 60
ethical hacking, 301
ETSI, 474
EUI (extended unique
identifier), 59
EUI-48 (extended unique
identifier-48), 59
EUI-64 (extended unique
identifier-64), 59
EV-DO (CDMA2000/Evolution
Data Optimized), 348
event management, 280–282
EventSentry SIEM, *281*
evil twins, 444–445
Evolved High Speed Packet
Access (HSPA+), 348
exclusions, DHCP, 229
Expedited Forwarding traffic
class, 285
explicit deny, 457
explicit TLS (FTPES), 252
exploits, 298
exporter, NetFlow, 289
extended service area (ESA),
351, 353
Extended SSID (ESSID), 351
extended unique identifier
(EUI), 59
extended unique identifier-48
(EUI-48), 59

extended unique identifier-64
(EUI-64), 59
Extensible Authentication
Protocol (EAP), 309–310,
368, 459
Extensible Authentication
Protocol over LAN (EAPoL), 456
extensible markup language
(XML), 429
Exterior BGP (EBGP), 161
Exterior Gateway Protocol
(EGP), 157, *157*
external DNS zones, 242–243
external threats, 300
external virtual switch, 472

F

facilities and infrastructure
support, 427–428
fire suppression, 427–428
HVAC, 427
factory reset, 412
Far End Crosstalk (FEXT), 91
Fast Ethernet, 22–23
fast link pulse, 23
fat AP, 355
fault, 425
fault tolerance, 425–426
FC. *see* Fiber Channel (FC)
FCS (Frame Check
Sequence), 59
ferrule, 38
FEXT (Far End Crosstalk), 91
FHRP. *see* first hop redundancy
protocol (FHRP)
fiber, Ethernet standards over,
37, *37*
fiber distribution panels,
45–46, *46*
fiberglass rods (strength
members), 34
fiber light meter, 93
Fiber Optic Association
(FOA), 180
fiber optic cable, 20–21
connector types, 35–37
considerations, 34
dirty, 93
Ethernet standards, 37, *37*
installation, *38*, 38–39, *39*
multimode fiber, 35

single mode fiber, 35
testing tools, 93
types, 34–40
fiber optic patch cords, 38, *38*
Fiber to the Curb (FTTC), 377
Fiber to the Home (FTTH), 377
Fiber to the Node (FTTN), 377
Fiber to the Premises (FTTP), 377
Fiber to the X (FTTx), 377
Fiber to the x (FTTx) multiple subscriber networks, 38
Fiber Channel (FC), 475
over Ethernet (FCoE), 475
Switched Fabric (FC-SW), 475
field devices, 417
file and print services, 253
File Transfer Protocol (FTP), 251–252
active *vs.* passive, 251, *251*
Trivial File Transfer Protocol (TFTP), 252
filter, 379
filter expressions, 62
filter syntax, 62
fingerprinting, 220
attacks, 440
fingerprint reader, 305
finishing type, 38–39, *39*
FIN segment, 210, 212, 213
fire extinguishers, 427
fire safety standards, 30
fire-stopped, 30
fire suppression, 427–428
fire triangle, 427
firewall chain (forward), 457
firewalls
access control list, 7
chains, 457–458
misconfigured, 332–333
in Network Function Virtualization, 473
in network layer, 6
packet filtering, 320–321
ping tests, 137
rules, ACL configuration and, *457*, 457–458
selection and placement, 321–322, *322*
in SOHO router, 13

stateful inspection, 251, 321, *321*
in transport layer, 7
uses and types, *320*, 320–321
firmware
automatic garbage collectors, 413
management, 460
updating (flashing the chip), 460
first hop redundancy protocol (FHRP), *435*, 435–436
Hot Standby Router Protocol (HSRP), 435, *435*
Virtual Router Redundancy Protocol (VRRP), 436
fixed address assignment, 229
fixed switches, 66, *66*
flags
TCP, 210
UDP, 210
flapping, 157, 198, 290, 353
flash devices, 412, 413
flashing the chip, 460
flash memory, 413, 460
flooding, 68, 276
flow control, 71
flow label, 140
Fluorinated Ethylene Polymer (FEP), 30
FOA (Fiber Optic Association), 180
foiled twisted pair (FTP) cable, 26
foiled/unshielded twisted pair (F/UTP) cable, *23*, 26, *27*
foil outer shield/foiled twisted pair (S/FTP) cable, 26, *27*
Follow TCP Stream, 221
footprinting attacks, 440
forced proxy, 323
Foreign Exchange Office (FXO) gateway, 262, 263
forward (firewall chain), 457
forward proxies, 322–323
Fox and Hound, 90
fps (frames per second), 284
FQDN (fully qualified domain name), 233–234, 330
fragmentation, 154

Frame Check Sequence (FCS), 59
frame/framing, 5, 59, *59*
BIX distribution frame, 43
Data Link protocol frame, 154
distribution, 41–42, 398–399
errors, 291–292
Ethernet, 70–71, 291–292
Intermediate Distribution Frame (IDF), 399
length, 60
Main Distribution Frame (MDF), 398
PAUSE frames, 71
SSID broadcast and beacon frame, 351
Type II frames, 60
WAN, 291
frames per second (fps), 284
FreeRADIUS, 311
free space path loss, 358
frequency band, 343
FTPES (explicit TLS), 252
FTPS (implicit TLS), 252
FTP servers, 440
FTTC (Fiber to the Curb), 377
FTTH (Fiber to the Home), 377
FTTN (Fiber to the Node), 377
FTTP (Fiber to the Premises), 377
FTTx (Fiber to the X), 377
F-type connectors, 31, *31*
full mesh, 189
full- or half-duplex operation, 68
full tunnel, 385–386, *386*
fully qualified domain name (FQDN), 233–234, 330
fusion splicing/splicer, 45–46
F/UTP (foiled/unshielded twisted pair) cable, *23*, 26, *27*
FXO (Foreign Exchange Office) gateway, 262, 263

G

gain, 360
Gateway Load Balancing Protocol (GLBP), 435
gateway/next hop (routing entry), 150

gateways
    default, 108
    DHCP, 126, 127, 131, 134, 135, 136, 137
    IP configuration, 126, 127, 131, 134, 135, 136, 137
    IPv4, 107, 107–108, 108
    unreachable, 442
    VoIP, 262
    VPN, 385
GBIC (Gigabit Interface Converter) form factor, 47
Gbps (gigabits per second), 21
general attacks, 440–441
General Packet Radio Services/ Enhanced Data Rates for GSM Evolution (GPRS/EDGE), 347
General Positioning System (GPS), 271–272, 272
general purpose (nonplenum) cabling, 30
Generic Routing Encapsulation (GRE), 99, 146, 384, 389, 482
Generic Security Services Application Program Interface (GSSAPI), 269
geofencing, 459
GeoIP, 332
Get/Get Next commands, SNMP, 277, 277
giant frame errors, 291
Gigabit Ethernet
    auto MDI/MDI-X, 68, 92
    CAT cable standards, 27
    fiber optic connectors, 36
    Gigabit Interface Converter (GBIC), 47
    standards, 23, 23
    switches, 55
Gigabit Interface Converter (GBIC) form factor, 47
gigabits per second (Gbps), 21
GLBP (Gateway Load Balancing Protocol), 435
global addressing, IPv6, 141–142, 142
global configuration mode, 66
Global System for Mobile Communication (GSM), 347
goodput, 85, 358
Google
    App Engine, 466

public DNS server, 243, 243
time source, 272
Workspace, 466
GPRS/EDGE (General Packet Radio Services/Enhanced Data Rates for GSM Evolution), 347
GPS (General Positioning System), 271–272, 272
graphical user interface (GUI)
    database services, 254
    IP configuration, 126, 128
    IP scanning, 217
    remote desktop protocol, 271, 386
grayware, 447
GRE (Generic Routing Encapsulation), 99, 146, 384, 389, 482
greenfield mode, 345
group authentication, 367
GSM (Global System for Mobile Communication), 347
GSSAPI (Generic Security Services Application Program Interface), 269
guest network isolation, 459
guest OS, 471, 471, 472
GUI. see graphical user interface (GUI)

H

hacking the human. see social engineering
half-open scanning, 219, 220
hard disk drives (HDDs), data remnant removal form, 412
hardening, 297, 453–461
    control plane policing, 458
    device and service, 453–454
    endpoint security and switchport protection, 454–456
    firewall rules and ACL configuration, 457–458
    IoT access considerations, 459–460
    patch and firmware management, 460
    secure configuration, 453–454
    security policies, 402

VLAN and PVLAN best practices, 456
hardware
    access control, 408
    addresses, 5
    control, 408
    failure issues, 133–134
    problems, 80, 87
    redundant, 433–434, 434
    VoIP PBX, 259
hashes, cryptographic, 305–306, 306, 389, 449
hash function, 390
HCCs (horizontal cross-connects), 42
HDDs (hard disk drives), data remnant removal form, 412
HDLC (High-level Data Link Control), 291, 378
headends, VPN, 388–389
headers, 140, 248–249, 249
health policy, 326
heating, ventilation, and air conditioning (HVAC), 30, 417, 427
heat maps, 353, 353
Hertz, 284
heterogeneous networks, 6
hexadecimal notation, 15–16, 16
hex digits, 16
HFC (hybrid fiber coax), 380
hierarchical star-mesh topology, 192
hierarchical star topology, 191
high availability, 431–437
    availability, defined, 424
    described, 424, 424–425
    first hop redundancy protocol (FHRP), 435, 435–436
    link aggregation/NIC teaming, 432, 432
    load balancers, 433, 433
    Maximum Tolerable Downtime (MTD) metric, 424, 424–425
    multipathing, 431
    redundant hardware/ clusters, 433–434, 434
High-level Data Link Control (HDLC), 291, 378

HMIs (human-machine interfaces), 417
holddown timer, 179
home/residential networks, 187
honeypots, 326
hop, 131, *131*
    count, 153, *153*, 157, 179
    limit, 140
    next, 143, 150
    Per Hop Behavior (PHB), 285
horizontal cabling, 41–42, *42*
horizontal cross-connects (HCCs), 42
horizontal/scaling out, 464
host, 233, 234, 243
    address, 237
        IPv4, 104, *104*
        IPv6, *134–135*
    bus adapter (HBA), 475
    discovery, 216, 217, 219
    hypervisors, 471, *471*
    IDs, 6
    key, SSH, 268, *269*
    name, 233–234
    nodes, 5
    number (host ID), 100
    OS, 460, 471–472
    port, 202
    receiving, 7
hosted private cloud infrastructure, 465
hosting packages, 249–250
host-to-host layer, 7
hot site, 427
hotspots, 187, 370
Hot Standby Router Protocol (HSRP), 435, *435*
HR (Human Resources), 402
HSPA+ (Evolved High Speed Packet Access), 348
HSRP (Hot Standby Router Protocol), 435, *435*
HTML (HyperText Markup Language), 248
HTML5 VPN, 387
HTTP. *see* HyperText Transfer Protocol (HTTP)
HTTP Secure (HTTPS), 250, *250*
    captive portal issues, 370
    firewall rules, *457*

forward proxies, 322
Internet Message Access Protocol (IMAP), 258
    management interface, 392
hub, 5, 53–54, *54*, *55*, 92, 416
hub and spoke, 189, *388*, 388–389, 482
human and environmental attacks, 450–451
    phishing attacks, 450, *450*
    piggybacking, 451
    shoulder surfing attack, 451
    tailgating, 451
human factor, 305
human-machine interfaces (HMIs), 417
Human Resources (HR), 402
humidity, monitoring, 276
HVAC (heating, ventilation, and air conditioning), 30, 417, 427
HWMONITOR, *275*
HWMP (Hybrid Wireless Mesh Protocol), 356
hybrid cloud infrastructure, 465
hybrid fiber coax (HFC), 380
hybrid protocol, 156, *157*, 159
hybrid topology, 191–192, *192*
Hybrid Wireless Mesh Protocol (HWMP), 356
HyperTerminal, 391
HyperText Markup Language (HTML), 248
HyperText Transfer Protocol (HTTP), 4, 7, 13, 248–250
    described, 248
    headers and payload, 248–249, *249*
    Secure Sockets Layer (SSL), 250
    Transport Layer Security (TLS), 250
    web servers, 249–250
    see also HTTP Secure (HTTPS)
hypervisor, *471*, 471–472, *472*

I

IAM (identity and access management), 304, 402

IANA (Internet Assigned Numbers Authority), 15, 99, 161, 208
IBGP (Interior BGP), 161
IBSS (Independent Basic Service Set), 355
ICANN (Internet Corporation for Assigned Names and Numbers), 15, 234
ICMP (Internet Control Message Protocol), 99, 130–131, *131*
ICMP Echo Request, 177
ICMP Time Exceeded error messages, 179
ICS (industrial control system), 417, 419
ICV (Integrity Check Value), 389, *389*
IDC (insulation-displacement connection), 42, 43, *43*, 45, 398
identification, in IAM, 304
identity and access management (IAM), 304, 402
IDS (intrusion detection system), 7, 70, 326–327, *327*
IDs, VLAN, 200–201
IEC (International Electrotechnical Commission), 26, 27, 35
IEEE 802 standards, 342–347
    802.1ax, 432
    802.1p, 286
    802.1Q, 201–203, *202*, 286, 291–292, 443, 456
    802.1Qbb, 71
    802.1X, 310, 368, *368*, 455–456
    802.3, 21, 342
    802.3ad, 432
    802.3af, 71
    802.3at, 71, 92
    802.3bt, 71
    802.3x, 71
    802.11, 261
    802.11a, 343
    802.11ac, 346–347
    802.11ax, 346–347
    802.11b/g, 344, *344*
    802.11n, 344–345
    802.11r, 353
    802.11w, 445

IETF (Internet Engineering Task Force), 15, 250, 288, 479, 480
ifconfig, 128, 128–129, 129
I/G bit, 60, 60
IGMP (Internet Group Management Protocol), 99, 112, 137
ignore, in troubleshooting methodology, 81
IGP (Interior Gateway Protocol), 157, 157, 159–160
IKE (Internet Key Exchange), 390, 391
images, policy violations and, 478–479
IMAP (Internet Message Access Protocol), 258, 449
imperative tools, 468
implicit deny, 457
implicit TLS (FTPS), 252
in-band management, 392
incident response plan, 401
incineration, 412
incorrect pin-out, 90
incorrect termination, 90
Independent Basic Service Set (IBSS), 355
indicator of compromise (IOC), 300
industrial control system (ICS), 417, 419
Infoblox, 216
informational messaging, in ICMPv6, 144
information gathering attacks, 440
infrastructure
    as code (IaC), 467–468
    layer, in SND, 479, 480
    node, 5
    as a service (IaaS), 466
    topology, 350–351, 351
ingress/egress traffic, 70, 321
initiator, 475
input (firewall chain), 457
input/output (I/O), 274
Instant Secure Erase (ISE), 413
Institute of Electrical and Electronics Engineers (IEEE). see IEEE 802 standards
insufficient wireless coverage, 360–361

insulation, 25, 29, 30, 31, 42, 44
insulation-displacement connection (IDC), 42, 43, 43, 45, 398
integrity, in CIA Triad, 296
Integrity Check Value (ICV), 389, 389
Intel's PROSet Wi-Fi configuration utility, 362
interactive logon, 306
intercepting proxy, 323
interface, 150
    identifier, 67, 141, 142
    ID/EUI-64, 142
    monitoring metrics, 289–290 (see also interface statistics)
    status issues, 134
    testing, IPv6, 143–144
interface configuration
    autoconfiguration, 143–144
    connectivity issues, troubleshooting, 87, 88
    switches, 66–68, 67
interface errors, troubleshooting, 291–292
    cyclic redundancy check (CRC), 291
    encapsulation errors, 291
    frame errors, 291–292
interface statistics, 289–290
    discards/drops, 290
    duplex, 290
    error rate, 290
    link state, 289
    per-protocol utilization, 290
    resets, 289–290
    retransmissions, 290
    speed, 290
    utilization, 290
interference issues, 90–91, 363–364
    absorption, 364
    electromagnetic interference (EMI), 364
    reflection/bounce (multipath interference), 363
    refraction, 363
Interior BGP (IBGP), 161
Interior Gateway Protocol (IGP), 157, 157, 159–160

intermediate cross-connects, 42
Intermediate Distribution Frame (IDF), 398, 399
intermediate system, 5, 6, 10
    connectivity issues in, 86
internal DNS zones, 242–243
internal firewall, 319
internal port, 11
internal routers, 173, 173–174, 174
    layer 3 capable switch, 174
    subinterfaces, 173, 174
internal threats, 300
internal virtual switch, 473
International Electrotechnical Commission (IEC), 26, 27, 35
International Organization for Standardization (ISO)
    11801 standard, 35
    cabling standards, 26, 27, 28
    ID card standard, 408
    Open Systems Interconnection (OSI) reference model, 2
Internet, 6
    cloud connectivity, 467
    SOHO network connected to, 14–15
    standards, 15
Internet Assigned Numbers Authority (IANA), 15, 99, 161, 208
Internet Control Message Protocol (ICMP), 99, 130–131, 131
Internet Corporation for Assigned Names and Numbers (ICANN), 15, 234
Internet Engineering Task Force (IETF), 15, 250, 288, 479, 480
Internet eXchange Points (IXPs), 14
Internet Group Management Protocol (IGMP), 99, 112, 137
Internet Key Exchange (IKE), 390, 391
Internet layer, in Internet model, 15

Internet Message Access Protocol (IMAP), 258, *449*
Internet model, 15
Internet of Things (IoT), 416–420
  access considerations, 459–460
  consumer-grade smart devices, 416
  described, 416
  industrial control system (ICS), 417
  mesh topologies, 356
  networks, 418
  physical access control system (PACS), 417
  placement and security, 419
  smart buildings, 417
  supervisory control and data acquisition (SCADA), 417
Internet of Things (IoT) botnet, 446
Internet Printing Protocol (IPP), 253
Internet Protocol (IP)
addresses, 12–13, 15
  /22 and 24, *104*, 163, *163*, 164
  autoconfiguration, 143
  base numbering systems in, 15–16, *16*
  classful, *116*, 116–117, *117*
  configuring
    address ranges reserved for special use, 118
    Automatic Private IP Addressing (APIPA), 118
    classful addressing, *116*, 116–117, *117*
    IPv4 address scheme design, 119–120
    loopback addresses, 118
    private IP addresses, 117
    public IP addresses, 117
  IP Address Management (IPAM), 216, 329
  IPv4 (*see* IPv4 addressing)
  IPv6 (*see* IPv6 addressing)
  local, 5, 59, 118, *142*, 142–143
  loopback, 118

multicast, *111*, 111–112, 144
  networking address services, 226–232
  (*see also* Dynamic Host Configuration Protocol (DHCP))
  private, 117
  public, 117
  ranges reserved for special use, 118
  troubleshooting
    duplicate IP and MAC address issues, 135–136
    incorrect IP address, 134–135
  unicast, 109–111, *110*, 141–142, *142*, 146
  universal, 59–60
Internet Protocol (IP) networks, 259
  configuring, 115–121
    ARP cache utility, 129–130, *130*
    Automatic Private IP Addressing (APIPA), 118
    ICMP, 130–131, *131*
    ipconfig, 127, *127*
    ipconfig and ip, *128*, 128–129, *129*
    issues, 134–135
    ping utility, 130–131, *131*
    tools to test, 126–132
    virtual LANs and subnets, 115, *116*
    in Windows, 126
  filtering, 320
  header, 98
  helper, 230
  IPFIX IETF standard, 288
  packets, 4
  protocol types, 99
  scanners, 216–217
  spoofing, 441
  troubleshooting, 133–138
    duplicate IP and MAC address issues, 135–136
    hardware failure issues, 133–134
    incorrect DNS issues, 137
    incorrect IP address, 134–135

    incorrect subnet mask, 135
    interface status issues, 134
    IP configuration issues, 134–135
    multicast flooding issues, 137
    power issues, 133
    problem isolation, 136–137
  VoIP PBX, 259
Internet Protocol Security (IPSec), 384, 390, *391*, 449
    Authentication Header (AH), 389
    Encapsulating Security Payload (ESP), *389*, 389–390
    extension headers, 140
    remote network access, 390, *391*
    transport mode, 390
    tunnel mode, 388, 390, *391*
Internet Service Provider (ISP), 14, 161
    multipathing, 431
    Point of Presence (PoP), 380
Internet Small Computer System Interface (iSCSI), 476, *476*
Internet Systems Consortium (ISC), 244
internetwork, 6, 106, *182*, 182–183, *183*
intrusion detection system (IDS), 7, 70, 326–327, *327*
intrusion prevention system (IPS), 327
inventory management, 397, *397*
inverse-square rule, 358
I/O (input/output), 274
IOC (indicator of compromise), 300
iOS
    Remote Desktop Protocol (RDP), 271, 387
    Web Services for Devices (WSD)/AirPrint, 253
IOS Software Checker, 460
IoT. *see* Internet of Things (IoT)
ip, *128*, 128–129, *129*

IP addresses. *see* Internet Protocol (IP) addresses
IP Address Management (IPAM), 216, 329
ip command, 128
ipconfig, 127, *127*, 134, 136, 137
iperf, 287, *287*
IP Flow Information Export (IPFIX) IETF standard, 288, 289
IP networks. *see* Internet Protocol (IP) networks
IPP (Internet Printing Protocol), 253
IPPS protocol, 253
iproute2, 128, 219
IPS (intrusion prevention system), 327
IPSec. *see* Internet Protocol Security (IPSec)
iptables, 457
IPv4 addressing, 98–105
    28-bit, 107
    32-bit, 100
    address format, *100*, 100–101, *101*
    address ranges, 104, *104*, 118
    broadcast addressing, 109–111, *110*
    datagram header, 98–99, *99*
    designs, 119–120
    DiffServ, 285
    forwarding, 106–113
        anycast addressing, *111*, *112*
        ARP, 108–109, *109*
        default gateways, *107*, 107–108, *108*
        layer 2 *vs.* layer 3 addressing and forwarding, *106*, 106–107
        multicast addressing, *111*, 111–112
        unicast and broadcast addressing, 109–111, *110*
    host address ranges, 104, *104*
    host name, 233, 237
    IPv6 *vs.*, 139–140

network masks, 101–102, *102*
subnet masks, 102–103, *103*
transition mechanisms, 145–146
IPv4 Link-local (IPv4LL), 329
IPv6 addressing, 139–147
    64-bit network ID, 141
    128-bit, 139
    address format, 140
    address prefixes, 146, *146*
    DiffServ, 285
    global addressing, 141–142, *142*
    host name, 233, 237
    ICMPv6, 144
    interface autoconfiguration and testing, 143–144
    interface ID/EUI-64, 142
    IPv4 *vs.*, 139–140
    link local addressing, *142*, 142–143
    multicast addressing, 144
    ND protocol, 143
    network prefixes, 141, *141*
    reverse DNS querying, 239
    SLAAC, 143–144
    stateless address autoconfiguration (SLAAC), 230–231
    transition mechanisms, 145–146
    unicast addressing, 141–142, *142*
IPv6 Rapid Deployment (6RD), 145
ISC (Internet Systems Consortium), 244
iSCSI (Internet Small Computer System Interface), 476, *476*
ISE (Instant Secure Erase), 413
ISO. *see* International Organization for Standardization (ISO)
isolated port, 456
ISP. *see* Internet Service Provider (ISP)
IT contingency planning (ITCP), 401
iterative lookup, 235
ITSCP (IT service continuity planning), 401

IT service continuity planning (ITSCP), 401
IXPs (Internet eXchange Points), 14

J

jackets, 25, 30, 34, 39, *39*, 44, 88
JavaScript Object Notation (JSON), 280
JetDirect, 253
jitter, 285
JSON (JavaScript Object Notation), 280
jumbo frames, 70–71
    errors, 292
Juniper Networks Steel-Belted RADIUS, 311

K

KDC (Key Distribution Center), 307
Kerberos, 269, 306, *307*, 307–308, *308*, 313
Kevlar (Aramid) strands, 34
Key Distribution Center (KDC), 307
Key Performance Indicators (KPIs), 425
knowledge factor, 305
KPIs (Key Performance Indicators), 425
Krone distribution frame, 43
Kubernetes orchestration platform, 468

L

L2TP (Layer 2 Tunneling Protocol), 385
Label Edge Router (LER), 483
Label Switched Path (LSP), 483
LACNIC (Latin America and Caribbean Network Information Centre), 15
LACP (Link Aggregation Control Protocol), 69, 432
LAG (Link Aggregation Group), 432
LAN. *see* local area network (LAN)

Lansweeper, 397
laser optimized MMF (LOMMF), 35
latency, 85, 285
    problems, 130
Latin America and Caribbean Network Information Centre (LACNIC), 15
layer 2. *see* data link (layer 2), of OSI model
Layer 2 Tunneling Protocol (L2TP), 385
layer 3. *see* network (layer 3), of OSI model
layer 4. *see* transport (layer 4), of OSI model
layer 5. *see* session layer (layer 5), of OSI model
layer 6. *see* presentation layer (layer 6), of OSI model
layer 7 (application layer), of OSI model, 8, *8*, 13, 15, 400, 433
LC (Local Connector), 36, *36*, *37*
LDAP (Lightweight Directory Access Protocol), 311, *311*
LDAPS (LDAP Secure), 313
leased line provider links, 377–378, *378*
lease time, DHCP, 227, 228
least privilege, 302
LED status indicators, 87, 93, 133–134
legacy (non-HT) mode, 345
legacy modems, 376
legacy systems, 298–299
Length field, 98, *99*
LER (Label Edge Router), 483
licensed feature issues, 335
Lightweight Access Point Protocol (LWAPP), 355
Lightweight Directory Access Protocol (LDAP), 311, *311*
    LDAP Secure (LDAPS), 313
Line of Business (LoB), 337
link aggregation, 69, 432, *432*
Link Aggregation Control Protocol (LACP), 69, 432
Link Aggregation Group (LAG), 432
link aggregation/NIC teaming, 432, *432*

link layer, in Internet model, 15
link local addressing
    IPv4, 118
    IPv6, *142*, 142–143
Link Local Multicast Name Resolution (LLMNR), 330
link state, 156, *157*, 289
Link State Advertisement (LSA), 160
link state database (LSDB), 160
Linux
    ARP cache, 130
    arping tool, 135
    authentication, 307
    dhclient to release lease, 228
    DHCP issues, 329
    DNS server addresses recorded in, 137
    DNS service, 241
    duplicate IPs, 135
    FreeRADIUS, 311
    hdparm utility, 412
    host as iSCSI target, 476, *476*
    ICMP and ping, 130
    ifconfig and ip, *128*, 128–129, *129*, 134–135
    incorrect DNS issues, 137
    iproute2 suite of tools, 128, 177, 219
    legacy net-tools package, 128
    link local address, 118, 143
    login, 305
    name resolution, 243
    netstat, *218*, 218–219
    net-tools package, 219
    Nmap Security Scanner, 217
    ntp package, 272
    ping, 130–131, *131*
    route command, 175, 176–177, *177*
    as router for VM network, configuring, 474
    Secure Shell (SSH), 268, 307
    tcpdump, 61–62
    traceroute, 177
    tunneling, 146
    VoIP PBX, 259
LLMNR (Link Local Multicast Name Resolution), 330

LMR/HDF/CFD 200 cable, 361
load balancers/balancing, 236, 237, 241, 433, *433*
LoB (Line of Business), 337
local address, 5, 59
    link, 118, *142*, 142–143
    resolution, 143
local area network (LAN), 10, 186–187
    configuring, using DHCP on wireless router, 12, *12*, *13*
    enterprise, 187
    examples, 187
    Extensible Authentication Protocol over (EAPoL), 456
    network types, 186–187
    ports, 10, 261
    SOHO network, 10–16
    switches, 195
    wireless controllers, 354, *354*, 354–355, *368*
    see also virtual LAN (VLAN)
local authentication, 305–307
    Linux, 307
    single sign-on (SSO), 307
    Windows, 306
Local Connector (LC), 36, *36*, *37*
local loop, 378
locally administered address, 60
local privileges, 405
Local Security Authority (LSA), 306
local sign-in, Windows, 306
location factor, 305
locking cabinets, 410, *410*
locking racks, 409
logging level, 281
Logical (IP/Layer 3), 400
logical bus topology, 191
logical network diagrams, 400, *400*
logical topology, 5, 188
logical unit number (LUN), 475
logon/login, 305–307
logs
    application, 278
    audit, 278, *279*
    collectors, *279*, 279–280
    network device, 278–279
    performance, 279
    reviews, 282, *282*

Syslog, 279–280, *280*
system, 278
traffic, 279
LOMMF (laser optimized MMF),
35
Long Term Evolution (LTE), 348,
418
loopback adapter (or loopback
plug), 87
loopback addresses, 118
loopback tool, 87
loops, 157
loss budget/calculator, 180
lossless Ethernet, 475
low optical link budget
issues, 180
LSA (Link State Advertisement),
160
LSA (Local Security Authority),
306
LSDB (link state database), 160
LSP (Label Switched Path), 483
LTE (Long Term Evolution), 348,
418
LTE Advanced (LTE-A), 348
LTE Machine Type
Communication (LTE-M), 418
LUN (logical unit number), 475
LWAPP (Lightweight Access
Point Protocol), 355

M

M2M (Machine to Machine)
communication, 416
MAC. *see* media access control
(MAC)
Machine to Machine (M2M)
communication, 416
    see also Internet of Things
    (IoT)
macOS
    Bonjour, 118
    Nmap Security Scanner, 217
    Remote Desktop Protocol
    (RDP), 271, 387
    Secure Shell (SSH), 268
    Web Services for Devices
    (WSD)/AirPrint, 253
MACs (moves, adds, and
changes), 43

magnetic media, methods of
destroying, 412
mailbox access protocols,
257–258, *449*
    configuring, *258*
    Internet Message Access
    Protocol (IMAP), 258
    Post Office Protocol (POP),
    257–258, *258*
Mail Exchange (MX), 237, 256
Main Distribution Frame (MDF),
398
malware
    attacks, 447
    protection, 405
managed switches, 65
ManageEngine, 216
management and
orchestration (MANO), 474
Management Frame Protection
(MFP/802.11w), 445
Management Information Base
(MIB), 276
management plane, 286, 480
management port, 391–392,
392
Man-in-the-Middle (MitM)
attacks, 441–442
MANO (management and
orchestration), 474
MariaDB platform, 254
massive MIMO, 348
master, 241
master key (MK), 368
master router, 436
MAU (multistation access unit),
191
maximum hop count, 179
Maximum Tolerable Downtime
(MTD) metric, *424*, 424–425
maximum transmission unit
(MTU), 60, 70, 154
MDF (Main Distribution Frame),
398
MDI. *see* medium dependent
interface (MDI)
mDNS (multicastDNS), 330
Mean Time Between Failures
(MTBF), 425
Mean Time to Failure (MTTF),
425–426

Mean Time to Repair (MTTR),
426
Mechanical Transfer Registered
Jack (MTRJ), 37, *37*
media
    access control and collision
    domains, 21–22, *22*
    bounded, 4
    cabled, 4
    converters, 5, 46, 52, *53*
    encryption key (MEK), 413
    magnetic, methods of
    destroying, 412
    network, cable standards
    for, *27*, 27–28
    sanitization, 412
    unbounded, 4
    wireless, 4
media access control (MAC),
21–22, *22*
    48-bit address, 59
    address format, 59–60, *60*
    Address Resolution
    Protocol (ARP), 108–109,
    129
    address table, 55, 68–69, *69*
    arp utility, 129–130
    broadcast storm, 198
    data link layer functions, 11
    derived addresses, 142
    duplicate address issues,
    135–136
    filtering, 454–455
    MAC-derived address or
    interface identifier, 142
    multicast addressing, 112
    spoofing, 441
    unicast and broadcast
    addressing, 111
    virtual NIC, hypervisor for
    configuring, 473
medium dependent interface
(MDI), 53, 68
    auto-MDI/MDI-X, 68, 92
    crossover (MDI-X), 53
MEF (mission essential
function), 298
megabits per second (Mbps),
21
membership, VLAN, 200–201
memorandum of
understanding (MOU), 406

memory, 274
Men & Mice, 216
Mesh Basic Service Set (MBSS), 356
mesh topology, *189*, 189–190, 356
Message Digest v5 (MD5), 449
message length, UDP, 213
message submission agents (MSAs), 257
message transfer agents (MTAs), 257
Messaging Application Programming Interface (MAPI) protocol, 258
Metageek inSSIDer, 353, *359*
Metro Ethernet, 37, 380
metro-optical provider links, 380–381
    E-LAN, 381
    E-line, 381
    Ethernet over copper, 380–381
    Ethernet over fiber, 380
metropolitan area network (MAN), 187
MFP/802.11w (Management Frame Protection), 445
mGRE (multipoint GRE), 482
MGT port, *92*
MIB (Management Information Base), 276
microsegmentation, 53
Microsoft
    Active Directory, 238
    APIPA, 329
    Azure, 466
    cloud services, 466
    Exchange mailboxes, 258
    Internet Information Server (IIS), 250
    logon or sign-in, 305
    Office 365, *404*, 466
    Outlook, 257
    Point-to-Point Tunneling Protocol (PPTP), 385
    Remote Desktop Protocol (RDP), 386–387
    route command, 175–176, *176*
    Secure Socket Tunneling Protocol (SSTP), 385

SQL Server, 254, 466
virtual switch in Hyper-V virtualization platform, 472–473, *473*
Visio, *399*, 400
microwave radio reflection sensors, 412
microwave satellite, 381
millimeter wave (mmWave), 348
milliseconds (ms), 85, 154, 260
MIMO (Multiple Input Multiple Output), 344–345
mini-GBIC, 47
minimum point of entry (MPOE), 377
mirror port, 61
mismatched standards, 90
missing route issues, 178
mission essential function (MEF), 298
MitM (Man-in-the-Middle) attacks, 441–442
MK (master key), 368
MLD (Multicast Listener Discovery), 144
MMF (Multimode Fiber), 21, 35, *37*, 52, *53*
mobile device management, 335
modem, 5, 10, 14
modular switches, 66, *66*
modulated electrical signal, 4
modulation, 376
modulation scheme, 4, 342
monitor, SNMP, 277, *277*, *278*
motion-based alarms, 412
moves, adds, and changes (MACs), 43
Mozilla Thunderbird, 257
MPLS (Multiprotocol Label Switching), 286, *482*, 482–483
MPO (multi-fiber push-on) termination, 47
MSA (Multi-Source Agreement), 47
MTBF (Mean Time Between Failures), 425
MTD (Maximum Tolerable Downtime) metric, *424*, 424–425

MTRJ (Mechanical Transfer Registered Jack), 37, *37*
MTTF (Mean Time to Failure), 425–426
MTTR (Mean Time to Repair), 426
MTU (maximum transmission unit), 60, 70, 154
multicast addressing
    IPv4, *111*, 111–112
    IPv6, 144
multicastDNS (mDNS), 330
multicast flooding issues, 137
Multicast Listener Discovery (MLD), 144
multifactor authentication, 305, 310
multi-fiber push-on (MPO) termination, 47
multilayer switches, 7, 433
Multimode Fiber (MMF), 21, 35, *37*, 52, *53*
multipathing, 431
multipath interference, 363
multiple access area network, 21
multiple access OFDM (OFDMA), 346
Multiple Input Multiple Output (MIMO), 344–345
multiplexer/demultiplexer (mux/demux), 48
multipoint GRE (mGRE), 482
Multiprotocol Label Switching (MPLS), 286, *482*, 482–483
Multi-Source Agreement (MSA), 47
multistation access unit (MAU), 191
multitenant (or public) cloud infrastructure, 465
Multiuser MIMO (MU-MIMO), 346–347, 348
mutual authentication, 390
mux/demux (multiplexer/demultiplexer), 48
MX (Mail Exchange), 237, 256
MySQL, 254, 466

N

NA (neighbor advertisement), 143

NAC. *see* Network Access Control (NAC)

NAK or NACK (Negative Acknowledgement), *210*, 216

name resolution
DNS configuration issues, 330–331
methods, 330
services, 233–239 (*see also* Domain Name System (DNS))
services to support internal/external DNS, 242–243
troubleshooting, 243–244
using DNS, 235, *235*

Name Server (NS) records, 236

NAP (network access point), 310

NAPT (Network Address Port Translation), 325

Narrowband-IoT (NB-IoT), 418

narrowband link, 377

NAS (network access server), 310

NAS (network attached storage), 253

NAT (Network Address Translation), 117, 180, 323–324, *324*, 473

National Electrical Code (NEC), 30

National Fire Protection Association (NFPA), 427

National Institute of Standards and Technology (NIST), 403

native IP protocol, *157*, 160

native VLAN, 456

NAT overloading, 325

NB-IoT (Narrowband-IoT), 418

ND (Neighbor Discovery), 143–144, 217, 455

NDA (non-disclosure agreement), 406

NDR (non-delivery report), 257

Near End (NEXT) crosstalk, 91

NEC (National Electrical Code), 30

Negative Acknowledgement (NAK or NACK), *210*, 216

neighbor advertisement (NA), 143

Neighbor Discovery (ND), 143–144, 217, 455

neighbors, 131

neighbor solicitation (NS), 143

NetBIOS, 253

netcat tool, 62

NetFlow, 288–289, *289*

NetIQ eDirectory, 312

netstat, *212*, *218*, 218–219

network
adapter, 6
card, 188
client-server *vs.* peer-to-peer, 186
device backup management, 429
host (*see* host)
icons, 400, *400*
Internet of Things (IoT), 418
links, 426
logon/login, 305–307
mask (or netmask), 101–102, *102*
performance issues, 331–332
prefixes, 141, *141*, 230–231
segmentation enforcement, 318–319
SOHO, 10–16, 65, 187
tiered switching architecture, 194–199
untrusted, 405
virtual LANs, 200–204
visibility, 216

network (layer 3), of OSI model, 6, 6–7, *12*, 12–13
addressing and forwarding, IPv4, *106*, 106–107
Generic Routing Encapsulation (GRE), 384
Internet Protocol Security (IPSec), 384
packet filtering firewall at, 320–321
routers at, 6, *6*
switches, 195
WAN, 376, 381

Network Access Control (NAC)

defense in depth, 326
IEEE 802.1X Port-based, 310

network access point (NAP), 310

network access server (NAS), 310

Network Address Port Translation (NAPT), 325

Network Address Translation (NAT), 117, 180, 323–324, *324*, 473

network attached storage (NAS), 253

network availability, ensuring, 274–293
bandwidth management, 285–286
bottlenecks, 274
environmental monitoring, 275–276
event management, 280–282
interface errors, troubleshooting, 291–292
interface monitoring metrics, 289–290 (*see also* interface statistics)
log collectors, *279*, 279–280
log reviews, 281–282, *282*
NetFlow, 288–289, *289*
network device logs, 278–279
network metrics, 284–285
performance baseline, 275
performance metrics, 274
Simple Network Management Protocol (SNMP), 276–277, *278*
Syslog, 279–280
traffic analysis tools, 287–288
traffic shaping, 286

network data transmission, 20–21
copper cable, 20
fiber optic cable, 20–21

network device logs, 278–279
audit logs, 278, *279*
performance/traffic logs, 279
system and application logs, 278

network devices, deploying, 52–57
    bridges, *54*, 54–55, *55*
    hubs, 53–54, *54*, *55*
    layer 2 switches, 55–56, *56*
    repeaters and media converters, 52, *53*
network diagrams
    logical, 400, *400*
    physical, 398–399, 400, *400*
    rack, 399, *399*
    wiring, 398
network function virtualization (NFV), 473–474
network ID (network number), 100
networking address services, 226–232
    see also Dynamic Host Configuration Protocol (DHCP)
network interface, 4, 6, 57–64
    Ethernet frame format, 59, *59*
    frame length, 60
    maximum transmission unit (MTU), 60
    media access control (MAC) address format/extended unique identifier (EUI), 59–60, *60*
    packet sniffers and TAPs, 61
    tcpdump, 61–62
    Wireshark, 62, *63*
network interface card/controller (NIC), 6, *58*, 58–59
    link aggregation/teaming, 69, 432, *432*
    virtual, 472–473, *473*
Network Interface Unit (NIU), 377
Network Layer Reachability Information (NLRI), 161
network management services, 268–273
    Network Time Protocol (NTP), 271–272, *272*
    Remote Desktop Protocol (RDP), 271
    Secure Shell (SSH), 268–270
    Telnet, 270, *271*
    terminal emulator, 268

network media, 4, 6, 27–28, 61, 187
network metrics, 284–285
    bandwidth, 284
    jitter, 285
    latency, 285
    Quality of Service (QoS) protocols, 284
network number (network ID), 100
Network Policy Server (NPS), 311
network protocol, 3
network services
    disabling unneeded, 454
    Domain Name System (DNS) services, 241–245
    name resolution services, 233–239
    networking address services, 226–232
Network Time Protocol (NTP), 230, 271–272, *272*
    issues, 335
    time synchronization, 335
network topology, 187–192
    bus, 190–191, *191*
    hybrid, 191–192, *192*
    logical, 188
    mesh, *189*, 189–190
    physical, 187
    point-to-point link, 188
    ring, 190, *190*
    star, 188–189, *189*
network types, 186–187
    local area network (LAN), 186–187
    personal area network (PAN), 187
    size and scope, 186
    wide area network (WAN), 187
NEXT (Near End) crosstalk, 91
next header, 140
next-hop determination, 143
Next Hop Router Protocol (NHRP), 388–389
Nexus platform, 65
NFPA (National Fire Protection Association), 427
NFV (network function virtualization), 473–474

nginx, 250
ngrep, 62
NHRP (Next Hop Router Protocol), 388–389
NIC. *see* network interface card/controller (NIC)
NIST (National Institute of Standards and Technology), 403
NIU (Network Interface Unit), 377
NLRI (Network Layer Reachability Information), 161
Nmap Security Scanner, 217, *217*, 219, *220*
$n(n$-1)$/2$ (in mesh topology), 188, 189
nodes, 475
noise, 86, 358
nominal bit rate, 85
non-delivery report (NDR), 257
non-disclosure agreement (NDA), 406
nonpersistent route, 151, 177–176
nonplenum (general purpose) cabling, 30
non-transparent server, 323
Non-Volatile Memory Express (NVME), 475
no reply (request timed out), 131
north-south traffic, 478
NOS platforms, 268
NoSQL (not only SQL) database, 254
notifications, 281
NPS (Network Policy Server), 311
NS (neighbor solicitation), 143
nslookup, 243, *243*
NS (Name Server) records, 236
NT LAN Manager (NTLM), 306
NTP. *see* Network Time Protocol (NTP)
NVME (Non-Volatile Memory Express), 475

O

OADM (optical add/drop multiplexers), 48

Object Identifier (OID), 276
octets, 12, 15, 100–103, *103*, 110, 116–117, *117*, 119
OEO (optical-electrical-optical) repeater, 52
OFDM (Orthogonal Frequency Division Multiplexing), 343, 346
OFDMA (Orthogonal Frequency Division Multiple Access), 346, 348
offboarding, 402
OID (Object Identifier), 276
OLT (optical line terminal), 381
OM (Optical Multimode) categories, 21, 35, *37*
omnidirectional antenna, 360, *360*
onboarding, 402
one-to-many NAT, 325
on-path attack, 330, 441–442
ONT (optical network terminal), 381
ONU (optical network unit), 381
OOB management methods. *see* out-of-band (OOB) management methods
open authentication issues, 370
OpenLDAP, 312
Open Shortest Path First (OSPF), 99, *157*, 160–161, *161*
OpenSSH, 268, 270
OpenStack, 466
Open Systems Interconnection (OSI) model, *2*, 2–3, *3*
    layers, 4–8, *8* (*see also individual layers*)
        data link (layer 2), *5*, 5–6, 11, *11*
        mnemonic for remembering, 3
        network (layer 3), *6*, 6–7, *12*, 12–13
        packets, 4, 5, 6, 7, 13
        physical (layer 1), 4–5, 10, *11*
        transport (layer 4), *7*, 7, 13
        upper, 7–8, 13
    top-to-bottom/bottom-to-top, 79–80, *80*

wide area network (WAN), 376
open WLANS, 187
operating plans and procedures, 396–397
    change management, 396–397
    configuration management, 396
    standard operating procedure (SOP), 397
operation, full- or half-duplex, 68
operational technology (OT) network, 418
OPNsense security appliance, *277*, *279*, *280*, *311*, *321*, *323*, *390*, *391*, *457*
optical add/drop multiplexers (OADM), 48
optical-electrical-optical (OEO) repeater, 52
optical line terminal (OLT), 381
Optical Multimode (OM) categories, 21, 35, *37*
optical network terminal (ONT), 381
optical network unit (ONU), 381
optical power meter, 93
optical source, 93
optical spectrum analyzer (OSA), 93
optical time domain reflectometer (OTDR), 93, 180
options, TCP, 210
options configuration, DHCP, 228–229
Oracle
    Database, 466
    SQL*Net, 254
    Virtual Box, 471
orchestration, 468
organizational documentation and policies, 396–407
    agreements, 405–406
    data loss prevention, 404
    hardening and security policies, 402
    logical *vs.* physical network diagrams, 400, *400*
    operating plans and procedures, 396–397

physical network diagrams, 398–399
    rack diagrams, 399, *399*
    remote access policies, 405
    security response plans and procedures, 401
    system life cycle plans and procedures, 397–398
    usage policies, 403–404
Organizationally Unique Identifier (OUI), 59–60, *60*
Orthogonal Frequency Division Multiple Access (OFDMA), 346, 348
Orthogonal Frequency Division Multiplexing (OFDM), 343, 346
OSA (optical spectrum analyzer), 93
OSC Radiator, 311
OSes, 177, *471*, 472
OSI model. *see* Open Systems Interconnection (OSI) model
OSPF (Open Shortest Path First), 99, *157*, 160–161, *161*
OSSIM SIEM dashboard, *301*
OTDR (optical time domain reflectometer), 93, 180
OT (operational technology) network, 418
OUI (Organizationally Unique Identifier), 59–60, *60*
outages, 465
out-of-band (OOB) management methods, 391–392, *392*
    AUX port, 391, *392*
    console port, 391, *392*
    management port, 391–392, *392*
output (firewall chain), 457
overcapacity issues, 363
overlap issues, 362–363
overlay networks, 479
overloaded service, 332
overwriting, 412, 413
ownership factor, 305

P

PaaS (Platform as a Service), 466
packet

analysis, 221
filtering firewall, 320–321
forwarding, 152–153
hop count, 153, *153*
maximum size, UDP, 237
in OSI model layers, 4, 5, 6, 7, 13
sniffers, 61
Time to Live (TTL), 153
traffic flow, 289
traffic shaping, 286
packets per second, 85, 290
packet-switched technologies, 347–348
PACS (physical access control system), 417
Page Description Language (PDL), 253
pairwise master key (PMK), 367, 368
PAKE (Password Authenticated Key Exchange), 367
PAM (pluggable authentication module), 307
PAM (privileged access management), 301–302
PAN (personal area network), 187
Pan-Tilt-Zoom (PTZ) controls, 411
parabolic (dish or grid) form factors, 360, *360*
parallelism, 347
Parallels Workstation, 471
partial mesh, 189
passive FTP, 251, *251*
passive infrared (PIR) sensors, 412
passive optical network (PON), 38, 381
passphrase issues, 369
Password Authenticated Key Exchange (PAKE), 367
passwords
    aging and history, 403
    attacks, 448–449
    change default, 453
    common, avoiding, 453
    complexity/length requirements, 403, 453
    cracking, 449

cryptographic hashes, 305–306, *306*, 449
    database dumps, 453
    policy, 403
    in SSH client authentication, 269
PAT (Port Address Translation), 325, *325*
patch bay, 43
patch cable, connectivity issues in, 86
patch cords, 38, *38*, 45
    connections, connectivity issues in, 86–87, *87*
    crossover, 92
    straight through, 91
patch management, 460
patch panel, 43, *43*, 44
path selection, 156
path vector, *157*
PAUSE frames, 71
payload, 248–249
    classifications, 447
    data, 390, 449
    length, 140
PBX (private branch exchange), 43, 259, *260*, 377
PC (Physical Contact), 38
PCL (Printer Command Language), 253
PD (powered device), 71
PDL (Page Description Language), 253
PDS (Protected Distribution System), 412
peak utilization, 290
peer-to-peer network, 186
penetration testing (pen test), 301
performance
    baseline, 275
    logs, 279
    metrics, 274
    network issues, 331–332
    website checkers, 288
    wireless assessment, 358–359
Per Hop Behavior (PHB), 285
perimeter network, 319
perimeter security, 325
permanent link, connectivity issues in, 86

PE (provider edge) router, 171, 291, 376
per-protocol utilization, 290
persistent route, 151, 176–177
personal area network (PAN), 187
personal assets, returning, 402
personal authentication, 367–368
    WPA2-PSK, 367, 368
    WPA3-SAE, 367–368
personal identity number (PIN), 305
PFC (priority flow control) mechanism, 71
pharming, 440, 442
PHB (Per Hop Behavior), 285
phishing attacks, 450, *450*
phones, VoIP, 261
PHP, 466
physical (layer 1), of OSI model, 4–5, 10, *11*, 376, 400
physical access control system (PACS), 417
physical address, 59
    see also media access control (MAC)
physical bus topology, 190–191
Physical Contact (PC), 38
physical interface, 4
physical layer (layer 1) of OSI model, 52
physical network diagrams, 398–399, 400, *400*
    distribution frame, 398–399
    floor plan, 398
    wiring diagram, 398
physical security methods, 408–415
    alarms and tamper detection, 411–412
    asset disposal, 412–413
    badges and site secure entry systems, 408–409
    detection-based devices, 410–411
    employee training, 402, 413–141
    for server systems, 409–410
physical starlogical bus topology, 191
physical topology, 4, 187

PID (Process ID) number, 218

piggybacking, 451

PIN (personal identity number), 305

ping utility, 130–131, *131*
  basic use, 130–131, *131*
  ping error messaging, 131
  ping sequence for identifying connectivity issues, *136*, 136–137
  ping switches, 131

pin-out, 398

PIR (passive infrared) sensors, 412

pixels, 284

PJL (Printer Job Language), 253

plain old telephone service (POTS), 259, 262, 263

plaintext
  authentication, 305–306, *306*, 313
  cryptographic concepts, 161, 449

plan of action to repair/replace/ignore, 81–82

Platform as a Service (PaaS), 466

PLCs (programmable logic controllers), 417

plenum-rated cable, 30

plenum space, 30

plug-and-play, 253

pluggable authentication module (PAM), 307

PMK (pairwise master key), 367, 368

PNAC (Port-Based Network Access Control), 455–456

PoE (Power over Ethernet), 27, 71, 92, 261, 352, 355, 411

pointer (PTR) record, *238*, 238–239

point of failure, 52, 61

Point of Presence (PoP), 380

point-to-multipoint links, 482

point-to-point link, 188, 189

Point-to-Point Protocol (PPP), 291, 378, 384

point-to-point wireless bridge connections, 360

poisoning, DNS, 442–443, *443*

polarization, 360

policy violations, 478–479

polyvinyl chloride (PVC) jackets and insulation, 30

PON (passive optical network), 38, 381

PoP (Point of Presence), 380

POP (Post Office Protocol), 257–258, *258*

POP3S (secure POP), 258

port, 208
  active *vs.* passive FTP, 251
  aggregation, 69, 432
  assignments, documenting, 208
  disabled, 87
  file and print services, 253
  filtering/security, 320
  mirroring, 69–70, *70*
  naming convention, 399
  numbers, 320
  POP3, 257
  Port Address Translation (PAT), 325, *325*
  Port-Based Network Access Control (PNAC), 455–456
  range (-p) scan, 219
  root (RP), 197
  scanners, 219–220, *220*
  security, 69
  security/IEEE 802.1X PNAC, 455–456
  Session Initiation Protocol (SIP), 261
  standard TCP/IP port (9100), 253
  switch, 86, 454
  tagging, 202
  TCP, 213–214, 248, 250–254, 257, 258, 261, 268, 270, 271
  Telnet Daemon, 270
  transport layer, 208–209, *209*
  UDP, 213–214, 252, 254, 261, 277

Port Address Translation (PAT), 325, *325*

Port-Based Network Access Control (PNAC), 455–456

port range (-p) scan, 219

port security/IEEE 802.1X PNAC, 455–456

PostgreSQL platform, 254

Post Office Protocol (POP), 257–258, *258*

PostScript (PS), 253

posture assessment, 297

potentially unwanted applications (PUAs), 447

potentially unwanted programs (PUPs), 447

POTS (plain old telephone service), 259, 262, 263

power
  capping, 71
  injector (or midspan), 71
  issues, 133
  levels, 362, *362*, 459
  management, 428–429
    battery backups, 428
    generators, 428–429
    power distribution units (PDUs), 428
    uninterruptible power supply (UPS), 428
  sourcing equipment (PSE), 71
  sum crosstalk calculations, 91
  supply unit (PSU), 399
  surges and spikes, 133

powered device (PD), 71

Power over Ethernet (PoE), 27, 71, 92, 261, 352, 355, 411

PPP (Point-to-Point Protocol), 291, 378, 384

preamble, 59

precursor to spoofing, 441

prefix
  discovery, 143
  IPv6 address, 146, *146*
  network, 141, *141*, 230–231
  in routing table, 162

presentation layer (layer 6), of OSI model, 8, *8*, 15

preshared keys (PSKs), 367, 368, 459

primary VLAN, 456

primary zone, 241

principals, 307

printer, 253

Printer Command Language (PCL), 253

Printer Job Language (PJL), 253

printer sharing, 253
priority flow control (PFC) mechanism, 71
privacy extensions, 131
private branch exchange (PBX), 43, 259, *260*, 377
private cloud infrastructure, 465
private-direct connection/ colocation, 467
private IP addresses, 117
private (inside local) network address, 324
private virtual switch, 473
private VLAN (PVLAN) best practices, 456
privileged access management (PAM), 301–302
privileged mode, 276
    EXEC mode/enable mode, 66
probes, 217, 219, 220, *220*
problem isolation, 136–137
process assessment, 298
Process ID (PID) number, 218
programmable logic controllers (PLCs), 417
promiscuous port, 456
Protected Distribution System (PDS), 412
protocol
    analyzer, 61, 221, *222*, *223*
    data unit (PDU), 4, 59
    disable unsecure, 454
    field, 99, *99*
    filter expression, 62
    ID, 70
    quality of service (QoS), 284
    real-world, 4, 7
    routing entry, 150
    VoIP, 260–261
provider edge (PE) router, 171, 291, 376
proxy server, 322–323
    configuration, *323*
    forward proxies, 322–323
    private addressing, 117
    reverse proxies, 323
PS (PostScript), 253
PSACRF, 91
PSACRN, 91

PSKs (preshared keys), 367, 368, 459
PSNEXT, 91
PSTN (public switched telephone network), 14, 182, 259
PTR (pointer) record, *238*, 238–239
PTZ (Pan-Tilt-Zoom) controls, 411
PUAs (potentially unwanted applications), 447
public address, 324
public cloud infrastructure, 465
public IP addresses, 117
public key, 268, 269
    authentication, 269
    cryptography, 308–309
    infrastructure (PKI), 308, 309
public switched telephone network (PSTN), 14, 182, 259
pulling cable, 44
pulverization, 412
punchdown block, 42, 43
punchdown tool, 45, *45*
Puppet orchestration platform, 468
PUPs (potentially unwanted programs), 447
PuTTY, 92, *269*, *271*, 391
PVC (polyvinyl chloride) jackets and insulation, 30
PVLAN (private VLAN) best practices, 456

Q

QoS. *see* quality of service (QoS)
QSFP+ (enhanced quad small form-factor pluggable), 47
quad small form-factor pluggable (QSFP), 47
quality of service (QoS)
    distribution layer, 195
    management, 140
    mechanism, 71, 473, 475
    protocols, 284
    stack, 458
    VoIP protocols, 260, 261

R

rack diagrams, 399, *399*
rack-mounted switches, 66
radio chain, 344–345
radio frequency (RF) attenuation, 358
Radio Frequency ID (RFID), 411
radio frequency interference (RFI), 91, 352
Radio Grade (RG) standard, 31
RADIUS (Remote Authentication Dial-in User Service), *310*, 311, *311*, 368, 385, 456, 459
RA (Router Advertisement) Guard, 455
RAID array, 426, 428
Random Early Detection (RED), 286
random period (backoff), 21
range extender, 360
ransomware attacks, 447, *448*
Rapid STP (RSTP), 198
RAS (remote access server), 383
RAT (remote access Trojan), 447
RDBMS (relational database management system), 254
RDP (Remote Desktop Protocol), 271, 386–387
read-only access, 276, 313
read-write access, 276, 313
Real-time Transport Protocol (RTP), 261
real-world protocols, 4, 7
reauthentication, 311
Received Signal Strength Indicator (RSSI), 359
receive (Rx) wires, 38, 53, 87, 90
receiving host, 7
Recovery Point Objective (RPO), 425, *425*
recovery sites, 426–427
recovery time objective (RTO), 425, *425*, 426
recursive lookup, 235
recursive querying, 235
RED (Random Early Detection), 286
redirection, 143

redundancy
  cyclic redundancy check (CRC), 59, 291
  disaster recovery, 426
  email servers, 237
  first hop redundancy protocol (FHRP), *435*, 435–436
  hardware/clusters, 433–434, *434*
  mesh networks, 190
  multiple primary servers for, 241
  secondary name servers for, 236
  Virtual Router Redundancy Protocol (VRRP), 436
redundant spares, 426
reflection/bounce (multipath interference), 363
refraction, 363
Registered Jack (RJ) connectors, 28
  Mechanical Transfer Registered Jack (MTRJ), 37, *37*
  RJ-11, 28–29, *29*
  RJ-45, 28, *28*
  smartjack, 377
relational database management system (RDBMS), 254
relational databases, 254
relative distinguished name, 312
relay, DHCP, 229
reliable delivery, 7
remnant recovery, 413
remote access server (RAS), 383
remote access Trojan (RAT), 447
Remote Authentication Dial-in User Service (RADIUS), *310*, 311, *311*, 368, 385, 456, 459
Remote Desktop Protocol (RDP), 271, 386–387
remote network access, 383–393
  authentication and authorization, 383–384
  client-to-site VPNs, 385–386

configuration, 386
desktop connections, 386
desktop gateways, 386
host access, 386–387
hub and spoke VPNs, *388*, 388–389
Internet Key Exchange (IKE), 390, *390*
Internet Protocol Security (IPSec), 389–390, *391*
logon/login, 305–307
meaning of, 383
out-of-band management methods, 391–392
policies, 405
policy restrictions, 383–384
port scanners, 219–220, *220*
print protocols, 253
remote access server (RAS), 383
remote host access, 386–387
sign-in/sign-on, 305–307
site-to-site VPNs, 387
tunneling and encapsulation protocols, 384
VPN headends, 388–389
renewable power sources, 429
repair, in troubleshooting methodology, 81
repeater, 4, 52, *53*, 191
replace, in troubleshooting methodology, 81
replication, 254
reputational threat research, 300
Request for Change (RFC), 396–397
Requests for Comments (RFCs), 15
request timed out (no reply), 131
Request to Send (RTS), 342
research, threat, 300
reservations, DHCP, 229
resets, 289–290
reset (RST) segment, 212
residential cabling standard, 30
residential networks, 186, 187
Resolve-DnsName, 244

resolvers for name queries, 228, 235
resource pooling, 464
resource records, 236, *236*
resource units (RUs), 346
retransmissions, 86, 290
reverse DNS querying, 238–239
reversed pair, 90
reverse lookup zones, 239
reverse proxies, 323
RF (radio frequency) attenuation, 358
RFC (Request for Change), 396–397
RFC 1542 compliant routers, 229
RFCs (Requests for Comments), 15
RFI (radio frequency interference), 91, 352
RFID (Radio Frequency ID), 411
RG (Radio Grade) standard, 31
ring topology, 190, *190*
RIP (Routing Information Protocol), *157*, 157–159, *158*, *159*
RIPE Network Coordination Centre (RIPE NCC), 15
RIPng (next generation), 159
RIPv1/RIPv2, 159
riser cabling, 30
risk, 296, *297*
  enterprise risk management (ERM), 297
  security assessments, 297–298
risk posture, 297
RJ connectors. *see* Registered Jack (RJ) connectors
roaming, wireless, 353–354
rogue access point, 444
rogue DHCP, 442
role-based access, 302, 454
rollback, 460
rollover cable, 92, 391
rootkit, 447
root ports (RP), 197
round robin DNS, 237
Round Trip Time (RTT), 130, 285
route flapping, 157
route once, switch many, 195

route processor (RP) attack, 458

router
  advertisement (RA), 143, 144, 230, 231
  backup, 436
  branch office, 388
  configuration, 174–175, *175*
  customer edge (CE), 171, 291, 376
  DiffServ-compatible, 285
  edge, 151, 161, 171–172, *172*, 173, *173*
  implementation, 390
  installation and troubleshooting, 171–183
    asymmetrical routing issues, 179–180
    edge routers, 171–172, *172*
    internal routers, *173*, 173–174, *174*
    low optical link budget issues, 180
    missing route issues, 178
    route, 175–177, *176*, *177*
    router configuration, 174–175, *175*
    routing loop issues, 178–179, *179*
    traceroute, 177
    tracert, 177–178, *178*
  internal, *173*, 173–174, *174*
  Label Edge Router (LER), 483
  master, 436
  at network layer (layer 3) of OSI model, 6, *6*
  provider edge (PE), 171, 291, 376
  RFC 1542 compliant, 229
  screening firewall, 319
  SOHO, 10–16
  SOHO, firewall in, 13
  solicitation (RS), 143, 144
  at transport layer (layer 3) of OSI model, 7
  Virtual Router Redundancy Protocol (VRRP), 436

wireless, configuring management interface on, 13, *14*
Router Advertisement (RA) Guard, 455
routes, 175–177, *176*, *177*
  adding, 176
  directly connected, 151
  static and default, 151
routing, 106, 150–155
  branch office internetwork, designing, *182*, 182–183, *183*
  fragmentation, 154
  loop issues, 178–179, *179*
  packet forwarding, 152–153
  path selection, 156
  protocol updates, 71
  routing tables, 150–152, *151*
  static and default routes, 151
  see also dynamic routing
Routing Information Protocol (RIP), *157*, 157–159, *158*, *159*
routing table, 108, 150–152, *151*
  entries, 150–151, *151*
  example, 152, *152*
  static and default routes, 151
RP (root ports), 197
RP (route processor) attack, 458
RPO (Recovery Point Objective), 425, *425*
RSSI (Received Signal Strength Indicator), 359
RSTP (Rapid STP), 198
RST (reset) segment, 212
RTCP (RTP Control Protocol), 261
RTO (recovery time objective), 425, *425*, 426
RTP (Real-time Transport Protocol), 261
RTP Control Protocol (RTCP), 261
RTS (Request to Send), 342
RTT (Round Trip Time), 130, 285
Ruckus, 355
runt frame errors, 291

RUs (resource units), 346
Rx (receive) wires, 38, 53, 87, 90

S

SA (Security Associations), 390
SaaS (Software as a Service), 466, 469
SAE (Simultaneous Authentication of Equals) protocol, 367–368
Salesforce, 466
SAM (Security Accounts Manager), 306
Samba software suite, 253
SAN. *see* storage area network (SAN)
sanitization, 412
SANITIZE command, 413
SAS (Serial Attached SCSI), 412, 413, 475
SASL (Simple Authentication and Security Layer), 313
SATA, 412, 413, 475
satellite, 381
SAWs (secure administrative workstations), 478
SC (Subscriber Connector), 36, *36*, *37*
SCADA (supervisory control and data acquisition), 417, 419
scalability, 464
scope, 228
scope exhaustion, 329
scope id, 143
screened subnets, 319
screened twisted pair (ScTP) cable, 26
screening firewall or router, 319
scripting, automation using, 468
scripting languages, 468
SCSI, 475, 476
ScTP (screened twisted pair) cable, 26
SDN. *see* software defined networking (SDN)
SDSL (Symmetrical DSL), 379
SD-WAN (software-defined WAN), 483–484, *484*
SE (Secure Erase), 412–413

sealing, 313
secondary zone, 241
Secure Access Control Server, 311
secure administrative workstations (SAWs), 478
secure configuration, 453–454
  deploying systems in (see hardening)
  policies that make up, 453–454
  protocols, disable unsecure, 454
  role-based access, 454
  unneeded network services, disabling, 454
  see also passwords
secure connection protocol, 392
Secure Digital slot for firmware updates, 92
Secure Erase (SE), 412–413
secure file transfer protocol (SFTP), 252, 252, 268
Secure Hash Algorithm (SHA), 449
secure POP (POP3S), 258
Secure Shell (SSH)
  client authentication, 269
  commands, 270
  Daemon, 270
  host key, 268, 269
  Linux authentication, 307
  management port, 391
  remote configuration of network appliances, 386
  router configuration, 174, 175
  Secure FTP (SFTP), 252
Secure Sockets Layer (SSL), 250
secure version of SIP (SIPS), 261
security, 296–303
  appliances, 318–328
    defense in depth, 325–326
    firewall selection and placement, 321–322, 322
    firewall uses and types, 320, 320–321

intrusion detection system (IDS), 326–327, 327
intrusion prevention system (IPS), 327
Network Address Translation (NAT), 323–324, 324
network segmentation enforcement, 318–319
Port Address Translation (PAT), 325, 325
proxy servers, 322–323
screened subnets, 319, 319
cloud, 468–469
concepts, 296
Confidentiality, Integrity, and Availability (CIA) Triad, 296
controls, 297
exploits, 298
information, 405
log, 278
penetration testing, 301
privileged access management (PAM), 301–302
response plans and procedures, 401
risk assessments, 297–298
risks, 296, 297
Security Information and Event Management (SIEM), 300
security risk assessments, 297–298
server systems, physical security for, 409–410
threats, 296, 297, 300
vendor assessment, 302
vulnerabilities, 296, 297, 298–299
see also firewalls; passwords
Security Accounts Manager (SAM), 306
Security Associations (SA), 390
Security Information and Event Management (SIEM), 300
SEDs (self-encrypting drives), 413

segments, 4, 7
self-encrypting drives (SEDs), 413
Sender Policy Framework (SPF), 238
sending host, 7
sensors, environmental, 275–276
separation of duties, 326
sequence number
  TCP, 209
  UDP, 213
Serial Attached SCSI (SAS), 412, 413, 475
serial (or null modem) link, 92
server
  in AAA architecture, 310
  configuration
    DHCP, 227–228
    DHCPv6, 231, 230–231
    DNS, 241–242
  message block (SMB), 13, 253, 449
  systems, physical security for, 409–410
    locking cabinets, 410, 410
    locking racks, 409
    smart lockers, 410
  types, DNS, 241–242
service hardening, 453–454
service level agreement (SLA), 405–406, 468
service loop, 44
Service (SRV) record, 238, 238
Service Set Identifier (SSID), 351, 369
session, 8
session control protocol, 260
Session Initiation Protocol (SIP), 260–261
session layer (layer 5), of OSI model, 8, 8, 15, 321
SFD (Start Frame Delimiter), 59
SFP+ (enhanced small form-factor pluggable), 47
SFP (Small Form Factor Pluggable), 32, 47, 47
SFTP (secure file transfer protocol), 252, 252, 268
S/FTP (shielded/foiled twisted pair) cable, 23, 26, 27

SHA (Secure Hash Algorithm), 449

shadow IT, 419

shared hosting, 249

SHDSL (single-pair high-speed DSL), 380

shielded/foiled twisted pair (S/FTP) cable, 23, 26, *27*

shielded twisted pair (STP) cable, 26

short, problem of, 89

shortest path first (SPF), 160

shoulder surfing attack, 451

show commands, 67

show config, 67

show interface, 67, 71

shunning, 327

SIEM (Security Information and Event Management), 300

signal strength, 358–359, *359*

signal-to-noise ratio (SNR), 86, 91, 359

signing, 313

sign-in/sign-on, 305–307

SIM (subscriber identity module) card, 347, 348

Simple Authentication and Security Layer (SASL), 313

simple bind authentication, 313

Simple Mail Transfer Protocol (SMTP), 13, *256*, 256–257

Simple Mail Transfer Protocol Secure (SMTPS), 257

Simple Network Management Protocol (SNMP)
    agents, 276, *278*
    IP scanners, 217
    management plane, 458
    monitor, 277, *277*, *278*
    secure, implementing, 454

Simple Network Time Protocol (SNTP), 272

Simultaneous Authentication of Equals (SAE) protocol, 367–368

Single Mode Fiber (SMF), 21, 35, *37*
    to Multimode Fiber (MMF), 53, *53*
    to twisted pair, 52, *53*

single-pair high-speed DSL (SHDSL), 380

single-pass zero filling, 412

single sign-on (SSO), 270, 307

SIP (Session Initiation Protocol), 260–261

SIPS (Session Initiation Protocol Secure), 261

site resiliency, 427

site secure entry systems, 408–409
    access control hardware, 408
    access control vestibule, 409

site survey, 352–353, *353*
    report, 399

site-to-site VPNs, 387

SLA (service level agreement), 405–406, 468

SLAAC (stateless address autoconfiguration), 143–144, 230–231

slave, 241

sleep states, 71

small and medium-sized enterprise (SME) networks, 187

Small Form Factor Pluggable (SFP), 32, 47, *47*

small office/home office (SOHO) networks, 187
    configuring, 10–16
    connecting to Internet, 14–15
    switches on, 65

small office/home office (SOHO) routers, 10–16, 171
    application layer functions of, 13
    data link layer functions of, 11, *11*
    Dynamic Host Configuration Protocol (DHCP), 226
    firewall functionality, 322
    network layer functions of, *11*, 12–13
    physical layer functions of, 10, *11*
    security functions of, 13, *14*
    transport layer functions of, 13

WAN interface of, to connect to Internet, 14–15
WAN IP address, 15–16

smart buildings, 417, 419

smart card login, 305, 307

smart devices, 416

smartjack, 377

smart lockers, 410

SME (small and medium-sized enterprise) networks, 187

SMF. *see* Single Mode Fiber (SMF)

SMS (text message), 281

SMTP (Simple Mail Transfer Protocol), 13, *256*, 256–257

SMTPS (Simple Mail Transfer Protocol Secure), 257

snagless cable, *28*

snips, 44

SNMP. *see* Simple Network Management Protocol (SNMP)

snooping
    DHCP, 455
    IGMP, 137
    Internet Group Management Protocol (IGMP), 137

snowflake topology, 192

SNR (signal-to-noise ratio), 86, 91, 359

SNTP (Simple Network Time Protocol), 272

SOA (Start of Authority) record, 236

social engineering
    authentication, 305
    definition of, 450
    eliciting information, 450
    in external *vs.* internal threats, 300
    footprinting, 440
    password policy, 403
    phishing, 450
    security awareness training, 402, 413–141
    spoofing, 440

socket, 209

software
    automated vulnerability scanning, 299
    BIND DNS server, *236*, 244, *244*

downgrading or rollback, 460

firmware vulnerabilities, 460

HTTP application data processing, 4

interface for, 7, 8

IP Address Management (IPAM), 329

network mapping, 400

Nmap Security Scanner, 217

password cracking, 449

problems, 80
   determining, 80
   diagnostic software, 78
   installation of unauthorized software, 82
   software patch, 82
   upgrading software, 81

PUPs/PUAs, 447

Samba, 253

SIEM, 300, *301*

throughput testers, 287, *287*

virtual appliances, 474

VoIP PBX, 259

vulnerabilities, 298–299

Wi-Fi analyzer, 359

wireless LAN controller, 354

Software as a Service (SaaS), 466, 469

software defined networking (SDN), 479–480
   architecture, 479–480, *480*
   controller, 479
   management plane, 480

software-defined WAN (SD-WAN), 483–484, *484*

SOHO networks. *see* small office/home office (SOHO) networks

SOHO routers. *see* small office/home office (SOHO) routers

SolarWinds, 216

solicited-node address, 144

solid state drives (SSDs), 412, 413

Something/Anything/Everything as a Service (XaaS), 465

SOP (standard operating procedure), 397

source port, 208
   TCP, 209
   UDP, 213

spam, 238

SPAN (switched port analyzer), 61, 70

spanning tree blocking, 87

spanning tree protocol (STP), 196–198, *197*, 332

spanning tree traffic, 456

spatial diversity, 345

spatial multiplexing, 345

spectral attenuation, 93

spectrum analyzer, 364

spectrum bands, 348

speed
   autonegotiate, 68
   in Ethernet terms, 85–86
   interface, 290
   mismatch, 87
   wireless performance assessment, 358

SPF (Sender Policy Framework), 238

SPF (shortest path first), 160

spine and leaf topology, 480–481, *481*

splash page, 370

splices, loss budget and, 180

split horizon, 179

splitter, 379

split tunnel, 385, *385*

spoofing, 440–445
   ARP, 441–442, *442*
   attack, 136
   deauthentication attack, 445
   disassociation/deauthentication attacks, 369–370
   distributed DoS (DDoS), 446
   DNS poisoning, 442–443, *443*
   evil twin, 44
   MAC and/or IP, 441, 455
   on-path attacks, 441–442
   phishing attacks, 450
   VLAN hopping, 443

sprinkler systems, 428

spyware, 447

SQL. *see* structured query language (SQL)

SRV (Service) record, 238, *238*

SSDs (solid state drives), 412, 413

SSH. *see* Secure Shell (SSH)

SSID (Service Set Identifier), 351, 369

SSL (Secure Sockets Layer), 250

SSL/TLS, 250, 252, 261

SSO (single sign-on), 270, 307

STA (stations), 350

stackable switches, 66, 67

standard operating procedure (SOP), 397

standby generator, 428

standby group, 435

standby power supplies, 426

star of stars topology, 192

Start Frame Delimiter (SFD), 59

Start of Authority (SOA) record, 236

star topology, 188–189, *189*

STARTTLS command, 257, 313

star with topology, 192

state/bare metal backup, 429

stateful inspection firewall, 251, 321, *321*

stateless address autoconfiguration (SLAAC), 143–144, 230–231

stateless protocol, 249

stateless/stateful mode, 230–231

static address, *13*, 229

static routes, 151

static tunnel, 388

static VLAN, 201

stations (STA), 350

status indicators, 87

ST (Straight Tip) connectors, 35, *36*, *37*

steady state, 157

stencils representing vendor equipment, 399

storage, 274

storage area network (SAN), *474*, 474–476
   connection types, 475
   fiber Ethernet standards, 37

Internet Small Computer System Interface (iSCSI), 476, *476*
jumbo frames, 70, 292
multipathing, 431
STP (spanning tree protocol), 196–198, *197*, 332
STP (shielded twisted pair) cable, 26
straight through patch cord, 91
Straight Tip (ST) connectors, 35, *36*, *37*
structured cable, 41–42, *42*, 86
structured query language (SQL), 254
  Azure SQL Database, 466
  Microsoft SQL Server, 254, 466
  MySQL, 254, 466
  Oracle SQL*Net, 254
  PostgreSQL platform, 254
stub resolvers, 235, 242
subnets
  addressing, 102–103, *103*
  configuring
    address ranges reserved for special use, 118
    Automatic Private IP Addressing (APIPA), 118
    classful addressing, *116*, 116–117, *117*
    IP networks, 115, *116*
    IPv4 address scheme design, 119–120
    loopback addresses, 118
    private IP addresses, 117
    public IP addresses, 117
    virtual LANs and subnets, 115, *116*
  masks
    incorrect, 135
    IPv4, 102–103, *103*
  screened, 319, *319*
Subscriber Connector (SC), 36, *36*, *37*
subscriber identity module (SIM) card, 347, 348
substitute known working hosts, 87
supernetting, 162
supervisory control and data acquisition (SCADA), 417, 419

supplicant, in AAA architecture, 310
switched port analyzer (SPAN), 61, 70
switches, 6
  authenticator, 456
  Cisco, 65, *67*, *69*, *70*
  configuring MAC filtering on, 454–455
  core/distribution, 195, *195*
  data, 195
  deploying network devices, 55–56, *56*
  desktop, 66
  desktop *vs.* rack-mounted, 66
  Fiber Channel (FC), 475
  Gigabit Ethernet, 55
  interface configuration, 66–68, *67*
  LAN, 195
  layer 2, 55–56, *56*
  layer 3, 195
  layer 7, 433
  modular *vs.* fixed, 66, *66*
  ping, 131
  private virtual, 473
  route once, switch many, 195
  stackable, 66
  top-of-rack (ToR), 481
  trunks, 201–202
  unmanaged *vs.* managed, 65
  virtual, 472–473
switching. *see* Ethernet
switching, deploying
switching loop, 198
switch port
  connectivity issues in, 86
  disabling unneeded, 454
  protection, 454
symbols, 85
Symmetrical DSL (SDSL), 379
symmetric cipher, 390
symmetric session key, 308
SYN/ACK packet, 446
SYN flood attack, 446
SYN segment, 210, 211, 213, 219
Syslog, 279–280
system life cycle, 398

system life cycle roadmap, 398
system logs, 278

T

T1/T2 timer, 228
T11 ANSI standard, 475
T568A/T568B standard, *29*, 29–30, *30*, 91–92
TACACS+ (Terminal Access Controller Access Control System), 310, 311, 368
tactics, techniques, and procedures (TTPs), 300, 440
tagged VLAN ports, 202–203
tagging mechanism, 286
tail drop, 286
tailgating, 451
tamper detection, 411–412
TAP (test access point), 61
target, 475
TCP. *see* Transmission Control Protocol (TCP)
TCP connect (-sT) scan, 219
tcpdump, 61–62
TCP/IP (Transmission Control Protocol/Internet Protocol) suite, 98, 248, 250, 253
TCP segment (window), 210
TCP SYN (-sS) scan, 219, *220*
TCP/UDP port number, 70
TDM (Time Division Multiplexing), 259, 377
TDMA (Time Division Multiple Access), 347, 348
TDR (time domain reflectometer), 89
teaming, 69, 432, *432*
TeamViewer, 387
teardown, 212
telecommunications company (telco), 14, 376
Telecommunications Industry Association (TIA), 26, 27, 28, 29, 30, 38, 39, 41
telecommunications room, 42, *42*
telephony features, 259
teletype (TTY) device, 268
Telnet, 270, *271*, 391
Telnet Daemon, 270
temperature, monitoring, 276

Temporal Key Integrity Protocol (TKIP), 366

temporary interface ID or token, 142

tenants, 465

TERA connectors, 27, *27*, 28

Terminal Access Controller Access Control System (TACACS+), 310, 311, 368

terminal emulator, 268

termination tools, 45

Tesla's Powerpack, 429

test access point (TAP), 61

text message (SMS), 281

Text (TXT) record, 238

TFTP (Trivial File Transfer Protocol), 252, 460

TGS (Ticket Granting Service), 307–308

TGT (Ticket Granting Ticket), 269, *307*, 307–308, *308*

theory of probable cause, 79–80

thin AP, 355

threat, 296, *297*, 300
   actor, 296, 300
   data, 300
   external *vs.* internal, 300
   research on, 300

3CX, 259

three-factor authentication, 305

three-tiered hierarchy, *194*, 194–196
   access or edge layer, 195
   core layer, 196
   distribution or aggregation layer, 195

three-way handshake, TCP, 211, *211*, 446

throughput, 85–86, 274, 345, 358

throughput testers, 287, *287*

TIA (Telecommunications Industry Association), 26, 27, 28, 29, 30, 38, 39, 41

TIA/EIA IS-95 (cdmaOne)-based handsets, 347

Ticket Granting Service (TGS), 307–308

Ticket Granting Ticket (TGT), 269, *307*, 307–308, *308*

ticket system, 82–83, *83*

tiered switching architecture, 194–199
   broadcast storm, 198
   spanning tree protocol, 196–198, *197*
   switching loop, 198
   three-tiered hierarchy, *194*, 194–196

Time Division Multiple Access (TDMA), 347, 348

Time Division Multiplexing (TDM), 259, 377

time domain reflectometer (TDR), 89

Time Exceeded message, 177, 179

Time Service, 272

time synchronization, 228, 272, 335, 474

time to live (TTL), 131, 153, 177, 242

timing out, 446

timing/synchronization, 4

tip and ring wires, 28

TKIP (Temporal Key Integrity Protocol), 366

TLD (top-level domain), 233, 234–235

TLS. *see* Transport Layer Security (TLS)

T-Mobile, 347

tone generators, 90

tone probe, 90

top-level domain (TLD), 233, 234–235

top-of-rack (ToR) switches, 481

top talkers/listeners, 287, *288*

top-to-bottom/bottom-to-top OSI model, 79–80, *80*

TP-LINK SOHO, *367*

TP-LINK wireless access point, *227*

traceroute, 177

tracert, 177–178, *178*

traffic
   analysis tools, 287–288
   bandwidth speed testers, 288
   throughput testers, 287, *287*

top talkers/listeners, 287, *288*

class, 140, 285

flows, 478–479

logs, 279

shaping/shapers, 286, 473, 483

training/policies, 402, 413–141

transceivers, 4, 46–47, *47*
   in connectivity issues, 86
   incorrect, 93
   QSFP/QSFP+, 47
   SFP/SFP+, 47

transition mechanisms, in IPv6, 145–146

Transmission Control Protocol (TCP), 4, 7, 13, 209–212
   connection teardown, 212, *212*
   flags, 210
   LDAP messaging, 312, 313
   main fields in header of TCP segment, 209–210
   ports, 213–214
   in Protocol field, 99
   remote print protocols, 253
   SYN flood attack, 446
   three-way handshake, 211, *211*, 446

Transmission Control Protocol/Internet Protocol (TCP/IP) suite, 98, 248, 250, 253

transmit (Tx) wires, 38, 53, 87, 90

transparent proxy, 323, *323*

transparent server, 323

transport (layer 4), of OSI model, 7, *7*, 13, 433

transport layer, in Internet model, 15

transport layer protocols, 207–224
   IP scanners, 216–217
   netstat, *218*, 218–219
   Nmap Security Scanner, 217, *217*
   ports and connections, 208–209, *209*
   protocol analyzers, 221, *222*, *223*
   remote port scanners, 219–220, *220*

Transmission Control Protocol (TCP), 209–212, 213–214
User Datagram Protocol (UDP), 212–214
Transport Layer Security (TLS), 250, 252, 257, 261, 384, 449
  digital certificates, 308
transport mode, 390
transpositions, 90
trap, SNMP, 277
tree topology, 191
triple homed, 319
Trivial File Transfer Protocol (TFTP), 252, 460
Trojan, 447
troubleshooting
  connectivity issues, 85–94
    attenuation and interference issues, 90–91
    cable application issues, 91–92
    cable issues, 86–87
    cable testers, 88–89, *89*
    complete loss of connectivity, 91
    crosstalk issues, 91
    distance specification and limitations, 85–86
    fiber optic cable testing tools, 93
    interface configuration, 87, *88*
    loopback plugs, 87
    reference points, 90
    status indicators, 87
    tone generators, 90
    wire map testers, 89–90
  IP networks, 133–138
    duplicate IP and MAC address issues, 135–136
    hardware failure issues, 133–134
    incorrect DNS issues, 137
    incorrect IP address, 134–135
    incorrect subnet mask, 135
    interface status issues, 134

    IP configuration issues, 134–135
    multicast flooding issues, 137
    power issues, 133
    problem isolation, 136–137
  methodology, 76–84
    actions, documenting, 82–83
    changes, determining, 78
    divide and conquer approach, 80
    duplicate the problem, 78
    escalation, 81, 82
    findings, documenting, 82–83
    full system functionality, verifying, 82
    gather information, 77
    identify symptoms, 78
    identify the problem, 77–79
    multiple approaches in, 79
    multiple problems, approaching individually, 79
    outcomes, documenting, 82–83
    plan of action to repair/replace/ignore, 81–82
    preventive measures, implementing, 82
    question the obvious, 79
    question users, 78–79
    reestablish new theory, 81
    solution, implementing, 82
    steps to resolve problem, determining, 81
    test the theory to determine cause, 81
    theory of probable cause, establishing, 79–80

    top-to-bottom/bottom-to-top OSI model, 79–80, *80*
  service and security issues, 329–338
    BOYD challenges, 335
    DHCP issues, 329–330
    licensed feature issues, 335
    misconfigured firewall and ACL issues, 332–333
    name resolution issues, 330–331
    NTP issues, 335
    scenarios in, *337*, 337–338
    unresponsive service/network performance issues, 331–332
    untrusted certificate issues, *333*, 333–334, *334*
    VLAN assignment issues, 331
trunking, 201–202, *202*
Tshark, 63
Ttcp, 287
TTL (time to live), 131, 153, 177, 242
TTPs (tactics, techniques, and procedures), 300, 440
TTY (teletype) device, 268
tunneling, 145–146, 384–391
  certificate-based, 370
  client-to-site VPNs, *385*, 385–386, *386*
  compulsory, 387, *387*
  full tunnel, 385–386, *386*
  Generic Routing Encapsulation (GRE), 384, 389
  hub and spoke VPNs, *388*, 388–389
  IPSec tunnel, 388, 390, *391*
  Point-to-Point Protocol (PPP), 384
  site-to-site VPNs, 387, *387*
  split tunnel, 385, *385*
  static tunnel, 388
  VPN headends, 388–389
tuples, 289, 457
turnstile, 409

twinaxial (or twinax) cable, 32, *32*

twisted pair connectors, 28–29

twisted pair copper cabling, 20, 22, *25*, 28–29

two-factor authentication, 305

TX/RX reverse (crossed pair), 90

TXT (Text) record, 238

type (filter expression), 62

Type II frames, 60

Type I/Type II hypervisor, *471*, 471–472, *472*

Type of Service field, 285

U

Ubiquiti, 355

UDP. *see* User Datagram Protocol (UDP)

UDP scans (-sU) scan, 219

U/L bit, 60, *60*

Ultra Physical Contact (UPC), 38

UMTS (Universal Mobile Telecommunications System), 348

unbounded media, 4

unicast addresses
    /48s, 146
    IPv4, 109–111, *110*
    IPv6, 141–142, *142*, 146

Unicode, 7

unidirectional antenna, 360, *360*

UniFi Wireless Network management console, *355*

Uniform Resource Indicator (URI), 248, 260
    SIP, 260–261

uninterruptible power supply (UPS), 133, 399, 426, 428

universal address, 59–60

Universal Mobile Telecommunications System (UMTS), 348

UNIX, 268

unmanaged switches, 65

unpatched systems, 298–299

unreachable default gateway, 442

unresponsive service issues, 331–332

unshielded twisted pair (UTP) cable, *23*, 26, *27*, 28

untagged VLAN ports, 202–203

untrusted certificate issues, *333*, 333–334, *334*

untrusted networks, 405

UPC (Ultra Physical Contact), 38

uplink, 288
    link aggregation, 432
    MU-MIMO (UL MU-MIMO), 347
    port, 68, 91–92, 195, 288, 481
    speeds, 288, 379, 380

upper levels (layers 5-7), of OSI model, 4–5, 10, *11*

UPS (uninterruptible power supply), 133, 399, 426, 428

Urgent Pointer, 210

URI. *see* Uniform Resource Indicator (URI)

URL (web address), 140

usage policies, 403–404
    acceptable use policy (AUP), 403
    BYOD policies, 403, *404*
    password policy, 403

user agents, 260

User Datagram Protocol (UDP), 212–214, *213–214*
    Domain Name System (DNS), 237
    LDAP messaging, 312, 313
    maximum packet size, 237
    ports, 213–214
    port scanning for enumerating, 440
    in Protocol field, 99

user EXEC mode, 66, 67

username/password, in SSH client authentication, 269

UTC (Coordinated Universal Time), 271

utilization, 290

UTP (unshielded twisted pair) cable, *23*, 26, *27*, 28

V

variable length subnet masking (VLSM), 164–167, *165*, *166*, *167*

VCSEL (Vertical-Cavity Surface-Emitting L), 35

VDI (virtual desktop infrastructure), 467

VDSL (Very high-speed DSL), 377, 380

vendor assessment, 302

vendor management, 302

Version field, 98, *99*

Vertical-Cavity Surface-Emitting L (VCSEL), 35

vertical cross-connects, 42

vertical/scaling up, 464

Very high-speed DSL (VDSL), 377, 380

very high throughput (VHT), 346

very small aperture terminal (VSAT), 381

vestibule control, 409

VHT (very high throughput), 346

video teleconferencing (VTC), 259, 260

virtual appliances, 474

Virtual Carrier Sense flow control mechanism, 342

virtual desktop infrastructure (VDI), 467

virtual extensible LANs (VXLANs), 479

virtual IP, *343*, 434

virtualization, 471–474
    hypervisor types, *471*, 471–472, *472*
    network function (NFV), 473–474
    virtual NICs, 472–473, *473*
    virtual switches, 473

virtual LAN (VLAN), 56, 200–204
    assigning nodes, 201
    assignment issues, 331
    automated pooling, 355
    best practices, 456
    black hole, 454
    configuring IP networks, 115, *116*
    default, 200, 456
    extensible (VXLANs), 479
    hopping attacks, 443
    ID (VID), 202, 456

IDs and membership, 200–201
multicast traffic, 137
primary, 456
private (PVLAN), 456
static, 201
subnets, configuring, 115, 116
tagged and untagged ports, 202–203
traffic management on local networks, 286
trunking and IEEE 802.1Q, 201–202, 202
voice, 203
virtual machine (VM), 249
infrastructure, 468
monitor (VMM), 471, 471–472, 472
network function virtualization (NFV), 473–474
virtual NICs and switches, 472–473, 473
virtual network computing (VNC), 386–387
virtual network function (VNF), 474
virtual NIC (vNIC), 472–473, 473
Virtual Private LAN Service (VPLS), 291
virtual private network (VPN), 99, 384
clientless, 387
client-to-site, 385–386
cloud connectivity, 467
dynamic multipoint (DMVPN), 388–389
gateway, 385
headends, 388–389
hub and spoke topology, 388, 388–389
multifactor authentication, 310
open authentication, 370
remote sign-in, 306
site-to-site, 387
Virtual Private Server (VPS), 249
Virtual Router Redundancy Protocol (VRRP), 436
virtual switches, 472–473
virtual terminal, 391

viruses, 447
visiocafe.com, 399
VLAN. see virtual LAN (VLAN)
VLSM (variable length subnet masking), 164–167, 165, 166, 167
VM. see virtual machine (VM)
VMware
ESXi Server, 472
vSphere, 473
Workstation, 471
VNC (virtual network computing), 387
VNF (virtual network function), 474
vNIC (virtual NIC), 472–473, 473
voice and video services, 259–263
see also voice over IP (VoIP)
voice gateways, 261–262, 262–263
voice or auxiliary VLAN, 203, 203
voice over IP (VoIP), 259–263
phones, 261
plain old telephone service (POTS), 259
private branch exchange (PBX), 259, 260
protocols, 260–261
resource units (RUs), 346
response times measured in ms, 260
voice gateways, 261–262, 262–263
VoIP. see voice over IP (VoIP)
VoIP-enabled PBX, 259, 260
VPLS (Virtual Private LAN Service), 291
VPN. see virtual private network (VPN)
VPS (Virtual Private Server), 249
VRRP (Virtual Router Redundancy Protocol), 436
VSAT (very small aperture terminal), 381
vSphere, 473
VTC (video teleconferencing), 259, 260
vulnerabilities, 296, 297, 298–299

Common Vulnerabilities and Exposures (CVE), 299, 299
software, 298–299
unpatched and legacy systems, 298–299
vulnerability assessment, 299
zero-day, 298
VXLANs (virtual extensible LANs), 479
VyOS-based software router, 151, 175

W

WAN. see wide area network (WAN)
WannaCry ransomware, 448
warm site, 427
wavelength division multiplexing (WDM), 47, 48, 93
WDS (wireless distribution system), 353–354
weak authentication, 405
wear-leveling routines, 413
web conferencing, 259
web portal, remote sign-in, 306
web servers, 249–250
Web Services for Devices (WSD)/AirPrint, 253
website performance checkers, 288
WebSockets, 387
WEP (wired equivalent privacy), 366
wet-pipe sprinklers, 428
wide area network (WAN), 10, 187
enterprise, 376
framing, 291
interface of SOHO routers, 10, 13, 13, 14, 15
links, 115
OSI model, 376
Physical layer, 376
provider links, 377–382
cable, 380
demarcation point, 377
digital subscriber line (DSL), 378–379
Fiber to the X (FTTx), 377

leased line, 377–378
metro-optical, 380–381
microwave satellite, 381
T-carrier system,
377–378
termination equipment,
377, 378
WIDS (wireless intrusion
detection system), 445
Wi-Fi 4, 344–345
Wi-Fi 5, 346–347
Wi-Fi 6, 346–347
Wi-Fi Alliance, 342
Wi-Fi analyzer, 359
Wi-Fi encryption standards,
366, 367
Wi-Fi Protected Access (WPA),
366, 368
WPA2, 366, 367
4-way handshake, 367
enterprise
authentication, 368
PSK mode, 367, 368
WPA3, 366, 367
enterprise
authentication, 368
Personal Transition
mode, 368
SAE, 367–368
Wi-Fi security configuration
issues, 369
window (TCP segment), 210
Windows
Active Directory, 238, 241,
242, 307, 312, 312, 313
arp utility, 129–130, 130
authentication, 306
cmdlets, 126, 244
connecting to iSCSI target
using iSCSI initiator, 476,
476
Device Manager, 133
DHCP, DNS, and IPAM (DDI),
216
DHCP issues, 329
dig, 244
DNS name resolution,
243–244
dual stack, 145, 145
duplicate IP address, 135
hardware failure issues, 133
IBSS, 355

incorrect DNS issues, 137
ipconfig, 126, 127, 127,
134–135, 136, 137, 228, 243,
330
LDAP, 312, 312, 313
MAPI protocol, 258
name resolution methods,
330
netsh, 126, 127
netstat, 218–219
Network Policy Server
(NPS), 311
Nmap Security Scanner, 217
nslookup, 243, 243
NTP issues, 335
ping, 130–131, 131
PowerShell, 126, 127, 244,
468
Remote Desktop Protocol
(RDP), 271
as router for VM network,
configuring, 474
Secure Shell (SSH), 268
sign-in, 306
Time Service, 272
tracert, 177
tunneling, 146
VoIP PBX, 259
Web Services for Devices
(WSD)/AirPrint, 253
WIPS (wireless intrusion
prevention system), 445
wired equivalent privacy (WEP),
366
wireless distribution system
(WDS), 353–354
wireless intrusion detection
system (WIDS), 445
wireless intrusion prevention
system (WIPS), 445
wireless local area network
(WLAN), 13, 187
configuration in
infrastructure mode,
350–351, 351
controllers, 354, 354–355
open, 187
wireless media, 4
Wireless Mesh Network
(WMN), 356
wireless network
access points, 350–351

adapter, 353
attacks, 444–445
client isolation, 459
installing, 350–357
ad hoc topology, 355
infrastructure topology
and wireless access
points, 350–351
mesh topology, 356
site surveys and heat
maps, 352–353, 353
wireless LAN controllers,
354–355
wireless roaming and
bridging, 353–354
wireless site design,
351–352
PAN (WPAN), 187
performance assessment,
358–359
attenuation, 358–359
signal strength, 358–359,
359
speed, 358
throughput, 358
security, configuring and
troubleshooting, 366–372
client disassociation
issues, 369–370
enterprise/IEEE 802.1X
authentication, 368, 368
features, 459
open authentication and
captive portal issues,
370
personal authentication,
367–368
Wi-Fi encryption
standards, 366, 367
Wi-Fi security
configuration issues, 369
wireless intrusion
detection system (WIDS),
445
wireless intrusion
prevention system
(WIPS), 445
site design, 351–352
speed and distance
requirements, 352
SSID broadcast and
beacon frame, 351

standards, 342–349
   cellular digital communications standards, 347–348
   IEEE 802.11 standards, 342–347
troubleshooting, 358–365
   antenna types, 360, *360*
   channel utilization and overlap issues, 362–363
   insufficient wireless coverage issues, 360–361
   interference issues, 363–364
   overcapacity issues, 363
   signal strength, 359, *359*
   wireless performance assessment, 358–359
wireless local area network (WLAN), 13, 187, 350–351, *351*
Wireless Mesh Network (WMN), 356
wireless PAN (WPAN), 187
wireless roaming, 353–354
wireless router, 13, *14*
wireless survey tool, 353
wire map testers, 89–90
Wireshark, 62, *63*
   Protocol Hierarchy tool, 222
   Statistics menu, 221, *221*

wiring
   diagram, 398
   distribution components, *42*
   tools and techniques, 44
WLAN. *see* wireless local area network (WLAN)
WMN (Wireless Mesh Network), 356
work area, 41, *42*
workgroup, 186
Work Recovery Time (WRT), 425, *425*
WorldWide Names (WWN), 475
WorldWide Node Name (WWNN), 475
WorldWide Port Name (WWPN), 475
worms, 447
WPA. *see* Wi-Fi Protected Access (WPA)
WPAN (wireless PAN), 187
WRT (Work Recovery Time), 425, *425*
WSD (Web Services for Devices)/AirPrint, 253
WWN (WorldWide Names), 475
WWNN (WorldWide Node Name), 475
WWPN (WorldWide Port Name), 475

X
X.500 series of standards, 312
XaaS (Something/Anything/Everything as a Service), 465
XEN Server, 472
Xirrus Wi-Fi Inspector, *444*
XML (extensible markup language), 429
xrdp, 271

Y
Yagi, 360, *360*
YAML ain't markup language (YAML), 128

Z
Zenmap, 217
zero-day, 298
zero filling, 412, 413
zero trust, 302, 479
Zigbee Alliance, 418
zombie hosts, 446
zone
   DNS, 241–242
   index, 143
   namespace, 241
   network, 318
   records, 235, 241, 242
   transfer, 241
Z-Wave Alliance, 418